P9-DDK-654

WHAT THE IRS DOESN'T WANT
YOU TO KNOW

WHAT THE
IRS
DOESN'T WANT YOU
TO KNOW

A CPA Reveals the Tricks of the Trade

Revised for 2001

MARTIN S. KAPLAN, CPA,
AND NAOMI WEISS

VILLARD · NEW YORK

Visit the *What the IRS Doesn't Want You to Know* website.
Read selections from the book.
Ask Marty a question about your taxes.
Read the tax tips newsletter.
http://www.irsmaven.com

This publication is designed to provide accurate and authoritative information in regard to the subject matter covered. It is sold with the understanding that the author and publisher are not engaged in rendering legal, accounting, and other professional services. If legal advice or other expert assistance is required, the services of a professional should be sought.

The author and publisher specifically disclaim any liability or loss that is incurred as a consequence of the use and application, directly or indirectly, of any information presented in this book.

Copyright © 2000, 1999, 1998, 1997, 1996, 1995, 1994
by Martin S. Kaplan, CPA, and Naomi Weiss

All rights reserved under International and Pan-American Copyright Conventions. Published in the United States by Villard Books, a division of Random House, Inc., New York, and simultaneously in Canada by Random House of Canada Limited, Toronto.

VILLARD BOOKS is a registered trademark of Random House, Inc.
Colophon is a trademark of Random House, Inc.

This work was originally published as a trade paperback by Villard Books, a division of Random House, Inc., in 1994. Revised and updated editions were published in 1995, 1996, 1997, 1998, and 1999.

Library of Congress Cataloging-in-Publication Data

Kaplan, Martin S.
What the IRS doesn't want you to know:
a CPA reveals the tricks of the trade / Martin S. Kaplan
and Naomi Weiss.—Rev. for 2001
p.   cm.
Includes bibliographical references and index.
ISBN 0-670-78358-X (alk. paper)
1. Tax administration and procedure—United States.
2. Tax auditing—United States. 3. United States. Internal Revenue Service.
I. Weiss, Naomi. II. Title.
KF6300.Z9K37   2001
343.7304—dc21   97-35509

Villard Books website address: www.villard.com

Printed in the United States of America on acid-free paper

2 4 6 8 9 7 5 3
Seventh Edition

I would like to dedicate this book to Harriet, my wife and best friend, for her love and unselfish support of all my endeavors, and for always being there for me. Also to Sharon, Jason, Hillary, and Bruce, children that any parent would be proud of. A special note to my granddaughter, Lindsay: It's never too early to begin tax planning.

—Martin S. Kaplan

During the time it took to write this book, one person consistently expanded my range of resources by tracking down information, photocopying, reading and rereading, double-checking calculations, and performing financial analyses. That person is my husband, William Halpern, and I dedicate this book to him.

—Naomi Weiss

NON SEQUITUR/ by Wiley Miller

Non Sequitur copyright © 2000 by Wiley Miller. Dist. by Universal Press Syndicate. Reprinted with permission. All rights reserved.

ACKNOWLEDGMENTS

I would like to thank Anthony Viola, CPA, the tax partner at Geller, Marzano and Co., CPAs, for his valuable insight and assistance with this revised edition. Thank you also to George K. Greene, CLU, for being such a good sounding board, Marvin Cohen, CPA, for his sound advice on technical matters, and Shelley Davis, former IRS historian, for helping us get organized in the early stages of research.

The authors wish to acknowledge the publicity department at Villard Books for spreading the word about our unique message and how important this material is for every taxpayer.

—Martin S. Kaplan

I wish to thank all the staff at the IRS who promptly answered my calls, mailed me information, and remained consistently courteous and patient, especially Sandy Byberg in the Statistics of Income office and those in the departments of Media Relations, Public Affairs, and Communications and Campaign Development. I also want to thank David Burnham and Susan Long, cofounders of the Transactional Records Access Clearinghouse (TRAC) at Syracuse University (http://www.trac.syr.edu/tracirs/), and Chuck Rappaport for introducing us to Alan Weiner, president of the New York State Society of Certified Public Accountants, and the crew at Holtz Rubenstein & Co., who gave us a wonderful head start.

I also acknowledge my friend and neighbor Sondra Gregory for her ability to zoom in on all the minute details when proofreading the bibliography, footnotes, index, and galleys; and Dottie Hook for always being there despite being an ocean away.

Finally, I thank my daughter, Micayla, for her steadfast support, respect, and love.

—NAOMI WEISS

Both authors wish to thank David Cay Johnston of *The New York Times* for his timely and comprehensive reporting on the IRS, and Sybil Pincus at Random House, our copy editor almost from the start, for her patience, eagle eye, guidance, and sunny disposition.

CONTENTS

CONTENTS

Cathy copyright © 2000 by Cathy Guisewite. Reprinted with permission of Universal Press Syndicate. All rights reserved.

WHAT THE IRS DOESN'T WANT
YOU TO KNOW

Ziggy copyright © 1998 by Ziggy and Friends, Inc. Reprinted with permission of Universal Press Syndicate. All rights reserved.

1

Why Every Taxpayer Must Read This Book

Welcome to the new millennium.

At the IRS, there's a new commissioner and what looks to be a solid effort to completely reorganize the agency into an organization focused on customer service. Dramatic steps have already been taken that may surprise taxpayers, steps based on new legislation designed to give you a more substantial footing in dealing with the IRS than ever before. It will take years for the project to be completed, but positive changes are taking place—along with some dramatic repercussions. Meanwhile, when it comes to paying taxes and dealing with the IRS, what really has changed? We're going to tell you—leaving nothing out.

Each year hundreds of reputable books are written about taxes, audits, and the Internal Revenue Service (IRS). No-nonsense, definitive, and powerful, the titles practically scream out ways that we can deal with the IRS: Fight, Win, Battle, Negotiate. Words such as *The Only* or *The Best* followed by *Audit, Tax Forms, Small Business*, or *Corporate Tax Guide Book You'll Ever Need* appear more than enough to guarantee results. Worried about the IRS, or in doubt about your personal tax situation? The confidence and warm cozy feelings titles such as these bring give a clear and unmistakable message to the taxpaying public: "Buy me," these books say, "and all of your tax problems will be resolved." So each year thousands buy these books, or select them off library shelves, hoping to discover the secret to keeping their tax payments low and their returns away from the scrutiny of the IRS.

Unfortunately, the information taxpayers really need to satisfy these goals rarely, if ever, surfaces. No matter how much information taxpayers read, hear, or research on the subject, they still remain easy targets for the IRS. In the IRS ballpark, despite living in a megatechnology environment, and with periodic promises about a more consumer-oriented IRS, some things have changed, but very little.

The time has come to deal with some clear-cut, shocking truths about what's behind the unsettling phenomenon that perpetually keeps blinders on the taxpaying public. This requires exploring the overall phenomenon, and then examining why those in the know aren't talking.

Let's face facts: Traditionally, the IRS has had a reputation for being all-knowing, all-powerful, and ruthless (many would say vicious). It is seen to have extensive manpower and technological resources, and the law is on its side. Without actually knowing what the IRS is and how the organization really works—or, perhaps more important, how it *doesn't* work—the public remains in the no-holds-barred grip of the IRS's reputation as the Big Bad Wolf.

Millions of taxpayers live with the fear that one day an IRS agent will single out an item from their tax return, decide an audit is in order, and come after them. In fact, the IRS is often referred to as an agency out of control—and with good reason. Once it selects its culprits, it chooses the punishment and proceeds to administer it with very little containment from any other governmental or nongovernmental agencies. So it's really not surprising that most taxpayers envision the IRS as harassing and abusive, using its power in an uncaring, even brutal way to possibly destroy their careers and families.

Taxpayers are consistently so fearful of dealing with the IRS that they rank it as an event as traumatic as divorce or having their house burn down. This paranoia shows how enormously successful the IRS has been in creating its all-powerful-and-untouchable image. By sustaining these fears, the IRS maintains a status quo that actually prevents taxpayers from

- Questioning how much of the IRS's reputation is actually true.
- Considering why a never-ending body of information, designed by well-meaning authors and "tax experts" to help them pay less in taxes and better manage the demands of the IRS, never genuinely helps them accomplish those goals.

Now let's talk about those who know exactly what is going on and find out why they aren't talking. Any good Certified Public Accountant (CPA) or tax professional knows how to beat the IRS at its own game. **But an unwritten law among tax professionals has traditionally prevented this vital information from being revealed publicly.**

What is this law based on? It's based on tax professionals' healthy fear that the IRS will turn against them.

When filling out their clients' tax returns, tax professionals use information they have gained as experts in their field. **But these very same professionals do not traditionally disclose, in anything resembling a public forum, information in three crucial areas that can make a huge difference in the lives of the millions of taxpayers who aren't their clients:**

1. What the IRS really is and how it thinks, responds, and operates, or, more precisely, *doesn't* operate.
2. Endless loopholes in our tax laws that can be used in the preparation of an individual tax return.
3. How *both* of these can be used consistently to benefit taxpayers.

Tax professionals have made it a practice NOT to reveal such information—and with good reason: They've seen firsthand how people can be destroyed by both warranted and unwarranted IRS attacks. Why would CPA's, or any professionals in the tax field, put their lives, families, careers, and futures on the line? The answer to this question has traditionally prevented tax professionals from publicly explaining why the right kind of information never gets to the taxpaying public. It also keeps them from revealing that information on a broad scale.

So, to prevent an all-out personal conflagration and probably endless repercussions, tax professionals continue to offer whitewashed material that promises to tell taxpayers how they can disappear from the IRS's view. In fact, much of this information is correct and does work. **But it is not the whole story. Too much information is left out, and no one knows this better than the authors themselves.**

After almost 35 years as a CPA, I have consistently watched how the IRS can financially ruin all kinds of people: rich, middle-class, the average working family—people exactly like you.

A few years ago a fascinating case involving IRS wrongdoing hit the newspapers. It had begun simply enough.

Mrs. Carole Ward accompanied her son to an audit of their family business, three children's clothing stores in Colorado Springs. Because the audit was going poorly, Mrs. Ward spoke up to the female IRS revenue agent, saying, "Honey, from what I can see of your accounting skills, the country would be better served if you were dishing up chicken-fried steak on the interstate in West Texas, with all that clunky jewelry and big hair."

Four weeks later, IRS revenue agents raided the family's stores, padlocked all three of them, and posted notices in the windows that implied that Mrs. Ward, who was 49, was a drug smuggler. The IRS then imposed a tax bill in the amount of $324,000.

Mrs. Ward hired two attorneys and sought press coverage to publicize her plight. The IRS countered with a publicity campaign that included sending a letter to the editor of the local newspaper giving details of Ward's case and providing a fact sheet about it to the TV show *Inside Edition*.

Three months after the raid, the government settled the tax dispute for $3,485, but a week later the IRS district director appeared on a radio show detailing the IRS's position against Ward but failing to mention that the bill had already been settled for little more than 1 percent of the original amount.

At this point, Ward sued the IRS for disclosing confidential information from her tax return. Until the case was brought to trial, Ward's daughter had to quit high school because the IRS statements led students to believe the family was engaged in drug smuggling. The family went from having no debts at the time of the raid to owing $75,000. The lease on one of the stores was lost. And only two thirds of the goods and equipment seized in the raid were returned, much of that badly damaged.

During the nine-day trial the IRS and the Justice Department, which defended the lawsuit, denied any wrongdoing. In a harshly worded 17-page opinion, Judge William Downes of the federal district court in Denver found that one of the IRS agents had been "grossly negligent," had acted with "reckless disregard" for the law, and had made three false statements in a sworn declaration. The judge awarded Mrs. Ward $4,000 in damages for improper disclosures, $75,000 in damages for the emotional distress the IRS caused her to suffer, and $250,000 in punitive damages, giving "notice to the IRS that reprehensible abuse of authority by one of its employees cannot and will not be tolerated." The judge also criticized the IRS district director who had made the radio appearance.

"I never should have spoken condescendingly," Ward later said, "but what they did to me for mouthing off was criminal."

Never forget—the amount awarded by the judge, and the fact that such a case was settled in the taxpayer's favor, is the result of almost 20 years of private citizens' fighting for retribution in thousands of similar cases but receiving nothing except bureaucratic doors slammed in their faces.

Here's another case that demonstrates the blatant and unmitigated arrogance of the IRS.

A high-level executive in a nationally known insurance company was the subject of an extensive IRS investigation. Allegedly he owed $3,500. The taxpayer agreed to admit to tax evasion, and the IRS promised, in a written agreement, to keep the matter out of the public eye. When the executive informed his employer of his tax problem, he was told that the one thing he must avoid was a public scandal. Since the agreement with the IRS seemed to preclude this, the matter should have ended there. But it didn't. About three months into the investigation, the IRS issued to more than 21 sources news releases that included the taxpayer's name, his address, and the name of his employer. The taxpayer promptly lost his job, had to move out of town, and never again regained his prominent position.

Why was the IRS so interested in pursuing a case in which the tax liability was less than $3,500? The answer was revealed about two years later at a trial resulting from a suit the executive brought against the IRS. Here's what really happened:

Initially, when the taxpayer found out that the IRS was investigating him, he asked the agent assigned to the case what he had done wrong. He was told that his wife had made some bookkeeping errors in managing his records, resulting in the amount owed. But a transcript from the trial showed the real reason for the extensive investigation. "The only publicity that is good for the IRS is when it brings a big one down," were the agent's words. Since the taxpayer was a prominent figure in his area, he satisfied that need, although the agent admitted that he didn't think there was any real proof that the taxpayer even owed the IRS money. In April 1998, after a 20-year battle, the case was settled to the tune of $3 million for the much maligned insurance executive.

I know many cases like these, but I have also come to learn and fully understand which words, style, techniques, and knowledge can effectively make the IRS come to an abrupt standstill in a lot less time.

What's more heartening is that recent tax legislation, the Taxpayer Relief Act of 1997 (TRA '97) and the Restructuring and Reform Act of 1998 (RRA '98), contain laws designed to limit the unbridled power of the IRS and restore certain rights to taxpayers.

In December 1994, an IRS collection agent entered the tax preparation office of Mr. Richard Gardner in Tulsa, Oklahoma, and demanded that he turn over $20,000 for nonpayment of income and Social Security taxes withheld from the paychecks of his seven employees. Mr. Gardner said that he would pay the amount in a few weeks, after receiving payment from his clients. The collection agent then threatened a "jeopardy assessment," in which cash, bank accounts, and property can be seized. To stall the IRS collection action, Mr. Gardner, who is the sixth-largest income tax preparer in Oklahoma, placed his two businesses, the second being a store selling used books and comics, in bankruptcy. Days later, he paid the overdue taxes and canceled the bankruptcy actions. Three months after that, armed agents raided Mr. Gardner's tax preparation office, seizing all the computers and files. That very night, Mr. Gardner purchased new computers, and the next morning he was back in business when an IRS agent from the Criminal Investigation Division telephoned. Hearing Mr. Gardner's voice, he said, "I'm surprised you're open. We thought we'd put you out of business."

In January 1998, the Justice Department withdrew the charges made against Mr. Gardner and, without admitting wrongdoing, paid $75,000 to Mr. Gardner's lawyer for the cost of the case. The two men had sought $102,000. This made Mr. Gardner the first person to have his legal defense fees paid by the Justice Department under a 1997 law intended to curb prosecutions that are "vexatious, frivolous, or in bad faith."

Mr. Gardner's lawyer has stated that the IRS took what were lawful, routine business actions on the part of his client as a personal affront and set out to destroy his client's business. Mr. Gardner believed that the charges made against him were essentially "unlawful actions" designed to punish him because he had the temerity to exercise his constitutional rights as a way of delaying payment of back taxes. What has made this case particularly extraordinary is that once an indictment is handed up in a tax matter, the Justice Department routinely insists on either going to trial or obtaining a guilty plea to at least one charge. It is inordinately rare for such a case to be withdrawn.[1]

Although examples such as this one, where a taxpayer wins out over the IRS, may occur more frequently these days, over the years, as I continued to witness the seemingly uncontrollable behavior of the IRS, I realized that I could no longer keep silent.

I have been collecting the information contained in this book for over 20 years. Am I afraid of repercussions from the IRS? Yes. But this information is too important *not* to be told. The value of the assistance it can bring to every U.S. taxpayer will, I hope, minimize my risk.

In *What the IRS Doesn't Want You to Know* I will

- Tell taxpayers why they have been kept in the dark for so many years.
- Present a point of view that can make taxpayers more powerful than they ever thought possible.
- **Give the taxpaying public new information, legal and legitimate, that is traditionally presented only by CPA's to clients in low voices and behind closed doors.**
- Let taxpayers know *in advance* what they need to watch out for and how to protect themselves from new IRS onslaughts.

This information will allow taxpayers to

- View the IRS from an entirely new and realistic perspective.
- Learn how to use glitches, crevices, and loopholes in our tax laws to their benefit.
- Recognize the shortfalls of the IRS so that the scales of justice are tipped in the taxpayers' favor.

I have decided to make this information available so that you, the average taxpayer, can be armed with the same tools of the trade that I use every day. You will learn how to use these tools to

- Avoid an audit.
- Minimize your tax assessment.

- Dramatically improve your business and tax situation, especially if you are self-employed, a service provider, or an independent contractor.
- Increase your tax-deductible expenses without drawing attention to your return.
- Dramatically reduce your personal tax liabilities by learning little-known techniques used in the tax trade.
- Make the IRS consistently work for you, once and for all reversing a long-standing trend.
- Learn what to watch out for as the IRS undergoes its enormous reorganization.

These commonsense tools, rarely divulged to the average taxpayer, represent specific legal steps you can take to shield yourself from the far-reaching clutches of the IRS.

It's rare to find this information anywhere else, even if the titles of a bevy of books suggest that they contain it. They don't.

Furthermore, the idea that only wealthy individuals, those who hire expensive tax attorneys, or those in the know can avail themselves of aggressive tax information is false. Anyone has the right to receive the same kind of information and advice on how to best handle the demands of the IRS, particularly the average taxpayer. **No one is too small to DEAL SUCCESSFULLY with the long, powerful, and often ruthless and arbitrary arm of the IRS.**

I intend to set taxpayers free by offering them a brand-new foundation from which they can deal with the IRS, one based on expert knowledge never before revealed publicly. For example, did you know the following?

- Despite spending billions of dollars, most of the technological advances the IRS predicted for the year 2000 did not happen.
- In 1994 the IRS restated its statistical tables back to 1988, to make the percentage of audited returns appear higher than it actually was.
- Each year the IRS loses files on which audits have commenced; the audit is then abruptly terminated.
- Travel and entertainment are still the first areas that are examined by an IRS auditor, because a partial disallowance of deductions is virtually certain.
- You should never represent yourself at an IRS audit. Such an ego trip usually ends up costing taxpayers dearly.

- In the past, the IRS has claimed responsibility for almost 50 percent more prosecutions than recorded by the Justice Department and more than twice the number of individuals sentenced to prison.
- You probably have a greater chance of being audited if you live in a certain part of the country.

With this information, and a great deal more like it, taxpayers will not only have a fighting chance in dealing with the IRS but can actually come out winners.

CPA'S GRADE CLIENTS

Now, let's enter a CPA's inner sanctum, a place most taxpayers are not privy to.

Over time it has become customary for tax professionals to "grade" their clients. Clients who make the highest grade from the tax professional's view pay less in taxes, are rarely audited, and have more money in their pockets. I would venture to say that in our profession we deal with three types of clients. Let's call them Type A, Type B, and Type C. Here's how this works.

Type A are the "good" clients. A good client is a person who heeds the professional's advice most of the time, but especially when the professional presents the advice in the form of a strong recommendation. The ideas presented in this book are strong recommendations, and nothing irks a tax professional more than when a client doesn't follow strong recommendations and ends up paying higher taxes or, worse, is audited.

Let's skip Type B clients for a moment and discuss Type C. Type C clients, because of their difficult behavior and negative attitudes, are at the bottom of the totem pole. The fee that they are charged is never commensurate with the time that is spent with them, both at face-to-face meetings or on the telephone. They are usually terrible listeners who refuse to hear much-needed information, which must therefore be continually repeated. Type C's often argue against the recommended course of action because they usually have a know-it-all mentality. Type C's also receive the greatest number of notices from the IRS, simply because they do not follow the tax professional's instructions. In short, a Type C client causes the professional the greatest amount of aggravation, the professional earns the lowest hourly rate, and Type C's are usually the first to complain that the bill is too high.

Type B represents all the clients who don't fit into Type A or C categories. As you might suspect, the majority of people are Type B's. Although Type B's aggravate you once in a while, they may overcome this by paying bills promptly. They may complain a lot, but they may also be a source of client referrals.

The dilemma faced by tax professionals concerning their client base should be becoming clear to you: Wouldn't it be great if we could drop Type C's from our client roll, and have Type B's gradually mend their ways and work themselves up to Type A's? But, alas, this is a tax professional's fantasy. In reality, clients drop down from Type A or B to become a Type C, but a Type B or C rarely moves up to become a Type A.

Now that you are aware of this aspect of the tax business, I'd like you to benefit as fully as possible from it by incorporating what you have just discovered into your own thinking and behavior from this moment on, **while you are reading this book.** Here's how.

Most of the advice, recommendations, and tips contained in *What the IRS Doesn't Want You to Know* has not been made available to the average taxpayer before. Therefore, to receive the full value of what I am revealing, you need to respond like a Type A client. In fact, I'd like each of you to become a Type A client by the time you have completed this book. The closer you come to being a Type A client, the easier it will be for you to understand how your own thinking and behavior can positively or negatively affect how your return will ultimately be handled by the IRS. **Behaving like a Type A or B instead of a Type C client can actually make the difference between an unnoticed return and an audit.** Here's what I mean:

A Type C client, Mr. Richards, came to me with a problem. He had received a fee of $35,000, for which the payer issued a 1099-Misc form (Miscellaneous Income) listing him as the recipient. Mr. Richards claimed that the fee was actually earned by his son. I suggested that he contact the payer of the fee and obtain a revised 1099 in his son's name. Without any further explanation, Mr. Richards instead asked me if he should prepare a 1099 in his son's name showing that he paid the $35,000, acting as the boy's agent. I strongly advised against this course of action. If this was noticed and subsequently questioned, the IRS would ask for full documentation, including a contractual agreement and canceled checks. But Mr. Richards, acting like the perfect Type C, insisted that he knew better and refused to heed my advice. I knew it would be useless to argue further. He prepared the 1099 form showing the $35,000 payment to his son.

Six months later, when the IRS detected the existence of two apparently related 1099 forms, both belonging to Mr. Richards, they contacted him and, not satisfied with his explanation, proceeded with a full-scale audit. The audit encompassed all of Mr. Richards's personal and corporate activities, which were substantial, since he was a highly paid executive. An audit lasting more than three years culminated with Mr. Richards's paying the IRS $140,000 in tax, interest, and penalties, plus $25,000 in accounting and legal fees. To this day, Mr. Richards still insists that he knows best, and his behavior has not changed one iota, despite the fact that if he had listened to me in the first place, I could have made his life a lot easier and saved him thousands of dollars.

Finally, the most crucial ability for taxpayers to have, which they cannot acquire on their own, is **the ability to understand how the IRS thinks, operates, and responds.** This is definitely something you as a taxpayer want to learn about and put into practice, yet it is rarely, if ever, made available.

In my interactions with countless clients and with the IRS, a great deal of unofficial information surfaces that is often more important than a specific tax law. **In fact, quite often what is most important is not what a tax law says, but how the IRS interprets and acts on it.** This knowledge, which tax pros gain from years of working in the field and interacting at all levels with the IRS, is what enables them to complete your return and know how the IRS will respond to each individual item recorded. This is the kind of information I will be revealing in this book. Here is a typical case:

Early in 1998, a Mr. Graham, who owned an interior design business, came to me for the preparation of his 1997 tax return. In reviewing his file, I saw that both his 1995 and 1996 returns had been audited. On the basis of what I knew about how the IRS thinks, it seemed to me that the audits were triggered by two items: First, Mr. Graham's gross income for each year was over $100,000, which in itself increases the chances of an audit. Second, in both years Mr. Graham claimed about 30 percent of his gross income, an unusually large amount, for entertainment, auto expenses, and travel, as reported on his Schedule C, Profit or Loss from Business (Sole Proprietorship). IRS regulations require anyone who is an unincorporated sole proprietor to file this schedule.

I knew that my approach would have to be based on presenting Mr. Graham's expenses from one perspective: in case he was audited. Any good CPA employs this kind of thinking automatically, but in this case it was more crucial because of the two previous audits. In addition, I had to eliminate, or reframe, whatever I could that had been previously questioned.

When my client and I set to work examining his business diary for 1997, one thing consistently kept showing up: Meal expenses on most days were for breakfast, lunch, and dinner. There is a rather obscure IRS regulation that some meals must be considered personal in nature. In other words, the IRS does not take kindly to three meals a day taken as a business expense. Mr. Graham was operating under the illusion that because these meals were business expenses, he would be able to reduce his overall tax bill by listing them that way. But he did *not* know that he was treading upon a favorite IRS attention getter: entertainment expenses.

I told my client about this regulation and promptly reduced Mr. Graham's business-related meals to two a day. To offset this loss, I also told him of another IRS regulation that would allow him to expense meals *under* $75 *without a receipt* if his business diary noted the person, place, and date of the meal, along with a brief description of what was discussed. With these additional diary entries, entertainment expense was back to its previous total, but because of the way it was presented on his return (and in backup material), I knew he would be safe if he was audited. I also insisted that my client substantiate every entertainment item *above* $75 with a receipt or canceled check, a practice he had previously been lax about.

Next, Mr. Graham's business diary showed $10,000 for out-of-pocket expenses but only $6,000 worth of checks made payable to himself. With his history, I knew the IRS would grab this in a flash. With a little investigation, I uncovered the source of the missing $4,000—cash gifts from his parents made during the year. In this case I used as documentation a section from the *Internal Revenue Code (IR Code)* that allows each taxpayer to personally give $10,000 annually to any other person without filing a gift tax return. Now we could prove the source of the $4,000, and best of all, gifts of this nature are *nontaxable*. However, to clear him even further, I advised my client to have his parents write and sign a one-sentence letter that documented the fact that they had given him the money during the year as a gift.

Finally, to save Mr. Graham from ever having to file a Schedule C again, where his entertainment, automobile, and travel expenses would be placed under continued scrutiny, I strongly recommended that he change his business from a sole proprietorship to a new small business corporation, an S corporation. By doing this, Mr. Graham accomplished the following: He substantially reduced his chances of being audited (i.e., his $100,000 in personal income would not light up the IRS computers). As an S corporation, he had available to him new techniques for reducing Social Security costs that he didn't have as a sole proprietor. And he had all the other advantages of being incorporated (e.g., limited liability to creditors). The end result was exactly what I had hoped for: Mr. Graham's personal and business tax returns since 1997 have not been selected for audit by the IRS.

YOUR TAX-SAVING STRATEGY.

Although the IRS no longer requires receipts for business transportation and entertainment unless the expense exceeds $75, detailed entries in your business diary are a must. Expenses for lodging require detailed receipts regardless of the amount.

Now, I have two requests of all taxpayers who read this book. First, I would like you to extract from the material all the points that have some relevance to your own situation. Then bring these points to the attention of your tax professional and ask for comments. If your tax professional says, for example, that you are too small to become an S corporation, ask for specific reasons to support that conclusion. If you are not satisfied with the response, find another pro for a second opinion. ·

My second request can be applied only after you have finished reading. When that time arrives, go back to your tax professional and ask what it will take to make you a Type A client. Encourage your tax pro to let you know how successful you have been in following his or her advice. I'm sure he or she can pull some specific examples out of the files. Walk through one or two together to assess how your behavior held up. Were you cooperative? Did you listen carefully? Follow instructions? As a result of your way of responding to your tax professional's advice, did you gain a stronger tax position, or did you end up with a loss that could have been avoided?

If your tax professional claims that he or she doesn't know what a Type A client is, tell that person to read this book.

A note on IRS statistics: As we went to press, the most recent source of IRS statistics was limited 1999 IRS data and the advance draft of the *IRS 1998 Data Book*, the latest one available because the IRS publishes it later and later each year, to the growing frustration of writers (like us), reporters, financial analysts, researchers, accountants, and more. More recent statistics come from the Transactional Records Access Clearinghouse (TRAC) at Syracuse University, and the fine work of Susan Long and David Burnham.

2

—

The IRS Personality:
Playing It to Your Advantage

Each of us who pays taxes to the U.S. government is involved in a relationship with the IRS. The good news is that we have choices for influencing how that relationship will turn out. We can behave like sheep, following IRS dictates and threats as if they were gospel. We can take a middle-of-the-road approach and, amidst our complaints, begin to ask why and how the IRS does what it does. Or we can choose to work with and beat the IRS from a sound foundation built upon experience, knowledge, and an understanding of who the IRS is and how it operates.

Imagine that you've just met someone new and that you're very interested in finding out what that person is like. Naturally, you're curious about family history, aspirations, career, and key incidents that have shaped that person's life. You can use the same principle of learning what you can about someone to become familiar with the IRS.

EVENTS THAT SHAPED THE IRS PERSONALITY

I believe it is time for taxpayers to recognize that the IRS is an entity with a distinct personality that affects you each time you fill out your tax return.

The significant events that make the IRS what it is today are clear-cut and straightforward. Through these the IRS personality unfolds.

THE EVENT: Establishing the Right to Collect Taxes
THE PERSONALITY: Stubborn. Tenacious. Undaunted.

Significance to Taxpayers

The U.S. government's privilege to levy taxes was incorporated into the Constitution in 1787. The responsibility for creating the machinery for collecting taxes was given to the Treasury Department (where it has remained ever since), under the supervision of the assistant to the secretary of the Treasury. In 1792 that position was replaced with the Office of the Commissioner of Revenue.

By 1817 the issue of taxes was abandoned because the government's revenue needs were met by customs duties (taxes on imports). The outbreak of the Civil War 45 years later and the government's need for massive financing led to President Lincoln's signing the Revenue Act of July 1, 1862, establishing the nation's first real income tax and re-establishing the Office of the Commissioner of Internal Revenue via a legislative act in which the commissioner was to be nominated by the president and approved by the Senate. The IRS was officially born.

Shortly after the war ended, Lincoln's wartime revenue system began to be dismantled and, as before, the government's fiscal needs were met by customs receipts collected on imported goods and taxes on alcohol and tobacco. With nearly 90 percent of internal revenue coming from these sources, by 1872 the income tax was again repealed until 1913 with the enactment of the Sixteenth Amendment to the U.S. Constitution. (See page 22.)

The table opposite charts tax revenues in key years, starting with the first year tax was collected on a formal basis and continuing until the present time. This two-century span shows a great deal more than numbers on a page. Stretches of stability and the depths of a country's economic depression are reflected here. So, too, are the strife and nationalistic fervor of war years, the growing pangs of a new nation, and periodic transitions as the United States moved from an agriculture-based economy to an industrial one. When the government's need for more income suddenly escalated, usually as a result of a war, taxes on products and/or income were imposed. Probably most impressive are the enormous sums the IRS has collected during our lifetimes.

How Taxes Are Raised Without Taxpayers' Noticing

Tax Bracket Creep

Congress, together with the IRS, continues to introduce new taxation policies to keep up with changing times.

One phenomenon that increases taxes without a change in tax law is known as tax bracket creep.

Fiscal Year	Gross Revenue Collected
1792	$208,943
1814	$3,882,482
1863	$41,003,192
1866	$310,120,448
1900	$295,316,108
1917	$809,393,640
1918	$3,698,955,821
1932	$1,557,729,043
1941	$7,370,108,378
1944	$40,121,760,232
1965	$114,434,633,721
1970	$195,722,096,497
1980	$519,375,273,361
1990	$1,056,365,652,000
1995	$1,390,048,000,000
1998	$1,769,408,739,000
1999	$1,917,642,000,000

Source: Shelley L. Davis, *IRA Historical Fact Book: A Chronology, 1646–1992* (Washington, D.C.: U.S. Government Printing Office, 1992), Appendix 3, pp. 245–47. The figures from 1992 on are from the *IRS 1992 Annual Report*, p. 25; advance drafts of the *IRS Data Book* from 1993 to 1998, Table 1; and preliminary 1999 IRS data.

Until 1986, there were 15 tax brackets into which taxpayers could fall on the basis of taxable income. The lowest bracket started at $2,390 and the highest was $85,130 and over. Each year, owing to inflation, our taxable income typically increases. This increase eventually puts us into a new, higher tax bracket, forcing us to pay higher taxes. Voilà! This takes place without any change whatsoever in the tax law. Although currently there are only five tax brackets instead of 15, the principles of bracket creep remain the same.

Softening the blow of tax bracket creep are cost-of-living increases in the bracket ranges, designed to prevent you from creeping upward into the next-higher bracket. For example, a married man with taxable income of $40,000 was in the 15 percent tax bracket in 1999. His taxable income increased to $43,500 in 2000, but he remained in the 15 percent bracket because the top of the 15 percent range was raised from $43,050 in 1999 to $43,850 in 2000.

But Congress has been selective, perhaps even manipulative, in other areas where taxpayers can use some relief. For example: The limit on 401(k) contributions was stuck at $9,500 for three years, reaching

$10,000 only in 1998. Anyone taking a deduction for entertainment and meal expenses needed to produce a written receipt when the expense reached $25. It took Congress about 35 years to increase that threshold to $75. As for IRA's, you and your working (or nonworking) spouse can generally contribute up to $2,000 each, annually. If the $2,000 were indexed for inflation (i.e., adjusted to reflect increases in the cost of living), the maximum contribution would have been raised to $3,500 years ago, giving taxpayers who want to save more money in a tax-deferred investment a much-needed break. (See 1997 Tax Legislation, pages 283–284.)

Isolated Ploys Raise Taxes

Congress and the IRS frequently create new ways of raising funds that actually go *unnoticed* by the taxpaying public. Here is an example. When the Bush administration extended unemployment benefits—a laudable measure—where was the money, about $2 billion, supposed to come from? From pension fund distributions. Beginning on January 1, 1993, anyone taking a lump-sum distribution from his or her corporate pension is subject to a 20 percent withholding tax. Many people who leave companies before 59½ years of age prefer to take their corporate pension, on which taxes aren't paid, in a lump sum rather than keep it with their company until they retire. By taking it this way they keep the money under their control—they determine the monthly payout, they're certain that they will receive it, and they don't have to worry about companies going bankrupt or investing their money unwisely.

Let's assume that your distribution entitled you to $100,000, which you took in 2000 (you actually held the check *payable to you* for the full or partial amount in your hands). Twenty percent, or $20,000, was withheld and you received only $80,000.

Now, the $100,000 had to be rolled over into *another tax-exempt qualified plan*, such as an IRA, within 60 days if you wanted to avoid paying tax. But since you did not have the $20,000 that was withheld, that shortfall is considered taxable income. **You may also be subject to a 10 percent early-withdrawal penalty.** (As most taxpayers know, the actual penalty amount is based on age restrictions. With a pension plan or a traditional IRA, a penalty is generally incurred if you withdraw money before the age of 59½. Anytime after age 59½, you may start drawing out your pension dollars without penalty. (See page 286 and Misconception 7, pages 219–220.)

How many taxpayers do you suppose know that this 20 percent tinkering around was earmarked to fund the unemployment extension? How many also realize that all Congress did in this case was create an illusion that it was paying for unemployment benefits without increasing the deficit? In fact, the $2.1 billion expected for 1993 never fully materialized. It all boiled down to an accounting gimmick that simultaneously produced several loopholes for avoiding the tax altogether.[1]

Alternative Minimum Tax (AMT) Snares the Unwary

The alternative minimum tax was designed in the late 1970's as a leveling device to ensure that everyone, especially upper-income people, ends up paying some tax no matter how savvy they may be in reducing their income through such devices as tax shelters and itemized deductions. In other words, the government wants your money no matter what—even if you are able to reduce your taxable income to zero. But here's the problem. The AMT has only two tax brackets: the first for those whose AMT income (taxable income plus add-ons) is $175,000 or less, and the second for those with AMT income above $175,000. Furthermore, to make sure the government doesn't leave anyone out, when filling out the AMT Form 6251 (Alternative Minimum Tax—Individuals), you are required to add back to your taxable income certain "adjustments and preferences." These include many items listed on Schedule A (Itemized Deductions), such as some medical and dental expenses, miscellaneous deductions and all taxes, plus personal exemptions. Taxpayers must then compute their taxes using both the regular IRS tax table and the AMT rates, and pay the higher of the two. (See pages 216 and 262–263.)

According to the IRS, 828,000 individual returns were hit by the AMT for 1998, up 40 percent from 1997, representing $4.43 billion. By 2010, the AMT is expected to snare up to 17 million unsuspecting middle-class taxpayers, a group never intended to be caught up in this trap.[2] These taxpayers are guilty of nothing more than having high deductions for such routine items as state income tax and unreimbursed business expenses, or simply because they have large families.

Support for reforming this dinosaur is coming from many sources. Some of the suggestions put forth are to create AMT tax bracket ranges that are indexed for inflation, thereby reflecting cost-of-living increases over the years since the AMT was initiated, and to reduce the number of adjustments and preferences. In any case, you'll want to watch out for this one.

Phasing Out Itemized Deductions and Personal Exemptions

Itemized deductions, listed on Schedule A, Form 1040, are a group of expenditures you are entitled to deduct from your adjusted gross income that reduce your taxable income. Some examples are home mortgage interest, real estate taxes, state and local taxes, and charitable contributions.

An exemption is not an expenditure but an amount of your income not subject to taxation at all—for example, a certain amount of income for each dependent. The effect of exemptions is also to reduce taxable income.

Beginning January 1, 1991, and continuing through today, in a nifty way to pick taxpayers' pockets that generally slips by unnoticed, itemized deductions can be phased out. (Excluded are medical expenses, investment interest, and casualty and theft losses, which each have their own unique limitations.)

It begins with your Adjusted Gross Income (AGI), which is a collection of all income items less a small number of adjustments to income, such as the deductions for self-employed pension deductions (Keogh plans) and alimony. AGI is typically the last line of page 1 of Form 1040 (U.S. Individual Income Tax Return).

If your AGI is more than $128,950 (married, filing jointly, or single), the IRS can disallow, or increase your taxable income by, as much as 80 percent of your total itemized deductions, at the worst leaving you just 20 percent. Working in real numbers, things might look like this. For the year 2000, Jay and Sharon Jennings have these itemized deductions:

Real estate and state income taxes	$15,000
Contributions to charities	2,000
Mortgage interest on their home	15,000
Total	$32,000

If their combined AGI for 2000 is $178,950, it means that $1,500 of their deductions is lost ($178,950 − $128,950 × .03), leaving net deductions on Schedule A of $30,500.

If they had a combined AGI of $278,950 and the same starting deductions, then they would lose $4,500 of their deductions ($278,950 − $128,950 × .03), leaving net deductions on Schedule A of $27,500.

In short, the more you earn, the more you lose in itemized deductions. Where does the money from this loss on itemized deductions go? It goes out of the taxpayers' pockets into the government's hands. In 1998, 4.8 million taxpayers were unable to deduct $25 billion, an increase of 14 percent in 1 year. What better way to disguise a tax increase!

At the same time as the phaseouts for itemized deductions were initiated, a new barrage of phaseouts involving personal exemptions was introduced.

A personal exemption is a deduction, determined annually by law, that reduces your taxable income. Personal exemptions are taken on Form 1040 and usually include the taxpayer, the taxpayer's spouse, and anyone else who meets the *Internal Revenue Code* dependency and support requirements. These phaseouts start at $193,400 for married couples filing jointly and $128,950 for singles. When the AGI exceeds the threshold level, the taxpayer loses 2 percent of the total exemption amount for every $2,500 or fraction thereof for AGI that exceeds the threshold.

Thus, for example, when your AGI reaches $125,000 more than your AGI threshold of $193,400 (or $128,950), you lose 100 percent of your personal exemptions.

Mathematically it works like this: $125,000 \div $2,500 = 50. Then 50×2 percent = 100 percent of lost exemptions. This is clearly a three-Excedrin explanation, so let's look at it again.

Carl and Judy Jimson file jointly and their AGI for 2000 is $255,900. They have three children and claim five exemptions, each one worth $2,800. Subtracting the $193,400 threshold from the $255,900 leaves $62,500. Dividing $62,500 by $2,500 equals 25. Multiplying 25 by 2 percent gives a 50 percent loss of exemptions. Because of the phaseout, the Jimsons' deduction for their five exemptions will be slashed in half—from $14,000 to $7,000.

But wait. It could be worse. Suppose the Jimsons had $5 more added on to their AGI. Under the phaseouts, they would lose another 2 percent of their total exemptions, or an extra $280 in deductions down the drain. The temporary phaseouts of both personal exemptions and itemized deductions were made a permanent part of our tax law with RRA '93.

Despite the current IRS reorganization, and its emphasis on customer service, taxation policy will continue to get more intricate, more sly, and more creative as it subtly reduces the income it lets you keep.

THE EVENT: Income Tax Becomes a Favorite Child
THE PERSONALITY: As stubborn, tenacious, and unmoving as the government's right to levy and collect taxes. Also highly effective. You'll find it shifty, unfair, and subject to changing times. But be aware that it can be flexible and workable as well.

Significance to Taxpayers

The Sixteenth Amendment, which was passed on February 3, 1913, states:

> The Congress shall have the power to lay and collect taxes on incomes, from whatever source derived, without apportionment among the several states, and without regard to any census or enumeration.

This amendment made it legal for Congress to impose a direct tax on the net incomes of both individuals and corporations, overruling an 1895 Supreme Court ruling that asserted that the income tax was unconstitutional because it was a direct tax rather than one apportioned among the states on the basis of population.

The right of Congress to levy an income tax, and the right of the IRS, as part of the U.S. Treasury Department, to collect taxes, periodically comes under fire from people who believe, mistakenly, that these functions are illegal or who fall prey to tax evasion schemes.

Do not be fooled by the latest: a variety of "tax kits," many available on the Internet, costing anywhere from $900 to $2,000, that promote the bogus philosophy that individuals are not part of the United States or aren't taxpayers, as defined by the federal tax code, but sovereign entities.[3] A sovereign entity is someone who exercises supreme authority within a limited sphere. Have no doubt, no matter how many dependents these kits recommend you take (often up to 98), or how many W-4 forms (Withholding Exemption Certificate), W-8 forms (Certificate of Foreign Status), "Affidavits of Citizenship and Domicile," or "Affidavits of Claims for Exemption and Exclusion from Gross Income of Remuneration, Wages, and Withholding" they include, any sucker who tries will eventually discover that the IRS is much more sovereign than you or I. A U.S. citizen is subject to U.S. law, and that includes paying taxes.

Following its passage, the income tax very quickly became the favorite of the federal government, producing more revenue than anyone could ever have thought possible, surpassing all other sources of revenue.

Despite its past and current inequalities, the goal of the income tax is to establish a close connection between a person's income and his or her ability to pay taxes. In theory, a progressive income tax aims to ensure that those with a greater income pay more taxes than those who earn less. In reality, things don't work that way. The rich hire the best tax lawyers and accountants, which works to shift the taxpaying burden downward. Since the poor have little ability to pay any taxes at all, the tax burden tends to fall on the middle class, thus undermining the theory.

As Americans, we are allowed to express opinions about the income tax. Once we express them, however, the numbers speak for themselves. Twenty years ago, out of a total of over $519 billion in federal revenues collected (gross dollars), 55.4 percent, or over $287 billion, came from individual income taxes.[4] By 1990, that figure rose to almost $540 billion, and in 1998 it was $928 billion.[5] Income tax dollars continue to represent 50 percent or more of federal revenues collected—the largest piece of the pie.

But don't give up completely on finding a way to use the income tax to your advantage. Because income tax continues to be a function of who you are and how you earn your money, there is room within its bounds to determine how you report that income.

In 1997 (the latest calendar year for which the following figures are available), the Spring 1998 IRS *Statistics of Income Bulletin* reported that out of approximately 120.7 million individual tax returns, 103 million indicated salaries or wages earned. Taxpayers in this group are typically more limited in how they report income than the 16.5 million who filed as sole proprietorships and the 1.8 million who filed as partnerships during the same year. (Choices regarding income tax reporting for straight wage earners do exist, and will be discussed further on.)

The basis of our system of taxation lies in something the IRS likes to call compliance. I'd like you to view compliance as having two components: **Part of compliance relies on the honor system and the other part relies on knowing how to report what you earn so that your return goes unnoticed by the IRS.** Accomplishing this goal will render your return audit-proof, and that's the goal you want to achieve. You'll learn how as you read on.

THE EVENT: Rise of Lobbying and Special Interest Groups
THE PERSONALITY: Highly focused, egotistical, frenzied, calculating, and determined to the point of being obnoxious. Can also be vociferous, well connected, and generally very organized.

Significance to Taxpayers

Politics and tax-making policy were intricately and inseparably intertwined when reviving the income tax became a cause célèbre at the turn of the century. Immediately after the income tax law became official in 1913, affecting both individuals and corporations, the IRS scurried to organize a Personal Income Tax Division and create a structure to handle the instant rush of telephone calls and correspondence.

Simultaneously, virtually every business trade association set up a tax committee or hired a full-time person to keep abreast of tax changes.[6]

So what was intended to be a discreet, rather insular process performed by the House and Senate was gradually transformed into a kind of free-for-all through which politicians, political parties, businesses, and private interest groups exerted their own brand of influence.

Once begun, these influences quickly became so widely accepted as part of tax-making policy that whenever a tax bill was in the process of becoming a law, widespread lobbying efforts were a given. Though they probably don't realize it, millions of taxpayers are affected.

Although one likes to believe that there are some principles left in the tax-making process, there is no doubt that organized interests are at the origin of most tax provisions. There is some pluralism here, some interest group bargaining there, some special versus general interest over here, some politics of principle over there, some sacred cow pleading its cause to attentive ears in that corner, some politics of indignation in another one, some strange bedfellows over there, someone tuning his political antenna over here, and so on.[7]

Today it is the norm for Congress to be consistently bombarded with hordes of lobbyists representing individuals, corporations, foreign governments, and trade associations representing diverse industries (agriculture, oil, banking, real estate, dairy), all demonstrating why tax laws should be structured to accommodate their special needs.

Although this might sound like a more modern, democratic way of having the American people influence the voting, unfortunately it usually isn't. What happens is that the groups with the greatest financial resources, who are well connected, have greater access to the media, and are savvy in the communications process, are the more powerful, and they win out over the rest. The end result doesn't usually benefit most taxpayers.

THE EVENT: Tax-Making Policy Permanently Changed
THE PERSONALITY: Capricious and easily swayed, leading to favoritism and inequities. Grows increasingly more complex each year but offers substantial rewards to those who can decipher and manipulate the ins and outs.

Significance to Taxpayers
The Constitution states that a tax or revenue bill must be introduced in the House of Representatives. In making this determination, our Founding Fathers created a direct link between the creation of tax laws and

the American people who directly elect members of the House. The actual step-by-step process was a clear-cut, sound model. But the rise of interest groups, which created a new set of linkages between government and its citizens, altered that model by opening up and actually distorting the process. As concessions or exceptions became introduced into our tax law because of pressure from special interest groups, innocent taxpayers got caught in the cross fire. Now we are forced to reckon with three types of tax traps:

- Tax laws that favor one segment of the population over another.
- An increase in the complexity of our tax laws.
- A rapidly expanding number of loopholes for avoiding or manipulating tax laws.

Each of these has a tremendous impact on taxpayers and their pocketbooks.

Tax Laws Play Favorites
A tax shelter is a way to protect your money from being touched by the IRS. (The politically correct phrase for this is "reducing your tax liability.") Essentially the tax shelter generates tax benefits in the form of investment tax credits, depreciation, and business losses, which allow taxpayers to save more in taxes than they had invested in the shelter. A person investing in a tax shelter is called a *passive investor*, with no say in the management of the actual operation of the investment; the investments are known as *passive investments*; and losses are referred to as *passive losses*.

But the term *tax shelter* has become a dirty word, because thousands of people use them not as legitimate investments but as a device to reduce their taxes, in that they offered substantial write-offs or deductions. Through the 1970's and into the '80's, these forms of abusive tax shelters grew geometrically, from $5 billion to $10 billion to $25 billion in write-offs.

Eventually the IRS was successful in pressuring Congress to outlaw most tax shelters (passive investments) through tax legislation—with one exception: **Taxpayers could continue to direct their money into tax shelters involving oil and gas investments.**

Who or what was behind this exception? A well-organized, well-connected, and especially strong oil and gas lobby.

Although some sound reasons for allowing the exception were put forth—such as, if people stopped investing in this field, it would drastically reduce oil and gas exploration—the bottom line was indisputable: The two groups that made out well were the IRS, and oil and gas interests.

One of the largest groups to take advantage of tax shelters over the years was the real estate industry. But by the late 1980's, and through tax legislation, if a taxpayer was a participant or owner in an active business, losses were legitimately allowed, *except in the field of real estate.* No investments in real estate that threw off losses could be used to offset other income by passive investors, or even owners or others who were *legitimately* in the real estate business. (This does look like a clear-cut case of the IRS getting even.)

But the real estate lobby fought hard, eventually gaining an amendment to this tax law before its effective date that allows active owners in the real estate business to take the first $25,000 of operating losses as a deduction against other income if their Adjusted Gross Income is less than $100,000.*

Yes, this was a minor compromise, considering the thousands of people legitimately engaged in the real estate business who did not fit into the under-$100,000 category. But look at what happened to this group because of the Revenue Reconciliation Act of 1993 (RRA '93). Instead of giving the real estate advantage back to everyone, it gave the tax breaks back to the real estate professionals who should not have been excluded to begin with. Beginning in 1994, taxpayers engaged full-time in real estate activities (not passive investors but those who spend more than 750 hours per year in the activity) were once again able to use real estate losses to offset other sources of income, but passive, inactive investors are still excluded.

People are quickly learning that real estate is again a great investment. Why? You can often make a relatively small cash investment that may produce enough tax write-offs to keep your current income taxes at a minimum while providing a good opportunity for long-term capital gain at favorable income tax rates. Here's an example:

You purchase a multifamily residential unit for $1 million, put $100,000 down, and obtain a 9 percent, 15-year mortgage for $900,000, which calls for payment of interest only for the first five years (many other variations of mortgages are available if you look hard enough). Annual income and expenses are assumed to be:

*This advantage is phased out as AGI exceeds $100,000. When AGI reaches $150,000, the benefit disappears entirely.

Rental income		$160,000
Less:		
Mortgage interest	81,000	
Real estate tax	20,000	
Repairs and maintenance	26,000	
		127,000
Net income before depreciation		33,000
Depreciation (building cost—$890,000)		
(27.5 years write-off)		32,360
Net income		$640

This is a tax shelter in its simplest form. The income is sheltered from current income tax by the depreciation. If the property is sold five years later at a gain of $200,000, the first $161,800 of gain (depreciation taken) is subject to a 25 percent maximum capital gains tax. The balance of the gain, $38,200, will be subject to a maximum capital gains tax of 20 percent. The investor will have received an annual tax-free cash flow of $33,000, which means he recovers his down payment in just three years and pays tax at low capital gain rates when the property is sold.

IRS officials have already caught on to the recent proliferation of tax shelter arrangements being taken by corporations, and they're not pleased! Efforts to combat them have thus far been on an ad hoc basis. (See pages 258–259.)

YOUR TAX-SAVING STRATEGY.
If you are engaged almost full time in a non–real estate occupation, there are severe restrictions on the amount of real estate losses you can deduct. However, if your spouse, for example, obtains a real estate broker's license and actively works at it, she or he is considered to be a "real estate pro." This will generally entitle you to deduct your full real estate losses on your joint tax return.

Another group that benefits through favoritism is the very wealthy. They have money to spend, political connections, influence, and bargaining power. Working to reduce their share of the tax burden is part of their life.

Amway Corporation, the international sales giant, has worked hard to culti-vate friends in Washington.

In April 1997 Richard DeVos, the company's founder, and his wife wrote two $500,000 checks to the Republican party to help erase campaign debts. That came on top of donations from Amway and Mr. DeVos totaling $416,000 in the 1996 election—putting the company and its founder among the party's top donors.

Their reward? Senate Majority Leader Trent Lott (Republican of Mississippi) and House Speaker Newt Gingrich (Republican of Georgia) shepherded a last-minute addition to TRA '97—long sought by Amway—that eases the tax bite on Amway's two Asian affiliates under foreign tax rules. The provision allows Amway to avoid having these affiliates categorized as passive investment com-panies, which have more stringent tax rules for shareholders, and it will ease pressure on Amway to move manufacturing operations overseas.

Senator Lott contemplated raising the proposal when the Finance Committee first convened in June 1997 to consider the bill, but backed away. In the interim, Roger Mentz, a former GOP Treasury official who lobbies for Amway, was able to secure a letter from Don Lubick, the Treasury's acting assistant secretary for tax policy, that said the administration "would not oppose" the tax change. Mr. Mentz says that he asked Mr. Lubick for the letter at the urging of Mr. Gingrich's office, and he has said that the provision was inserted because "it is good policy, not be-cause of the company's political connections or campaign contributions." During the same interim, some research was done that showed that a handful of other firms would benefit from the provision as well but that those firms didn't apply the heat that motivated Senator Lott and Congressman Gingrich to action.[8]

The Amway provision stands out because it wasn't in either of the tax bills pro-duced by the House or the Senate. But it wasn't the only favored tax break in-corporated into the $95 billion tax-cut bill.

A host of key members of Congress, especially members of the two commit-tees responsible for tax legislation, the House Ways and Means Committee and the Senate Finance Committee, negotiated some 80 other narrowly written tax breaks. These included the following, along with their projected dollar cost to the American people over a period of five years: apple growers in the North-east received a reduction in the tax on draft cider from $1.07 per gallon to 22 cents (cost: $3 million); the Big Three Detroit automakers received an exemption from the 8 percent luxury tax on electric, low-pollution cars whose development costs raised the cars' price tag above $30,000 (cost: $2 million); Amtrak was granted a tax refund dating back to 70 years before it existed, by claiming losses accrued by the bankrupt private railroad companies that Amtrak replaced (cost: $2.3 billion); and county clerks in Mississippi (Lott's home state) were given the go-ahead to deduct business expenses not already deductible (cost: too small to calculate).

Tax Laws Become Increasingly Complex

Creating exceptions for special groups has resulted in a steady stream of new and revised tax laws, which have lengthened the *Internal Revenue Code* to over 4,500 pages and rendered it virtually unreadable. Often one section can run up to several hundred pages. A special tax service used by tax professionals (there are many), which explains the meaning and application of each part of the code, is contained in another 12 volumes!

The end result is an increasingly complex tax code that tries to please everyone but pleases no one. It is barely understandable to even the most experienced tax professionals. The harder Congress tries to simplify it, the more complex it becomes.

What does all this mean for you, the taxpayer? Preparing your tax return, delving into a tax law, if you need to, and strategizing how to keep more of your hard-earned dollars in your pocket become increasingly difficult with each passing year.

Even tax professionals with years of experience—trained and steeped in tax preparation—must religiously attend tax seminars and read myriad journals, magazines, and monthly tax tips, among other things, to correctly interpret the tax code and gain the advantage over the IRS.

Finding and Using Tax Loopholes: An Industry in Itself

Exemptions created in the tax-making process have led to the birth of an entire industry dedicated to searching out tax loopholes and using them to the searchers' advantage. **One of the most effective ways you can get the IRS before it gets you is to learn how to find and manipulate to your advantage loopholes in the tax law—before the IRS uses those same loopholes against you.**

Loopholes in the Lump-Sum Distribution Laws

Ten years ago, President Bush tried to pay for the extension of unemployment benefits by instituting a 20 percent withholding tax on lump-sum distributions from corporate pension plans, which is still in effect today. Let's take a few minutes to examine the loopholes you can make use of that were created as a result of that seemingly insignificant gesture.

One loophole lets you out of paying the 20 percent if you arrange to have your distribution transferred from the financial institution that currently has your pension money directly to another financial institution (such as your own IRA). This procedure, known as a trustee-to-trustee transfer, in which you do not touch the money in any way, absolves you of paying the withholding tax and dispenses with the 60-day rollover period and the required one-year waiting period between rollovers from one IRA into another. Just make sure to follow up and verify that the transfer agent or financial institution handling the transfer has actually transferred the money to an equivalent retirement account within 60 days. If transferred to a regular, *taxable* account in error, the IRS will consider this a taxable distribution plus penalties, with *no* exceptions allowed.

Here's a loophole within a loophole for a taxpayer who wants to keep the distribution but does not want any money to be withheld. If you want to take the distribution early in, say, 2000, and use the proceeds—*not* roll it over—you can be adequately covered by following these steps:

- First transfer the lump sum from your pension plan to your traditional IRA via the trustee-to-trustee transfer.
- After the transfer is complete, you can make a cash withdrawal from your traditional IRA, which will not be subject to a 20 percent withholding.

There are a few trade-offs: Although you have avoided withholding, you cannot avoid the fact that any proceeds you take from an IRA or retirement plan distribution are fully taxable, just like any other income. You are also subject to an additional 10 percent penalty if you take money out prematurely from a traditional IRA (before you reach the age of 59½). (See Misconception 7, pages 219–220.)

Let's examine this situation one step at a time.

In 2000 you are eligible to receive a $9,000 distribution from your employer's pension plan and you need $7,500 to buy a new car. You arrange to have the $9,000 transferred directly to your traditional IRA account. You then withdraw the $7,500 you need for the purchase of the car. (Note: You can transfer an unlimited amount of money into your traditional IRA from another qualified plan, such as a pension. This is not to be confused with the $2,000 limit on new IRA contributions.)

YOUR TAX-SAVING STRATEGY.

- Since the distribution was taken from your traditional IRA, there is no 20 percent withholding tax requirement.
- If you change your mind and decide not to buy the car, you have 60 days to put the money back into the IRA (to roll it over).
- In April 2001, you can withdraw the final $1,500 from your IRA and use it to help pay the extra income tax and the 10 percent penalty for the earlier withdrawal. You'll now be responsible for the income tax and penalty on the last $1,500 withdrawal, but this is a small amount and you should be able to handle it. You have a whole year to plan for it.

If you choose this ploy, you have gained an extra 12 months—from April 2000 to April 15, 2001—to utilize your money and to pay any possible additional tax caused by the inclusion of the pension distribution in your 2000 income.

If there is a balance due when you file your return, you *might* be charged a penalty. Even if no balance is due, you could still incur a penalty if you did not pay estimated taxes on the distribution taken in four equal installments. In other words, you cannot arbitrarily wait until you send in your return to pay a large balance due. The IRS wants the money throughout the year. **The bottom line is, you can take your distribution, but you must be aware of some of the pitfalls, which actually aren't that terrible.**

Of course, it is impossible to define and report on all the loopholes that occur in our tax laws, although many will be explored in this book. So my advice is: Be aggressive. Ask your tax professional to advise you of any loopholes you can take advantage of to make your burden easier. If you do not assert yourself, your tax pro could mistakenly conclude that you don't know loopholes exist, or that you are too conservative in your thinking to use them to your advantage.

If you don't have a tax professional (or even if you do), it's a good idea to contact a local CPA firm, one that issues a monthly or quarterly tax newsletter and perhaps even a year-end tax tips letter. Ask to be added to the firm's mailing list; usually you'll find a great deal of valuable tax help here. You don't have to feel as if you're using the information without giving something back. Most firms expect that one day you'll become a client, or that at the very least you will give them free publicity by circulating their newsletters and telling others what you have learned.

THE EVENT: The IRS as a Criminal Watchdog
THE PERSONALITY: Macho, showy, tough. Glib yet dangerous.

Significance to Taxpayers

In 1919 the commissioner of internal revenue was given official responsibility for investigating and enforcing infringements relating to the National Prohibition Enforcement Act, which rendered illegal literally any activity connected with intoxicating beverages: manufacturing, selling, buying, or transporting. To best get the job done, a group was created in the bureau that was first labeled the Intelligence Unit, then, in 1954, renamed the Intelligence Division, and ultimately, in 1978, renamed the Criminal Investigation Division (CID).

Back when the Intelligence Unit was created, it was the Roaring Twenties, a scene packed with notorious gangsters, mob violence, and organized crime. Just imagine it! The Office of the Commissioner of

Internal Revenue, established by our Founding Fathers as a revenue producer to meet federal needs, had grown into a full-fledged criminal investigation arm of the government characterized by tough guys, shootings, and its own private war against organized crime. The IRS's bad-guy image was born.

Very few would question the fact that investigating and bringing to light people who commit tax fraud or engage in criminal activities that affect our country's revenue is work that needs to be done. Furthermore, there is no doubt that the Criminal Investigation Division was and still is made up of dedicated people, some of whom lost their lives during those early Prohibition years.

But the contrast between what the agency set out to do and what it ended up doing shows us an agency that is certainly out of bounds, if not out of control.

This part of the IRS personality hits taxpayers hard. First there is the initial training IRS personnel receive, which brands taxpayers as criminals and cheats. This "us against them" philosophy, reported on by IRS personnel who work there today and by those who worked there over 20 years ago, allows the IRS to do its job with the requisite aggressive mind-set: If you're dealing each day with taxpayers labeled as lying, dishonest cheats, you need to be suspicious, unemotional, inflexible, ruthless, and determined.

THE EVENT: Tax Payment Act of 1943—Withholding and the W-2 Form
THE PERSONALITY: Efficient, slick, savvy, and extraordinarily dependable. It is also highly inflexible, unless you know the key.

Significance to Taxpayers
The next milestone to influence the personality of the IRS was the Tax Payment Act of 1943, which made the withholding of taxes from wages and salaries a permanent feature of our tax system. It also introduced the W-2 form (Wage and Tax Statement). Under this system, the employee files a W-4 form (Employee's Withholding Allowance Certificate) with his or her employer that indicates name, address, Social Security number, marital status, and the number of exemptions claimed. By law, the employer then withholds specified amounts from each employee's salary, correlated to an income rate scale, and periodically remits these amounts to the IRS. Annually, employers must also report to the Social Security Administration the total annual amount withheld on a W-2 form (Wage and Tax Statement) and provide their employees with this information. Taxpayers fulfill their reporting obligations by attaching the W-2 to their 1040 (U.S. Individual Income Tax Return) and mailing

both to the IRS, hopefully before April 15. This information reflects income for the preceding year.

People who are subject to withholding taxes work for a company or an organization and are paid a salary by that entity. According to the IRS Statistics of Income office, about 85 percent of those who mail in a 1040 form receive a salary from an employer. That's a lot of W-2's. (Taxpayers who work at more than one job receive multiple W-2's.)

Today, withholding continues to be lucrative for the IRS. In 1996, 35.9 percent of gross tax dollars collected by the IRS represented withholding by employers. The actual dollar amount collected was over $533 billion. For 1998 that figure was over $646 billion.[9]

The collection process flows relatively easily; money comes into the government's coffers automatically from over six million employers across the United States. With this device, the IRS learns exactly how much employees are paid and how much is withheld from their earned income for federal, state, and Social Security taxes. Getting employers to do the dirty work was not only smart, it was also a real plus because it makes the IRS look terribly efficient. With good reason, withholding has been called the backbone of the individual income tax.

The attitude of taxpayers toward withholding is predictable: You never see it; it is a chunk that is taken out of each paycheck; there is nothing one can do about it. Most employees just accept it and forget it.

With the W-4's information from the employee and the W-2's wage and salary information submitted directly from the employer, the IRS figured that the government couldn't lose. But loopholes in tax laws weakened that position, providing opportunities for taxpayers to rescue tax dollars in the area of withholding.

YOUR TAX-SAVING STRATEGY.
What happens if the company you worked for during the year went out of business and never prepared W-2 forms? Obtain Form 4852 (Substitute for Form W-2, Wage and Tax Statement) from the IRS, and by using your pay stubs and deposit slips, do the best job you can in stating your gross income and withheld taxes for the year. You can then attach Form 4852 to your tax return, which is acceptable by the IRS a majority of the time.

Loopholes in the Withholding Law and How to Benefit

There is one important loophole in the withholding law available to many taxpayers; unfortunately, many are not versed in how to manage it to their benefit.

An employee's paycheck reflects the amount of withholding taken out. However, if your deductions are high, and you know they will remain so—for example, you filed your 2000 tax return and will receive a ridiculously high refund—it makes sound tax sense to reduce the amount of your income withheld.

To accomplish this, you need to engage in a balancing act between your deductions and exemptions. If you know that your itemized deductions (deductions that are allowable on a 1040 form) are going to be high for a given year, you should submit a revised W-4 form to your employer. The revised form should indicate a higher number of exemptions than you would ordinarily be entitled to. More exemptions will reduce your withholding, which in turn will result in your taking home more money each payday.

If, when you file your W-4, it turns out to be overly optimistic (for example, you closed on your new house six months later than anticipated and therefore estimated your itemized deductions too high), you can recoup. Just submit a revised W-4 to your employer requesting larger withholding payments from your paychecks in the last few months of the year. The amount will be sent to the IRS with the fourth-quarter 941 form (Employer's Quarterly Federal Tax Return, the form used by companies to pay withholding) and will increase your "federal income tax withheld," box 2 on your W-2. The end result is that the W-2 system will record your withholding tax as being paid evenly throughout the year. In fact it wasn't, but you've made the system work for you.

(By the way, you do not want to overwithhold early in the year, because in effect you would be lending money to the IRS without collecting interest from them. This is a real no-no!)

How to Put More Money Back into Your Pocket
Throughout the Year

A first-time homeowner exemplifies what happens when it's time to use this loophole to put more money back into your pocket. For the most part, first-time homeowners, who have never before had very high deductions, suddenly have enormous deductions for mortgage interest and real estate taxes. All new homeowners who are wage earners (both partners in a couple) should revise their W-4's immediately by balancing their exemptions to reduce their withholdings.

When you use this approach you may end up owing a few dollars, but don't worry. No penalties are involved as long as your total payment for the current year (withholding and estimated taxes) comes to at least 100 percent of the total tax liability for the previous year, 90 percent of the current year's tax, or 106 percent if your prior year's AGI exceeds $150,000. Here's how this one works:

Amy and Charles Lynfield had a joint 1993 income of $80,000 per year, $50,000 for Amy and $30,000 for Charles, and lived with their one child in an apartment that they purchased in January for $80,000. The purchase was financed with a $70,000 mortgage.

I determined their deductions to be $5,600 interest (8 percent mortgage), $5,500 real estate taxes, $5,900 state income tax, and $3,000 in contributions—a total of $20,000. Before they bought the apartment, the Lynfields were taking three exemptions (the husband one, and the wife two). After revising both W-4's, Amy could take six exemptions, and Charles could take four, a total of 10. This change reduced Amy's withholding and put $37 more per week in her paycheck, an increase of $1,924 for the year. And Charles saw a paycheck increase of $1,092 for the year, or $21 more per week.

As a result of rising real estate prices, the apartment doubled in value after four years, to $160,000, so the couple decided to buy a house. The new house cost $150,000, with a mortgage of $100,000. Based on the new itemized deductions (see the chart below), the Lynfields legitimately increased the number of their exemptions from 10 to 12. Their deductions now equaled $23,600, and they gained two extra exemptions. Since they bought their first home, the added exemptions provided Amy with $44 per week, or an extra $2,288 for the year, and Charles with an increase to $28 a week, or another $1,456 per year.

	Apartment	House
Mortagage interest	$5,600	$8,000
Real estate tax	5,500	6,700
State taxes	5,900	5,900
Contributions	3,000	3,000
	$20,000	$23,600

Total increase in itemized deductions: $3,600

Computing the formula to fit individual needs should be performed on the worksheet on the back of the W-4 form. This advises taxpayers how many exemptions they are entitled to on the basis of their dollar level of itemized deductions. Additional help can be found in IRS Publication 919, *Is My Withholding Correct?*, and in a new interactive W-4 calculator available on the IRS website in the "Tax Info for You" section at www.irs.gov.

How to Use the Withholding Loophole
If You Pay Estimated Taxes
Estimated taxes are paid by self-employed taxpayers who don't receive a W-2 and therefore can't use withholding to control their tax payments.

Estimated taxes must also be paid by taxpayers who earn the majority of their money from W-2's but also receive extra income *not* covered by withholding. This includes a mélange of miscellaneous money earned on anything from interest and dividend income to serving as a member of a board of directors to prize and award money to royalties or gambling winnings. In cases such as these, and there are many more, if federal tax amounts to more than $1,000 a year, quarterly estimated taxes must be filed to avoid penalties.

Estimated payments are made by people who fall into this category for two reasons:

1. So you're not stuck with an unusually large amount of taxes to pay all at once with your return.
2. To avoid penalties for failure to pay at least 100 percent of the previous year's total tax liability, 106 percent if your prior year's AGI exceeds $150,000.

Determining the correct amount of estimated tax and working through whatever overruns or underruns result at year-end is a complex process. This is because anyone who uses the estimated tax method must generally calculate and pay the amounts in four equal installments to avoid penalties. However, this is only a general statement, a ground rule. In practice, often a taxpayer's itemized deductions and income will, like the Lynfields', vary during the year. When this occurs, although the required amount of estimated taxes will also vary, the taxpayers must still try to pay the four installments in equal amounts.

To do this successfully, you must determine how many changes in itemized deductions or income reductions affect your total estimated tax for the entire year. Then you simply reduce the second, or third, or fourth, or any combination of estimates, to achieve the same goal—to avoid overpaying income taxes. Regarding estimated taxes and filing an extension, if you miss the deadline (April 15), you may not have a clue as to the amount due with this first-quarter current year estimate. So, you can intentionally overpay the amount you mail in with your extension. When you ultimately file the prior year's return, you can apply the overpayment (if any) to the following year and you may completely eliminate penalties for failure to pay the estimated taxes in a timely manner. In effect, last year's overpayment becomes your required first and possibly second and third payments for the current year.

What if you forget to mail in the second or third estimated installment? Do not wait until the next installment is due to make up the shortfall. Unlike most IRS penalties, which are computed in 30-day cycles, interest on estimated tax shortfalls is computed on a weekly basis. For example, if you should have paid $10,000 on September 15, but you do not send in the check until September 22, at 10 percent annual interest the charge will be around $2. My opinion is that there is even a two- or three-day informal grace period before any interest at all is charged.

This is an area best handled by a tax pro. The worksheet contained in the Form 1040-ES (Estimated Tax for Individuals) booklet also provides assistance.

YOUR TAX-SAVING STRATEGY.
When applying part of this year's refund to next year's estimated taxes, try not to overestimate. If you are having a bad year and need the money from your applied estimates back quickly, you will have to wait until you file your next year's return.

How to Use the Withholding Loophole If You Earn W-2 Income and Have Extra Income

A client of mine filing as single who earned an annual salary of $64,000 recently inherited $150,000, which produced $9,000 a year in interest. To cover the extra tax liability of $2,500 on the interest income, I instructed my client to prepare and submit to her employer a revised W-4 that reduced her exemptions from three to zero. The result produced an additional $2,500 being withheld from her paycheck. Simply by increasing her withholding, she extinguished the possibility of incurring a new tax burden on April 15, avoided any underpayment penalties, and eliminated any nasty surprises—at least in this area—that the IRS could hit her with at tax time.

How to Manage Withholding If You're an Employer
The concept of managing withholding also applies to small, closely held businesses that can massage withholding laws to their benefit. Here's how.

Small business owners often wait until the end of the year to take a bonus, since up until that point they're not certain about how much profit they'll have. As a small business owner, you can rely on your accountant to come in toward the end of the business year to determine your profit, which will in turn dictate your bonus.

True, this is manipulation of the withholding law because this same owner/taxpayer may have been taking loans from the business throughout the year in lieu of salary and paying no withholding to the IRS. (The payments are considered loans, not salary.)

If you continue to take these loans in the place of salary, the IRS will interpret this as a mechanism to avoid paying taxes. On an audit the IRS can easily see through this. However, during the year you *can* treat the money as a loan. When you, the owner/taxpayer, know the amount of salary you can take as a bonus at the end of the year, you convert the loans into "salary"—and "salary" is how it will be reported on your books. This technique is allowable as long as it is temporary.

One cannot continue to operate this way on a permanent basis, because in practice loans must be validated by having fully executed corporate minutes, and promissory notes that have stated maturity dates and bear federal statutory rates of interest. But the loan-to-salary conversion process is perfectly acceptable if performed within a time frame of one year.

In fact, the IRS does not normally question why withholding was or wasn't paid out during the year. To be sure, employers are required to report to the IRS any W-4's indicating more than 10 withholding allowances and when any employee claims that he is exempt from withholding on wages that exceed $200 per week. The IRS always has the right to request W-4's. But the fact is, they don't.

This brief withholding exposé can offer some real, albeit temporary, benefits to taxpayers. For example, if you can increase your monthly take-home pay by as little as $300 a month, you can afford to move up to a larger apartment, or pay the interest on an equity loan that you use to buy a new, medium-priced car, or add a room to your home.

If you choose to use this device, you must find out how quickly your employer can process the necessary paperwork. When you fill out the W-4 form and indicate the amended number of exemptions, it should be recorded on a company's payroll system almost immediately, but some organizations don't work quite that fast. Obviously the element of timing is key if everything is to run smoothly.

Earned Income Credit

The Earned Income Credit (EIC) is a refundable credit for low-income working families. To qualify, a taxpayer must

- Have a job.
- Earn less than $26,473 if there is one qualifying child (essentially the child must live with you for more than six months of the year in a U.S. home).
- Earn less than $30,095 if there are two or more qualifying children.
- Earn less than $10,030 if there are no children, with an adjusted gross income of less than $10,030, and you or your spouse must be between 25 and 64 years old.

The best thing about the EIC is that it's the only credit the IRS makes available even if a taxpayer doesn't pay any tax. Moreover, *if taxpayers have zero taxable income, they are still eligible to receive part or all of the EIC credit, which is granted as a refund.* The requirements for the EIC credit are not affected by itemized deductions.

The EIC has had an interesting history: In 1991 the IRS sent out refunds on the basis of its assumption that some categories of low-income families were entitled to the EIC even though they had not filed a claim for it. In fact, a majority of these taxpayers did not even qualify. This error allowed 270,000 nonqualified filers to get the EIC credit, and it cost the government $175 million in erroneous refunds, an average of $650 per return.

The following year the IRS reached out to more than 300,000 taxpayers, notifying them that they had not taken the EIC, and suggested that they review their returns to include it.

Then the IRS had a change of heart. A study of returns filed between January and April 1995 showed that approximately $4.4 billion or 25.8 percent of total EIC claims were in error. EIC noncompliance is at unacceptably high levels, with over one fourth of the amount paid out going to taxpayers who are not eligible to receive benefits, says the IRS. Based on this, the IRS is supposed to be developing new profiles of potentially erroneous EIC claimants to select for pre-refund audits. During the 1998 filing season, the agency said it would earmark substantial resources for this intensified compliance effort.[10]

Most CPAs know that poor EIC compliance is the result of involved paperwork, confusing definitions, and the fact that EIC rules have been changed 10 times since 1976.

Still, the number of taxpayers who take the EIC continues to rise, from 14.8 million in 1994 to 19.8 million in 1998, which represents $23.2 billion in refunds issued since 1982.[11]

Tightening Restrictions on the Earned Income Credit

Starting with the 1996 passage of the Welfare Reform Act, anyone applying for the Earned Income Credit must use a taxpayer identification number (TIN), i.e., a Social Security number, on the return. If the applicant is married, the spouse's TIN must also be included. This requirement aims to deny the EIC to anyone not authorized to be employed in the United States.

Two other restrictions concern disqualified investment income (taxable and tax-exempt interest, dividends, net rent and royalties) and adjusted gross income. An individual is *not* eligible for the EIC if disqualified income exceeds a certain amount, and that threshold is

$2,350 in the year 2000. Further tightening comes from a new definition of disqualified income expanded to include capital gains (except investment income from sales of business assets) and passive income (e.g., tax shelters, rents). It would appear that a person receiving income from interest, dividends, capital gains, rent, and royalties is not one who fits the EIC profile.

In addition, certain losses that a taxpayer could once apply to lower his adjusted gross income to qualify for the EIC have been disallowed. Some of these include net capital losses, net losses from trusts and estates, and net nonbusiness rents and royalties. Lastly, three quarters of any net losses from Schedule C (Profit or Loss From Business) and Schedule F (Farm Income and Expense) are disallowed and added back to your adjusted gross income. But watch out. If you recklessly, intentionally, or fraudulently claim the EIC, you become ineligible to claim it again for a period of 2 to 10 years.

Clearly, Congress is tightening the reins on the money it had heretofore been almost happy to give away under the EIC.

What conclusions can the average taxpayer draw? Make sure you qualify before you apply, and fill out the Earned Income Credit form, Schedule EIC, very carefully.

THE EVENT: The IRS Meets Corruption Head-on
THE PERSONALITY: Ever-present and inescapable. From its darkest self, the IRS can be sneaky, defiant, and too smart for its own good. But eventually everyone learns what's going on.

Significance to Taxpayers

The Founding Fathers were quite savvy in recognizing the potential for corruption in the tax collection process. Section 39 of the *Public Statutes at Large* for March 3, 1791, lists penalties for crimes that duplicate almost down to the letter those indulged in periodically since the inception of the IRS by its employees, public officials, and businesspeople. Although many IRS publications downplay or eliminate these crimes altogether, scandal built to volcanic proportions during the early 1950s. Unfortunately, the IRS was ripe for corruption.

Since its inception, the IRS had grown geometrically. Existing tax rates went up, new taxes were added, and the force of employees required to keep up with the workload jumped from 4,000 to 58,000 between 1913 and 1951.[12] A low point in the history of American tax collection came in the post–World War II period, when collections soared by 700 percent as the number of taxpayers rose from 8 million to

52 million.[13] By the early 1950s, the IRS was plagued with deplorable processing operations and a corrupt patronage system stemming from the presidential appointment of all 64 collectors of internal revenue. The system became so inbred that favor after favor was passed up and down the line, and bribe taking, influence peddling, and widespread defrauding of the government through payoffs, extortion, and embezzlement of government funds were endemic. Settling a large tax bill of $636,000 with a payment of $4,500 was commonplace.[14] So was having a case worth $2 million in tax claims somehow mysteriously disappear, preventing the government from collecting on it.[15]

After a three-year housecleaning, initiated in 1949, hundreds were let go at all levels, resulting in a major reorganization of the bureau in 1952 as recommended by President Harry Truman and incorporated into legislation passed by Congress.

In an effort to reduce the possibility of misconduct and corruption exerted through political influence, all employees except the commissioner of internal revenue would henceforth be under the civil service.

The bureau became a strongly decentralized organization in which a district office and its local branch offices were set up as self-contained operating units. Here taxpayers filed their returns, paid their taxes or got their refunds, and discussed and hopefully settled their tax problems. In short, the district offices became the focus in the organization where the primary work of the service was carried out. (Years later much of this work was taken over by IRS service centers.)

This new arrangement successfully reduced the power of IRS personnel in Washington, but it left regional commissioners and district staff, from directors to auditors and collections people, with considerable discretion to wield their powers. The situation eventually produced a new slew of problems. Instead of corruption being removed from the top and eliminated completely, it resurfaced at a new level. "While the data appears [sic] to indicate an increasing effectiveness and control of the integrity problem," writes one historian of the IRS, "IRS officials are the first to admit that internal criminal activity has by no means been wiped out."[16]

Despite the vigilance of an internal inspection service independent of the rest of the bureau, the IRS is periodically consumed with corruption and scandals.

The task of keeping on top of the integrity problem in the IRS is compounded not only by the magnitude of its fiscal operations, but also by the fact that the daily work of employees consists of their making constant value judgments that can expose them to opportunities for graft.

There is no easy way for someone reviewing a revenue agent's work to determine whether a monetary favor from a taxpayer influenced the agent's determination on certain issues.

The IRS's Internal Security Program typically uncovers a steady stream of corruption: from 159 convictions in 1994, to 229 in 1997. For 1997, bribe payments received amounted to $144,930, and embezzlement theft funds recovered amounted to $938,384.[17] One wonders how many other cases were soft-pedaled or overlooked altogether.

THE EVENT: Information Gathering and the Matching Program
THE PERSONALITY: A technological whizbang that excels in some areas but fails in others. Shows unpredictable future potential because it is dependent on budget dollars and strong management skills.

Significance to Taxpayers

The final event to influence the personality of the IRS probably had its antecedents in that seemingly innocent W-2 form, a by-product of the withholding process, initiated in 1943.

The W-2 provided the IRS with a new source of information on how much money employers paid to employees. Comparing information submitted by the taxpayer with information reported by outside sources would put the IRS in a strong position to

1. Catch taxpayers who have underreported or failed to report an amount.
2. Catch nonfilers, taxpayers who have submitted no return.

The possibility of catching underreporters or nonfilers by matching information on individual tax returns to information received from a wide range of outside sources soon whetted the IRS's appetite for more of the same. Propelled by the information age and the introduction of new technologies, the IRS went full steam ahead to create a situation whereby increasing amounts of information must, by law, be reported to the IRS from an expanding range of sources for the sole purpose of verifying if taxpayers, and those who should be taxpayers, are playing by its rules (see also pages 102–107). For tax year 1998, employers, banks, mortgage companies, and other financial institutions filed over 1.1 billion information documents, or third-party reports, with the IRS.[18] Through the magic of IRS technology, these were matched to the 123 million individual income tax returns filed.

Through its document-matching program, for the last three years the IRS contacted an average of 3.4 million taxpayers per year because of underreporting of income or nonfiling. This generates an average of $2 billion per year in additional taxes and penalties.[19]

But not all of the IRS's technology efforts are aimed at matching items of income. Because computers are an increasingly visible part of IRS operations, a separate chapter explores the subject. In that chapter you will discover what very few will tell you about what the IRS *can* do and, much more important, what it *can't* do with its current technological capabilities.

NEVER FORGET!

Throughout this book I will be reiterating several themes. It is to your benefit to absorb these points until they become second nature:

- Don't be scared by the IRS image. Learn what's really behind it.
- You *can* become audit-proof. Managing and reporting income so that you reduce or eliminate your chances of being audited is a function of knowing certain tax information and techniques. These will be explained throughout this book.
- Our tax laws are enormously complex, with loopholes large and numerous enough so that taxpayers can understand and use them to their advantage.
- There are many reasons why the IRS may be unable to verify certain aspects of your income. It has operated and will continue to operate under budget and to be understaffed, disorganized, and mismanaged.
- Despite its technological successes, the IRS is still overburdened with paper and not technologically up to speed.

ACKNOWLEDGING DEDICATED IRS PERSONNEL

Many people working for the IRS are committed and hardworking and are concerned with doing their jobs properly, improving taxpayer service, and making the agency's operations more effective and responsive.

But no matter how much we may want to view the agency employees as nice guys, inevitably the IRS can be counted on to go so far off course in the process of collecting the ubiquitous tax bill that lives and families have been and continue to be severely disrupted, even destroyed, in the process.

Peeking behind the scenes of the IRS and describing what really goes on there is my attempt to tip the scales in the taxpayers' favor.

3

Who Runs the Show: What You're Up Against

THE IMAGE

How the IRS Gets You Where It Wants You
How much of the IRS's all-powerful and heartless reputation is truth and how much is fiction? The IRS's Public Affairs Department at the National Office and IRS public affairs officers at local levels work hard to establish good relationships with print and broadcast media. Even state tax departments get into the act. **It is no coincidence that a rash of articles publicizing IRS enforcement activities, investigations, and convictions typically begins to appear in January and February (to set the correct tone for the new year), and again in early April, before D Day for taxes.**

These cases tend to involve high-profile taxpayers: entertainment and sports figures like Willie Nelson, Pete Rose, and Darryl Strawberry; or attorneys, accountants, and political and religious figures like Lyndon LaRouche, Jr., and Jerry Falwell; and even John Gotti and Harry and Leona Helmsley, whose tax evasion charges hit newspapers just before April 15.

Then, as tax time approaches, in addition to the scare stories, the IRS becomes Mr. Nice Guy. "Trust us" is the message in Sunday tax supplements that appear in national newspapers during early March just as taxpayers are beginning to deal with the fact that tax season is upon them. These supplements usually contain valuable information about recent tax news, tax tips, and even human interest stories about how the people at the IRS are ready to help you.

Image creation is how chic Madison Avenue advertising firms make their money. But do taxpayers know that the IRS also secures the image it wants without incurring expensive advertising fees? How? By counting on taxpayers to spread the word, tell their friends, neighbors, and business associates how an ordinary audit over something as simple as a padded expense account was turned into a horror story by the machinations of the IRS. An expensive public relations firm couldn't do nearly as good a job of getting the message out as taxpayers themselves.

So, which will it be? The good, the bad, or the ugly? Only time will tell, now that the winds of change have arrived buoyed by several forces:

- Taxpayer testimony before the Senate Finance Committee from September 1997 to early 1998 of IRS abuses.
- The frustration and critical outpouring of key political leaders.
- Legislative recommendations by the National Committee on Restructuring the IRS.
- Charles O. Rossotti, cofounder of a management consulting firm specializing in information technology, handpicked as the current IRS commissioner to put the IRS's house in order—the first person to head the agency since World War II who is not a tax lawyer.

Together, these forces have led to the passage of the IRS Restructuring and Reform Act of 1998 (RRA '98), resulting in the most significant changes to the structure and operations of the IRS in the past 40 years. Anyone who comes in contact with the IRS, from professionals working in the field to taxpayers, will be directly affected by the ongoing changes.

Will the new legislation rock the very foundation of the IRS, as alleged? Will a new reorganized IRS ever be totally realized? And most important of all, will we be alive to see it?

To say that confusion and upheaval, mixed with a good dose of IRS resistance, abound is an understatement. Estimates are that the full payoff—better service, provided by a totally revamped IRS—may not come for 10 years.

Meanwhile taxpayers need to know what's going on inside the IRS *now*.

WHAT IT LOOKS LIKE FROM THE INSIDE OUT

The IRS cares a great deal about how it is perceived by its own employees. By contrast, how many taxpayers do you think ever give a thought to what IRS employees think of U.S. taxpayers? They don't see us as hardworking, compliant citizens who are trying to scrape together annual tax dollars from a salary that never seems to be enough. In fact, if IRS employees are to do their jobs correctly, they must see taxpayers as cheaters and themselves as getting the government its due. Changing this view to one that makes the IRS responsible for informing taxpayers about their rights and options regarding tax compliance is already part of the new IRS agenda.

To the IRS employee, the image of us, the taxpayers, as the bad guys and them as the tough but strong and righteous good guys served as a motivational tool that won't be easily altered.

A former attorney who worked for the IRS for over 10 years brazenly said to me, "During an audit we used to watch taxpayers squirm, and the more they squirmed and dug themselves into a deeper hole, the more we'd laugh at them later on."

THE ORGANIZATION

From its inception the IRS has operated under the U.S. Treasury Department. With over 97,530 employees during peak season and almost 85,000 the rest of the time, the IRS is the largest law-enforcement agency in the U.S. Taken together, the police departments in New York City, Los Angeles, Chicago, Detroit, and Philadelphia don't even come close to the number of those working for the IRS. The IRS has more employees than each of these major corporations: Xerox, 3M, Texaco, American Express, and Continental Airlines and TWA put together.

IRS headquarters, in its National Office in Washington, D.C., has about 7,900 administrators. From this base the organization reaches across the nation through its 4 regional and 33 district offices and 10 service centers. But that setup is beginning to shift as the new IRS organization is phased in, based on serving four distinct groups of taxpayers. (See page 317.)

The IRS also has nine foreign posts open to the U.S. taxpayers living and working abroad, plus an office each in Puerto Rico and Guam.

Regional offices execute broad nationwide plans and policies, tailor specific procedures to fit local needs, and evaluate the effectiveness of current programs. Each regional office also oversees a number of district offices and service centers.

Each district office, which is a self-contained unit that serves specific geographic areas, is responsible for four distinct operations: examination, collection, criminal investigation (tax fraud), and taxpayer services. District offices also manage two volunteer programs: Volunteer Income Tax Assistance, and Tax Counseling for the Elderly.

This three-tiered organizational setup has allowed IRS employees to wield extraordinary power in functions that dealt intimately with taxpayers.

Furthermore, the decentralization makes it almost impossible to understand the real parameters of specific jobs. Confusion is one of the strategies the IRS uses to keep taxpayers at a distance.

The service centers serve as the local data-processing arm of the IRS. These offices are where the bulk of the work associated with the IRS occurs. Service centers across the U.S. receive individual and business returns, process them (open, sort, record the data, check the arithmetic, credit accounts), match returns with third-party reports, mail out refunds, and communicate with taxpayers regarding their tax situation by fax, letter, and/or telephone. Because of the range of work they do, service centers have areas or divisions (depending on their size) devoted to examination, collection, and criminal investigation.

One of the largest service centers is the Brookhaven Service Center (BSC) located in Holtsville, New York, which processes tax returns for the five boroughs of New York City and nearby counties. Brookhaven employs about 5,200 people during peak filing season, April and May, and maintains a permanent workforce of about 2,700, including data transcribers, tax examiners, computer operators, technicians, and clerical workers. For the 1999 filing season, Brookhaven received and processed 7.9 million tax returns as of June 30.[1]

Additional technological support is provided by the IRS's National Computer Center in Martinsburg, West Virginia; a data center in Detroit, Michigan; and another in Memphis, Tennessee.

Where the Taxpayer Fits In

Taxpayer involvement begins and usually ends at the district level, where all of the four major IRS functions (examination, collection, criminal investigation, taxpayer services) are carried out. If you're going to stand your ground and deal with the IRS face-to-face, after becoming familiar with the IRS personality, the next skills you want to add to your repertoire are knowing where your district office is and learning about its main functions. Knowing what each function entails will give you a running start on when to call "Halt" if somebody gets out of line.

Martin S. Kaplan, CPA, and Naomi Weiss

What You Need to Know About the Examination Division

What They Say They Do

Currently, the Examination Division has 20,700 employees, of whom almost 13,200 are revenue agents and 2,000 are tax auditors. The size of the division peaked in the late 1980's with nearly 32,000 employees, a decline of 35 percent compared with today.

The number of revenue agents and tax auditors also declined, about 23 percent, from a peak of just under 20,000 in 1999 to 15,200 currently. Both of these declines reflect the shift of examination and other IRS staff to customer service areas in accordance with new tax laws passed in 1998, which emphasize taxpayer assistance. More than one fifth of IRS employees are currently being used to shore up this area, which leaves fewer people to do other work, such as examining returns and collecting tax due.

Until the new IRS reorganization falls into place, the actual responsibility and authority for examining specific returns remains in the hands of IRS employees in the district offices in each state.

DIF Scores

The majority of returns are selected for audit by a computer program that uses mathematical parameters to identify returns that are most likely to generate additional revenue. The method of scoring, called the Discriminate Information Function (DIF), is kept top secret by the IRS. No one outside the IRS and few insiders know how it really works.

We do know that every return filed receives a score in which a number of DIF points are assigned to key items included on or omitted from the return. The higher the DIF score, the greater the likelihood of an audit.

The DIF process that examines data from your tax returns is carried out at the Martinsburg Computing Center. Once selected, the "score cards" (cards representing tax returns whose scores fall into the audit range for one or more of the categories) are returned to the service center, where they are matched with the actual tax returns (hard copy). DIF selection represents the start of the audit selection process. (The actual step-by-step procedures of the audit selection process are discussed in chapter 7.) In the final analysis, currently only 1 to almost 1.3 percent of all individual tax returns filed, or about 1.5 million, are actually audited.

What's Behind the IRS Audit Strategy

Another very different type of audit is the Taxpayer Compliance Measurement Program (TCMP). Unlike the DIF system, TCMP chooses only about 50,000 returns for each audit year chosen. Although this is a comparatively small number for the IRS, the data collected is crucial. Here's why.

The TCMP has one major objective: to measure the effectiveness of the tax collection system by evaluating if taxpayers are voluntarily complying with the law. To make this kind of determination, detailed data must be developed on selected groups of taxpayers, on the basis of which norms of all kinds are established. That's what the TCMP audits accomplish. TCMP information is gathered directly from one-on-one sessions with taxpayers whose responses are then compared to established national or regional norms or averages. As a result, the TCMP effectively shows the IRS where people are cheating and telling the truth on their tax returns. It also tells where voluntary compliance is at its highest and lowest levels in terms of income groups and other categories.

Gathering raw data from taxpayers across the nation through the TCMP is a crucial device used by the IRS to update the DIF scores.

Although we know that DIF and TCMP data are highly confidential, we *can*, by comparing tax returns that have been audited, identify some of the items within the DIF database that can trigger IRS computers to raise an audit flag. They probably include

- Expenses that are inconsistently large when compared to income, e.g., if a taxpayer shows $25,000 of expenses and only $15,000 of income on the Schedule C (Profit or Loss from Business). Other triggers could include itemized deductions (interest, taxes, contributions) that are much higher than "average" returns with the same level of income.
- Required schedules or forms that are missing.
- Reporting installment property sales (sales in which the seller receives the proceeds over more than one year, and interest for the unpaid balance accrues to the seller) but failing to report related interest income.
- Reporting the sale of a stock but failing to report dividend income from that stock.
- Married couples filing separate returns that contain large itemized deductions, perhaps with one or more duplications.

A TCMP audit is an all-encompassing, excruciatingly long (at least four times longer than an office audit), intense examination of your tax return where every dollar and deduction must be documented.

Since the IRS's position on TCMP audits has changed repeatedly, it seems unlikely that too many taxpayers will receive an audit notice with the letters TCMP. If you do, go directly to a tax professional for guidance. In late 1995, Congress reduced the IRS's manpower budget for 1996, indefinitely postponing TCMP audits of 153,000 taxpayers. The General Accounting Office (GAO) the investigative arm of Congress, responded by suggesting a trimmed-down TCMP of 34,000 taxpayers, conducted over a number of years, rather than in one shot. But even this suggestion has been rejected by Congress. As of mid-2000, TCMP and its audits have not been resumed.

The IRS also uses supplemental systems to identify tax returns for audit. These systems address specific noncompliance areas such as tax shelters, tax protesters, returns containing deductions for unallowable items, and returns in which certain income amounts do not match with amounts reported by third parties.[2]

What's really behind the IRS audit strategy continues to fascinate. A new study conducted by the GAO reported that for 1992–1994, the examination of 1.1 million audits found that 59 percent of returns were selected as a result of the DIF formula. Furthermore, it was determined that the remaining returns were selected as a result of

- Referrals from other government agencies.
- Being prepared by a return preparer targeted as "questionable" by the IRS.
- A return identified by the IRS as "questionable."
- Criminal investigations and bankruptcy proceedings.[3]

In contrast, a nongovernmental agency, the Transactional Records Access Clearinghouse (TRAC) at Syracuse University (www.trac.syr.edu), sees things differently. TRAC agrees that the primary reason a return is chosen for a formal, face-to-face audit is a result of the DIF formula. However, they reported that data tapes from the IRS indicated that DIF is playing a diminishing role in the audit process. For example, in 1992 DIF was cited as the initiating factor in just under half the audits, about 46 percent of returns. Furthermore, in 1998, only a little more than one quarter of individual tax returns (29 percent) selected for audits at an IRS district office were triggered by DIF.

According to TRAC, the second reason a return might be selected is that in one way or another it was related to a second return that was already being audited. When the IRS finds a tax problem in a return filed by an individual in one year, it may go back and look at the returns that the same individual filed in previous years. Correspondingly, if the IRS identifies a problem in the tax return of one partner, it often examines the filing of the other partners.

The third-largest reason for an audit occurs when someone decides not to file any tax return at all. In 1996, this factor was cited as the trigger in 20.4 percent of the face-to-face audits. The next likely returns selected are those the IRS believes may present certain compliance problems, such as those taking the Earned Income Credit, or those in the underground economy who might, for example, be involved in a cash-intensive business.

To further improve the tax collection process, TRAC has reported that IRS administators from time to time conduct special audit studies of various categories of taxpayers. In 1992, there were 39,039 of these information-gathering audits, 5 percent of all audits undertaken by the IRS that year. By 1998, there were 70,380, almost 13 percent of the total. For 1998, it appeared as if the IRS were relying somewhat less on the DIF formula and somewhat more on these information-gathering projects, especially for individual tax returns.

An interesting contrast is what triggers the IRS to audit income tax returns filed by corporations. Tax shelters are by far the number one reason (63.8 percent), followed by having a return related to one already selected (22.5 percent). Then, in much lesser amounts, come a DIF-like formula and claims for refunds.[4]

With new legislation enacted July 22, 1998, specific laws are supposed to take the guesswork out of why a return is selected for audit. (See 1998 Tax Legislation, page 307.) To read about the IRS's return selection process, you can access the GAO website at www.gao.gov/reports.htm. You can also access TRAC at www.trac.syr.edu/tracirs/.

What IRS Auditors Really Do

If you receive official notice that you are to appear for a formal audit, you need to know that examinations or tax audits are conducted on one of three levels:

- Office
- Field
- Correspondence

Recent auditing initiatives include economic reality or financial status audits and the new Market Segment Specialization Program (see pages 57 and 174–178).

A nonbusiness audit is generally conducted as an *office audit* by a *tax auditor* in an IRS district office. In addition, some small-business audits are done as office audits, but generally these involve few complex accounting or tax issues.

Tax auditors are generally trained by the IRS and have no other special qualifications in tax law or accounting. As a result, they handle the less-complicated types of audits, which tend to be office audits.

Some tax auditors are pretty good at what they do. The nature of their work is highly repetitive, and the auditing routine is second nature to them. The items they audit are very specific, and often the same, whereas in a field audit, *any* line of income and expense is open for exploration.

After a while, tax auditors have seen and have asked questions about every possibility for the items they are continually auditing. The IRS recognizes that this process of assigning tax auditors to repeatedly audit the same issues increases the effectiveness of the audit process. To ensure that this remains the case, the IRS has devised a series of kits on different aspects of conducting a district office audit, which are presented in "Pro-Forma Audit Kits—Office Examination," in the *Internal Revenue Manual*—the IRS's "bible"—page 4231-11. Specific audit kits instruct the auditors on what to look for, what questions to ask, and how to proceed regarding the following examination items:

Miscellaneous
Taxes
Medical
Interest
Casualty Loss
Moving Expense
Contributions
Rental Income and Expenses
Employee Business Expense

Although the use of the pro-forma aids is mandatory for all office examinations, the *Internal Revenue Manual* does remind the auditors that the kits suggest the *minimum* amount of work to be completed and are *not* designed to include all possible audit procedures. Accordingly, the auditor is encouraged to use his or her judgment in deciding what extra steps should be taken in each case.

Now, while the repetitiveness of an office audit can make tax auditors more efficient, it can also make them unreasonably shortsighted by encouraging them to stick too closely to the rules while ignoring the bigger picture. Obviously, efficiency benefits the IRS, while shortsightedness benefits the taxpayer.

The *field audit*, or on-site examination, generally occurs at the tax-payer's place of business, where the books and records pertinent to the examination are kept. It involves the examination of individual, partnership, and corporate tax returns. Corporate or partnership returns are audited *only* in the field. In addition, some individual returns are field-audited, especially those thought to involve complex accounting or tax issues.

In my experience the *only* individuals who are field-audited are

- Self-employed people who fill out a Schedule C and have significant income. Even a corporate wage earner who earns between $100,000 and $200,000 is not as great an attraction to the IRS as a self-employed person who earns over $100,000.
- Those with multiple rental properties, especially properties that throw off net losses that can be deducted in full by taxpayers who are involved full-time in real estate.
- People who are self-employed in a service business (no product/inventory) can be assigned to *either* an office or a field audit. If a service business has a large gross income, over $100,000 annually, it will probably end up field-audited. However, sometimes the IRS makes mistakes in assignments and a case that should have been audited in the field may be assigned to an office audit or vice versa.

An often overlooked benefit to having an IRS agent conduct an audit at your office is that you have the psychological advantage. Although agents are used to going to all sorts of locations to dig into all sorts of returns, as the business owner you will feel more comfortable in your own territory. A request for an on-site examination is often granted by the IRS if it is too difficult to bring the books, records, and other materials needed for the audit to the IRS district office. Also, the IRS usually considers a field audit if a taxpayer has other valid circumstances, such as someone being a "one-man" operation or being physically handicapped, that necessitate conducting the audit on-site.

Field audits are typically conducted by a *revenue agent*, also referred to as a *field auditor*. These are the most experienced of all audit personnel. The revenue agent will usually have a minimum of 24 credits of college-level accounting courses, and will have received advanced audit training by the IRS.

With ongoing changes in our economy, the IRS continues to attract people to accept jobs as revenue agents who have college degrees in accounting *and* prior work experience in private industry. (See There's a Varied Audit Mix, page 83.) This has introduced an interesting phenomenon into the examination function; if you are assigned an agent with this background, be prepared for the worst. Whereas someone from the "younger set" may overlook an issue, even a substantial one, a revenue agent with previous corporate experience, familiar with special accounting nuances, probably will not.

I try to learn early on whether or not the person assigned to a case of mine has had prior corporate or public accounting experience. I no longer assume that these people are lifetime civil service employees.

Correspondence audits are conducted primarily through the mail between taxpayers and the Correspondence Audit section of their service center. Although not technically audits, these are an attempt to resolve certain issues, or complete areas of your tax return, simply by having you mail specific information or documents requested. This type of audit is a recent attempt by the IRS to allow taxpayers to bypass the bureaucracy.

Often a correspondence audit is generated through the Automated Correspondence Procedure, the most common one resulting from a mismatch between your W-2 or 1099 or on a third-party report with what appears on your tax return. For example, if a third-party report indicates you received interest income of $1,000 and that amount did not appear on your return, you will receive a CP-2000, Notice of Proposed Changes to Your Tax Return. The taxpayer's reply may clear up the situation, or a bill may be sent for the amount due. The CP-2000 letter, often referred to as a "matching letter," is *not* a bill. It is a request for information that, hopefully for the taxpayer, will resolve the mismatch. At this point, a taxpayer has the right to request an office audit, to be conducted at his or her local district office.

CP-2000 letters are used when a tax return cannot alone be used to make a determination of the tax due. CP-2000's are spit out by computers and sent to literally millions of taxpayers annually.

For the fiscal year 1997, 33 percent of all individual audits were done at the IRS district offices, 14 percent were conducted in the field—usually at a taxpayer's business or a tax professional's office—and 53 percent were done through correspondence audits at the service centers. What the statistics reveal is that since 1994 the IRS has placed a tremendous emphasis on having the service centers examine returns, a more judicious use of manpower and technology.

Here's what the dollar amounts show:

Tax Dollars Collected by Type of Audit of Individual Returns, 1998

- Office audits, conducted by tax auditors, averaged $3,372, a decrease of 2.5 percent "Per Tax Return" (previously stated as "Average Tax and Penalty Per Return," a reflection of the IRS deemphasizing quotas).

- Field audits, conducted by revenue agents, averaged $17,849 per tax return, a decrease of 7.7 percent.
- Correspondence audits generated on average additional monies of $2,760 per taxpayer, a decrease of 6.9 percent over last year.[5] (For an explanation of the decline, see pages 60 and 184–186.)

Total Dollars Recommended in Additional Taxes and Penalties

For audits that have been completed (individual, corporation, etc.), the IRS computes the total amount of additional taxes and penalties owed on the total number of returns audited. In 1997, that amount was almost $29 billion. In 1998, that figure dropped to $23 billion. However, preliminary 1998 IRS data traced only "Recommended Additional Tax," whereas previously "Recommended Additional Tax and Penalties" was also reported. So the $6 billion drop probably reflected the change in reporting. This figure may no longer be made available because of Commissioner Rossotti's intention to draw attention away from any resemblance of a quota system, which could involve the tallying up of penalties, liens, seizures, and more.

Most recently, financial status auditing and the Market Segment Specialization Program have been used by the IRS to increase auditing dollars from its favorite place, the underground economy.

Financial Status Auditing

Financial status auditing, formerly known as economic reality or cost-of-living audits, is a new name for an old technique.

Whereas the standard method of uncovering unreported income and other possible taxpayer irregularities focused on verifying information on the tax return, the IRS's financial status audits training modules emphasize investigating the "whole taxpayer." This approach is supposed to provide revenue agents and tax auditors with an economic profile that will help them to reach certain assumptions regarding what is reflected on the return versus the taxpayer's actual lifestyle. How a taxpayer spends money can be a better indication of income than the tax return itself.

The program allows agents to use aggressive interviewing techniques that could include such questions as: Do you own any large asset (over $10,000) besides autos and real estate? What is it and where is it kept? Is it paid for, and if not, what is the payment? Do you ever take cash advances from credit cards or lines of credit? How much and how often? What cash did you have on hand last year, personally or for business, not in a bank—at your home, safe-deposit box, hidden somewhere, etc.?

Whereas in the past these and similar questions might have been routinely asked in audits where fraud was suspected, many taxpayers have been facing barrages of this nature at the onset of an ordinary audit examination.

During an audit, if it soon appears that you're facing an inquisition with implications that fraud is suspected, this is what you should do:

For the best preventive medicine, read chapter 8, "How to Avoid an Audit Completely," so that you will be in the strongest position possible.

If you're already involved in an audit, and the auditor wants to interview you without an adviser, you can request a delay until you have a professional representative. My feeling is that if you are alone, stop the audit immediately and postpone it for as long as possible. This way, the caseloads will pile up and the IRS may be forced to cut back on imposing economic reality audits, at least for a while.

If the notification of the audit arrives with Form 4822 (Statement of Annual Estimated Personal and Family Expenses), which requires you to estimate all personal living expenses paid during the audited tax year (the total cost of food, housing, vacations, clothing, etc.), you are in a no-win situation. An overestimate of expenses will possibly increase your taxable income, while a low estimate could possibly be rejected by the examiner. It's hard to figure out why the IRS requests this information to begin with, unless it is to use against you at a later time. Anyway, can you really remember off the top of your head what your annual expenditures were—two or three years ago—for such items as groceries, clothing, and vacation? Probably not. *So, remember that you are not required to fill out the form, and your refusal cannot be used against you during an audit.* Consult with your representative. Be informed, however, that the tax examiner can search out additional data about you from external sources, such as social service agencies, motor vehicles databases, credit bureaus, trade associations, and court records. The examiner can also interview landlords, employers, and financial institutions. However, the IRS must notify you in advance if it intends to contact third parties for information about you.

Once you are working with a tax professional or attorney, you will need to proceed honestly. Ask your tax pro for a pre-audit evaluation to determine if a situation exists that might generate significant interest to an IRS tax examiner during an audit. Disclose as much as you can concerning what an examiner would be interested in. Consider your "global lifestyle," including your standard of living, overall yearly consumption versus costs, and method of accumulating wealth. What does your economic history look like? Do business profits or wages match your standard of living and wealth accumulation? Are your assets and liabilities consistent with your net worth? Also be prepared to answer questions about loans, large purchases (real estate, stock transactions, personal items), lender's source of funds, and possible cash hoards, gifts, or inheritances.

Ask your tax pro to request the IRS file on you, if this hasn't already been done, to assess the basis for the investigation and to send a message to the IRS that your tax pro intends to monitor the procedure.

During the audit, if the examiner asks financial status questions, your tax pro can challenge them by asking if there is any suspicion of unreported income.

Finally, remember that an examiner cannot conduct a civil examination as if it were a criminal fraud investigation. If indication of fraud is suspected, the audit must be suspended and a fraud referral report submitted through the ranks. The case then proceeds to the Criminal Investigation Division (CID).

Although the IRS claimed that financial status audits came into play in only about 20 percent of all audits, the outcry, not only from bruised taxpayers but particularly from the American Institute of Certified Public Accountants (AICPA), has had a positive effect.

Congress has determined that the financial status audit technique is unreasonable and overintrusive. Accordingly, the IRS is now prohibited from using financial status or economic reality examination techniques to determine the existence of unreported income of any taxpayer unless the IRS already has a reasonable indication that there is unreported income. This was made effective July 22, 1998.

Market Segment Specialization Program

Traditionally, revenue agents were trained to examine compliance problems within a particular geographic region, focusing on income ranges for individuals or asset ranges for corporations. Sometime in mid-1995, this technique became subservient to the Market Segment Specialization Program (MSSP), where the focus shifted to investigating taxpayers in specific industries.

With this initiative, the IRS believes it can significantly strengthen its audit capability as more of its examiners become trained industry experts able to uncover as yet undreamed-of sources of income. The IRS has isolated over 100 such industries and has kept quite busy developing and publishing a series of industry-specific guidebooks that address key issues and concerns, set guidelines for audits, and provide concrete, in-depth background information such as balance sheet accounting, components of sales and other income sources, costs of goods sold, and typical expenses. So whereas tax auditors in the district offices are guided by the Pro-Forma Audit Kits contained in the *Internal Revenue*

Manual, field auditors (revenue agents) are now guided by the material prepared for the MSSP. (For a more complete discussion of the industries targeted and what to do if you are in the line of fire, see pages 174–178.)

An Examiner's Personality

In general, the procedures that revenue agents and tax auditors are supposed to go through appear logical and well ordered when one reads them in the *Internal Revenue Manual.*

Under the heading "Research of Unfamiliar Items," the *Manual* (page 4231-10) advises revenue agents that "an examiner cannot perform adequately unless he is familiar with the issues on the return which scrutiny raises. . . . The tax law, regulations, Treasury decisions, rulings, court cases, the published services, and a myriad of other sources of information are the tools of the trade. No one can work without tools, and no one can improvise substitutes for such tools."

What really happens, however, is that this IRS "bible" can become virtually irrelevant as an agent's personality often supersedes, modifies, and even rewrites any procedures that should have been followed.

Often, I've walked into an audit genuinely concerned for my client, only to find that because of the personality of the agent assigned, not only does the audit go smoothly, but most of the information I was concerned about was never even touched upon. (Of course the reverse can also happen, as you will see in chapter 4, when Mr. Fields, the IRS revenue agent, audited my client, an exporting agency.) Here's an example of how the revenue agent assigned to your case affects the course of the audit process.

Mrs. Price was the president of a closely held corporation dealing in wholesale medical supplies. After she received notice that her company's return would be audited, she called me to handle the audit and to review the tax work done by the company's corporate controller. I immediately saw several major audit issues that required more research. I secured additional backup data and prepared myself for some difficult negotiations. But I knew the final determining factor, the IRS revenue agent, could turn the whole thing around. In this case, he did.

The agent, Mr. Stores, was a pleasant young man who did not have much experience handling complicated audits. I determined this early on by his manner and the questions he began with.

On Day 1, Mr. Stores routinely inquired about how my client's corporation conducted business: Who its customers and suppliers were, and the names and addresses of the banks the business used. He also went through the standard routine of examining paid bills for two random months and verifying them against cash disbursements journals. Then he verified two random months of sales invoices and traced them to cash receipts journals.

He worked so slowly that he didn't complete his work on a reconciliation of bank deposits until the close of Day 3.

At this point, I was waiting for him to raise a few of the larger issues that were part and parcel of this corporation's return, issues that would be quite evident to any trained professional, such as:

Officers' loans. A balance of $400,000 was owed to the corporation by Mrs. Price. Although the money had been advanced over a six-year period, interest had been accrued only on the books; Mrs. Price had never actually paid any interest or principal. Moreover, the corporation's earnings were sufficient to pay Mrs. Price dividends, but she had never been paid any. Clearly, the IRS would strongly argue that some of the loans be reclassified as dividends, which are not deductible by the corporation. Therefore, they would be considered taxable income for Mrs. Price.

Officers' salaries. In the corporation's year-end accounting journal entry, the corporate controller recorded $50,000 of officers' salaries, which was paid to Mrs. Price 45 days after the close of the corporate year. In a closely held corporation, salaries are deductible *only* in the year paid, not in the year they are accrued or recorded on the books.

Officers' life insurance. During the year, $30,000 of officers' life insurance was paid and was deducted as an expense on the corporate tax return. However, it was not listed as a separate item; it was buried in the category of "General Insurance." The problem with this is that officers' life insurance is *not ever* deductible.

Instead of stopping to discuss even one of these issues, the revenue agent made additional requests for more information to support bills paid for entertainment, travel, auto expense, and commissions. These areas are old standbys that revenue agents seem to fall back on especially when they have decided not to delve into other issues that are more complex. At the next meeting, Mr. Stores wasted half the day verifying the expense information he had previously requested. He also verified a schedule of bank interest that was nothing more than a reprise of two items per month that represented interest for two corporate bank loans. He pulled all 12 bank statements to verify that the interest was listed on our schedule accurately.

Why did Mr. Stores choose to engage in this painstakingly slow and practically redundant exercise? In my opinion, he was padding his work papers by including a schedule of bank interest to let his group chief know he hadn't omitted anything.

Toward the end of Day 4, he finally got around to insurance. I submitted paid bills for all ordinary insurance such as auto, worker's compensation, and health insurance, plus the bills for officers' life insurance totaling $30,000.

Finally he asked for promissory notes covering the officers' loans, which I gave him. He dropped the matter entirely without ever asking why interest had never been paid on the loans.

The audit was concluded with the agent disallowing the $30,000 in officers' life insurance. He also disallowed approximately $15,000 of travel and entertainment.

The issue of the officers' salaries paid in the wrong year was never discussed. This alone could have meant an additional tax liability of $25,000. Since the agent had my client's 1040's for several years, he could have traced the salaries if he had chosen to. He didn't.

If you're reading this and are awestruck, don't be. This kind of audit is not unusual. I know that Mr. Stores fully believed he was performing conscientiously. Revenue agents with more experience think and act differently (they get through the routine information more quickly), and stand a better chance of uncovering larger issues.

You never can predict how the audit process will go because so much depends on the kind of revenue agent assigned to your case. Even reading up on the subject probably won't help you much, although you can pick up a lot of very worthwhile and specific information. The key is to focus on preventive medicine: **Make sure you never receive that audit notice**—by following the advice in this book. If you do receive an audit notice, get the best professional you can find, one who has had plenty of experience facing IRS agents at audits, to represent you.

What You Need to Know About the Collection Division

What They Say They Do

In 1996, the Collection Division had over 17,500 employees, a drop of 1,800 from 1995. But by 1997, that figure dropped rather dramatically to about 10,900 and rose somewhat in 1998 to 11,600. A close look at the IRS personnel summary for that year shows that the "missing" 6,500 people, nonrevenue officers, were shipped into a customer service area, along with another 4,000 others from Taxpayer Services. This boosted customer service from 1,777 people to 12,216 in one year!

In 1999, we learned for certain that this shift reflected one of the major directives of RRA '98—to better serve taxpayers. Using examination and collection people to temporarily help in the area of customer service is an ongoing effort.

As with the Examination Division, policies and procedural guidelines for collecting delinquent taxes and securing delinquent tax returns are established in the Office of the Assistant Commissioner of Collection in Washington, D.C. Carrying out those policies and guidelines becomes an enormous decentralized operation managed at the district level.

Collection deals with people who owe tax who say they cannot pay, those who never filed, and the innocent, victimized taxpayer who unfortunately falls into the IRS's "I made a mistake" category.

IRS personnel from Collection are the ones who can wipe out your possessions and, until RRA '98, could do so with few limitations.

Collection has three major components: the service center, the Automated Collection System, and the district office.

What Collection Really Does

Since all tax returns are mailed to a taxpayer's appropriate service center, the actual collection process begins in the collection areas in each of the 10 service centers across the country.

To resolve balance due or delinquent tax matters, the service center routinely sends up to four "balance due" or "return delinquency" notices.

501 is Reminder of Unpaid Tax
503 is Urgent—Payment Required
504 is Final Notice
523 is a Notice of Intent to Levy

If you receive a 504 letter, this is really not the "final" notice, just the final notice from the service center. If you don't pay in full within 30 days of receiving this notice, the IRS can begin the enforced collection process. After this, the process can take on a life of its own. After the 523 notice is received, the IRS can seize your assets. So you must give this notice immediate attention.

In 1983, the amount collected from taxpayers on the first notice was close to $2 billion. In 1993, the average first notice from the IRS claiming money due brought in over $7.4 billion from taxpayers who were probably relieved to get the IRS off their backs simply by writing one check. By 1997, the figure rose to almost $9.2 billion, and increased slightly for 1998 to almost $9.5 billion.[6] You can see the IRS's progress in this area alone.

The initial mailings of notices for tax due should include certain publications. *Your Rights as a Taxpayer*, IRS Publication 1, commonly referred to as the "Taxpayer Bill of Rights," is usually mailed with the first notice, and *The IRS Collection Process*, IRS Publication 594, is mailed prior to enforced-collection action. The latter will answer many of your questions and explain clearly and objectively what you need to do when you receive a bill from the IRS. Both of these publications have been revised in keeping with 1998 tax legislation, so their focus is much more customer oriented, detailing your rights and your options, and describing the most recent procedures as well as safeguards for taxpayers. If you don't receive the publications, call the taxpayer assistance telephone numbers in your state and ask to have them sent. (See Appendix C.)

If a taxpayer has not responded after receiving the last notice, or if the situation looks as though it may not be easily resolved, the Automated Collection System (ACS) takes over.

Automated Collection System (ACS)

ACS has offices around the country staffed with employees responsible for collecting unpaid taxes and securing tax returns from delinquent taxpayers who have not responded to previous service center notices. Their work is carried out strictly through the mail or over the telephone. Chances are, no matter how many people you speak to from ACS, you will never meet with any of them in person.

The work that goes on in the ACS offices is quite focused. Personnel trained to locate errant taxpayers are supported in their efforts by computer links to a range of information resources. These include state tax files and local offices, and other records, such as the registry of motor vehicles, voter registration office, and membership in union, trade, professional, or other organizations. They also use telephone books and post office records and can easily obtain unlisted phone numbers. ACS employees also routinely write letters of inquiry to your employees, next-door neighbors, and schools that you or your family have attended. All of this is performed as part of their vigorous attempts to locate Mr., Mrs., Miss, or Ms. taxpayer who owes the government money.

Once the contact is made, the IRS says what will happen next:

> When taxpayer contact is made, either through an outcall or in response to an ACS letter or enforcement action, the ACS employees will discuss how best to resolve the tax matter. Where there are unpaid taxes, the IRS has written guidelines for considering an installment agreement to pay the tax over a period of time, for adjusting incorrect tax bills and reducing or eliminating penalties, and for determining situations where the case should be reported currently not collectible.[7]

If and when the ACS fails to get as far as it should and/or it looks as if the taxpayer is not cooperating, and/or it appears as if the situation is not easily going to be resolved, the service center sends the case to the district office for further investigation.

District Office Collection

When ACS has determined that nothing else has worked and that it's time to take enforcement action, you've reached the final step in the collection process.

What happens at the district level is the all-too-familiar nightmare of the "surprise visit" to your home or office, where the revenue officer (or officers) will ask lots of questions and arrange for a more formal interview. During the formal meeting, the officer will fill out a detailed financial report on an IRS form with the information you supply. Then the two of you will work through the methods and means you will use to pay the money you owe. These might include certain routes the revenue officer decides you must take no matter what, such as producing immediate monies to pay the bill, selling specific assets, or strongly suggesting that you pay a visit to your bank to secure a bank loan. Payment could also be made via a carefully detailed installment plan, Form 9465, which, compared to the other choices available, begins to sound good. But be wary of this. (For more information, see chapter 10, pages 354–356.)

If none of these are workable for the taxpayer, the situation literally deteriorates right before your eyes and things are, for the most part, taken out of your hands.

To fully realize the extent of authority vested in the Collection Division, each taxpayer should know the major steps Collections can take to, as the IRS says, "protect the government's interest in the tax matter, or if the taxpayer neglects or refuses to pay, or fails to help resolve a tax matter."[8]

A *summons* simply requires that you must appear at a given time and place and offer specific information as you are grilled by IRS revenue officers.

A *lien* is a much more dangerous weapon. First of all, it means that the IRS is going to publicly notify all your creditors and business associates that the IRS has a claim against your property and your rights to property, including property that you might acquire even after the lien is filed.

Second, you will, in effect, lose your credit rating because notice of a lien is filed with all the appropriate official and legislative channels, the secretary of state, and the county clerk. If this happens, it can take years to stabilize your financial standing, even if you have the best tax attorney on your side. IRS Publication 594, *The IRS Collection Process*, makes this misleading statement under the heading "releasing a lien": usually 10 years after a tax is assessed, a lien releases automatically if we have not filed it again.

A lien is a notice to creditors that the government has a claim against your property for a tax debt. A *levy* gives the IRS *control* over your assets, so that it can literally, physically, take the property out of your possession to satisfy your debt. A levy encompasses property that you hold (home, boat, car) or property held for you by third parties (wages, savings accounts). The principle behind this is that your possessions are no longer yours but rather belong to the government.

Some relief is given to taxpayers under the IRS Restructuring and Reform Act of 1998 regarding liens and levies. Beginning January 23, 1999, the IRS must notify you in advance of all the steps it intends to take throughout the lien and levy process. The IRS must also allow you ample time to retain professional help and hopefully to remedy the situation. (See 1998 Tax Legislation, pages 304–307, for additional safeguards.)

Under the levy (and seizure), you should be aware that the IRS is required to leave something behind. This includes unemployment benefits, workmen's compensation, fuel, provisions, furniture, and personal effects for a head of household with a total value of $6,250, and books and tools used in your trade, business, or profession worth up to $3,125, and a minimum weekly exemption for wages, salaries, and other income. Because the previous limits were so small, the IRS was able to take cars and other personal belongings from individuals with limited means. These new exemptions will allow taxpayers at least to retain more of their belongings. Beginning January 1, 1999, both amounts are subject to inflation adjustments. The full list is in *The IRS Collection Process*, IRS Publication 594.

When taxpayers fail to make arrangements to resolve their tax debts, the IRS goes a step further. After the levy and seizure, the IRS will sell any real or personal property that a taxpayer owns or has an interest in. Seizure of a primary residence used to only require approval from a district or assistant district director. Now, of course, that situation has changed dramatically.

A jeopardy assessment is an emergency legal procedure that allows the IRS to swiftly seize, *at any time*, the assets of taxpayers if the IRS suspects that they may flee the country. People who intend to travel for a long distance usually secure plane tickets, something the IRS should have no trouble verifying. Beyond this, however, how can anyone determine with any certainty if a person is going to leave the country? No doubt, we want the IRS to enforce the jeopardy assessment when drug dealers jam $500,000 into an expensive attaché case or brown paper bag and hop on a plane to Brazil. But in and of itself, this emergency procedure is open to unverifiable assertions that could be used purely for harassment purposes and could prove especially dangerous to taxpayers in the hands of certain IRS revenue officers.

Other collection techniques involve the IRS's making a special arrangement with

- Your employer to collect money owed, by initiating payroll deductions from your wages.
- Anyone who pays you interest or dividends, to withhold income tax at the rate of 31 percent.
- The IRS's own Collection Department, to apply your annual tax refund to offset any balance due.

Let me emphasize that all of these actions, which have been part of the tax collection process and which occurred across our nation, were standard operating procedures. Before any other law enforcement agency so radically disturbs a citizen's peace and lifestyle, it must by law obtain a court order. The IRS Collection Division was exempt from this procedure until RRA '98. Taxpayers should now have a much better chance at due process when dealing with the once strong-arm tactics of the IRS Collection Division.

In fact, given shifting staffs, a decrease in tax collectors, an increase in tax returns, and what appears to be a backlash against the 1998 laws that affect collection procedures, plus learning or not learning how the new laws need to be applied, collections in all areas—seizures, liens, levies—have dropped significantly. (See pages 336–338.)

Forms and More Forms

Each of the procedures just described—and there are even more of them—consists of very specific steps that the taxpayer and the IRS are supposed to go through before an actual collection action can be made. Enter IRS forms, those things that have become second nature to the IRS since its inception: forms that tell taxpayers what is about to happen "unless"; forms that rescind the threats; forms that announce that the IRS is going to proceed with the action after all, no matter what; forms that give the taxpayer one last chance; forms that repeal or dismiss the action because the taxpayer is ready to settle the bill.

The paperwork, telephone calls, and correspondence required both to set these actions into motion and to stop them are unbelievably intricate, voluminous, even ridiculous. Add to this the tricks and techniques tax professionals extract from their "what-to-use-against-the-IRS-Collection-Division" repertoire to stall, delay, or reverse decisions already put into action via the forms, and we could go on forever. I prefer to focus first on how to deal with the human element in the IRS if you do get involved, and second, on how you need not get involved in these quagmires at all.

Collection People Mean Business

IRS collection staff mean business, and they have always had a great deal of power and substantial leeway to exercise it. Here's what I mean:

Anthony was the owner of a business with about 100 employees that contracted cutting clothes for the men's garment industry in New York City. Because of intense competition that resulted in small profit margins, Anthony made a dangerous mistake: In a six-month period, he fell behind in paying $58,000 of payroll taxes to the IRS.

When Anthony hired me in early 1998 to help him out of this mess, the first step I took was to make sure current payroll taxes were paid. To do this, Anthony borrowed $12,000 from relatives. Next, I called the telephone number shown on the collection notice to arrange an appointment with a revenue officer with the intention of settling the case by negotiating an installment agreement. One week later I met with a Mr. Michaels and explained that Anthony was in a position to pay off the existing $58,000 liability at the rate of $10,000 a month while continuing to pay current payroll tax obligations. I submitted Forms 433-A (Collection Information Statement for Individuals) and 433-B (Collection Information Statement for Businesses) to show the agent Anthony's current personal and business financial situation and to make clear his willingness to meet his IRS obligations. Though he had no assets of value or any equity in his business, Anthony wanted to clear his debt because he was only 40 years old and the company was his sole livelihood. Hoping I had set the stage for negotiation, this was Mr. Michaels's reply, verbatim:

"I don't care what your client's intentions are, and it doesn't matter to me that he's paying his current obligations promptly. Let me just close him down and put him out of his misery."

To counter any further steps in that direction, I immediately asked Mr. Michaels if he would bring his group chief to the "negotiating" table, which he did.

Only after I handed her a bank check for $10,000 as a down payment (more money that Anthony had borrowed from relatives) did she reluctantly agree to approve an installment agreement of $8,000 a month stretched over a period of six months.

If you think the objective of every IRS revenue officer is to maximize collections, think again. Collection people mistakenly rely on prior cases of delinquent and tardy taxpayers and then do their best to make life miserable for average people like Anthony. So be forewarned. (The IRS is clamping down on payroll tax abusers more harshly than ever before.)

In another collections case, the owner of a hardware store owed $22,000 in payroll taxes. Twice before he had broken agreements to pay on an installment basis. The revenue officer on the case obtained a warrant from the court, showed up in the store, seized the entire contents of the store, and sold it at an auction a short time later.

In both these cases, the taxpayer was in trouble and the revenue officers assigned were doing their jobs—brutal, but expected. **In payroll tax cases, revenue officers are instructed to be especially forceful because the IRS holds employers to a greater degree of responsibility (they must pay employees' taxes) than an individual taxpayer who owes only his or her own taxes.**

Often, in collections, the end does not so pointedly justify the means.

A new chief of collections appointed in the Manhattan district office immediately placed a great emphasis on raising the level of collection of old cases. The new chief met with the revenue officers assigned to the district and told them to go out and get the job done, no holds barred. One story came back from this group about a taxpayer who had just undergone brain surgery. He owned a dry-cleaning establishment and owed $14,000 in payroll taxes. After agreeing to an installment plan, he had paid the agreed-upon $600 per month right on time, until illness struck. The new chief approved the seizure of the man's business, which was liquidated within a few weeks while the taxpayer was in a coma and his wife and family literally stood by helplessly.

Revenue officers are out to get what they can from you because you owe the government. If they can get all you owe, that's great for them. But they will also settle on taking whatever they can get their hands on. If this sounds brutal, I advise you that they and the process are supposed to be.

Despite the more equitable approaches legislated in RRA '98, how long do you think it will take for the IRS collection mentality to change its entrenched attitudes? Without a doubt, it will take many years.

A recent variation to offset the hard-core collection scenario was initiated toward the end of 1997 amidst the furor to overhaul the IRS. On Saturday Problem-Solving Days, the IRS invited taxpayers into all 33 district offices across the United States to meet with collection officers in an attempt to resolve tax disputes, some of which were ongoing for years.

The initial responses were so successful, the IRS says it will continue the effort at least once a month. Call your local district office if you think it would be helpful for you to participate. Check Martin Kaplan's website, www.irsmaven.com, for a current list of Problem-Solving Days.

What You Need to Know About the Criminal Investigation Division

What They Say They Do

If you are the subject of a criminal investigation, you'll be involved with the IRS's Criminal Investigation Division (CID), also referred to as Tax Fraud and Financial Investigations. This division formerly conducted investigations in five areas: abusive compliance (investigations involving violations in commodity futures, options, government securities transactions, excise taxes, illegal tax protesting, fraud schemes, or abusive/illegal tax shelters), narcotics crimes, organized crime, public corruption (investigations involving violations of public trust of or by government officials and employees), and white-collar crime. Of these, abusive compliance and narcotics accounted for more than 80 percent of the cases initiated. Accordingly, in 1995 the program was restructured into only two areas, fraud and narcotics, which contain data from the former categories though not labeled as such. In 1998, this division had almost 3,000 special agents, out of over 4,400 employees.

Although very powerful in its own right, CID does *not* have the power to determine tax liability. It does have the responsibility of scaring taxpayers into compliance with the tax laws, stopping criminal acts involving tax violations, and punishing violators.

The heaviest caseloads for CID vary between tax fraud, drugs, and illegal activities involving money laundering, and white-collar crime committed by stockbrokers, investment bankers, money managers, and organized crime. As a general rule, the average amount of taxes owed by a taxpayer when the IRS files criminal charges is over $70,000. Because of the nature of their job and whom they deal with—organized-crime figures, very wealthy individuals, drug dealers, executives, professionals—special agents have a certain untouchable aura about them that goes back to CID's establishment in the 1920's.

Where CID Receives Its Leads
Cases in which criminal activity is indicated or suspected are sent to CID from various sources:

- Revenue agents and other auditors refer cases while conducting routine audits. This is usually the most common way that criminal cases get started. Therefore, while you are involved in a regular audit, do not get caught in a lie that will arouse suspicion. It will increase the chances of your case being referred to the CID.
- CID employees search through newspapers, articles, broadcast media, and other public sources for specific circumstances, such as lifestyles that might indicate fraud; items reported stolen (to see if they match up to a taxpayer's reported income); other branches within the IRS.
- The Justice Department—Refers primarily narcotics and organized-crime cases. The number of special agents who work on organized crime and narcotics cases is not publicized because it represents a very high percentage of the total cases handled by CID.
- Law enforcement agencies—FBI, DEA (Drug Enforcement Agency).
- Regulatory agencies—the Department of Consumer Affairs, Securities and Exchange Commission, Food and Drug Administration, Federal Communications Commission.
- Banks and other financial institutions—All are required to report a cash transaction of $10,000 or more, as well as any other "suspicious" transactions, on Form 8300 (Report of Cash Payments over $10,000 Received in a Trade or Business).
- Undercover agents—CID has its own staff who nab unsuspecting taxpayers. The undercover agent can even be part of illegal activity with the taxpayer as long as the agent does not induce the taxpayer to commit a crime that he would not otherwise have

committed. To prevent the taxpayer from using a defense that he was a victim of entrapment, the government's lawyer must show that the crime was exclusively the taxpayer's idea.

- Independent CID leads from paid informants—*The Internal Revenue Code* has a provision for paying informants 15 percent of tax that is recovered as a result of a tip (see pages 163–164); CID also has people on its payroll who regularly provide tips about criminal activities.

- Voluntary informers—Lovers left in the lurch, vindictive ex-wives or ex-husbands, former employees, and more are very willing to "tell all" to the IRS. The best advice is not to brag about how you fooled the IRS. Don't make statements in public such as, "I live off cash and never file a return." You may regret saying it.

If CID doesn't think a case will end up with a conviction, it will turn it back to the referring party. Special agents don't waste time. They are diligent, focused, and well trained, and they perform meticulous, detailed investigations.

A criminal investigation can be initiated by either the IRS, known as an administrative investigation, or by a grand jury. In an administrative investigation, a summons issued by the IRS is the vehicle that gets the taxpayer and any other witnesses to the investigation. Enforcement in this instance tends to be more difficult, and long delays are common. In a grand jury investigation, which employs the subpoena, witnesses show up faster and the U.S. attorney immediately enters the picture. Subpoenas are easier to obtain, and the process is quicker and more effective compared to an administrative investigation.

Another difference is that in an administrative investigation CID is in charge, but with a grand jury, the U.S. attorney, who works for the Justice Department, is in charge and the IRS plays second fiddle. So although a grand jury investigation is quicker and more efficient and thus an easier task for CID and its agents, it is common knowledge that the IRS doesn't like taking orders from anyone. But since a large percentage of cases are referred to CID from the Justice Department, CID doesn't have a choice. A case referred by the Justice Department automatically receives a grand jury investigation.

From a taxpayer's perspective, all I would say here is that an administrative investigation might be slightly more preferable (although being in a position of having to undergo a criminal investigation of any sort is completely *not* preferable), simply because it works much more slowly than a grand jury.

Once CID is convinced that prosecuting a citizen is in order, the case moves up through CID to the district counsel, then to the Department of Justice, Tax Division, Washington, D.C., and on to the U.S. District Court. The case must garner approval each step of the way, or it will be thrown out. This approval process normally takes two to six months.

After a criminal investigation is completed, the evidence and facts are contained in the special agent's report. The examination auditor will probably use this report when imposing civil penalties. If you are the person under investigation, obtain a copy of the report by writing to the attention of the disclosure officer at the IRS district office where the criminal investigation took place and mention that your request is "pursuant to the Freedom of Information Act."

If at the conclusion of its investigation CID decides it doesn't have a case against the taxpayer, the case will be dropped. But that's not the end of it. The case then finds its way back to an auditor, who examines it for civil penalties, which can run as high as 75 percent of what is owed. Even when a person is prosecuted and found guilty, civil penalties are likely to be imposed as well.

When CID builds a case against a suspected tax criminal, the work it performs is very thorough and precise. By the time you, your friends, your family, or neighbors are contacted by a special agent, the case gathered against you will be pretty solid. The special agent will have already reconstructed approximately how much the suspect has spent during a given year and compared that amount with available cash from taxable and nontaxable sources, such as gifts and loans. The search will also include payments made with unreported income, i.e., cash used to pay off credit cards, college tuition, cars, newly insured jewelry, and more.

When a taxpayer falls into the criminal category, he or she stands to receive a fairer deal than a taxpayer caught up in the collections area. **That's because in the Criminal Investigation Division, the burden of proof is on the government: The taxpayer is innocent until proven guilty. For every case handled by any other division of the IRS, the reverse is true.** The only recent change comes from RRA '98 regarding noncriminal proceedings that reach the level of Tax Court or Federal Court. In these instances, the burden of proof may shift to the IRS if the taxpayer meets certain conditions. (See 1998 Tax Legislation, pages 297–299.)

In summary, putting people in jail is the job of the Justice Department. When it comes to tax violations, it's the IRS that gets Justice headed in the right direction.

In 1998, CID referred over 3,500 cases for prosecution, resulting in almost 3,000 sentences; 2,413 of these received prison terms. At that rate, 81 percent of those sentenced went to prison.[9]

What is significant in these findings is that

- The number of criminal tax cases the IRS gets involved with is relatively low, less than .002 percent of the total population of taxpayers sending in tax returns, or, for 1998, a little over 4,650 CID investigations initiated out of almost 225 million returns filed.
- Although CID has the smallest staff of all the four major district-level operations (examination, collection, criminal investigation, and taxpayer services), it has the best reputation because of its ability to secure convictions.

You see, the decision to launch an investigation is made by CID with great care. True, CID may not always have a choice: If a person is well known and the IRS wants to make an example of him, or if the U.S. attorney insists that CID pursue a specific case in the area of organized crime, CID must follow up. But given the time and expense it takes to reach the stage where the IRS recommends a case to the Justice Department for prosecution, you can be sure that that case will stand a good chance of winning.

What CID Really Does Regarding Fraud

The *Internal Revenue Manual* clearly defines what conditions must exist for fraud, a criminal offense, to be indicated:

> Actual fraud is intentional fraud. Avoidance of tax is not a criminal offense. All taxpayers have the right to reduce, avoid, or minimize their taxes by legitimate means. The distinction between avoidance and evasion is fine, yet definite. One who avoids tax does not conceal or misrepresent, but shapes and preplans events to reduce or eliminate tax liability, then reports the transactions.
>
> Evasion, on the other hand, involves deceit, subterfuge, camouflage, concealment, some attempt to color or obscure events, or making things seem other than they are.[10]

But here's the problem: **Because the final determination is made by CID, the gap between what is criminal and what is civil allows for significant leeway, which can be and has been used against the taxpayer.**

Let's say a taxpayer files Form 4868 (Application for Automatic Extension of Time to File U.S. Individual Income Tax Return), on which he underestimates his tax liability, and then does not file the completed return. CID could hold that this seemingly innocent action involved intent to commit fraud, or criminal behavior.

In another case, suppose a taxpayer willfully lies to a special agent. This is a clear indication of intent, is it not? This makes it criminal.

Don't for one second think that criminal violations involve only organized crime, narcotics violations, and money laundering. The majority of taxpayers would never even *think* about getting involved in these kinds of vice activities. But that's all right. The IRS gives you lots of chances to be charged as a criminal violator anyway.

How to Tell If Your Behavior Borders on Criminal
Taxpayers are at risk of criminal exposure when they

- Understate income, such as denying receipt of income and then not being able to offer a satisfactory explanation for the omission.
- Conceal accounts with a bank, brokerage firm, or other property.
- Repeatedly fail to deposit receipts to business accounts.
- Use fictitious names on bank accounts.
- Manipulate personal expenses to appear as business expenses.
- Take excessive religious and charitable contributions.
- Show substantial unexplained increases in net worth, especially over a period of years.
- Show substantial excess of personal expenditures over available resources.
- Fail to file a return, especially for a period of several years, while receiving substantial amounts of taxable income.

Are You Exhibiting "Badges" of Fraud?
If you are being examined for a civil or criminal violation, there are certain kinds of behaviors, referred to as "badges" of fraud, which according to the IRS could indicate fraud. As listed in the *Internal Revenue Manual,* some of the more common badges of fraud are as follows:

- False statements, especially if made under oath. For example, taxpayer submits an affidavit stating that a claimed dependent lived in his household when the individual did not.
- Attempts to hinder the examination. For example, failure to answer pertinent questions or repeated cancellations of appointments.
- Testimony of employees concerning irregular business practices by the taxpayer.
- Destruction of books and records, especially if it's done just after an examination was started.
- Transfer of assets for purposes of concealment.

Are You Exhibiting "Willful Intent"?
The *Internal Revenue Manual* goes on to explain that in and of themselves, these actions by the taxpayer usually are not sufficient to estab-

lish fraud. However, when these are combined with other items they may be taken to indicate a willful intent to evade tax. These other items include

- Refusal to make specific records available.
- Diversion of a portion of business income into a personal bank account.
- Filing the return in a different district.
- Submitting false invoices or other documents to support an item on the tax return.
- Lack of cooperation by taxpayer.

In short, the most common areas of interest to CID are:

- Tax evasion.
- Filing a false tax return.
- Failure to file a tax return.

These indicators are behaviors thousands of taxpayers exhibit with good reason during examination proceedings. Now that you know them, you realize that if you act in any of these ways, you could set off a lightbulb in some examiner's head that will then place you in the category of exhibiting a "badge" of fraud.

Attorneys strongly recommend that the moment taxpayers know a case is criminal they should *stop talking* and get a lawyer immediately. The lawyer should be a criminal attorney who is familiar with tax matters, and not a tax attorney who is familiar with criminal matters.

How a Tax Professional Spots an Audit Case Turned Criminal

Just as the IRS has defined certain taxpayer behaviors that indicate fraud, tax professionals have learned to stay finely tuned and spot corresponding "triggers" on the part of the IRS that could indicate that one of our audit cases is being considered as a criminal violation.

I have had several clients whose cases I suspected might be recommended to CID. As each new audit meeting arrived, I carefully watched the revenue agent to see if I could detect any change in his attitude: Was he being overly cooperative? Or, perhaps, suddenly very uncooperative by keeping a tight lid on his comments? Was he beginning to request new information unrelated to the issues we had been discussing all along? In the end, settlements of the cases in question were made either with the revenue agent or at an appeals conference. None were turned over for criminal action.

An important piece of information for taxpayers regarding the possible change in classification of a case from civil into criminal is this: During a regular audit proceeding, you can ask the revenue agent if your case is being considered as a criminal matter. The agent is required to answer truthfully. If, however, the case is *subsequently* deemed to be a criminal one, the agent is *not* obliged to voluntarily reveal this information, *even though* you previously asked that question. Of course, you are still in your rights to ask the same question again, but this could in itself be interpreted as a "badge" of fraud, especially if the agent has already decided that your case is criminal or has, in fact, turned it over to CID.

A CPA colleague described the case of a taxpayer, Mr. Lockwood, with a janitorial services business whose customers were primarily large corporations. Mr. Lockwood's business was a sole proprietorship. During an audit of his tax return (Form 1040, Schedule C), the revenue agent had a problem reconciling Mr. Lockwood's books with his tax return. The agent appropriately began to request additional backup data and to ask a lot of questions.

Immediately Mr. Lockwood berated the auditor for being a clock-watcher and accused him of being "just like all the other civil servants—people without real feelings or regard for the taxpayer." At the end of the day the auditor requested a list of items, including customer invoices and vendor-paid bills for a two-month period, to be brought in to the next audit session.

My colleague told his client not to do any talking. Even though he had an appalling filing system, he was also told to show up with every item the auditor requested. The auditor was only following a set routine of selecting several test months for closer scrutiny. But my colleague had a full-fledged Type C client on his hands, as described in chapter 1. The fact that he was losing his audit seemed less important to him than being right.

Several days later, when Mr. Lockwood finally produced the information requested, almost 50 percent of the items were missing. During the session he looked the auditor straight in the eyes and told him that the other items had been misplaced.

Three weeks passed, which made my colleague uneasy. When an audit is in full swing as this one was, a sudden break without any apparent reason is cause for suspicion. The CPA telephoned the auditor to ask him if he could set up another date. It was then that the agent said he was turning the case over to CID.

Before the CID person began the investigation, she sent a letter to each of Mr. Lockwood's customers on CID letterhead. The letter stated that Mr. Lockwood was under criminal investigation for tax fraud and requested verification of payments from each customer made to the taxpayer during the year under audit. After this, the CID agent checked Mr. Lockwood's bank records, and guess what? Mr. Lockwood was able to clearly explain away all of the agent's questions. The investigation then ended—at least as far as the IRS was concerned.

Within six months of this rather minor debacle, Mr. Lockwood lost over 30 percent of his clients and half of his annual revenue. As a postscript, the IRS never did send a follow-up letter to his customers explaining that no criminal activity had occurred.

Now Mr. Lockwood decided to sue the IRS under Section 6103 of the *Internal Revenue Code*, which allows a taxpayer to bring suit if the IRS "wrongfully revealed confidential tax information," which Mr. Lockwood claimed did occur in the letter the IRS sent to his customers.

The case arrived in U.S. Tax Court, where the judge agreed with the taxpayer and added that the agent should have attempted to resolve the discrepancy by examining bank and other records *before* sending out a letter to parties not directly involved in the investigation.

Not satisfied with this decision, the IRS appealed the case to the circuit court of appeals, which, unfortunately for Mr. Lockwood, overruled the lower court's decision, stating that although the agent could have used better judgment, the IRS had caused no liability to the taxpayer.

In a farcical attempt to mitigate the harshness of the decision, the circuit court added that it did not want people to think that the IRS could investigate anyone it wanted to on a whim, since this kind of investigation could devastate a small business in a local community. Well, that's exactly what it had done. Mr. Lockwood ended up devastated by the ruling, which almost cost him his business plus attorney fees.

The REAL Reason CID Contacts Third Parties

The three real reasons CID summons witnesses or third parties in an attempt to prove its case against taxpayers are

1. To obtain information that will incriminate the taxpayer.
2. To scare the very same people being contacted into never violating tax laws themselves (the deterrent mission).
3. To use the contact as an opportunity for the IRS to spread its tough-guy image.

Once CID discovers incriminating evidence, there are no statutes anywhere that forbid or prohibit this information from being used against the taxpayer. Many careers and reputations have been destroyed because some of this stuff just happened to leak out.

Unspoken Problems in the Criminal Investigation Division

Despite the positive reports reflecting the level of CID work, there are problems with CID and the entire CID process that often go unspoken.

- The cost of building a criminal case and nabbing the suspect is high. In 1993 the total amount spent for tax fraud investigations cost the IRS $343.5 million; by 1997 it rose to almost $378 million, then dropped slightly to $372 million for 1998.[11]
- The number of fraud cases initiated is surprisingly low, averaging

around 3,603 between 1996 and 1998, with narcotic initiations averaging only 1,500 for the same period.[12] However, 89 percent of narcotics suspects who were sentenced in 1998 were sent to prison.[13]

- Even though tax criminals go to prison and are assessed a given amount of tax and penalties, the IRS has *not* been successful in collecting the full amount of tax dollars owed.

See page 225 for a discussion on the major misconception taxpayers have regarding criminal cases and client-accountant confidentiality.

What You Need to Know About the Taxpayer Services Division

What They Say They Do

According to the IRS, the staff in Taxpayer Services traditionally hovered between 6,000 and 7,000 until 1997, when Commissioner Rossotti began to take action and a new Customer Service area was formed, comprising over 12,500 people. By the following year, this new group had essentially melded with Taxpayer Services so that currently, according to the IRS, more than 16 percent of its overall staff time is devoted to taxpayer services. In 1999, the people in this division numbered 15,891, a jump of 21 percent over 1997. In general, Taxpayer Services provides guidance and assistance to taxpayers who write, telephone, or visit an IRS district office inquiring about their federal tax obligations. It also disseminates tax information, publications, films, and other educational materials, conducts tax workshops, and generally helps people untangle IRS red tape. The programs it offers are fairly extensive, and much of the material is worthwhile and helpful.

Taxpayer Services' toll-free assistance telephone numbers consist of various toll-free answering sites in all states as well as the District of Columbia and Puerto Rico. You can call your local IRS district office for this list, or see Appendix C for state filing authority phone numbers.

There has also been a sharp increase in staff who answer these toll-free assistance telephones. According to TRAC, personnel assigned to this function jumped 27 percent, from 6,840 in 1997 to 8,669 in 1999. One of the most obvious results of this enlarged effort has been a great improvement in the ability of taxpayers to get through when they call IRS toll-fee assistance lines. In 1995, six out of every seven taxpayer calls met with a busy signal. In 1998 this is supposed to have dropped to one in ten, but there's still a lengthy up-front waiting period until you do get through, and even then, you may not reach the person you wanted to talk to.

There is also a "TeleTax" service, which provides recorded tax information tapes on over 150 topics. A complete listing of the topics available, automated refund information, and the local telephone numbers for TeleTax are in IRS Publication 910, *Guide to Free Tax Services*, and in the 1040, 1040A (U.S. Individual Income Tax Return), and 1040EZ (Income Tax Return for Single and Joint Filers with No Dependents) tax packages, all of which are free of charge.[14] (See also Appendix B, page 483.)

Other programs provide free tax information and tax return preparation for taxpayers 60 years or older; educate high school students about their federal tax rights and responsibilities; support student tax clinics, staffed by graduate accounting students and second- and third-year law students; and assist taxpayers who would not normally obtain counsel in audit, appeals, and Tax Court cases.[15]

What Taxpayer Services Really Does

Taxpayer Services is a good place to begin if you have a general tax question or need information that only the IRS can provide. The fact is that the Taxpayer Services Division, like the rest of the IRS, is traditionally understaffed. Still, getting through to a live person over the telephone requires time and persistence.

This division exists to service taxpayers' general tax needs and to educate people regarding U.S. taxes. On the basis of what IRS Commissioner Rossetti plans, we can expect better service from this area, but who knows when?

Interestingly enough, in 1995 and 1996 this division secured almost $16 million worth of free advertising, with an estimated 97 million viewers/listeners. For 1997, the value of free advertising dropped significantly to about $5 million, yet the estimated viewers/listeners remained a steady 97 million.[16] How these numbers are derived is anybody's guess! The "Taxpayer Information Program," a responsibility of this division, is what the IRS does to place information in the print and electronic media, as well as to assist taxpayers and increase voluntary compliance. If you were to conclude that a great deal of this material is image-sensitive, you would be correct. Thus, the news releases, fact sheets, and question-and-answer promotional pieces that the IRS prepares on diverse tax topics and offers to newspapers, local network and cable TV stations, radio stations, and others give the IRS the opportunity to spread its image—the omniscient IRS and the caring IRS helping befuddled taxpayers through another tax season.

In the theater, an empty stage slowly comes to life with scenery, lights, actors. Now that the background and the structure of the IRS are in place, let's bring up the curtain on the people who work there.

4

IRS People

Whom You Need to Know
What They're Really Like
How to Work with Them
Standard Operating Procedures

At the writing of this edition, the IRS is facing the second-largest overhaul since its inception (one might, perhaps, justly refer to it as an assault). At this time, all we can be sure of is that things are moving slowly and the new organizational structure will take years to put into place. (See chapter 13.)

The existing organization, however, is what will keep the IRS going until each new function is phased in. Until then, this is what you need to know about people at the IRS.

THE IRS CHAIN OF COMMAND

According to the latest IRS organization chart, at the top of the IRS chain of command are the commissioner and deputy counsel, both of whom are currently appointed by the president and report to the Treasury Department. The chief inspector, who is responsible for keeping the agency and its employees honest, is also at this level, along with the National Taxpayer Advocate and the National Treasury Employees

Union Advisor (NTEU). (See the new IRS organization chart on page 318.) Constant reorganizations make it difficult to analyze or keep track of the IRS organizational structure.

WHO RUNS THE SHOW?

What had been unique about the commissioner's job was its short term. IRS commissioners typically reigned for only brief periods of time, generally because

- A new one has been appointed every four to eight years, reflecting our political process.
- Offers from law and accounting firms often seduce them away even sooner.

The author David Burnham has calculated that "since the end of World War II, the average tenure at the top position has been only 37 months."[1] How much can a person really learn about the workings of the largest bureaucracy in the world in three years? More important, how much can that person ever really be held accountable for the agency's failures or successes? With RRA '98, the commissioner's term has been made permanent for a five-year period, with the possibility of reappointment to another five-year term.

At the field organization level are the district directors and, on the same functional level, the service center directors, all of whom report to the regional commissioners.

Since the reorganization in 1952 and decentralization, power was handed down to the lower levels in the IRS hierarchy. According to Burnham, "The long-term effect of this sweeping reorganization has been that although the assistant commissioners who surround the commissioner in Washington are free to issue policy memos, testify before congressional committees, prepare charts, and hold meetings, they have little real authority over the tens of thousands of investigators, auditors, and clerks who actually go about the job of collecting taxes."[2]

THE EXAMINATION DIVISION

What People in the Examination Division Are Really Like

One constant I kept hearing during my interviews for this book was "Years ago there were better people in the IRS," or "Things were better in the old days," or "Things have really gone downhill." All are accurate statements describing the standard IRS performance, specifically that of the Examination Division.

Abusive Tax Shelters Monopolized the Audit Function

In the late 1970's and throughout the 1980's, when the IRS realized the extent to which people were using tax shelters, hundreds of auditors and revenue agents were removed from their normal work assignments and assigned to ferret out and destroy tax shelters listed on individual and corporate returns. In fiscal year 1979, tax shelter exams accounted for only 1.7 percent of a revenue agent's workload, but by fiscal 1984 this percentage had grown to 19.1 percent.[3]

According to tax law, if an investment is not intended to make a profit, deductions and credits and certainly the huge write-offs generated by tax shelters are not allowable.

Here's what used to take place with a typical tax shelter:

For $10,000 a taxpayer would purchase the rights to a well-known performer's unreleased record album that had been professionally appraised at $100,000. The balance of the acquisition costs, in this case $90,000, was regarded as a loan from the seller, to be paid down from earnings derived from sales of the record album.

What is the overall effect of this simple procedure? If the taxpayer was in the 50 percent tax bracket, the $10,000 investment would have allowed him to reduce his taxes in the first year by about $15,000, including the investment tax credit. In the second year, without the taxpayer investing any additional funds, that initial $10,000 investment would still have functioned as a vehicle for a major tax write-off of about $19,000. This system of gaining substantial tax reductions annually would continue until the asset was fully depreciated—in about six years in the case of a record album. By then, the initial investment would have saved the taxpayer an estimated $58,000 in taxes.

Tax shelters rob the government of money and divert investments into frivolous assets.

The Tax Reform Act of 1986 put an end to tax shelters by 1990 and made the rules retroactive as far back as 1980. Many of the cases involving audits of tax shelters took years to complete and lasted into the mid-1990's. About 24 percent of pending Tax Court cases at one point in 1985 involved tax shelters.[4] The impact of all this on the Examination Division was practically irreparable. The shift weakened the function so severely that the percentage of taxpayer audits dropped steadily for the next 10 years from 1.77 percent in 1980 to about 1 percent in 1990. This drop translated to about 800,000 fewer individual tax returns audited each year. In 1998, I was still working with several clients to settle their tax shelter cases. Abusive tax shelters are on the rise again, but this time the abusers seem to be coming from the corporate sector. (See pages 358–359.)

Outdated Management Practices Stymie Results

Typically, the turnover in entry-level positions at the IRS is quite high. This group usually stays two to three years and then leaves for a private accounting firm or tax law practice, where they are likely to double their salary. According to a former compliance officer, the absence of talented young agents has really frustrated the IRS because it takes from three to five years to adequately train a revenue agent to handle complex cases.[5]

At the other end of the spectrum are the IRS career professionals, those 20-year employees who really know how to slow down the quality of work. This group represents a sizable number who are *not* interested in moving up the career ladder. They want job security (it is very difficult to get fired from the IRS), they are content to follow orders without asking questions, and they want to get through the day with minimum amounts of aggravation, mental dexterity, and energy. They think the way the IRS wants them to (middle-of-the-road), they do what they have been trained to do (not to rock the boat, conform at any cost), and they try hard to maintain the status quo.

A good example of the 20-year professional is a friend of mine who was finally promoted from revenue officer to revenue agent. After four months on the job he requested a transfer back to being a revenue officer. Why? He specifically told me that the tax issues were just too complicated and he was mentally exhausted at the end of each day. As a revenue officer, life was much easier. You just chased after delinquent taxpayers. No new issues were involved, and you didn't have to "tax" (pardon the pun) your brain.

Now add two more ingredients: Advancement at the IRS is almost strictly limited to people within the organization, which strips the lower ranks bare as the talented people are moved into supervisory roles; simultaneously, the overall level of supervision has dropped dramatically. According to a former IRS agent, revenue agents in the field used to review cases fairly thoroughly with their supervisors. These days if something doesn't get resolved in the time it takes to have a brief conversation, it just doesn't get resolved. (The extended four-day audit of my client Mrs. Price, the president of the wholesale medical supplies corporation discussed in chapter 3, pages 58–59, proves my point.)

IRS Auditors Always Operate Two Years Behind the Times

Unbeknownst to the majority of taxpayers, the following scenario is the norm: Tax returns are selected for audit 12 to 18 months after the filing date. By the time you, the taxpayer, have received notice of an audit appointment, it is often a year and a half after the year that your tax return under question covers. What's wrong with this picture? The revenue agent you will be working with on your old return, prepared almost two years ago, is still auditing issues using the old laws while he is simultaneously trying to learn the new laws. For example, in 1998 the Examination Division was still auditing 1996 returns, whereas on January 1, 1998, sweeping changes enacted with TRA '97 were put into effect. And in 1999, with passage of the IRS Reconstructing and Reform Act, the Examination Division was still concentrating on 1997 returns.

In contrast, tax pros have already mastered the new laws. We have to because of the nature of our work. Our clients need us to advise them about how *today's* tax laws, as well as past laws, are affecting them, particularly if there's an audit.

This confusing situation translates into some important information for taxpayers:

- Given our complex tax laws, and the pressured situation of learning new tax laws while having to perform as an "expert" in past tax law, revenue agents tend to stick to the old standbys when conducting an audit. These include travel and entertainment, real estate, matching of income, and verification of cash and bank balances.
- From this we can infer that more complicated issues such as officers' loans, excessive compensation, aggressive inventory valuation methods, or accounting for the deferral of revenue from one year to another stand a good chance of not being scrutinized.

A revenue agent friend of mine admitted the following: **In a good-sized IRS district office, there are usually only one or two people who are familiar with tax law involving capitalization of inventory costs or passive losses to an extent that they could teach it to other employees.** Now just pause for one moment and look at the significance of this. Thirteen years later, after they were created by TRA '86, there are many complex issues involved in these aspects of that tax law still virtually undigested by IRS agents who work on the front lines with taxpayers.

IRS Commissioner Charles Rossetti has quickly caught on to what had been this self-perpetuating flaw by directing an enormous amount of the IRS budget and manpower toward a hurculean training effort. A major goal of this effort is to bring IRS employees up to speed with the provisions of RRA '98. (See pages 340–341.) It may still take a few years to do it.

There's a Varied Audit Mix

Today's auditors come from very different segments of the population. The first—these are in the majority—is the younger set with three years or less of auditing experience.

The next group is a constantly changing mix of people resulting from downsizing in the private sector where experienced people, in good positions (e.g., corporate controllers), 50 to 55 years old, who have been let go from corporations are drawn to the IRS because they want to continue working. There are also college-educated women, some of whom are CPA's, who want a secure job, good benefits, and shorter working hours (agents in the field are usually freer), without feeling the need to put in overtime.

If one of these people is subsequently hired by the IRS as a revenue agent, his or her greatest asset is knowing what deserves further scrutiny on a return. This kind of business experience, as opposed to book learning and IRS training courses, dramatically improves someone's chances of being an effective IRS auditor.

But here's the rub. There aren't enough of these people to make a real difference in the quality of auditing at the IRS.

Finally, with the IRS push to educate its auditors about specific markets, an entire new group has become MSSP specialists (see pages 57–58 and 174–178).

In short, taxpayers often encounter the following when they become involved with the audit level in the Examination Division:

- IRS auditors are generally not thorough and certainly are not interested in opening a can of worms. They just want to get the job done, move caseloads off their desks, and go home.
- Some of the new IRS auditors have become experts on how to avoid answering a question.
- Some auditors have become especially efficient at shuffling taxpayers from one IRS person to another in an effort to push the work on to someone else.
- If you were to describe their work ethic, to say that auditors are clock-watchers is putting it mildly.
- During the transition from the old to the new IRS, some auditors can't wait to leave, some are accepting transfers to do the same job

in a new location where auditing functions are being moved to, and others are volunteering for new assignments entirely.

How to Work with the Examination Mentality

The auditor, therefore, has become the biggest unknown factor when a taxpayer is facing an audit. Sometimes the most difficult cases escape scrutiny because the auditor was not experienced, was not interested, or did not care enough to do a thorough investigation, like Mr. Stores in chapter 3. On the other hand, sometimes the easiest, most uncomplicated audit will turn into a nightmare.

A recent case of mine involved a corporation that exports foodstuffs such as soybean oil and sugar to Central and South American countries. Although this may sound intriguing, even complicated, the guts of the audit were straightforward. The revenue agent, Mr. Fields, was a typical IRS hire with only two years' experience. After Day 3, I knew I was in for a long haul.

Obviously Mr. Fields didn't read the part of the *Internal Revenue Manual* that tells him to become familiar with the issues of his assigned audits, because he quickly made it clear that he knew absolutely nothing about exporting foodstuffs, freight forwarding, letters of credit, or international banking transactions.

As the audit proceeded, a number of issues required documentary proof: documents from court cases and excerpts from published tax services. Although I did all the research and had the data ready, something most auditors would accept at face value, Mr. Fields disregarded them. He was also unfamiliar with the documentation we were dealing with.

Slowly, it also became apparent that this agent did not have a strong accounting background. My client, Mr. Grant, often buys goods from his customers and sells them other items. For practical reasons, my client's bookkeeper simply offsets the balances between accounts receivable and accounts payable so that only the new net balance owed to or from the person remains on the books. This simple accounting approach was completely unintelligible to Mr. Fields.

At the end of each day Mr. Fields would hand me a list of items to have on hand for the next meeting. The list contained many items I had already showed him. In my opinion the agent was either too lazy, too inexperienced, or too frightened to go to his supervisor for some direction. It was clear that he was in way over his head.

The professional fees were mounting and I saw no end in sight, so I insisted that we use the next meeting to finalize things. We agreed on four routine issues—travel and entertainment, auto expenses, insurance, and bad debts—out of a total of six. This amounted to $50,000 of disallowed expenses, which translated to a tax assessment of $17,000 plus another $7,000 in penalties and interest. As a condition of the settlement, Mr. Fields agreed to discuss the offsetting of receivables and payables with his group chief.

Six weeks later, Mr. Fields got back to me. We settled on a disallowance covering the final issue amounting to $5,000, resulting in an additional assessment of $3,000 in tax, penalties, and interest. Considering Mr. Fields's inexperience, he most likely believed that he had done a good job, and my client also was satisfied.

Handling the Auditor

Friend or Foe?

I have read accounts by professionals in the tax field who recommend making the auditor your friend. I can't say that's a reality for me; everyone involved is fully aware that an audit implicitly involves an adversarial relationship. That shouldn't mean that anger or aggression have to be a part of the audit process.

The approach I use and recommend for working with examination staff, especially auditors, is to be polite, friendly, and cooperative. You don't have to go so far as to offer information or documents unless asked, but civility is de rigueur. Be focused on reading the auditor's personality (that's usually not too difficult to do) and providing the auditor with the information requested.

Be in Control

It is also very important for you and your representative to be extremely prepared, neat, and precise. Receipts, cash register tapes, journals, bank files, and the like are better indications of integrity than dog-eared, discolored papers and containers of disorganized data. Know and look as if you are in full control. My friends in the IRS tell me this can put off the auditor, which usually works to the taxpayer's advantage. It also helps to appear relaxed.

Offer Direction

During an audit situation, things can go awry for various reasons. When an audit seems unfocused, presenting your position in a strong, clear, and affirmative way usually helps. With Mr. Fields, for example, I felt he needed a structure, since he couldn't create one for himself. Regarding the documentation that I submitted, which he kept refuting, I finally told him: "You can either accept what I am submitting or come up with new research yourself." That successfully worked to extinguish that part of his behavior. He knew that I knew I was right and he was floundering.

Handling a Clash

There may also be a clash of personalities. The auditor may become angry and challenge you. I have also known auditors to lie, bluff, and manipulate. Don't blow these things out of proportion. With all the pressure and heavy workloads that auditors face regularly, you may just be the one they've decided to take a stand against. It may pass if you stay calm.

Yes, there's a fine line between standing up for your rights and being pushed around, but it works to approach each situation individually. If you and the auditor are stuck on a few points, you can request to have the supervisor's input. I've gotten some positive responses using this method. Choices are available each step of the way, but they can and often do change at a moment's notice.

If an auditor is showing complete incompetence, the audit is getting nowhere, or the auditor is not agreeing to anything you say for reasons you may not be aware of, you have the right to request another auditor (a request not granted very often). Even if it is granted, it could all backfire, since you could end up with a competent person who may locate items that the disagreeable auditor never could have found.

If the point of disagreement is a large dollar amount and the auditor's supervisor doesn't agree with you, or if the auditor takes an entirely unreasonable position and the supervisor agrees, you can begin to move up the line to the IRS Appeals Office. (You could bring in a CPA or tax attorney at this point if you haven't already done so. To go it alone, see the discussion of the appeals process, pages 94–97.) The argument could end there in your favor, or the case could continue to escalate, depending how far you choose to push.

Obtaining Your Tax File in a Disputed Case

Preparing an appeal takes time and can be costly if you are using a tax professional. Before you bother to take this step, be aware of the following: **There is an often overlooked IRS policy regarding protested and disputed tax cases.** Previously the IRS kept its enforcement strategies and litigation approaches secret and consistently maintained that this information should not be released to the public. As usual, the IRS didn't want to give away anything it didn't have to. In several cases, however, the federal court ordered the IRS to comply with individuals' Freedom of Information Act requests for all relevant documents in their tax files. (See the discussion of the Freedom of Information Act on page 116.) Although the IRS does not like to admit giving way to pressure, the change in policy, as the IRS calls it, seems to have been a direct result of these cases. So a new precedent has been set: **The Examination Division must now provide taxpayers with the IRS's rebuttal position regarding issues under conflict in cases that are being forwarded to Appeals.**

The good news is, you get to see in black and white what positions the auditor has taken, and an idea of how much and what information is being sent to the appeals officer.

The bad news is the auditor's work papers are often incomplete, which could lead you to believe the auditor has a weak case. Don't assume. He may know more than he's written down. You can disregard any incompleteness, but be sure to review the auditor's assumptions and the accuracy of his calculations. If you uncover an error in your favor, you are not obligated to bring it to the auditor's attention. No matter what, prepare your best case for presentation at the appeals conference.

Calling a Halt to the Audit

Finally, you can terminate an audit at any time by stating that you'd rather not continue, since it appears that nothing further can be accomplished. Usually the auditor will write up the case as being "unagreed" and pass it up to the supervisor. Perhaps a new auditor or the Appellate Division will offer a solution.

THE COLLECTION DIVISION

What People in the Collection Division Are Really Like

IRS *revenue officers*, also referred to as *collections officers*, are traditionally focused, determined, and unemotional. They face taxpayers one-on-one to carry out the actual collection process and are trained to think and act quickly and efficiently. Though the latest statistics show dramatic decreases in collection activity due, to a large extent, to newly legislated taxpayer safeguards, it is the job of collection officers to get the equivalent of your house, your car, your savings, and more into the pockets of the federal government to pay your tax debt. (See pages 336–338.)

How Revenue Officers Differ from Auditors and Other IRS Employees

- First of all, revenue officers like what they do, or they wouldn't be in that division.
- Second, their personalities combine with their work to make a perfect fit. If people get into collection who don't belong there because they have too much heart, they leave. The ones who remain are diehards.
- Revenue officers, at least the ones who go on-site to do the actual negotiations and confiscations, are unquestionably more ambitious than those in auditing or examination. They want to be noticed.
- Until recently, the IRS tradition was to reward employees with

plaques, honors ceremonies, and rapid promotion to higher grade levels if they used their power to achieve the desired results.

How to Work with the Collection Mentality

Part of the collection mentality is formed and predicated on quotas, even though they may not be called that. This is something the IRS vehemently denies, but quotas nevertheless seem to exist, according to several former auditors and revenue officers I have spoken to. With the pressure to levy, place liens, seize property, and turn in a better weekly or monthly performance than those at desks to the left and right of them, how would you expect revenue officers to behave? (All of this is starting to change with RRA '98; see pages 334–336.)

The best way to work with collection people is to avoid ever having to deal with them. But if you get this far down the road and end up in a tax jam in which you have to face one or more collection officers, don't mess with them. Do what they say. Follow your part in the collection process. Answer their queries. Don't ignore the letters you keep receiving. Be clear. Stick to your story.

Because there are different stages in the collection process, you are likely to encounter different personality sets common to each stage. No one tells taxpayers that. For example, quite often a lot can be cleared up at the ACS (Automated Collection System) level just by dealing with a collection representative over the telephone. Sometimes things can even be sorted out with revenue officers *before* they visit your home or office. The point is, just because you find yourself under the jurisdiction of the collection department doesn't mean you have to panic.

Here's a fairly representative case involving the beginning stages of the collection process, what you're likely to encounter, and how to deal with it.

One day, I received a call out of the blue from one of my corporate clients, who told me that the securities firm he does business with had received a letter from the IRS notifying him that his brokerage account had a $2,500 levy placed on it.

My client, a medium-sized and very successful corporation, very much in the black, was and has always been an A client. The firm's brokerage account in question did a sizable amount of securities trading and at that time contained a portfolio of stocks and bonds valued at over $600,000. A levy placed on this brokerage account was very serious. It meant the corporation was unable to engage in any securities activities; the securities firm would in turn be highly fearful of doing business with them while their account had a levy placed on it by the IRS.

I knew my client had done nothing wrong and that the IRS had messed up. The challenge was to find out where the problem was, to get the IRS to recognize what they had done wrong, and to work with them to correct it. Gearing up for the utterly outrageous and unexpected, I telephoned the revenue officer from the local district office who had signed the letter.

Within two minutes things became clearer, at least from my end. "We never received any notices," I said.

"We sent all four of them [the 500 series, remember them?]," the revenue officer replied.

"Where to?" I asked.

"To ———," he said.

"The company moved from that address almost four years ago," I answered, rather blatantly disgusted.

"Well, you should have had the mail forwarded," he said.

"We did," I replied, "but the post office only forwards mail for one year. Why didn't you look on your computer for the 1998 file, which has the new address on the corporate return?" I asked.

"No returns were showing for that year," he said. "The corporation didn't file a return."

"Of course we filed a return," I said. Now I knew that this guy was too lazy to look for it.

"Look," the revenue officer replied, totally avoiding my points because he knew that I knew that he hadn't looked for the return, "you owe us $2,500 for 1996 payroll taxes."

"If you look on your computer, you'll see you owe us a $38,000 refund due from an overpayment on corporate income tax," I replied.

"That has nothing to do with it," he said. "You still owe us $2,500."

At this point I decided to go for a compromise and fight the $2,500 later. "Since the $38,000 is due to be received by us within the next few weeks, why don't you just deduct the $2,500 from the $38,000 credit and release the levy from the stock account."

"We can't do that."

"Why not?"

"It's too much trouble. I don't have time to check into all the details. Pay us with a bank check and then we'll release the levy."

"We can't wait that long," I said. "You know that will take over a month and my client can't leave that account dormant all that time."

"Hold on a minute. I'll be right back."

"O.K. Now," I thought, "maybe something will happen because he is obviously going to speak to his group chief."

Next I hear a new voice from the other end of the phone, obviously the group chief, although he didn't introduce himself. Some IRS people don't always have the time, inclination, or awareness to recognize that it's helpful to know whom you're speaking to. They often prefer to remain anonymous, and withhold their names so they don't have to become involved or incur blame.

"We don't have the facilities to arrange for the $2,500 to be offset against the $38,000. If you want the levy released, just pay the $2,500 with a bank check."

Although I could have continued to argue that my client in no way owes $2,500, I knew I was speaking to two people who would continue to parrot each other and the only solution was to agree to do it their way, at least that time.

So we sent the bank check the second week in April, and the levy was released two weeks later. The way this works is that the IRS sends a release of levy form to the brokerage firm so that the firm knows everything has been cleared up and activity begins again.

A brief analysis will clue in taxpayers about the collection mentality. (Note: Any perceptible overlaps with the Examination Division are actually common threads that link all IRS divisions to the IRS personality.)

- Collection staff are inflexible.
- Collection staff generally take the easy way out.
- Lying, bluffing, and deceiving are common practices.

Another entrée into the mentality of revenue officers in Collection is this: Most whom I have met are always worried about their jobs. (This is also true for many revenue agents in the Examination Division.) If they make too many mistakes, will they be fired? Or demoted? Or put last in line for a promotion? If they disagree with the tactics that are used and do not take an aggressive line of action, which is expected, will they fall from grace? The answer used to be yes.

In some ways, the situation regarding their concern remains the same, but now the reasons for dismissal stem from RRA '98 and the "10 deadly sins" for which collection agents can be fired. (See page 337.) In no uncertain terms, these new laws, designed to modify unwieldy and often unjustified collection tactics, represent a step toward fairness in the collection process and a gain for taxpayers. Although collection agents may currently seem at a loss as to how to operate, or they may resent the changes they are faced with, in the long run the outcome should be positive, though it may take several years for this to be manifest.

Above and beyond all of this, revenue officers have been trained to provide answers for every question, and to fill in every blank on the preprinted IRS collection procedures forms. In this division, as in Examination, it's paperwork that counts.

Sometimes when I watch revenue officers filling in line after line, page after page of IRS forms, it just seems downright stupid under the circumstances. But my conclusions fall by the wayside as they follow some IRS voice inside their head (which I certainly don't hear), which tells them to fill in the blanks, no matter what. Here's what I mean:

Similar to the tone of the last case describing the collection mentality (I know it sounds more like a bad dream), I received a notice from the IRS that a client of mine hadn't sent in the IRS federal payroll tax form for the first quarter of 2000, and that currently, with penalties and interest, the amount due had reached $30,000.

I knew this was not plausible. This client had sold her business to a big conglomerate and moved to New Mexico two years before. The revenue officer refused to hear any explanations over the telephone and insisted that I come to the district office to settle things.

At our cozy one-on-one, there sat the revenue officer with a pile of forms one inch thick on his desk. He explained that the 1999 quarterly payroll tax was missing. "But the company was sold in 1998. The last quarterly payroll tax you received was for 1997."

"It was," the revenue officer agreed, "and we've been sending notices ever since, but haven't heard anything."

There were obviously three irritants that prompted this situation: First, the client's bookkeeper who sent in the last form neglected my directions to properly notify the IRS that this would be the final quarterly payroll tax form.

Second, the notices were going to nowhere. Where was the post office in all of this? (Are you beginning to realize that given the nature of the tax collection process, the post office is a vital, albeit somewhat uncontrollable, link in the process?)

Finally, because the IRS did not know the company was extinguished, and because it did not receive the next quarterly payroll tax form, some clerk in the examination department checked the amount of the last payroll tax and entered a made-up figure based on the last amount entered on the quarterly form and came up with $25,000.

Once this occurs **you are face-to-face with a problem that materializes out of the vacuum created from missing information the IRS expected to receive but didn't.** Since there is no response, penalties and interest accrue, no matter what. By the time I was contacted, the amount due had reached $30,000.

Now let's return to the face-to-face meeting at the district office. I calmly repeated to the revenue officer that my client had sold her company and had been out of business for over two years. This is what happened next: Appearing to have heard every word, the revenue officer, staring at his topmost form, pen poised for action, responded by firing a string of questions at me. "What is the new location of the business? How many employees are there? What are the taxes owed in the current year?" To jolt him out of his "fill-in-the-blank" reverie, I grabbed his arm and said rather loudly, "I already told you, my client is out of business. This is a self-generated liability. The IRS computer created it."

"No," the officer said. "It's a tax due."

"No, it's not. It's an estimate."

At that point he got up and left the room, actually another good sign, probably a trip to his group chief.

When he returned, there was good news. The group chief agreed with me. The revenue officer was told to void the liability entirely. He assured me that he'd fill out the necessary forms and send the credit. Approximately six months later, the credit was finally issued.

The fact that IRS employees are taught to leave no line blank has become a double-edged sword. Yes, there is the possibility for completeness on the one hand. But on the other, this same revenue officer, diligently performing as he was taught, becomes so focused on the line information that he fails to ask for or recognize that there are a lot of other more important things going on. It appears that group chiefs will scold someone on their staff more easily for a piece of missing information because an empty line is particularly visible.

THE CRIMINAL INVESTIGATION DIVISION

What People in the Criminal Investigation Division Are Really Like

Special agents employed in the Criminal Investigation Division are involved in the kind of investigation work and chasing down the bad guys depicted in the movies. Involvement at this level means possible criminal offenses levied against you, leaving you subject to a possible jury trial and imprisonment.

Special agents are highly skilled in locating hidden assets and unreported sources of income and identifying false records and fraudulent tax returns. Working with a full array of the latest in police and crime detection technology, they interrogate, untangle intricate transactions, obtain corroborating statements, make third-party investigations, conduct raids, use electronic surveillance, and decide whom to summons.

The agents who work in this division are extraordinarily thorough, painstakingly patient, and tough. They have to be—it's their job to build a case against the unsuspecting taxpayer.

But they are also calm, at least initially, and have a way about them that says to the taxpayer, "You can trust me. I'm easy to talk to." Part of their job is to instill this feeling in taxpayers. But once you open up to a special agent, well, their case is made, and your fate could be sealed. That's why, if that special agent comes to your door, anything you say could be an open invitation or a recrimination. Neither does you any good. Reach for your phone and dial a good tax attorney.

While other areas of the IRS may be haphazardly run, the process involved in catching big- and small-time tax criminals is tedious and time-consuming. Completion of a good case in the space of a year is considered a satisfactory performance for a special agent. The work may be hazardous, and advancement is generally faster here than in other IRS divisions.

How to Work with the Criminal Investigation Mentality

Recently, I was a witness before a grand jury relating to a CID investigation of one of my clients. It was there that I learned how meticulous the CID can be. The IRS typically has a great deal of trouble locating a taxpayer's past returns, especially returns that are five years old or older. When I was on the stand, the prosecutor showed me not only the last ten 1040's filed by my client, but the original ones at that!

After that, the CID subpoenaed all my client's books and records (he owned and operated several corporations). When the records were returned to the corporation, CID inadvertently also included a large portion of the work papers it had created and assembled for the case, an obvious mistake by CID but a golden opportunity to examine their work firsthand. No, it's not illegal. Their mistake was fair game to us.

The work papers showed a complete analysis of all corporate bank accounts and the client's personal bank accounts, including every deposit slip, canceled check, and debit and credit memo. In our profession, that level of work is highly impressive. Coming from the IRS, it is astounding!

In the end, my client wound up having no charges brought against him. Ultimately the grand jury investigation was terminated and my client was not brought to trial. Therefore, I concluded that no damaging evidence had been uncovered.

When you are working with CID, the message is clear: CID is thorough and determined. Don't underestimate them or their abilities.

THE UPPER ECHELONS

What People in the Upper Echelons Are Really Like

A large group that stands out and apart from IRS employees is what I call the upper echelons. These are IRS attorneys, accountants, and specially trained people with advanced educational degrees. In 1997, the chief counsel's office had over 2,600 employees. The majority of them are in the upper echelons and their work exposes them to a very full range of legal matters, from appeals and criminal tax cases (including the kind that end up in the Supreme Court) to all sorts of other litigation (Freedom of Information Act opinions, unfair labor practices, bankruptcies) and international tax matters.

Never for a moment forget: **Every time you get in the sights of the IRS there is an enormous legal infrastructure ready to fire.**

What's even more interesting is that this group, which reports up through the chief counsel's office, is separate and distinct from another IRS upper-echelon function, the Legislative Affairs Division, which reports up through the deputy commissioner, directly under the IRS commissioner.

The Legislative Affairs Division is heavily focused on developing, coordinating, and monitoring plans to implement new or pending legislation; developing legislative proposals for the IRS; communicating legislative information to the IRS commissioner and throughout the

IRS; working with Public Affairs on press releases and media strategies relating to new legislation; and coordinating IRS responses to the General Accounting Office (GAO), the investigative arm of Congress.[6]

All of these upper-echelon people are treated as a rather elite group of which the IRS is particularly proud and which it handles with kid gloves.

To keep updated on their specialties and on policy and procedural changes within the IRS, upper-echelon employees periodically attend rather high-level training courses. The nature of their work keeps them together in a sort of specialized clique. In turn, they tend to stay among themselves and are looked up to by everyone else at the IRS.

Their salary levels are fairly competitive with (but not equal to) those in the private sector, and the on-the-job experience they can gain on the basis of the volume and range of cases that they are exposed to can be truly superb. Many at this level stay an average of five to ten years before they go off to a specialized law or accounting firm, where they command larger salaries and are considered prized property, having come from the IRS.

How to Work with the Upper-Echelon Mentality

Taxpayers rarely, if ever, come in contact with this level of IRS personnel. If you do, what you'll find are highly educated professionals, many attorneys who know their stuff. They are hardworking, focused, and operate essentially like trial lawyers, doing research, interviewing, preparing legal papers, appearing in court cases.

The only time taxpayers might meet someone from the IRS upper echelon is if they go to Tax Court or the Appeals Office (formerly referred to as the Appellate Division). At both of these levels, your representative will talk to his or her person and that's where you'll get some inkling of how these people operate. The chart on page 95 gives an overview of the process described in the following pages.

You and the Appeals Process

The IRS Appeals Office has the authority to settle cases, partially or wholly, on the basis of its assessment of the IRS's chances of winning. In other words, the ultimate objective for an appeals officer (who may be a lawyer or someone trained by the IRS to handle appeals) is to prevent a case from going to Tax Court. The Tax Court calendar has a huge backlog of cases, and the process of going through it is extremely trying for both sides. Even after a case has left the audit level and is filed with the Tax Court, to avoid going to Tax Court the Appeals Office can inter-

Income Tax Appeal Procedure

Internal Revenue Service

At any stage of procedure:
You can agree and arrange to pay.
You can ask the Service to issue
you a notice of deficiency so you
can file a petition with the Tax Court.
You can pay the tax and file a claim
for a refund.

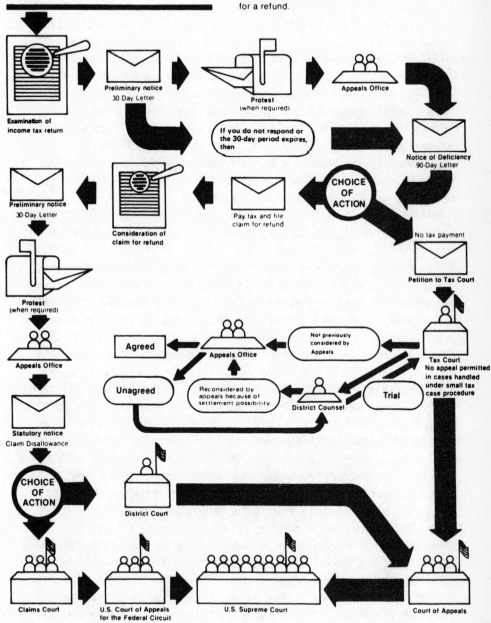

Examination of income tax return

Preliminary notice 30 Day Letter

Protest (when required)

Appeals Office

If you do not respond or the 30-day period expires, then

Notice of Deficiency 90-Day Letter

CHOICE OF ACTION

Pay tax and file claim for refund

Consideration of claim for refund

Preliminary notice 30-Day Letter

Protest (when required)

Appeals Office

Statutory notice Claim Disallowance

CHOICE OF ACTION

No tax payment

Petition to Tax Court

Tax Court No appeal permitted in cases handled under small tax case procedure

Not previously considered by Appeals

Trial

District Counsel

Reconsidered by appeals because of settlement possibility

Appeals Office

Agreed

Unagreed

District Court

Claims Court

U.S. Court of Appeals for the Federal Circuit

U.S. Supreme Court

Court of Appeals

95

vene and offer the taxpayer an additional four-month period to settle the case in Appeals.

Appeals categorizes the cases it hears into small cases and all others. Small case disputes involve $10,000 or less. With RRA '98, beginning July 23, 1998, that amount has been raised to $50,000 or less per tax year, excluding interest. Small cases are initiated by the taxpayer but must be concurred with by the Court. The trial for small cases is conducted informally, with taxpayers typically representing themselves, though they can also choose anyone admitted to practice before the Tax Court. Briefs, oral arguments, and rules of evidence are not applied. Furthermore, any decisions rendered in small case procedures may not be cited as precedent in future cases and may not be appealed to a higher court by the government or the taxpayer. The Court will usually agree to the taxpayer's election of a small case unless the dispute will exceed the small case dollar amount, or if justice requires that the case be heard by a regular division of the Court, i.e., if the decision would have an impact on other cases. Then a full trial is preferable.

NOTE: Small cases are normally decided by a brief statement by the Court, often orally, with only a summary of the reasons for the decision.[7]

The settlement ratio that Appeals has with small cases is an impressive 98 percent and a success ratio of 90 percent of all docketed cases. **Regarding all other cases, the IRS doesn't go to Tax Court unless it believes that it has a better than 50 percent chance of winning.**

If the appeals officer in the Appeals Office determines that the IRS may have a tough time winning the case, he'll recommend coming to a settlement. To achieve this he will probably concede an issue to induce the taxpayer to settle without delay. Even if it looks as if the IRS will win, the appeals officer might still offer a small concession simply to avoid the time and expense of going to Tax Court. At this point it was wise for the taxpayer to settle because if the case went further, the Tax Court automatically presumed that the IRS position was correct. Now that the burden of proof has shifted to the IRS in noncriminal court proceedings regarding a taxpayer's liability, the question of should you settle or fight still remains. (See 1998 Tax Legislation, page 297.)

The IRS has in place a program to help taxpayers prepare and file protest letters in resolving undue delays in getting a case through the appeals process. To take advantage of this service, speak to an Appeals Office representative by calling your local district office. You can also send for IRS Publication 5, *Your Appeal Rights and How to Prepare a Protest If You Don't Agree.* In any case, a filing must be made with the

Tax Court no more than 90 days after the mailing date of a tax deficiency notice. Forms can be obtained from the Clerk of the Court, U.S. Tax Court, 400 Second Street NW, Washington, D.C. 20217. The Tax Court website is: www.ustaxcourt.gov.

OFFERING A BRIBE—WHAT ARE THE CONSEQUENCES?

Accepting bribes has been against the rules of conduct for anyone working in the IRS, *at any level or division,* from its inception, as the U.S. Constitution clearly states. That doesn't mean, however, that the practice doesn't exist.

A quiet bribe between a revenue officer (or even a revenue agent or tax auditor) and a taxpayer who owes tax money (or has obviously fiddled around on a tax return) is not and has never been unique. There are two primary issues to be considered here. What constitutes a bribe, and did you offer one?

Generally a bribe involves an offer to an IRS employee whose purpose is to persuade or encourage that person not to take a certain action against you, the taxpayer. The bribe can be anything from a fancy lunch to a gift, a flight to Santa Fe, money, and lots more. But essentially a bribe is anything that sounds as if it is a bribe to the IRS person whose mind and actions you are trying to bend your way.

The Office of Government Ethics issues *Rules of Conduct* that apply to all governmental agencies, including the IRS. Furthermore, there is a standard procedure regarding the taking of bribes that IRS collections officers, revenue agents, and anyone else having intimate contact with a taxpayer must follow. The procedure, which is drilled into the heads of these IRS personnel, is very precise, and goes something like this:

PROCEDURE FOR REPORTING BRIBES

- If a revenue agent believes he or she has been offered a bribe, nothing is done or said at that time, while the taxpayer is present.
- As soon as the meeting with the taxpayer is over, the agent is to immediately notify the Inspection Division, whose job it is to keep tabs on corruption within the IRS.
- If the Inspection Division decides to take the next step, and in most cases it probably does because it accepts the agent's word, the taxpayer is set up with the same agent at another meeting—except

this time the agent is wired and has been rehearsed so that he or she knows how to get the taxpayer to repeat the bribe offer.

- If this occurs, someone from the Inspection Division will appear at the right moment and the taxpayer will be placed under arrest.
- The worst scenario: The U.S. attorney's office will get involved and prosecute the case, and the taxpayer could face a jail sentence. The best scenario for the taxpayer is if the bribe offer proves to be inconclusive. However, the items under audit will surely be disallowed in full.

I would never advise any client of mine to offer a bribe or anything that sounds like a bribe to anyone employed by the IRS. You may feel bad about paying an enormous tax assessment. But compare that to a stay in prison.

STANDARD OPERATING PROCEDURES

If anyone in the tax field were given two minutes to come up with a handful of epithets to characterize the behaviors we often face at the IRS, I am certain the list would include the following:

- Out-and-out lying
- Bluffing
- Threatening
- Sheer incompetence
- System breakdown
- The "IRS shuffle"
- Offering misleading or erroneous information

Watch how the first three weave in and out of a client audit that began in 1997 covering 1995 and lasted over two years.

Some background: An IRS analysis of my client's 1995 checking account showed that out of a total of $500,000, only $100,000 was accounted for. My client attributed the other $400,000 to the sale of an art collection that he had accumulated over a 40-year period. The sale of the art was conducted by an auction house that had gone out of business about six months after completing the sale.

Things began to heat up as auditor number two entered the scene toward the end of 1997. The first auditor, assigned to us by the IRS for over nine months, had been in way over her head. Her replacement was a shrewd middle-aged woman who told us she had 15 years with the IRS. She was also extremely busy, with a full workload at the IRS and college teaching besides. It became common for her to cancel meetings, be out of the office for weeks at a time, and be difficult to reach.

For the final meeting she promised to bring in an IRS "art expert" to refute the sales prices and/or costs we were submitting. She also said that the case would drag on unless my client accompanied me. Clearly she was hoping he would make some admission that she could use against him. How did I counter her threats? By showing her documented costs of the art, a 45-page inventory list packaged with canceled checks and receipts (vendors' bills) that were from one to 30 years old (some of the paper looked quite antique). The checks and receipts total came to $90,000.

Next I counseled my client so that he said nothing of use to her. I actually liked the idea of his being there because he was, in effect, the resident art expert.

Our auditor never did bring in that IRS expert (it was a big bluff) because, I believed then and still do, she was in an enormous hurry to finish with us (you'll see why), and requesting an expert can require a lot of lead time.

By the end of the day, we submitted the following data:

Total sales price	$400,000
Costs we claimed (total inventory list)	210,000
Taxable capital gain (profit)	$190,000

Since the inventory records were meticulous and authentic, the IRS auditor agreed to allow us all of the $90,000 plus half of the cost for which we had no paperwork, i.e., half of $120,000, or $60,000. (In audits of this nature, actual receipts are requested but are not an absolute requirement to win your case.)

In summary, these were the figures:

Total gross proceeds		$400,000
Less allowable cost (justified with receipts)	$90,000	
Extra as agreed (our deal)	60,000	150,000
New capital gain		$250,000

In 1995, the maximum long-term capital gains rate was 28 percent. Hence, we argued long and hard for any unreported income to be considered from the art sale (capital gain) rather than being considered as ordinary income, since my client was in the highest tax bracket of 39.6 percent.

The proposed settlement was a tax liability of $70,000 plus approximately $22,000 of penalties and interest.

We decided to accept the proposal, and the auditor said she would write it up and, as is customary, submit it to her group chief for approval.

Four weeks later I called her to ask when we could expect the papers. At this point she informed me that she was allowing $90,000 for our costs (only the amount we could prove), but she did not mention the extra $60,000 she had agreed to. She insisted that she never agreed to it and as far as she was concerned, there was nothing more she could do.

I called her group chief and told him that she had lied to me and my client. He took it under advisement for a couple of days and called me back to say that he believed her story and that if we were not happy, we should take the case to the Appeals Office, so we did. As was her style, she managed to drag out the meeting with the appeals officer by not forwarding her work papers until six months later, which of course meant an additional six months of interest tacked on to the bill.

The Appeals Office will carefully examine the merits of a case. If they don't believe there will be a clear-cut victory in Tax Court, the IRS will strike a bargain, and that's exactly what happened after a two-hour meeting.

The appeals officer allowed the original cost of $90,000 plus $50,000 of the extra $60,000. This meant that my client had "regained" $14,000 (28 percent of $50,000 equals $14,000) plus accumulated penalties and interest.

P.S. Within two months after the conclusion of the audit, our shrewd auditor was promoted to the Appeals Office, a rather significant promotion for a revenue agent.

Many questions remain open: Was the revenue agent in a big rush because she expected a promotion? (In a friendlier moment, she did actually mention to me that she was expecting it.) After agreeing to allow us half of the $120,000, did she realize that she had given up too much, which was not her normal performance? Or, remembering that she was brought in as a relief quarterback, did she want to avoid showing weakness (giving a taxpayer too much), which would hurt her chances for that promotion to Appeals?

Now watch as the IRS easily and predictably produces the last few items of behavior that often show up during an audit.

In early September 1997, out of the blue, I received a copy of a check that a client received from the IRS in the amount of $40,000. As I scanned it, the particulars of her case came back to me.

On her 1040 form for 1996, we requested that the IRS carry over $40,000 to her 1997 return. The money represented an overpayment that would do my client more good if carried forward to the following year. This was because by the time her 1040 was expected to be filed, June 15, 1997, she already owed $40,000 in estimated taxes for 1997, so we proceeded as if the carryover had taken place. (As planned, her 1040 for 1996 was filed June 15, 1997.) Although we thought the IRS had honored our request, three months later, when we looked at the check in hand, we saw that obviously something had gone wrong.

The first question was "What should we do with the check?" The problem was that now my client would begin to incur penalties for not paying the April and June 1997 quarterly estimated income taxes in a timely manner.

After mailing a power of attorney to the IRS district office, I called a revenue officer at the district office (taking the number directly from the letter in hand) and asked why the IRS had sent the check. The revenue officer's response was typical: "I don't know, and I can't tell you. The 1996 return is not showing up on the computer."

"Well, what about the 1997 return? Can you locate any estimated payments?" I asked.

"No, I can't. I'm too busy right now. I've got too much to get through. You'll have to call back later."

"But then I'll have to start all over again."

"Just call the same number," the revenue officer said. "You'll get someone to help you."

"Can't you just take a minute to look it up?"

"I have to go. Call back," he said and hung up.

A few hours later I called back and, surprisingly, ended up with the same revenue officer. Again I asked him to locate my client's 1996 return. Guess what? After a few minutes, he found it. "Oh, yes," he said. "Here it is. The income listed is $732,000, but no tax is due."

Now I was fully aware that my client's taxable income was $732,000. I was also aware that the tax paid on that return was $225,000. Here I was, faced with an IRS revenue officer in the Collection Division telling me that my client had no tax due. "How could there be no tax due on $732,000?" I asked, totally astonished.

"Well," the person replied, "maybe there were a lot of deductions." I actually held my breath wondering if in a few weeks my client would receive another refund, this time for $225,000. "Oh, wait a second," he said. "I've got another screen that says there is an assessment on this return of $225,000."

"That's not an assessment. That's the tax we paid on the account."

After a few more minutes of banter, the revenue officer became convinced that I was correct, and we proceeded to find an answer to the $40,000 check by going over the payments one by one. "The tax was entered in the wrong place," he said.

"That's impossible," I answered.

"Oh, not by you. On my screen." I guess an IRS entry clerk made the error.

Now a plan of action became clear. I would instruct my client to return the original $40,000 check to the IRS with a cover letter explaining that the money should have been credited to her 1997 estimated tax account.

The Secret to Finding Your Way Through the IRS

I am not interested in taxpayers understanding what each individual section of the IRS does in isolation. **You have to be able to make connections, to see literally the whole of what the IRS does, so that things take on meaning within this framework.** Those who have become experts in working with the IRS say one of the secrets to their success is the ability to grasp, even superficially, what goes on from one end of the agency to the other. Taxpayers who can afford it flock to these specialists, who know how to "find their way through" the IRS because of their ability to view the agency from a larger perspective.

Taxpayers also need to recognize where the power of the IRS comes from above and beyond the never-ending process of collecting, enforcing, and processing billions of tax dollars. Dissecting this power into its component parts, then learning how to manage it, is the next hurdle to jump.

5

Neutralizing the IRS's Power

THE IRS POWER BASE

The IRS power base comes from several sources. The IRS has unique

- Information resources
- Legal standing
- Role as a law enforcement agency
- Legislation-originating authority
- Ability to make mistakes without consequences
- Freedom to do what it wants

POWER FROM INFORMATION RESOURCES

Information gathering, with state-of-the-art equipment, has imbued the IRS with more power than any other bureaucracy in the world. This fact goes hand in hand with other, more disturbing realities: IRS computer centers have questionable security; there is significant evidence of periodic leaks for political purposes; few, if any, independent private or governmental bodies review IRS operations or management processes. "Thus," comments David Burnham, "it has come to pass that the IRS has developed into the largest, most computerized, and least examined law enforcement agency in America."[1]

What Information Is Gathered About You?

Did you know that the IRS is legally entitled to collect information about you from the following sources:

- Your employer or anyone who pays you over $600 for services rendered
- Institutions that provide pensions and annuities to the elderly
- Casinos and racetracks
- Banks or corporations
- Barter deals or exchanges of property
- Real estate agents, when you buy or sell a property
- Any organization granting you a loan
- Your state unemployment office

In fact, the IRS receives information from such a wide range and number of sources that if it wanted to, it could easily discover what you earn, how you live, how many homes you own, the type of car you drive, where you spend your free time, where you go on vacation, and on and on.

Did you know that once it has the information, the IRS can do the following:

- Label you as a someone who owes the government money, never filed a return, earns above a certain dollar amount, has high audit potential, and more.
- Allow thousands of IRS agents across the country easy access to your tax return.
- Share the information on your tax return regularly with other states, cities, and federal agencies.

It seems as if each new piece of legislation designed to provide additional information from third parties about how taxpayers live whets the IRS's appetite even further. Since 1994, any charitable contribution of $250 or more must be acknowledged in writing by the organization receiving the money in order for it to be deductible by the giver.

What Are Your Legal Rights Against Misuse of the Information?

There is a body of law that protects private citizens by prohibiting misuse of financial information. One is the Privacy Act of 1974; another is the Computer Matching and Privacy Protection Act of 1988, Public Law 100-503.

Generally speaking, preventing misuse means making certain that only those who are allowed by law to access the information can in fact do so. It means using the information for its designated purpose—for example, to verify that someone's annual income can support a specific mortgage loan amount, or to answer taxpayers' questions about their tax returns. It means ensuring that the information used is up to date. The fact that someone has declared bankruptcy, for example, must be cleared from a person's record after a period of 10 years.

If these laws are broken private citizens can legally seek redress. What if, for example, a seller accepted your bid to buy a new home and an independent private agency that verifies credit standing notified all parties concerned that your credit was unacceptable? Suppose that wasn't true. Suppose your credit rating was fine. With a credit agency, you have the right to demand a printout of the information, or to follow specific procedures to update or correct it. **With the IRS this is not possible.**

Who Is Guarding Your Privacy?

Information protection for taxpayers regarding the information collected about them and overseen by the IRS must come from two sources: the technology, which stores and manipulates the information, and the people who have access to it.

Scrupulous and precise rules for accessing information should be in place in IRS data centers to protect your interests and prevent leaks and misuse. However, there really aren't such rules.

Part of the problem, according to the IRS, is lack of resources. It takes funding to track down what systems networks within the IRS are being linked to what other IRS systems networks, and to close any gaps through which information can be accessed or "leaked." It takes time and effort to sweep each system clean of passwords used by former employees so that at least these entry points are locked. And, yes, it is expensive to install security-oriented software and to conduct periodic security audits.

Timely reports by the GAO, one in April 1997, continue to point out "serious weaknesses" in the controls used to safeguard IRS computer systems and protect taxpayer data.

Here's some comforting news: In a 1997 report, after visiting five IRS facilities, the GAO said that some 6,400 computer tapes couldn't be properly accounted for and that some might contain thousands of taxpayer files. Three months later, an IRS spokesperson was quoted in *New York Newsday* as saying that 5,700 of the tapes had been located.

Why were the tapes lost? Where did they go? Who had access to them, where are the rest of them, and how much, if any, information about *you* leaked out?

To reveal or not to reveal information disclosed on an individual's tax return has been debated since President Lincoln signed the first income tax into law in 1862. Almost from the beginning there were two opposing camps.

Congress's position at that time required that tax returns be published in at least four public places and for at least 15 days. (Can you imagine it!) In this way it was hoped that everyone would be kept honest. In 1914 the Supreme Court ruled that returns of individuals shall not be subject to inspection by anyone except the proper officers and employees of the Treasury Department.[2]

The battle over confidentiality raged on. Each time a new revenue act was proposed, proponents of disclosure argued for the people's right to know, while the opposition argued that people have a right to privacy concerning their business affairs.

The real kicker came with the Nixon administration's abuses of individual privacy through misuse of IRS information during the early 1970's. Section 6103 of the *Internal Revenue Code* was eventually approved by Congress several years later to prevent political use of IRS-generated information by limiting the number of people and governmental agencies that could access tax information. But the IRS is still plagued by "snooping," or unauthorized inspection of tax returns by the agency's own employees.

In 1997, the Taxpayer Browsing Protection Act (new *IR Code* Section 7213A) was passed. The act imposes criminal penalties up to $1,000 or imprisonment of not more than one year or both for the unauthorized inspection of tax returns and tax information by any federal employee or IRS contractor as well as any state employee or other person who acquired the tax return or return information under the provisions of Section 6103. The bill also provides that offended taxpayers may bring a civil action for damages against the government in a U.S. district court.

Thus far, the IRS has defined two approaches for implementing the Taxpayer Browsing Protection Act. The first is through modernizing its automated systems, which will allow the IRS to restrict employees' access to taxpayer records that need to be looked at only if there is a work-related reason to do so, and to enable the IRS to detect unauthorized access almost as soon as it happens. As you know, systems modernization of any nature at the IRS is years in coming, so in the meantime the agency has taken other steps. These are to provide briefings to all employees on unauthorized access, and to create a unit to track proven access violations that would also help to administer penalties.

Between October 1997 and November 1998, the IRS identified 5,468 potential instances of unauthorized access, and completed preliminary investigations of 4,392 of those. In 15 cases, the IRS has determined that employees had intentionally accessed taxpayer data without authorization. These employees either resigned or were fired.[3]

But programs that seem to ignore taxpayer privacy continue to be launched by the IRS. Unofficially called "the lender project," developed after a two-year test period, here's how this one works:

When you apply for a home loan, the lender typically asks for copies of your income tax returns to verify your income. It is not uncommon for taxpayers to try to increase their chances of success by inflating their income on a 1040 specifically "revised" for the mortgage lender. In the new IRS program, participating lenders in California fax the income information to the IRS, and within 48 hours the IRS replies with tax data—typically the applicant's AGI for one or more years.

If the income on the application doesn't match the income on the tax return, not only may you be rejected for the loan, you also stand to face an audit, since the IRS assumes you either underpaid taxes or filed a false loan application.

The prime targets for this effort allegedly are self-employed borrowers who have a high degree of flexibility regarding how much income they report. Among 31,985 loans for which the IRS was asked to verify income, differences were found on 1,687, or 5.27 percent. Five hundred of these have been selected for audit.[4]

It seems as if the IRS has decided that mortgage lenders are a perfect vehicle to police taxpayers' returns, especially those of the self-employed.

If the IRS goes national with this program, lenders will e-mail authorizations by home-loan applicants to the IRS, and the agency will e-mail back the tax data as a matter of course.[5]

Now, we should always be accurate in reporting our income, but is this an issue of catching tax cheats, as the IRS claims, or is it a gross manipulation of privileged information? Although Section 6103 is on the books, given the IRS's controlling, secretive nature, the reality is that an elaborate set of barriers discourages taxpayers from seeking legal redress in the courts. The misapplication of the well-intentioned privacy law, says Burnham, has led to a situation where "lawyers are blocked from obtaining information they need to initiate suits challenging genuine IRS abuses. . . . A congressional committee empowered to investigate the IRS is partially blocked from investigating serious allegations of IRS corruption by a tortured application of the same law. The IRS has repeatedly initiated audits, leaked information, or otherwise harassed individual citizens, both in and out of government, who raised valid questions about its performance."[6]

POWER FROM THE IRS'S UNIQUE LEGAL STANDING

If you are a taxpayer suspected of violating our tax laws, you are guilty until you prove that you are not. No other area of our government operates upon this premise. In fact, the entire foundation of our civil law is based upon the assumption that one is innocent until proven guilty—except where the IRS is involved. The IRS can accuse taxpayers of an infringement, garnishee their paychecks, put a lien on their homes, and seize their cars and businesses, with minimal court approval. Unfortunately, the accused taxpayer is fully responsible for proving his or her innocence. Limited relief is now available if your case reaches the U.S. Tax Court. (See 1998 Tax Legislation, page 297.)

POWER FROM ITS UNIQUE ROLE AS
A LAW-ENFORCEMENT AGENCY

A look, even a rather cursory one, at IRS operations since its reorganization in the early 1950's reveals an indisputable trend: the continuous expansion of the IRS's authority to penalize taxpayers for a growing laundry list of freshly created tax-related violations. In the early 1960's there were about six penalties that the IRS regularly imposed on taxpayers due to, for example, filing late, paying late, and underestimating income. **Now the IRS has the authority to penalize taxpayers and business entities for some 150 types of violations.**
    Taxpayers are penalized when they

* Write checks to the IRS that bounce.
* Don't provide a Social Security number for themselves, their dependents, or other persons.
* Don't file a complete return.
* Don't report their tips to their employer.
* Are considered negligent in the preparation of a tax return.
* Overvalue a deduction by more than 20 percent.

An entire new slew of violations and consequent penalties has been created by the phenomenon of information reporting, or, rather, inadequate information reporting. Who is liable? People or organizations that do not provide the IRS with information that Congress has deemed necessary for collecting taxes. This includes

- Tax preparers who fail to enter their federal ID number on a return they have prepared.
- Banks, real estate agencies, and securities houses that don't provide the IRS with accurate and timely information about money they are paying to taxpayers. (Fines can be stiff, up to $100,000.)
- Any business or organization that employs independent contractors or consultants and fails to file 1099 forms for payments of $600 or more per year.

Congress and the courts have also granted the IRS powers that have been specifically denied traditional enforcement agencies. For example, when the FBI investigates drug-related crimes or money laundering, its actions are rooted in strictly defined criminal laws. If a person's civil rights are proved to have been violated, even if the target is a major drug offender, FBI agents involved suffer the consequences.

Too often with the IRS's Criminal Investigation Division, however, the actions guiding its special agents are what the IRS determines they should be.

The IRS and its employees are carefully protected in carrying out a range of activities that no others in the field of law enforcement would dare attempt for fear of losing their jobs or being jailed.

POWER FROM ITS UNIQUE LEGISLATION-CREATING AUTHORITY

The majority of taxpayers do not know that the IRS plays a major role in influencing and actually creating legislation through several distinct vehicles, including

- Technical advice memoranda
- Revenue rulings
- Private letter rulings
- Regulations

In addition, there are several not-so-well-known arenas in which the IRS has the ability to affect a tax bill *before* it becomes a law, and also literally to sponsor its own tax legislation.

As taxpayers, we should be cognizant of the IRS's capacity to affect and create legislation that has an impact on each of us. Most of these are powers that have been granted to the IRS by Congress and authorized by the *Internal Revenue Code*.

Technical Advice Memorandum

A technical advice memorandum arises from a request by an IRS district office or the Appeals Office concerning a technical or procedural question that can arise from several sources: during the examination of a taxpayer's return; in consideration of a taxpayer's claim for refund or credit; or in some other matter involving a specific taxpayer under the jurisdiction of the Examination Division or Appeals Office.[7]

A technical advice memo is highly specific in its focus and is binding only upon a particular issue in a given case. If the IRS feels it has unearthed an issue that could have broader appeal, it can be developed into a revenue ruling. (For an example, see page 208.)

Since 1993, the IRS has made decisions on an average of 290 technical advice memoranda per year.[8]

Revenue Rulings

A revenue ruling is an official interpretation of the *Internal Revenue Code* issued to provide guidance to taxpayers and the agency itself. The subjects of revenue rulings can originate in many areas, such as rulings to taxpayers, technical advice memos, court decisions, tax articles, news reports, and suggestions submitted by tax organizations and industry specialists.

Revenue rulings are published weekly in the *Internal Revenue Bulletin* (an IRS publication) and various other tax services. They also often show up in trade publications or monthly tax newsletters, where taxpayers can read about them. Specific rulings are selected for publication because

- They answer questions commonly asked by taxpayers on specific tax matters.
- The IRS believes the information presented has fairly widespread application to taxpayers in general.

Thus, without any congressional involvement, the IRS is freely empowered to interpret how a specific area of the tax law

should be applied. The IRS decides, "This is the law. This is how we see it."

Since 1993, the IRS has made decisions on an average of 379 revenue rulings per year.[9]

Private Letter Rulings

Private letter rulings are written statements issued to a taxpayer that interpret and apply the tax laws to a taxpayer's specific set of circumstances.[10] These rulings are initiated because a company or individual is considering a specific action and needs to know how the IRS would treat any tax implications involved. A company, for instance, may need to know how substantial sums should be treated on its books, e.g., as tax deductions, legitimate losses, or tax savings. The transaction in question is generally outside the normal range of categories described in the *Internal Revenue Code.*

Because they are elicited by a specific request, the rulings may be applied only by the taxpayer who receives the ruling. They cannot be relied on as precedents by other taxpayers or by IRS personnel in examining other returns.[11]

In reality private letter rulings are well known to and mainly used by businesses, especially major companies that are advised by experienced and handsomely paid tax attorneys. They are often willing to take a chance by relying on another taxpayer's private letter ruling on circumstances similar to their own particular case. These attorneys also know that the IRS often gathers several private letter rulings on a similar subject and molds them into a revenue ruling.

The IRS states that with a few exceptions, all letter rulings are available for public inspection after the deletion of all data that could identify the taxpayer.[12] **But since most people are not aware that private letter rulings exist, they are not likely to ask to see one, even though these rulings can affect broad segments of unsuspecting taxpayers.** On those occasions when the IRS hands down a negative conclusion to a taxpayer's question in a private letter ruling, watch out. The IRS will warn the taxpayer when the unfavorable ruling is about to come out, and the taxpayer can change or withdraw the original request altogether. However, the IRS notifies the taxpayer's local district office to inform them that research on the ruling is available from the IRS National Office. Those who requested the ruling should not be surprised if their tax return is later audited.

Private letter rulings allow the IRS broad discretion in handing down final decisions related to tax law, often to function de facto like the

Supreme Court. Sometimes Congress eventually gets involved in more important cases, but it is likely to be years after the impact of the letter has been felt.

Since 1993, the IRS has decided on an average of 3,157 private letter rulings per year.[13]

Regulations

Once a tax bill is signed into law by the president, the bill is passed to the IRS. In essence, Congress says, "Here's the law, IRS. Now work out how it's going to be administered."

Regulations, or "regs," as they are known in the business, accompany about 80 percent of every new tax law. They are written by IRS attorneys and other staff who work directly with the chief counsel's office to interpret, clarify, and advise taxpayers and tax professionals about how to comply with the new law. "Regs" can appear soon after a revenue act is passed or, because the process of developing final regs is so complicated, years later. Since regulations are law, when they do appear they automatically become retroactive and taxpayers are required to file amended tax returns accordingly.

Because regulations can be hundreds of pages long for any given piece of tax law, they appear first as "proposed," then "permanent," then "final." Once issued in either temporary or final form, they are binding on all taxpayers and employees of the IRS.[14]

All regulations appear in the *Federal Register* (a daily publication of all governmental proceedings) and some commercial publications. Then they are thrown open for public comment. Most often CPA's and lobbyists send written replies to the IRS National Office suggesting how to reword or reframe them. The IRS also offers the opportunity for a public hearing on proposed regulations if a hearing is requested.[15] The IRS is supposed to consider the comments it receives before a final regulation is developed.

What do taxpayers and tax professionals use as a guide between the time when a reg is proposed and when it is finalized? They have a kind of guessing game during which they interpret the law and worry about the consequences later.

Sometimes an aspect of a new tax law may require a quick fix, especially if delaying the issuance of the final regulation(s) would mean a hardship to those affected by the new law. In this case, the IRS does not wait for the regulation process to be completed. Instead, it issues *temporary regulations* that short-circuit the usual opportunity for public comment.

Given the situation, wouldn't most taxpayers ask, "Isn't the system of creating tax laws and applying them to the taxpaying public a chaotic and virtually unregulated situation?" The answer is a definite no because basic tax laws that affect the majority of taxpayers get "fixed" right away.

Waiting is the norm, however, in more complicated areas of the tax law—for example, allocations of partnership income and loss, distribution of money and property, or the intricate machinations involving how certain expenses can be recorded—regulations have been in the process of being finalized for years. In 1999 the IRS was still writing final regs for the 1986 reform act. This hard-to-believe situation, where proposed regulations have yet to be finalized after 10 years or more, was confirmed by testimony presented by the American Institute of Certified Public Accountants at a public hearing of the National Commission on Restructuring the IRS, a bipartisan panel created by Congress in 1997.

The favorite statement from Congress at the end of a new tax bill is "Regulations to be promulgated by the IRS." Usually no timetable is attached.

I hope the present system regarding preparation of regulations by the IRS continues. Tax professionals usually enjoy trying to think how the IRS thinks, making decisions accordingly, and patting ourselves on the back when the outcomes are confirmed by final regs.

Since 1993, the IRS has made decisions on an average of 223 regulations per year.[16]

The Role of the IRS Before a Bill Becomes Law

Many Americans are familiar with how a revenue bill becomes a law. **But do they also know the extent to which the IRS is involved in shaping tax legislation before a bill becomes a law?**

The IRS Legislative Affairs Division is brought in to analyze and contribute to the development of pending legislation long before it comes up for a vote in Congress, and to ensure effective implementation of new legislation after it is enacted. This is actually sound management practice. But taxpayers must learn to recognize the extent to which the IRS becomes involved with new tax legislation, especially legislation the IRS doesn't like, and more, the extent to which it can massage, refine, or downright change, oppose, or block legislation to protect its own point of view, or maintain the status quo.

Here's a specific example of how this works:

In 1987, when Senator David Pryor (D., Arkansas) introduced the Omnibus Taxpayer Bill of Rights legislation, the first of its kind that describes the rights private citizens should have when dealing with the

IRS, he knew what he would be up against: major opposition from the IRS. He has even gone on record saying it was very difficult indeed to find members of Congress to support the bill. "I saw real fear of the possible IRS retaliation among many members of the Senate and the House of Representatives," he said at the time.[17] **In other words, other elected officials believed that if they supported his bill, the IRS would get after them in one way or another.** (For more on the "Taxpayer Bill of Rights," see page 167 and Appendix D.)

When it comes to "shaping" or even rejecting new legislation that the IRS doesn't want to see enacted into law, it is not shy. It labels the legislation as unnecessary, says it will interfere with the normal tax collection process, claims it would involve too great an imposition on the administration, and asserts it doesn't have the budget or staff to comply.

IRS-Sponsored Legislation

Ensuring even greater clout in the legislative arena is the IRS's ability to sponsor legislation and to lobby Congress for IRS-backed proposals to become law. **Currently, this is the highest rung the IRS has reached in its ability to gain legislative powers almost equal to those of the U.S. Congress.**

During the hearings on the Revenue Act of 1962, the IRS uncovered the phenomenon of companies claiming large deductions for vacations, club dues, theater tickets, sports activities, business gifts, etc., from an audit of 38,000 returns. The IRS recommended remedial legislation to Congress, including substantial limitations on deductions for travel and entertainment expenses. Congress enacted the legislation, which became Section 274 of the *Internal Revenue Code* and ended up filling three pages of fine print.[18]

On January 1, 1993, newly signed legislation eliminated unreimbursed travel expenses as a deduction for taxpayers in the construction, engineering, computer, and other fields who were sent by their employers for one- to two-year assignments. Henceforth, employees in these categories could no longer claim work-related meal, lodging, and travel expenses as deductions against their income. Any payments these workers received for living costs become taxable income after one year. The IRS has had a consistent track record of voicing its displeasure and fighting taxpayers on this issue. No doubt the IRS pointed out that by eliminating this deduction, Congress could expect to increase tax revenues by $131 million over five years.

In another example, the IRS fought to make punitive damages taxable. Although some district courts ruled in favor of taxpayers (that proceeds of punitive damages were not taxable in some cases), the IRS continued to fight it until it got its way in the 1996 tax law.

In 1792, the Office of the Commissioner of Internal Revenue was established to levy and collect taxes. **Today, the IRS frequently goes head to head with Congress, creating and shaping tax legislation and challenging new and existing tax laws.**

POWER TO MAKE MISTAKES WITHOUT CONSEQUENCES

When people find themselves chatting about the IRS, one remark that inevitably surfaces is the fact that the audit rate for individual tax returns hovers between 1 and 1.6 percent. This remark is phrased to imply a certain comfort level, almost a gift to the American taxpaying public. Nothing could be further from the truth.

One percent of individual tax returns audited in 1998 translates into over 1,230,000 people. Now that percentage doesn't sound so small, does it?

Just extrapolate this same thought to the numbers of taxpayers affected each year by IRS mistakes. Let's say an IRS computer mistakenly sends out a past due tax notice to only 0.5 percent of the taxpayers in New York City. The letter charges them with penalties for failing to pay their quarterly estimated taxes in a timely manner. In fact, the computer program was malfunctioning, and most of these people did make their payments correctly.

Most taxpayers (imagine you are one of them) would naturally respond by calling their local service center, writing the necessary letter, even double-checking with their tax professional. Weeks go by, all to no avail. More letters and telephone calls later still haven't succeeded in short-circuiting the process, and now you are faced with a large collection of new IRS notices announcing dollars and penalties due.

No matter what you do, eventually your case reaches the Collection Division, where you personally fit the bill as the "cheating" taxpayer that the IRS teaches its employees about. You are trapped in IRS Problem City. The thing is—this is not happening only to you. It is *simultaneously* happening to 30,000 others, because that's 0.5 percent of the taxpayers in New York City!

The IRS does not keep records of how many taxpayers it has abused. IRS computers can be highly effective in catching a mismatch between 1099's and 1040's. But the same technology isn't at all interested in slowing down because of IRS mistakes made along the way.

POWER FROM THE FREEDOM TO DO WHAT IT WANTS

Another aspect of IRS power comes when it decides to ignore the federal government, our judicial system, Congress, individual rights of citizens, or its own job requirements and chooses, instead, to do just exactly what it wants.

The IRS Defies the Judicial System

Dr. Nader Soliman, an anesthesiologist, who worked in three hospitals a total of 30 to 35 hours a week during the year, also set up a home office in his McLean, Virginia, apartment to maintain records, consult with doctors and patients, perform billing and scheduling activities, and study medical journals. The doctor entered the public's view when the IRS, during an audit, denied his $2,500 home-office deduction (Section 280A of the *Internal Revenue Code*) on his 1040 form for the tax year 1983, alleging his home office wasn't his "principal place of business." Dr. Soliman appealed the IRS's decision in the U.S. Tax Court and won.

To say that the IRS was furious (because the decision was more lenient toward taxpayers than any previous home-office interpretation in that it allowed taxpayers to deduct home-office expenses even when they do not spend a majority of their time working at home) is an understatement. The IRS decided to fight, taking the case to the U.S. Court of Appeals for the Fourth Circuit in Richmond, Virginia, which upheld the Tax Court's decision.

Because this was a substantial expansion of the home-office rule as it traditionally stood, it would automatically result in a large chunk of lost tax dollars. The IRS was going to fight this to the finish, and it did, right up to the Supreme Court.

On January 19, 1993, in *Commissioner v. Soliman*, the Supreme Court reversed the two lower-court rulings and strongly reinforced the long-held IRS position, established in the Tax Reform Act of 1976, that to take a home-office deduction the site had to be used exclusively and regularly as the principal place of business.

The new ruling actually strengthened existing IRS guidelines. The Supreme Court gave the IRS an unexpected bonus because the ruling went so far in the other direction. (See page 152 for the latest home-office rules.)

The IRS Defies the Federal Government

During the Watergate investigations, Senate Watergate Committee investigators accused the IRS of obstructing the panel's continuing inquiry by defying the Senate's resolution to provide tax returns and other data to the committee, and by refusing to provide tax data and investigative files on more than 30 individuals and corporations.[19] The IRS's underlying motivation, consistent since its inception, is tenacious and simple: **When the IRS doesn't want to do something, no matter who or what is telling it what to do, the IRS will fight long and hard to get its way.**

The IRS's ability to do what it wants despite directives from governmental bodies, individuals, and the law brings into play two particularly important laws specifically devised for and suited to the American way of life. These are the 1966 Freedom of Information Act (FOIA) and the 1974 Privacy Act, both enacted to formalize a citizen's right to request records from federal agencies.

Before enactment of the FOIA, the burden was on the individual to establish a right to examine these government records. There were no statutory guidelines or procedures to help a person seeking information, and there were no judicial remedies for those denied access.

With the passage of the FOIA, the burden of proof shifted from the individual to the government. According to a guide published by the House Committee on Government Operations, those seeking information are no longer required to show a need for information: "Instead, the 'need-to-know' standard has been replaced by a 'right-to-know' doctrine. The government now has to justify the need for secrecy."[20]

All taxpayers should know their rights in these matters, as explained in the *Citizen's Guide on Using the Freedom of Information Act and the Privacy Act of 1974 to Request Government Records*, available from the U.S. Government Printing Office, Washington, D.C. Regarding what records can be requested under the FOIA:

> The FOIA requires agencies to publish or make available for public inspection several types of information. This includes (1) descriptions of agency organization and office addresses; (2) statements of the general course and method of agency operation; (3) rules of procedure and descriptions of forms; (4) substantive rules of general applicability and general policy statements; (5) final opinions made in the adjudication of cases; and (6) administrative staff manuals that affect the public.[21]

The IRS Defies Private Citizens

The *Internal Revenue Manual* is a major weapon against the often ludicrous situations that the IRS is known to suck taxpayers into, yet it is something most taxpayers don't know a thing about—for very good reasons. It contains IRS policies, procedures, job descriptions, and more that explain what the agency is made of. This information is exactly what the IRS hopes you won't get your hands on. You see, it is especially useful for verifying the functions of each division, for providing the parameters of specific jobs, or for spelling out specific instructions to employees on how a specific task is supposed to get done, such as seizing your assets.

In my quest to receive the *Internal Revenue Manual*, I learned firsthand how the IRS regards the FOIA and the Privacy Act. What follows describes my attempt, as Mr. Nice Guy Taxpayer, to follow the rules so that I could glance through, in the words of the FOIA, this "administrative staff manual that affects the public."

Obtaining the Internal Revenue Manual

In a book about taxes, *Tax Loopholes,* a former director of the Albany and Brooklyn IRS district offices, George S. Alberts, states that someone can request a copy of the *Internal Revenue Manual* under the Freedom of Information Act from the IRS Reading Room in Washington, D.C. Furthermore, Mr. Albert says, you don't have to tell the IRS why you want the material; the fee to obtain the book is reasonable; and your action will not trigger any other actions by the IRS.[22]

Another popular tax book confirms that "each IRS District Office maintains a 'reading room' where the *Manual* is available. Copies of specific provisions of the *Manual* can also be obtained by contacting the Disclosure Officer in each district."[23]

My first step was to go to the Federal Information Center at Federal Plaza in downtown Manhattan, where I purchased the *Citizen's Guide on Using the Freedom of Information Act and the Privacy Act of 1974 to Request Government Records.* According to this publication, each act contains a provision for obtaining IRS materials, and suggests writing a letter to the agency stating that "I am willing to pay fees for this request up to a maximum of X dollars. If you estimate that the fees will exceed this limit, please inform me first."

I took no chances. I wrote two letters, one following a format suggested by Mr. Alberts, and the other following the government publication. My letters were mailed July 21, 1994; a response is required *by law* within 10 days.

I sent follow-up copies of my letters on August 21 and September 21. As of November 21, 1994, I had received no replies whatsoever.

After 30 days, on December 21, I visited the IRS district office in Manhattan and asked the person at the information desk where the IRS reading room was. The woman began to laugh hysterically. When she caught her breath, she told me there was no reading room. There was never a reading room; she had been at her job for over 15 years and had never heard of such a thing. There was, she said, a small room upstairs where IRS employees *only* could find IRS publications. Furthermore, she informed me that she had never even heard of the *Internal Revenue Manual.*

Next I made several phone calls to IRS headquarters in Washington, D.C. No one in the IRS or the Treasury Department could find a phone number for the reading room, nor did anyone know how I could obtain a copy of the *Internal Revenue Manual.*

About this time I attended a tour of the Brookhaven Service Center in Holtsville, New York. My ulterior motive was to make contact with someone who could help me in my quest to obtain this elusive book. A disclosure officer there was surprised at my tale. He immediately called the IRS in Washington, D.C., and handed me the phone, whereupon I gave my name, address, and phone number to a person responsible for filling these kinds of requests. She said that within three hours she would have an answer.

Fourteen days later I still hadn't heard a thing, despite periodic phone calls to that woman, who seemed to have disappeared.

Now I turned to the IRS historian, which, someone said, was a newly created position. This person said the *Internal Revenue Manual* was in the building next to hers (in Washington, D.C.) and if I could give her a few days, she would see what she could do.

Several days later she called me back and said the staff in the Office of Disclosure couldn't find any of my correspondence, but that if I'd send another letter, along with a check for $11, they'd send the *Manual*.

Two weeks later my check had cleared, and still no *Manual*. Finally, a full month later, some photocopied pages arrived, with "Internal Revenue Manual, Tax Audit Guidelines for Internal Revenue Examiners" written across them, along with a three-hole-punched preprinted booklet entitled *Examination*.

A "Cost for copying certain Internal Revenue Manual Sections" was included in the package. Here I discovered each section of the *Internal Revenue Manual* outlined, and the corresponding cost for copying each one.

As a CPA, I can access the *Internal Revenue Manual* or something very close to it, with commentary, published not by the IRS or Government Printing Office but by a tax service, in a professional library closed to the public. Unfortunately, the average taxpayer will not find the task that easy. Parts of the Internal Revenue Manual are now available at the IRS website, www.irs.gov/search/site_tree.html. If you're going to represent yourself at an audit, this section is required reading.

Finally, I want to pass on to my readers information that the IRS has obviously deemed important enough to issue as an *Internal Revenue Manual Addendum:* **"In the event of a nuclear attack, to guide the conduct of all IRS employees, operations will concentrate on collecting taxes which will produce the greatest revenue yields."**[24]

I've described my epic somewhat lightheartedly, but it is not a funny story. The Freedom of Information Case List, published annually by the U.S. Department of Justice, shows the number of U.S. citizens trying to get their hands on information that can help them deal with the IRS, only to get a door slammed in their faces year after year.

Some have made the difficult decision to legally battle whatever allegations the IRS has made against them, and some of these have made a real name for themselves and become recognized experts on how the

IRS administratively and otherwise resists making any information available. Most people never get very far and are forced to give up. Others do succeed in suing the IRS, winning a judgment, and getting charges against them dropped, but it takes an enormous toll in time, and often tens of thousands of dollars in legal fees.

THE BOTTOM LINE

Why has all of this been allowed to continue? There are several reasons.

The IRS Manages to Get the Job Done

In 1999 the IRS collected over $1.9 trillion in gross tax dollars, an increase of more than $130 billion over the previous year. It also examined over 1.23 million returns and recommended over $19 billion in additional taxes.[25] All this at a cost of about only one half of 1 percent of the over $1.9 trillion it brings in.

According to one account of the development of U.S. tax policy, "In the early 1940s, many people—even highly placed officials of the Internal Revenue Service—doubted that an income tax covering almost everyone could be administered effectively."[26] Although there are enormous problems up, down, and across the organization, the job is being done.

The dollars collected are done so at an overall cost of about $8.11 billion, the IRS budget. For 2001, President Clinton requested an increase in that figure to $8.84 billion. "The increase includes $174 million this year and next to hire 1,633 more people, including 633 more auditors and 33 more tax collectors."[27]

The IRS Is Backed by the Government—Usually

Congress and our legal system (the courts, judges, district attorneys) have consistently supported the IRS

- By legitimizing or ignoring the growing powers of IRS personnel.
- By seeking to punish taxpayers through a growing list of tax violations.
- By demanding ever-increasing amounts of information from an ever-growing range of third-party sources.
- By ensuring that Americans obey the IRS or face stiff consequences and penalties.

In addition, Congress has repeatedly taken the IRS under its wing,

- To protect the IRS, despite repeated cases of wrongly abused citizens, valid findings about its poor performances, and corrupt misdealings.
- To ignore instances when the IRS has skirted and gone beyond the law into realms it has no business being in.
- To give the IRS more protection from citizen suits than any other federal agency.[28]

The IRS Has the Support of the American People—Usually
Despite Americans' never-ending grumblings about, resistance to, and enormous fear of the IRS, the fact that federal taxes are an inescapable part of our lives is widely accepted. It is also true that the majority of Americans willingly complete and mail in their returns, and pay their taxes, giving the U.S. one of the highest tax compliance rates in the world—about 83 percent.

The Winds of Change Are Here
The level of disgust expressed by the media at the time of the Senate Finance Committee hearings in late 1997 comes as no surprise to myself, to anyone working in the tax field, to a great many taxpayers, and to those who have read past editions of this book. The following conclusion is what those witnessing the hearings on taxpayer abuses discovered:

"Many IRS foot soldiers are frequently rude, arrogant, dismissive of taxpayers, lazy and mouthy—basically about as unprofessional as one encounters in government. Some are so high on the power granted them under the law that they violate or ignore taxpayer rights. And they do so with impunity—protected by a Treasury employees union unresponsive to the feelings of voters or taxpayers in this country, concerned only with its entrenched power and seemingly unanswerable to no one."[29]

A change is due, and that is exactly what is happening.

Sizing Up the IRS as an Opponent
As a general rule, a taxpayer never wants to get crossways of the IRS. **What you do want to aim for is the ability to manipulate the power of the IRS through the income tax process.** You have to take extreme care doing this. It cannot be accomplished haphazardly or without sufficient knowledge. In the martial arts a small person can bring down a much heavier, stronger one. By the same token, I and thousands of other tax professionals like me continue to witness taxpayers accomplishing similar feats when dealing with the IRS.

6

IRS Technology

What Works
What Doesn't Work

It hasn't been easy for the IRS to design and implement its systems to keep abreast of an ever-expanding workload and advancing technology. Until the mid-1980's a great deal of the work—assembling millions of tax returns by year, organizing them geographically, and comparing them with third-party reports—was still being done manually. Sacks filled to the brim with tax return information sat for years in IRS corridors; massive amounts of incorrect information were disseminated to taxpayers en masse; huge numbers of tax returns would disappear, never to be found again; annually thousands of letters from taxpayers remained unanswered because they couldn't be matched up to their corresponding files; and enormous time delays for a range of requests were the norm (75 days or more instead of a promised 30).

Today the IRS computers housed in the National Computer Center (NCC) in Martinsburg, West Virginia, contain trillions of bits of information on millions of U.S. taxpayers. Do images of huge storage tanks of electronic information housed in shining silver eight-foot-tall containers fill taxpayers' visions? That's exactly the image the IRS would love to have.

The current IRS technology behemoth, called the Tax Systems Modernization (TSM), was initiated in the early 1990's at a cost of $8.3–10 billion. (This was on top of a previous $11-plus-billion technology project.) The system was, among other things, supposed to

- Execute the IRS's Information Returns Program, or matching program, in which information on all 1040 forms (Individual Tax Return) is matched up or compared with all W-2's (Wage and Tax Statement) and the full range of 1099 documents that are sent to the IRS by third parties (i.e., employers, banks, real estate agents, loan companies, and more). This process enables the IRS to isolate underreporters and nonfilers.
- Eliminate millions of unnecessary contacts with taxpayers.
- Provide copies of tax returns to taxpayers who have lost their copies and to IRS employees who are conducting audits in less than one day rather than the current 45-day average.
- Reduce by one quarter the time it takes to process cases.
- Tailor correspondence to the taxpayer's account rather than issue generic form letters.

These were strong indications that the IRS was serious regarding its efforts to build, manage, and employ technology. By now, however, it is clear that relatively few of the IRS's technology efforts have been successful. But that's something the IRS would rather taxpayers not know.

THE PROCESSING PIPELINE

What Happens to Your Return in the Processing Pipeline
The IRS "processing pipeline" is a process your tax return goes through from the time it is dropped into the mail until a refund is issued.

Where *does* all the "other stuff" take place? Where are tax returns selected for audit? Where is the matching program run? Where are people targeted for a criminal investigation? These all take place in a vast IRS-land that has come to be called the "nonprocessing pipeline."

The problem is, for the most part this phase is not fully revealed to taxpayers. **Even explanatory material sent out by the IRS labeled "nonprocessing pipeline" is not complete. By not telling the whole story, the IRS triumphs over the taxpayer, because what transpires in the nonprocessing pipeline holds tremendous importance for anyone who files a tax return.**

First, let's take a brief look at what happens to your return in the normal processing pipeline.

Millions of mailed returns are delivered to the service centers, where they are fed into computerized equipment that reads the coding on the envelopes, opens the envelopes, and sorts them by type—married, single, business. (Uncoded envelopes take longer to open and sort; using a properly coded envelope will speed things up.) Next, clerks manually remove the contents of the envelopes and sort the returns further into those with or without remittances. Payments are credited to taxpayers' accounts and are separated from the returns, totals are balanced, and the checks are sent to the service center's bank for deposit, eventually to end up in the U.S. Treasury.

All returns are then verified for completeness of information (the filer's signature, Social Security number, the proper forms), and coded to assist in converting the raw data directly from the return into an electronic language for computer processing. IRS personnel transcribe the data directly from the tax returns to computer disks, then the computer analyzes the information and enters error-free returns onto magnetic tapes.

If errors are encountered, they are printed on a separate report and passed on to tax examiners in the service center, who check the error records against the appropriate returns and correct what errors they can. If the errors are not easily corrected, the error is coded, indicating that the taxpayer will be sent an error notice requesting clarification.

Now the magnetic tapes containing data from all the accurate tax returns are shipped to the National Computer Center and added to the master directory of all taxpayer accounts, and updated records are sent back to each service center for further processing.

Refund tapes are sent to the Treasury Department for issuance of refund checks directly to taxpayers, and the processing pipeline ends. The total time from mailing your return to receiving your refund generally runs about six to eight weeks.

THE NONPROCESSING PIPELINE

What Happens in the Nonprocessing Pipeline
Taxpayers are kept in the dark about many phases of the nonprocessing pipeline that are quite important for them to know.

• The first round of letters is cranked out by IRS computers *only* because of missing information. If someone forgot to sign a return, if a schedule is missing, if the W-2 is not attached, these issues are handled within the first month after the return is mailed in. (All of the time periods given in these examples are for tax season, February 1 to April 15. At other times of year the turnaround time is probably shorter.)

• The next round of letters is sent to correct purely arithmetical errors. **There are generally some 6 million of these errors each filing season.** Letters of this nature are sent anywhere from two to three months after a taxpayer has mailed in his or her return.

- The Information Returns Program (IRP), or matching program, is not part of the normal tax-return-processing routine. It is run as part of the nonpipeline processing.
- The W-2, which taxpayers attach to the 1040, doesn't actually get matched to the 1040 until approximately one and one half years after it is submitted.
- Audit letters don't usually get sent out until six months to one year after the return is filed.
- No matter how spiffy the matching program sounds, the IRS itself admits that it is still a labor- and paper-intensive operation.
- **In 1992, only 2 percent of the data maintained in tax accounts was readily available on-line.** The other 98 percent was in paper files—returns filed in federal records centers or in databases without on-line retrieval capability.[1] There has been some, but not much, appreciable improvement in this area since then.

Here's the full story of what happens in the nonprocessing pipeline.

Enter W-2's
W-2's, from private and public entities that report employees' salaries, are due in to the IRS the last day of January, and 1099's, from business owners, are due February 28.

Enter Inquiry Letters
It's early July and tax season has been over for about three months. Initial inquiry letters are being sent out by the service centers requesting that taxpayers send in information they inadvertently left out, and/or to correct mathematical errors. Once these situations have been corrected, one to two months later, the service centers reenter the information and create a good tape, which is then fed into the Martinsburg computer system.

Enter Audit Selection
The initial process selects tax returns whose DIF scores (Discriminate Information Function, discussed in chapter 3) mean that they fall in the audit range for one or more of the DIF items or categories. This amounts to about 3 percent of all individual returns, or about 3.7 million, that have audit potential. These returns are sent by Martinsburg via tape back to the corresponding service centers, where the computer data is matched up with the hard copy, the actual tax return.

Staff in the Examination Division at the service centers manually review and select only returns that indicate the greatest potential monetary yield. As a result, at least another 80 percent of the original 3 percent are discarded, leaving approximately 750,000 individual tax returns chosen for audit as a result of the DIF selection process. At this point, the tax returns targeted for correspondence audits are turned over to the Examination Division at the service centers. The balance of the tax returns are distributed to the district offices, which send out letters to taxpayers notifying them that they are being audited. This entire process takes from six months to one year after the tax return is filed.

While audit selection is taking place, so is another entire range of activities.

Enter the Social Security Administration
Did you know that the first link between you, your W-2's, and the matching process is the Social Security Administration (SSA)? Here's how this one works: The first copy of the W-2 is sent to the SSA by employers so that wages can be added to a taxpayer's lifetime earnings account. The SSA then forwards the W-2 information to the IRS on magnetic tape, where it is matched to the 1040 form and, along with the 1099's, initiates the nonprocessing pipeline.

Now the matching program can be run. The sequence of events goes something like this:

Enter Mismatches
On the basis of the data in Martinsburg, all 1040 forms (individual tax returns) are matched with W-2's and compared with over 1 billion 1099's and other third-party documents. All mismatches are downloaded onto a separate tape, which goes back to the service centers. The assigned sections in the service centers then analyze the data (see below). When a discrepancy exists indicating a mismatch among 1099's, W-2's, and 1040 forms, the case enters the collection area at the service-center level.

Enter Underreporter Notices
The service centers send out mismatch notices, "underreporter notices," or CP-2000 letters, triggered when there is a disagreement between what a taxpayer reported on the 1040 and what was reported about that person's income by one or more third-party reports. These notices propose a change to income, payments, or credits and are sent to taxpayers about one and a half years after the tax return was filed. Apparently, the fact that the SSA uses the information first contributes to the enormous delay. In 1997 the IRS generated almost one million notices for underreporting.[2] This was a drop of almost one million contacts over the previous year. Was this due to IRS computer downtime as technology experts scramble to fix the year 2000 bug? Supporting this

assumption is the fact that the matching process brought in almost 50 percent less in recommended taxes and penalties for 1997, a drop of $1.4 billion (see below).

Enter the Collection Division

After this, depending on how the taxpayer does or does not respond to IRS correspondence, tax assessments are made or taxpayer explanations are accepted. In any case, the collection cycle is now triggered, and the case makes its way up through the collection process, as discussed in chapter 4.

Enter the Criminal Investigation Division

At this point the Criminal Investigation Division (CID) takes center stage.

CID staff trains service center personnel to identify typical characteristics of false and fraudulent returns and potential criminal violations. If a return of this nature is recognized by someone in the service center, the case is brought to the attention of CID. From there it might head up the line, or be dismissed for lack of potential to produce either big bucks and/or a conviction.

THE REST OF THE PROCESSING PIE

Individual taxpayers are *not* the sole focus of IRS processing, so if some of the delays that occur in both pipelines seem inordinately long, one of the major reasons involves the rest of the IRS tax return–processing pie.

In 1998, the over 123 million individual tax returns the IRS processed represented 50 percent of total net dollars collected, the majority in the form of withholding. Employment taxes represented 34.2 percent, and corporation taxes were 11.6 percent of total dollars collected.[3]

The scope of the entire processing cycle is arduous, tedious, and enormous. But there is a major lesson for all taxpayers: **There are so many levels the IRS must get involved with in processing tax returns that if you learn how to prepare an unobtrusive return, chances are in your favor that it will pass through the system unnoticed.**

If you look at the three areas in the IRS that are responsible for bringing in tax dollars, you can get a good perspective on the agency's technological capability.

In 1998,

- Matching recommended $1.6 billion in additional taxes and penalties.
- Examination recommended over $23 billion.
- Collection yielded almost $40 billion on a combination of collections on delinquent accounts and assessments on delinquent returns.[4]

The matching program, which is dependent on technology, offers the IRS widespread coverage across the taxpayer base. Nevertheless, people-dependent Examination and Collection, where IRS staff do most of the work, actually bring in far more tax dollars because of their selectivity: They select only those cases with the greatest potential for tax dollars.

So just exactly where is IRS technology performing well, and what information is still sitting around or just completely unreachable, as in the old days?

WHERE THE IRS TECHNOLOGY WORKS

W-2's (Wage and Tax Statements) and 1099's (Third-Party Reports) Matched to the 1040 Form (Individual Income Tax Return)

As you know, the Information Returns Program (IRP), or matching program, allows the IRS to match up third-party information—wages, interest, dividends, and certain deductions—with the amounts taxpayers report on their 1040 form. In addition, the IRS also uses the IRP to identify nonfilers, people who have received some income (as indicated by one or more third-party reports) but nevertheless did not file a return. **The current estimate is that about 6 million people are nonfilers.** (The reasons why this segment is so large are discussed in chapter 7, "IRS Targets and What to Do If You're One of Them.")

Mismatches result from a variety of factors: mathematical errors or negligence (taxpayers do make honest mistakes), unreported name and address changes, as well as downright cheating.

Implications for Taxpayers

If you do not properly report your W-2 earnings, there is little doubt that the IRS computers will pick it up through the matching process. Therefore be honest here, to the letter.

Social Security Number Cheating Schemes

Several years ago a rash of taxpayers tried to avoid paying taxes by manipulating Social Security numbers. The incidence of fooling around with Social Security numbers increased to the point where the IRS was successful in having a law passed that requires all third-party payers to obtain corrected Social Security numbers from taxpayers when the IRS provides the payers with a list of mismatches that affects them. If a taxpayer does not comply with the third party's request for the corrected Social Security number, the institution or third party will be instructed by the IRS to begin to withhold tax from payments that person is receiving from business owners, as well as from any other third-party payments such as interest and dividends.

Starting January 1, 1993, the rate of withholding tax from this type of situation, called *backup withholding*, was 31 percent. Previously, the amount was only 20 percent, but when George Bush was president he had it raised to generate additional tax revenue from the American public without announcing a tax increase.

Among others, the requirement targets taxpayers who provide an erroneous Social Security number on their bank accounts to avoid including the sums as taxable income. This produces a mismatch on IRS computers and triggers the backup withholding mechanism.

Once the mismatch is identified, the IRS notifies the bank, and after a two-year period, if the taxpayer hasn't stepped up to resolve the issue or offered a corrected Social Security number, the bank will automatically take 31 percent out of the account in question. So if the account earns $3,000 in yearly interest, $930 will immediately be sent to the IRS as backup withholding.

Pension Plan Distributions

The IRS's matching program regarding pension plan distributions used to have some real holes in it. With approximately half a million pension plan distributions disbursed annually, the common practice is to roll over pension funds, or place them in a qualified investment that entitles the money to remain nontaxable according to IRS requirements. If the rollover isn't followed to the letter of the *Internal Revenue Code*, the distribution is considered taxable income and the taxpayer is generally subject to income tax and added penalties if the distribution is taken before the taxpayer reaches age 59½.

Implications for Taxpayers

According to the *Internal Revenue Code*, when the organization holding the distribution turns it over to the taxpayer it must issue a 1099-R (Distribution from Pensions, Annuities, Retirement or Profit-Sharing Plans, IRA's, Insurance Contracts, Etc.), which spells out the amount disbursed, and send this information to the IRS. For the most part, this reporting requirement is adhered to by companies making the pension distributions, especially since IRS computers are now fully capable of matching up the pension-plan distribution with the rollover amount. (For an update, see pages 290–291.)

Form 2119 (Sale of Your Home) and Schedule D (Capital Gains and Losses)

When you sell a house, you generally receive a 1099-S (Proceeds from Real Estate Transactions) from the real estate broker or attorney, which shows the gross sale price of your house. If no tax is due on the transaction, probably because your gain on the sale is $500,000 or less for married couples, or $250,000 or less for a single person, you are no longer required to file Form 2119. If your gain exceeds these limits, report the entire gain on schedule D (Capital Gains and Losses) and then subtract the exclusion.

YOUR TAX-SAVING STRATEGY.

Even if no forms must be filed on your home sale, keep complete cost and sales records regarding your residence. Tax laws change. You never know when the current amount you are allowed to exclude from gain will be raised, affecting a future home sale. Or, conversely, Congress could scale back the amounts, leaving you with unforeseen tax to pay.

If you sell investment rental property, your return must include the sale on Schedule D (Capital Gains and Losses). Omitting this information could lead to an audit because the IRS has increased its search capabilities of real estate transactions and is matching that data with sales shown on Schedule D. For planning opportunities, see pages 291–294.

Disposition of Investment and Schedule D

If you have been receiving dividends from an investment and the dividend income disappears, you must show a disposition of the investment on Schedule D or be ready to prove that the company ceased the payment of dividends.

Auditors are also instructed to account for investments appearing on the previous year's tax return that have suddenly disappeared, or are not accounted for on a subsequent Schedule D. If a rental property appears on a taxpayer's 1040 one year and does not appear on the subsequent year's 1040, the auditor will suspect that you sold it and did not report the taxable gain on your 1040.

Overreporting Income

When a taxpayer submits an overpayment of tax on a check enclosed with the 1040 form, the IRS is thoroughly honest and in almost all cases will return to the taxpayer the appropriate refund. But what happens to the thousands of taxpayers who innocently overreport income?

Implications for Taxpayers

Just as underreporting income is easily detected through the matching program, so, now, is overreporting. **However, when it comes to over-reporting income, the IRS does not behave as honestly as when there is an overpayment of tax.** When taxpayers overreport their income, *and* the IRS records it, the IRS doesn't tell taxpayers that they've made an error. If you pay more taxes than you owe, you will receive a refund from the IRS, but not when you overreport income.

Matching Form 941 (Employer's Quarterly Federal Tax Return) with Total Wages and Taxes Withheld on W-2's

The 941 form, filled out by employers and sent quarterly to the IRS, shows total wages, taxable Social Security wages, taxable Medicare wages, federal income tax withheld, and Social Security and Medicare taxes. Since these items all appear on each employee's W-2 at year-end, the totals reported on the employer's four quarterly 941's for the year *must* agree with the grand totals of all W-2's, also reported by the employer. **The IRS meticulously matches the W-2 totals with the 941's to ensure that businesses have legitimately paid their tax liabilities to the government in a timely manner.**

Discrepancies arise between W-2's and 941's for these reasons:

- Many 941's, year-end reconciliations, and W-2's are filled out by employers manually, not with a computer.
- Many employers do not fully understand the requirements for making payroll tax deposits.

Implications for Taxpayers

This matching process is at once a safeguard for the taxpayer (your company is not allowed to play around with money it has deducted from your salary, such as Social Security and withholding), a deterrent for the employer, and also a deterrent for taxpayers who believe they can cheat the government on taxes withheld from wages earned.

It also prevents little games from being played—for example, creating a fictitious company and issuing oneself a false W-2. So why not send in a mathematically correct return with a phoney W-2 from a fictitious company, which will result in a large refund, after which the taxpayer disappears fast? Forget it. It's a major criminal offense. No one gets away with it.

As for the genuine companies and employers, those who fail to make timely payments are subject to strictly enforced penalties. They are also held personally liable for any Social Security or federal withholding taken from employees' wages that are not transmitted to the IRS. If the tax liability and required payments as shown on the 941's do not match up with the actual payments made by the employer, the IRS contacts the employer immediately.

The IRS has completely revised the 941 requirements several times over the years to cut down on deposit errors. (There was a great deal of confusion about when to send in the money.) The goal was to make depositing easier for approximately 5 million employers and eliminate most of the deposit penalties. Errors on the 941 form probably accounted for more than 80 percent of IRS discrepancy letters received by employers.

Another benefit to how the IRS has managed Form 941 is this. The program places on-line account data in front of IRS employees. So when the tax professional or taxpayer calls, the problem is usually resolved then and there. In my experience, this is one program the IRS can be proud of.

YOUR TAX-SAVING STRATEGY.
When a taxpayer is ready to collect retirement benefits, the Social Security Administration will use a specific formula to determine that person's monthly Social Security benefit, based on the total amount of earnings accumulated over the years.

My advice to all wage earners is to obtain a printout of your earnings account every three years by writing to your local SSA office. Verify it with the entries from your W-2's. Errors are easier to correct this way than by waiting until an error is inadvertently discovered by the Social Security Administration.

WHERE MISTAKES ARE MADE IN THE IRS MATCHING PROGRAM

Just because the technology in these areas is impressive doesn't mean that mistakes can't be made. (By the way, these mistakes are separate from instances where the IRS technology falls short, discussed further on in this chapter.) Here are the most common mistakes:

Mismatching Information on W-2 Forms with Information on the 1040 because of Nonstandardized W-2's
A tax professional who prepares personal tax returns knows that it is standard operating procedure for W-2's to be in a nonstandardized for-

mat. But have taxpayers even noticed, much less asked themselves, why the W-2, a key player in the IRS's third-party reporting system, arrives in the taxpayers' hands in all varieties of forms? Here's the answer: Employers with 250 or more employees must submit W-2 information on magnetic tape, which all appears in a standard IRS format. Almost all other employers submit the information on paper, in a format either prescribed or approved by the IRS but, unfortunately, not followed often enough. Although the requirement to use magnetic tape is strict, the format of the printed W-2, which goes directly from employers to taxpayers, was not subject to formal guidelines until March 1993, when the IRS issued instructions for the placement of the federal wage and tax data. **The end result for taxpayers was and still is a ludicrously simple situation of wrongly copied information:** Even though some of the W-2 information has to be placed in predetermined positions, the rest of the information placement and the design of the forms still vary wildly. If I had one cent for each time a taxpayer miscopied information from a W-2 to a 1040 form, because the information presented on the W-2 was not in a standardized format, I'd be living in Australia and scuba-diving on the Great Barrier Reef right now. Surely the resulting error rate causes thousands of taxpayers to receive CP-2000 letters and collection notices each year because of IRS computer mismatches.

The goal of every taxpayer should be to stay out of the clutches of the IRS; any minor recording error can in a flash destroy a taxpayer's ability to fulfill this mission.

NOTE: Corporations are still allowed to design and print their own W-2 forms, but regulations in effect require data for W-2's to be presented in the exact order as on the preprinted IRS form. Even though these regulations break a well-entrenched pattern, we'll see how long it takes for companies large and small to completely implement the changeover.

YOUR TAX-SAVING STRATEGY.

Take care when you transfer your wages information from your W-2's to the "Wages, Salaries" line of your 1040 form. Doing it incorrectly could mean problems; e.g., by transposing FICA wages (Box 3, on the W-2) and gross wages (Box 1, on the W-2), you may be reporting more income than you should. This will attract unnecessary IRS scrutiny.

Mismatching Information on 1099 Forms with Information on the 1040

For self-employed persons who receive 1099's for income earned from a sole proprietorship and file Schedule C, it is inappropriate to list each

1099 separately on Schedule C. Some of my clients receive 50 or more 1099's. However, you must be absolutely sure that the total gross income from the self-employed business that you report on line 1 of Schedule C equals or exceeds the total dollar amount of the 1099's that you receive. Otherwise you will be flagged for underreporting income.

Mistakes Made Through Social Security Numbers

An incorrect Social Security number will immediately trigger a mismatch. The error might come from someone who created a bogus Social Security number that turned out to be yours. When *you* opened your last bank account, did the bank employee ask for your Social Security card to prove the validity of the Social Security number you provided to him or her? Probably not, because this isn't common practice—so a person could quite easily give an erroneous Social Security number. If some devious person just happens to give a false Social Security number to a bank or elsewhere and it turns out to be yours, you will receive a mismatch notice. The IRS will eventually notify the bank (or source) to obtain a corrected Social Security number from the person who gave yours. Unfortunately, you've been contacted by the bank or the IRS and been annoyed by unnecessary correspondence through no fault of your own.

Exempt Income Items

The IRS will sometimes select for a mismatch notice income items bearing your Social Security number that should have been excluded from your taxable income; such items might be interest earned on IRA's, interest on tax-exempt bonds, and transfers between your IRA and pension plan. An erroneous match of these exempt-income items may occur if the third-party payer submitted the information on the wrong magnetic tape.

Keypunch Errors

Sometimes an error occurs simply because of one incorrect keypunch by an IRS operator: a misspelling of your name or address or one wrong digit in your Social Security number.

WHAT TO DO IF YOU RECEIVE AN IRS "MISMATCH LETTER"

Promptly answer the IRS mismatch letter with full documentation in your first reply. Failure to do so keeps your return in front of an IRS employee unnecessarily. For example, if in the mismatch notice your income was increased by an IRA distribution that you properly rolled over within 60 days, document your answer with the statement from the financial institution that shows the receipt of the rollover money plus a copy of the canceled check, if you have it. Do not assume that the IRS employee understands the data you are sending. Include a cover letter stating all the facts.

Now that you know which areas of the IRS technology work, and also where the most common mistakes are made, let's focus on several of the IRS's sore points.

WHERE THE IRS TECHNOLOGY FALLS SHORT
ON THE INCOME SIDE

We are first going to concentrate on items that show up as "income" on the 1040 form: distributions from partnerships, corporations, estates, and trusts; capital gains; and gifts and inheritances.

Schedule K-1

K-1's are schedules issued by partnerships (which report income on Form 1065), S corporations (Form 1120S), and estates and trusts (Form 1041), on which these entities show distributable amounts of income and expense that have been allocated to each partner, shareholder, or beneficiary. Information on K-1's must be reported on the partner's, shareholder's, or beneficiary's Form 1040.

Tax preparers for entities that issue K-1's are responsible for placing income and expense items on the proper line. This is not always straightforward because of the factor of *basis*. Basis is a dollar amount that represents the cost of a taxpayer's investment in an entity. Because of continuous adjustments to each taxpayer's basis in that particular entity, **the income or loss as shown on the K-1 may not reflect the true amount that must be recorded on the taxpayer's current-year Form 1040.**

If you are the recipient of a K-1 from an entity, you cannot take for granted that the income or expense as shown on the K-1 is ready to be transferred to Form 1040 as it is stated; you should rely on your tax pro to determine the correct information.

Once taxpayers are sure that they have the proper income or loss amount, they are then faced with the arduous task of transferring the K-1 information onto their Form 1040. Several lines on the K-1 are easy to comprehend, and their counterparts on Form 1040 and its schedules are easily located. These include interest income and dividend income, lines 4A and 4B, respectively, which transfer to Schedule B of Form

1040; and net short-term capital gain or loss and net long-term capital gain or loss, lines 4D and 4E respectively, which transfer to Schedule D (Capital Gains and Losses). For 1997 and 1998, Schedule D was revised to reflect gains and losses based on varying holding periods (the amount of time an asset is held) as well as the new capital gains law in RRA '98 as determined by 1997 legislation. (See page 291.) But Schedule D remains as complex as ever. (See page 262.)

Then there are complicated items that have their own deductibility limitations, such as Section 179, depreciation "Expense Deductions" (discussed in chapter 7, "IRS Targets and What to Do If You're One of Them"), investment interest, and low-income housing credit (Form 8586, Low-Income Housing Credit, discussed under Rule 5 in chapter 11).

To prepare a proper return, taxpayers really have to dig deeply into K-1 form instructions—which are often 10 pages long—and also examine additional schedules that explain the more complicated items being reported. Imagine it! The K-1 has up to 48 lines, some of which baffle even tax professionals. When that information is transferred to a 1040, it can appear in a number of different places on various 1040 schedules besides Schedules B and D, such as Form 6251 (Alternative Minimum Tax—Individuals), and Form 8582 (Passive Activity Loss Limitations).

Implications for Taxpayers

Clearly, Schedule K-1 is inherently complex. Add to this the necessity of transferring a great deal of detailed information to the 1040 in a variety of different places, and you can understand how difficult it would be even for computers to organize, digest, and store information from the K-1 and then match it properly to the 1040. I am aware of several specific cases that demonstrate this point.

On April 15, 1995, a colleague of mine received a call from a client who said that without fail her return had to be filed on time. He told her that he couldn't do that because it was missing a partnership K-1 form. "I don't care," the client said. "What was the amount from last year?"

"It was a three-thousand-dollar loss," he replied.

"Take the same loss," she said, "and file the return on time." He did. Four months later, the K-1 arrived from the partnership indicating a $1,000 loss. Her job was transferred overseas for the next few years, and she never filed an amended tax return. She has never heard a word from the IRS.

In another case, an elderly taxpayer filing on October 15, under the latest extension possible, was missing two S corporation K-1's. The return was filed as if it were complete, except it was not noticed that the information from the K-1's was totally omitted. Three months later, the two K-1's arrived showing several items of additional income. As was his way, the elderly taxpayer buried the forms in a pile of unopened mail. An amended return should have been filed but never was, and no inquiry was ever received from the IRS.

Before we leave the K-1, I'd like to inform readers about one more thing: **K-1 reporting by the entities (the partnerships, corporations, estates, and trusts) that issue the K-1 forms is not standardized.** K-1's issued by nationally syndicated partnerships are so complicated that they tend to be accompanied by a brochure generated by each partnership explaining how taxpayers should transfer K-1 information to their 1040. Although the explanations say precisely where on the 1040 specific information should be entered, the words "Consult your tax adviser" are almost always present. For taxpayers, this is a rather indisputable indication of the difficulty of the task at hand.

Very little about the K-1 standardization predicament is news to the IRS. In 1992, during a meeting of the National Society of Public Accountants (NSPA), representatives of the Society and the IRS Tax Forms Coordinating Committee exchanged ideas and information regarding form changes. The IRS agreed that lack of K-1 standardization presents a considerable problem for both the agency and the taxpayer/practitioner communities. It also went on record as stating that the issue remains under review, and progress is likely to come only *after* the standardization of W-2/1099 reporting is complete.[5] It has been almost six years since the IRS issued new regulations regarding the standardization of W-2 forms. In early 1999, the IRS announced that additional improvements to the W-2 format will not occur until it issues tax-year 2001 forms, after it gets over the hurdle of potential Y2K problems. So it appears that not until 2002 at the earliest will the IRS get a better handle on K-1 reporting, matching, and standardization.

Capital Gains—Sales Price of a Stock Transaction

When a person sells a stock or any type of security, the broker who sold it is required to report the sale on a 1099-B form (Proceeds from Broker and Barter Exchange Transactions). The form contains pertinent information such as the broker's name, the recipient's name and Social Security number, the trade date, gross proceeds, and a brief description of the sold item, e.g., "100 shares of XYZ Corporation stock." This information is reportable by the taxpayer on the 1040, Schedule D (Capital Gains and Losses).

There are billions of securities transactions annually, so taxpayers can understand how vital it is for the IRS to receive 1099-B information on magnetic tape from the thousands of brokers who are members of securities and commodities exchanges. Once on magnetic tape, the information is easily transferred to the IRS computer center.

There's the background. Now let's look at the reality.

The IRS requires that each security sold by a taxpayer be reported on a separate 1099-B, but it allows a great deal of latitude in how the information from the 1099-B is reported back to taxpayers. Although the IRS does have its own standardized 1099-B form, the form is used infrequently.

Essentially, reporting brokers create their own forms, so there is little if any uniformity. It is not uncommon for brokers to issue substitute 1099-Bs, which can be monstrous creations that list all the securities an individual taxpayer sold in a given year on letter-size paper. Sometimes up to 40 transactions are squeezed onto a single sheet, often excluding the number of shares sold. This forces taxpayers who are looking for more detailed information to search for their original trade confirmations from their brokers. How are taxpayers to report the amount of money they receive from the sale of securities and transfer the proper information compiled by the financial institution onto Schedule D? With difficulty.

Further complications arise when a block of shares purchased as a single lot is sold at different times, or when companies split their stocks to take advantage of an opportunity to offer a lower market price to the public. For example, how does one monitor the sale of 1,000 shares of IBM purchased as a single lot, then sold on five different dates? Twenty percent of the cost would have to be assigned to each sale of 200 shares. Perhaps this sounds easy, but what if there were two or three stock splits during the time you owned the stock? You could end up with a complex math problem that might take a taxpayer hours to sort out.

Implications for Taxpayers

The information that is now being reported to the IRS by the securities industry is the sales proceeds of the transactions. Determination of the cost basis, or matching what the taxpayer paid for the security, is another matter entirely. Because this task often requires intricate and complex record keeping, computers would have to monitor detailed cost information for each taxpayer and deal with ongoing adjustments caused by stock splits and dividend reinvestment plans. It is not a surprise, therefore, that taxpayers generally do not receive notices of mismatches originating from 1099-B's. **Any technology system would be hard-pressed to sort out the quagmire of matching a 1099-B with the information on Schedule D.**

During an audit, revenue agents do not always verify the buys and sells of securities transactions. It is interesting to note that in the training materials for conducting office audits that the IRS has developed on frequently examined items, there is no pro-forma audit kit on the verification of securities.

One reason for a seeming complacency by the IRS in its examination of securities transactions could be that it has discovered in its TCMP (Taxpayer Compliance Measurement Program) examinations (the ones used to compile the Discriminate Information Function scores) that the public has been generally honest in its reporting of securities transactions and further audit measures are therefore not required.

This isn't to say that the IRS doesn't use or can't access security transaction information. It certainly does. For example, if the Criminal Investigation Division is investigating a taxpayer, special agents will track down a list of any securities transactions made by that taxpayer and trace them accordingly. But this is done as part of another or secondary investigation. It is not normally done as part of the IRS matching program. Also, based on information from third-party reports, the IRS sends notices to taxpayers who haven't filed prior years' returns, reminding them that they have stock sales that must be more fully reported on Schedule D (Capital Gains and Losses).

To be perfectly frank, the entire area of securities transactions is too important a revenue source for the IRS to turn its back on. Four years ago I said that the IRS will begin to solicit the assistance of financial institutions, brokerage firms, and other companies in the securities business on this issue. As of 2000, more and more brokerage companies are matching cost data associated with securities transactions of their clients, but because there is no requirement to do so, they are not generally reporting it to the IRS.

I suppose readers next want to know when all this additional reporting is going to become a requirement. That I don't know. But I do know that what I just described is probably the strongest means by which the IRS could get a good, solid grip on securities transactions.

Estate and Gift Taxes/Lifetime Exclusions

Reporting inheritances and gifts—inheritances passed on through decedents' estates and assets received as gifts from living individuals—is another area difficult for the IRS to get its arms around. In addition to cash, the more common forms of inheritances and gifts are land, homes, jewelry, autos, and marketable securities, or stamp, art, and coin collections.

Reporting requirements for inheritances and gifts usually fall into three major categories:

- If a decedent's estate exceeds $675,000 in 2000 or 2001, Form 706 (U.S. Estate Tax Return) is required.
- Taxpayers who give gifts of more than $10,000 in one calendar year to one person must file Form 709 (U.S. Gift Tax Return). If a married person gives a gift of $20,000, it can be treated as a split gift, i.e., $10,000 from each spouse.
- Taxpayers who receive gifts and inheritances and ultimately dispose of the items in a taxable transaction must report them as gains or losses on Form 1040, Schedule D (Capital Gains and Losses).

When taxpayers try to determine the value or cost of a gift or inheritance, they find themselves confronted with a complex problem. The following rules are used to determine the cost basis of inherited or gifted assets: In figuring gain *or* loss of an inherited asset, generally use the fair market value at the date of death of the decedent. For gifts disposed of at a *gain*, use the donor's original cost basis. For gifts disposed of at a *loss*, use the donor's original cost basis *or* the fair market value at the time of the gift, whichever is lower.

Implications for Taxpayers

There is not a lot of information going into the IRS computers regarding the cost basis of gifts and inheritances. Therefore, in this area the IRS has to rely almost solely on taxpayer compliance. The situation has several rather far-reaching implications.

When a federal estate tax return, Form 706, is filed, the assets of the estate will be listed along with their fair market values. In this case a taxpayer could easily prove the cost of the inherited property, especially if these items are questioned during an audit, by producing the estate tax return of the decedent. Pay particular attention to stock splits and dividend reinvestment plans, which will make tracing individual stocks somewhat difficult.

YOUR TAX-SAVING STRATEGY.

If you find yourself the recipient of an inheritance where there is *no* accompanying estate tax return, you should get an appraisal of the asset unless it is a marketable security whose value is readily obtainable. This will establish the fair market value of the item, which will allow you to properly compute gain or loss when you dispose of the asset.

Also, it is generally *not* wise for a relative to transfer assets just before passing away; rather, the assets should be in the will. This way, the cost basis of the assets you receive as a beneficiary of the estate will be valued at current fair market value, thereby reducing your tax bite when you sell.

If the transfer is made while the relative is still alive, it is classified as a gift, and upon the disposal of the asset, you will often be burdened with a significant taxable gain, since the cost basis of a gift when computing gain is the original cost to the donor and not the fair market value.

Mr. Davis's mother *gifted* her son a Florida condominium, which she had purchased for $25,000. One year later, Mr. Davis sold the apartment for $40,000. The cost basis for the gift is the original $25,000 and now results in a $15,000 taxable capital gain. *On the other hand,* if Mr. Davis had *inherited* the condo after his mother's death and then sold it a few months later for $40,000, his cost basis would be $40,000 (fair market value at date of death) and there would be no taxable gain or loss.

The question is, "How can the IRS keep track of and catalog the value of bequests from an estate and gifts?" For example, could the IRS require that every person, when asked to prove the cost of inherited property, produce the estate tax return of the decedent? Although this is requested during an audit, it is not feasible to include this step in routine practice because of the relative scarcity of estates with assets that are valued in excess of $675,000, hence of estate tax returns. Sounds like another mission impossible.

It is up to the taxpayer to produce an appraisal or other proof to show fair market value, or to show a paid bill or canceled check to prove cost. Other than estate and gift tax returns, the IRS computer contains no information that will refute the documented proof that you are presenting.

To clear up a major misconception regarding tax implications of gifts and inheritances, see pages 217–218 and 294–295.

WHERE THE IRS TECHNOLOGY FALLS SHORT ON THE EXPENSE SIDE—MORTGAGE INTEREST AND REAL ESTATE TAX

Mortgage interest and points paid in a mortgage transaction of $600 or more are reported to taxpayers by their mortgage lenders on Form 1098

(Mortgage Interest Statement). Others besides mortgage lenders who must file this form are taxpayers who pay out $600 or more of mortgage interest in the course of conducting their trade or business, even if the taxpayer is not in the business of lending money. At tax preparation time, the taxpayers must transfer this amount to line 10 of Form 1040, Schedule A (Itemized Deductions).

Taxpayers often make errors when entering or transferring information onto their 1040. In the area of mortgage interest the chances for error are extremely high. From the taxpayer's perspective, this is extremely understandable. There are several reasons why this area has such a high error rate. Although home mortgage interest can be copied from Form 1098, most taxpayers copy both mortgage interest and real estate tax information from the annual mortgage expense statement that they receive from financial lending institutions, because Form 1098 does not contain real estate tax information. Besides information on mortgage interest and real estate taxes, other information found on annual expense statements is interest earned on tax escrows, homeowner's insurance, water charges, and late charges.

These annual statements, like the W-2 and K-1, are *not* standardized. Most are computer-generated by the reporting institutions. **As a result, when taxpayers transfer the figures to their 1040, they often transfer real estate taxes as mortgage interest and vice versa.**

Another common error is to use homeowner's insurance and water charges as a valid deduction, which of course they are not. The end result is a mismatch between the figure(s) the taxpayer entered on Schedule A, and the figure(s) supplied by the third party reporting the mortgage interest and real estate tax information.

Sounds like a simple situation and a simple mistake, and indeed, this is a *very* common error. Of course things could be clarified and subsequently made easier for the taxpayer if the IRS were to revise the 1098 form to include a line for real estate taxes. Then these two figures would at least be broken out on the same sheet of paper, which would reduce or even eliminate this particular problem altogether.

The tracking of real estate taxes is further complicated by the fact that real estate taxes are not reported only on the annual expense statement received from the lending institution.

• A taxpayer with no mortgage on his home pays his real estate taxes directly to the municipalities. In this instance, no annual expense statement is received by the taxpayer. Furthermore, since the taxpayer now has four to six checks to sort through at tax time, he will often include in his total real estate tax deduction the payment for water charges or rubbish removal (nondeductible items), because they are paid to the same payee, the municipalities.

Many homeowners have been successful in having their real estate tax burdens reduced due to unequal or incorrect assessments in this way. If you receive a lump-sum check from your municipality, you should reduce your real estate tax deduction in the year you receive the check.

• Mortgage interest for the short period, from the date of purchase to when the first new mortgage payment will be paid, is paid at the closing. Since this amount has been paid *before* the new account is set up, it is often not included on the annual expense statement or the 1098, both issued by the lending institution. The knowledgeable taxpayer will add up the total payments for the year, including interest and real estate taxes shown on the closing statement, and disregard the interest amount entered on the 1098. Too often, though, taxpayers forget to claim deductions for mortgage interest or real estate taxes that they are legitimately entitled to.

The IRS recognizes this problem and is trying to persuade Congress to issue regulations that would require lending institutions to include these adjustments on their annual expense statements. Once this happens, taxpayers will receive more complete and understandable information from the lending institutions, which will help them claim their proper deductions.

Other possible sources of disagreement between mortgage interest as shown on Form 1098 and the deduction on Schedule A is the inclusion of late charges on the annual expense statements, incurred because the mortgage was paid after the usual 15-day grace period, and prepayment charges that accrue when you pay off your mortgage early. These charges are considered to be extra interest, *not* penalties. Accordingly, taxpayers can add the late and prepayment charges to the regular mortgage interest paid during the year.

Note that information regarding late and prepayment charges on mortgage payments is allotted three sentences on page 4 of IRS Publication 936, *Home Mortgage Interest Deduction.* Wouldn't you like to know how much revenue has been generated by the federal government because thousands of taxpayers did not realize that both of these charges were a valid deduction?

Implications for Taxpayers

If you receive a mismatch notice on mortgage interest, don't panic. Often there is just as great a chance that the error comes from the reporting institution. Answer the inquiry promptly with full documentation, including copies of your original Form 1098 and, for new home buyers, the closing statement from the purchase of your home. This will show the IRS where the extra mortgage-interest deduction can be found.

WHERE THE IRS TECHNOLOGY FALLS SHORT— NONFILERS AND UNDERREPORTERS

The General Accounting Office (GAO) does periodic studies of the IRS and usually makes specific recommendations as to how the IRS can improve its performance. The GAO studied IRS effectiveness in the area of nonfilers and underreporters, with these results:

- Nonfilers with incomes over $100,000 could more easily escape detection than those with lower incomes.
- When high-income nonfilers are pursued and they *do* file their returns, the IRS needs to scrutinize these late returns very carefully. It appears that the GAO made this very same suggestion in prior reports, but the IRS ignored it.
- The IRS should hire more employees to investigate high-income nonfilers.
- To reduce the time spent on reviewing underreporter cases that result from mistaken entries and not genuine underreporting, the IRS should change the matching program to search for reported income on as many different tax return lines as possible.
- The IRS should report to the Social Security Administration errors in wage data it finds in underreporter cases.[6]

Implications for Taxpayers
It does appear that the IRS is reducing the number of nonfilers. It remains to be seen how many of these delinquent taxpayers were contacted by the IRS because of its increased technological capabilities of the matching program versus how many voluntarily filed because they believed the IRS was on their trail; or how many were pulled in by the IRS nonfiler program, or the media hype regarding leniency and so-called taxpayer amnesty.

WHERE THE IRS TECHNOLOGY FALLS SHORT—LACK OF REPORTING REQUIREMENTS FOR CORPORATIONS

The biggest gap in the IRS technology infrastructure concerns payments to corporations of income, interest, dividends, rents, royalties, and capital gains. There is currently no requirement that any corporation receiving such payments be sent 1099's. (There are several limited exceptions, such as for companies performing legal services.) According to a 1991 IRS study, small corporations voluntarily reported 81 percent of the tax they owed on such payments in 1981, but by 1987 the compliance rate dropped to only 61 percent. The GAO and the House Government Operations Committee have consistently pushed for legislation that would require entities that pay dividends, interest, and other payments to corporations to file 1099's with the IRS. The IRS would then attempt to catch corporations that understated income or failed to file returns.

NOTE: There are no reporting requirements for financial institutions to send records of IRA payments to the IRS, according to an IRS spokesman.[7]

Implications for Taxpayers

There are several valid reasons why the IRS has been dragging its feet on bringing in corporate recipients under the 1099 reporting umbrella:

• It would enormously increase the IRS processing burden of the already overworked IRS computers and staff. I estimate that more than 100 million new pieces of paper would be generated annually by payments to corporations. Also, the proponents of this arduous task have not considered the added cost to businesses, which may be as much as $1 billion annually.

• The IRS is going through an extremely difficult time strategizing, building, and managing its computer capabilities. The added burden of corporate reporting would set back the very much overexpensed and underperforming program even further.

• The task of matching bits of corporate income data to the multiple income line items that exist on Forms 1120 (Corporate Income Tax Return) and 1120S (U.S. Income Tax Return for an S Corporation) will be more formidable than matching individual income with lines on Form 1040.

• Many corporations base their books on years that end anytime between January 31 and November 30, while fiscal 1099 reporting is calculated on a calendar year. Thus, many 1099's will contain income that spans two corporate years. The only way to eliminate this problem is to require *all* corporations to convert to a calendar year. When Congress attempted exactly this procedure for S corporations in 1987, tax professionals revolted to an extent not seen since the Boston Tea Party. Being able to do fiscal year closings of books for corporations during off-peak times for accountants saves me (and no doubt countless numbers of other tax professionals) from an early death. Ultimately, Congress scaled back the calendar-year requirement just enough so that the revolt died down.

The House Government Operations Committee proposal urged the IRS to initiate corporate document matching, but it was cut from the final version of RRA '93. The report said that matching could bring in significant tax revenues and have a *minimal* impact on the payer community and corporations. Based on the points just made, you can see that whoever wrote this report must have had no corporate experience or must not have been in touch with reality.

WHERE THE IRS TECHNOLOGY FALLS SHORT— THE AUDIT LEVEL

The IRS continues to have trouble accessing specific information from their own computers. Information retrieval for a given year, a given tax return, or a specific piece of information may be readily available, but one never knows what will happen once a request is made. Basic tax return information takes more than a year to reach IRS computers in a readable form, and IRS technology is still too slow to meet the needs of either IRS employees or taxpayers.

Implications for Taxpayers
Despite state-of-the-art technology, there is still too much information and not enough people and/or systems to process it. **In conclusion, it seems there are and probably always will be gaps and lags in IRS computer capabilities.**

TECHNOLOGY OVERHAUL A FIASCO

In 1988, during the planning stage, an overhaul of the computer system was expected to have been completed by 2000 at a cost of *only* $8 billion! The job did not get done, and even with recently approved budget cuts, the total cost for such an overhaul continues to grow—in excess of $20 billion, including maintenance and operations expenses. The sums are so enormous they don't seem real, but they are, all U.S. tax dollars.

Arthur Gross, former assistant commissioner for modernization, appointed early in 1997 to help sort out the mess, said, "Customer service representatives must use as many as nine different computer terminals, each of which connects to several different data bases, to resolve problems."[8] His admission that the Tax Systems Modernization effort has failed was made before the National Commission on Restructuring the IRS. Some systems, one costing almost $3 million, have been "killed," and there is talk of scrapping the entire project altogether, starting over, or even outsourcing the entire process. "For the foreseeable future," Mr. Gross said, "the IRS must continue to work with dozens of antiquated computer systems that cannot trade information with one another."[9] Everyone agrees that modernization is vital "to bring in the $1.6 trillions of dollars needed annually to pay for the government, to restore public confidence in the service's ability to resolve taxpayers' problems quickly and to increase the use of electronic filing of returns."[10] But no one seems to have the answers as to where or how to begin.

The biggest problems are the choices of software, security, and lack of integration across the IRS's vast computer network. With outdated equipment that prevents systems from sharing files—there are 70 different operating systems—the agency continues to rely on magnetic tapes transported between offices via trucks and planes. The basic tax and accounting systems were never designed for modern financial management. The failure of the technology effort means that taxpayers in a dispute with the IRS could face years of frustration. With records kept on two or more computer systems, being able to retrieve necessary information in a timely manner becomes difficult, if not impossible.

Parts of the new system that are working, besides the matching program or Information Returns Program, are electronic filing, on-line filing, and 1040EZ filing (see pages 333–337), where taxpayers can file their returns with only a brief phone call. TeleFiling, too, is a continued success, along with the establishment of the IRS websites.

Technological successes on the business side would be the electronic Federal Tax Payment System and the "one-stop-shopping" benefits for Form 941 (Employer's Quarterly Federal Tax Return).

The primary force behind improving IRS technology appears to be Charles Rossotti. When he showed up, everything changed, including the blueprint for the initial stage (design phase) of another modernization effort presented to Congress in 1998. That year, under Rossotti's charge, the IRS issued a request for a proposal for a prime systems integration services contractor. By December the IRS awarded a contract that could be worth some $5 billion to a division of Computer Science Corp. (CSC). The setup now is for CSC to lead a consortium of contractors that include Northrup Grumman, KPMG Peat Marwick, Unisys, IBM, Lucent Technologies, and Science Applications International Corp.

This enormous initiative will focus on business modernization, the new organizational changes as well as the much-needed systems modernization.

Although some of the newest systems ease processing, speed requests, and provide more across-the-board information on tax returns, I don't see the technology situation changing much for years to come.

7

IRS Targets and What to Do
If You're One of Them

The tax compliance rate—the rate at which taxpayers willingly (although perhaps not contentedly) pay their taxes in the United States—hovers around 85 percent.[1] Even so, only $83 of every $100 due in income tax is collected.[2] So despite the fact that the tax collection process brings in what seems like extraordinary sums (over $1.9 trillion in gross collections for 1999), each year the federal government continues to be shortchanged an estimated $195 billion. (Even this is an understatement because it excludes an additional $300 billion or so of taxable income produced through drug sales, organized crime, and other illegal activities.) But really, who knows for sure?

In this realm of extraordinary tax evasion, very little has changed over the decades except the amounts owed and never paid, which continue to rise. Beginning in the late 1980's, however, the IRS seriously began to focus on breaking open the phenomenon that has come to be called the *underground economy*, whereby a substantial number of people, businesses, and organizations do not pay their proper share, or any share at all, of their taxes.

Without a doubt the underground economy is a serious problem—for the IRS, for our society, and for honest taxpayers. **However, the IRS has taken such an aggressive position on exposing the underground economy that it is punishing innocent taxpayers and wiping out entire sectors of the independent business community.** This chapter is written for the people who are being wrongly and often unlawfully pursued.

ARE YOU IN THE LINE OF FIRE?

Individuals are responsible for about 75 percent of each year's tax shortfall, while corporations account for only 25 percent. How does the IRS identify the groups who are not paying their fair share of taxes? These groups overlap, duplicate, and even meld as players in the underground economy glide through avenues that facilitate evading or avoiding taxes. Easiest for the IRS to identify are

- The self-employed
- People who work out of a home office
- Independent contractors
- Cash-intensive businesses
- Nonfilers

Within each group, the two primary methods for evading tax dollars are hiding income and overstating or manipulating expenses or deductions.

TARGET: THE SELF-EMPLOYED

At the top of the IRS hit list for breaking open the underground economy are the self-employed, whether a sole proprietorship or a corporate entity. People who own a business and work full time for themselves probably have the greatest opportunities not only to hide money but also to overstate deductions.

What makes matters even more embarrassing is that the IRS knows just exactly which segments of the self-employed are the worst offenders. According to the GAO, service providers lead the list of underreporters. At the top are auto dealers, restaurateurs, and clothing store operators, who underreport nearly 40 percent of their taxable income, according to the IRS. Telemarketers and traveling salespeople have a shortfall of about 30 percent. Then come doctors, lawyers, barbers, and accountants, who understate about 20 percent of their income.[3] In the Northeast, my recent experience strongly indicates that lawyers and doctors head the list of service providers who are being audited.

To more easily conquer this segment, as I see it, the IRS has subdivided the self-employed into three smaller groups:

- Sole proprietors
- Those who work out of a home office
- Independent contractors

Target: Sole Proprietors

A sole proprietor is defined as an unincorporated business or profession in which net income is reportable by only one person. The gamut of the self-employed runs from people who own a service business (beauticians, home services and repairs, tutors) to professionals (doctors, lawyers) to insurance agents and computer programmers and more.

How the IRS Attacks Sole Proprietors

Integral to the definition of sole proprietors is the necessity to file a Schedule C with a 1040 form. While Schedule C requires you to define the type of business you are in and/or your occupation, it also functions as a wonderful device for deducting business expenses dollar for dollar against business income (see also Rule 3, page 246). As a sole proprietor, via Schedule C you have every opportunity to underreport your income and lots of other opportunities to convert personal expenses to business expenses.

For these two reasons, the IRS sees the sole proprietor as a double enemy: a cheat in the underground economy *and* a prime audit target.

What Sole Proprietors Can Do to Protect Themselves

Although Schedule C affords full deductibility of business expenses, a heavy concentration of expense items is a valuable indicator for the IRS, so the IRS is naturally going to focus on what you've listed. However, the IRS is *not* necessarily focusing on aggressive stances taken on expense items unless certain items jump out, such as travel being $25,000 out of a $50,000 income. **The IRS *is* focusing on the *type of business* for which the Schedule C is filed, particularly if the business type falls into one of the IRS target areas: service providers, professionals, or cash-intensive businesses.**

What will the auditor ask you to provide? A review of Form 4700 (IRS Examination Workpapers) indicates that the examiner will request from you

- A description of the business and the number of years you have been in business.
- The number of employees and the bookkeeper's name.
- The amount of cash in the business at the beginning and end of the year.
- The name and address of your bank.
- What method of accounting you use—cash or accrual.
- Outstanding loans due to or from the owners of the business.

- Business expenses verification.
- Copy of tax return from prior year.

This is the minimum information that the auditor will require. Make sure you review the data carefully before you hand the auditor anything.

Here's an amazing story, the sort of thing that pops up every once in a while in the tax field, about a taxpayer who without realizing it discovered the secret to resolving the "double enemy" predicament— legally.

Sam grew up working in his father's hardware store, which was left to him after his father passed away. The normal tax procedure for this process would have been to close the estate by filing a final estate return, then to begin reporting the ongoing operations of the store on a Schedule C attached to Sam's 1040. However, the operations of the store were reported as part of a U.S. Fiduciary Income Tax Return (Form 1041), not on a 1040, and the store's net income was passed through to the son on a K-1 form (Beneficiary's Share of Income, Credits, Deductions, etc.), which is a schedule of Form 1041.

Sam continued to report income from the store through the estate on the K-1 of Form 1041 until he retired. At no time did the IRS ever inquire why the operations of the store were included in the fiduciary income tax return. This unusual tax setup kept Sam's business virtually unnoticed by the IRS.

If you are a sole proprietor *and* are at a high risk for audit, the perfect solution, which Sam used without ever realizing it, involves the *way* you report your business activities to the IRS. By extracting yourself from the sole proprietorship/Schedule C category and transforming your business to, for example, a partnership or corporation, you can successfully remove yourself from the IRS hit list. However, in a surprising update, it seems the IRS has detected a "sharp increase" in the number of trust returns, e.g., Form 1041 (U.S. Income Tax Return for Estates and Trusts) with a Schedule C attached. IRS officials fear that taxpayers are taking advantage of the low audit rate for Form 1041 returns by using this form to report and file their business taxes. IRS focus on this area is long overdue. What took them so long? Taxpayers, beware.

Because this subject is so closely linked to the audit component, the entire area will be discussed at length in chapter 8, "How to Avoid an Audit Completely."

Target: People Who Work Out of a Home Office

As many as 40 million people work at least part-time at home, with about 8,000 home-based businesses starting daily. Of these, almost 1.7

million claimed home-office deductions on their 1997 tax returns, amounting to over $3.8 billion.[4]

How the IRS Attacks People Who Take
the Home-Office Deduction

Inspired by Compliance 2000, an IRS initiative from the early 1990s to ascertain why at least 10 million individuals and businesses do not comply with tax regulations, the IRS decided that taxpayers who take the home-office deduction represented too large a segment of the underground economy. After all, a great many items taken as home-office expenses that would ordinarily be for personal use, like telephone, utilities, repairs, maintenance, and depreciation of certain items in the home, were being transformed to deductible business expenses on the 1040 form. (Home-office expenses are contrasted with out-of-pocket business expenses such as office supplies or postage, which would be incurred by a business whether it was located in a home or not.)

New Home-Office Rules

Beginning January 1, 1999, the home-office deduction was rolled back to pre-Soliman days based upon an expanded definition of "principal place of business." (See page 115.) New rules allow you to take a home-office deduction if your principal place of business is where you perform administrative or management activities provided there is no other fixed location to perform those activities. This revised interpretation means that people who conduct their business from a home office but perform the majority of their work elsewhere will be able to take the deduction even though the home office may be used "only" for routine administrative tasks such as billing, keeping books and records, writing reports, and ordering supplies. As with prior law, taxpayers will still be obliged to prove that their home office is used exclusively on a regular basis, and if you are an employee, you can take the deduction only if such use is for the convenience of your employer.

Here's a case involving one of my clients affected by the new home-office rules:

Ellen Stedman is an employee of a corporation whose only office is in Chicago, Illinois. But she lives in Newark, New Jersey, and uses her apartment as a home office. There she arranges customer contacts, speaks with suppliers, and performs administrative functions such as writing up sales orders and expense reports, which she mails to her employer in Chicago. Her normal workday keeps her out of her home office and on the road from nine A.M. to four P.M.

Beginning January 1, 1999, Ms. Stedman's home office qualifies as her principal place of business for deducting expenses for its use. It's where she conducts administrative activities, and she has no other fixed location where she performs these same functions. The fact that she does some administrative work at her clients' locations does not disqualify her home office as her principal place of business as it would have before these new rules went into effect.

Form 8829

Form 8829 is an IRS weapon for getting a grip on taxpayers taking the home-office deduction. Anyone who chooses the deduction must submit the form with Schedule C, Profit or Loss from Business (Sole Proprietorship), together with the 1040.

Although the IRS consistently denies it, Form 8829 can single out your tax return for scrutiny. But just as with all other IRS forms, there are ways to interpret and fill this one out without quivering.

How to Solidify the Home-Office Deduction and Avoid Audit Traps on Form 8829

First, make sure you maintain a separate telephone number for business purposes only. Also, make sure your business correspondence is sent to your home-office address rather than to some other convenient place, like one of your biggest clients.

Finally, make sure you understand what benefits the home-office deduction offers and how to make the best use of them. You can deduct depreciation on the business portion of your principal place of residence; depreciation on equipment and furniture; the business portion of your transportation expenses; an amount for self-employment tax; a range of benefits that accrue when you are able to reduce your AGI; and certain computer and record-keeping expenses. Here's what you need to know about each of these:

PERCENT OF HOME SPACE USED AS AN OFFICE.
The percentage of expenses for business use of your home—insurance, utilities, repairs and maintenance, and rent, if you are a renter—that you can deduct is based on the total square footage of the residence that is used for business. Take a sensible approach in computing the percentage or you'll be caught in an audit trap. It is entirely acceptable for your business space to occupy 20 to 25 percent of your total home space, but a figure of 40 percent or more is unreasonable unless you store merchandise in your home.

NUMBER OF SQUARE FEET.

You probably should not go over the 40 percent mark regarding square footage; on the other hand, too many taxpayers operate under the wrong assumption that every piece of office furniture and equipment must be squeezed into a tiny space.

Be sure to include space you use for storage shelves, file cabinets, and other equipment. The tax allowance that provides deductions for items pertaining to space allocated on a regular basis in the taxpayer's home office includes storage of product samples. This is particularly beneficial to businesses whose inventory and samples take up substantial space.

NOTE: Taxpayers should remember to make a distinction between product samples and inventory, the latter being already allowable in the existing home-office deduction. Also keep in mind that merchandise inventory is not always stacked up in neat piles. With all that tax auditors have to do, it's rare for one to visit your home to verify square footage information, so utilize the greatest amount sensibly available.

DEPRECIATION OF THE HOME OR PRINCIPAL PLACE OF BUSINESS.

Depreciation for the portion of your home used for business, referred to as "nonresidential rental property" on Form 4562 (Depreciation and Amortization)—Part Two, is based on a write-off period of 39 years. The basis for depreciation is the original cost of your residence (excluding land cost) plus additional costs for permanent improvements, or fair market value at the time of conversion to business use, whichever is *less*.* **If you use fair market value, a common mistake, your depreciation figure will show up as unnecessarily high because fair market value is generally much higher than original cost. This may attract IRS attention.**

DEPRECIATION ON EQUIPMENT AND FURNITURE.

You can depreciate the cost of new equipment and furniture over a five- or seven-year period (depending on the item as defined and explained in the instructions for Form 4562). In addition, anyone taking the home-office deduction can also depreciate office machines, equipment, and furniture that have been converted from personal (not new) to business use. The basis for depreciation is original cost or fair market value at the time of conversion to business use, whichever is *less*. The IRS will not be surprised to see depreciation of this kind and will not hound you for bills covering original items purchased, since they assume you purchased them some time ago, probably as personal items.

*Real estate tax bills show the assessed amount of land value.

You have several methods of depreciation to choose from:

- The *straight line method* allows you to ratably depreciate business capital assets evenly over the assets' useful life.
- The *200 percent declining balance method* gives taxpayers twice the amount of depreciation in the earlier years. The process is described in IRS Publication 334, *Tax Guide for Small Business*, and Publication 534, *Depreciation.*
- Section 179 of the *Internal Revenue Code* allows taxpayers to write off *current-year purchases* of automobiles (with limitations) and business equipment and furniture up to $19,000 annually for 1999, $20,000 annually for 2000, and $24,000 annually for 2001, regardless of the item's useful life (use Form 4562). Section 179 write-offs will increase in steps to $25,000 by 2003. So if you experience high net taxable income and can make a major purchase of office equipment or furniture in the same year, utilizing Section 179 will increase your expenses and reduce your net taxable income. Say you purchase a $15,000 copier that is normally deductible over five years according to the *Internal Revenue Code* for depreciation on office equipment. Under Section 179, you can deduct the entire $15,000 in the current year. The benefit gained is an extra $13,500 of expenses in a year when you have high taxable income. In the 31 percent tax bracket, the savings is $4,185. **Once you write off items under Section 179, you cannot depreciate them further.**

Be aware that the election to use Section 179 can be made only on the originally filed tax return. You cannot use an amended return filed after the normal due date of the return to make or modify the election. Furthermore, the full extra depreciation of $20,000 for 2000 is available only if you purchase no more than $200,000 of eligible business assets. If your purchases exceed this amount, you lose part of the $20,000 depreciation dollar for dollar. Plan your purchases carefully. You might think about leasing some equipment instead of making an outright purchase in order not to exceed the $200,000 amount.

YOUR TAX-SAVING STRATEGY.
The Section 179 deduction cannot be used to reduce your taxable income below zero (taxable income includes the aggregate net income or loss from all businesses you and your spouse conducted during the tax year, *plus* any wages earned as an employee). If a Section 179 deduction would reduce your taxable income below zero, your alternative would be to use normal depreciation methods. You must depreciate autos,

typewriters, computers, copiers, calculators, and the like over five years. (Computers are subject to special dollar limitations, as described below. Automobile depreciation is discussed on pages 252–253 and 255.) The write-off period for office furniture (desks, files, and fixtures) and carpets is seven years.

Remember, when taking depreciation for office equipment and furniture,

- You don't need a receipt for every last cent, since you might have purchased the items a while ago.
- An IRS auditor would not be surprised to see depreciation for a desk, chair, couch, and carpeting.
- Estimates, if they are reasonable, are acceptable by IRS auditors.

YOUR TAX-SAVING STRATEGY.
If you inadvertantly did not claim the allowable amount of depreciation for prior years, you previously could not deduct missed depreciation in the current year. One way to recoup deductions you failed to claim was to file amended returns for the years missed, but not beyond three years. An easier solution is now available based on IRS Revenue Procedure 97-27, which allows you to file Form 3115 (Application for Change in Accounting Method) at any time during the year in which the proposed change is to be made.

TRANSPORTATION EXPENSE DEDUCTION.
If your residence is your principal place of business, you may deduct daily transportation expenses incurred in going between your home and another work location in the same trade or business, regardless of the distance and whether or not the work location is regular or temporary. For various ways to report mileage expenses, see pages 252–253. For salespeople particularly, whose first and last trip of the day may be lengthy, the transportation deduction is substantial and reason enough to fill out Form 8829.

DECREASED SELF-EMPLOYMENT TAX.
Because the home-office and transportation expense deduction usually reduce self-employment income, self-employed taxpayers receive a benefit of reducing their self-employment tax, which is computed at a rate of 15.3 percent of self-employed income (12.4 percent for FICA and 2.9 percent for Medicare.) Even moonlighting taxpayers whose income exceeds the FICA maximum wage of $76,200 from a full-time job can

obtain a reduction in the 2.9 percent Medicare portion of their self-employment tax.

TAX BENEFITS CORRRELATED TO YOUR ADJUSTED GROSS INCOME.
To the extent that deductions for home-office and transportation expenses decrease your adjusted gross income, you may find that certain other tax benefits become available. For example, by taking these deductions, you may reduce your joint AGI below $150,000, which would make you eligible to make a full contribution to a Roth IRA.[5] By reducing your AGI, you can also benefit by an increase in a whole slew of other deductions and expenses that are subject to AGI limitations. These can include increased itemized deductions for medical expenses (see page 257) and casualty and theft losses, along with exclusions for adoption expenses, Social Security benefits, deductions for rental expenses, student loan interest, the AMT exemption, eligibility for traditional IRA's, and more.

REDUCED COMPUTER RECORD-KEEPING REQUIREMENTS.
A computer is generally considered "listed property" and is subject to more stringent rules than other office equipment in order to claim any part of its cost as depreciation on a business return. To be eligible for depreciation, business use must exceed 50 percent, and only that attained portion can be expensed. Where some personal usage is involved, use of a daily log to substantiate the business use is required by the IRS. However, if the computer is kept and used in your home office, it is assumed to be business property and therefore not subject to the special rules.

But be forewarned. You don't want to push any of these too far. You could risk triggering an audit trap in Form 8829.

Disadvantage of the Home-Office Deduction
Probably the biggest disadvantage of taking the home-office deduction kicks in when you are ready to sell your home. If you took a home-office deduction and then plan to sell your home, you will be prevented from taking the full exclusion of $250,000 for singles, $500,000 for married couples filing jointly on the gain from the sale of your home. To qualify for the full exclusion, you must have owned and used the entire property as your principal residence for at least two out of the five years preceding the date of sale. That's because the business portion being used for the home office is not eligible for the $250,000/$500,000 exclusion, and the gain, which accrues to the taxpayer by taking the home-

office deduction, is subject to a maximum long-term capital gain rate of 20 percent. Furthermore, any depreciation taken on the house after May 6, 1997, is subject to a maximum tax rate of 25 percent.

However, there is a way to avoid or at least minimize this disadvantage by using some forethought. If you are planning on selling your home, the best thing to do is to not utilize the home office for at least two years prior to the date of sale. For further information, see page 291.

Taking the allowable amount of business deduction for depreciation of your residence subjects you to capital gains tax when you sell your home after May 6, 1997. If you correctly claimed a deduction of $2,500 on your 1040 Schedule C over a period of five years, for example, when you sell your home you must pay capital gains taxes on $12,500, even though the balance of gain on your residence will probably not be subject to tax because of the available $250,000/$500,000 exclusions.

If you are an employee and are taking a deduction for the home office, do not use Form 8829, which is meant for self-employed individuals. Instead, use the work sheet contained in IRS Publication 587, *Business Use of Your Home.* You then transfer the total home-office deduction from line 32 to Form 2106 (Employee Business Expenses) or Form 2106-EZ (Unreimbursed Employee Business Expenses). The employee business expenses end up as miscellaneous expenses on Schedule A (Itemized Deductions) and are subject to a deductible equal to 2 percent of your adjusted gross income.

Here is a final comment on Form 8829. At an American Institute of Certified Public Accountants (AICPA) seminar, an IRS presenter told the crowd that it would take an hour and a quarter to fill out Form 8829 and seven minutes to study the rules. This was followed by an outburst of laughter.[6]

I say there isn't a person alive who could learn anything useful about the *Internal Revenue Code* provision that governs this form in that time period. It more likely would take an entire day at a minimum.

Loopholes in the Home-Office Deduction
The biggest loophole regarding the home-office deduction is available to anyone who owns an S corporation, is a member of a limited liability company or a partner in a partnership, *and* uses a home office.

Owners of S corporations report income and expenses on Form 1120S (U.S. Income Tax Return for an S Corporation) whereas LLCs and partnerships report income and expenses on Form 1065 (U.S. Partnership Return of Income). **There is no special form to identify the home-**

office deduction. This means that you can be the owner of an S corporation, operating fully out of your home, and there is no distinction made between your home-office expenses and any other business expenses. You avoid the home-office IRS hit list altogether. This is more fully explained in the discussion of S corporations in chapter 8, "How to Avoid an Audit Completely" (see pages 192–200).

Target: Independent Contractors

What began with millions of laid-off workers refashioning their experience and marketing themselves as one-person operations to be hired out on an as-needed basis spawned a new way to earn a living—being an independent contractor. To the IRS, the nature of how independent contractors are paid is evidence enough that some of them have joined the ranks of the underground economy. Their tax impact is an estimated shortfall of $10 billion a year.

Reclassification of Independent Contractors

By law, the IRS is entitled to receive from employers the following taxes for each employee:

- FICA tax (Social Security and Medicare), which comes to 15.3 percent of the employee's salary up to $76,200, covered equally by the employer *and* the employee, 7.65 percent each, 1.45 percent each on salary above $76,200.
- Federal withholding tax or the amount deducted from your gross wages on the basis of income level and exemptions.
- Federal unemployment insurance tax of 0.8 percent of only the first $7,000 in wages, paid by the employer. The federal unemployment insurance tax rate can be as high as 6.2 percent, which may vary according to the amount of state unemployment insurance tax paid by the employer. The rate differs in each state.

When employers hire independent contractors, these requirements and others disappear. Employers

- Are *not* required to include the contractor on the quarterly payroll tax reports. So business owners save at a minimum the employer portion of the FICA tax, or 7.65 percent of each independent contractor's gross earnings (1.45 percent on earnings above $76,200).
- Aren't subject to state unemployment insurance premiums or even increases in these premiums when a contractor is let go, since business owners who hire independent contractors are not subject

to state unemployment laws. This alone represents a major consideration when deciding whether to hire an employee versus an independent contractor.

- Reduce their compliance costs, since the federal Age Discrimination in Employment Act and the Americans with Disabilities Act of 1990 do not apply to independent contractors.
- Are *not* required by law to cover an independent contractor for worker's compensation insurance (accidents or sickness on the job), or disability insurance (accidents or sickness away from the job).
- Do *not* include independent contractors in the company's pension plan (this item alone is often as high as 10 percent of an employee's gross wages), sick leave or vacation benefits, medical coverage, or stock options.

All the business owner is required to do is file a 1099-MISC and send it to the IRS at the end of the year.

When workers choose to be classified as independent contractors and/or employers choose to get rid of employees and instead hire independent contractors, the IRS is shortchanged in two ways because independent contractors can

- Deduct on their tax return many items that would otherwise be considered personal: travel, entertainment, office supplies, insurance, and home-office expenses (subject to the key tests discussed earlier in this chapter). This could reasonably amount to 20 percent of one's net income.
- Set up their own pension plan, which is deductible against their income.

In turn, independent contractors *must* fulfill these obligations to the IRS:

- Pay their own FICA tax, which is about 15.3 percent of their net taxable income up to $76,200 and 2.9 percent above that, on Form 1040, Schedule SE (Self-Employment Tax).
- Pay withholding tax on their net taxable income.

The growing numbers of independent contractors surging through our economy present many opportunities for workers not to pay the IRS all the money it is legislated to receive.

Are you beginning to get the picture? **Every additional worker**

classified as an independent contractor means the IRS loses tax dollars through unpaid FICA, withholding, and unemployment taxes, and through income tax deductions as well.

The IRS would be delighted if all workers became classified as employees and the category of independent contractor disappeared. In its attempt to make this a reality, the IRS has initiated an all-out nationwide attack on independent contractors. One of its claims is that 92 percent of the companies it called in for a worker classification review during one recent period were assessed a higher Social Security tax, with an average assessment of $67,000 per audit.[7]

The GAO has reported that between 1988 and 1995, the latest study available, 12,983 employment tax audits resulted in $830 million of proposed assessments and reclassifications of 527,000 workers as employees.[8]

With the IRS paying so much attention to "misclassified" employees, it is more crucial than ever for businesses and independent contractors to recognize the IRS's aggressive tactics and how to stand protected.

IRS Attack Methods Against Independent Contractors

RECLASSIFYING INDEPENDENT CONTRACTORS.
To detemine whether a worker is an employee or an independent contractor, the IRS gives the greatest weight to the degree of control exercised by the employer in three specific areas:

- Control of behavior (instructions and directions—what to do and how to do it).
- Control of finances (financial risks of the worker and opportunities for profit).
- Relationship of employer and worker (how they view each other in their written contract).

Besides the issue of control, the techniques used by the IRS to turn independent contractors into employees include:

- A 20-factor control test
- Third-party leads (nothing more or less than informers)
- A shift in IRS Examination Division resources
- Unannounced audit blitzes by the Collection Department

Twenty-Factor Control or Common-Law Test

The factors are taken from a 1987 guide, *Revenue Ruling 87-41*, in which 20 statements are offered as a test to determine if a worker is an employee. On the basis of this criteria, workers are generally employees if they

1. Must comply with employer's instructions about the work.
2. Receive training from or at the direction of the employer.
3. Provide services that are integrated into the business.
4. Provide services that must be rendered personally.
5. Hire, supervise, and pay assistants for the employer.
6. Have a continuing working relationship with the employer.
7. Must follow set hours of work.
8. Work full-time for an employer.
9. Must do their work on the employer's premises.
10. Must do their work in a sequence set by the employer.
11. Must submit regular reports to the employer.
12. Receive payments of regular amounts at set intervals.
13. Receive payments for business and/or traveling expenses.
14. Rely on the employer to furnish tools and material.
15. Lack a major investment in facilities used to perform the service.
16. Cannot make a profit or suffer a loss from the services.
17. Work for one employer at a time.
18. Do not offer their services to the general public.
19. Can be fired by the employer.
20. May quit work at any time without incurring liability.[9]

The more control the worker has over the performance of the work and the hours worked, the less integrated the worker is in the regular routine of work. Similarly, the more the worker is motivated by profit and the less by having a long-term working relationship, the more likely that person is to be classified as an independent contractor.

There are, however, measures a business owner and an independent contractor can take to strengthen their respective positions.

The contract created between the business owner and the independent contractor is regarded by the IRS as a key item in assessing classification. When drawing up the contract, business owners can take several precautions.

How to Draw Up a Foolproof Independent Contractor Contract

- Specify the services to be rendered.
- Insert a starting and completion date.
- Make sure that the independent contractor is controlling the procedures necessary to accomplish the agreed-upon services. This would mean that the contractor hires additional employees of his or her own choosing to carry out the job, provides work tools, and sets payment schedules on the basis of the completion of the work, not simply on the passage of time.
- Make it clear that the independent contractor is in complete charge of supervising and directing how the work will be performed.
- Indicate that all insurance—liability, fire and theft, worker's compensation, and disability—will be provided by the independent contractor.
- Payment methods should be sporadic and vary over time, to justify treating the worker as an independent contractor.
- Do not separately state an allowance for overhead costs, such as meals and transportation; these should be included in the contract price.
- Spell out that training of workers is the full responsibility of the independent contractor.
- Do not include a provision that grants the independent contractor office or working space on the business owner's premises. This implies an employer-employee relationship. If the contractor needs office space, he'll use it. There is no need to put it in black and white.
- Avoid paying a bonus or any fringe benefits such as vacation pay or medical insurance, since that isn't the nature of an independent contractor's arrangement.
- Tell the contractor that if things slow down, he will not be given other work to do. The business owner's obligation is only for the work originally assigned and agreed upon.

In addition to the contract, business owners should make it clear to independent contractors that their responsibility is to complete the contract; they can't be fired, nor can they quit the job, without being at risk of a lawsuit for nonperformance of the contract.

Business owners should avoid making two common mistakes:

- Do not fill out both 1099's and W-2's for anyone working for you. An independent contractor must have payments reported by the business owner on the 1099—Miscellaneous Income—while an employee has wages filed on a W-2. Each business owner must make the decision up front as to how the payments for the worker are to be filed.

- Do not give even limited benefits to an independent contractor. It's a sure indicator that the worker is more an employee.

In a recent corporate audit of a client's return, IRS auditors uncovered workers who were treated as *both* employees and independent contractors within the same calendar year. This occurred because the employer was "trying out" the employees, so for the first three months they were treated as independent contractors, to keep paperwork to a minimum and to allow for the possibility that they might not work out. After the (unofficial) trial period was over, the workers were given employee status. This is a no-no! The workers should have been classified as employees *from the first day* they began working.

The results of the audit were expensive: The employer had to pay FICA, Medicare, and Federal Unemployment taxes of approximately 16 percent of the wages earned during the first three months, plus penalties and interest.

In a case that was decided by the Ninth Circuit Court of Appeals (*Microsoft* v. *Vizcaino*, 7/99; 1/99), the court has ruled that Microsoft cannot withhold benefits from workers it had classified as independent contractors. Workers classified by Microsoft as independent contractors are entitled to participate in the company's Employee Stock Purchase and 401(k) plans. These workers had worked at the company for years and performed the same work as permanent employees. The court used the phrase "common law employees" in referring to this group of independent contractors employed by Microsoft.

How to Strengthen Your Status If You Are an Independent Contractor

- Independent contractors should always be able to take on assignments from other companies.
- The contract drawn up should never appear to be an exclusive agreement.
- Independent contractors should be able to prove that they receive income from other sources. This will help to legitimately determine their tax status as a self-employed person filing a Schedule C.
- Incorporate yourself. There is no obligation to issue a 1099 form to

a corporation. As the IRS homes in on independent contractors by reviewing 1099 forms, you will no longer be included in this group.

USE OF INFORMERS.

The IRS encourages both disgruntled workers and companies that use employees rather than independent contractors to tattle on companies that use independent contractors via a "snitch sheet." This snitch sheet was distributed by an IRS official at a taxpayer association meeting in California. Reportedly the official asked technical service firms to act as "snitches" by filling out the sheet and returning it anonymously in a plain envelope. The official promised that all such leads would be followed up.[10]

The revenue officers whom the IRS turns loose for these snitch assignments are from the Collection Division. They come on sincere and act as though they're on your side. They may promise that if you help them by providing the right information, they'll help you by allowing you to retain the classification of independent contractor or by allowing your company to continue to employ independent contractors.

Once you give in, and the case is open for audit, don't be surprised if these agents tell you they have acquired new information that they didn't have at the beginning of the audit and that is being used against you. The case could conclude with the agent's saying, "Even though you did as we suggested, all of your independent contractors have been reclassified as employees, and you owe $50,000 in additional FICA, withholding, and federal unemployment taxes."

Another information pool is large national firms that have actively and aggressively cooperated with the IRS in going after local firms in the same industry that treat workers as independent contractors. One national health-care agency has regularly contacted the IRS National Office regarding what it considers to be withholding-tax abuses involving the use of independent contractors in the supplemental nurse staffing industry.[11]

Now, however, larger businesses are hiring independent contractors with the same regularity (and gaining the same benefits) as smaller firms. For example, it is not unusual for large multinationals to hire new computer workers as independent contractors.

Despite the shift, the IRS continues to seek out independent tattletales. According to the agency, outside tips brought in over $167 million in 1999, representing almost $8 million paid to informers. Form No. 211 (Application for Reward for Original Information) allows you as an informer a maximum reward of $2 million and keeps your identity secret. The reward for informing is 15 percent of the amount collected. In the past 10 years, the IRS collected $1.56 billion on approximately 89,000 tips and paid out $35.6 million, which represents a pretty good return on their investment. For more information, see IRS Publication 733, *Rewards and Information Provided by Individuals to the Internal Revenue Service.*[12]

Warning: The IRS is not legally required to pay fees to informers. In several recent cases, the IRS has gone back on its word by refusing to pay promised rewards. In fact, 19 informants who have sued IRS to obtain reward money have all lost. The IRS offers reasons for not paying informers, which the courts go along with:

- The IRS already had the information. (How could you refute that?)
- The information was not valuable.
- The informer was a party to the criminal activity.
- The informer was a government employee and was just performing his normal duties.

WHAT TO DO IF YOU'RE PRESSURED TO INFORM.
If you are involved in a reclassification audit and you have every reason to believe your involvement was the result of undue pressure from a revenue agent, and the agent begins to pile up "new" information that could have been gained only through other snitches, you have every right to cease the audit and gain professional advice. If you already have a professional on your side, your best bet is not to discuss the case any further with the auditor. Let your professional do it.

If you feel the auditor has lied in addition to applying pressure on you to inform, you can request that the auditor's group chief review the case. You can then ask the group chief to replace the auditor.

From here, you can move up the line in the appeals process. If you and your professional feel that you have a strong case, go for it. Taxpayers tend to do better at the appeals level, where they face more levelheaded, educated people.

SHIFT IN EXAMINATION RESOURCES.
In the Examination Division, the IRS has instructed revenue agents to look for misclassifications in the course of regular audits and has developed special training programs and audit techniques to help them do this.[13] In addition, the IRS admits to assigning several hundred revenue officers from the Collection Division to run special audits for the purpose of uncovering misclassifications. The focus of this group is businesses with assets of less than $3 million.

These investigations are nothing more than employment tax audits that are being carried out by the Collection Division instead of the audit personnel from Examination—who are *supposed* to be assigned to these tasks. Reports of incidents in the business world suggest that the way the IRS collection staff is handling these tax audits is nothing short of illegal. RRA '98 has placed new restrictions on revenue officers from Collection, such as prohibiting them from acting without supervisory authority. Hopefully, this will keep revenue officers in check from now on, along with *Your Rights as a Taxpayer*, IRS Publication 1, or, as it is generally called, the Taxpayer Bill of Rights.

THE TAXPAYER BILL OF RIGHTS.

Originally passed in October 1988, with Senator David Pryor, Democrat from Arkansas, as its major supporter, the goal of this bill is that tax-payers be treated fairly, professionally, promptly, and courteously by Internal Revenue Service employees.

Part of this fair treatment involves being handed *Your Rights as a Taxpayer* upon *initial* contact by Examination, Collection, or any other IRS personnel, as required by law. Sometimes these pamphlets *are* given out. But too often they are handed to the taxpayer, particularly independent contractors or employers who hire them, at the *end* of a collection agent's visit, when it's too late to know which of your rights the IRS has abused.

Since its initial passage, the bill has gained increasing clout (more ammunition for the taxpayer) with the passage, in 1996, of the *Taxpayer Bill of Rights 2* (TBOR 2).

Because the majority of the 40 taxpayer rights in TBOR 2 have been legislated into TRA '97 and further strengthened and expanded in RRA '98, in effect TBOR 2 has been superseded by a newly revised TBOR 3, called *Your Rights as a Taxpayer*. (See Appendix D.)

THE AUDIT BLITZ.

Once the IRS revamped its audit and collection resources, it came up with a new attack technique: an unannounced visit from the Collection Division. Often these officers do not explain the purpose of their visit or what they are looking for. If they do provide an explanation, be wary. The real reasons for the visit are to uncover people who are legitimately working as independent contractors but whom the IRS would like to classify as employees, to verify the level of compliance regarding a specific reporting requirement, or to gather incriminating information on a particular industry or individual organization. The blitz is an all-purpose weapon used by the IRS to audit whichever businesses or organizations strike its fancy.

How would you feel if an IRS officer came into your company unannounced and demanded information from you, such as how the company distinguishes individual contractors from employees? **This act in and of itself is against the law and in full violation of a taxpayer's rights.**

Don't try to handle the audit blitz yourself. When revenue officers know you are afraid, they will use that fear to get as much information out of you as they can. **You have the right to ask them to leave and not to answer any of their questions.** When asked, they generally do leave. They are, after all, trespassing.

Then call your tax professional, CPA, or attorney immediately. I tell my clients that the definition of an emergency is when the IRS is at your door, or inside, ready to close your business down. An unannounced audit is an emergency. Since my career began over 30 years ago, I have had only two such calls, and in both cases they were triggered by revenue officers from Collection.

LONG-AWAITED RELIEF—REAL OR NOT?

With continued pressure from the business community, and a congressional subcommittee examining the independent contractor issue at a White House Conference on Small Businesses, here's what's new.

First, the Classification Settlement Program (CSP) has been initiated by the IRS to help businesses currently being examined to settle their employee classification issues by offering deals based on a graduated settlement scale ranging from a 25 to a 100 percent discount on a single year's back payroll tax liability. The offer is made using a standard closing agreement, and participation is voluntary. A company can decline to accept a settlement and still have the right to appeal an IRS ruling. The CSP was originally tried for a two-year test period and was so successful, it's been extended indefinitely.

Second, an early referral of employment tax issues to the Appeals Office allows a business to hasten settlement and allegedly cut short the prohibitive penalties that can build up while a case is being disputed.

Third, a new training manual has been published to provide explicit guidance to field agents on the difference between an employee and an independent contractor. The manual does not preempt the 20-question control test. Instead, it is designed to simplify and explain it, and in so doing, introduces areas that the IRS has conceded for the independent contractor.

Revised IRS Stance on Independent Contractor Status

The manual presents these new IRS positions:

- Changes over time: The IRS admits that factors in determining worker status change over time. For example, uniforms previously indicated an employer-employee relationship. Today the IRS concedes that a uniform may be necessary for an independent contractor to perform the job.
- Control: The IRS admits that even in the clearest cases, an independent contractor is not totally without control, and conversely, employees may have autonomy, previously deemed a clear indicator of independent contractor status.
- Home offices: The manual strikes a blow at using a home office as a characteristic to prove independent contractor status. Renting an office is viewed as more concrete proof because it indicates a "significant investment."
- Financial dependence: The manual points out that Congress and the Supreme Court have rejected the argument that focuses on whether or not the worker is economically dependent on or independent of the business for which services are performed and warns agents not to apply this standard.
- Hours and location: Given the current environment, the IRS no longer considers part-time versus full-time, temporary or short-term work, on- or off-site locations, or flexible hours as indicative of a worker's status.[14]

The manual also reinforces the importance of Section 530 of the Revenue Act of 1978, often referred to as a "safe harbor."

Safe Harbor—Section 530

In the Revenue Act of 1978, Congress enacted *Internal Revenue Code* Section 530. It became known as a "safe harbor" because it was supposed to prevent the IRS from retroactively reclassifying workers as employees if an employer consistently and in good faith classified them as independent contractors.

An employer whose workers are under scrutiny by the IRS for reclassification from independent contractors to employees can apply Section 530 if the employer has

- Not treated the workers as employees in the past.
- Consistently treated the workers as independent contractors on all returns filed (including Form 1099).

- A reasonable basis (reliance on judicial authority, prior IRS audit, a long-standing industry practice, or advice from an accountant or attorney) for treating the workers as independent contractors.
- Not treated anyone else holding a substantially similar position as an employee.[15]

Any company meeting these provisions cannot be held liable for taxes not withheld after a worker is found to have been an employee rather than an independent contractor. The IRS often uses Section 530 as a bargaining tool, agreeing to its applicability only if a business re-classifies a worker. Faced with costly legal battles, which most small businesses can't afford, many accept the IRS offer.[16]

1996 LEGISLATION MODIFYING SAFE HARBOR RULES FOR TREATMENT OF EMPLOYEES AND INDEPENDENT CONTRACTORS.
What the IRS had previously suggested to revenue agents regarding Section 530—that they advise taxpayers undergoing a worker classification audit (independent contractor or employee) that the safe harbor rules exist—has now become, in the Small Business Job Protection Act of 1996, obligatory. IRS agents *must* inform taxpayers of the existence of the provisions in Section 530. This material is available to taxpayers in IRS Training Manual 3320-102, *Independent Contractor or Employee?* This 160-page manual can be downloaded from the IRS website at www.irs.gov/plain/businfo/training.html.

In another safe harbor change, on a more negative note, a taxpayer undergoing a worker classification audit could previously rely on *any* previous income tax audit to use as an example of worker status. In the new law, a prior audit may be used as proof of status *only* if that audit discussed whether or not the worker was treated as an employee of the taxpayer. The somewhat saving grace is that taxpayers may still rely on the prior audit rule if the audit began before 1997, even if it was not related to employment tax matters.

After years of quibbling about what degree of industry practice could be relied on to prove the necessity of using independent contractors as workers (instead of hiring full-time employees), the 1996 law clearly states that no fixed percentage of the industry in question must be shown, and in no case will an employee undergoing a worker classification audit be required to show that the practice of hiring an independent contractor is followed by more than 25 percent of that industry. This lowers the percentages necessary to constitute standard practice. In addition, to determine if an industry practice is long-standing enough for the employer to rely on its classification of workers, no fixed length of time is required. The IRS was pushing for a 10-year requirement, which it will accept automatically; however, a shorter period may also be considered as "long-standing," depending on the facts and circumstances. Both of these new laws represent genuine wins for independent contractors and employers who hire them.

In a recent case, a used-car dealer who established that a significant segment of the used-car sales business treated salespeople as independent contractors, rather than as employees, demonstrated a reasonable basis for such treatment. Thus he was entitled to safe harbor relief under Section 530.[17]

And finally, if an employer has established a reasonable basis for treating a worker as an independent contractor, the burden of proof shifts to the IRS to prove otherwise. Now, although this may sound like a major breakthrough, it isn't; the law sets up several conditions, simultaneously stringent yet vague, that leave IRS behavior too open-ended.

A company that employed direct sellers on a contract basis scrupulously followed the rules to qualify the sellers as independent contractors. When the IRS stepped in to prove that the workers were employees, it conceded that the company provided all of its workers with the required 1099's and that its treatment of similar workers was consistent, thereby meeting the first two tests of Section 530. Furthermore, the workers' status had been upheld in two prior audits and the use of contract workers in the business is an industry practice, proving double validation of the third test of Section 530.

Despite this, the IRS auditor claimed that the company could not shift the burden of proof to the IRS. Even after the CPA in the case showed the auditor the new law, and demonstrated that the company's requirements for relief were met, the auditor said, "I don't believe it."

When the CPA asked for the written audit report to see why the auditor did not find Section 530 applicable, the report stated that the IRS agreed that the taxpayer met the reporting and consistency requirements, but that it didn't have any basis for claiming independent contractor status.

Further proof of independent contractor status was presented via an *Internal Revenue Code* section that allows direct sellers of services, such as this company had, to statutorily qualify as independent contractors. However, the auditor turned down this argument as well.

Now the CPA spoke to the auditor's group manager. But guess what? The manager had not yet taken the new IRS training program on worker status cases, and besides, the manager considered the auditor to be an expert, since he had handled these cases for years. As a result the manager backed up every decision the auditor made.

Finally the CPA provided the manager with the relevant sections of the IRS's own training manual for employment tax audits. The manager's response was, "What is this? Where did you get it? Why did you give it to me?"

The CPA was confident that his client would eventually win its case after going to the IRS Appeals Division or into court, and the IRS will likely be tagged with some of the client's legal bills.

But the bottom line is, even though the laws are on the books, in the end you're up against the auditor and typical IRS behavior—stubborn, uninformed, and stymied thinking.[18]

WHAT ALL THIS MEANS

Settlement options aren't terrific. The taxpayer still has to fork over a large sum of money just to end the annoyance, and the IRS is getting backlogged with cases.

The 20-point test and Section 530 are rehashes of old concepts. If you qualify, you beat the rap and the IRS can't touch you even if you employ independent contractors who really appear to be employees. The safe harbor rules, however, appear to apply mainly to larger employers, and not to too many at that.

In short, there is still not enough reason for the IRS to do anything else but continue to employ its "pay up or else" tactics. The steps taken thus far appear to be in line with the agency's usual attempt to offer some leniency in the face of mounting criticism.

Target: Cash-Intensive Businesses

No doubt businesses in which large amounts of cash are routinely handed from consumers to business owners present the greatest opportunities to underreport income. These include everything from automobile dealers, check-cashing operations, jewelers, travel agencies, brokerage houses, and real estate businesses to hair salons, bars, and restaurants. So targeting this segment of the underground economy is naturally on the IRS's agenda. But it's another thing to treat legitimate cash-intensive businesses as if they are engaging in criminal activity.

IRS Attack Method Against Cash-Intensive Businesses—Form 8300

In a big push to enhance compliance, particularly among cash-intensive businesses, the IRS issued proposed regulations that expanded cash transaction reporting requirements. Using Form 8300 (Report of Cash Payments Over $10,000 Received in Trade or Business), anyone who in the course of trade or business receives cash (cashier's checks, traveler's checks, money orders, or bank drafts) in excess of $10,000 in one separate or two or more related transactions must report the transaction(s) to the IRS. The information must be reported within 15 days of the date the cash is received and a statement must be supplied to the payer by January 31 of the following year. Owners or operators of any trade or business who do not file this form face civil and criminal penalties, including up to five years' imprisonment.

Here are some examples of how the legislation works:

Through two different branches of a brokerage company, a person purchases shares of stock for $6,000 and $5,500 cash on the same day. Each branch transmits the sales information to a central unit, which settles the transactions against the person's account. The brokerage company must report the transaction because it fits the definition of being a single receipt of over $10,000 from one person.

A man buys a Rolex watch from a retail jeweler for $12,000. He pays for it with a personal check for $4,000 and a cashier's check for $8,000. The personal check is not considered cash. Thus, the amount of cash received is not more than $10,000, and the jeweler does not have to report the transaction.

Using the audit blitz, IRS agents swooped unannounced into businesses across the country. The goal—to secure so-called delinquent 8300 forms and the penalties assessed for the unpaid sums.[19] To enhance its coverage the IRS next shifted responsibilities onto the taxpaying public by requiring that businesspeople must report cash payments of over $10,000 in these kinds of situations:

For example, a travel agent receives $8,000 in cash from a customer for a trip, and the next day receives another $8,000 from the same customer to take a friend on the trip. If a customer makes two or more such purchases within a 24-hour period totaling more than $10,000, it is considered a related transaction and therefore reportable.

The IRS is also encouraging businesses to report transactions of less than $10,000 *if they appear to be suspicious,* and smaller related or multiple-cash payments that total over $10,000 in one year. Pause for a moment and think what this represents:

- The IRS is asking the private sector to do work that should be assigned to the Criminal Investigation Division.
- The business owner must now be a detective, a mind reader, and an expert administrator with systems that can track these kinds of multiple payments.
- Given the volume of business common to most of the companies that fall into this reporting category, it's probable that some transactions that should be reported would be missed, a fate not likely to be discovered until audit time, when the businessman gets hit full force in the pocketbook.

According to the IRS, in 1986 only 1,200 Forms 8300 were received from taxpayers. By 1992, when enforcement efforts increased, that number jumped to 142,000. Since then, it has hovered around 132,000 annually.

What to Do If You're in a Cash-Intensive Business

Stay within the law and report to the IRS cash transactions that exceed $10,000. Use as guidelines the information outlined in the instructions to Form 8300.

When the IRS carried out its audit blitzes, most of the violations uncovered were straight cash transactions that exceeded $10,000. In other words, they were blatant violations of the *Internal Revenue Code* for which the taxpayer had no defense.

Don't worry that you might miss some suspicious chain of transactions because of the volume of cash transactions in your day-to-day business operations. There is no case law that sets a precedent that you should or could know that a series of transactions are related or suspicious.

TARGET: INDUSTRIES IN THE MARKET SEGMENT SPECIALIZATION PROGRAM

The Market Segment Specialization Program (MSSP) (see page 57) was instituted by the IRS in 1993 to assist IRS revenue agents to shift from functioning as generalists to specialists when examining tax returns of a variety of unrelated businesses. The IRS claims that the objectives of the program are to "share MSSP expertise through educational efforts with taxpayers, involve representatives of key market segments who can deal with the underlying cause of noncompliance, and conduct tax audits using examiners skilled and knowledgeable in a particular market."[20] With the experience it provides, the program is also supposed to allow an agent to conduct audits more quickly and efficiently.

To support these goals, Audit Technique Guides are being developed by the IRS with input from industry representatives, covering almost 100 industries identified so far.

What to Do If Your Industry Is Targeted

Let's be honest. The MSSP is designed to tell agents whether taxpayers are paying what they should. However, the agency does appear to be going about this in a spirit of cooperation.

The guides themselves can serve as valuable assets for taxpayers. So

Market Segment Specialization Program (MSSP)
Guide Order Form

Guide	Stock No.	Price
Air Charters (See Aviation Tax)		
Alaskan Commercial Fishing: Catcher Vessels—Part I	02357-1	10.00
Alaskan Commercial Fishing: Processors & Brokers—Part II	02358-0	7.50
Alternative Minimum Tax For Individuals*	02423-3	9.00
Architects	02350-4	3.25
Artists & Art Galleries	02388-1	4.25
Attorneys	02375-0	8.50
Auto Body & Repair Industry	02363-6	13.00
Aviation Tax (former title: Air Charters)	02409-8	8.50
Bail Bond Industry	02387-3	4.75
Bars & Restaurants	02355-5	8.50
Beauty & Barber Shops	02362-8	4.00
Bed & Breakfast	02345-8	4.25
Car Wash Industry*	02399-7	8.00
Carpentry/Framing	02410-1	7.00
Cattle Auction Barns	out of print	
Child Care Providers (Coursebook)*	02427-6	3.25
Coal Excise Tax	02393-8	8.50
Commercial Banking	02382-2	26.00
Commercial Printing	02379-2	9.00
Computer, Electronics and High-Tech Industry	02394-6	8.00
Construction Industry	02398-9	15.00
Drywallers	02402-1	5.00
Entertainment—Important 1040 Issues	02365-2	12.00
Entertainment—Music Industry	02364-4	7.00
Farming—Specific Income Issues & Farming Cooperative	02420-9	5.00
Furniture Manufacturing	02383-1	20.00
Garden Supplies*	02426-8	7.50
Garment Construction	02391-1	8.00
Garment Manufacturers	02378-4	10.00
Gas Retailers	02353-9	7.00
General Livestock*	02428-4	14.00
Grain Farmers	02359-8	28.00
Hardwood Timber Industry	02392-0	9.00
Independent Used Car Dealer	02371-7	17.00
Low-Income Housing Credit*	02421-7	24.00
Manufacturing Industry*	02396-2	21.00
Masonry & Concrete Industry*	02400-4	3.25
Ministers	02343-1	3.50
Mobile Food Vendors	02356-3	14.00
Mortuaries	02344-0	16.00
Net Operating Loss For Individuals*	02407-1	9.50
Oil and Gas Industry	02372-5	18.00
Passive Activity Losses: Reference Guide	02354-7	23.00
Pizza Restaurant	02346-6	5.00
Placer Mining Industry*	02417-9	6.50
Port Project	02360-1	14.00
Reforestation Industry	02361-0	14.00
Rehabilitation Tax Credit	02373-3	22.00
Resolution Trust Corporation: Cancellation of Indebtedness	out of print	
Retail Liquor Industry	02389-0	7.50
Scrap Metal Industry	02408-0	7.00
Sports Franchises*	02418-7	13.00
Taxicabs	02348-2	3.00
Tobacco Industry	02374-1	13.00
Tour Bus Industry	02390-3	3.50

Market Segment Specialization Program (MSSP)
Guide Order Form (cont.)

Guide	Stock No.	Price
Trucking Industry	02349-1	12.00
Veterinary Medicine	02406-3	10.50
Wine Industry	02352-1	10.00

* New for 2000

Advance payment is required, and some guides are not reprinted after the initial supply is exhausted.

Mail your order to: Superintendent of Documents
P.O. Box 371954
Pittsburgh, PA 15250-7954
Tel.: 202-512-1800
Fax: 202-512-2250

the first thing to do is to send for the guide appropriate for you. Then become familiar with it. The more familiar you are, the more you can be on the alert to assess the direction of the audit and to work successfully with your tax pro.

On the facing page is the most current list of Market Segment Specialization Program (MSSP) guides available, including the stock numbers and prices, and where to send your order and check. Note that advance payment is required. You can also find most of the guides at www.irs.gov ("Tax Information for Business").

The guides are thorough and well researched. Here are several examples from already published guides to show you what to expect regarding specificity and completeness.

The Beauty & Barber Shops Guide states, "The [hairdressing] industry is cash intensive, . . . the majority of the workforce had a high school education and were graduates of a cosmetology school. . . . It was important to compare the type of services and the number of appointments to the income reported," and it provides a specific technique to calculate unreported tips.[21]

The Architects Guide gives a rule of thumb that architects "will generally be paid about 10 percent of the project cost for small jobs while for larger jobs, that may drop to 4 or 5 percent of the project cost." It points out that billings will generally be progressive rather than in lump-sum payments often tied to completion of various phases. It also notes that the plans "represent the only real leverage the architect has to secure payment of fees and, therefore, will normally have billed 80 to 90 percent of the fees by the start of the construction phase."[22]

The Attorneys Guide says, "The businesses with one person having the majority of internal control have the most audit potential, i.e., there is more opportunity to manipulate the books. . . . Furthermore, certain areas of attorney specialization are more productive than others. The personal injury area produces adjustments through the advanced client costs adjustment since, by nature of the specialty, significant client costs may be advanced prior to settlement. Criminal attorneys have more access to cash receipts than most other attorneys."[23]

The Garment Manufacturers Guide focuses on problem areas such as inventory, write-downs, costing errors, improper purchase accruals, and unallowable reserves for sales discounts, returns, and allowances. Under the section Related Entities, it says, "It is not uncommon for individuals to own interests in more than one garment manufacturing company. Sometimes these entities will have intercompany transactions or similar issues that require the examiner to open another examination."[24]

Under the Contractors section, it says, "A significant number of contractor returns have been spun off from examinations of a manufacturer's return, as potential unreported income cases." Further on it states that "cases can be developed using the canceled checks of the manufacturer under examination. Civil or criminal fraud penalties may be applicable and should be considered."[25]

The Bars and Restaurants Guide urges IRS auditors to "determine the number of seats in a restaurant, multiply that figure by how many times per day the seats are occupied, and multiply again by the average 'check per seat' to arrive at the average daily sales."[26] In a "probing first interview," the auditor will gather information about markup percentages and the cost of food and alcohol and then use indirect methods to ensure accuracy. The auditor may also obtain records of purchases from local wine and beer distributors.

Newest MSSP Guides

Three more MSSP audit technique guides have just been released, covering the garden supplies industry, net operating loss (NOL), and alternative minimum tax (AMT) for individuals.

The information in the garden guide is based on the findings of a team of IRS agents who conducted individual and business audits to determine that industry's characteristics, potential issues, and compliance problems. The guide looks at garden centers and equipment dealers, greenhouses, mulch, tax considerations, and accounting methods, and concentrates on the retail and wholesale aspects of garden supplies rather than the service aspect, such as lawn and landscaping services.

The content of the NOL guide includes, among other things, an overview of both net operating loss and net operating loss deduction, audit procedures, statute of limitations on claims and assessments, carryback and carryover periods, effects of changes in marital and filing status, and bankruptcy.

The AMT guide offers line-by-line guidance on the calculations involved on Form 6521 (Alternative Minimum Tax—Individuals), along with the various adjustments that go into the basic computation.[27]

Will the MSSP snare more taxpayers into the audit net, or will the audit guides provide the right information for taxpayers to prepare their returns?

In conjunction with the MSSP is the Market Segment Understanding (MSU) Program. According to the IRS, this is supposed to "identify a particular area of tax noncompliance where the facts, law or both are unclear, or noncompliance is widespread."[28] What is unique about the MSU is the establishment of a working group consisting of IRS and industry representatives who, together, will discuss how tax law applies to the area in question and produce a document clarifying issues that will then be made available to the public or IRS personnel.

An MSU can be initiated either by the IRS or at the request of an industry. One drawback appears to be the directive that MSU's require several levels of IRS review and approval wherever meetings are held. It is hoped that MSU's won't end up bogged down in political positioning and paperwork.

Now available on the IRS website at www.irs.gov are MSU's on Classification of Workers Within the Limousine Industry, Van Operators in the Moving Industry, and tip reporting in the food service, hairstyling, and gaming industries.

Coordinated Issue Papers

Similar to MSSP guides are Coordinated Issue Papers (CIP). Each of these papers focuses on a specific tax issue that may be relevant to one or more businesses. These tax issues may include meal allowances, employment contracts, and deductibility of illegal bribes and kickbacks—a total of about 80 papers. Each issue is examined in detail and explains how IRS auditors are to handle it. To help you better understand the audit process, check if your industry is mentioned and obtain a copy at www.irs.gov/plain/bus_info/tax_pro/coord.html.

TARGET: NONFILERS

An estimated 6 million people across the United States do not file any income tax returns whatsoever, down from the 9 to 10 million of about four years ago. About 64 percent of nonfilers are self-employed people who deal primarily in cash. They have been out of the system an average of four years, are in their peak earning years, and live affluently. On average, less than 25 percent of their total income is reported to the IRS by an employer, bank, or broker.

As a group, nonfilers account for almost $14 billion a year in lost revenue to the IRS and cost each of us at least $600 extra at tax time. The good news is that when it comes to the nonfiler, the IRS has for the most part proved itself to be rather trustworthy. (See also chapter 11, Rule 2, page 245, and "How to Pay What You Owe," page 351.)

The IRS Approach for Bringing In Nonfilers

The IRS's overall thinking is that as many nonfilers as possible should be brought into the system not by threats but by cooperation. The IRS believes that once they take the first step, nonfilers will feel all the better for filing, since many are not really willful violators. It's just that they've been out of the tax collection loop for so long that they're afraid of the amounts they might owe.

The IRS has developed a nonfiler program based on this assumption. While taxpayers theoretically could be prosecuted for failing to file income tax returns, if they come forward under this program, the IRS promises

- Not to prosecute, but only to charge for back taxes and interest owed, and possibly penalties.
- To work out installment payments.
- To expand its "offer in compromise" terms, whereby the IRS settles for only a portion of back taxes owed, depending on the taxpayer's ability to pay.
- That the approximately 24 percent of nonfilers who are due refunds will get them if they come to their local IRS office to claim the money within three years after the due date of their tax return.

By the end of January 1993, more than four million delinquent returns from businesses and individuals were filed under the nonfiler program. Nearly 45 percent of those filing received refunds."[29]

By late 1996, according to the IRS Media Relations Department, the strong focus on nonfiler compliance was being phased out because it was so successful. Now all that has changed, and there is a new, all-out concerted effort by the IRS to again bring in nonfilers. (See pages 359 and 361.)

Another often overlooked way to catch nonfilers is via Form 8300 submitted by financial institutions. (See page 172.) This document is used to report currency transactions over $10,000, and when this information is run through the IRS matching process, it has great potential to identify nonfilers and unreported income.[30]

What to Do If You're a Nonfiler

Nonfiler cases are often unique, simply because when a nonfiler walks into a tax professional's office, you never know what to expect. About 10 years ago a new client came to me with this story:

Mr. Frammer was a used-auto-parts dealer who also refurbished autos for resale. He worked out of a junkyard, was foreign born, and had come to the United States about 15 years before.

He had *never* filed an income tax return and sought my advice because he thought he was in trouble with the IRS. Mr. Frammer believed this was so because the previous year, a lawyer he knew had convinced him to set up a corporation so that he could limit his personal liability in selling used autos. Now the IRS was sending him notices that his corporate income tax return was past due. Incorporating had established a direct link between Mr. Frammer and IRS computers.

I filed the past-due return for him but then was curious. How could he have escaped detection for 15 years? He owned a business and he had eight children. The answer was easy.

Although Mr. and Mrs. Frammer had Social Security numbers, they never used them. They had no bank accounts, no charge cards, no bank loans, nothing that would put them within the scope of any type of third-party reporting whatsoever. His children's Social Security numbers were never used, since he didn't take them as dependents on a 1040 form.

Mr. Frammer maintained a business checking account through which he paid monthly overhead items such as telephone, electricity, and rent, but he paid all other personal and business expenses in cash. As far as the IRS was concerned, the Frammer family did not exist.

This scenario would be hard to duplicate today.

In another case, two nonfilers ended up surprisingly pleased; in the words of the IRS, they were permanently brought back into the fold.

A man and a woman, both professional lawyers, came into my office saying they hadn't filed income tax returns for the past three years and now were ready to do so. Using their tax data, I computed the balances owed and refund due. The couple were quite pleased when I told them that the second year resulted in a refund of $1,000, and in the first and third years, the balances due were only $2,500 for each year.

We filed the first two years immediately and the last year a month later. On the refund return, we instructed the IRS to carry the balance over to the following year. The reason we delayed the filing of the third year was to ensure that the tax return containing the $1,000 refund had already been processed into the IRS system. When we filed the last year, we remitted only $1,500 ($2,500 minus the $1,000 refund carried forward).

When the entire process was completed, I thought I'd never see this couple again. But they have been my clients ever since, and their returns are always filed on time.

If this sounds simple, it was because the clients were able to supply me with all the necessary information. With nonfilers this is generally not the case. Much information is usually missing, which too often serves as a great deterrent for the taxpayer. Nonfilers are often motivated to file again when they understand what is required:

- Go to a tax professional.
- The tax professional will contact your local IRS office and inform it that he or she has a case of a nonfiling taxpayer who wishes to file.
- The tax professional will explain that information for the past three (or whatever) years is missing or lost because of illness, divorce, natural disaster, etc.
- The revenue officer will probably cooperate by providing the professional with income data entered under the matching program from the IRS computer listed under the taxpayer's Social Security number. This would include W-2's, 1099's for miscellaneous, interest, and dividend income, and possibly information from 1098's showing mortgage interest paid by the taxpayer. Most important, the W-2 would show the amount of federal tax that was withheld each year.
- Next, the tax professional will reconstruct the 1040, enlisting the taxpayer's support to fill in information such as estimates of contributions, medical expenses, and other deductions. Revenue officers have been accepting reasonable estimates in cases like this.
- This entire process could take as little as a few weeks or as much as a few months, if items can't be found immediately.
- The IRS will add up to 25 percent in penalties plus interest to the balance due. That is to be expected. However, perhaps you will be one of the 25 percent of nonfilers who are due a refund.

The IRS continues to stress that nonfilers who do not come forward will be pursued to the point of criminal prosecution. All in all, the process of moving from being a nonfiler to a filer is not difficult. In my experience it is a great relief for taxpayers.

No one will deny that so far, the majority of the IRS's attempts to pursue the underground economy have been successful. But if you are unjustly attacked, you will be in the strongest position to hold on to what you're entitled to if you understand how the IRS moves in and out of the underground economy, and if you learn your rights.

8

—

How to Avoid an Audit Completely

Learning what it takes to have your tax returns slide through IRS computers and past IRS scrutiny is not only possible, it's also uncomplicated. You simply must know the correct way to approach the situation. The correct way involves understanding which actions to take, and becoming familiar with the vulnerabilities and habits of the IRS. Once you know these, your fear of the IRS should drop significantly and you should be ready to proceed with a clear head and a regular pulse.

In this chapter you are going to learn how to avoid an audit through a set of clearly defined actions that apply to all taxpayers.

First a word on audit rates and how the IRS plays with them.

DON'T BE AFRAID OF AUDIT STATISTICS

The IRS selects its audits from 12 or so categories of types of returns, including those filed by individuals, corporations, and small businesses, as well as estate and gift tax returns. Individual and corporate returns typically receive the most media attention, as does the overall audit rate for all returns filed.

During most of its existence, the IRS audit rate for individual tax returns hovered between 1 and 2 percent. This may seem minuscule, but it isn't if you take into account that currently over 123 million personal returns are filed annually. Between 1980 and 1990, though, the audit rate for individual tax returns dropped rather steadily, from 1.77 percent, or 1.6 million individual returns, to 0.80 percent, or 883,140 individual returns.[1]

As of 1994, however, all of this changed because the IRS engaged in some substantial historical revisionism, as reported in the *IRS 1993 Annual Report*. Here's the significance of what was done:

All audit statistics were amended retroactively to include the service centers' correspondence audits. The immediate effect of this move increased the overall number of returns that the IRS claimed it audited. It also inflated the audit rate for all returns. Revisionist numbers in the *IRS 1993 Annual Report* therefore showed that the audit rate for individual returns fell below 1 percent for the first time *only* in 1993. The previous 1990 audit figure was restated as 1.04 percent audited, or 1,145,000 returns examined,[2] an increase, through some statistical manipulation, of 30 percent. How did the IRS accomplish such a herculean feat? By adding in almost 262,000 service-center correspondence contacts.[3] Imagine how this affects audit figures across the board, and think of how taxpayers, tax professionals, financial writers, and analysts have reacted. Sure does make the IRS look better than ever.

AUDITS OF INDIVIDUAL AND ALL RETURNS AT AN ALL-TIME LOW

There continues to be a steady decline in the audit rate for both individual and all returns. For individuals, the audit rate dropped from 1.57 percent in 1988 to 0.99 percent in 1998. Similarly, the audit rate for all returns declined from 1.26 percent in 1988 to 0.85 percent in 1998.[4] This decline was reversed for a brief period in 1995, with the addition of a thousand new auditors, which temporarily raised the audit rate for all returns to 1.36 percent and individual audit rates to 1.67 percent.[5]

As you can see from 1998 figures, the audit rate for individuals is now almost 36 percent below what it was 10 years ago, and for 1999, the audit rate for individuals has dropped even further to an all-time low of .90 percent. There also appears to be a change in the IRS's focus over time. Statistics show that "since 1988, audit rates for the poor have increased by a third, from 1.03 to 1.36 percent, while falling 90 percent for the wealthier Americans, from 11.4 to 1.1 percent."[6] Have audit rates really shifted from individuals with incomes of $100,000 and over to those earning less than $25,000?

IRS commissioner Rossotti has said that the only reason for the audit rates focusing on the working poor while the rate for wealthy taxpayers has declined was a mandate from the White House and Congress to closely monitor the Earned Income Credit. But this, too, may be questionable, since most of these audits are correspondence audits sent through the mail. And remember that all audits have declined across the board. Some reasons are as follows: There's been a decline in the IRS staff, some purely by attrition, some by the shift of examination and collection people to customer service areas. The current IRS staff numbers about 81,000, a drop of 30 percent from 1990, when that number was over 116,000. That means fewer IRS examiners to conduct audits for increasing numbers of tax returns, 225 million in 1998, compared to 201 million in 1990, a 12 percent increase. Furthermore, according to the Transactional Records Clearing House (TRAC), the IRS continues to rely on data from TCMP audits that are at least 11 years old on which to base its current audit selection. In so doing, the IRS ignores such recent phenomena as companies offering their employees stock options instead of cash, and taxpayers deducting interest on home equity loans and margin debt on stock purchases, which reduces the effectiveness of using TCMP data for discovering unreported income.

The TRAC website shows how much the percent of individual returns audited has declined over time. In 1981 it was about 75 percent higher than it was in 1998, or 1.77 (excluding the service center audits) versus 0.99 (which includes the service centers' audits).

For 2000, things are not improving. "Auditors closed only 98,000 cases in the first quarter of the year, down from 160,000 during the same period in 1999. And IRS auditors spent an average of 16 percent less time per case. Similarly, individuals with income over $100,000 incurred 35 percent fewer audits."[7]

For this year, fewer than one in 300 individual returns is expected to undergo a face-to-face audit with a revenue agent in the field or a tax auditor at an IRS district office. In 1981, one in 63 tax returns received such an audit.

The IRS does continue to get the biggest bang for its bucks with correspondence audits. When the service centers' correspondence audits are included in the audit selection, the audit rate more than doubles, to 0.99 percent, which means that approximately one out of 99 individual returns will probably be audited either through the mail or face-to-face.

Despite the steady decline in audit figures, the IRS still generates about $6 billion a year in additional taxes and penalties on individual returns.[8]

"LIVE" AUDITS ARE AIMED AT CORPORATIONS

The IRS had traditionally deployed its live resources to audit corporate returns with the highest dollar potential. If the IRS knew anything, it did seem to know where the money was, or could come from, in the business arena. In the early 1990's, the Coordinated Examination Program (CEP) was initiated, which focused on retraining revenue agents to audit 1,500 of the largest corporate taxpayers. Corporations having $250 million or more in assets have consistently been hit the hardest. In 1995, the IRS examined more than half of these (51.77 percent); in 1998, slightly more than one third (38 percent); and for 1999, this group continues to show the highest percentage of returns audited, despite the fact that the percentage of all corporations audited shows a steady decline. By comparison, **the highest audit rate ever for individual returns was 2.3 percent in 1975.**[9]

As you can see from the chart, the audit rate for small corporations ($1 million to $5 million) increased to almost 8 percent in 1997 but has dropped dramatically in 1999 to 4.86 percent. In fact, there's no hiding that the audit rate for all corporations has dropped consistently over the past three years. This much-publicized drop, which currently also holds true for individual and all returns, as mentioned above, can be attributed to RRA '98 and its focus on customer service. According to TRAC, in the last two years, personnel assigned to the phones in a taxpayer services capacity rose 27 percent. A look at the IRS staffing figures shows a customer service group of 12,216 people formed between 1997 and 1998 created by taking staff from examination, collection, and taxpayer services. (See page 60.) Fewer auditors and revenue officers means fewer people left to examine returns and collect taxes owed.

But for individual returns, particularly those of the self-employed, audit risk is a function not only of income level but also of the type of return filed. Self-employed taxpayers who own small businesses and report their income on Form 1040, Schedule C, have consistently attracted greater IRS attention. Until 1996, the focus on these "C filers" was on the group that earned under $25,000; then it shifted to C filers with incomes over $100,000; and for 1999, the focus has again returned to the lower income group. Despite a reduction of 19 percent in 1997 for all C filers, there is still an unusually high audit effort spent on C filers, and they continue to remain an IRS audit target.

Audit rates for partnerships, S corporations, and small C corporations, and what they tell taxpayers, are discussed later in this chapter.

Corporations' Balance Sheet Assets	Percent Audited			
	1996	1997	1998	1999
$1–5 million	6.64	7.78	6.40	4.86
$5–10 million	14.08	16.02	13.52	10.09
$10–50 million	19.88	20.10	18.02	14.75
$50–100 million	21.29	19.59	18.19	16.05
$100–250 million	27.57	22.88	19.61	18.51
$250 million and over	49.61	46.77	38.60	34.55

Individuals' Income as Shown on 1040	1996	1997	1998	1999
TPI under $25,000	2.00	1.28	1.06	1.36
$25,000–$50,000	.95	.70	.58	.36
$50,000–$100,000	1.16	.77	.62	.37
$100,000 and over	2.85	2.27	1.66	1.15

Income of Taxpayers Filing Schedule C	1996	1997	1998	1999
All filers	3.74	3.15	2.35	2.03
Under $25,000	4.21	3.19	2.37	2.69
$25,000–$100,000	2.85	2.57	1.82	1.30
Over $100,000	4.09	4.13	3.25	2.40

Source: Advance drafts of the *IRS Data Book* from 1996 to 1999, Table 11, and the TRAC website, www.trac.syr.edu/tracirs/.

There are ways, however, to minimize your audit risk, no matter what schedule you file, how much you earn, or even if you are on the IRS underground-economy hit list. Part of the answer comes from taking the proper preventive measures.

HOW TO PREVENT AUDIT PROBLEMS BEFORE THEY OCCUR

The first contact between your 1040 and the IRS is a computer. You can't reason with computers, so long before you get ready to fill out your 1040 or business tax return, there are certain steps to take so that your return is "prepped" to escape selection by the IRS's first technology go-around. Preventive medicine up front, or "covering your books" (CYB), can help you avoid an audit. Here's a rundown of the most effective measures for avoiding an audit and reducing its scope if you are selected.

1. Make sure that any third-party income and reports agree with your records. Verify that

- W-2's from all employers match your declared salary.
- Interest and dividend reports from your banks and securities firms match the actual interest and dividends you have received and entered on your return.
- Mortgage interest statements from your bank or lender match your mortgage interest deduction.
- Income from 1099 forms matches the appropriate income items on your return.
- If you discover an error on any of these forms, you should contact the issuer and request a corrected version immediately. If possible, try to get the information corrected before the IRS receives the incorrect version.

2. Make sure you have selected the correct forms and schedules to fill out. Ask yourself: Do the forms apply? Am I stretching the situation? Are there other credits that I am entitled to whose forms I haven't included but need to?

3. Make sure you have recorded all payments on your return. This is especially important for taxpayers who make estimated payments during the year.

4. Keep track of bank deposits so that all items will be easy to trace. Write the source of the check directly on each deposit slip, especially transfers between accounts, so that these are not inadvertently counted as income. The first thing tax auditors request are your checking, savings, and investment accounts. They then proceed to do a total cash receipts analysis, comparing the total to the gross income shown on your tax return. By marking every deposit slip, you know where to look for further documentation to support your notation, and the auditor will

have the trail in front of him or her for the source of unusual nontaxable receipts such as insurance recoveries, loans, gifts, and inheritances. It's not that much work.

Deposits into personal checking or savings accounts usually consist of one or two items, and most small- to medium-size businesses deposit a manageable number of checks on a daily basis. You would be amazed at how forgetful people can be regarding large receipts after two or three years have passed. You also need to keep copies of incoming checks that are unusual or very large.

5. Always keep your checking and savings accounts free of irregularities. Be sure you can explain large bank deposits and increases (especially sudden ones) in your net worth. At a minimum, the auditor will ask for verification of information on your return that is derived from an institutional account, including *every* item of interest income, dividend income, and capital gains and losses.

I recently heard about an audit covering a three-year period where the taxpayer, an attorney, had great difficulty recalling the source of two large checks: a $14,000 inheritance received from the estate of an aunt, and $28,000 from the sale of her mother's condo subsequently managed by her. Because this information was not available right away, the revenue agent scheduled another audit day so that these items and a few others could be resolved. During that extra day, the auditor uncovered travel deductions totaling more than $10,000 that could not be supported and a $3,000 payment for college tuition included in charitable deductions. The taxpayer was charged an additional $5,000 in taxes, which could have been avoided if her records had been in better shape.

Warning: If you have unreported income of more than 25 percent of your adjusted gross income, the auditor may turn your case over to CID. **If you suspect this may occur, do not provide any leads to the auditor regarding the sources of unexplained deposits.** The burden of proof is on the IRS. You don't have to provide leads that make their job easier.

6. Keep your business and personal bank accounts separate. Many taxpayers, especially those with sideline businesses, do not open a separate business checking account. This is a mistake. One's business account should be the depository for all business receipts and disbursements. Although there is no prohibition against paying for items that are strictly personal, they should be charged to your loan or drawing account as personal items. If you use your business account to pay for personal items on a consistent basis, an auditor will suspect that other personal items have been inadvertently, or purposely, charged to

business categories. This could lead to an expanded audit, which can easily be avoided. Although it may take some discipline, the reward for keeping your business account strictly business will be to dramatically eliminate hassles in case of an audit.

7. If you know that you're going to take a business deduction, pay for it by check. Although taxpayers can pay for these things in cash, why arouse the suspicions of an auditor who is going to ask you to prove the source of all that cash? Also, it is wiser to pay for routine personal items such as bills for electricity, telephone, rent, and clothing with a check or credit cards. If these payments do not appear, the auditor assumes you used cash to pay for them and you've opened yourself up to an expanded audit.

HOW LONG SHOULD TAXPAYERS KEEP RECORDS?

Generally the IRS has only three years from the date you filed to come after you for extra tax. These are the exceptions:

- If your return omits more than 25 percent of your income, the IRS has six years to audit you.
- If you file a false and fraudulent return with intent to evade tax, there is no time limit on your being audited.

However, from a practical viewpoint, this is how long I recommend that you hold on to your records:

Business Records
  Four years
    Sales invoices
    Purchases and expense bills
    Routine office correspondence
  Six years
    Bank statements and canceled checks
    Accounting journals and books
  Ten years
    Payroll tax returns
    Business income tax returns
Personal Records
  Four years
    Receipts, bills, and canceled checks that support all deductions
      on Form 1040

Records that support receipts of income, e.g., 1099's and K-1's
Until four years after an asset is sold
Brokerage records showing purchases or sales of investments
Records relating to IRA contributions and withdrawals, home ownership (buying and selling), including home-office depreciation and deductions, receipts for improvements, repairs, appliances, and landscaping
For multiple home sales, keep records including Form 2119 (Sale of Your Home) for all homes until four years after the last home is sold
Six years
Bank statements and canceled checks
Forever
Personal income tax returns and W-2 forms

For more information, check out IRS Publication 522, *Record-Keeping for Individuals*, available at the IRS website www.irs.gov.

HOW TO AVOID AN AUDIT COMPLETELY

The majority of taxpayers believe that the way to reduce taxable income safely is to exaggerate deductions. Wrong! Increased deductions can act as triggers that raise a taxpayer's risk for an audit.

The most important and essential step you can take to make yourself audit-proof, and the central theme of this chapter, is to remove as much information as possible from your 1040 to another place where the chances of audit are greatly diminished.

Wage earners receive their earnings primarily from W-2 income. If, in addition, they report only interest and dividend income *and follow the recommendations throughout this book*, they will successfully place themselves in a low-audit-risk category because by definition they are not on any of the IRS hit lists.

However, people who are self-employed are generally open to greater audit risk. If this group is to become audit-proof, taxpayers must choose a business entity that allows them other reporting options than, for example, a Schedule C, used by a sole proprietorship. **The most common choices of business entities available are an S corporation, a partnership, a C corporation and, gaining popularity, a limited liability company.**

Before we discuss the best form of business entity to choose, however, I would like you to review the charts at the end of the chapter. They compare tax and legal ramifications for four of the most common types of business organizations: sole proprietorship, partnership, S corporation, and C corporation. Pick out several items that are most relevant to your own operations. This should give you a good head start in deciding which business form will offer you the most favorable tax position. Then read the discussion on S corporations and partnerships and see why both of these are the most preferred way of doing business for small to medium businesses; larger businesses that have many owners and greater potential liability typically become C corporations.

SMALL BUSINESS CORPORATIONS (S CORPORATIONS)

An S corporation is a form of organization that offers its owner the advantages of a corporation along with the favorable tax treatment of the sole proprietorship or partnership.

S corporations were first introduced in 1958. The original intention was to give mom-and-pop operations the ability to gain the advantages of incorporation (limited liability, perpetual life) and at the same time enable them to avoid the double taxation that goes with being a corporation.

Two changes in our tax law prompted the growth of S corporations, making them extremely attractive as business entities. Initially a business choosing S status could not derive more than 20 percent of its gross receipts from passive investment income such as rents, royalties, dividends, interest, annuities, and capital gains from securities or stocks. This requirement was eliminated in 1982 (subject to certain limitations). So for the first time, owners of real estate could elect S status.

Then the TRA '86 repealed the long-standing doctrine that a C corporation would have only *one* tax to be paid by its shareholders when it distributes property in a complete liquidation of the corporation. The new law imposed a *double tax* on a liquidating sale and distribution of assets (one tax upon the corporation and a second on its shareholders) for C corporations but *not for S corporations*. From that time, C corporations flocked to S status as a way to ensure that *only one tax* would be imposed on their shareholders.

For many years it has been demonstrated to me again and again that from a tax perspective the S corporation is the best kind of business type **because it offers the many advantages of a corporation with the favorable tax treatment afforded the sole proprietorship or partnership.**

Avoiding an Audit by Setting Up an S Corporation

You are a prime candidate to be an S corporation if you

- Do not have to infuse large sums of capital into your business.
- Are a service business with modest requirements for investment in equipment.
- Invest in real estate or other rapidly appreciating assets.
- Expect to incur losses in the first year or two of operations.

Information No One Dares Tell Taxpayers About What They Can Gain by Operating an S Corporation

- The annual net income or loss of an S corporation passes through to each shareholder's 1040 on one line, which appears on Schedule E. Accordingly, no income or expense detail shows up on the 1040. You immediately avoid all the targets, triggers, and special programs that the IRS currently has in place to bring attention to taxpayers who file Schedule C's.
- There is no disclosure of home-office expenses. Although S corporations are subject to the rules regarding home-office expenses, **there is no special IRS form designed for an S corporation to list home-office expenses.** By contrast, a sole proprietor who operates out of a home office and files a 1040 must file Form 8829 along with Schedule C. You already know that Form 8829 is an audit trigger. S corporations report expenses incurred in home-office operations on the 1120S (U.S. Income Tax Return for an S Corporation). The appropriate allocations are combined with all other expenses and placed on their appropriate lines.
- The IRS does a good job of matching personal income, but corporate income reporting requirements are entirely different. **If a payment for goods purchased or services performed is made to a corporation, the entity making the payment is not legally required to file a 1099-MISC form reporting the payment.** A major exception is for payments made to any entity that performs legal services. Accordingly, when the IRS uses 1099's to audit independent contractors, you can avoid all this as an S corporation.
- Chances are that expenses that are typical audit triggers (travel, entertainment, automobile) will receive less attention on an S corporation simply because the audit rate for S corporations is considerably lower than for individuals. (See chart, "Examination Coverage of Returns Filed," page 215.)
- There has never been a better time to own a small corporation be-

cause the IRS audit function is paying the least attention to small corporations, partnerships, and LLC's. Currently, the potential for the IRS to extract tax dollars through the audit process is immeasurably greater with large corporations because of the Coordinated Examination Program (CEP), which focuses on auditing the largest corporate taxpayers in the country. But look what's happening to the rest of the business population. **The lowest percentages of business returns audited are for partnerships, S corporations, and small C corporations.** For calendar years 1996 and 1997, the percentage of S corporations being audited remained at 1.04 percent; it was only 23,898 out of 2,290,900, and 25,522 out of 2,449,900 respectively; for partnerships, only 10,082 out of 1,737,800, or 0.58 percent.[10] Partnerships continued to have the lowest audit rate, followed by S corporations and C corporations (with assets under $250,000). (See chart, page 215.)

• By controlling the amount of salary you take out of an S corporation, you can substantially reduce FICA taxes. For example, an S corporation with one owner-employee has a net income before salary of $50,000. If the owner takes a $50,000 salary reportable on a W-2, the combined FICA taxes for the corporation and employee will be 15.3 percent, or $7,650. But if the owner takes a reasonable salary of $30,000, the FICA taxes will be only $4,590, a savings of $3,060 to the corporation. The remaining corporate net income of $20,000 ($50,000 minus $30,000) is passed through to the owner on a K-1 form. As a result, his personal income tax remains unchanged.

• Owners of an S corporation are immune to double tax on an audit. If a C corporation is undergoing an audit, and travel and entertainment deductions are disallowed because they were found to be personal, or some officer's compensation is deemed by the auditor to be excessive, the IRS will assess a tax at both corporate *and* shareholder levels (i.e., the corporation will be charged one tax on the disallowed expense, and a second tax will be assessed upon the individual shareholder). In an S corporation, disallowed business expenses pass through to the 1040 and become taxable income to the recipients. But in this case, the IRS can levy only *one* tax—at the shareholder level. **It is my belief that this inability to double-tax an S corporation is a major reason why the audit rate is so low on S corporations.**

• There are some real advantages for S corporations that expect to incur losses in the first few years of operation. A new business usually experiences hard times initially. If you expect to incur losses in the first three months of operation, the best time to apply for or elect S corporation status would be the last three months of the calendar year. (S corporations must use the December 31 calendar year-end. There are a few exceptions but they are rarely granted.) In this way, losses pass through to the shareholders in the current year and shelter income from other sources. This is a common scenario for a taxpayer who was an employee for the first nine months of the year, and then incorporates as an S corporation, using his losses to shelter W-2 earnings.

• It is easier for the owners of an S corporation to sell the business because, unlike a C corporation, there is no corporate-level tax when the assets are sold. This makes for a preferred sale, since most buyers are interested only in the assets, not a corporation's potential liabilities.

Requirements for an S Corporation

- To have only individuals, estates, qualified pension and profit-sharing plans, and certain types of trusts used in estate planning as shareholders; no partnerships, corporations, or nonresident aliens.
- To have no more than 75 shareholders. This facilitates ownership in an S corporation by family members, employees, venture capitalists, and others.
- To have one class of stock.
- To be a "domestic corporation" created or organized pursuant to federal and state laws.

Furthermore, a corporation that decides to elect S status again, after not being one, can do so immediately, without the previous five-year waiting period.

And, an S corporation can own 80 percent or more of a C corporation as well as become an owner of other kinds of business entities, including wholly owned S corporation subsidiaries. NOTE: The subsidiary does not have to file its own corporate tax return but can file a combined return with its parent S corporation. In other words, the parent S corporation can own a "qualified subchapter S subsidiary" that will not be treated as a separate corporation for tax purposes. This opens up the field tremendously for S corporation owners to place separate operations in subsidiary companies with significant tax advantages to boot.

New laws are constantly changing to make it more beneficial than ever to become an S corporation. An S corporation is not only more attractive for investment purposes, it also offers greater estate-planning opportunities to reduce estate taxes. This is *not* the right time to switch out of S corporation status.

How to Set Up an S Corporation

1. Incorporate. Several choices are available. If you choose to use an attorney, the fees range from $600 to $1,000 depending on the size and location of the law firm. A second alternative allows you to incorporate yourself. The department of state in your home state will provide you with the required forms and fee schedule. In some states you can pay an optional "expediting fee" (about $10), which will get the paperwork returned to you in a week or two instead of three weeks to a month. Overall costs for this type of incorporation are approximately $375. For those who want a quick and more commercial route (without paying attorney's fees), there are incorporation services. At a very modest price, they offer step-by-step instructions and provide everything you need to know about legal aspects of forming your own corporation in any state of your choosing. (You can usually find these in the classified section of your Sunday newspaper.)

2. Obtain a federal identification number by filing Form SS-4 (Application for Employer Identification Number) with the IRS. You will receive your number about three weeks after you apply. If the wait is impractical because you need the number to open a commercial bank account, you can use the IRS Tele-Tin (Telephone Tax Identification) system. To do this, first complete the SS-4, then call your local IRS service center and ask for the fax number for the Tele-Tin system. Fax the SS-4, and within approximately 48 hours you will receive a phone call from the IRS and be given your new federal identification number.

3. File Form 2553 (Election by a Small Business Corporation) with the IRS. Generally you must apply for an S corporation, the S election, within two months and 15 days after commencing operations. For existing C corporations, the election must be filed no later than two months and 15 days after the elected year has begun. For example, if you commence operations in 2000, the election deadline is March 15, 2000.

Once your papers are in order you should send Form 2553 to your IRS service center by certified mail, return receipt requested. This is the best proof of mailing acceptable by the IRS, although you can also use Federal Express, United Parcel Service, Airborne Express, and DHL Worldwide Express. It is important to file as early as possible to avoid missing the deadline and to avoid other hassles and delays.

YOUR TAX-SAVING STRATEGY.
These days, state and local taxes take a significant chunk of tax dollars. Therefore, for tax-planning purposes, all taxpayers, even S corporations, must be concerned about taxation at the state and local levels.

Currently, at least 40 states recognize some form of S corporation status. New York State imposes an annual fee of $325 for S corporations, while Florida doesn't impose any. California and Illinois impose a 1.5 percent corporate tax rate on an S corporation's taxable income, but these rates are considerably less than the regular rates for non–S corporations. In participating states all the advantages that accrue to S corporations at the federal level are also recognized on the state and local levels.

New York City does not recognize S corporation status. Accordingly, the tax-planning opportunities for S corporations are limited within this jurisdiction. The optimum planning for states and localities that impose regular corporate rates is to reduce corporate net income of the S corporation to zero by increasing the salaries to the owners-employees whenever it is reasonable and proper. This results in minimal net corporate income subject to the regular corporate tax rates, and the increased salary is simply subject to individual income tax. **If at all possible, try to locate the business in an area where the S election is available at the state and local levels of taxation so that you can receive maximum benefits.**

Loopholes in the Timing of an S Election

Remember those myriad loopholes that arise out of our complex tax laws? Well, there are several that work to benefit owners of S corporations.

Let's say that you inadvertently let the 2½-month period pass, did not file the S election, and just made up your mind to actively operate as an S corporation. For the initial year of the corporation's existence ONLY, the 2½-month period does not start until the earliest of the following:

1. Date the corporation first had shareholders.
2. Date the corporation first had assets.
3. Date the corporation began doing business.

Therefore, to still elect S status, place a date that accurately represents the actual "starting" date of the corporation in Item H on Form 2553.

Let's say you recently incorporated and started doing business as a C corporation and it was more than 2½ months ago. Generally, that means you are precluded from taking advantage of the first loophole unless you follow certain explicit instructions in Revenue Procedure 97-40, which can be obtained from the IRS. But what you can do is close off your C corporation year immediately and elect S status for the remainder of the year.

For example, the business was incorporated and started on January 5, 2001, and now, on May 10, 2001, you want S status. File the S election immediately and simply indicate in your S election, Form 2553, Item C, that the election is to be effective for the tax year beginning March 1, 2001. You will be able to operate as an S corporation beginning March 1, 2001, because you are filing within the first 2½ months of the new, short year, which began March 1, 2001. The only disadvantage to this ploy is that you must file a C corporation tax return for the short period from January 5, 2001, to February 28, 2001.

YOUR TAX-SAVING STRATEGY.
As a new corporation, try to maximize the amount of C corporation short-year expenses as start-up expenses that can be amortized later on in S corporation years. Losses incurred while you are a C corporation will remain frozen as long as you are an S corporation.

Loopholes in the Early Stages of an S Corporation

Depreciation of Assets
New corporations usually purchase furniture and equipment at the outset. Under Section 179 of the *Internal Revenue Code* (see chapter 7, pages 154–155), you can elect to depreciate up to $19,000 of business furniture and equipment purchased anytime in 1999, $20,000 in 2000, and $24,000 in 2001 and 2002. Therefore, even if your initial S corporation year is but a few weeks in the current year, you can deduct the full Section 179 depreciation if the assets are purchased within that period.

YOUR TAX-SAVING STRATEGY.
Section 179 deductions cannot reduce your taxable income below zero. If the S corporation's net income is approaching zero, utilize only the amount that you need to reach zero income. Or you can delay your asset purchases until the following year, when presumably there will be greater income to be offset with this deduction.

Loopholes in Reporting Income or Losses for an S Corporation

Shifting Losses
For S corporations, there is a unique way of shifting losses to a desired tax year. This brings the element of *basis* into play. Basis is a dollar amount that represents the cost of a taxpayer's investment in an entity. It can be adjusted upward or downward. S corporation losses can be used only by shareholders who have sufficient basis in the stock. If you need the losses in 2000, lend the corporation sufficient money to cover your share of the losses. If 2001 is the year you can make better use of

the losses, make no additional loans until 2001. If need be, distribute loans to yourself before the end of 2000 so that your basis is minimized.

If you personally guarantee loans made to an S corporation, your basis is not increased. Therefore, borrow the money personally, and lend the proceeds to the S corporation. This will enable you to take greater losses if they become available. The key point is, S corporations provide many opportunities for the owner to handle losses.

YOUR TAX-SAVING STRATEGY.

If you own two S corporations and one loses money and the other makes money, you should restructure them as a parent and a subsidiary and file a combined return (see page 195). In this way, the loss of one corporation offsets the profit of the other, and you do not have to worry that the corporation with the loss does not have sufficient basis, as discussed above.

S Corporations Now and in the Future

For the past 10 years the IRS has been giving the public a consistent message about S corporations: "S elections and S status are cumbersome and fraught with dangers. If you are a small business person, you will be better off filing as a sole proprietor on Schedule C." **This is simply not true.** The IRS is pushing this line because it can more easily watch over the activities of small businesses using Schedule C's.

But in reality, there is a clear trend whereby existing laws and requirements pertaining to S corporations are consistently making it easier and wiser to choose this form of tax entity. For example, distributions of S corporation earnings are not and have never been subject to FICA or Medicare tax.

Then there was 1996 legislation easing S corporation restrictions (discussed above), and, in 1997, the IRS issued Revenue Ruling 94-43, which frees up S corporations to be partners in partnerships. Finally, a new Treasury regulation, known as the "check-the-box" regulation, allows you to indicate the type of business entity you have chosen for tax purposes from a corporation, partnership, or single owner by simply checking a box on Form 8832 (Entity Classification Election.)

True, the top personal tax rate is 39.6 percent, which is something S corporation owners should keep in mind, because earnings from S corporations (unlike C corporations) must be included in your personal income, which could land you in a higher tax bracket. Couple this increase with the phaseout of personal exemptions and itemized deductions, and if your taxable income exceeds $288,350, you are facing an individual tax rate as high as 41 percent. Does this mean that S corporations will flock to revoke their S elections in order to take advantage of lower C corporate tax rates? I would recommend against this course of action for several reasons.

First, for taxpayers who own S corporations with modest earnings, taxable income up to $161,450 on a joint return (up to $132,600 if single) is still taxed at 31 percent or less.

Second, you may be subject to the built-in gains tax if you revoke your S election and later decide to reelect to become an S corporation. This is a kind of corporate-level tax on appreciation of assets held by a former C corporation; it is imposed as these assets are disposed of during the first 10 years after you become an S corporation.

S corporations are more available and enticing than ever before, and the advantages being granted to S corporations are being accelerated on a regular basis.

LIMITED LIABILITY COMPANIES AND PARTNERSHIPS

A new type of entity, called a limited lability company (LLC), has emerged in the past few years. Because it is often set up in a partnership format, its name then changes to a limited liability partnership (LLP). Wyoming was the first state to enact an LLC statute in 1977. Each state now has an LLC statute.

An LLC combines two of the most important attributes that are important to business owners: pass-through taxation, where annual net income or losses pass through each shareholder's 1040 on one line, Schedule E (see page 193), and limited liability for business debts. Although these attributes are mentioned in this chapter in discussions of corporations and partnerships, for some types of businesses, setting up an LLC is more suitable. Here are some reasons why.

Whereas an S corporation must allocate income or losses in proportion to stock ownership, in an LLC agreement you can vary the sharing percentages of income and losses and not have to worry about being subject to undue scrutiny by the IRS. Also, an LLC may have foreign investors, while an S corporation cannot.

Furthermore, in a partnership, investors ordinarily become limited partners so that they are liable only for the amount of their investments. Because of this, they cannot take part in the active running of the business, which is left to the general partners, who *are* liable for all debts of the partnership. Under an LLP, *all* members can take an active part in the day-to-day operations of the partnership and *not* be subject to un-limited liability for the debts of the partnership.

In most respects, LLC members are treated for tax purposes like general partners and S corporation shareholders. For example, fringe benefits such as health insurance and group-term life insurance are gen-erally not deductible. Additionally, LLC owners and general partners are at a disadvantage in that they are subject to self-employment tax (15.3 percent on the first $76,200 of earnings and 2.9 percent over that amount).

The trickiest part of forming an LLC or LLP is to make sure that the IRS does not classify the entity as a regular corporation, which would stop you from being a pass-through entity. To begin with, you must fol-low the guidelines of the LLC statutes in your state. Next, the operating agreement must contain everything that any corporate agreement would contain plus other sections that are specifically designed for an LLC agreement.

To be recognized for tax purposes as a partnership, and to avoid being taxed as a corporation, an LLC or LLP must meet the IRS-imposed re-quirement of not having more (i.e., three or more) corporate character-istics than noncorporate characteristics. The four traits that the IRS considers as corporate characteristics are limited liability, continuity of life, centralization of management, and free transferability of interests.[11]

If an entity has only one or two of these corporate characteristics, it will be taxed as a partnership and be treated as a pass-through entity, which is desirable. In fact, an LLC should use Form 1065 (U.S. Partner-ship Return of Income) to meet its annual filing requirements with the IRS. It is important to work with an attorney who is knowledgeable in this area to set up the LLC operating agreement so that (1) it does not meet the corporate characteristics as defined by the IRS and (2) it con-forms with federal and state regulations.*

PARTNERSHIPS

A partnership is a good alternative to an S corporation.

This discussion focuses on only those general partnerships in which each partner is responsible for his or her share of partnership debts. (It does *not* include a limited partnership, which is subject to its own rules

*These characteristics are defined in the *IR Code Section* 7701-2 (a)(1), and IRS Revenue Procedure 95-10.

and regulations beyond the scope of this discussion. See also limited liability companies and partnerships, page 200.)

Advantages of a Partnership

• A partnership is easier to create than an S corporation. Two or more people just agree to be in business together. This union is made evident by a written agreement best prepared by an attorney.

• As with S corporations, a partnership has no double tax. Net income and other separately stated income and expense items, such as capital gains and contributions, are passed through to each partner via a K-1 form.

• If the partnership later decides to incorporate, the transfer will be tax-free as long as any property that is transferred to the corporation is exchanged for at least 80 percent of the corporate stock.

• It may be easier to obtain credit because one partner may provide expertise and additional net worth that could be used to guarantee partnership liabilities.

• Income or losses are allocated according to the partnership agreement, but the agreement can take into account the business efforts made by each partner. This means income can be allocated by a method that is not based on ownership percentages. But you cannot allocate income and loss merely to take advantage of the tax laws. Similarly, if you have a family partnership, you cannot allocate income to younger family members just to reduce taxes. The allocation must reflect the value of services rendered by each of the partners.

• As with S corporations, there is no special IRS form designed to list home-office expenses.

• As with S corporation shareholders, a partner's tax losses cannot exceed his or her basis (see definition on page 198).

A partner's basis

1. Increases when he pays money or contributes property to the partnership.
2. Increases by his share of income earned by the partnership.
3. Can increase or decrease as his proportionate share of partnership liabilities changes.
4. Decreases if the partnership reports losses, or if the partnership distributes money or property to the partners.

In an S corporation, basis is a more restrictive concept because it does not change as a function of the stockholder's share of general corporate liabilities.

Disadvantages of Partnerships

• A partner is personally liable for the debts of the partnership above and beyond his investment. This is characterized as unlimited liability, and it is the main reason why corporations are the preferred way of doing business. With a corporation, or an LLC, generally you can lose only the money and property that you contributed to the corporation.

• Although a partnership is easy to form, it is also easily dissolved, such as when a general partner who owns more than 50 percent of the entity withdraws. Thus, there is no "continuity of life." With a corporation, a withdrawing shareholder simply sells his stock to a new shareholder and the corporation continues to operate.

• Similarly, it is difficult to withdraw from a partnership if the remaining partners refuse to purchase the withdrawing partner's interest. A buy-sell agreement drawn up when the partnership is formed is highly recommended to avoid this situation. The agreement should contain a formula to measure the amount that a withdrawing partner receives, or the amount to be paid to a partner or his or her beneficiary in case of death or permanent disability.

BUSINESS VENTURES AND THE HOBBY LOSS RULE

If you're in an existing business or considering starting up a new business, besides choosing which legal entity will work best from a tax perspective, you'll also need to be aware of Section 183 of the *Internal Revenue Code*, "Activities Not Engaged In for Profit," or the Hobby Loss Rule, as it is commonly called. Ignorance or mismanagement of the Hobby Loss Rule can easily increase the chances of an IRS audit.

In order not to be subject to the Hobby Loss Rule, taxpayers need to show a profit in any three out of five consecutive tax years ending with the current tax year. This rule covers sole proprietors, partnerships, S corporations, and estates and trusts. If the IRS determines that your business activity is "not engaged in for profit," according to the Hobby Loss Rule your losses will be considered personal expenses and only expenses up to the amount of your hobby income will be deductible. Furthermore, these otherwise deductible hobby expenses will be transferred to Schedule A—Itemized Deductions (Other Miscellaneous Deductions), and be subject to a limit of 2 percent of your AGI. Mortgage interest and real estate tax are fully deductible as itemized deductions in any case. (See chapter 11, page 260, for additional information on the Hobby Loss Rule.)

What does this rule mean, and how does it affect the taxpayer? Many young businesses do, after all, legitimately experience operating losses in three out of five years. But the IRS created the Hobby Loss Rule to prevent taxpayers from using personal business ventures such as horse racing, farming, or stamp and coin collecting to throw off losses used to offset other income (salaries, interest).

How to Strengthen Your Position Regarding the Hobby Loss Rule

If you are a taxpayer who could fall under the Hobby Loss Rule, you have to be ready to prove that you had an intention of earning a profit. Theoretically you could operate a business for many years and never actually earn a profit, but still be entitled to a deduction for the losses.

To strengthen your position in this direction, become familiar with these nine factors used by the IRS to determine whether or not a profit objective exists:

1. Conduct the activity in a businesslike manner. This includes keeping accurate books and records, printing business stationery and cards, keeping a separate bank account for the business, and obtaining a federal identification number.

2. Obtain sufficient knowledge to operate a successful business. This is an indication that you are trying to increase the profitability of the business. Read trade journals and books on the subject, attend professional seminars and the like to gain expertise, and be able to show proof of these activities within reason.

3. Spend a sufficient amount of time in the activity so that it doesn't look as though you're dabbling (as with a hobby). If you have another full-time occupation that produces income, and most of your time is spent there, your new venture would appear to be secondary. To counteract this, you could hire competent qualified people to run the new business for you or consult with experts in the same field.

4. If you expect the product that you're working on to appreciate in value, this is proof that you have a profit motive. For example, if you purchase antique cars and can show that their value has risen, that in itself is proof of the profit motive.

5. Your success or lack of it in prior business ventures is a consideration. If you have previously turned an unprofitable business into a profitable one, you have proved that your mode of operation involves having a profit motive in mind even though you are currently losing money. Try to write a business plan for your business and include in it how you expect to be profitable. The IRS looks favorably on a written business plan and how you have followed through with it, even though all the goals you may have outlined were not met.

6. The IRS will examine your income track record in the startup busi-

ness. If you had a string of successively profitable years more than five years ago, that is an indication that you have the ability and intention to turn your loss into a profit. Similarly, you may be able to show that your current losses are due to events beyond your control such as depressed market conditions or natural disasters.

7. The IRS also looks at the existence of occasional profits, if any. Profits are compared to losses over the duration of the operation; how both relate to the value of assets invested in the business is examined.

8. The wealthier you are, the more likely that the activity will look like a hobby in the eyes of the IRS. If you don't have substantial income from other sources, the IRS will tend to look more favorably on your activity.

9. Does the business have a significant element of personal pleasure or recreation? This factor is probably the one that has caused the term *hobby loss* to come into being.

Sometimes, no matter what you do, the IRS will insist that your business is a hobby. For all of us who have seen pink Cadillacs cruising down the road, this next case reminds taxpayers that part-time salespeople seeking small returns and large deductions may soon be seeing red.

Mrs. Linde's business was selling cosmetics. In two consecutive tax years, she received the use of a luxury car and reported her activity on Schedule C, indicating losses in excess of $25,000 per year. These losses offset the substantial income earned by her husband on their joint returns.

Using the nine-factor test above, the tax court decided that the most important issue determining whether the business was a hobby or not was the manner in which the business was run. First, Mrs. Linde did very little to separate her personal and business activities. Although she presented mounds of records to prove the claimed expenses, some of the records proved that some of the deductions were taken for purely personal expenditures.

Mrs. Linde also produced summary sheets prepared by herself that the court called self-serving; it gave them no real weight. The actual books and records of her business were not organized well. After examining these, the court said it could not figure out how she computed the losses she claimed.

Lack of a profit motive was further evidenced by Mrs. Linde's failure to seek advice on how to run the business from people outside the cosmetics organization. This was particularly important because she had no prior experience in the business. The only evidence she cited to corroborate her time spent in the activity was her own testimony, which the court discounted.

Finally, the court observed that much of the time Mrs. Linde did spend in the activity involved taking people to restaurants and bars, which signified a substantial element of personal pleasure.

In summary, the court decided that Mrs. Linde's business was not a "for-profit" activity under Section 183, the Hobby Loss Rule. The result was that the taxpayer could deduct expenses only to the extent of the income from the hobby; expenses cannot reduce net operating income below zero (except for mortgage interest and real estate tax, which are deductible on Schedule A, Form 1040).

BUSINESSES THAT INCLUDE MERCHANDISE INVENTORY

If you file a business return and if you sell a product, as opposed to of-fering a service, one of the things the IRS computer (or audit reviewer) will focus on is the "Cost of Goods Sold" section on the statement-of-income section found on all business income tax returns. Generally the IRS will devote greater attention to a return showing a smaller gross profit than industry norms. The IRS gathers this information and reaches its conclusions by trying to identify the cost of the product being sold, or how much gross profit (sales less cost of goods sold) a business earned in a year.

There are a number of avenues the IRS can take to scrutinize this and come up with how much money it thinks a business has made on the basis of the cost of goods sold. If the gross profit percentage that you re-port on the business return is found to deviate greatly from what other taxpayers report in the same industry, there are some acceptable ex-planations.

With acceptable proof, you may show that you experienced

- More than normal returns of merchandise, which you were forced to sell at cost price or lower.
- Normal increases in the cost of acquiring or manufacturing your products, but you were unable to pass them on to your customers in the form of price increases.

How to Prepare an Ending Inventory Schedule
to Minimize Audit Risk

When a tax return showing a low gross profit is being examined, the IRS auditor will most likely ask for a detailed ending inventory schedule, or the inventory at the end of the company's fiscal year. In the Garment Manufacturer's Guide, it states: "The focus of the ending inventory ex-amination is to determine whether the inventory is understated. In other words: Have certain costs been omitted? Have units of inventory been omitted?"[12] Taking a physical inventory is a time-consuming task, especially if you are trying to service customers or sell products during the inventory process. On the basis of your past experience, you may be able to estimate some of the inventory quantities. In so doing, you must be aware of certain things:

- The method most widely used to value inventory is the "lower of cost or market." Use of this method allows you to assign below-normal values to inventory items that are collecting dust—or are obsolete, damaged, or unusable, or whose prices have dropped since you purchased them. Regarding write-downs, the MSSP Garment Manufacturers Guide states: "The most difficult write-down to locate in the audit is that which completely omits the item from the count and detail sheets. By doing so, the manufacturer is taking the position that the items are being written down to a zero value."[13]

- A majority of the items included in an inventory should be those purchased a short time before the closing date, generally not more than one year prior to the closing date. An exception would be hard goods, e.g., hardware, that can have a normal shelf life in excess of one year. The Garment Manufacturers Guide states: "The most recent purchases, that is, those made at year-end, are also commonly left out of the piece goods inventory. This omission is usually due to careless error."[14]

- The items included in the ending inventory should be traceable to subsequent period sales. For example, if December 31, 1999, is the closing inventory date, then a large percentage of items should have been sold in the first half of 2000.

Therefore, it is important that the closing inventory schedule be as current as possible and be based on gross profit percentages that are normal to your industry.

Audit Risk and Nonpayment of Payroll Taxes

If you own a business, here is something you should know regarding an audit triggered by nonpayment of payroll taxes. The IRS is required to notify a person it has identified as the "responsible person" (one who is responsible for paying certain FICA and withholding taxes in a timely manner to the IRS) at least 60 days before contacting that person for taxes and penalties owed. Previously, the IRS could contact a person without any notice and collect 100 percent from *any* "responsible person" without bothering to go after other guilty culprits. (This is similar to where the IRS chased an innocent spouse for all the tax and penalties incurred and owed by that spouse's guilty partner on a joint return; see page 300.) The IRS must disclose the identity of others deemed responsible for not paying payroll taxes to those already identified as culpable. The IRS must also commence an action against the other responsible parties to pay their share of the amounts owed. This ensures, for example, that a low-salaried employee who was deemed by the IRS to be the "responsible person" doesn't take the fall for the head of a company who may be the real culprit.

SECURING A TAX-ADVANTAGED LIFE

The fact is that if you are self-employed and you incorporate, you will have a tax-advantaged life that will be sheltered within a corporate environment. A technical advice memorandum, issued by the IRS, puts an interesting slant on the importance of choosing the right business format.

After 40 years of operating their farm, a husband, his wife, and their son created a corporation, selling their house, automobile, crops, and farming equipment to the corporation in exchange for stock. They then became employees of the corporation. Given this situation, the family declared that providing food and shelter was not taxable income because it was required by the job.

The primary tax question that arose, therefore, was "Can the corporation deduct these as a legitimate business expense?" Normally a farmer cannot take the cost of his home and food as an expense against farm income.

The IRS agent examining the case declared that this was an example of avoiding income tax. However, in a technical advice memorandum involving a lengthy analysis, the IRS ruled that *the taxpayers would have been entitled to the same deduction if a partnership and not a corporation had been formed*. It was also decided that the taxpayers were not evading or avoiding federal income tax because they were only obtaining benefits otherwise permitted under specified statutes as outlined in the *Internal Revenue Code*.

Legally, technical advice memoranda are not supposed to set any kind of precedent; as with private letter rulings, they apply only to the taxpayer who receives them, as discussed in chapter 5, page 109. But this case emphasizes the overriding principle that certain tax advantages can be gained by one's choice of a business format. The conclusions I offer taxpayers are these:

- If you want an environment in which most of your income is not reported to the IRS on a 1099 form, incorporate now.
- If you are self-employed, incorporate or form a partnership now.
- If you want to reduce IRS scrutiny of your business deductions, incorporate or form a partnership or LLC now.
- If you want to place your business income tax return in a category that is least susceptible to an IRS audit, incorporate or form a partnership or LLC now.

A Surefire Checklist for *All* Taxpayers Who Don't Want to Be Audited

- Know the proper time to file. You have learned that filing late is not the way to avoid an audit. IRS computers aren't programmed to review only those returns received on or before April 15. So who is to say that late returns, those filed after April 15, won't be audited, or will be audited less than returns mailed earlier? All returns, late or not, go through a secondary audit potential selection process at the district level. All tax professionals have clients who filed late but were audited anyway. The days of thinking you're immune because you file late are over.

- Be thorough. Don't leave out any information that applies to you. Sign where you are supposed to.
- Be neat.
- Be sure your mathematics is correct.
- Be consistently accurate. Are the proper entries on the proper lines? Have you provided your complete address and Social Security number? Did you leave any lines blank that should be filled in?
- Balance out your total deductions with your income. Excessive and elaborate business expenses that add up to a substantial percentage of your income are an audit flag.
- Adjust your stated exemptions as shown on Form W-4, filed with your employer, so that you don't end up receiving large refunds. Remember, they only amount to a free loan of *your* money to the IRS (discussed on pages 34–38 and 221).

Tax Considerations

	Sole Proprietorship	Partnership	S Corporation	C Corporation
Net operating income	Taxed directly to owner on 1040.	Passed through to partners' 1040 via Form K-1 whether or not distributed.	Passed through to shareholders' 1040 via Form K-1 whether or not distributed.	Double tax: once on C corporation, again when paid to shareholder as dividends.
Net operating losses	Reduces Adjusted Gross Income. Can be carried back 2 years (5 years for a farming business) and then forward 20 years (back 3 and forward 15 years for tax years beginning prior to August 5, 1997).	Passed through to partners' 1040 via Form K-1. Losses cannot exceed partners' basis in the partnership. Subject to at-risk rules and passive-loss limitations. Losses can be carried back or forward.	Passed through to shareholders' 1040 via Form K-1. Losses cannot exceed shareholders' basis in the corporation. Subject to at-risk rules and passive loss limitations. Losses can be carried back or forward.	Deductible only against net operating income. Losses can be carried back 2 years and forward 20 years (back 3 years and forward 15 years for tax years beginning prior to August 5, 1997).
Capital gains	Taxed directly to owner on 1040.	Passed through to partners' 1040 via Form K-1.	Passed through to shareholders' 1040 via Form K-1. Some gains are taxable under certain conditions for older S corporations.	Gains taxed at regular corporate rates.
Capital losses	Offset against capital gains + $3,000 per year. May be carried forward indefinitely.	Passed through to partners' 1040 via Form K-1.	Passed through to shareholders' 1040 via Form K-1.	Deductible only against corporate capital gains. Can be carried back 3 years or forward 5 years as a short-term capital loss.
Contributions to charities	Itemized deduction on 1040.	Passed through to partners' 1040 via Form K-1.	Passed through to shareholders' 1040 via Form K-1.	Limited to 10% of corporate taxable income, as adjusted by special items. Unused can be carried forward for 5 years.
Dividends received	Taxed directly to owner on 1040.	Passed through to partners' 1040 via Form K-1.	Passed through to shareholders' 1040 via Form K-1.	Can deduct from income 70% of dividends received from domestic corporations.

Tax Considerations (Continued)

	Sole Proprietorship	Partnership	S Corporation	C Corporation
Tax rates	Based on taxable income: 15%–36% on first $288,350 for singles ($283,150 for married); 39.6% on amount over $288,350 for singles ($283,150 for married)	Each partner pays individual tax rate.	Each shareholder pays individual tax rate.	Based on taxable income: 15% of first $50,000 25% of next $25,000 34% of next $25,000 See instructions for amounts over $100,000.
Fringe benefits (e.g., health insurance and group term life insurance)	Partially deductible on 1040, subject to limitations.	All partners are not eligible to receive tax-free benefits	Cannot receive tax-free benefits if shareholder owns more than 2%.	No restrictions.
Retirement plans	Keogh, SEP, Defined Benefit, or SIMPLE is available. Loans are prohibited.	Keogh, SEP, Defined Benefit, or SIMPLE is available. Loans are prohibited.	Profit-sharing, defined contribution plan, Defined Benefit plan, or SIMPLE is available. Loans to shareholders are prohibited.	Profit-sharing, defined contribution plan, Defined Benefit plan, or SIMPLE is available. Loans permitted up to ½ your vested benefits or $50,000, whichever is less.
Sale of ownership interest	Capital gain.	May be part ordinary income and part capital gain. Special election to step up basis of partnership's assets for purchaser.	Capital gain.	Capital gain.
Liquidation	N/A.	N/A.	Capital gain or loss to shareholder. Avoids double taxation. Exceptions if previously a C corporation.	Double taxation—first at corporate level, then at shareholder level.
Alternative Minimum Tax (AMT)	Subject to 26% or 28% Alternative Minimum Tax.	Partnership not subject. Preference items and adjustments passed through to partners' 1040 via Form K-1.	S corporation not subject. Preference items and adjustments passed through to shareholders via Form K-1.	Applies at corporate level—at Alternative Minimum Tax rate of 20%. Certain small corporations are exempt from AMT.

Tax Considerations (Continued)

	Sole Proprietorship	Partnership	S Corporation	C Corporation
Payroll taxes	15.3% self-employment tax on first $76,200 of taxable income, 2.9% above that. Half of tax is deductible.	Partnership income not subject. Passed through to partners' 1040 via Form K-1, subject to self-employment tax.	Undistributed income is not subject. However, some part of distributions may be subject to payroll taxes if salary is deemed insufficient by IRS.	Corporation and its employees each pay 7.65% of FICA wages up to $76,200 1.45% above that.
Items affecting basis	Not an issue.	(A) Income and gains increase partners' basis in partnership; losses decrease basis. (B) Capital put into partnership increases basis; distributions decrease basis. (C) General partners' share of partnership liabilities increases basis.	(A) Income and gains increase shareholders' stock basis. (B) Capital put into S corporations increases basis; distributions decrease basis. (C) Loans put into S corporation by shareholder increase stock basis. Other corporate liabilities have no effect on shareholder basis.	Not an issue.
Cash vs. accrual method for preparing taxes.	Cash or accrual method.	Cash or accrual method. Must use accrual method if inventory is a factor.	Cash or accrual—no limits on annual receipts. Must use accrual method if inventory is a factor.	Cannot use cash method if annual receipts are $5 million or more, or if inventory is a factor.
Splitting of income	Not an issue.	May be allocated by partners' agreement.	Allocated in proportion to number of shares owned.	Not an issue.
Tax year	Calendar year.	Must use same year as principal partners, which usually is calendar year.	New corporations must use calendar year (some limited exceptions).	Calendar or fiscal year.

212

Tax Considerations *(Continued)*

	Sole Proprietorship	Partnership	S Corporation	C Corporation
Accumulated earnings tax	Not subject.	Not subject.	Not subject unless S corporation was previously a C corporation	Unreasonable earnings above $250,000 ($150,000 for personal-service corporations) are hit with a special 39.6% tax.
Excessive compensation	Not subject.	Not subject.	Not subject.	If deemed excessive. Excess is deemed to be a nondeductible dividend.
Disallowed personal expenses on audit	Individual tax rate.	Each partner pays his individual tax rate.	Each shareholder pays his individual tax rate.	Double taxation—first at corporate level, than at shareholder level.
Personal holding company tax*	Not subject.	Not subject.	Not subject.	Subject to a special 39.6% tax under certain conditions.

All Other Considerations

	Sole Proprietorship	Partnership	S Corporation	C Corporation
Ease and cost of formation	No special actions.	No special actions. Usual arrangement is to prepare written partnership agreement.	Initial costs of $600 to $1000; $400 to $600 if you do yourself.	Same as S corporation.
Period of existence	Discretion of owner.	Termination if partners agree, or on partner's death or retirement.	Continues until dissolution. Not affected by sale of shares, unless sale is to ineligible shareholder.	Same as S corporation with no restriction on eligibility of shareholders.

*A corporation that is more than 50% owned by five or fewer individuals and 60% or more of whose ordinary gross income is derived from dividends, interest, royalties, and annuities.

All Other Considerations (Continued)

	Sole Proprietorship	Partnership	S Corporation	C Corporation
Continuing costs	Minimal.	Annual federal and state partnership tax forms. Approximately 50% increase in tax preparation fees over sole proprietor.	Annual federal and state S corporation tax forms subject to minimal taxes in some states. Approximately 50% increase in tax preparation fees over sole proprietorship.	Annual federal and state corporation tax forms plus payment of corporate-level income taxes. More tax planning is required. 50–100% increase in tax preparation fees over sole proprietorship.
Owners' exposure to business debts	Liable for all debts of business.	General partners are liable for all debts of business.	Shareholders liable only for capital contributions and debts that are personally guaranteed.	Same as S corporation.
Effect on organization upon withdrawal of taxpayer	None.	Dissolution of partnership.	After stock is disposed of, corporation continues.	Same as S corporation.
Transfer of ownership interest	N/A.	Addition of new partner requires consent of other partners.	Easy to do—just transfer stock shares to new owner.	Same as S corporation.
Limitations on ownership	N/A.	No limit on number of partners.	Limited to 75 eligible shareholders.	No limit on number and eligibility of shareholders.
Ownership control	N/A.	Owner serves as general partner. All others are limited partners.	Owner retains voting stock and transfers nonvoting stock to minority stockholders (generally those who own less than 50% of the stock).	N/A.

Examination Coverage of Returns Filed*

	Calendar Year 1996			Calendar Year 1997			Calendar Year 1998		
	Returns Filed	Returns Examined	Percent Examined	Returns Filed	Returns Examined	Percent Examined	Returns Filed	Returns Examined	Percent Examined
Partnerships	1,653,100	9,811	.59	1,737,800	10,082	.58	1,861,000	7,991	0.43
S corporations	2,290,900	23,898	1.04	2,449,900	25,522	1.04	2,599,800	21,169	0.81
C corporations (assets under $250,000)	1,587,000	18,846	1.19	1,561,600	11,654	.77	1,506,300	6,865	0.46
Schedule C (all filers)	7,375,700	232,463	3.15	7,593,900	178,628	2.35	7,690,100	155,786	2.03
Schedule C (gross receipts $100,000 and over)	1,770,700	73,049	4.13	1,835,500	59,728	3.25	1,876,000	44,945	2.40
Individuals (TPI** $100,000 and over)	5,260,500	119,575	2.27	6,004,700	100,079	1.66	7,025,000	80,038	1.14
All individuals	118,362,600	1,519,243	1.28	120,342,400	1,192,780	.99	122,546,900	1,100,273	0.90

*Chart reflects most recent figures available, tabulated by the IRS as of September 21, 2000.

**Total Positive Income is the sum of all positive income that appears on a return, excluding losses.

9

The Thirty-three Biggest Misconceptions
Taxpayers Have About Their Returns

1. Misconception: "If I am in the 31 percent tax bracket, it means that my tax liability is 31 percent of my income."

What You Need to Know

Taxpayers in the 31 percent tax bracket operate almost across the board under the mistaken belief that because they are in that tax bracket, 31 percent of their income is being taxed. This is absolutely not true. A taxpayer in that tax bracket is actually getting taxed *less* than 31 percent. Even though you're in a 31 percent tax bracket, you pay less than that percentage because you get the benefit of being taxed at lower rates on the amounts you earn in the tax brackets that precede the bracket you are in.

Thus, a single taxpayer with $65,000 of taxable income, in the 31 percent bracket, is taxed this way: The first $26,250 of income is taxed at 15 percent, or $3,937.50. The next $37,300 is taxed at 28 percent, or $10,444. Only the remaining taxable income of $1,450 is taxed at 31 percent, or $449.50, and it is here, at this person's top income figure, that this taxpayer's tax bracket is determined. So even though this taxpayer is in the 31 percent tax bracket, the tax this person pays is actually just under 23 percent of $65,000, or $14,831.00.

You see, your total income tax bill accumulates as you climb up the tax rate ladder. While you are on the lower rungs, the rates being charged against your income are correspondingly lower.

The tax bracket that you finally fall into is also referred to as the marginal tax rate. Things would become much clearer to taxpayers if they viewed their top income figure as the *outside* margin, because it is this top percent that the government uses to fit the taxpayer into the tax bracket system. In no sense, however, is that percent the only one used to figure the actual amount of tax one pays.

2. Misconception: "When I transfer money from one mutual fund to another within the same family of funds to secure a stronger investment, or if I sell my tax-exempt municipal bonds, I don't have to worry about any tax consequences."

What You Need to Know
Each time you move money around from one mutual fund to another, even if the funds are owned by the same company, it is a taxable event that requires the investment company to report your sales proceeds by sending a 1099-B to the IRS. The information on that form must subsequently be reported by you on Form 1040, Schedule D, whether it is a gain or a loss. So before you decide to transfer money within a fund family, be aware of the tax consequences.

Regarding tax-exempt municipal securities: These produce income that is generally not subject to being taxed at the federal level. However, when you sell tax-exempt securities, there is always a capital gain or loss that must be reported on Form 1040, Schedule D.

3. Misconception: "A company I invested in recently split its stock 2-for-1. How much tax will I owe and what form do I use to report it?"

What You Need to Know
When a stock splits 2-for-1, your cost per share has not changed. It is simply now spread over twice as many shares. You will generally experience a taxable transaction only when you dispose of part or all of the stock. So it is important to keep track of the cost of each new share to report the correct gain or loss in the future. For example, if you initially paid $5,000 for 100 shares, each share has a cost of $50. After a 2-for-1 stock split, you now have 200 shares at a cost of $25 per share.

4. Misconception: "When I receive my inheritance from Uncle Leo, the IRS will take out a chunk of it."

What You Need to Know
Many people mistakenly believe that when they receive a gift or an inheritance they have to pay tax on it. They don't. The provider does.

Gifts and inheritances are *not* taxable to the recipient until the asset is disposed of, at which point taxes are due on any capital gain. The taxpayer should obtain documentation for the cost basis of the gift or inheritance so that when he sells the item he can determine how much tax he owes.

YOUR TAX-SAVING STRATEGY.
A parent or grandparent can make tuition payments for children or grandchildren directly to a college or private school and not be subject to the $10,000 per year gift tax limit. Although this exception applies to tuition only, there is no limit on the amount.

5. Misconception: "If I use the preprinted label that the IRS sends me on my tax return, my chances of being audited will be greatly increased."

What You Need to Know
The purpose of the preprinted labels is to allow an IRS data transcriber to access an account and enter the data needed to process the return using one-third fewer keystrokes. According to the IRS, the preprinted label reduces the chance of error and saves time. Labels contain tax period information that is used to post remittances and return information to the IRS master file. As discussed in chapter 8, the Discriminate Information Function (DIF) is the primary method the IRS uses to decide the majority of returns selected for audit, along with the ever-changing audit triggers. If the IRS were to use its preprinted labels for audit selection, the average tax assessment per audit would decrease dramatically due to the absence of audit criteria on the label. In other words, those labels offer absolutely no indication of a taxpayer's audit potential to the IRS. With over 224 million returns filed in 1998, the IRS must get the biggest bang for its buck. Those preprinted labels aren't even in the ballpark when the IRS considers audits.

Opposite is the latest version and an explanation of the information it provides the IRS.

6. Misconception: "I've heard about the increase in the number of people subject to the Alternative Minimum Tax (AMT). But since the AMT is supposed to prevent the very rich from getting away tax free, I don't have to worry about it."

What You Need to Know
The AMT was originally designed to catch high-income taxpayers who were using loopholes to reduce their tax bills. (See pages 19 and 262.)

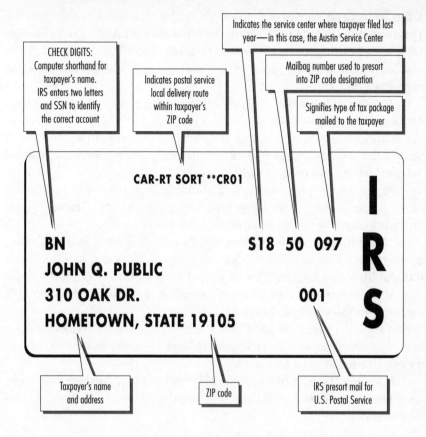

Indicates the service center where taxpayer filed last year—in this case, the Austin Service Center

CHECK DIGITS:
Computer shorthand for taxpayer's name. IRS enters two letters and SSN to identify the correct account

Indicates postal service local delivery route within taxpayer's ZIP code

Mailbag number used to presort into ZIP code designation

Signifies type of tax package mailed to the taxpayer

CAR-RT SORT **CR01

BN   S18 50 097
JOHN Q. PUBLIC
310 OAK DR.   001
HOMETOWN, STATE 19105

I R S

Taxpayer's name and address

ZIP code

IRS presort mail for U.S. Postal Service

Source: IRS, 1999 Tax Hints, Brookhaven Service Center, p. 30.

Although only 1 percent of all taxpayers are hit by this tax, the number of people being affected by it is rising at the rate of 30 percent a year, and it is predicted that by the year 2010, at least 17 million taxpayers will be subject to AMT. It is hoped that Congress will redesign the law governing the AMT to eliminate unintended victims, mainly middle-class America.

My advice is that you should fill in Form 6251 (Alternative Minimum Tax—Individuals) to determine if you are subject to the AMT. If you don't, the IRS will and you don't want that.

7. *Misconception: "If I make a withdrawal from my traditional or Roth IRA before age 59½, there is no way I can avoid the 10 percent penalty unless I roll it over to another IRA within 60 days.*

"The same holds true for my corporate or Keogh pension plan."

What You Need to Know

This is not necessarily true. There are other exceptions. You can take an early distribution from a traditional or Roth IRA without the penalty:

a. For certain medical expenses and for medical insurance. (See pages 287–289.)

b. If you make a series of equal annual payments that must continue for the longer of 5 years or until you reach age 59½. After that age, you can withdraw differing amounts without the 10 percent penalty. If you violate the payment schedule, all payments, past and present, will be subject to the 10 percent penalty.

c. If you have a physical or mental disability expected to last indefinitely (or until death) that stops you from performing the type of work you were doing before your condition arose.

d. If the distribution is tax-free and you never used it as a deduction against your income. This includes distributions from nondeductible traditional IRA's and distributions of annual contributions from Roth IRA's.

e. If the distribution is for higher education expenses of the account's owner, a spouse, a child, or grandchild.

f. If the distribution is used to buy a first home up to $10,000.*

g. For distributions of converted rollover amounts that have been in a Roth IRA for at least five years.

Concerning the corporate or Keogh pension plan, you can take early distributions from either of these without the 10 percent penalty in certain cases:

a. For certain medical expenses (see "a" above).

b. For certain annual payments (see "b" above), except that the payments must begin *after* you leave the company.

c. For a physical or mental disability (see "c" above).

d. If the distribution is taken after you leave the company and you are at least 55 years of age at that time.

YOUR TAX-SAVING STRATEGY.

Before incurring additional income tax and a 10 percent penalty by taking any distributions from your corporate pension or Keogh plan, it is a good idea to check with your employer regarding the possibility of borrowing from your pension plan account balance. The rates of interest are usually reasonable. (This option is not available to self-employed owner taxpayers, i.e., those with a Keogh plan.)

*A "first-time home buyer" is someone who hasn't owned a home in the past two years.

8. Misconception: "Isn't this great—I've just received a huge refund from the IRS. I sure know how to beat them at their own game."

What You Need to Know
Many taxpayers prefer to overwithhold and go for a large refund as a means of forced savings, or to ensure that they do not have to make any additional payments to the IRS on or after April 15. **The fact is, taxpayers who consistently receive large refunds are actually giving the IRS an interest-free loan, and the money the IRS is borrowing is *yours*.**

The most likely candidates to be sucked into this trap of overwithholding are taxpayers with unusually high deductions (mortgage interest, contributions, taxes) who haven't properly assessed how these deductions will affect their final tax bill. These taxpayers would be better served if they reduced the amount of withholding taken out during the year and got more money each week, which adds up to the same amount as the refund check.

One final tip regarding large end-of-year refunds: Although the IRS continues to maintain that its audit selection criteria are top secret, in my opinion one of the things IRS computers *do* look at is the size of a taxpayer's refund and how it was computed.

If an average taxpayer, married with two children, had a gross income of $75,000 with $13,000 of it withheld, and ended up with a $10,000 refund, the IRS is going to be very interested in the exemptions and deductions that caused this unusually large refund. In other words, that taxpayer has made himself or herself more susceptible to an audit. The solution? It's better to have less tax withheld and reduce that year-end refund.

9. Misconception: "It doesn't matter in what part of the country I live. All areas are considered equal in audit selection."

What You Need to Know
Sadly, this is so far from the truth that it has attracted increasing media coverage of late. Even the IRS admits huge variances in audit coverage and selection based on location; these are hard-to-explain differences in how the government treats taxpayers. Based on IRS data over the past five years, the Transactional Records Access Clearinghouse (TRAC) has ranked all 33 IRS districts from the most audited to the least. Here's what a selection of the figures tells you: The highest percentage of individual returns audited in the country was in the Los Angeles district.

From an auditing perspective, therefore, taxpayers would most likely not consider California to be the "golden west." The IRS district offices in California (Southern California, Los Angeles, Northern California) have consistently been the most aggressive in auditing individual tax returns, demonstrating an audit rate of 1 percent, roughly double the national average of 0.5 percent.

Conversely, district offices in the Northeast, including New England, New Jersey, and upstate New York, and parts of the Midwest—Ohio and Michigan—are the least aggressive regarding their audits of individual tax returns, with rates of about half the national average.

In general, rankings by IRS district offices remain stable. True, North Central moved from number 14 to number 5, as you can see from the chart, but overall the rankings for the past five years have remained consistent.

What one normally assumes are the money-center areas of the country—Los Angeles and Southern California, Houston and Manhattan—tend to rank high. But the Northeast and upper Midwest—Ohio, upstate New York, Michigan—tend to rank near the bottom.

Similarly, criminal enforcement of the tax laws also varies surprisingly based on 1998 figures of IRS criminal convictions of all kinds by location. (See IRS Criminal Convictions, opposite.) Brooklyn and Manhattan in New York City, Philadelphia, Newark, and Miami rank the highest, with the numbers descending to five convictions each in Anchorage, Alaska, and Sioux Falls, South Dakota, four in Washington, D.C., and zero convictions in Burlington, Vermont.

10. Misconception: "I want to retire to a warm climate. I expect that most states offer similar tax breaks."

What You Need to Know
The two most popular retirement states, Florida and Nevada, have no income tax, but neither do Alaska, South Dakota, Texas, Washington, and Wyoming. But remember that there are a variety of other taxes you would want to be aware of when moving to another state that could make up the difference even if there is no income tax. During your retirement years you will probably spend a large proportion of your total income on sales tax. The only states without sales tax are Alaska, Delaware, Montana, New Hampshire, and Oregon. You also need to factor in property and estate tax laws before making your final decision.

11. Misconception: "I can take more itemized deductions than I am entitled to (especially contributions and medical expenses) and not be audited as long as I stay under the national averages published by the IRS."

Percent of Individual Tax Returns
Audited by District Office (1995–1999)

IRS District	1995	1998	1999	Percent Audited*
Southern California	1	3	1	0.9
Los Angeles	2	2	2	1.0
Northern California	3	1	3	1.1
Central California	8	4	4	0.7
North Central	14	7	5	0.6
Manhattan	5	6	6	0.6
U.S. Average				0.5
New England	23	28	28	0.3
Illinois	24	17	29	0.5
New Jersey	32	24	30	0.3
Michigan	27	31	31	0.3
Upstate New York	30	26	32	0.3
Ohio	33	33	33	0.2

*Percent audited results by district are for 1998 only.

IRS Criminal Convictions
Districts in Rank Order

Federal Judicial District	City	Number Convicted	Rank
N.Y., S	Manhattan	70	5
Nevada	Las Vegas	21	8
Pa., E	Philadelphia	65	9
N.Y., E	Brooklyn	80	11
Ga., N	Atlanta	46	13
Fla., S	Miami	50	16
N.J.	Newark	64	25
S. Dakota	Sioux Falls	5	30
Hawaii	Honolulu	8	31

Source: Transactional Records Access Clearinghouse, Syracuse University. Copyright 1999.

What You Need to Know

Each year itemized deductions claimed by individuals on their tax returns, grouped by levels of adjusted gross income, are published by the Commerce Clearing House. These figures appear on page 224. Play this game and you'll end up playing audit roulette. To take a tax deduction, follow this simple rule: If you pay for a tax-deductible item, you can use it on your return as long as you can prove it with a canceled check or an itemized bill or receipt.

Average Itemized Deductions for 1997 by Adjusted Gross Income Ranges

Adjusted Gross Income Ranges	Medical Expenses	Taxes	Interest	Contributions
$15,000 to $19,900	$7,491	$2,119	$5,299	$1,368
$20,000 to $24,999	4,017	2,250	5,651	1,368
$25,000 to $29,999	4,893	2,249	5,262	1,493
$30,000 to $39,999	3,987	2,772	5,551	1,451
$40,000 to $49,999	4,002	3,285	6,346	1,616
$50,000 to $74,999	6,620	4,236	6,824	1,862
$75,000 to $99,999	8,413	6,200	8,387	2,477
$100,000 +	18,463	15,730	12,852	11,501

Derived from Commerce Clearing House, Federal Tax Guide Reports, *Tax Week*, April 23, 1999, p. 8.

Certainly, some reasonable exceptions are allowed. You don't have to prove the first $78 of cash contributions, and you don't need every last toll or taxi receipt if you are an outside salesperson. However, deductions for taxes and interest are straightforward—if you're lacking proof, you will owe money to the IRS when audited, no matter where you fall in the national averages.

12. Misconception: "Now that I have been audited by the IRS and had money due, I will be audited every year."

What You Need to Know

As already mentioned, tax returns are most often selected for an audit based on computer-generated criteria. The selection process is done on a year-by-year basis, with each new year standing on its own.

YOUR TAX-SAVING STRATEGY.

If one of the issues that caused a taxpayer to pay additional taxes resulted from an error, such as depreciation on a piece of office equipment, an auditor will know that this kind of error is often repeated. He or she will probably examine the prior year's return, if the statute of limitations has not expired and/or the following year's return if it is already filed. However, since these steps will normally take place immediately after the current year's audit is completed, it helps to keep your current year's return on extension while the audit is in progress (extending the filing date to October 15), if at all possible.

If the same taxpayer's return for the following year contains another red flag, such as very high travel and entertainment expenses, that return is again at risk for having a higher than normal audit potential.

13. Misconception: "I'm in big trouble with the IRS, so I'd better hire an attorney because I can only obtain the right of privileged communication from an attorney who practices before the IRS."

What You Need to Know

Beginning July 23, 1998, thanks to the IRS Restructuring and Reform Act, a taxpayer is now entitled to receive from advisers who are CPA's or enrolled agents the same confidentiality protection for tax advice as the taxpayer would have if the advising individual were an attorney. This coverage is for noncriminal tax proceedings before the IRS and federal courts. If you suspect that your case will become a criminal action, use only an attorney. (See page 299.)

14. Misconception: "Since I am a first-time home buyer, I can withdraw $10,000 from my IRA and put all of the money into my new house with no tax consequences to worry about."

What You Need to Know

Many people have the idea that the $10,000 withdrawn under these circumstances is tax free. Not true. It only escapes the 10 percent early withdrawal penalty but is subject to tax at ordinary income tax rates. Also, you have only 120 days to buy the home or return the money to the IRA without penalty.

YOUR TAX-SAVING STRATEGY.
A couple who buys a home jointly can increase the lifetime $10,000 limit to $20,000 if each one withdraws $10,000 from their own IRA's. To receive this break, both spouses must qualify as first-time home buyers. NOTE: You do not owe income tax on money withdrawn from a Roth IRA to buy the first home as long as the money has been in the Roth account for at least five years. If less than five years, you are taxed on the earnings from the Roth IRA.

15. Misconception: "By filing a timely Form 4868 [Application for Automatic Extension of Time To File U.S. Individual Income Tax Return], I will be excused from all penalties and interest as long as I file my tax return within the extension period and pay the balance of tax that is due."

What You Need to Know

By filing a timely Form 4868, the only penalty that you eliminate is for filing the return late (5 percent per month, 25 percent maximum). However, you do not eliminate the penalty on the tax that is paid late (½ of 1 percent per month) or interest on the late tax payment (currently 8 percent per annum).

YOUR TAX-SAVING STRATEGY.
Here's a related matter regarding refunds. If your tax return results in a refund, you will be charged *no* penalties or interest for late filing because late-filing penalties and interest are based on the balance of tax due. In fact, you can file your refund return up to two years late and receive your refund while not being subject to penalties and interest. (Sorry, no interest is given on the refund for the length of time it takes you to file the return.)

16. *Misconception: "I did not convert my traditional IRA to a Roth IRA in 1998, so I missed out on the benefit of spreading the tax over four years. Did I really lose a golden opportunity to reduce my taxes when I retire?"*

What You Need to Know
After 1998, conversions can be made in any amount as long as your adjusted gross income (AGI) remains under $100,000 (not including the amount of money you want to convert). The point is, you do not want to end up in a higher tax bracket as a result of the conversion. In the year that you make the conversion, however, you must pay the full amount of tax due. As long as your AGI remains under $100,000 for a given year, you can transfer just enough money so that your taxable income remains in the same tax bracket. In this way, you can spread the tax bite over a multi-year period. Keep in mind that you must take a distribution from your traditional IRA by December 31, 2000, to start the conversion process, and you must complete the transfer into the Roth IRA within 60 days.

YOUR TAX-SAVING STRATEGY.
Let's say you converted $50,000 from a traditional IRA to a Roth IRA in July 2000 but the investment has dropped in value to $25,000. Assuming you have already filed your 2000 return, you have until October 15, 2001, to "recharacterize" the conversion (a new term which means to change the character or type of your IRA) back to your traditional IRA by filing an amended return, Form 1040X (Amended U.S. Individual Income Tax Return). You will also need to attach Form 8606 (Nondeductible IRAs) to the amended return to claim your refund. This method is also available if you have not yet filed but have requested an extension of time to file until August 15 or October 15, 2001. And here's an added bonus:

After the recharacterization, if you wait at least 30 days, you have the option to convert your traditional IRA back into a Roth IRA. Do this only if you expect your 2001 AGI to be under $100,000. (See page 284.)

17. Misconception: "As the longtime owner of a business, I am better off with a company 401(k) plan than with a regular retirement plan."

What You Need to Know
Probably not. If you are older than 50 and the majority of your employees are 20 years or more younger than you, you can contribute much larger amounts if you adopt a defined benefit plan, which provides for specified benefits, typically in the form of a monthly retirement pension based on levels of compensation and years of service. Plan contributions are actuarially calculated to provide the promised benefit and are not allocated to individual accounts for the participants. Since you are closer to retirement than your younger workers and will require a larger pension, your annual contribution can be $50,000 or more in many cases, while your younger employees receive considerably smaller amounts. If they leave before they are fully vested, their contributions revert to the plan, leaving you with reduced future contributions.

True, employees who contribute to a 401(k) plan can reduce their taxable wages by the contributed amount for income tax purposes. However, these plans are generally expensive to administer, and if the employer does not match part of the employees' contribution, very few employees will join the plan, which will make the plan inoperable.

18. Misconception: "My spouse recently passed away, and he left me his company retirement money. I suppose the best thing is to take a lump sum and take control over the money."

What You Need to Know
Not necessarily. Any money you take immediately is fully subject to tax. If you took the money before January 1, 2000, you might be eligible for either 5-year averaging, if your spouse was at least 59½ years old, or 10-year averaging, if he was born before 1936. Otherwise, you can roll your spouse's retirement funds into a traditional IRA, which will maintain the tax deferral. If you don't need this money for many years, you could then convert part or all of the traditional IRA to a Roth IRA, discussed on page 284.

19. Misconception: "When I do a rollover from my traditional IRA to my Roth IRA, I might as well take advantage of the rising stock mar-

ket and use the check to buy some mutual funds and then deposit the shares into my new Roth IRA account."

What You Need to Know

When money or property is withdrawn from an IRA, you have 60 days to deposit the same money or property into a second IRA in order to complete a tax-free rollover. The purchase of mutual fund shares disqualifies the rollover and makes it taxable.

YOUR TAX-SAVING STRATEGY.
You can transfer money or property from one IRA to another via a trustee-to-trustee transfer (see page 29), where the trick is for you not to touch the money in any way. Once this is complete, you can make the stock purchases described above from your Roth IRA account, which will then be a tax-free rollover.

20. Misconception: "Since I can't afford to pay the balance due on my tax return, I'll hold up filing until I have all of the money."

What You Need to Know

This is the worst choice you can make in this situation, because you will incur one of the harshest IRS penalties: a failure-to-file penalty of 5 percent per month (maximum 25 percent) of the balance of tax due. This is in addition to a failure-to-pay penalty plus interest. (See pages 249–250 for better solutions to this problem.)

21. Misconception: "If I make an extra mortgage payment before this year ends, I can increase my deduction for mortgage interest on my 1040 return."

What You Need to Know

While it is true that you can make as many extra mortgage payments as you want in any calendar year, which does allow you to increase your interest deduction, this might not be the wisest thing to do. If you find that you consistently have extra money for this purpose, you would be better served by applying it against your mortgage principal. This not only pays down the loan faster, it also saves interest over the long haul. If you can, try to do this early in the year for maximum effect and always clearly designate the extra money as going toward principal.

22. Misconception: "Once I meet the Social Security guidelines of earning 40 credits (formerly known as quarters of coverage), I will be eligible for the maximum Social Security benefit. Also, it is great that my benefits will be based on the last five years of my employment."

What You Need to Know

Although it is not a tax item, I have heard this erroneous statement repeated by many people. The truth is that earning or meeting the Social Security guideline of 40 credits makes you eligible for retirement benefits at a cetain age, but it has *nothing* to do with the amount of your benefits. Benefits are based on average earnings over a 35-year span during which the worker earned the most money. The worker's actual earnings are then adjusted to account for changes in average wages since the year the earnings were received.

23. Misconception: "I'm an outside salesman and my employer reimburses me for all my travel, meals, and entertainment expenses. Of course these amounts will be added to the gross earnings on my W-2 form at the end of the year."

What You Need to Know

In most instances, not only will these amounts *not* be added to the employee's earnings, there will be no accounting for them whatsoever on your Form 1040. If you document the entire outlay of expenses on an expense report for trips during a certain period, and a balance may be due either from you to your employer or vice versa, once these are met you have satisfied the requirements for what is known as an accountable plan, which is acceptable by the IRS.

24. Misconception: "After my divorce, my wife still gets to take the tax exemption for my child who lives with her, even though I pay most of my child's support. I can't catch a break!"

What You Need to Know

If you are currently separated or divorced and you wish to claim an individual as an exemption, you must meet five dependency tests:

- The gross income of the dependent must be less than $2,800 in 2000 unless the child is either under 19 or a full-time student under 24 on December 31, 2000.
- You must be a relative or member of the household: almost any lineal relative of either spouse (children, parents, grandparents, inlaws, etc.) and any other person who resides in the taxpayer's household for the entire year.

- If married, the dependent must not have filed a joint return with his spouse.
- The dependent must generally be a citizen or resident of the United States, Canada, or Mexico at some time during the year.
- More than one half of the support must be furnished by the parent, or by both parents combined in the case of divorced or separated parents. Even if the noncustodial parent actually provides up to 100 percent of the dependent's support, the *custodial* parent is deemed to have provided more than half of the dependent's support and, accordingly, is entitled to the exemption. However, the custodial parent can release the exemption to the noncustodial parent by using Form 8332 (Release of Claim to Exemption for Child of Divorced or Separated Parents).

EXCEPTION: If a couple with a child have never been married to each other, only the parent who has provided more than half of the child's support can take the dependency exemption, providing the other four dependency tests are met. The qualifying parent *cannot* release the exemption to anyone else.

25. Misconception: "I didn't have any W-2 earnings this year, but at least I received unemployment compensation, which will allow me to make my $2,000 annual contribution to my IRA."

What You Need to Know
Unlike W-2 earnings or net income from a self-employed business, unemployment compensation is not considered income from personal services. Therefore, no IRA deductions of any kind are permissible.

26. Misconception: "I must add to my taxable income all federal and state income tax refunds that I received this year."

What You Need to Know
First, federal refunds are *never* considered taxable income on federal income tax returns.

Second, state refunds are income on your 1040 *only* if you deducted state taxes paid in a prior year, thereby reducing your taxable income. Once you use state taxes as a deduction to reduce your income, then you must declare that year's state tax refund as income on your federal tax return. Here's an example: If you used a federal standard deduction, i.e., one lump sum amount, instead of itemizing deductions on your 1999 return, you do *not* have to include the state tax refund as income on your 2000 return. But if you took itemized deductions, and state taxes were listed, then you must report the state tax refund as income on your 2000 federal return—i.e., if 2000 is the year you received the refund or you applied the 1999 refund as payment against your 2000 state tax liability.

27. Misconception: "It doesn't pay to transfer income-producing assets to my child, who is under 14 years of age. The income will still be taxed at my top income tax rate."

What You Need to Know
This statement is true only if the child's taxable investment income exceeds $1,400. The amount of tax charged is based on a three-tiered approach:

1. Zero to $700: Income produced at this level is wiped out, since the child is entitled to a standard deduction of $700. No tax is due and no tax form or return needs to be filed by the child.
2. $701 to $1,400: Investment income above $700 is not included in the parent's taxable income. However, it is taxed at a 15 percent rate using Form 8814 (Parents' Election to Report Child's Interest and Dividends). To report this, the child must file an individual tax return.
3. $1,401 and higher: After calculating the tax on the first $1,400 of investment income as outlined in 1 and 2 above, the balance of investment income is taxed at the parents' highest tax rate. The parents must fill out Form 8615 (Tax for Children Under 14 Who Have Investment Income of More Than $1,400) and attach it to their tax return. (See page 264.)

YOUR TAX-SAVING STRATEGY.
These rules cover investment income only. If your child earns other income, from salaries and wages, for example, that income is taxed at 15 percent to $26,250, which is the end of the 15 percent bracket for single taxpayers.

28. Misconception: "My company's corporate tax return is due March 15, 2001, but I do not have the money to fund my required retirement plan contribution before the filing date. I will have to delete the contribution from the tax return before I file it."

What You Need to Know
In order not to have to delete the contribution from your tax return, this is what you need to do: If the plan is new, make sure that you have the retirement trust documents prepared and signed by December 31, 2000. If a qualified pension, profit-sharing, or Keogh plan is already properly set up, you have until the due date of the company's tax return to make the 2000 contribution, plus additional time for extensions, which brings you up to September 15, 2001.

29. Misconception: "Since my wife is now eligible for a pension plan where she works, we are both prohibited from making a contribution to our traditional IRA's."

What You Need to Know
You may still be eligible to make tax-deductible contributions to your traditional IRA's if you do not exceed certain income levels. In the above scenario, if the taxpayers' adjusted gross income is $52,000 or less ($32,000 or less for a single taxpayer), they could each contribute up to $2,000 to their traditional IRA's. They would be eligible for a partial contribution between $52,000 and $62,000 ($32,000 and $42,000 for singles). Above $62,000 AGI ($42,000 for singles), they would not be eligible. Beginning January 1, 1998, a spouse's eligibility for IRA contributions has changed. (See pages 283–284.)

YOUR TAX-SAVING STRATEGY.
Even if you are ineligible to make a tax-deductible contribution to your traditional IRA, you might be eligible to make a nondeductible contribution up to $2,000 to a Roth IRA. (See pages 284–288.)

30. Misconception: "If my return undergoes a correspondence audit by an examiner from the IRS Examination Division, I can be sure that person will be highly skilled and trained, most likely even a college graduate."

What You Need to Know
Correspondence audits take place at IRS Service Centers and are conducted by clerks who often receive rudimentary training from the IRS, and they are required to have only a high school education. So, if you disagree with the results you receive in the letter from the IRS about your case, and you feel the facts are on your side, fight the decision by providing full details in your first response and reasons for your position. When a final solution is arrived at, if you subsequently receive

a bill, be sure to check the facts and figures because inaccuracies often occur.

Furthermore, because of continuing budget cuts, many tax auditors who handle face-to-face audits at district offices are not required by the IRS to have a college degree. They do make mistakes, so with careful preparation you can often sustain any deductions they may question.

31. Misconception: "If I am an employer who enrolls in the Electronic Federal Tax Payment System (EFTPS) to pay my payroll and corporate business taxes, the IRS will have immediate access to my business bank account, which means they could peruse privileged information or even take money from my account for other items that may be in dispute with the IRS."

What You Need to Know
If you enroll in the EFTPS, *you* decide the amount of taxes that needs to be declared. The IRS is prohibited from using the system for any other purposes. This position has been publicized so effectively that 400,000 businesses *not* required to use the system have voluntarily enrolled in it.

Remember—no special equipment is required. A simple telephone call to transfer funds takes less time than preparing the paperwork and going to the bank. EFTPS computer software is free. Call the U.S. Treasury at 800-555-4477 or 800-945-8400 for more information.

32. Misconception: "I'm glad that Congress changed the laws governing the sale of personal residences. Now I'll be able to deduct the loss from the sale of my house against other capital gains."

What You Need to Know
Losses incurred on the disposition of personal assets not used for business, such as your home or car, are *not* deductible on your personal income tax return. Although RRA '98 has raised the threshold on capital gains tax on the sale of your residence ($500,000 for married couples filing jointly, $250,000 for single filers), unfortunately losses are still not deductible.

33. Misconception: "Our current tax system is riddled with loopholes that wealthy taxpayers take advantage of. A flat tax will not only remedy this situation and level the playing field for the rest of us, it will also simplify things dramatically. Everyone will pay the same percent of income to the government, we can say good-bye to all those complicated tax forms, and we'll finally be able to do away with the IRS along with all those CPA's who are kept in business because tax laws are so complicated."

What You Need to Know

Proponents of the flat tax and value-added tax have argued that the current tax system taxes investments and savings too heavily, hurts the nation's competitiveness in international markets, and is just too complicated to administer. However, many of these same arguments were used in support of a major overhaul of the tax system, the Tax Reform Act (TRA) of 1986. The TRA '86, which was supposed to be an improvement over the existing situation, did wipe out the most abusive tax shelters, but it also severely limited taxpayers' ability to use real estate investments to shelter income. The result was that the real estate industry was brought to its knees. This new weak link, created under the guise of tax reform, contributed to a recession that lasted several years.

The lesson we need to learn and remember is this: **Major tax reform often has significant side effects that are not known until some of the laws get played out.**

The most often repeated argument against the flat tax is that it would destroy the progressive nature of the tax system—in which the amount of taxes owed rises according to income earned—and load the tax burden more heavily on the backs of the middle class. While there are economists who passionately debate both of these arguments, here are some of the potential results if a flat tax were to be enacted:

- With interest, dividends, and rental income no longer taxed, the wealthy would be able to add to their riches in a way similar to what the Vanderbilts and Rockefellers did prior to 1913; i.e., whatever interest and dividends they received from their investments, they kept—legitimately—because they were tax free.
- Tax shelters in the form of limited partnerships would lose their attractiveness, reducing needed capital sources for businesses, such as the real estate industry. This is exactly what happened with TRA '86.
- Mortgage interest and real estate tax deductions would disappear. Without these, home values would plummet.
- Sales of municipal bonds, which provide tax-sheltered interest income, would drop because with a flat tax all interest income becomes tax sheltered, thereby wiping out the advantages of municipals. The resulting shortfall in municipal revenue would be a

double whammy—local property taxes would rise, which would be an additional burden on middle-class home owners, *and* these taxes would no longer be deductible on a personal income tax return.

- Charitable contributions would be eliminated. Consider the effect this would have on the level of contributions by savvy taxpayers to charitable organizations across the country!

Now let's explore how the flat tax and value-added tax proposals would affect the nation's business community.

Under the flat tax, instead of depreciating certain assets over time or being held to certain limiting thresholds, as is the case under current tax law, businesses could *immediately* write off or expense the following:

1. Amounts paid for purchases of goods, services, and materials, whether or not these are resold by year's end.
2. All purchases of tangible real and personal property, such as land, buildings, and equipment (capital items).
3. Compensation, meals and entertainment, and several other limited expenses.

Sounds like a real free-for-all for the business community, doesn't it? If this should become the status quo, what do you think would be needed more than ever before? How about a watchdog, *like the IRS*, to ensure that businesses comply with the new tax rules? Why? Because the temptation to bend the law will be greater than ever, given the easy route open to every businessperson to avoid taxation or to defer taxes indefinitely simply by increasing the current year's purchases of goods or capital equipment and deducting the full cost. Even if this was done legitimately, the resulting loss of business tax revenues would transfer the tax burden right back to the middle class. Inevitably tax increases would soon follow to make up the differences.

As far as those CPA's are concerned, we are probably the largest, strongest, and most genuine group of taxpayer advocates, constantly putting ourselves on the front lines. We know the law and we also know how and where our clients, the taxpayers, are being hit the hardest by the IRS. CPA's, as I see it, are in the best position to save taxpayer dollars through their advice and daily scrutiny of individual and business returns. The American Institute of Certified Public Accountants (AICPA) and local state CPA societies have a solid track record for establishing a viable working relationship with the IRS. If positive changes are to occur in tax laws, with the taxpayer as the beneficiary, lobbying groups such as the AICPA will be the ones to start the ball rolling.

Concerning the question regarding the demise of the IRS: Think this one through! We would still need a system to administer the collection of over $1 trillion annually. In addition, taxpayers would still need to file information in some format—although a lot less paperwork would probably be required.

Let's face it. As long as the tax-making process is intricately tied to Congress and the political machinery, the chances of having a flat tax passed into law are pretty slim. Considering the potential ramifications of a flat tax, that may be fortunate.

10

How to Hold On to More Money—
Overlooked Credits and Deductions

1. Selling Securities from a Dividend Reinvestment Plan
When you sell a mutual fund or a security that had a dividend reinvestment plan, taxpayers typically recall the original cost of the item plus periodic cash investments made along the way. But they frequently forget about those reinvested dividends used to purchase additional shares that were taxable each year as dividend income. Although notice of these are sent annually as paper transactions, taxpayers often overlook them, but they can represent more money in your pocket. Here's how: Add the costs of these dividends to your total cost basis when you sell a fund or security and you'll reduce your taxable gain, or increase your loss.

2. Identifying Specific Securities That Are Sold
If you have purchased many shares or mutual funds over a period of time from the same company during a rising stock market, capital gain can be reduced if shares with the highest basis are sold first. (For a definition of basis, see page 134.) To accomplish this, you must keep track of each specific lot of shares you purchased, plus any dividend reinvestments that were generated from the specific lots. This is something most taxpayers fail to do. You must also notify the fund manager or broker in writing as to which shares are to be sold and request a written receipt. If you don't follow this procedure, you will be stuck with using other, less effective, methods for determining the cost of your purchase,

237

e.g., average costing, which will result in higher capital gains subject to tax.

A new technique for using specific identification was clarified in a 1999 Letter Ruling (LTR 9728021). The Letter Ruling stated that the requirements for adequate identification of specific securities were met when the client instructed the broker to sell shares with the highest cost basis first, when selling identical shares of stock, and for those shares with the same cost basis, to sell shares with the longest holding period.

3. Convert Ordinary Income to Capital Gain

If you're about to sell a mutual fund that you've held for more than one year, check when the fund will next pay out ordinary, fully taxable dividends, and how much it will be. Here's why: Immediately following all dividend payouts, the shares of a mutual fund generally decrease by the amount of the dividends. So, if you sell your mutual fund shares before the payment date of the ordinary dividends, which are taxable at your highest tax rate, you will lose the dividends but you will have received a higher share price on the total shares you sold. Voilà! You've just converted ordinary income into capital gains income, which is probably subject to a lower capital gains tax rate.

4. Unamortized Points on a Home Mortgage

With interest rates still very low, many taxpayers are refinancing their mortgages to obtain the lower rates. Points paid on an original home purchase can be deducted immediately, but points paid for a refinancing must be amortized over the life of the new loan per IRS instructions. Often overlooked when doing a second (or more) refinancing is that the balance of the unamortized points from the previous closing is deductible in full when the mortgage for the previous financing is paid off.

5. Deductible Interest on a Home Equity Loan

After you receive money from a home equity loan, the interest on the first $100,000 is fully deductible. But even if you reach that maximum amount allowed for deducting interest on a home equity loan, you may be able to go further. If the loan proceeds above $100,000 are used to run a business or for investment purposes, the interest on that portion of the loan can be deductible as well.

NOTE: Investment interest is deductible only to the extent that you have investment income such as dividend and interest income appearing on your 1040. Any unused deduction can be carried forward to the following year.

6. Unused Losses, Expenses, and Credits

To prevent taxpayers from bunching up deductions in a single year, Form 1040 contains numerous limitations on losses, expenses, and tax credits. Some of these items are lost forever, e.g., medical expenses that do not meet the 7.5 percent of AGI threshold cannot be added to next year's medical expenses. (For an exception, see number 7.) However, many other deductions, losses, and tax credits can be carried forward from prior years and then be deducted on your current year's tax return. For example, the law allows taxpayers to deduct only $3,000 a year in capital losses (after offsetting your capital gains). So if you had net capital losses of $8,000 last year, the unused portion, or $5,000, can be utilized this year as a deduction against your income. Other often overlooked "carry-forwards" are investment interest and charitable donations listed on Schedule A, home-office expenses and Section 179 Depreciation (see pages 154–155 and 198) on Schedule C (Profit or Loss From Business) and passive losses on Schedule E (Supplemental Income and Loss). So it pays to check last year's return for any unused losses or expenses that can be carried forward to this year's return and use them to put more money in your pocket. (There are also several tax credits available as carry-forwards, but it's best to ask a tax pro for assistance to know if you are eligible.)

7. Self-Employed Deduction for Health Insurance

Self-employed taxpayers who file their taxes using Schedule C or 1120S (U.S. Income Tax Return for an S Corporation) can deduct 60 percent of the annual health insurance premiums they have paid out in 2000 and 2001 against their adjusted gross income. For example, if your AGI is $100,000 and your health insurance premiums are $6,000, you can deduct $3,600 (60 percent of $6,000) on page 1, line 26, of your Form 1040, even though you fail to exceed the medical expense threshold of 7.5 percent of AGI on Schedule A. In effect, you are reducing your AGI and taxable income by $3,600 regardless of whether you meet the medical expense threshold.

8. Charitable Donations—Securities

You can increase the amount of your charitable deductions listed on Schedule A (Itemized Deductions) by handing over to your favorite charity marketable securities that you have held for more than 12 months that have appreciated in value. You, in turn, can take a deduction for the securities' fair market value on the date of the gift. If you sell the securities first, and then contribute the net proceeds to charity, you'll be stuck for the tax on any capital gain.

If you held securities for 12 months or less, and they went down in value, you can either donate the stock to charity or sell the stock and donate the proceeds. There is no tax difference.

9. Charitable Donations—Household Items

The cartons of clothing, old furniture, and appliances you give away have residual value. Most charities will gladly give you a receipt each time you make a donation, so don't be surprised if all together the sum comes to $500 or $600, without exaggeration. If you're in the habit of making these kinds of donations regularly, check the list of used property values issued by the Salvation Army, in Appendix A, Form 8283. The IRS should accept this list when determining the dollar value of secondhand items. The total of these receipts can translate into an unexpected windfall deduction on Schedule A, Form 1040, which can reduce your overall taxable income.

10. Social Security Tax Overpayments

Social Security tax paid by employees is deducted from gross wages up to $76,200. Therefore, if you worked at more than one job in 2000 and your combined W-2 earnings as shown in Box 3 of all your W-2's exceeds $76,200, you probably overpaid Social Security taxes. You can check this by adding up the amounts of Social Security tax shown in Box 4 of all your W-2's. Anything above $4,724.40 is an overpayment. Put the excess amount on line 62 of Form 1040 and you'll receive a dollar-for-dollar reduction taken against your tax liability that will either increase your refund or reduce the amount you owe. If your gross wages are from only one source and your total wages exceeded that amount, chances are your company did not take more Social Security taxes than necessary, but you should verify it anyway.

11. Job-Hunting Expenses

Remember to add up all job-hunting expenses such as résumé preparation, newspapers purchased, cabs and auto mileage taken, use of placement services, and even airline tickets, hotels, and meals if the interview was out of town and you were not reimbursed. Taxpayers typically lump these with other miscellaneous deductions on Schedule A, and together they are subject to a 2 percent deductible of your adjusted gross income. So do the computations and take what you are entitled to.

YOUR TAX-SAVING STRATEGY.

For job-hunting expenses to be deductible, you have to be searching for a job that is in the same field as the one you currently hold. The expenses are valid even if you don't get the job you applied for. However, first-time job seekers, e.g., college graduates, cannot deduct expenses when searching for their first job.

12. State Income Tax Deductions

If you pay estimated state taxes in four quarterly installments, the fourth scheduled payment is made around January 15 of the following year. This means that for calendar year 1999, you can deduct the January 2000 payment on your 2000 federal return as an itemized deduction on Schedule A. Another scenario, based on the same principle, is this: If the balance due on your 1999 state tax return was paid in 2000, usually around April 15, you can deduct this amount as an itemized deduction on Schedule A of your 2000 Form 1040. This gives you a solid deduction you might otherwise not be aware of.

13. Parental or Grandparental Support

If you provide more than half the support for your parent or grandparent, you may be entitled to a dependency exemption of $2,800. Keep these conditions in mind:

- The dependent can't have more than $2,800 of reportable income.
- Social Security benefits do not count as reportable income.
- Medical expenses paid by you count toward providing support.

14. Federal Income Tax Withheld on Forms 1099

The largest amount of income tax paid to the IRS is withheld from employee salary and wage payments, both of which appear on Form W-2, issued at the end of the year. However, income taxes are also often withheld from non-wage sources such as backup withholding (see page 128), or distributions from pension plans (Form 1099-R). Make sure to attach a copy of the appropriate 1099 form(s) to your tax return along with copy B of your W-2 so that you receive full credit for all taxes withheld from 1099 payments as well as from salaries and wages. Because this is an often overlooked tax credit, whatever you gain is found money.

11

—

Ten Ground Rules Never to Break
to Win with the IRS

Winning at taxes is not about finding the right piece of information. It *is* about knowing as much as possible about *your own, personal tax situation* and moving beyond your fears to clearly see that the IRS is simply a group of people who have an enormous job to accomplish.

To continue to keep the scales between you and the IRS tipped in your favor, you must always follow these 10 ground rules for winning with the IRS.

RULE 1. ALWAYS REPORT INCOME ON YOUR TAX RETURN THAT IS BEING REPORTED TO THE IRS BY THIRD-PARTY PAYERS.

The most common include W-2's, income items on K-1's, and the entire series of 1099 forms: distributions from pension plans and individual retirement accounts (IRA's); interest and dividend income; sales of stocks, bonds, and mutual funds; state income tax refunds; and Social Security and unemployment insurance benefits.

Some of the tax laws and requirements that govern third-party disclosures are

- Withholding law (Tax Payment Act of 1943).
- Requirement to report miscellaneous income totaling $600 or more in a year (1099-MISC).
- Requirement to report payments of interest and dividend income totaling $10 or more (1099-DIV, 1099-INT).

- Any of the other tax laws governing information reporting that bring into play the full series of 1099 forms, 13 in all.

But as usual, when it comes to obeying the law, people don't always meet their legal obligations uniformly. Exceptions occur because people misinterpret, manipulate, or simply ignore what is requested. As a result, you must pay attention to more than the letter of these laws and be prepared for the following circumstances in adhering to this ground rule.

Some Employers Report All Payments

Be aware that many business owners report *all* payments on 1099-MISC to the IRS, even if they are less than $600. What implication does this have for taxpayers? To follow the letter of the law, taxpayers should report all income received, even if the amount is below $600 annually.

In fact, taxpayers should learn to assume responsibility for keeping track of all their own earnings. At least then they can be certain that a comparison between what they say they earn and the 1099's provided by payers will be accurate.

Payment Methods

A worker can be paid "on the books" or "off the books." "Regular employees" and independent contractors are paid on the books. Regular employees receive a salary from the entity they work for and have their income reported directly to the IRS by that entity on a W-2 form. Independent contractors have their income reported to the IRS by the entity that pays them on a 1099-MISC if their remuneration is $600 or more per year.

All payment methods—cash, checks, barter—are treated equally under the law. **No matter what the form of payment, including barter, the business owner is legally bound to report the amount paid to the IRS on a W-2, on a 1099-MISC, or on any of the other twelve 1099 forms.** This information is carefully matched up on IRS computers, so if you don't report it, you place yourself at audit risk.

Workers who so choose or are talked into it are paid "off the books," in cash—and usually no reporting requirements are fulfilled by the entity to the IRS. This group usually believes they're getting a bargain. Not true.

When You Are Paid "Off the Books"

Fifteen or 20 years ago "off the books" meant taking your earnings home with no taxes deducted. Today all of that has changed because of information technology and reporting requirements. **Anyone who ac-**

cepts this method of payment becomes an independent contractor in the eyes of the IRS and is liable for all of the taxes independent contractors must pay.

If your teenage daughter tells you she'll be working part-time, "off the books," what is really going on is probably not the "classic" definition just described, but something more like this: Mr. and Mrs. Owner are the only "employees" listed on the company's payroll records. All others whom they employ are issued 1099's at the end of the year. Since 1099's represent payments to nonemployees, no taxes are withheld from these payments, and the worker is treated like an independent contractor. Thus your daughter could earn $5,500 with no taxes withheld but end up being liable for paying FICA taxes of $777.13.

If she were instead treated as an employee, the FICA tax deduction from her salary would be $420.75 (7.65 percent of $5,500), a net savings of $356.38. In both instances, she would owe no income tax because she would be earning below the $7,200 threshold for a single person. The $5,500 is wiped out by a personal exemption of $2,800 and a standard deduction for a single person amounting to $4,400.

In short, if you are a part-time or summer worker, insist you be paid "on the books," receiving full benefits, paying your share of taxes. A student is generally subject only to the withholding of FICA tax. If you are working full-time on a permanent basis and are not self-employed or are not inclined to file your tax return as a self-employed person, also insist that you be treated as a regular employee.

The Greed Factor

Dealing in cash presents temptations. Once you have been tempted, it's often difficult to overcome the *greed factor*. Problems arise when business owners pocket cash and fail to report it to the IRS, or get involved in schemes for hiding income. Why would a business owner report the *full* amount of cash payments made to workers on 1099's but report only *part* of the cash income to the IRS? To reduce the company's net taxable income. (If the income goes directly into the owner's pocket, the IRS can't tax it, right?) None of this is news to the IRS.

The only major reporting exception for business owners is something many tax professionals consider to be a major weakness in the IRS's reporting system: **The IRS does not require business owners to prepare 1099-MISC forms for payments to corporations except for legal services.** That means if you are an independent contractor or self-employed *and you incorporate*, anyone who pays you is *not* required to file a 1099-MISC with the IRS. (See also page 193.)

What Happens When You Don't Receive a 1099?

Some people actually believe that if they don't receive a Form 1099, it means that it was not mailed to the IRS and therefore they don't have to include that income on their tax return. Nothing could be further from the truth. It is vital that you follow Ground Rule 1 even if you do not actually receive your 1099 form telling you how much income you received from a particular job.

Why Business Owners Don't Send 1099's

Occasionally business owners are unfamiliar with the rules governing payments for labor and services and fail to prepare the required 1099 paperwork. Or sometimes they inadvertently forget to mail the 1099 to the recipient. But the primary reasons business owners "forget" to prepare 1099's are these:

- They are fearful that the independent contractors they use will be reclassified by the IRS as employees. What better way to avoid reclassification than by not mailing the 1099's to the IRS?
- They believe that the less the IRS knows about their operation in general, the better off they are. If they do get audited and the IRS discovers that they didn't file 1099's, they would rather risk paying the penalties ($100 per nonfiling of a 1099) than reveal more of their business operations to the IRS.

An IRS auditor does not often impose a penalty for failure to file 1099's. Even if one does, though, the $100 per item nonfiling penalty is small compared to the possible costly reclassification of some or all of the business owner's workers as employees. However, if the IRS can prove *intentional* disregard of the filing rules by the business owner, there is no maximum penalty per information return.

The bottom line for workers is this: If you do *not* receive a 1099, ask the business owner if one is forthcoming. Upon receiving a late 1099, if you become paranoid about the unreported income, you can file an amended tax return. In 1995 the IRS received 2.2 million amended individual returns, most probably the result of late notifications of income plus guilty consciences. Remember, for small amounts of additional tax ($100 or less), it can cost double that in tax preparation fees.

RULE 2. NEVER INCLUDE OTHER FORMS THAT ARE *NOT* REQUIRED WITH YOUR TAX RETURN. DO NOT VOLUNTEER ADDITIONAL INFORMATION.

This ground rule applies to a number of situations, some involving several specific (and many newly created) IRS forms, some applying to cases in which taxpayers owe the IRS money and negotiations are a possibility, and some applying to audits.

Form 8275 (Disclosure Statement) and Form 8275-R (Regulation Disclosure Statement)

The IRS would love it if all taxpayers used Forms 8275 and 8275-R more often because they are supposed to be filed with a 1040 if a taxpayer knowingly takes a position on the return that is questionable. Both forms look extremely harmless and provide minimal direction. Form 8275 states, "Do not use this form to disclose information that is contrary to treasury regulations." Form 8275-R states, "Use this form only to disclose items or positions that are contrary to treasury regulations." Following each sentence is blank space. The IRS designed Forms 8275 and 8275-R this way to give taxpayers enough rope to hang themselves.

In 1993, I said that by electing to use these forms, you are notifying the IRS that you're probably doing something wrong. In 1995, the IRS finally admitted it.

The instructions for Form 8275 and 8275-R require that you support your position through revenue rulings, revenue procedures, tax court cases, and the like. This means that you need to locate, from thousands of pages in our current tax code, previous laws and decisions that support your position.

According to the IRS there is a plus side to all of this: If you attach Form 8275 or 8275-R to your return, and if the return is subsequently audited, *and* the issue is decided against you, you won't have to pay any penalties. However, you will still have to pay additional tax, plus interest.

Form 8275 and 8275-R are nifty tools devised by the IRS to ease the burden of the Examination Department. **Instead of IRS personnel manually sorting through thousands of returns to come up with questionable issues, with these forms, taxpayers are now flagging questionable items for the IRS of their own free will.** Why should you be the one to start the ball rolling?

The fact is that you can disregard these forms entirely and still take the same position regarding income and expenses, and rely on the same rulings or procedures, which your tax professional may already be familiar with.

There's something else to consider when it comes to Forms 8275 and 8275-R. **The consensus of tax pros regarding both of these forms is that the IRS wants to make it tougher on tax preparers if they take aggressive positions on their clients' tax returns.** Existing

IRS regulations say that when a tax preparer takes a questionable position on a return, one that stands less than one chance in three of being accepted by the IRS, the tax preparer must describe the position taken and then include support for it by using Form 8275. If the use of a borderline justification is not disclosed in this way, and the return is found unacceptable, the instructions to Form 8275 indicate that the taxpayer is subject to additional tax, and the preparer can be charged with a $250 penalty as well.

Who's to judge whether the tax preparer has one in three chances that the position taken on a client's 1040 will be accepted? The regulation goes on to say that the final decision will be based on a "reasonable and well-informed analysis by a person knowledgeable in tax law." If you were to bet on which decision would win, the one taken by the IRS or the taxpayer, which would you choose?

My advice is that if your tax pro suggests including Form 8275 or Form 8275-R with your return, be sure that he or she justifies why the form is being used and convinces you that it is being used for your benefit and not just to cover your tax professional's own exposure.

Form SS-8 (Determination of Employee Work Status for Purposes of Federal Employment Taxes and Income Tax Withholding)

Form SS-8 was formerly called Independent Contractor Status. As explored in chapter 7, the IRS is currently very focused on reclassifying independent contractors as employees. As you recall, reclassification enables the IRS to recoup huge amounts of tax dollars.

To file an SS-8 would be to admit that there is some doubt in your status as an independent contractor or, if the form is being filed by an employer, the status of your workers. Based on what you have already learned about the IRS, why would you want to place doubt on your own working status, or on the working status of your workers? The form is also quite complicated and cumbersome, even for professionals.

If you do not file Form SS-8, your status, or your workers' status, will probably come into question *only* during an audit.

Form 8082 (Notice of Inconsistent Treatment or Administrative Adjustment)

Schedule K-1 is an information form that reflects your shares of income and expenses that are passed through to your individual tax return by partnerships, S corporations, limited liability companies, and estates and trusts (see pages 134–136). If you do not agree with an amount or the way an issue has been shown on your K-1, you do not have the option of changing the form on your own and reporting it a different way on your Form 1040. In this situation, the IRS suggests that you use Form 8082, which contains adequate space to explain why you are taking a different position on your Form 1040.

Now, wait just a minute. Common sense tells you that informing the IRS *in advance* that you are taking a contrary position is tantamount to requesting an audit of your entire return. Here's what to do instead: If you're in a partnership, for example, discuss the situation immediately with the partner who handles tax matters and is responsible for the content of the tax return. If he agrees with you that a mistake was made, and the return has not yet been filed, he may be willing to make the necessary changes. If the return has been filed (which is likely), an amended partnership return could be prepared and filed. If the partner who handles tax matters does not agree with the changes that you believe are necessary, then using Form 8082 may be your only alternative, but be sure you have a convincing argument in favor of your position just in case you have to explain it to an IRS revenue agent.

Form 5213 (Election to Postpone Determination as to Whether the Presumption That an Activity Is Engaged in for Profit Applies)

If you file taxes as an individual, a partnership, an S corporation, or an estate or trust (pass-through entities) that has incurred or is expected to incur net operating losses for three out of five years, you can elect to file Form 5213.

If an activity is presumed to be engaged in for profit, the activity must show a net profit for three out of five years. Conversely, if you have net losses for three out of the first five years, your activity will be presumed to be a hobby and on an audit deductions will be allowed only to the extent of income reported from the activity. That is, you will be able to reduce the income to but not below zero. Here is a case that demonstrates the use of 5213 and the tax rulings associated with it.

During an audit, a client of mine, a producer of small documentary films, showed a string of losses for five years amounting to approximately $15,000 per year. Although she had only small amounts of income and large expenses, she was still actively seeking distribution outlets for the films she produced. In her favor was the fact that three years prior to the five years showing losses, she showed a substantial profit in two out of three years.

During the past five years, however, she was living off her savings. Careful documentation provided to the tax auditor showed that she was making an honest attempt to sell her films. For example, many of the travel expenses charged to the business were in pursuit of this effort.

After a half-day audit that covered a two-year period, the agent concluded that my client had demonstrated an honest profit motive.

This goes to the heart of the Hobby Loss Provision. Losses in three out of five years merely *indicate* that you're not in it to make a profit. If you can *prove* the profit motive (time spent, investigation before starting, expertise, lack of other income to offset losses, etc.), then the losses will stand. (See page 203.) The IRS would have loved my client to have filled out Form 5213 when she began producing films. This could have led the IRS to believe that this occupation was a hobby—which in reality it wasn't.

The IRS is trying to sell you on Form 5213 by attaching a bonus to it: If you file Form 5213, you can postpone the determination by the IRS as to whether or not you are engaged in an activity for profit. That is, you cannot be audited during the initial five-year test period. **This may sound good, but it's not, for two reasons.**

First, there is nothing automatic about the Hobby Loss Provision. If you show net losses for three or four consecutive years, you may not hear from the IRS. **By filing the form you are actually informing the IRS that you are afraid that your losses will be disallowed.** Why put yourself on record that you might be subject to the Hobby Loss Provision? Let the IRS discover your losses on its own. If you don't file Form 5213, you still retain all your rights to refute the IRS that you have engaged in the activity not to make a profit.

Second, when you file Form 5213 you are also agreeing to extend the period for tax assessment (statute of limitations) for two years after the due date of the return in question for the first tax year of the five-year test period. For example, if the test period is 1995 through 1999, the IRS would normally have until April 15, 1999, to initiate an audit of the 1995 return. However, if you file a 5213, the IRS has until April 15, 2001, an extra two years. **This could mean giving the IRS five years to assess you for additional tax instead of the normal three!** It's better not to fill out the form.

Form 872 (Consent to Extend the Time to Assess Tax) and Form 872-A (Special Consent to Extend the Time to Assess Tax)

When an audit has been going on for six months or more and the statute of limitations, normally three years, will be up in one year or less, the auditor may ask you to sign Form 872 or 872-A. Before you even think about signing either one, you should consider that the wrong choice could hurt you badly.

After December 31, 1999, the IRS must notify you of your right to refuse. If you don't agree to an extension of the statute of limitations, the IRS will send you a Statutory Notice of Deficiency, which will force you to end up in Tax Court or at least have the IRS commence collection actions against you. In addition, if it looks as though you can't settle your case with the auditor at this point and you're thinking of taking your case to Appeals, signing an extension for at least one year is usually required.

So now the question is, which one do you sign? **Under no circumstances should you choose Form 872-A, which until RRA '98 left the extension date open-ended.** This gave the IRS an unlimited amount of time to complete your examination. The case would end up at the bottom of the pile and the clock would tick away as interest charges mounted up. I know of cases like this that have gone on for years. The new law provides a 10-year limitation and ensures other taxpayer rights. (See 1998 Tax Legislation, page 297.)

Therefore, when signing an extension, choose Form 872, which defines the end of the extension period. And you absolutely want to limit this period to one additional year.

One more thing: Make sure the agent doesn't "inadvertently" hand you the 872-A instead. I've had that happen to me.

The Fallacy of Giving the IRS Backup Data for Deductions

Many tax preparers suggest including backup data with your return when you have taken a larger than normal deduction. For example, they suggest that if you have sustained a large casualty loss, you should include repair bills and appraisals. My advice to you is this: **Do not include this data.** The only thing you accomplish by including backup data is to bring the questionable items to the attention of IRS reviewers. Also, if the return *is* selected for a review, by the time it reaches the reviewer your backup data may be incomplete after having gone through mail and sorting machines and being handled by lots of different people.

Let the IRS carry out its audit function its way. If your return is selected for a correspondence audit to verify one glaring item, you can submit all your documentary proof at that time.

RULE 3. IF ANY INFORMATION THAT YOU ARE PUTTING ON A TAX RETURN IS A "GRAY" AREA, GO FOR AS CLOSE TO FULL DEDUCTIBILITY AS POSSIBLE.

Often the data taxpayers are planning to include on a return is not a perfect fit for the category or line that they think it belongs on. For example, a variety of expenses can appear in more than one place on Form

1040. The secret is knowing which schedule to choose to gain the biggest tax advantage and how to support your claims. This also applies if you are filing as a partnership or an S or C corporation.

The majority of taxpayers choose to report expenses on three schedules, all used in connection with the 1040 form: Schedule C (Profit or Loss from Business), Schedule E (Supplemental Income and Loss [from rental real estate, royalties, partnerships, S corporations, estates, trusts, REMIC's, etc.]), and Schedule A (Itemized Deductions).

The essential differences among these is that many expenses listed on Schedule A are subject to formulas that limit deductibility such as percentage of adjusted gross income. In contrast, expenses listed on Schedule C and Schedule E are fully deductible, with the exception of certain restraints such as home-office expenses on Schedule C and passive loss amounts on Schedule E, both of which are sometimes not fully deductible on their respective schedules.

Form 1040, Schedule C (Profit or Loss from Business)

Form 1040, Schedule C (Profit or Loss From Business) is used to report the income from a business operated by a self-employed person, the income of someone who renders part- or full-time service as an independent contractor, or of someone who carries on a trade or business as a proprietor. In the audit chapter, taxpayers were advised to reduce their 1040 line items by eliminating Schedule C in its entirety. **If you must continue to use Schedule C, there are certain flexibilities you should know about.** (The following information can apply to all business entities, such as partnerships, LLC's, S corporations, and C corporations.)

Schedule C contains about 25 listed expense items and an unlimited amount of other miscellaneous expense categories, and it provides taxpayers with ample opportunities to increase business deductions. Some line items are more flexible than others.

Listed Items

    Advertising
    Car and truck expenses
    Legal and professional services

Other Expenses

    Telephone

You can use these items to your advantage.

Advertising

You're self-employed, and you decide to print up some résumés and place ads for your services in your local newspaper, at a total cost of $2,500. As a self-employed person you can report this as a business expense on Schedule C and take a full $2,500 deduction.

If these or other job-related expenses are incurred while you are an employee, they must be reported on Schedule A in a section titled "Job Expenses and Most Other Miscellaneous Deductions." Here, however, the total amount of your deductions is subject to a reduction of an amount equal to 2 percent of your adjusted gross income (AGI). If you are single with an AGI of $60,000 and in the 28 percent tax bracket, 2 percent is $1,200, so your deduction would be reduced by this amount, and would be only $1,300.

Car and Truck Expenses

No matter what type of business you are in, you probably use your car some of the time for business reasons. Taxpayers in this position have two choices for computing and reporting vehicle expenses.

The simplest and safest way to report these expenses is by using the *mileage method*. To do this, simply multiply business miles driven by the allowable mileage rate (currently 32.5 cents for 2000), add tolls and parking expenses, and you have your deduction. If you use your car for a mere 5,000 miles for the year, this will provide you with a $1,625 deduction.

Using the alternative *direct method*, you simply add up all your auto expenses—gas and oil, repairs, and insurance—plus depreciation. You then must factor in the number of days per week the car is used for business purposes. If it's Monday to Friday, then you can deduct five sevenths of the auto expenses. The remainder of the costs represent those incurred for personal use and are not deductible.

Since many business owners often use their cars on Saturdays and perhaps even on an occasional Sunday to greet an out-of-town customer or supplier, deduct six sevenths of the total car expenses and present your position if you are audited.

To decide which works best, compare the direct-method costs with the mileage costs and go with the one that offers the largest deduction. You should also factor in one further consideration: If you are audited, with the direct method you have to document every last item of expense with receipts, and maintain a diary that shows full details of your business miles. With the mileage method, a diary that shows your business miles is all that is required. If you lease your car, you can use either the mileage or the direct method. However, once you begin using direct-method costs, you must continue using it as long as you use that particular car for business. If you used mileage costs, you can switch to direct-method, but no switching back again. (See pages 272–274.)

Legal and Professional Services

The IRS wants you to apportion deductible legal and accounting fees to each appropriate schedule on your return: Schedules A, C, and E; or "Other Income," line 21 on page 1 of the 1040. Since a tax professional usually spends a considerable amount of time preparing the business part of your return, it is perfectly acceptable for you to request that the bill be weighted in favor of Schedule C, where it is deductible in full without limitations. If a legal fee is personal in nature and doesn't relate to the business, exclude it. For example, preparation of a will is personal, but tax advice that was part of a discussion with the attorney is deductible. The tax and investment planning portions of a bill from a financial planner would likewise be deductible. Speak to the attorney or the financial planner *before* the bill arrives and explain that you're tax-savvy and insist that the tax advice be clearly shown on the bill.

The greatest advantage for taxpayers is achieved by including expenses for legal and professional services in a schedule that offers 100 percent deductibility. This is what a detailed bill and its traceable deductions might include:

Where to List Legal and Professional Services for Maximum Deductibility

Item	Schedule
Professional fees in pursuit of back alimony	Line 21, page 1 of 1040
Audit fees to uncover hidden assets of ex-spouse relating to alimony	Line 21, page 1 of 1040
Attorney's fees on purchase of a new home	Add to cost basis of home
Legal fees to collect back rent*	Schedule E, Part 1
Tax preparer's fees for preparation of business payroll tax returns	Schedule C
Attorney's fees for setting up a new business	Schedule C

*Where to List Legal and Professional Services for Maximum
Deductibility (Continued)*

Item	Schedule
Planning advice in reference to a new business venture	Schedule C
Professional fees for representation at tax audits	Schedule C or Schedule A (Miscellaneous Deductions), if personal
Preparation of tax returns	Same
Financial planning	Same

*The last seven items are also generally deductible by partnerships and corporations.

Telephone Expenses

Generally speaking, you can take a more aggressive position if you use estimates to supplement actual receipts. For example, since there are no receipts available for coins put into public telephones, working people who spend a lot of time on the road can conceivably declare they spend as much as $30 a week on business calls from pay phones. Even if you have a telephone credit card or a cellular phone, it is more economical to use coins for calls under one dollar. Because items such as telephone calls are not a major expense, IRS auditors spend little time in this area, so reasonable estimates are usually accepted.

If you have a dedicated business phone, most IRS auditors will accept your deduction as a 100 percent business cost. Don't worry, auditors generally will not test your honesty by calling specific telephone numbers.

For a smaller business, where your previously personal telephone has been switched over to both business and personal use, you have to determine which portion is now business-related and which long-distance calls are to your Aunt Sylvia. However, an auditor will not usually compare your usage of the telephone now that you are in business to the time when your phone was strictly personal. So estimate generously in favor of business use.

Expenses for Business Use of Your Home

As you learned in the chapter on the underground economy, this is still a hot topic. Taxpayers were once able to deduct home-office expenses directly on Schedule C. Now all of this is done on Form 8829, a clever IRS device/weapon. (For a full discussion of how to obtain the maximum benefit from Form 8829, see page 153 in chapter 7.)

Form 1040, Schedule E (Supplemental Income and Loss)

Another useful schedule that allows taxpayers flexibility regarding the gray areas of deductions is Schedule E, Part 1. This schedule is used to report income or loss from real estate rentals and royalties.

Bear in mind that many of the considerations concerning expenses that taxpayers can place on Schedule C are also appropriate for Schedule E. An expense on Part 1 of Schedule E is fully deductible against rental income. So the IRS is on the lookout for expenses that may be more personal than business and that should rightfully be placed on Schedule A (Itemized Deductions) or some other schedule that, because of the threshold of the deductible, will reduce the expense to a meaningless amount. (See Legal and Other Professional Fees, page 256.)

Direct expenses that are deductible against rental income are easy to identify. These include cleaning, maintenance, utilities, commissions, insurance, mortgage interest, and real estate taxes. To give owners of rental property the greatest advantage, the following discussion focuses on items that are subject to interpretation, and how an aggressive position regarding these expenses may be possible.

Auto Expenses

To arrive at the maximum amount that you can deduct as a proper business-related auto expense on Schedule E, you have to ask yourself some questions that an IRS auditor would ask: Do you use your car to visit your properties? How often? How far is the round trip? Even if you do not run the day-to-day operations, do you drive to a specific location to meet with the managing agent, or sign new leases, or collect rents directly from tenants? Certainly, you would make a personal visit if one of the properties was sold or if you were purchasing a new rental property.

If you answer yes to some of these questions, you can deduct your auto expenses on Schedule E. You can determine how much to deduct by using the mileage method; total up the business miles and multiply by the allowable mileage rate. As usual, to back up your figures, keep a diary of trips associated with the rental property. (See also Car and Truck Expenses, page 252.)

Travel Expenses

Is your rental property in another state? Many residents of one state have rental properties in another and have to travel there periodically by air to buy or sell a property, or to take care of an existing problem. If you decide to stay a little longer and vacation for a few days, your air travel plus the cost of hotels and 50 percent of meals while you are involved in the business-related activities are still fully deductible against rental income. If your spouse is a co-owner of the property, then his or her expenses are also deductible if he or she accompanies you.

Keep an accurate diary of your business activities so that you have clear and convincing evidence that the trip was not solely personal in nature. Since a deduction like this is usually substantial, have all expenditures fully documented. Estimates are not appropriate in this situation.

Legal and Other Professional Fees

Sometimes it's hard to differentiate between a fee for ordinary legal services, which is deductible in one year, and a fee for legal services in connection with a purchase of property, which must be added to the cost basis of the property and depreciated over a period of years, or in connection with a sale of property when a legal fee decreases the capital gain generated from the sale.

Your attorney may be performing services for you on an ongoing basis, and your bill may not provide an adequate explanation of the services rendered. If this is the case, ask your attorney for a bill with the services listed. If you can't obtain a more descriptive bill, take an aggressive position by deducting a reasonable part of the entire bill as being applicable toward your business activities.

Repairs

The cost of repairs to a property used in a trade or business is deductible as an ordinary and necessary business expense. Capital expenditures must be depreciated over a period of years. Generally, improvements, additions, or replacements that extend the property's life or increase its value must be capitalized. How do you determine whether the property value increased or if the property's useful life was extended? You should approach your local real estate appraiser, who may provide you with an appraisal that indicates no change in the property's value, which allows you to write off the entire repair in the current year.

YOUR TAX-SAVING STRATEGY.
If you do not need additional write-offs, the best approach is to capitalize the expenditure (add to the property's cost basis), and depreciate it over 27½ years (residential) or 39 years (nonresidential). That way you avoid a potential argument with an IRS auditor, since a common IRS position is to push for capitalization of large items rather than expense the items in their entirety in the current year.

Form 1040, Schedule A (Itemized Deductions)

If you're not sure about what and how much to deduct on Schedules C and E, a more appropriate place for your expenses may be Schedule A. Relocating expenses from Schedule C or E to Schedule A will probably reduce the items' deductibility because of the many limitations. However, the trade-off is greater peace of mind and a decreased chance that you'll be audited.

The chart below lists the most common expenses taken on Schedule A and explains their limitations.

Typical Expenses on Schedule A Subject to Limitations

Description of Expenses	*Location on Schedule A*	*How It Works*
Medical and dental	Lines 1–4	Otherwise deductible medical and dental expenses must be decreased by 7½ percent of Adjusted Gross Income (AGI)* (see next page).
Investment interest	Line 13	Deductible only to the extent of net investment income. Unused portion can be carried over to future years.
Contributions by cash or check	Line 15	Donations to public charities are limited to 50 percent of AGI. Unused portion can be carried over for five years. A detailed receipt is required for items $250 or higher** (see page 259).

Typical Expenses on Schedule A (continued)

Description of Expenses	Location on Schedule A	How It Works
Contributions other than by cash or check	Line 16	Form 8283 (Noncash Charitable Contributions). If you make noncash charitable contributions in excess of $500, you must include Form 8283 with your return. If the noncash deduction exceeds $5,000, you will also have to include a separate appraisal on the item donated.
Casualty and theft losses	Line 19	Must be reduced by 10 percent of AGI *plus* $100.
Job expenses and most other miscellaneous deductions, including unreimbursed employee business expenses	Lines 20, 21, 22	The total of lines 20 through 22 must be reduced by 2 percent of AGI and the net amount entered on line 26.

*YOUR TAX-SAVING STRATEGY.

Self-employed people are allowed to deduct 60 percent of their health insurance premiums from their adjusted gross income. This deduction remains at 60 percent for 2000 and 2001, increases to 70 percent for 2002, and reaches 100 percent in 2003.

If you offer group health insurance to all of your employees, and your spouse is one of them, your spouse can elect family coverage, which will include you. This translates into a 100 percent health insurance deduction for your business as compared to the partial deductibility when you pay personally.

These are obvious pluses for anyone owning a business. They also make for a sweeter package of incentives currently available to the dramatically growing number of small-business owners as well as to those who work at home.

**YOUR TAX-SAVING STRATEGY.
Cash contributions of $250 or more require a detailed receipt from the charitable organization. Because of this rule, taxpayers are making these two mistakes: 1. After obtaining the detailed receipt, they are attaching it *to* the 1040. The only requirement is that you actually *have it* when the return is filed. 2. Taxpayers are obtaining detailed receipts if their *total* cash contributions are $250 or higher. You need the detailed receipt only for *single* cash contributions of $250 or higher.

What Wage Earners Can Do

Attention everyone out there who earns W-2 income from a salary: You can receive some of the financial benefits that come from loopholes in our tax laws by relocating income and expense items to Schedules E and C.

To do this, you should try to find a way to create self-employment income. As you know from the Hobby Loss Rule, the IRS is constantly monitoring "businesses" that don't have a profit motive and are carried on as a hobby. So there's no point in creating something that *looks* like a hobby. What I am suggesting here is the creation of a bona fide business that stems from a personal interest.

Some taxpayers actively pursue a hobby that can easily be turned into a business venture. For example, someone I know, Carl Jennings, a high school teacher, loved to tinker with clocks. He decided to put his free time to better use by beginning a clock-repair service. He began to visit local stores that both sold and repaired clocks and informed the store owners that he was "open for business." Three months later, he was so busy he had to turn down new work.

There's no reason why you can't do it too. Follow these guidelines:

1. Develop a new source of income, something you always wanted to do but never did. The tax benefits you will gain should give you plenty of motivation and incentive to pull this together.
2. Set up your new business so you can work when you want to.
3. If the business mushrooms, incorporate as an S corporation.
4. Make your home your full-time place of business where most of your relevant business activities occur, and follow the suggestions in this book, which allow you the complete array of home-office deductions.

5. Take out-of-pocket costs, such as supplies and tools that were previously considered personal items, as items fully deductible against your self-employment income.
6. When traveling to suppliers or customers, take deductions for the business use of your auto.
7. If possible, make contributions to a self-employed Keogh Retirement Plan, which will eventually supplement your retirement pay from your nine-to-five pension plan.

Before we leave this discussion of how to achieve full deductibility by using Schedules C, E, or A, there's something you need to be warned about: The IRS is constantly on the lookout for taxpayers who use Schedules C and E to load up on expenses that are not fully deductible elsewhere or not deductible at all. Because expenses listed on these two schedules are fully deductible against income, taxpayers tend to abuse this capability. **As a result, Schedules C and E have become popular audit triggers (C more so than E).** Going too far can get you into trouble. The IRS generally allows reasonable leeway when taxpayers estimate expenses, but you need to avoid crossing the line between a generous estimate of a deduction and downright abuse. Always be prepared with some reasonable explanation for why you have chosen to place your expenses on Schedule C.

Hobby Loss Rule

Also be aware that when it looks at Schedule C, the IRS is looking for personal expenses that taxpayers disguise as business expenses. One of the most significant measures the IRS uses to assess the distinction between what constitutes a business versus a hobby is known as the Hobby Loss Rule or Provision. (See also pages 203–205.)

Accordingly, the IRS scrutinizes Schedule C's that show large deductions that reduce gross income down to a minimal profit, or produce a net loss. If you can prove a profit motive, then your business expenses will be fully deductible even if they produce a net loss.

In a recent case, a couple took losses for horse breeding, rodeo activities, and an antiques store. Since the taxpayers had hired no experts for the antiques business, had inadequate record keeping, and the store was open only part-time, the Tax Court ruled in favor of the IRS. However, for the horse breeding and rodeo activities, the taxpayers sought out the advice of experts, kept good records, worked long hours, and had a business plan. Here the Tax Court ruled in favor of the taxpayers.[1]

Knowing when to be aggressive, especially regarding the opportunities available to taxpayers on Schedules C, E, and A, can save you money *and* hold up against IRS scrutiny. (See page 204.)

RULE 4. FILE YOUR PERSONAL TAX RETURN BY APRIL 15. USE AN EXTENSION ONLY IF ABSOLUTELY NECESSARY.

The idea that your return will slip by unnoticed because you file later than April 15 is no longer valid.

Computers are slaves. On April 10, they will process 100,000 returns each day at the same rate as on August 10, when they may process only 5,000 returns.

Some tax professionals argue that workloads are set and returns are selected for audit by the end of August, so if you file in September or October, your return will not be selected for audit. This is a fallacy. **A return can be selected for audit at any time.** Furthermore, if your return contains some unusually large deductions, the chances of its being selected for audit will not diminish simply because you wait until October to file.

Another theory suggests that the IRS likes to review a return for audit potential when it has leisure time. Therefore, if you file four or five months after April 15, you are giving the IRS what it wants—more time to make up its mind about your return.

There are other, more substantial reasons why you are *not* well served by delaying the filing of your return. For one thing, hiring a tax professional anytime in April or later is expensive: no doubt 25 to 30 percent higher than normal. This is because the taxpayer must still make a good-faith effort to compute and pay all taxes by April 15 even with the extension form in hand. For the tax professional, the extension requires an unavoidable duplication of effort. The tax professional must first go through all items of income and expense to prepare a reasonable guesstimate. Then, weeks or months later, the same job must be repeated in even greater detail.

Also, if you have a refund due, instead of receiving it on time, about six weeks after April 15, you won't receive it until six months after your extended filing date. So you lose four to six months' worth of interest.

Furthermore, for those who pay estimated quarterly taxes, filing late complicates the following year's payments. If you file on August 1, you have already missed the following year's estimated tax due dates of April 15 and June 15. Since you did not have accurate figures to work with, based on the previous year's return, you may have underpaid these estimates and may be subject to underpayment penalties.

RULE 5. DON'T WORRY ABOUT BEING UNABLE TO INTERPRET OR DECIPHER THE REALLY COMPLEX IRS TAX FORMS. MANY IRS AUDITORS DON'T UNDERSTAND THEM EITHER.

A great deal has been said in this book about the complexity of our tax *laws*. It is no surprise, therefore, that this same complexity characterizes many of our tax *forms*. Here are the most complex ones and what to do about them:

Schedule D (Form 1040—Capital Gains and Losses)

Who would have ever thought that a basic 1040 form like Schedule D would be so complicated that the thought of preparing it manually would be unimaginable. The confusion is widespread and includes sophisticated as well as ordinary investors. Tax preparers are blaming Congress for the complexity of the new Schedule D, which includes five different tax rates for capital gains, depending on the type of asset, length of time held, and when it was sold. Although RRA '98 made some positive adjustments in the capital gains areas, there are still going to be approximately 54 lines on the 2000 Schedule D. The IRS estimates that it will take the average taxpayer four hours, 19 minutes, to complete the schedule without professional help.[2]

Adding to the confusion early in 1998 was the failure of most mutual funds to provide adequate or timely information for 1997 transactions. Sometimes taxpayers received as many as three revised 1099's for the same transaction. Given the changes that had to be included because of TRA '97, plus the tight time constraints handed out by Congress, the IRS eventually did a wonderful job of rewriting Schedule D. It encompasses all the aspects of the overly complex capital gains law.

Good luck on this one, but I recommend that you do not try Schedule D without a computerized tax program.

Form 6251 (Alternative Minimum Tax—Individuals)

Computing taxable income is based on either the IRS tax table or the alternative minimum tax (AMT) method. The higher of the two is the tax you pay. **All taxpayers are supposed to compute their taxes on the basis of these two methods.** Determining who is subject to the AMT and who is less likely to be affected by it gets extremely complicated. But if you don't compute AMT, you're placing yourself at risk of being audited.

To complete Form 6251 using the AMT method, you start with your regular taxable income, then make adjustments on the basis of approximately 20 items that Congress has added on over the years. The more common add-on's are personal exemptions, standard deduction (if used), state and local taxes, certain interest expense, part of medical expenses, certain income from exercising Incentive Stock Options, and passive-activity losses. Then you add on "tax preference" items (about 10 in all), special tax deductions given to a select group of taxpayers, many of whom are partners in oil and gas enterprises and real estate investments, whose tax information is passed through via K-1's. If the resulting "Alternative Minimum Taxable Income" (AMTI) exceeds $45,000 for a joint return ($33,750 for single or head of household), then the AMTI is subject to tax at a rate of 26 percent on the first $175,000 and 28 percent on AMTI greater than $175,000.

The entire process is so complicated that the IRS has still not issued a publication devoted to an explanation of AMT. **But nowadays the computer does the work for them, so if you are subject to the AMT and it consists of routine add-ons that can be extracted directly from your tax return (e.g., from itemized deductions), and you fail to file Form 6251, you can be sure the IRS will recompute your tax as submitted on your 1040 and send you a bill for the difference.** (See Misconception 6, page 218.)

Form 8582 (Passive Activity Loss Limitations)

Form 8582 is another terribly complex form—10 pages of instructions—that affects hundreds of thousands of taxpayers. This form is used by people who have investments in any passive activity, such as oil and gas or real estate. The form measures available passive losses for the current year and the amount to be carried over to future years.

The process of filling out this form is a nightmare. First, data must be gathered from your current year and prior year's returns and grouped into two broad categories: "rental real estate activities with active participation" and "all other passive activities." Then activities with net income must be segregated from those with net losses.

Before reporting the information, you must first complete up to *six* preliminary work sheets preprinted by the IRS that accompany the form. Interestingly enough, the IRS does *not* require that you submit the work sheets with your return, but they must be made available if your return is subsequently examined. You see, unless the losses described on Form 8582 stem from unincorporated real estate activities that you operate yourself, much of the input for these work sheets originates from K-1's that taxpayers receive from partnership and S corporation investments. Remember that the IRS has difficulty matching this part of the K-1 to taxpayer returns.

The form determines the amount of passive losses you can deduct this year and how much has to be deferred to future years. So no matter what, if you are a passive investor, you really must go through this exercise and determine whether you are entitled to any current deductions.

Form 8586 (Low-Income Housing Credit) and Form 8582-CR (Passive Activity Credit Limitations)

Tax shelters may be a thing of the past, but investing in low-income housing increased at least 500 percent in the early 1990's and for 1999 and 2000 has again risen dramatically. Any taxpayer who owns part of a residential rental project that provides low-income housing is subject to two other complex nightmares, Form 8586 and Form 8582-CR. The investment is usually marketed through major brokerage firms, and like any other investment, it has advantages and disadvantages that should be fully researched before you invest.

Taxpayers who qualify for and choose to take the low-income housing credit will feel as if they're walking through an endless maze as they embark on the tax computation for it. Most tax credits begin with a base figure that is provided to you from the partnership as listed on Schedule K-1. To this base, you normally apply a percentage, which produces a tentative tax credit. Not in this case. As with passive-activity losses, you must first complete three preliminary work sheets to achieve the first required amount of credit.

Two stages and up to *six* more work sheets later, you arrive at the tentative current-year credit, which can be used *only* against regular income tax and not against the alternative minimum tax (AMT). Therefore if you do not plan in advance and you are subject to the AMT, you will lose part or all of the benefit of the low-income housing credit for the current year. In the end, if you add up the tax credit and cash distributions, a good investment will produce a 10 percent return on your investment. Therefore, it makes sense to fill out Forms 8586 and 8582-CR, and take a shot at the credit.

Form 8615 (Tax for Children Under Age 14 Who Have Investment Income of More Than $1,400)

The complexity of this form begins with the task of first determining if you are required to file it. (The answer is on page 231.) If you do, the plot thickens if your child has capital gain income, which mandates the use of a 54-line two-column monstrosity, part of Form 8615 called Capital

Gains Rates Tax Calculation Worksheet. Finally, if you have more than one child under 14 years old with investment income, you have to apportion the extra tax to each child by filling out up to five additional work sheets under one heading, also part of Form 8615—Net Capital Gain Worksheets.

The only plus side to complex forms such as these is this: **If you attempt to complete them, you can be confident that an IRS auditor will understand only a little more than you do.**

RULE 6. STRIVE TO BE NEAT.

I have been telling my clients for years that neat returns, especially computerized ones, are less likely to be audited than handwritten or sloppy ones. Even the IRS has gone on record stating that computerized returns are preferable and, as I see it, less likely to be selected for audit than hand-prepared returns, which often contain errors or are illegible, causing them to be selected for further review. Accordingly, a whole new industry now supplies computer software specifically designed for nonprofessional use, allowing taxpayers to produce extremely complicated schedules (e.g., passive losses).

There are several other areas where neatness and good organization can and should be applied.

When you have been asked to submit material to a tax auditor, the auditor should be handed well-organized records pertaining *only* to the matter being questioned, with an adding machine tape on the top. The more time an auditor spends on your case, the more pressure he or she is under to collect additional taxes.

Also, when submitting a diary intended to show a detailed log of your travels, be sure that the entries are as neat as possible. In most cases, where a diary is being used as evidence, adequate information contained in the diary will, for IRS purposes, support deductions for entertainment, auto expenses, airline travel, auto rentals, hotels, taxicabs, and local travel.

Records should be in perfect order for corporate audits as well. The IRS revenue agent usually reviews corporate records such as minutes, capital stock certificates, stockholder loan agreements, and related promissory notes. When the corporation has made loans, each disbursement should be covered by a separate promissory note and a set of corporate minutes of the meeting in which the loan was authorized, as well as complete details as to the rate of interest and repayment dates.

RULE 7: WHEN ALL ELSE FAILS, WRITE TO YOUR CONGRESS-PERSON.

Almost every congressperson has a contact in the IRS who is dedicated to being responsive to taxpayers. If you have been involved with an IRS issue that just isn't getting resolved, try writing to your congressperson. I have recommended this many times with good results. Typically, someone in the congressperson's office calls, followed by someone in the IRS, and in a matter of weeks the issue gets resolved.

Taking this route, however, has its pitfalls. In your first letter, you must fully document the case so that it is clear and accurate. The congressperson will forward your letter to his or her contact in the IRS.

After this the IRS will treat you strictly according to the letter of the law. The IRS is not particularly fond of this approach because it is both a pressure tactic and leaves them no way to wiggle out. However, this should get you the response you've been waiting for.

To learn the name or phone number of your member of Congress, call the U.S. Capitol switchboard: (202) 224-3121 for Senate inquiries; (202) 225-3121 for House inquiries. Tell the operator your ZIP code and she can give you the phone number of your senator or representative. Give your name, city, and state, and ask for the caseworker on staff.[3] Many representatives can be contacted via the Internet through the House of Representatives' home page at www.house.gov/ and selecting "Member Offices." To know who your representative is, go to the Write Your Representative website at www.house.gov/writerep/. By entering your state and zip code+4, you will be connected to the e-mail system of your member of Congress. You can also reach the Senate and senators from your state at www.senate.gov.

RULE 8. MAKE IT YOUR BUSINESS TO KNOW WHICH TAX LOOPHOLES APPLY TO YOUR PERSONAL TAX SITUATION.

By now you know that hundreds of loopholes in our tax laws exist. Creating a complete list of these is impossible. Tax newsletters, sent by subscription only, are full of them. Here are some loopholes that one doesn't often see elsewhere. They are arranged by general subject, and if any apply to you, take advantage of them.

You Want to Eliminate IRS Penalties

There are approximately 150 penalties that the IRS can impose on you, the most common ones being for late payment of taxes or late filing of tax returns. Before you try to get the penalties abated, complete the filing of past due returns and try to pay the amounts of tax and interest that are due. Interest charges cannot be waived. This will, it's hoped, put the IRS employee into a conciliatory frame of mind.

Although the IRS does not publicly disclose a list of acceptable reasons for lowering a taxpayer's penalties, here's the scoop on what the IRS may be moved by:

In my experience, health- and age-related reasons are accepted a majority of the time. This includes physical or emotional illness (including drug and alcohol abuse); health problems of family members, especially if you are a care provider; your advanced age; emotional problems caused by a divorce; and nonfiling or nonpayment caused by your ex-spouse, which, in turn, has prompted you to file for Innocent Spouse Relief (see page 300). Another excuse that has recently prompted the IRS to reduce a taxpayer's penalties involved a business owner who was having unusual business problems that kept him at the office an unreasonable amount of time, e.g., more than 14 hours a day, seven days a week.

Surprisingly, the IRS will not lower penalties if your tax preparer was sick, or even passed away. In this case, the IRS says you should have taken precautions to avoid late filing or late payments. Furthermore, someone with a chronically unreliable filing history would have diminished chances of having these excuses being accepted.

You're Facing Bankruptcy
According to bankruptcy law, taxpayers can file a bankruptcy petition, which must be done with the help of a professional. Although this can be expensive and complicated to execute, here's what it can do for you.

It can bring collection activities to a halt. The government cannot issue a notice of intent to levy, nor can the government seize your property and sell it for the payment of taxes.

In our current environment of easy credit, many taxpayers have been falling behind in paying their bills. Ultimately many file for personal and/or business bankruptcy. Since one of the ultimate creditors is bound to be the IRS, there are steps taxpayers can take to ease their burden if they fall on financially hard times. Even if your tax liability is insurmountable, be sure to file your return on time. In a federal bankruptcy court proceeding, filing in a timely manner could result in your tax liability being discharged in as little as three years. Even newly assessed tax liabilities, such as those caused by a tax audit, are dischargeable only 40 days after they have been assessed.

For Married Couples
If you are married, you and your spouse should file separate returns. With separate returns, each spouse is responsible only for his or her own tax liability. This allows at least one spouse to remain debt-free.

The disadvantages in this are that separate return rates are higher, and itemized deductions such as mortgage interest and real estate tax can be deducted only by the spouse who pays for them. But with a little forethought and planning, you can end up in a better place if the spouse who earns the highest income pays for these kinds of major deductions.

If you file jointly, the IRS can go after either spouse to collect any unpaid tax assessments, although relief is given to the innocent spouse if the innocent spouse can prove he or she had no knowledge or limited knowledge of the other spouse's misdeeds. (See page 300.)

YOUR TAX-SAVING STRATEGY.
Bankruptcy arrangements often result in a taxpayer selling his home to receive funds to pay off creditors. The IRS generally takes the position that the exclusion of gain from the sale of a primary residence ($250,000 for singles; $500,000 for married filing jointly) can be used only when the sale of the residence is made by the homeowner himself. However, in a recent case, a bankruptcy trustee, i.e., the person assigned by the court to handle the taxpayer's bankruptcy, sold the taxpayer's house and was allowed to claim any tax break on the home that would have been available to the homeowner. As a result of this decision, the trustee used the tax-free proceeds to pay off the taxpayer's creditors.

If you cannot pay your taxes promptly and cannot work out an installment agreement with the IRS, your IRA can be levied upon and seized. Furthermore, when the financial institution holding your IRA pays over the money to the IRS, it is considered a taxable distribution to the taxpayer and subject to a possible 10 percent early-distribution penalty if the taxpayer is under 59½ years of age. But effective January 1, 2000, the 10 percent penalty will not apply to distributions made on account of an IRS levy.

If you feel that the seizure of your IRA by the IRS is imminent, withdraw the money immediately and send in an estimated tax payment representing the income tax and penalty on the withdrawal. You then at least have control over the balance of the proceeds.

You Are Incorporated as a C Corporation and the Corporation Is Discontinued Because of Heavy Losses

A shareholder can take the loss of his capital investment on his 1040 as an ordinary loss and not as a capital loss by using Section 1244 of the *Internal Revenue Code*. On a joint return, you can deduct losses from the sale or worthlessness of Section 1244 stock up to $100,000 ($50,000 on separate returns). Any excess above the threshold is a capital loss. This provision is limited to companies whose original capitalization is under $1 million and covers only regular operating businesses, not tax shelters or real estate. NOTE: There are no disadvantages to using this provision. If your business does well, Section 1244 will be forgotten.

You Are Disposing of Your Entire Interest in a Passive Activity

Any taxpayer in this situation has a wonderful opportunity to take advantage of one of the few possibilities for double tax benefits. To begin with, both current and deferred losses come to the surface and the accumulated losses wipe out any gain you are recognizing on the disposition of the investment. Then the balance of unused losses can be used to offset other nonpassive income such as salaries and interest income. If the gain on the disposition is higher than the accumulated losses, you can use passive losses allocated to other activities to reduce the gain even further, until you reach zero gain. Therefore, if you fully dispose of a passive investment, make sure you deduct all the losses that you are entitled to.

The next part comes into play if the gain on the disposition is a capital gain. If this is so, the gain is both capital gain and passive income at the same time. This entitles you to further benefits. Not only can you take passive losses to offset the passive income, but if you have unused capital losses (because of the $3,000 annual limitation), you can offset these capital losses dollar for dollar against the capital gain as well. For example, if you have a capital gain of $25,000 recognized upon sale of a passive activity, $25,000 in passive losses will be allowed to offset the gain. Because the character of the income is capital gain, up to $28,000 in capital losses, if available, can also be deducted currently.

You Are Drawing Salaries from Two or More Corporations Under One Roof

This situation is referred to as a *common paymaster* because although the corporations may be involved in different businesses, all payrolls are derived from the same source and are usually paid by the same accounting department. Identical ownership of the companies is not mandatory. One company must own 50 percent or more of the other, *or* you need to be sharing only 50 percent of officers *or* 30 percent of employees. The taxpayer can take advantage of the little-known common paymaster rule, the privilege of withholding FICA taxes from one salary only.

The general rule for FICA tax is that 6.2 percent of the first $76,200 of salary is withheld for the Social Security portion of the tax, and 1.45 percent of all salary, no limit, is withheld for Medicare. The corporation must match these withheld amounts and remit the total to the IRS. The common paymaster rule cannot be used to avoid reaching the maximum FICA tax, but it can be used to avoid the payment of a double FICA tax. Here's how this works:

Mr. Jones receives annual salaries of $175,000 from ABC Corporation and $150,000 from DEF Corporation. He owns 100 percent of both corporations. Both salaries are paid from the same office location by the same bookkeeper. Using conventional withholding tax rules, the bookkeeper is obligated to withhold 6.2 percent of the first $76,200 from *each* salary ($4,724.40 × 2, or $9,448.80), *and* Medicare tax of 1.45 percent of both salaries—1.45 percent of $325,000, or $4,712.50. The bookkeeper then matches the total of $14,161.30 and remits $28,322.60 to the IRS ratably over the year as the salaries are paid.

When the common paymaster rule is used, ABC Corporation pays the entire $325,000 to Mr. Jones and withholds from his salary the same 6.2 percent of $76,200 or $4,724.40 for just one salary, and 1.45 percent of $325,000 ($4,712.50), a total of $9,436.90. The bookkeeper matches this total and remits $18,873.80 to the IRS. Thus, the common paymaster method produces a savings of $9,448.80 ($28,322.60 − $18,873.80).

DEF Corporation reimburses ABC Corporation for its share of Mr. Jones's salary and all taxes. In the end, DEF Corporation receives an immediate saving of $4,724.40, representing the employer's share of the FICA tax. And Mr. Jones has avoided the double withholding of FICA tax in the amount of $9,448.80.

YOUR TAX-SAVING STRATEGY.
Assuming that you otherwise qualify, choose one company among your group of corporations to be the "common paymaster," and assign it the responsibility for handling all payroll.

You Operate as a Sole Proprietorship or S Corporation and You Want to Hire Your Dependent Child

The major advantage to hiring your dependent child (under 18 years of age) to work in your sole proprietorship is that you don't have to pay FICA and Medicare taxes. (Of course the salary must be paid for actual services rendered.) Remember that the first $4,400 of wages paid is not subject to income tax because that is the standard deduction for single taxpayers. As of 2000, the next $26,250 is taxed at 15 percent.

You and your child can save some additional money if he or she contributes $2,000 to a traditional IRA—for example, to save for college. (Even though taxes and a penalty would have to be paid when the money is withdrawn early—before your child reaches retirement age— the benefit of the current deduction still makes it worthwhile.) Assuming the child's taxable income is not more than $26,250, you will be able to save about $300 on federal taxes, because no tax will have to be paid on the $2,000 in the IRA. You can also put $500 annually into an Education IRA. (See pages 279–280.) Or a Roth IRA may be a better solution. (See pages 284–286.)

This discussion concerns wages, or earned income, of a dependent. Don't confuse this scenario with the "kiddie tax," which is a tax on the investment income (interest and dividends) of children under age 14 and is based on the parents' tax rates. (See page 264.)

If you pay wages to your children from an S corporation, you must pay FICA and Medicare taxes, because all corporate wages are subject to these taxes. But there is another advantage with an S corporation: You can reduce your tax bill by splitting income with other members of your family. This is accomplished by allowing each family member to own stock in the corporation. Each person reports his or her share of income on the 1040, including children who will probably be in the lowest tax bracket.

Warning: This arrangement works best with children over 14 years of age, who are not subject to the "kiddie tax."

Warning: In this situation, parents/owners cannot take an unreasonably low salary to reduce personal taxable income because if this is discovered during an audit, the IRS can reallocate income among family members.

You Operate as a Sole Proprietorship or Partnership and You Want to Choose the Best Pension Plan

People in this situation who have few or no employees might want to forget about the more cumbersome profit-sharing or Keogh pension plans and take a good, hard look at a Simplified Employee Pension (SEP) plan. The advantages are numerous:

- To set up a plan, you need to fill out only a one-page form.
- No additional reports or annual tax returns need to be filed.
- Setup of the plan can be done *and* deductible contributors can be made up until the extended due date of your return, e.g., October 15, 2001. Most other plans have to be in place by year's end.
- You can skip a contribution altogether if you have a bad year.

- In 2000 you can contribute up to approximately 10 percent of self-employed earnings, but not more than $25,500.
- Even though you have a SEP, you can still contribute another $2,000 to a traditional or Roth IRA if you qualify.

Disadvantages: If you have employees, you'll have to contribute the same percentage of their pay that you do for yourself. Also, if your earnings are under $50,000, you will probably achieve a higher deduction by setting up a SIMPLE pension plan (see page 290).[4]

You Want to Lease an Automobile for
Business Purposes Instead of Buying One
Over the years the IRS has set up special tables for the annual depreciation of an auto used for business. In 2000, an automobile costing more than $15,500 is considered to be a "luxury car." For luxury cars "placed in service" in 2000 (any automobile used for business purposes), you can take maximum depreciation of $3,060 for the first year, $4,900 for the second year, $2,950 for the third year, and $1,775 for each succeeding year. These dollar caps are applicable if the automobile is used 100 percent for business.

If you lease a luxury car that has a fair market value in excess of $15,500, you are required to include in your W-2 income an amount specified for that market value. You can find these values in IRS Publication 463, or call 1-800-TAX-FORM, or go to the IRS website at www.irs.gov. Theoretically this additional W-2 income treats leased autos the same as purchased autos for tax purposes. **In actual practice, though, you obtain a much greater tax savings when you lease an auto, especially if the lease is for at least four years.** For example, if you leased a car in 2000 valued at $27,000 for four years at a rate of $400 per month, over four years you'd pay a total of $19,200. According to the IRS's "leasing inclusion table," assuming the car could be claimed as 100 percent business use, you would have to add back to your income $965 over the four-year period. Therefore, your net tax deduction for the four years is $18,235.

If instead you purchased the car for $27,000, your monthly payments would be considerably higher and the depreciation deductions on your business tax return would be only $12,685. The extra write-off ($18,235 − $12,685) is $5,550, and if you are in the 31 percent tax bracket, this is a tax savings of $1,720.50.

One downside to leasing is that if you put on high mileage, you will have to pay a hefty 10 to 20 cents per mile for excess mileage over the typically allowable 15,000 miles per year. On the other hand, buying a high-priced car usually requires a substantial down payment while leasing requires only a deposit equal to one or two monthly payments. Also, a leased car cannot be taken by creditors, whereas an owned car can. If you buy a new car, you can probably use it for seven or eight years, but the paramount advantage of leasing is that you get the luxury of driving a new car every four years, along with a substantial business lease deduction that is more advantageous than if you bought a vehicle.

If the auto is used 100 percent for personal use, leasing and buying end up costing about the same, assuming you sell the auto just after you finish paying the last installment. But if you keep the personal-use auto for a long time, leasing is more expensive. Also, if you drive a luxury vehicle such as a sports car, those vehicles often depreciate very quickly in the first few years, which means a purchase would make more economic sense.

You Want to Lease a Sport Utility Vehicle

Cars weighing more than 6,000 pounds are not considered to be "luxury cars." Some sport utility vehicles and some Mercedes, Lexus, and Cadillac models exceed that weight limit. Therefore full depreciation is allowed as follows:

Year 1	20	percent	Year 4	11.52 percent
Year 2	32	percent	Year 5	11.52 percent
Year 3	19.20	percent	Year 6	5.76 percent

Like most other business equipment, a heavy luxury business car is also eligible for additional first-year depreciation—Section 179 depreciation—in addition to the regular depreciation. For 2000, the allowable amount is $20,000. Accordingly, the depreciation deductions for heavy luxury business cars can be enormous in the first few years. For example, if you bought a new luxury car for $30,000, you take a write-off of $26,000 on your business tax return in the first year.

You Want to Trade in a Car Used for Business Purposes

When an old car that has been used for business purposes is traded in for a new business car, no gain or loss is recognized. The basis of the old car (generally cost less accumulated depreciation) is added to the net cost of the new car, and a new depreciation period begins. This can produce positive results if you would have ended up with a gain on the sale of the old car, since no gain will be recognized for tax purposes until the vehicle is sold. But if your old car was expensive and its sale would re-sult in a recognized tax loss if sold outright, what you can do is sell the car for cash and buy a new car with the proceeds. In that way, you will have a deductible business loss that you can use on this year's return.

If the car costs $15,500 or less, it can be depreciated using the regu-lar depreciation rates listed above, and you can take Section 179 depre-ciation. If you are leasing, there is no amount to be included in your W-2 income. See IRS Publication 463, *Travel, Entertainment, Gift, and Car Expenses*. If the car weighs 6,000 pounds or less, the vehicle is sub-ject to "luxury car" rules, if applicable.

RULE 9. USE TO YOUR ADVANTAGE THE FACT THAT THE IRS SYS-TEM FOR DOCUMENT RETRIEVAL IS ARCHAIC.

Given what you already know about the massive failure of the IRS's Tax Modernization System, if should be no surprise that the IRS still faces grave problems when it comes to retrieving tax returns.

The negative implications of these problems continue to be far-reaching. **Hundreds of thousands of individual taxpayers, as well as IRS staffs from Examination, Collection, and CID who work directly with taxpayers, are all stymied by the situation.** But prob-ably the most visible person who has to deal with this embarrassing mess, aside from the taxpayer and the taxpayer's representative, is the IRS auditor who is preparing for an audit, or who is in the midst of one. Not being able to locate a specific tax return consistently affects an au-ditor's role, behavior, and performance.

Mrs. Raymond hired me as her accountant in 1994 and asked whether I could assist her in obtaining a home equity loan. This was not an easy task, since the IRS had placed a lien on her house and I have not yet come across a mortgage lender who will provide a borrower with any funds if the IRS has a lien on that person's property.

I discovered that the IRS had disallowed a tax shelter deduction from Mrs. Raymond's 1985 tax return. After the tax was assessed, the IRS filed the lien in October 1990.

Further investigation made me increasingly suspicious. Each time I phoned the IRS, all I got were indirect answers. I also wondered why the IRS had not sent Mrs. Raymond even one collection letter during the past three years. I did find out that the tax Mrs. Raymond owed, including penalties and interest, amounted to over $100,000.

I finally reached an auditor at the IRS office in Mrs. Raymond's hometown who had been assigned to the case and who admitted to me that Mrs. Ray-mond's entire file had been lost! He had turned the situation over to his super-visor because it was "too hot to handle." The supervisor delayed for another three months while he insisted on a thorough search of the storage warehouse where Mrs. Raymond's file might have been sent in error—a warehouse in Passaic, New Jersey.

When the search proved fruitless, the supervisor would not take the responsibility of excusing a $100,000 case simply because a file had been misplaced. He forwarded the case to the regional Problem Resolution Office (PRO), obviously hoping for a miracle. Nothing was solved, but at least the matter was out of his hands.

Everyone I dealt with at the IRS tried to hide this information trail from me as long as they could.

After only 30 days—PRO is the most efficient unit in the entire IRS—a credit was put through for the entire $100,000. A short while later, Mrs. Raymond's equity loan cleared.

Auditors *like* to have some independent corroboration of items of income so they can verify what the taxpayer has previously included on the tax return being examined. After all, they are trained to look for information that may be missing, altered, or omitted intentionally, and part of their job is *not* to accept automatically what the taxpayer or the taxpayer's representative is handing over.

But any IRS auditor knows that when a request for a copy of a tax return is made, the return may not be received until *after* the audit is completed, or too late in the audit process for it to be useful.

A successful self-employed sales rep, Mr. Joseph, was being audited for 1996. His business operations were filed on Form 1040, Schedule C, and an 1120S (Income Tax Return for an S Corporation), since he also owned part of an S corporation in a separate business.

During the audit, the agent requested copies of Mr. Joseph's 1040's for 1995 and 1997 and the 1120S's for 1995 and 1996. I gave the auditor Mr. Joseph's 1040 for 1997 and the 1120S for 1996 (which was the final return filed for this corporation), and said we didn't have copies of the 1040 or 1120S for 1995. The returns were destroyed in a flood that Mr. Joseph had at his former office. The auditor naturally said he'd try to retrieve them from the IRS system.

Expecting that the IRS would take a minimum of 45 days to get the copies, if they ever got them, I made my next and final date with the auditor less than 30 days later. At that meeting, the auditor still had not received the requested tax returns, so he proceeded with the audit, disallowing $9,500 of items on Mr. Joseph's Schedule C business return (specifically insurance and entertainment), and then closed the case. If the missing returns contained any information that could have been damaging to Mr. Joseph, the IRS will never know.

How to Take Advantage of the IRS's Ancient Retrieval System

The implications of this situation for taxpayers are particularly important if you are facing or involved in an audit. *Take your time* locating a copy of an earlier return if you think that a prior return will

- Contradict any information on the return being audited.
- Provide reasons for the auditor to examine additional areas for which you have less than adequate proof.

You are playing for time here, because time is most likely on your side, as we just discussed. For example, you may know that something on a past or current return will show up as an inconsistency—a K-1 from a rental property that no longer appears, or dividend income on an investment for which the dividend is no longer reported *and* there is no reported sale of the investment. There may be adequate explanations for these inconsistencies, but you should conclude the audit as soon as possible *before* the auditor receives the requested information from the IRS.

RULE 10. IF YOU ARE INVOLVED WITH IRS PERSONNEL IN ANY WAY, BEHAVE DECENTLY.

When dealing with revenue officers in particular, do not make them angry by complaining about the IRS in general terms, by treating them rudely, lying to them, or insisting that you're being treated unfairly. If you do, they will be more prone to use their arsenal of weapons—liens, levies, seizures, and sales of property—in an arbitrary and capricious manner.

If you receive any correspondence from the IRS, answer it promptly. If you have received a notice of tax due and you do not agree with it, or if you know for a fact that the IRS is wrong, do not disregard the notice or the IRS. Send a letter to the IRS with the notice explaining why you feel the tax is incorrect. If you can't pay the tax, send in a token payment and say that more money will be coming shortly.

This way you are appealing to the human side of the person who reads your response. You can appease that person for a while as long as he or she does not think that you are a renegade. You also have ample opportunity to restate your case to his or her supervisor or to an appeals officer, if you choose.

This is the perfect place for me to reinforce one of the major themes of this book: learning about the IRS personality. Don't forget, with an IRS auditor you're usually dealing with a civil service employee who is just trying to get through the day without making waves. Most often, these IRS staff members are not ambitious enough to go through the extra effort required to make life miserable for you. But if you anger them with a poor attitude, they will probably try harder to get the added proof needed to show that you are not telling the truth.

12

—

New Tax Legislation—
What to Watch Out For, How to Benefit

1997 TAX LEGISLATION

The biggest federal tax cut in 16 years, the Taxpayer Relief Act of 1997 has been hailed as a tribute to bipartisanship between a Democratic president and a Republican Congress. It was an eleventh-hour measure (signed only days before Congress was to recess for August) to balance the budget, reduce the deficit, and secure a favorable political platform. Here's what the bill does for the average taxpayer.

The sections of the law with the greatest significance to taxpayers are devoted to the Child Tax Credit and tax incentives for education, pension and retirement, home sale, estates and gifts, and small businesses. These areas are discussed below; other existing tax situations affected by these new laws are updated throughout the book.

Child Tax Credit

Beginning January 1, 1998, a parent can take a $400 nonrefundable tax credit for each qualifying child under the age of 17 ($500 for taxable year 1999 and beyond). A child qualifies if the taxpayer can claim a dependency exemption for that person and he or she is a son or daughter, stepson or stepdaughter, or a foster child. The credit begins to phase out at AGI of $110,000 for married taxpayers filing joint returns. For taxpayers filing single or head of household, the threshold is $75,000. For married taxpayers filing separate returns, the threshold is $55,000. Any unused Child Tax Credit cannot be carried forward to future years.

If you exceed the AGI thresholds, determining partial credit is a nightmare without a computer program.

The IRS has issued "IRS helps taxpayers with child tax credit claims," available on the IRS website, www.irs.gov.

Education Tax Incentives

One of the features of the 1997 legislation was in the area of education, specifically a range of tax relief in the form of credits and educational savings accounts modeled after IRA's. These are provided for students and their families from the first year of college onward, making higher education somewhat more affordable. There are also opportunities for self-employed taxpayers and employees who want to take courses to improve job skills or simply to learn more about their job or occupation.

HOPE Scholarship Credit

A nonrefundable HOPE Scholarship tax credit can be taken beginning January 1, 1998, against federal income taxes for qualified tuition and related expenses for a taxpayer, a spouse, and any dependents up to $1,500 for each of the first two years of college if the student attends on at least a half-time basis. The $1,500 credit can be taken as follows: 100 percent of the first $1,000 of tuition and fees required for enrollment or attendance, or $1,000, and 50 percent of the next $1,000, or $500 paid for each of the first two years. These credits can be taken by families with AGI up to $80,000 a year and are gradually phased out for families with AGI up to $100,000 ($40,000 to $50,000 for single filers). After the year 2001, the HOPE credit will be indexed for inflation. Any unused HOPE credit cannot be carried forward to future years.

YOUR TAX-SAVING STRATEGY.
The HOPE credit is computed on a per-student basis, i.e., a separate credit is allowed for each eligible student in a taxpayer's family.

Lifetime Learning Credit

Individuals are allowed to claim a nonrefundable Lifetime Learning Credit (LLC) against federal income taxes equal to 20 percent of up to $5,000, i.e., $1,000, of qualified tuition and fees paid during the taxable year on behalf of the taxpayer, the taxpayer's spouse, or any dependent ($10,000 for tax years beginning after 2002, or up to a maximum credit *per taxpayer return* of $2,000). In other words, the LLC does not vary based on the number of students in the taxpayer's family. The student can be enrolled in an undergraduate or graduate degree program on at least a half-time basis, or take courses at an eligible institution to acquire or improve job skills even if enrolled on a less-than-half-time basis.

The credit is phased out according to the same income ranges that apply to the HOPE credit, but, in contrast to the HOPE credit, the Lifetime Learning Credit may be claimed for an unlimited number of taxable years. Any unused LLC cannot be carried forward to future years.

The Lifetime Learning Credit is available for expenses paid for education furnished in academic periods beginning after June 30, 1998.

YOUR TAX-SAVING STRATEGY.

Taxpayers who have more than one student in college should elect the HOPE credit over the Lifetime Learning Credit. Furthermore, until 2003 taxpayers can maximize the tax credits they can take for education on their tax return by electing the HOPE credit for the first two years of a student's college education and the Lifetime Learning Credit thereafter. As you can see, each family has to spend some time to determine which credit benefits it the most.

NOTE: Beginning January 1, 1998, there are two forms you will need to use to apply for the Child Tax Credit, the HOPE Scholarship, and the Lifetime Learning Credit. These are Form 8812 for the Child Tax Credit and Form 8863 for the other two. See IRS Publication 970, *Tax Benefits for Higher Education*, for more details about these credits and other tax benefits for taxpayers who paid higher education costs.

Education IRA

Beginning January 1, 1998, a new IRA allows parents to shelter earnings on college savings. The Education IRA has been created exclusively for the purpose of saving tax-free dollars that will eventually be used toward a child's higher education expenses. Parents will be able to contribute $500 per child annually until each child reaches the age of 18. The deduction is phased out at certain AGI levels—between $150,000 and $160,000 for couples filing jointly, and $95,000 and $110,000 for other filers. If your AGI exceeds the threshholds, gift the $500 to another family member, such as a grandparent, who can then make the deposit. No contribution can be made in any year that the beneficiary is receiving contributions from a qualified state tuition program.

Education IRA contributions are not tax-deductible, but accumulated earnings are tax-free; so are withdrawals if the money is used for undergraduate- or graduate-level room, board, books, or tuition. If the beneficiary doesn't attend college, or a remainder of the earnings is left, the money must be withdrawn, generally subject to a tax and a 10 percent penalty, within 30 days after the child turns 30. However, *before* the beneficiary reaches 30, the account balance can be rolled over or transferred tax-free to another Education IRA for another member of the family who is under 30 years old.

NOTE: Unlike contributions to other IRA's, which can be made up until April 15 of the following year, contributions to an Education IRA must be completed by December 31. Furthermore, in the year in which you exclude from your income a distribution from an Education IRA to pay education expenses, no HOPE Scholarship credit, LLC, or any business-related education deduction is allowed.

Deductions for Interest on Student Loans

For interest due and paid on qualified education loans beginning January 1, 1998, individuals may claim a deduction up to a maximum of $2,500 per year. The maximum deduction is phased in over four years with a $1,000 maximum deduction in 1998, $1,500 in 1999, $2,000 in 2000, and $2,500 in 2001 and thereafter. The deduction is phased out at certain AGI levels—between $60,000 and $75,000 for couples filing jointly and between $40,000 and $55,000 for other filers. A deduction cannot be taken if you are a dependent of another taxpayer or if your filing status is married filing separately.

The deduction is allowed only for interest paid on a qualified education loan during the first 60 months in which interest payments are required (which may not begin until after a student graduates from a four-year program). The deduction is allowed whether or not the taxpayer itemizes other deductions on Schedule A, Form 1040. Expenses paid with the loan proceeds generally include tuition, fees, room and board, and related expenses. The indebtedness must be incurred exclusively to pay for higher education expenses, and the student must be enrolled at least half-time.

One option to maximize the new education benefits is to take the HOPE credit for the first two years, the Lifetime Learning Credit for the next two years, followed by the student loan interest deduction for the next five years.

If you take the HOPE Scholarship or Lifetime Learning Credit, that amount must be reduced by certain other tax-free educational benefits you may also receive, such as scholarships, fellowships, and any employer-provided educational assistance. In other words, cheating the government by taking double tax benefits simultaneously is a no-no.

Parents who take out a student loan to pay education expenses are entitled to the interest deduction. However, if your AGI exceeds $75,000, here's a better plan: If possible, use the proceeds of a home equity loan for the education expenses. This will provide you with a full mortgage interest deduction on Schedule A (1040).

Qualified State Tuition Programs (QSTP)

To save for a family member's college education, you can participate in a qualified state tuition program. This has been around for years and although the plans are administered by the states, not the federal government, it has expanded greatly since the federal rules were spelled out in 1996. This is how it works: You can contribute to two types of state plans and make cash contributions to an account for a designated beneficiary that are earmarked to cover that person's costs of higher education. When the student begins postsecondary education, you can take distributions from the account to cover the qualified education expenses. Almost all the states now offer tax-favored tuition savings plans, although program features vary considerably. All plans fall into one of two categories: prepaid tuition plans or savings plans.

- *Prepaid tuition plan.* A state-operated trust offers residents a hedge against tuition inflation by agreeing to pay future tuition at a public university or college pegged to current tuition levels. The state's contractual promises may or may not be guaranteed.
- *College savings plan.* Here, the basic idea is that contributions will grow over time in a state-sponsored mutual fund, hopefully keeping pace with rising tuition costs. Since this is not guaranteed, there is the possibility that there will be a shortfall when college time rolls around. Most new QSTP's are savings plans because they are more flexible than prepaid tuition plans and have upside potential from its investments in the stock market.

Several states have plans that are open to both residents and nonresidents, and in some states the student can attend college anywhere in the world. There are no income restrictions to these plans for the donor; contributions can be made by parents, grandparents, or anyone else. Some states have maximum limits on total contributions, but they are generous, well over $100,000 per student in several states. Many states allow a current deduction for state income tax purposes for part of the contributions; earnings only (not principal) are taxed at the federal level when withdrawals are made and are taxed to the student, not to the parent/owner, and some states exempt the amounts from state income tax. Balances are transferable to another child in the family, but if you withdraw the money for other uses, you will be subject to taxes, penalties, and withdrawal fees.

If someone in your family plans to attend college, check this out so you can start saving now. For further information, visit the College Savings Plans Network website at www.collegesavings.org or www. savingforcollege.com.

Employer Educational Assistance Exclusion

The educational assistance exclusion is available to employees who receive reimbursements from their employers for undergraduate education costs, including tuition, fees, books, and related costs. Up to $5,250 per year can be deducted on the employer's business return yet is not taxable income to the employee. This is a substantial tax-free benefit for the estimated 800,000 people who receive educational assistance from their employers. Interestingly, shareholders of an S corporation who own 2 percent or more of the corporation are generally subject to income tax on fringe benefits, but they can receive educational assistance tax-free.

The current extension of this law is good for all expenses paid by an employer for courses that begin no later than December 31, 2001.

Educational Business Expenses

If your employer does not have an educational assistance exclusion plan, you have two remaining choices if you are taking a business-related course:

Take the Lifetime Learning Credit (LLC), which is available even if you enroll on a less-than-half-time basis, or, as under prior law, take a miscellaneous itemized deduction on Schedule A (1040). Remember, if you choose the latter, you must first reduce the total of your miscellaneous deductions by 2 percent of your AGI.

If you are self-employed, you would take your deduction on Schedule C and it would be fully deductible. To be eligible for either of these deductions, the expenses must be used to maintain or improve your skills in your current line of business or be required to maintain your job status. Both the HOPE credit and interest on student loans would normally not be available for business purposes because of the requirement that attendance be on at least a half-time basis.

Here is a possible sequence of educational benefits to consider. Of all the programs, the *best* is the employer educational assistance because nothing beats a course you can take for free. For the self-employed, unless the HOPE credit is available, which is unlikely, a deduction on Schedule C would provide the greatest benefit, since self-employment tax as well as federal and state taxable income is reduced. Next in line, for those who can take a *full* itemized deduction on Schedule A, the benefit is greater than taking the LLC because the LLC is limited to 20 percent of $5,000 of educational expenses, or $1,000, while the Schedule A deduction has no upper limit for expenses. Just as significant is that if this itemized deduction reduces income subject to a 28 percent or higher rate, the *minimum* savings would be 28 percent of $5,000, or $1,400, which is $400 more than the LLC.

Penalty-Free Withdrawals from Traditional IRA's for Higher Education Expenses
In addition to the educational incentives just described, TRA '97 has given the traditional IRA a new look. Beginning January 1, 1998, taxpayers can withdraw money penalty-free from an existing IRA if the money is to be used for higher education expenses (including graduate-level) for a taxpayer, a spouse, or any child or grandchild. (See also Roth IRA, page 284.) A child does not have to live with you or qualify as your dependent for you to receive the tax break.

YOUR TAX-SAVING STRATEGY.
Penalty-free educational distributions are *not* allowed to be taken from a qualified retirement plan. So you might want to consider transferring funds to an IRA and then making a penalty-free education distribution.

Pension and Retirement Incentives

Individual Retirement Accounts (IRA's)— Allowing Full IRA Deduction for Nonworking Spouses
The maximum amount allowable for an IRA contribution for a spouse who did not work outside the home had been $250.00. Legislation passed in 1996 raised that maximum to $2,000, which made the contribution equal to that of the spouse who works outside the home. Now, a broader range of choices are available because of the Taxpayer Relief Act of 1997.

It was especially difficult for active participants in employer-sponsored retirement plans to make tax-deductible contributions to IRA's. The active participation of one spouse in an employer-sponsored plan triggered possible limitations on IRA deductions for both spouses if certain AGI limits were exceeded, i.e., the deduction was phased out for married taxpayers with a joint income of $40,000 to $50,000 and $25,000 to $35,000 for singles and heads of households.

Beginning January 1, 1998, these AGI ranges are increased to $51,000 to $61,000 for married couples ($52,000 to $62,000 in 2000) and $31,000 to $41,000 for single and head-of-household taxpayers ($32,000 to $42,000 in 2000). Furthermore, these limits are increased each year until they are double the present limits—i.e., until the phase-out range is $80,000 to $100,000 for married taxpayers and $50,000 to $60,000 for single taxpayers.

Even if the other spouse participates in a retirement plan at work, the new law allows a working spouse not participating in a retirement plan, or a nonworking spouse, to contribute a fully deductible $2,000 to a traditional IRA. This is subject to phase-out at a joint AGI level of between $150,000 and $160,000, far greater than previous levels.

This obviously represents significant changes to the old law. The previous income limits were in place for more than 10 years without allowing indexing for inflation, and lawmakers seemed not to consider the severity of limiting contributions when only one spouse was a member of a pension plan.

Roth IRA

The Roth IRA is new for 1998, and aims to shelter earnings from federal taxes. In a sense it is the "opposite" of the traditional IRA. In the latter, investors deduct annual IRA contributions from their taxable income, and the taxes on IRA earnings are deferred. When the money is withdrawn, generally after age 59½, taxes are paid at the ordinary income tax rates. However, with the Roth IRA, investors are not given an upfront deduction, but *all* earnings from contributions made are exempt from federal taxes—with some exceptions. The earnings can be withdrawn after a five-year period beginning with the first tax year in which a contribution was made. A subsequent conversion from a traditional IRA will not start the running of a new five-year period. In general, qualified distributions include any money taken after age 59½, upon death or disability, for purchasing a first home up to a lifetime limit of $10,000, and to pay for college expenses.

There is a full deduction for AGI's under $150,000 for joint filers and $95,000 for singles. The phaseout range for joint filers is from $150,000 to $160,000 and from $95,000 to $110,000 for singles.

The Roth IRA is a boon to middle-income and upper-income taxpayers who thus far have been unable to make deductible IRA contributions because they participate in a company retirement plan and have income above certain levels. The Roth IRA also gives married couples earning less than $160,000 and individual taxpayers with incomes below $110,000 the chance to invest $2,000 a year in stock funds or other investments and avoid all federal tax as long as the money is used as directed.

The biggest benefits are

- People who earned too much to qualify for deductible IRA's can now qualify for a Roth IRA.
- Tax benefits remain intact in later years even if the holder's income rises way above contribution limits.
- There are no requirements, as with a deductible IRA, for distributions to begin at age 70½.
- Although you pay regular income tax when you roll over money from an existing IRA into a Roth IRA, you escape the 10 percent tax imposed on withdrawals before 59½. (Rollovers are allowed only for taxpayers with an AGI below $100,000, either single or married.) The taxable portion of the conversion is not taken into account when calculating the $100,000 AGI limit. Whether it is a one-year rollover or a four-year conversion, initiated in 1998, any rollover to a Roth IRA raises your income tax bill because you will be incurring taxes on existing IRA balances. But you have choices for how to minimize paying taxes on the additional income resulting from the rollover. You could transfer just enough each year so that you do not push yourself into a higher tax bracket. The lower your other taxable income is for a given year, the more you can transfer without jumping into a higher tax bracket. Or, you can increase your withholding from wages or estimated taxes to cover the shortfalls. (See page 227.)

If in 1998 you chose to spread the rollover amount over a period of four years and you withdraw any of the converted dollars before year 2001, you will have to include this "accelerated distribution" in your income immediately. It will also generally be subject to a 10 percent early withdrawal tax. (A surviving spouse who is the sole beneficiary of the Roth IRA may elect to continue the four-year deferral period.) Also, if you make a conversion from a traditional IRA into a Roth and then discover you made some sort of mistake, e.g., your AGI was too high to allow the conversion, you may correct the error without penalty. Here's how: You arrange for the contribution and any earnings on the contribution to be transferred to another IRA via a trustee-to-trustee transfer (see page 30) by the due date of your return for the year of the contribution (including extensions). If you decide to change your mind about the way you filed a Roth IRA, you have until October 16, 2000, to file an amended return for 1999, and until October 15, 2001, to file an amended return for 2000.

NOTE: The most anyone can contribute to any type of IRA remains $2,000 a year, plus another $500 per child for the Education IRA. The new option to pull out money early for education and first-home buying without penalty applies to all retirement IRA's.

When you make withdrawals from a Roth IRA, the first money withdrawn is considered to come from annual contributions, which will be free of tax and penalties. The next will be considered converted amounts, which are generally free of tax and penalties, and finally, you'll tap earnings that may be subject to tax and penalties if they are taken before you reach 59½.

How do you decide which IRA is for you? It may appear that a tax-free growth in the future can be more valuable than getting a tax deduction today and withdrawing money at a later date at ordinary income tax rates. But the determining factor is the tax bracket you are in. If you expect to be in a lower tax bracket in retirement, it probably makes better sense to take the deduction now using a traditional IRA, because you will get more of a tax break. If your desire is to lower your tax bite, the deductible IRA is also preferable, since you can take the tax write-off reducing the cost of funding the account.

Changing When to Begin Withdrawals from Tax-Deferred Retirement Accounts

Prior to 1997, anyone participating in a qualified tax-deferred retirement plan had to begin to withdraw the money by age 70½. Under new legislation, you can begin to withdraw the money at that age or you can keep your money in the account as long as you're employed, i.e., until you retire. This change does *not* apply to distributions from traditional IRA's. The only exception is for someone who is at least a 5 percent owner of the company, in which case the money must begin to be distributed no later than April 1 of the calendar year following the year in which that person reaches age 70½.

This is clearly a boon for those tens of thousands still earning salaries who don't need their pension money. Now their money can remain untouched, tax-deferred, and growing.

NOTE: If you have already elected to begin taking pension money and want to take advantage of the new law, your pension plan will be permitted to stop your distributions until required to do otherwise. Some good advice that anyone can give regarding this new law is to immediately start making careful plans about how you want to take and manage the money.

IRA Beneficiaries

Do not take for granted that the financial institution that holds your IRA also holds your beneficiary designations. Because there has been such a large number of bank and brokerage mergers over the years, many beneficiary forms have been misplaced or lost completely. So you must keep a copy of all IRA beneficiary designations with your other important papers.

If the form cannot be found and you were not yet receiving distributions, your estate will receive the proceeds and be required to pay out the entire amount within a relatively short five years. This is why you should never name your estate as any kind of beneficiary. Even worse, if distributions had already begun, the entire IRA would have to be paid out by December 31 of the year following the taxpayer's death.

If there have been changes in your family circumstances, such as the birth of children, marriage, divorce, or a death, you may want to change beneficiary selections. When making these changes, other pitfalls arise if you name minor children, or multiple or contingent beneficiaries. It is important to seek professional help with your IRA's especially regarding this issue.

Offering Penalty-Free Withdrawals from IRA's for Medical Expenses and Medical Insurance

Under the new law, a taxpayer can take early distributions from an IRA without the previous 10 percent penalty as long as the distributions are for medical expenses that exceed 7.5 percent of the taxpayer's adjusted gross income and are used for the taxpayer, the taxpayer's spouse, or dependents. Among other things, the money can be used to hire a nurse, to pay for prescription drugs, and even to purchase eyeglasses, hearing aids, and dentures. These penalty-free withdrawals are available beginning in 1997.

NOTE: The amount withdrawn will be subject to income tax that can be offset by taking a corresponding medical expense deduction if it is itemized on Schedule A (Itemized Deductions).

Early distributions can also be made from IRA's penalty-free to pay for medical insurance for the taxpayer, the taxpayer's spouse, or dependents *without regard to the 7.5 percent minimum of adjusted gross income* if the individual has received federal or state unemployment compensation for at least 12 weeks, and the withdrawal is made in the year the unemployment compensation is received or in the following year. Although self-employed taxpayers generally do not receive umemployment benefits, they do qualify for this penalty-free tax break. All those who qualify continue to withdraw from their IRA's to pay for health insurance for up to 60 days after they find a new job. (Also see page 220.)

Setting Up Tax-Favored Medical Savings Accounts

An interesting pilot program running from 1997 to 2002 has made a limited number of self-employed people, and those covered by a small employer's high-deductible or catastrophic health plan, eligible for a medical savings account (MSA). A small employer is defined as having no more than 50 employees. Under the program, taxpayers are allowed to make tax-deductible contributions, with certain restrictions, to an MSA if they satisfy various requirements. Taxpayers with other health insurance plans generally won't be able to establish an MSA. This rule does not apply to plans that provide coverage for specific items such as worker's compensation benefits, dental, vision, long-term care, etc.

Contributions to an MSA for employees are tax-deductible, tax-free, and not subject to payroll tax withholding as long as they are made by the taxpayer's employer and the amount does not exceed the individual's compensation. In the case of the self-employed, contributions are deductible from adjusted gross income, they are not subject to any percentage of income limitations, and they cannot exceed that person's earned income. Earnings on contributions for both employees and the self-employed are tax-free, and amounts could be withdrawn tax- and penalty-free if used for specified medical purposes. The maximum annual contribution is 65 percent of the deductible for individuals and 75 percent of the deductible for families. At the time of the contribution, self-employed individuals must be under age 65.

Here's how this works: The qualified consumer elects the MSA as a health insurance plan with an insurance company that carries a high deductible, between $1,550 and $2,300 annually for an individual, and $3,050 to $4,600 for a family in 1999 and 2000, and indexed for inflation after 2000.

The policyholder then establishes a medical savings account at a participating bank or mutual fund company. Payments can be made in monthly installments or in a lump sum at the beginning of the year.

Using checks drawn on those accounts, policyholders pay medical bills and submit claims to insurers. At the end of the year, any money remaining in the account is carried over to the next year. All contributions are deductible on federal tax returns, and interest accumulates tax-deferred up to age 65 and in most cases is entirely tax free if used for medical care. After 65, the money can be withdrawn with no penalty. If the money is withdrawn early for nonmedical expenses, there is a 15 percent penalty and income taxes must be paid. Once the deductible is met, plans often pay up to 100 percent.[1]

After three years of the pilot, there are some unexpected results:

- A profile of the participants proved to be few small businesses but more self-employed and empty-nesters starting businesses at home.
- The pluses and minuses of the MSA became clear. If you remain healthy and can afford the deductibles, you build up tax-free savings. But, the worst scenario, if you need the money for medical expenses, and your deductible has not yet been met, those costs must be paid by you, out of pocket.
- Problems surfaced involving the complexities of administering the program, the high deductibles, and the cap of testing only companies with 50 employees and not larger companies, which generally lead the way.

On the whole, the MSA has not been as successful as expected, although Congress is currently addressing some of these issues. For those who have sincerely tried to apply for it, the MSA has proven to be more complicated and convoluted then its overall value. The pilot allowed as many as 375,000 people to participate by April 1, 1997, but the Treasury Department estimates that only 100,000 accounts were initially established, though they are now becoming more widespread. The MSA program has been extended to December 31, 2002. For 2000, contributions must be completed by April 16, 2001. You must use Form 8853 (Medical Savings Accounts and Long-Term Care Insurance Contracts) to report information about MSA's established in 2000. Taxpayers can request IRS Publication 969, *Medical Savings Accounts: Understanding MSA's.*

NOTE: Unlike flexible spending accounts, where an employee must use the full dollar amount for medical purposes by a certain time or lose it, MSA's do not contain this negative provision.

SIMPLE

In an effort to increase the flexibility of retirement plans, the 1996 law established a retirement plan for small businesses called the Savings Incentive Match Plans for Employees (SIMPLE). In short, this is a new kind of simplified IRA or 401(k) plan. SIMPLE plans can be adopted by self-employed individuals, and employers having 100 or fewer employees who received at least $5,000 in compensation for the preceding year and who do not maintain another employer-sponsored retirement plan. Employees who earned at least $5,000 from the employer in any two preceding years before the SIMPLE plan was offered and who also are expected to receive at least $5,000 in compensation for the current year are eligible to participate. Employees' contributions, which are generally matched by the employer up to 3 percent, cannot exceed $6,000 per year. The SIMPLE can be adopted as an IRA or as part of a 401(k) salary-deferral plan, and, as such, it involves typically intricate and sometimes confusing rules for employers matching specific sums, vesting, and how contributions and distributions are made, including associated tax implications.

It is important to review the fine print for this plan, but generally it is a good incentive for small businesses and their employees. Some benefits for both employees and employers are:

- SIMPLE plans are not subject to the nondiscrimination rules as other qualified pension plans are. This means that the amount of money an individual earns or a person's ownership percentage of a company does not control or limit the amount that person can contribute to the plan.
- Contributions are deductible by the employer and are excludable from the employee's income.
- Contributions are immediately vested, i.e., the money is yours to keep even if your employment is terminated.

NOTE: Unlike other Keogh and 401(k) plans, 40 percent of all eligible employees do *not* have to elect to participate. An employer may establish a SIMPLE even if no employees wish to participate, but the employer *must* notify employees of their right to do so. Generally speaking, this is an easier plan for employers to adopt and administer, and less expensive as well.

A significant drawback for employees is that if you withdraw money in the first two years, you are subject to a 25 percent withdrawal penalty (on SIMPLE IRA's only), which is 15 percent more than normal IRA's.

For employers, a major drawback is that they must continue to match at least 1 percent of employees' compensation even if the business is doing poorly. There are many other intricate benefits and drawbacks that need to be examined before you make a choice.

In my experience, the SIMPLE has proven itself to be generally unpopular with employers, particularly those having smaller companies, because of their reluctance to offer the amount of matching contributions necessary to establish the plan. Though these employers receive a deduction off their corporate taxes, when the numbers are added up, the difference between opening the SIMPLE even with the amount subsidized by the government doesn't seem to be enough of an incentive. For self-employed individuals and partners in partnerships, see pages 271–272 for a discussion of a Simplified Employee Pension (SEP).

The SIMPLE was made available after January 1, 1997. Use Form 5304–SIMPLE, or Form 5305–SIMPLE: the first if all contributions go to a financial institution designated by the employer; the second if eligible employees are permitted to choose their own financial institution.

SIMPLE plans must have been set up by October 1, 2000, for 2000 contributions to be deductible on your 2000 tax return.

Tax-Planning Opportunities for Selling Your Home
TRA '97 affords homeowners, especially those with primary residences valued above certain dollar amounts, a wonderful new variety of tax-planning strategies. Here are a few:

Capital Gains Provisions—Home Sale
Before TRA '97, a homeowner paid no tax on profits from the sale of a home if within two years of the sale those profits were "rolled over" by buying another home costing at least as much as the one that was sold. With TRA '97, a married couple can exempt up to $500,000 of profit on the sale of a home if the house or apartment has been the primary residence of one spouse for at least two of the last five years; a single homeowner can exempt up to $250,000. This replaces a much more limited home-sale exclusion of $125,000 for those over 55 years of age. In effect, the new law means most homeowners (with homes worth under $500,000) will now be able to avoid paying taxes when selling their primary residence.

Those who have profits above the exclusion amounts, either because the price of the home rose from the time it was purchased, or because the homeowner "bought up" (i.e., owned and sold several homes over the years, each one increasingly more expensive), could, even with the new law, end up owing a large tax bill—20 percent on the accumulated profits over and above the exclusion—due at the sale of the current home even if the home is sold at little or no profit, or at a loss.

NOTE: **The new tax exemptions on profits of a home sale can be used repeatedly, so long as the seller lives in the home for at least two years.**

The real estate industry is generally positive about the new capital gains law because it has stimulated business, especially in the lower price ranges, and brought product into the market by those who want to sell their homes but don't plan to buy more expensive ones. It also helps that mortgage rates are at historically low levels.

As with the previous law, when a home is sold at a loss, no deductions or other tax benefits are available to the seller.

Vacation Homes Versus Primary Residences

People who own a vacation home often declare it as their primary residence to gain the tax advantage of living in a new state, such as Florida or Texas, which has no personal income tax. However, there may be bigger benefits available if you can arrange your affairs so that your former primary residence is your tax home when it comes time to sell. The tendency is to sell an original primary home before the vacation home. This could mean having to pay the full capital gains tax and losing the exemption, $500,000 for married couples and $250,000 for singles. The solution: At your first inclination of selling your home, switch your permanent residence back to the original home, the sooner the better. The requirement is to live there at least 183 days a year. Other proof of residency is to change your voting address, get a driver's license in the state where you want to demonstrate a principal residence, and file your federal or state returns from that location. True, you may lose the savings of living in a tax-free state, but after two years you can move back to the vacation home *and* you have up to three years to sell your original primary residence and take the exemption. If your home doesn't sell after the fifth year, switch your permanent residence back and start over. This works no matter what state your second home is in.

If Marriage Is in the Picture

If you intend to marry and are facing a home sale with a large built-in gain, don't sell before the wedding. From a tax perspective, it's really best if you marry and have your spouse move in with you, live in that house for two years, then sell the home and take the $500,000 exemption for married couples.

If you are lucky enough to have a spouse who also owns a home, after you've lived in your home and sold it, move into your spouse's home, making that your primary residence for the next two years, then sell it and take the exemption. If this sounds somewhat calculating, just think of how much you'll be calculating into your bank account.

Renting Counts

Something that might make the above situation and others like it more feasible is to rent one of the houses. The law allows you to move into your next home before you sell the one you own and rent it out while you're waiting for a buyer. To take the exemption on the old home when it's sold, you must prove to the IRS that you were actively trying to sell the home at the time you moved out. Sound proof would be having the home listed with a broker.

This scenario also works well for anyone who owns a principal residence and a rental property. Assume that a single person has lived in the current house for at least two of the previous five years at the time of the sale. He uses the capital gain exclusion of $250,000 and then moves into the rental unit, which is now his principal residence. After two years, he sells the rental unit at a substantial gain, of which $250,000 can be excluded under the law. It makes no difference that most of the appreciation on the second property was realized when it was a rental unit and that he had been taking depreciation for the entire time it was rented. The only part of the gain subject to tax, at a maximum rate of 25 percent, is any depreciation taken after May 6, 1997.

If Divorce Is in the Picture

Under the new tax law, a spouse who acquires a partial interest in a house through a divorce settlement and becomes single can move out and still exempt up to $250,000 of any taxable gain, even if he or she has not lived in the home for two of the last five years. The divorce decree must state that the home will be sold later and the proceeds split. The spouse staying on can also exempt up to $250,000 in profit.

Can the spouse who moved out buy another principal residence and qualify for the exemption? Yes, but the new home must be sold either two years before or two years after the one involved in the divorce is sold. Remember, you can take the exemption repeatedly so long as the seller lives in the home for at least two years, or in this case, one exemption to a homeowner every two years.[2]

Falling Short of the Two-Year Requirement

Here's a feature that helps you pay less tax when selling your home (as amended in RRA '98, and retroactive to May 7, 1997). If, for certain reasons such as a job relocation, illness, or some other "unforeseeable event," you are unable to stay the required two years, you can still receive a partial exemption to apply against the profits from the sale of the home. To figure this out, take the number of months you used the home as a principal residence and divide by 24 months. For example, if you are married and lived in the home for 18 months and then you had a job transfer, you could take eighteen twenty-fourths of the $500,000, or $375,000. Even if the same taxpayer lived in the primary residence for as little as one year, he or she would qualify for a $250,000 exemption, which, in most cases, would probably be sufficient to cover any taxable gain.

Estate and Gift Taxes/Lifetime Exclusions
Prior law has allowed individuals to exempt from federal income taxes $600,000 on the value of their estate upon the taxpayer's death, or to use any part of the $600,000 as gifts that could be given away tax-free during the owner's lifetime—a clean-cut way to reduce estate and gift taxes. (See pages 138–140.) The $600,000 amount, however, had been in place since 1987 and was never indexed for inflation. Therefore, it never kept up with the steady rise in the overall net worth of individual estates. Currently, only 1 percent of Americans who pass away each year are hit with the combined estate and gift tax, because most don't have estates worth more than $600,000 or because they have set up a good estate-planning package with a tax pro. But if rising real estate and stock values of our current economy continue to enhance the value of individual estates, more people will be subject to the tax, unless they plan properly.

TRA '97 gradually increases the lifetime amount exempted from federal estate and gift taxes to $1 million. The time table is as follows:

1998	$625,000	2004	$850,000
1999	$650,000	2005	$950,000
2000 and 2001	$675,000	2006	$1,000,000
2002 and 2003	$700,000		

Small Business Tax Incentives
Small family-owned businesses and farms were given some tax relief that should facilitate passing business ownership to younger family members. For individuals who passed away in 1999, if the family business makes up more than 50 percent of a person's estate, the executor may generally elect to deduct up to $650,000 of the value of the family business from the taxable estate. In 1999, the deduction of $650,000 plus the regular exemption of $650,000 will provide a total deduction and exclusion of $1.3 million. While the regular exemption rises each year, the

small business deduction goes down, but the maximum combined deduction and exemption stays constant at $1.3 million.

Here are some other requirements small-business owners will need to know: The principal place of business must be in the United States; there must be at least 50 percent ownership by one family, or 70 percent by two families, or 90 percent by three families, as long as the decedent's family owns at least 30 percent. There can be no public trading of business stock or securities within three years of the decedent's death, plus there are various ownership and participation requirements for the decedent and qualified family members both before and after the decedent's death that you will need to know. Get the advice of a tax pro.

There is a special exception: A family business can be left to someone who is not a family member if the person is actively employed in the business for 10 years prior to the decedent's death.

NOTE: It is a good idea to review your existing will and testament so you can make changes wherever the former $600,000 exemption amount is mentioned. It may also be wise to use percentages of assets rather than exemption amounts (dollar amounts) so that the will won't have to be rewritten every year, saving time and money.

Individuals who own small businesses and farms will have even more work to do, especially if your current will calls for the business to go to one child and other kinds of assets to another child.

YOUR TAX-SAVING STRATEGY.
Since it takes nine years for the full estate and gift tax exemption to take effect, eat a healthy diet, exercise accordingly, and plan to be around until 2006 to maximize your bequests to your heirs.

1998 TAX LEGISLATION

Like most tax laws, the IRS Restructuring and Reform Act of 1998 (RRA '98), signed into law by President Clinton July 22, 1998, is complex (about 800 pages long) and affects a broad cross section of taxpayers in many significant ways.* It has two focuses: first, to restructure the IRS/taxpayer relationship to hopefully rein in the agency and eliminate at least some of the pain taxpayers have always had in dealing with the

---

*Unless otherwise stated, the discussion of the RRA '98 is based on *1998 Tax Legislation, IRS Restructuring and Reform Law, Explanation and Analysis*, Chicago: Commerce Clearing House, 1998.

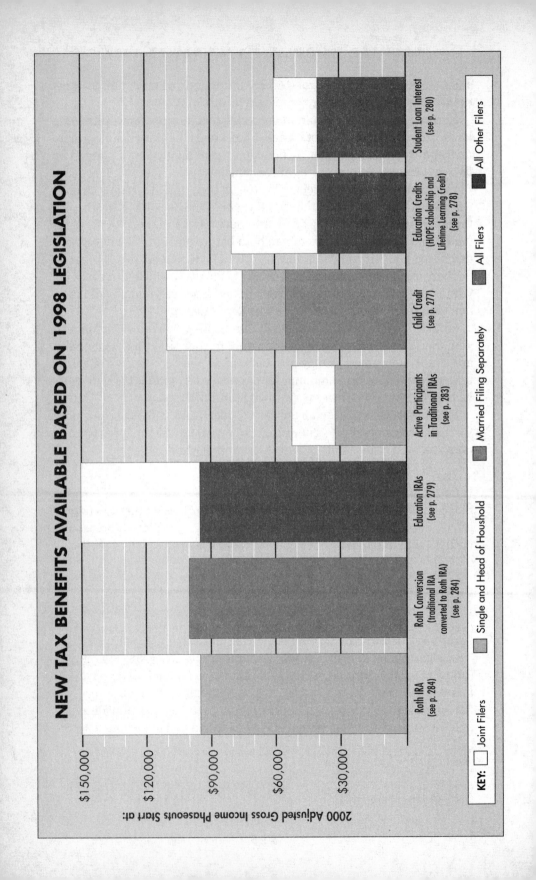

NEW TAX BENEFITS AVAILABLE BASED ON 1998 LEGISLATION

2000 Adjusted Gross Income Phaseouts Start at:

$150,000
$120,000
$90,000
$60,000
$30,000

Roth IRA
(see p. 284)

Roth Conversion
(traditional IRA
converted to Roth IRA)
(see p. 284)

Education IRAs
(see p. 279)

Active Participants
in Traditional IRAs
(see p. 283)

Child Credit
(see p. 277)

Education Credits
(HOPE scholarship and
Lifetime Learning Credit)
(see p. 278)

Student Loan Interest
(see p. 280)

KEY:
Joint Filers
Single and Head of Household
Married Filing Separately
All Filers
All Other Filers

IRS, and second, to resolve and fine-tune answers to many of the open questions raised by the Taxpayer Relief Act of 1997 (TRA '97).

The new provisions of RRA '98 are presented here with the technical corrections or updates included in 1997 tax legislation. Because the majority of these laws are effective in 1998, you need to know what you're entitled to. Keep reading. It's easy to get it.

Capital Gains Legislation

The maximum tax on net long-term capital gains has generally been lowered to 20 percent (10 percent for taxpayers in the 15 percent tax bracket). To qualify, you must hold the asset for more than 12 months. If you hold the asset for one year or less, you will be subject to tax at your ordinary income tax rate, ranging up to 39.6 percent. The 18-month holding period required to take advantage of the lowest capital gains tax rates has been eliminated.

While these changes are positive, there continue to be two unfavorable exceptions:

1. The maximum tax on net long-term capital gains of collectibles such as artwork, stamps, and coins will continue to be taxed at 28 percent even though they need only be held for more than 12 months.

2. Net long-term capital gains attributable to real property will be taxed at two rates. To the extent depreciation has generally been taken on the property, the maximum tax rate will be 25 percent. The balance of capital gain, if any, will be taxed at the lower, favorable rate of 20 percent.

TAXPAYER PROTECTIONS AND RIGHTS

Many of the new laws set forth in RRA '98 deal with one extremely important issue, essentially what all the recent hullabaloo has been about—taxpayer protections and rights. These are intended not only to help those already caught in the IRS audit and collections process, but also to help taxpayers avoid having problems with the IRS in the first place. The most significant provisions included in this section include a shift in the burden of proof from the taxpayer to the IRS, adjustments in awards, costs, and civil damages granted to taxpayers, taxpayer confidentiality privileges, innocent spouse relief, a variety of audit and collections safeguards designed to impede heavy-handed IRS tactics, and a new approach regarding offers in compromise.

Shift in Burden of Proof

Do you think that the burden of proving who is right in a tax dispute with the IRS can make the difference between winning and losing? One would think so. In the past, if you went to court to fight the IRS about the amount of taxes you owed, the IRS was presumed correct until you proved otherwise. The new law shifts the burden of proof from the taxpayer to the IRS in noncriminal cases that reach the U.S. Tax Court. However, once taxpayers get their day in court, they must comply by

- Substantiating any item of income, deduction, or tax credit, or other tax items.
- Keeping appropriate records as required by law or regulation. (Both of these existed before the 1998 act.)
- Meeting net worth limitations, i.e., the burden of proof remains on corporations, trusts, and partnerships whose net worth exceeds $7 million.
- Cooperating with reasonable IRS requests for meetings, interviews, witnesses, information, and documents, even if these are not under the taxpayer's control.

The burden of proof rules apply to court proceedings arising in connection with examinations after the July 22, 1998, date of enactment.

Awards, Costs, and Civil Damages

If the IRS takes a position against you that is not substantially justified, this is what you can recover: reasonable administrative and litigation costs, including fees and expenses you incur from the date on which the first letter of proposed deficiency was issued, plus expenses, costs, and fees related to persons who represent you if you win your contest with the IRS.

To determine if the IRS position is unreasonable, the court must take into account whether the IRS has lost on this point in other U.S. Courts of Appeal.

If you make a qualified offer to settle and the IRS turns you down, and then obtains a judgment against you, you can still collect reasonable costs and attorneys' fees even if the IRS wins an amount that is equal to or less than your offer (not counting interest accrued). This provision is to encourage taxpayers to offer a reasonable amount for settlement of taxes owed and for the IRS to act reasonably in accepting such offers.

Civil damages may be awarded for the unauthorized inspection or disclosure of your tax returns or any information on your return. If this occurs, you are entitled to collect attorneys' fees.

If an IRS employee negligently disregards the law in connection with collecting your income tax, you can collect up to $100,000 in civil damages, and up to $1 million if an IRS employee willfully violates the law governing collections.

The effective date of the civil damages applies to costs incurred and services performed beginning January 18, 1999.

Impact

Now that the much-sought-after burden of proof switch has been made, there are questions as to how it will play out. Taxpayers, will you get the measure of relief and control from IRS collection and court officials who knew they, not you, were always in the right? Will you become bogged down complying with IRS administrative requests to prove their case? Will the law encourage the IRS to be more aggressive and intrusive, which will directly lead to more extensive costs, or will the IRS be more understanding and sympathetic, as Commissioner Charles Rossotti has proposed? More time will have to be spent on cases to ensure "full cooperation," as set down in the new law. What this means is that taxpayers must comply fully with IRS requests for information if they expect the burden of proof to shift to the IRS. Because of this, you can expect more stringent IRS audit procedures that will include many more requests for documents in the hope that taxpayers will not respond, in an effort to prevent the burden of proof from shifting. This could easily increase litigation costs. Perhaps taxpayers who have control of information will fare better by awaiting trial before disclosing that information. Or perhaps where they do not have control of information and the IRS cannot obtain that information on its own, these taxpayers may do better by doing nothing, even though the burden of proof is on their side. Be sure to get good representation—someone who has experience trying cases before the IRS.

Confidentiality Privilege

Whereas a taxpayer always enjoyed the privilege of confidentiality between him- or herself and his or her attorney, you are now entitled to the same protection of confidentiality with respect to tax advice received from any "federally authorized tax practitioner" such as a CPA or enrolled agent. The privilege applies in any noncriminal tax proceeding before the IRS or federal courts. Interestingly enough, it does not extend to written communication between a tax practitioner and a corporation in connection with the promotion of any tax shelter.

Impact

CPA's and enrolled agents should be diligent in reviewing the rules regarding this law because there are limits to the privilege. For example, the privilege usually does not apply to the preparation of tax returns, giving accounting or business advice, or tax accrual work papers.

If your civil, noncriminal case becomes a criminal case, the IRS could use a summons to compel your tax adviser to reveal details of past conversations he had with you that you would prefer left unsaid. It is also known that the IRS has threatened to implicate the tax adviser as a co-conspirator in tax evasion cases if the adviser refuses to cooperate. Despite this, the new law should prove a great help to taxpayers and CPA's working together in a tax audit situation.

Innocent Spouse Relief

Anyone who signs his or her name to a joint return immediately becomes liable for possible tax misdeeds of the other filer. Innocent spouse relief is intended to help spouses caught in IRS collection actions because of all understatements of tax attributed to the other spouse. To avoid this situation entirely, of course, married people always have the choice of filing separate returns. But once that joint return is filed, it was very difficult until recently for an innocent spouse to become free of tax liabilities unlawfully incurred by the erring spouse. Even if a divorce decree states that a former spouse will be responsible for any amounts due on previously filed tax returns, both spouses are still liable.

Both the Treasury Department and the General Accounting Office reported on what has come to be called the "joint and several liability standard" wherein joint filers are liable for one another regarding the information they submit on their 1040. Their objective was to assess how the existing law protected the rights of innocent spouses, particularly if they were separated or divorced. In early 1997, the GAO recommended no changes, but IRS Commissioner Rossotti did the opposite. He pushed for new legislation to help innocent spouses and for a new form, Form 8857 (Request for Innocent Spouse Relief). These changes, in much stronger language, were incorporated into RRA '98.

At last married taxpayers who file a joint return are protected from wrongful tax liabilities of their spouses under the following conditions:

Innocent spouses will be liable for tax on only their own income if, in signing the joint return, they did not know, and had no reason to know, that there was an understatement of tax. Even partial relief is available, based on this same criterion.

Separate Liability Election or Separation of Liability

In addition to choosing innocent spouse relief, if you filed a joint return and became divorced, widowed, legally separated, or simply have not lived in the same household for the past 12 months, you can still limit your tax liability through a separate liability election. This election would limit your liability only to the items on the return that specifically pertain to you. In other words, for those items, the innocent spouse would be treated as if he or she had filed a separate return.

This election may be partially or completely invalid if the electing spouse had actual knowledge of incorrect items on the joint return or if there was a fraudulent transfer of assets between spouses with the intention to avoid payment of taxes.

If it can be shown that you had knowledge of your spouse's misstatement of tax liability, you will be held responsible unless you can prove you signed it under duress.

Both innocent spouse and separate liability elections are available up to two years *after* the IRS begins collection activities, and the two-year period will not begin until collection activities alert the spouse that the IRS intends to collect the joint liability from each spouse.

YOUR TAX-SAVING STRATEGY.

The criteria in a separate liability election are based on the standard of "actual knowledge." This means that taxpayers electing separate liability could do so if they did not have actual knowledge of the specific event that created the liability. For the IRS to prove this claim, they must establish actual knowledge based on the evidence. Accordingly, the separate liability election, though offering more narrow relief, might be easier for the taxpayer to prove. In contrast, the innocent spouse election, where the criterion is that the taxpayer "knew or should have known," may offer broader relief but be easier for the IRS to disclaim. If the IRS claims that your spouse had unreported income, you can try to prove that you had no knowledge of the omission by showing that your standard of living did not change by some mysterious infusion of newfound money. To prove your case you will need to gather at least two years' worth of bank deposits and check and credit card expenditures, which you'll have to show to the IRS. Hopefully, this should do it.

Equitable Relief

In drawing up the legislation, it became obvious that other circumstances not included in the first two sections of the innocent spouse provision would prevent taxpayers from obtaining relief. To deny these people help related to the wrongdoing of their spouses would be unfair. Therefore, the equitable relief provision was born. Accordingly, you may be relieved of responsibility for taxes, penalties, and interest if you fit into these categories:

- Your circumstances make you ineligible for innocent spouse relief or separation of liability. For example: You file a joint return with

Three Types of Innocent Spouse Relief at a Glance

Factors	Rules for Innocent Spouse Relief	Rules for Separation of Liability	Rules for Equitable Relief
Type of Liability	You must have filed a joint return that has an understatement of tax due to an erroneous item of your spouse.	You must have filed a joint return that has an understatement of tax due, in part, to an item of your spouse.	You must have filed a return that has either an understatement or an underpayment of tax.
Marital Status		You must be no longer married, legally separated, or have not lived with your spouse in the same house for an entire year before you file for relief.	
Knowledge	You must establish that at the time you signed the joint return you did not know, and had no reason to know, that there was an understatement of tax.	If IRS establishes that you actually knew of the item giving rise to the understatement, then you are not entitled to make the election to the extent of actual knowledge.	
Other Qualifications			You do not qualify for innocent spouse relief or separation of liability.
Unfairness	It must be unfair to hold you liable for the understatement of tax taking into account all the facts and circumstances.		It must be unfair to hold you liable for the underpayment or understatement of tax taking into account all the facts and circumstances.
Refunds	Yes, your request can generate a refund.	No, your request cannot generate a refund.	Yes, for amounts paid between July 22, 1998, and April 15, 1999, and for amounts paid pursuant to an installment agreement after the date the request for relief is made.

Source: IRS Publication 971, *Innocent Spouse Relief.*

your spouse where the liability is $12,000 and you pay $7,000 when you file the return. To meet your obligations, you then borrow $5,000 to pay the balance, but without your knowledge, your spouse spends the $5,000 on himself or herself.

- It would be unfair to hold you liable for an understatement or underpayment of tax given all the facts and circumstances of your situation. To decide if it is unfair, the IRS would, for example, try to determine if you received any significant benefit from the understatement of tax. Another reason deemed to be unfair circumstances would be if you were later divorced or deserted by your spouse.

There is a second new IRS form that indirectly relates to the innocent spouse situation. By filing Form 8379 (Injured Spouse Claim and Allocation), you may prevent the IRS from taking your share of any refunds on a joint return. This form is specifically designed to help when the injured spouse was not even married to the delinquent spouse at the time the tax liabilities were incurred.

All of the innocent spouse provisions apply to any tax liability arising after July 22, 1998, *and* any tax liability arising before July 22, 1998, that is unpaid as of July 22, 1998.

Impact
In addition to these new laws, the IRS is required to

- Alert married taxpayers to the legal consequences of filing a joint return.
- Send any deficiency notice relating to a joint return separately to each name on the return.
- Establish procedures to notify taxpayers of their innocent spouse relief and/or separate liability options.

Telephone representatives specifically trained in the innocent spouse provision are available through the IRS's toll-free numbers.

By easing the former restrictions on innocent spouse relief, which were completely arbitrary and had a disproportionate effect on low-income taxpayers, determining eligibility for such relief should be simpler and more just. The impact of this law is expected to save a lot of headaches for a great number of taxpayers innocently burdened with debts they had nothing to do with and, often, didn't even know existed. Complete information is contained in IRS Publication 971, *Innocent Spouse Relief*. (Also see pages 338–340.)

Collection and Audit Safeguards
New lien, levy, and collection safeguards have been legislated to protect taxpayers from unscrupulous treatment by the IRS:

Seizures of Residences and Businesses
The greatest power revenue officers have had is their ability to file federal liens and levies and to seize property belonging to taxpayers without obtaining prior approval. (See page 61.) This is where the IRS gets you. RRA '98 strikes at the core of this power, and the changes here are dramatic.

Now, not only is supervisory approval generally required before *any* lien or levy action can be taken, but the supervisor must completely review the case, taking into consideration all the facts and circumstances, including the value of the asset subject to the seizure as it relates to the tax debt due. If the revenue officers and/or supervisors fail to follow the prescribed procedures, both are subject to disciplinary action. As taxpayers, you need to be informed of these steps:

- A seizure of a residence requires the written approval of a U.S. District Court judge or magistrate.
- A seizure of a residence generally cannot take place to satisfy a liability, including penalties and interest, of $5,000 or less.
- A seizure of personal or real property used in a taxpayer's trade or business generally requires the written approval of an IRS district or assistant district director, after it is determined that no other assets are available to pay the amount due.
- The IRS cannot sell *any* seized property for less than a previously agreed-upon minimum bid price. If sold for less, the taxpayer can sue for civil damages.
- For all sales of seized property, the IRS must provide to the taxpayer full details of the sales, including seizure and sale dates, expenses of sale, and how the net proceeds were applied to the taxpayer's tax liabilities.
- The revenue officer who is recommending the collection action has to verify your liability, determine that you will have sufficient equity in the property to yield net proceeds to apply against that liability, and give thorough consideration to other collection methods available, such as an offer in compromise or installment agreement.

Collection "Due Process"—Liens and Levies
This part of the law adds several "due process" safeguards in reaction to IRS collection abuses.

Within five days of filing a lien on, or at least 30 days prior to levying, a taxpayer's property, the IRS must notify the taxpayer and provide the following information in simple, nontechnical language:

- The amount of unpaid tax.
- That a hearing can be requested within 35 days after receipt of the notice of lien, within 30 days for a levy.
- Available administrative appeals and procedures.
- Procedures relating to release of the lien, or alternatives that could prevent the levy on the property (e.g., installment agreements).

And in case of a levy, two additional notifications include

1. The proposed actions the IRS will take and the rights the taxpayer has with respect to those actions, and
2. IRS provisions and procedures relating to the levy, sale, and redemption of the property.

If you receive a Notice of Federal Tax Lien filing, a Notice of Intent to Levy, or a Notice of Jeopardy Levy, you should obtain Form 12153 (Request for a Collection Due Process Hearing) from the IRS if they haven't already included it. Fill out the form within 30 days and return it to the IRS.

All of these forms are new, a result of RRA '98. According to the new law, the forms and the subsequent procedures they initiate are intended to provide taxpayers with a stronger chance for due process if they are in the difficult position of facing a lien or levy. The complete list of publications and forms sent free by the IRS regarding collection can be found in IRS Publication 594, *The IRS Collection Process.*

YOUR TAX-SAVING STRATEGY.
Notices of liens and levies generated by the Automated Collection System (ACS) will not be covered by these new provisions until December 31, 2000, probably because of the technology upgrades involved. Therefore, if you receive a notice generated by the ACS, bring it to the attention of IRS personnel immediately so that you can receive the protection of the new, more stringent rules.

Right of Appeal
With either a notice of lien or intent to levy, a taxpayer is entitled to a hearing conducted by an impartial person who had no prior involvement in the case. By filing Form 12153 (Request For A Collection Due

Process Hearing) with the Appeals Division of the IRS, you can bring up any new appropriate issues concerning collection activity such as innocent spouse status, an offer in compromise, or an installment agreement. However, you generally cannot challenge the underlying tax liability. If you lose, you have another 30 days to appeal to the Tax Court or a higher court if appropriate.

NOTE: Under prior law, if you lost in Appeals, your case was returned to collection, leaving you with no alternative. Because you can now appeal to higher courts, you can expect greater consideration from the Appeals officers, who are also obligated to consider all alternative collection procedures you may make to settle your liability.

Third-Party Involvement

Another of the most damaging aspects of liens and levies occurs when the IRS notifies third parties concerning examination or collection activities targeting a taxpayer. In this book alone you have read many true stories of people whose careers and reputations have been destroyed or whose businesses and personal assets were severely weakened for years because the IRS spread the word, often without cause, and almost always refusing to make amends, about a taxpayer's alleged unlawful behavior.

Now some level of safeguard has been put in place that gives taxpayers a way to fight back. Generally, in civil cases, before the IRS contacts third parties in connection with the examination of a taxpayer or the collection of any tax owed, the taxpayer must be notified of the service of a summons on a third party within a reasonable time before the date of service. This at least gives taxpayers the chance to resolve issues and volunteer information to the persons about to be contacted before the IRS gets to them.

These laws became effective January 18, 1999. In chapter 13, read about the impact these laws are having.

Interest and Penalty Relief

To aid taxpayers who owe money to the IRS, some interest and penalty adjustments have been made as follows:

If the IRS does not provide a notice of a tax deficiency within 18 months after the timely filing of a return, beginning with returns for the year ending December 31, 1998, some interest and penalties for adjustments made by the IRS will be suspended. However, interest and penalties can resume 21 days after the notice is sent. What does this mean? It means that interest and penalties will not accumulate if the IRS is lazy about pursuing a taxpayer for money owed.

If you are paying taxes after 1999 that you owe under an installment agreement with the IRS, you do not have to pay interest on the amount you still owe. This applies only to those who filed on time the tax return to which the agreement relates.

Explanation of Taxpayer's Rights in Interviews and Disclosure of Audit Selection Criteria

The IRS is required to rewrite and to more clearly inform taxpayers of several audit safeguards.

Taxpayers have the right to be represented at interviews with the IRS by someone authorized to practice before the IRS, and to suspend the interview once they say they wish to have representation.

Along the same lines, a relative "sleeper" and accordingly a self-contained section of RRA '98 turns out to be a surprise for taxpayers, and an important one at that. In chapter 8, you read that a return is selected for audit based on a variety of criteria—DIF scores, TCMP audits, the matching process, various IRS audit triggers, and the latest IRS targets. But none of us ever really knows why our particular return is chosen. Surprise.

Now the IRS is required to inform taxpayers of the methods used to select their tax returns for examination unless such information would be detrimental to law enforcement. Also, the IRS had to put both of these procedures into effect and rewrite Publication 1, *Your Rights as a Taxpayer*, to include a taxpayer's rights of representation and the disclosure of audit selection criteria. This has been done. (See Appendix D.)

Impact

At first, I wondered if these new laws regarding taxpayer protections and rights would be another case of empty promises that few will remember in a year or two. I don't think so. Not this time. The audit and collection safeguards combine to form some very serious protections against what has been unfair and often brutal treatment imposed by the IRS. Once these procedures are put into action, they should make a foreseeable difference in the lives of taxpayers. Congress has finally turned on the IRS and in doing so has revamped the examination, collection, and appeals processes. Beginning with the first letter a taxpayer receives informing him or her of an audit or collection problem, all the way—possibly through the federal courts—the taxpayer will be informed of his or her rights and should be able to make informed decisions. No longer will revenue officers be able to arbitrarily and capriciously slap an unwarranted lien or levy on an unsuspecting taxpayer without following prescribed protocol. Though they may continue to try these tactics, the fear of reprisals, now part of the law, should reduce unwarranted and erratic behavior considerably.

The guidelines aimed at the IRS Collection Department to maintain flexibility when negotiating a taxpayer's installment agreement or offer in compromise should not only ease the situation from the IRS's perspective but also ease the minds of thousands of taxpayers who want to unburden themselves of their tax debts. For the first time, taxpayers are given specific statutory protections against enforcement action by the IRS while they are attempting to settle their tax obligations. To see the impact these laws have already had on the IRS collection process, see pages 336–338.

Regarding disclosure of audit selection, if the IRS, by either letter or a live auditor, ever really explains why a return was chosen for audit, it will provide taxpayers with some genuine benefits. First, it will offer clues regarding issues that the IRS might raise during their audit, and this, in turn, should help taxpayers and their representatives present a stronger defense.

Staying informed is key. If the IRS tries to take shortcuts, you need to recognize which steps are being left out, and how to proceed.

Offers in Compromise and Installment Agreements

To ease the situation for taxpayers who want to settle their tax liabilities for less than 100 percent of the amount owed, new guidelines will be developed by the IRS based on case-by-case decisions rather than on formerly imposed national and local standards for housing and living allowances. It was not uncommon, when abiding by those standards, for the IRS to force taxpayers into unrealistic agreements that would not allow for certain necessities. From the IRS's perspective, the primary obligation for the taxpayer was the payment of taxes; expenses for educating a child and paying off a credit card were deemed less important. So when a low-income taxpayer, for example, offered a minimum amount to settle liabilities, the offer might be rejected even though it represented that person's maximum ability to pay.

Impact

Revenue officers are now encouraged to base their decisions on the facts and circumstances of each taxpayer and to be flexible in finding ways to work with taxpayers who are sincerely trying to meet their tax obligations. Accordingly, any offer in compromise or installment agreement submitted by a taxpayer that is rejected will first go through an independent administrative review before the taxpayer is notified.

During the period of negotiating for either an offer in compromise or an installment agreement, the IRS must cease all collection activities, i.e., a levy may not be placed on that person's property. This prohibition extends for 30 days after an offer in compromise is rejected or an installment agreement is terminated, and during the pending of any appeal provided the appeal is filed within 30 days of the rejection. Neither can any levy be made when an installment agreement is in effect.

Generally these laws apply to offers in compromise and installment agreements submitted after July 22, 1998.

Most recently, taxpayers can make arrangements for installment agreements in person, by phone, or by correspondence. This applies to both individual and business income taxes.

Instead of waiting for a contact from an IRS collector, you may initiate a request for an installment plan by attaching Form 9465 (Installment Agreement Request) to the front of your tax return, listing the proposed monthly payment amount. You can also choose to have the payments taken automatically from your bank account.

Beginning July 1, 2000, the IRS must provide annual statements to taxpayers under installment agreements. These statements must show the balance at the beginning of the year, payments made, and the balance at the end of the year.

In my recent experience, the IRS is still pressuring taxpayers for full up-front payments before granting an installment arrangement. With businesses, there continue to be many revenue officers who are hell-bent on forcing the sale of business assets to achieve some payment even if the taxpayer is put out of business in the process.

But the latest news from the IRS's Office of Electronic Tax Administration is the rollout of a self-help application that either taxpayers or practitioners can use on the Web. The application offers an interactive installment agreement featuring a dramatically simplified financial statement questionnaire, or Form 433A or 433B (Collection Information Statement for Individuals or Businesses), along with the request for an installment agreement or Offer in Compromise. The user enters the data while the program guides you through. When the application is complete, the user downloads the information, prints it out, and sends it to the IRS. But remember, before locking yourself into this kind of agreement, there are other ways to pay your tax bill. As of October 2000, the interactive installment agreement is operational.

Extension of Statute of Limitations

Remember Forms 872 and 872-A, whereby the taxpayer gives the IRS more time to assess taxes owed, because the three-year statute of limitations is drawing near? For years I have been advising you never to sign 872-A, which gives the IRS an unlimited amount of time to complete an audit examination. (See pages 249–250.)

Impact

If the IRS wants to extend the three-year statute of limitations on assessments made after December 31, 1999, it must now notify you of your right to refuse extension or to limit the extension to specific issues through Form 872 (Consent to Extend the Time to Assess Tax). **This notification must be provided each time an extension is required.**

In another area, the IRS has 10 years to collect a properly assessed tax by levy, or in a court proceeding. Generally, effective after 1999, it will be very difficult for the IRS to obtain an agreement from a taxpayer to extend the 10-year limitation period on collections except in connection with an installment agreement.

Fair Debt Collection Practices Act

The goal here is for the IRS collection people to treat tax debtors with at least the same respect and dignity as is generally common with private-sector debt collectors. Thus, the IRS may not communicate with you

- At any unusual or inconvenient time or place unless you agree.
- At your place of employment if the IRS knows or has reason to know that such communication is prohibited by the employer.
- If the revenue officer knows you have obtained representation from a person authorized to practice before the IRS and it can readily obtain that person's name and address.

This went into effect after July 22, 1998.

Impact

If this works, what can be bad?

Tax Law Complexity

The National Commission on Restructuring the IRS found a definite correlation among tax law complexity, difficulty in administering the tax law, and taxpayer dissatisfaction with the tax system. Complexity also increases taxpayer contact with the IRS as well as training costs necessary to teach IRS employees what all these new laws are about, and how to best enforce them. To ease the complexity burden, RRA '98 calls for some interesting and major changes in how tax laws are currently passed.

Beginning January 1, 1999, any amendments to the *Internal Revenue*

Code must include a tax complexity analysis, which is defined as "a report on the complexity and administrative difficulties of each tax law provision that has widespread applicability to individuals or small businesses."[3] The analysis must include the number of taxpayers affected and their income level, requirements for new or revised tax forms, additional taxpayer record-keeping costs, and a complete impact analysis on IRS personnel training, reprogramming of its computers, and revisions to the IRS manual. With these changes, Congress will no longer be permitted to consider tax legislation that is not accompanied by a tax complexity analysis.

Also, the IRS commissioner must prepare an annual report for Congress that will "include any recommendations for reducing the complexity of the administration of federal tax laws and for repeal or modification of any provision the commissioner believes adds undue and unnecessary complexity to the administration of the federal tax laws."[4]

Impact

Will this legislation minimize the creation of complex laws, or will it merely add more paperwork to a process and an agency already buried in forms? Even if the idea is sound, I don't really see all that complex analysis getting done with each new amendment to tax code. But lots of brave ventures are being made to change things for the better. We'll have to see how this one plays out. It may remain, or quickly disappear.

2000 LEGISLATION

Repeal of Social Security Limit on Earnings

Our economy is booming and America could use more workers who don't command large salaries that could tip the scales by raising inflation. Hiring retired people, those 65 years of age and older, may be the perfect solution. Congress seems to have agreed, as a new law signed by President Clinton on May 19, 2000, ends the earnings limit placed on Social Security recipients. For the first time since the Social Security Administration began sending out checks in 1940, people who have reached full retirement age—65 or over—may earn unlimited amounts of income without having their Social Security benefits cut. Previously, the law allowed people 65 through 69 who were receiving Social Security benefits to earn up to $17,000 in 2000. If they earned more than that, they were to lose $1 of benefits for every $3 earned, and pay Social Security tax on their earnings even though doing so would not enhance their future benefits. All of this was in addition to paying income tax. As a result, many capable, healthy, vibrant Social Security recipients worked a few months and then quit their job.

The situation has always been different for retirees 70 and older who, since 1983, have never had earnings limitations tied to their Social Security benefits.

Although there is no longer a cap on earnings for retired people, this group is still subject to paying federal income tax on part of their Social Security benefits. Retirees with an income over $25,000 for an individual, and $32,000 for a married couple filing jointly, will owe federal income tax on up to half of their Social Security retirement benefits. Single taxpayers with income over $34,000 and married couples filing jointly with income over $44,000 owe tax on as much as 85 percent of Social Security retirement benefits.[5] The new law is being made retroactive to January 1, 2000, meaning that about 415,000 seniors who lost Social Security benefits this year will receive a refund that will average $3,500. The new law will also mean an additional $6,700 in payments for some 800,000 recipients who are working and another 100,000 who haven't sought benefits because they already have jobs.[6]

You might want to check the Social Security Administration website at www.ssa.gov, which provides examples of how you can come out ahead.

Proposed Tax Legislation—The Marriage Penalty

Many taxpayers took it for granted that new 1998 tax legislation would include at least partial relief from the so-called marriage penalty, which forces millions of two-income couples to pay higher taxes than they would if they were single.

The problem Congress faced was how to replace the billions of dollars of lost revenue that any new provisions would cost. The answer was to obtain funding from the anti-tobacco bill that once seemed assured of passing. But on June 17, 1998, the anti-tobacco legislation went up in smoke in the Senate, and the marriage penalty provisions were also snuffed out.

Currently, the so-called marriage penalty has been back in play since the Senate passed a bill that would reduce income taxes for approximately 45 million couples, including about 25 million two-earner households that incur something like $1,380 more in taxes annually than they would if they were single.

Here's the story: Do you believe that the "married-joint" filing status allows you to pay less in taxes than a "single" filing status, or that the "married-joint" tax rates and exemptions are double those of the "single" filer? Wrong. The marriage penalty often kicks in whenever both spouses work and end up paying more taxes as a couple than they would if each of them were single. This generally happens when both spouses have relatively equal incomes. For example, if Bruce and Hillary each earned $32,500 in 2000, and each filed as a single taxpayer without other income such as interest, dividends, and capital gains, and each used the standard deduction $4,400 for a single filer instead of itemizing deductions, each would have to pay federal tax in the amount of $3,795. That means their total tax bill together, using the single filing status, would amount to $7,590. If Bruce and Hillary had the exact same income but they were married and filed a "married-joint" tax return for 2000, their tax bill would amount to $8,874. In other words, as a married couple, they would have to pay $1,284 in additional taxes, almost 17 percent more.

How did this come into being? First, the standard deduction for a single taxpayer is currently $4,400, while the standard deduction on a joint return is $7,350. Shouldn't the deduction on the joint return be at least double that of the single return, or $8,800? The fact is, it's not, and therein lies the penalty for married folks. Second, federal tax brackets, which delineate taxable income ranges and the percent they are taxed at, are not set up in a logical fashion. For example, if a single person has taxable income of $25,350 and files a single return, he or she is taxed at a rate of 15 percent. Wouldn't you expect that the taxable income of a married couple would be double the $25,350, or $50,700, at that same 15 percent rate? As before, it simply doesn't work that way, because the top end of the 15 percent rate for a joint return is only $43,850, significantly less than twice the single top end amount. As a result, some of the joint return taxable income is taxed at the next highest rate of 28 percent, while the two single returns are not taxed above the 15 percent rate.

The situation becomes more complex the more you examine it. There are other penalties that affect married people besides the standard deduction and the bias in tax rates. For example, couples generally face a quicker phase-out of itemized deductions and personal exemptions, and lower deductions regarding rental property and capital losses. (See pages 19–22.) But in a more favorable light, a tax "bonus" (reduction in taxes) might be realized by couples who file jointly but have a wide discrepancy in their earnings, or couples with only one spouse working.

For any married person who thinks it's possible to avoid the marriage penalty by filing "married-separate" tax returns, think again. When married couples file separately, they cannot use the "single" tax rates used for unmarried people; they must use the "married-filing separate" rates.

True, these rates are exactly half of those for the "married-filing joint" tax brackets, but they are still less favorable than the "single" rates. So the marriage penalty is generally not eliminated. As with every tax situation, there are upsides and downsides regarding possible options available for couples who want to avoid the marriage penalty.

The bill passed by the Senate in July 2000 advocated changing the tax brackets and the standard deductions so that married couples filing jointly would receive future tax savings. Specifically, whereas the tax deduction for a single taxpayer is $4,400, the bill would allow married couples a deduction of $8,800 instead of what it currently is—$7,350. The tax brackets would also change as follows: The 15 percent and 28 percent income tax brackets for married couples would gradually be expanded until they are approximately double those of single filers.

The cold, hard truth for Congress, however, is that once the marriage penalty is eliminated, billions of dollars will be lost. Other complications are that Democrats claim these tax cuts benefit primarily upper-income people, and President Clinton wants Congress to include in the bill a provision that provides a Medicare prescription drug benefit to help millions of older Americans.

As of August 4, President Clinton vetoed the bill on the grounds that it was too generous in giving tax breaks to all married couples, even those who would not normally be subjected to a marriage penalty, and that the bill abandoned fiscal discipline. On August 14, the House failed to override the President's veto.

To see how the marriage penalty affects you, you can go on-line at www.cwfa.org/action/marriage-tax.shtml.

Attempts to Repeal the Estate and Gift Tax
Besides the marriage penalty, the Republican Congress is pushing legislation that will repeal the estate and gift tax in its entirety by the year 2009. That means that inheritances and/or gifts (land, jewelry, homes, autos, and marketable securities, or stamp, art, and coin collections) passed down from one family member to others, through the generations, will be done so tax-free. Concurrently, the exemptions and deductions on the estate and gift tax would become defunct. (See pages 138–140.)

During World War I, estates were taxed at the rate of 10 percent. That rate climbed to 77 percent in 1941 and is now at a top rate of 55 percent. The current legislation calls for an estate and gift tax exemption that would start to gradually lower the rates as early as 2001.

The estate and gift tax used to be a primary concern for wealthy taxpayers, but with a soaring stock market and surging home prices, net household wealth has risen to almost $42 trillion from $22 trillion in the past eight years.[7] As a result, more taxpayers than ever before, including those in the middle class, are now faced with paying this tax. Those on the side of repeal, therefore, have gained a broader base of support. This is what they say:

The estate and gift tax produces only a small amount of revenue, less than one percent of federal revenue. In fact, it costs almost as much to collect the tax as it brings in. Second, the wealthy are very savvy about using whatever vehicles and devices are available to them to reduce the amount of money they know they can't take with them, or pass on to their relatives. Many of them manage to avoid paying the tax altogether. Finally, taxpayers whose estates are mainly comprised of a small business or farm can be forced to sell or liquidate the business or farm in order to pay the tax as it is now legislated.

If the estate and gift tax is repealed, those who will benefit the most are the families of women who were widows and were left large estates by their late husbands. The families of these widows pay an average tax bill of $294,000, verses only $70,000 for the families of men who died with large estates.[8]

Critics point out that the proposed legislation would increase capital gains tax on inherited assets in the year 2010. That means that heirs would have to pay a 20 percent capital gains tax measured by the original purchase price of an asset when it is sold, not on the market value upon the death of the decedent. Currently, for example, if you inherit 1,000 shares of IBM now worth $100,000, and the decedent paid $5 for each share, your per-share cost when you sell the shares is $100, not the original cost of $5. This reduces your capital gains tax substantially. But with the proposed legislation, heirs will pay capital gains tax on the appreciation that has accumulated since the original owner acquired the asset.

Critics also say that repealing the estate and gift tax will discourage a wide range of philanthropic gestures that Americans have benefited from since the time of Andrew Mellon, Andrew Carnegie, the Rockefellers, and more. After all, look at what Bill Gates has done. On August 31, President Clinton vetoed the bill that would have repealed the estate tax.

Changing Pension Laws

As baby boomers begin to reach the age of 50, it seems that they're beginning to wonder whether they'll have enough money when the time comes for them to retire. This question has spurred a review of our current pension laws to the point where the House of Representatives has passed a bill that would boost the maximum annual contribution to an individual IRA to $3,000 next year from the current $2,000, and then to $5,000 by 2003. Wage earners aged 50 and older could begin putting in the full $5,000 in 2001. The bill would also raise the limit on annual contributions to 401(k) plans, 403(b) annuities—the savings plans for employees of nonprofits—and certain small-business retirement plans from $10,500 to $15,000, to be phased in between 2001 and 2005. Certain other provisions would make it easier for workers to do such things as take their savings-plan balances with them when they retire.

The current administration insists that it will veto these proposals, and instead it has proposed a system of government-subsidized retirement accounts for lower- and middle-income workers.

The good news is that people are beginning to realize that if IRA contributions had kept up with inflation originally, the contribution would have already reached $5,000. Although different groups of people have differing abilities to save at different times in their lives, for those who do have the money, this bill would be a terrific savings incentive.

13

The New IRS

In a sweeping overhaul that has been compared to the reorganization under President Truman in 1952 (see pages 40–41), regulations under the IRS Reconstruction and Reform Act of 1998 have spurred a "new" IRS.

NEW IRS MISSION

Here's a first glance at what it's going to look like, beginning with a new mission statement: *Provide America's taxpayers with top-quality service by helping them understand and meet their tax responsibilities and by applying the tax law with integrity and fairness to all.*

This contrasts with the former mission, which begins: *The purpose of the IRS is to collect the proper amount of tax revenue at the least cost.*

It is easy to spot the difference in intent between the two. The first emphasizes fairness, the second, collecting revenue. Ponder that.

SERVNG FOUR GROUPS OF TAXPAYERS

For almost fifty years, the IRS has been organized as a geographically based structure where each taxpayer is served by at least one service center and a district office with the entire operation driven by the function it performs, i.e., examination, collection, tax return processing.

In comparison, the backbone of the new IRS will be built upon serving four distinct groups of taxpayers who have similar needs:

INTERNAL REVENUE SERVICE
(New Organization)

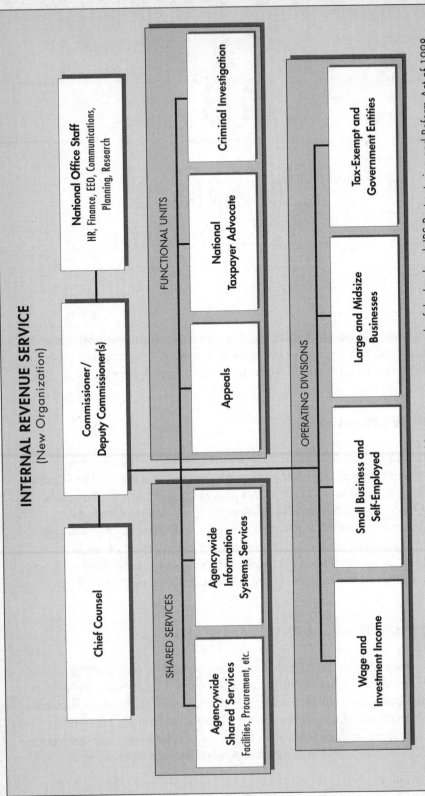

Chief Counsel

Commissioner/ Deputy Commissioner(s)

National Office Staff
HR, Finance, EEO, Communications, Planning, Research

SHARED SERVICES

Agencywide Shared Services
Facilities, Procurement, etc.

Agencywide Information Systems Services

FUNCTIONAL UNITS

Appeals

National Taxpayer Advocate

Criminal Investigation

OPERATING DIVISIONS

Wage and Investment Income

Small Business and Self-Employed

Large and Midsize Businesses

Tax-Exempt and Government Entities

The IRS's new focus on the needs of specific taxpayer groups and better service is a result of the landmark IRS Restructuring and Reform Act of 1998.

Source: *Journal of Accountancy*, March 2000

- Wage and investment income taxpayers who file 1040A, 1040EZ, and simple 1040's.
- Small business, self-employed, and supplemental income tax-payers who file C, E, F, or 2106 schedules; some, if not all, partnerships and S corporations; and corporations with assets under $5 million.
- Midsize and large corporate taxpayers, defined as corporations with assets between $5 million and $250 million. Large corporations are defined as having assets greater than $250 million.
- Tax-exempt, including employee plans, exempt organizations, and state and local governments. (See the new IRS organization chart on page 318.)

The shift is a dramatic one. The four groups or business units are intended to replace the IRS's four regional offices and much of the national office, leaving the remaining national office structure to focus on overseeing the IRS and broad policy concerns rather than operations. According to the IRS, regions and districts, in their current format, will no longer exist. However, the service centers will probably continue much the same as they do today. The work that goes on there, from processing to customer service, is considered crucial, though some of the service center work may be realigned to the individual business units. The service centers, along with the toll-free IRS sites and the Automated Collection System sites, will, however, be customized to better deal with segments of customers and their questions.

Commissioner Rossotti has said that the overall concept for this new subdivision is based on proven established practice throughout most of the private sector. Instead of one institution doing everything for everybody, now, within that organization, there will be different operating divisions working for different kinds of customers.

Let's see where each of these buiness units stands:

Wage and Investment Income (W&I)
The one division that will directly touch the lives of most taxpayers is Wage and Investment Income (W&I). According to the IRS, about 47,000 employees currently working in National Headquarters, Customer Service, district walk-ins, electronic filing, and taxpayer education will offer improved service to 123 million taxpayers. The taxpayers in this segment have only wage and investment income, most of which is reported and withheld by third parties. The division headquarters will be located in Atlanta, Georgia, and there will be seven area headquarters offices, eight Submission Processing field sites, five Accounts Man-

agement field sites, and five Compliance Services sites. The division will be divided into four major components, the Headquarters Office and three operating units: Communications, Customer Assistance, Research and Education (CARE); Customer Account Services (CAS); and Compliance.

The Headquarters Office will be staffed with about 470 employees involved in human resources, finance, business systems planning, Equal Employment Opportunity, and electronic tax administration (ETA), which is building an account management organization to increase the use of IRS e-file. (See pages 344–345.)

CARE will be staffed with about 5,000 employees who will be involved with media and publications, taxpayer education and communications, and field assistance. CARE focuses on prefiling needs and on developing a variety of customer-focused needs, such as forms and publications, and educational programs, as well as providing face-to-face assistance and resolving wage and investment compliance issues at walk-in sites.

CAS will be staffed with about 400 in the headquarters, with another 34,700 employees who will be involved in submission processing and accounts management. The primary function of this area includes processing tax returns, issuing refunds, and resolving wage and investment taxpayer accounts.

Compliance headquarters will be staffed with about 130 employees who will manage examination and collection activities. About 6,000 employees will be responsible for telephone and correspondence transactions.

As you can see from this setup, W&I literally pulls apart the essence of what is required to process individual tax returns and deal with taxpayer compliance and problems.

Remember, Commissioner Rossotti is using a flexible approach to establishing these business processes, meaning that if a job or function assigned to a given area or division doesn't prove effective, it will be shifted to where it would work better.

The preliminary time line calls for W&I headquarters to be established and its senior leaders selected during the year 2000. By early 2002, customers will begin filing in five centers dedicated to W&I customers.

Small Business and Self-Employed (SB/SE)

The 47,000 IRS employees in the Small Business and Self-Employed Division will be broken out into 31,000 at headquarters and the field, and another 16,000 from service centers. It will provide one-stop service for small companies ranging from one-person start-up companies to established businesses, including taxpayers who file Schedule C and E, Partnership, S corporation and C corporation returns with assets of less than $5 million. This group, about 45 million of them, has more frequent and complex filing requirements and must often interact with the IRS up to 60 times a year regarding monthly tax deposits, quarterly employment returns, and more.

Headquarters will be in New Carrollton, Maryland, and there will also be 14 field organizations across the country. The division will be organized around three major processes:

- Taxpayer Education and Communication will provide prefiling help for taxpayers and will work closely with industry groups and tax practitioners.
- Customer Account Services representatives from W&I will help this division process returns and manage accounts over the telephone, by E-mail, and by correspondence.
- Compliance will handle postfiling activities. SB/SE will also handle U.S. taxpayers who live overseas, estate and gift, excise, and employment returns. Plans call for operations to begin in 2000.

Large and Midsize Business (LMSB)
The Large and Midsize Business Division consists of some 210,000 corporations, subchapter S corporations, and partnerships with assets of over $5 million. That group pays about $712 billion in taxes annually. The division will be served by about 8,500 IRS employees and will be functionally aligned around five industry groups:

- Financial services and health care, headquartered in Manhattan, will serve 5,000 large businesses and 41,600 midsize businesses. This sector will consist of commercial banks, savings and loan institutions, securities and financial services, health care, and insurance.
- Food, retail, and pharmaceutical, headquartered in Chicago, will serve 1,000 large businesses and 28,200 midsize businesses. This group will include food and beverage, retailing, pharmaceuticals, agricultural commodities, and farms.
- Natural resources, headquartered in Houston, serves 1,300 large businesses and 16,100 midsize businesses. This group will consist of oil and gas, mining, forest products, and utilities, including chemical engineering, energy-related industries, and all natural resources.

- Communications, technology, and media, headquartered in the San Francisco Bay Area, is responsible for 500 large businesses and 13,600 midsize businesses. This group will consist of producers of computers and related equipment, including communications and software, broadcasting, publishing, sports franchises, and recreational services.
- Heavy manufacturing, construction, and transportation, headquartered in central New Jersey, will serve nearly 103,000 taxpayers. This group will include tax law specialists in the areas of air and ground transportation, aerospace, motor vehicles, shipping, construction, and real estate.

Leadership for the Large and Midsize Business Division is currently being recruited. Its headquarters, staffed by about 315 employees, will be located in a newly constructed building in Washington, D.C. Operations in this division began in early 2000 in selected cities around the country, making it the second of the four divisions to roll out.

Tax Exempt and Government Entities
The Tax Exempt and Government Entities Division, with about 1.6 million filers, will serve three customer segments:

- Employee Plans will serve over a million private and public retirement plans, controlling assets of over $4 trillion.
- Exempt Organizations will cover more than a million tax-exempt organizations and 350,000 religious organizations. This segment controls more than $1.3 trillion in assets.
- Government Entities will serve 86,000 federal, state, and local governments and oversee more than 220,000 outstanding tax-exempt bond issuances valued at $1.3 trillion. They will also address issues related to 559 federally recognized Native American tribes.

The focus of the first two will be to determine that their constituencies meet the criteria for tax-exempt status and comply with regulations. The focus of the latter will be to examine the exempt status of bonds issued by state and local entities.

This division will be headquartered in Washington, D.C., and the current 2,800 Employee Plans and Exempt Organizations staff throughout the IRS will form the core of the new division. This is the first of the four divisions to begin operation. The rollout was in December 1999.

All of the four main divisions—Wage and Investment Income, Small

Business and Self-Employed, Large and Midsize Business, and Tax Exempt and Government Entities—will have a common structure. This is how it will work, managerially: The person who heads each division will be supported by a management team within the division. The team will include the division's deputy commissioner and representatives from the Chief Counsel's Office, Appeals, Taxpayer Advocate, Criminal Investigation, and Information Systems. Each division will also have its own Examination Function and an Industry Research and Relations function, which will study market trends and gather and refine data about the needs of the industry and its taxpayers.

From the way things stand now, it appears as if the power of the IRS will rest in these four operating divisions. According to the IRS, the idea is to promote end-to-end accountability by making the divisions responsible for designing, developing, and implementing their own programs and procedures. Each management team will have the knowledge, responsibility, and authority to set policies and take the actions that best address the needs of the specific group it serves. Being the closest to its customers and most familiar with their needs, it will become the expert, for that taxpayer base, controlling policies, resources, and technology. In turn, this setup is expected to reduce the total number of management layers by about half the number found today, and hopefully speed decision making.

The IRS expects that by reorganizing by type of taxpayer, rather than by geographical area, the organization will have a greater ability to develop technical and industry expertise. As these changes become operational, remember that when you fill out your return, the IRS will have increasing industry expertise. In a way, the agency is extending its existing Market Segment Specialization approach.

The IRS believes that the new structure will encourage the practice of recruiting executives from the outside, something that has been uncommon, especially for IRS top management levels.

Benefits to Taxpayers
At least on paper, it seems clear that IRS Commissioner Rossotti has aligned the heart of the new IRS organization to fulfill taxpayers' needs. Though genuine benefits will only begin to play out once most of this is in place, there are several positives that bode well.

Since each of the four groups will be run by management teams solely dedicated to meeting the needs of the taxpayers they serve, this seems a vast improvement. In the current system, IRS officials are responsible for handling a wide variety of problems that typically arise in a district office or a service center. Logically, IRS employees in each of the four new groups should acquire much-needed expertise in recognizing *what* to do and *how* to do what's best for the taxpayers in their population. In other words, they will move from being generalists to being specialists. And if Mr. Rossotti has anything to say about it (and he does), each will be held accountable for meeting productivity, satisfaction, and solution-oriented requirements.

Finally, the most dramatic departure from the existing IRS structure, and, indeed, thinking, is the change of emphasis from collecting revenue to providing service.

Shared Services and Information Systems
The agencywide Shared Services Division will provide common services across the IRS. Shared Services will provide facilities management, personnel services, procurement, and Equal Employment Opportunity and Diversity Field Services. Formerly called Support Services, the new service will be set up like a business, where each of the four operating divisions will establish agreements that outline the services to be performed, their cost, and how to measure successful delivery. Plans call for implementation by mid-2000.

Given the continued emphasis on the IRS's systems modernization, the new IRS will have a revamped Information Systems (I/S) Division. Computer support staffs are being centralized under the Chief Information Officer, along with groups of non-I/S employees who perform key I/S work, such as systems development, systems operations, network management, telecommunications, and more. These groups will make the transition to the I/S function before December 2000. Then, over the next few years, the function will become a shared service that will fulfill tailored systems needs of the operating divisions. It will also have a single help desk to improve responsiveness to internal IRS customers.

Communications and Liaison Division (C&L)
This is a very interesting division, to be made up of 585 employees both in the field and at its Washington, D.C., headquarters. The division will be divided into Communications, Governmental Liaison and Disclosure, Legislative Affairs, and National Public Liaison. The role of Communications is to create an understanding or to market to the IRS staff and to taxpayers the IRS's corporate visions, mission, and goals. The mission of Governmental Liaison and Disclosure is to ensure protection of taxpayer and employee confidentiality rights while addressing the public's right to access information and to partner with federal, state,

and local governments to help taxpayers. Creating two specific areas to handle these two distinct sets of responsibilities speaks directly to RRA '98 and to much of the work that preceded it, not forgetting the IRS war stories presented by taxpayers to the Senate Ways and Means Committee. It also seems to encompass the enduring work of David Burnham and Susan Long, who fought for years for taxpayer privacy and fair treatment under the Freedom of Information Act.

According to the new IRS, the mission of Legislative Affairs is to help the IRS achieve its legislative objectives by building ongoing positive relationships with members of Congress. However, as mentioned before, the IRS has always been forceful in its relationships with Congress and, historically, has done a good job of getting its desires turned into law. So, essentially, this "new" law was working effectively long before it was passed.

The mission of National Public Liaison is to enhance the IRS's external relationships with professional groups and the business sector to improve voluntary compliance and reduce taxpayer burden. The idea of having a separate group devoted to reaching out to practitioners, i.e, tax professionals, taxpayer assistance groups, business and trade associations, and government groups, is quite innovative, and so far, at least, it looks good on paper. My experience is that tax practitioners listen carefully and adjust quickly to new legislation, while it typically takes the grass-roots level of the IRS at least two years to catch up to changes handed down by its own policymakers.

Service Centers Become Campuses

In moving toward the new organization, the 10 existing IRS service centers will become 10 "campuses." Each campus will have staff performing functions of Accounts Management, Compliance Services (currently Customer Service), and Submission Processing for the Wage and Investment (W&I) and Small Business/Self-Employed (SB/SE) divisions.

This is the first time that Customer Service and Submission Processing operations have been aligned under two distinct management structures. The Customer Service sites will specialize in assisting taxpayers by telephone and correspondence and helping them on matters from tax laws to resolving problems with their accounts. Submission Processing will specialize in processing tax forms, payments, and deposits. This should allow employees in this area to focus on improving quality and productivity as well as customer service by, it is hoped, eliminating the need for follow-up contacts with taxpayers.

The IRS expects that this alignment will make it easier to manage its Customer Service facilities and to respond quickly to changes and unforeseen emergencies. For example, if one site is unable to handle calls due to bad weather, such as a hurricane, the work can easily be shifted to another site. The realignment also makes sense regarding the ability to train personnel on a timely basis, especially for the filing season. It will also allow for consistent procedures and technology across the agency. Each of the 10 individual sites will have its own director.

The move from the service centers to the campuses is expected to continue throughout the next two years, during which time special teams will examine site-specific issues, including personnel, training, and facilities.

The Transition
A great deal of private, up-front consulting studies and analysis went into what has thus far been conceived. Time lines, phases, and teams assigned very specific tasks have brought the work through the "implementation planning" stage into the design phase, and for some areas, such as Tax Exempt and Large and Midsize Business, into the rollout stage.

What will happen to the IRS, and perhaps, more importantly to us, the taxpayers, while this enormous shift takes place from the existing organization to the new one? It appears that it will be "business as usual." What has run the organization thus far will continue to run it. The new law makes that infinitely clear. Whatever proceedings, cases, payments due, lawsuits filed, or actions are in the process of being handled now will continue. This also applies to appeals taken. The IRS has made it clear that phasing in the new organization means that some new units will become operational while districts, regions, and the National Office are still operating. In other words, don't expect a clear-cut IRS organization chart in the near future!

The IRS Commissioner
As before, the IRS commissioner continues to be appointed by the president, and may be removed at any time by the president. The commissioner reports to the secretary of the Treasury, who delegates to the commissioner the responsibility for administering the tax laws. Tax policy, however, is the domain of the assistant secretary of the Treasury.

Whereas in the past the IRS commissioner was out of a job each time a new president came into office, the new law makes the commissioner's term permanent for a five-year period with the possibility of being reappointed to another five-year term.

Furthermore, several specific functions of the commissioner have been categorized and spelled out:

- To administer, manage, direct, and supervise the execution and application of the tax laws and tax treaty provisions.
- To recommend to the president candidates for, or the removal of, chief counsel, as well as have some control over the same for high-level executives.
- To appoint and direct personnel necessary for the administration and enforcement of the tax laws, and to assign posts of duty.

Benefits to Taxpayers

The constant turnover at the top of the IRS has made it consistently difficult if not impossible for anyone to "run the show." How much could anyone learn about the operation of an organization having the size and scope of the IRS in four years, much less make valuable managerial strides? The situation has been clearly out of hand for some time now. The five-year term should result in a greater degree of continuity and accountability, as well as minimize political interference.

Furthermore, because the commissioner came and went but a body of senior executives stayed on, often 15 years or more, similar to the ones described previously in the Examination Division, these entrenched executives have made it extremely difficult to implement new management approaches of any kind. With more defined responsibilities and some control over the hiring and firing practices of upper-level executives, the commissioner should be in a better position to direct the IRS and make management and operational changes as necessary.

The Chief Counsel

As before, the chief counsel, who is also appointed by the president, reports to the IRS commissioner. However, in the new law there has been an important division of labor in the chief counsel's functions:

Regarding legal advice, interpretation of tax law not relating to tax policy, and tax litigation, the chief counsel reports to both the commissioner and the general counsel for the Treasury Department.

Regarding legal advice or interpretation of tax law relating solely to tax policy, the chief counsel reports only to the general counsel.

The biggest change in the Chief Counsel's Office is that it will be reorganized to provide legal support to each of the four new operating units, though staff will continue to report to the chief counsel. The thinking is that most of the counsel's field attorneys will remain in their current posts but will be aligned to meet the specialized needs of one of the four divisions. The Chief Counsel's National Office technical experts will remain in Washington, D.C.

Implementation will proceed in stages, with the field attorneys being coordinated with the schedule for establishing the new IRS operating divisions.

Appeals

Officers in the new Appeals organization will have some settlement authority to work with taxpayers and examiners on factual disputes, the goal being to resolve cases in an average of 14 days. The work and Washington, D.C., location of the 2,100 appeals employees will stay more or less the same, except there will be only one layer of management between headquarters and employees who interact with taxpayers. As with the Chief Counsel's Office, Appeals will be similarly divided into units to support the Wage and Investment Income, Small Business and Self-Employed, Tax Exempt and Government Entities, and Large and Midsize Business divisions.

Legislation ensures that the reorganized IRS will have "an independent appeals function," which will prohibit "ex parte" communications, the exchange of information between Appeals officers and other IRS employees, especially auditors, so as not to inadvertently or intentionally color the facts presented in an appeal. As far as anyone can tell, this is the first time an attempt has been made to legislate this important facet of taxpayer rights into existence.

Benefits to Taxpayers

This dual reporting relationship is designed to ensure that the chief counsel connects to the commissioner on matters relating to the IRS's day-to-day operations. But it preserves the traditional separation of the IRS commissioner from influencing tax policy.

National Taxpayer Advocate

Perhaps you recall the Taxpayer Ombudsman Office, the Office of the Taxpayer Advocate, the Problem Resolution Office, and the Taxpayer Advocate. For nearly 20 years the IRS has provided some form of assistance to taxpayers who have had problems with the agency. Unfortunately, most of the time taxpayers were not aware these services existed and, for the most part, the services themselves were generally understaffed, overburdened, and therefore not generally effective.

Now there will be a National Taxpayer Advocate (NTA) appointed by the Treasury Secretary. The NTA must have a background in customer service and tax law along with experience representing individual taxpayers. This person may or may not have been an officer or employee of the IRS.

The responsibilities of the NTA are to

- Assist taxpayers in resolving problems with the IRS.
- Identify the areas in which taxpayers have problems in dealing with the IRS.
- Propose changes to administrative practices and identify possible changes in the law to minimize such problem areas.
- Issue Taxpayer Assistance Orders.
- Supervise local taxpayer advocate offices.
- Prepare detailed semiannual reports for use by Congress that stress solutions such as identifying the primary areas of tax law that impose compliance burdens on taxpayers or the IRS and identifying the most litigated issues, with recommendations for mitigating these disputes.

In a move designed to provide taxpayers a greater voice inside the IRS, Commissioner Rossotti has set up a network of Taxpayer Advocates. There will be 74 Taxpayer Advocates located across the country, at least one in each state, as well as one at each of the 10 IRS service centers or campuses. The local advocates will report to nine Area Taxpayer Advocates serving under the National Taxpayer Advocate, a total of 2,300 employees nationwide, says the IRS. Four more advocates will be added when the new IRS operating divisions are put in place. These four will be specialists responsible for making suggestions about improvements in the divisions. New positions will include Associate Advocates, who will handle routine taxpayer problems, and Senior Associate Advocates and Technical Advisors, who will be forwarded more complex taxpayer cases. Furthermore, caseworkers handling taxpayers' cases through the National Taxpayer Advocate's Problems Resolution Program will now be assigned full-time to the job. Previously, their time was split between Taxpayer Advocate cases and other IRS casework.

When an advocate meets initially with any taxpayer, the advocate must explain that the Taxpayer Advocates operate independently of any other IRS offices and that they report directly to Congress through the National Taxpayer Advocate. The local Taxpayer Advocate has the discretion *not* to inform the IRS of any contact with that taxpayer or of any information provided to the local office by the taxpayer. It is also not intended that the local advocates report to a district director or other IRS official. These issues of trust and the viability of keeping the Taxpayer Advocates insulated from the rest of the IRS are important ones if the TA function is to work.

NOTE: Each local TA office must have a separate telephone, fax machine, and post office address, as well as other electronic communication access that is independent of the IRS.

Regarding visibility—the local Taxpayer Advocate will no longer be a well-kept secret. The telephone numbers of the TA offices must be published on statutory notices of deficiency sent to taxpayers as well as in traditional media such as telephone directories. You can now call the TA at a toll-free hotline, 877-777-4778.

This part of RRA '98 also sets forth new rules for determining the issuance of Form 911 (Application for Taxpayer Assistance Order to Relieve Hardship), generally referred to as a Taxpayer Assistance Order (TAO). The form originally appeared in the Taxpayer Bill of Rights, and it became effective January 1, 1989. It is designed, as the instructions indicate, "for a significant hardship situation that may have already occurred or is about to occur if the IRS takes or fails to take certain actions. A significant hardship normally means not being able to provide the necessities for you or your family." While the application for a TAO is being reviewed, any enforcement actions are suspended and only the Taxpayer Ombudsman, through the Problem Resolution Office, has the authority to issue it.

The problems with the TAO were that the IRS made it very difficult to prove "significant hardship" and even when you did, though relief, or suspension of an IRS action, was supposed to be upcoming within 48 hours, collection officers nevertheless often went ahead with collection activity anyway. In time, tax pros would resort to other measures that could be just as effective, so use of the TAO has never become exactly overwhelming.

However, the new law broadens the use of the TAO that can now be issued by the National Taxpayer Advocate and supervising local taxpayer offices. A TAO can be issued if there is

- An immediate threat of adverse action.
- A delay of more than 30 days in resolving a taxpayer problem.
- An incurring by the taxpayer of significant costs (attorneys' or accountants' fees) if relief is not granted.
- Irreparable injury or long-term adverse impact on the taxpayer if relief is not granted.[1]

Benefits to Taxpayers

A TAO can be a tremendous help if a taxpayer, or the tax pro or attorney handling the hardship case, is able to secure one. I have had clients whose lives, along with their homes and possessions, have literally been saved by a timely TAO. If the law is applied as intended, hundreds or thousands of new TAO's will be authorized, saving taxpayers who desperately need this level of help. If you are in an emergency situation, call the Taxpayer Advocate office directly and someone there will help you fill out Form 911.

IRS Headquarters

One major concern about the current IRS National Office is its distance from taxpayers. To be more responsive to taxpayer needs and to the needs of employees in the field, the new model gives IRS headquarters greater responsibility for and involvement in operations for other departments. The new National Office staff will be smaller than it is today and will include the Commissioner's Office, Management and Finance, Communications and Liaison, and Equal Employment Opportunity and Diversity. The staff will also handle Human Resources, Research, and Statistics of Income.

Oversight Board

In an attempt to rebuild public confidence in the IRS, and to maintain it, a special board is in place to oversee the functioning of the IRS. Although there are currently several other groups in existence designed to advise the IRS on policy and management, the Oversight Board has actual authority to control certain actions within the IRS.

The board consists of nine members, six of whom (known as private-life individuals) are not federal officers or employees, plus the secretary of the Treasury (or deputy secretary of the Treasury), the IRS commissioner, and one person who is a full-time federal employee or an employee representative. The private-life members and the employee representative are appointed by the president.

Qualified candidates have a range of professional experience and expertise in one or more of the following: management, customer service, federal tax laws, and the needs and concerns of small businesses. The length of the terms is staggered and vary from two to five years.

The board's role is quite broad. Among other things, it is to ensure that taxpayers are being treated properly by IRS employees, and to review and approve IRS strategic plans, performance standards, reorganizations, operational functions (modernizing the tax system), and training and education. It can also make recommendations to fill high-level IRS positions as well as evaluate whether officers in those positions should be removed. The IRS budget prepared by the IRS commissioner is subject to review and approval by the board.

However, the board has no authority to develop tax policy or interfere in law enforcement activities of the IRS, including audits, collection, or criminal investigations.

The private-life members receive $30,000 in annual compensation, as does the employee representative if that person is not also a federal officer or employee.

Mr. Rossotti is optimistic when he says, "If capable and enthusiastic board members are chosen who are truly committed to getting to know the agency and take their jobs as seriously as those sitting on the boards of Fortune 500 corporations, the IRS will finally have a truly independent advisory board that can help guide the agency into the twenty-first century."[2]

Benefits to Taxpayers

The date of enactment for beginning the reconstruction of the IRS as described here was July 22, 1998, when the law was signed. But what cannot be stressed enough is this: Restructuring the IRS is an enormous undertaking. There's the new organizational vision, the technology behemoth to sort out, the about-face focus on customer service versus collection, and finally there's the IRS—the people, the employees, and the staff to deal with.

Mr. Rossotti is to be congratulated for his courage in not only taking the job of IRS commissioner, but actually using his years of management and technology expertise toward getting as far as he has. RRA '98 is the work of many, but the push behind it all is Rossotti, who must have the political savvy equivalent to some of the finest politicians we have ever known. But the reorganization is happening in stages with lots of different balls being juggled in the air simultaneously. That is exactly how a professional executive works.

So far, IRS people are being shifted and moved into place, and new divisions are continuing to roll out. Yes, there are major downturns in certain areas, but the IRS is in the thick of being reorganized. If Mr. Rossotti and his staff at the IRS continue in this fasion, heading toward the goals of RRA '98, taxpayers as well as the IRS should be the better for it.

14

—

Where the IRS Is (or Isn't) Going
and What *to* Do,
or *Not* Do, About It

What more comforting gift than a glimpse into the future could someone give to taxpayers who want every assurance possible when it
comes to the IRS? An educated look could successfully extend a taxpayer's horizons far beyond the pages of this book. Our attempt to establish a new approach for taxpayers regarding their relationship with
the IRS now leaves us at the door to the future. At this junction, there
are obstacles the IRS must overcome, directions the IRS is taking, and
new trends appearing on the horizon.

DIRECTION—REFORM

During the seven years this book has been published, the IRS has attempted a variety of plans to "reinvent" itself, each with similar, laudable
goals. Now the situation has been taken out of the agency's hands.
Though political posturing is rife and the pressure on the new IRS commissioner, Charles Rossotti, to make everything happen now must be
overwhelming, let's remain calm and look at some of Mr. Rossotti's intentions.

Overall, he aims "to bring corporate know-how to an antiquated
agency and upgrade its seriously outmoded technological systems."[1]

He has parceled the work to be done into five components:

- Organizing the IRS into four distinct operating groups, each having
  responsibility for serving taxpayers with similar needs and compli-

ance requirements—individual taxpayers, small businesses, large corporations, and tax-exempt organizations.

- Creating cohesive management teams for the four operating groups, each focusing on the particular needs and problems of the units it serves.
- Gearing business practices toward customer service, so that IRS staff would understand, solve, and prevent taxpayer problems.
- Establishing new measurements of an employee's performance to create a balance between customer service and fair enforcement of the tax law.
- Upgrading existing technology through central professional management, common standards, and partnerships among all those involved—business units, information technology professionals, and outside contractors.

This, Mr. Rossotti says, is not simply a reorganization. It is more of a stabilization and refocusing. Given this neatly designed process, the commissioner still has several other major issues to contend with.

OBSTACLES TO OVERCOME

Quotas Versus Customer Service

Do quotas exist at the IRS? Many believe they always did, though the IRS has consistently denied it, stating that at least as far back as 1988, collection quotas were outlawed.

However, during the Senate Finance Committee hearings, it appeared that IRS agents levied unwarranted tax assessments and unfairly seized property to prove they were doing their jobs. Furthermore, IRS agents struggling to meet collection quotas were targeting lower- and middle-income taxpayers who couldn't afford to fight back. In a six-month study, it was also found that tax assessments were being levied to raise the individual statistics of an IRS employee, and that there was a commonplace use of tax collection quotas to rate agents or officers.[2]

So although the IRS says there are no quotas, when performance measurements are based on statistical information connected to enforcement activities, isn't that the same thing as having a quota? If your employees' performance, productivity, and achievements are based on statistical results, well, the message is clear. Performance measures are what this is all about, and Mr. Rossotti has zoomed right in on the situation.

His immediate measures were aimed at rooting out abuse and stopping the practice of linking employee performance to tax collection. Accordingly, he conducted an internal audit of the IRS's general policy on quotas and other key issues. To review the findings, he created a panel consisting of high-ranking IRS staff and executives outside the IRS.

The results regarding the quotas: There would be no more ranking the 33 IRS district offices on the basis of how closely they met their goal of tax collections. An in-house guide for tax collectors would be rewritten to emphasize customer service over productivity. Goals related to revenue production in the field would be suspended. Enforcement results would not be used to evaluate employees. And penalty amounts and revenue collected would no longer be included in statistical results.

It seems that, by following this route, Mr. Rossotti is positioning the IRS in no uncertain terms for its new role as taxpayer advocate.

Evaluating Job Performance

A new system, referred to as a balanced measurement system, is to encompass three ways to evaluate employee job performance—business results, customer satisfaction, and employee satisfaction—while downplaying statistical enforcement goals. These measures are to be aligned from the top of the organization down to the frontline employees. But guess what! Preliminary results of an ongoing review of the IRS's employee evaluation systems tended to emphasize efficiency and revenue over customer service. I'm sure that comes as no surprise. It will be enormously difficult to develop a new performance-based system that will offer new ways to measure business results that do not rely on enforcement. Enforcement statistics have been used to rank the performance of IRS district offices and have played an important part in the evaluation of the performance of managers in those offices. Although those measures are now prohibited, further IRS studies show that employees continue to perceive that enforcement statistics affect evaluations despite the prohibition. Creating this "disconnect," as the IRS calls it, is going to be tough, and it may not be completely realized at least until all the old-timers are retired.

Closely tied to evaluating performance is having a baseline for measuring business results. You can't do one without the other. The Taxpayer Compliance Measurement Program (TCMP) audits once offered what the IRA felt was a reliable measure for voluntary compliance. But those audits have been suspended because of the burden they placed on the taxpayer. It appears, however, as if the IRS is musing about a modified version of the TCMP that's easier on taxpayers. How it's going to manage that is anyone's guess.

Meanwhile, for other directions the IRS is moving toward in the near future, this is what you need to know.

Whistle-blowers and Reprisals

Amidst the hard work and genuine effort going into the creation of new ways to evaluate an employee's performance comes news of the backlash directed at IRS employees who spoke up before the congressional investigation that led to RRA '98. It appears that these whistle-blowers are suffering on the job. How far, really, can the IRS possibly advance into the new millennium, with all of its defined goals and initiatives, if this kind of Stone Age attitude still surfaces within its ranks? In spite of IRS assurances that there would be no retaliation against employees, the jobs of most of the agents who testified before the Senate Finance Committee in 1997 are being threatened, according to Senator William Roth, Jr. (R-Del.) and William Nixon in their book, *The Power to Destroy.*

According to Roth, a vast majority of employees report that the agency has a "kill the messenger" attitude, and more than 70 percent of the almost 100,000 employees polled said that there are not adequate protections against retaliation for employees who come forward with reports of abuses against taxpayers or fellow employees. Commissioner Rossotti has promised to get to the bottom of the reprisal issue.[3]

Slowdown in IRS Collections

From the passage of RRA '98 until now, the news regarding the results of the IRS Collection Department has been quite astonishing. In the six months ending March 31, 1999, the IRS says it seized taxpayer property for overdue taxes approximately 110 times. This represents a sharp decrease from the same period in 1998, when there were more than 1,150 seizures, and a dramatic drop from 5,000 only two years ago. "The outlook for the last 10 years showed a drop of 98 percent, from about 10,000 seizures annually to 161 in 1999."[4] Liens on property also fell from 272,000 to 98,000, as did levies. In 1999 there were only 504,403 levies, a drop of 86 percent in two years. The IRS continues to say that these sorts of decreases are partially due to a mandatory allocation of IRS staff to implement new RRA '98 provisions, and using its existing budget—somewhere around $8.1 billion—for new computers and training. It is true that the IRS has shifted large portions of its employees, about 21,000 people, including those in collection and examination, to temporarily bolster customer service efforts, i.e., answering phones, working at counters in walk-in centers, and participating in Saturday Problem-Solving Days, and with the agencywide training effort, time usually spent on regular assignments is further eaten away.

But IRS officers in six states said in interviews with *The New York Times* that the biggest reason for the retreat was their fear of being dismissed for running afoul of the new law intended to protect taxpayers from overzealous collectors.

The IRS Restructuring and Reform Act of 1998 states that agency employees must be dismissed if, following an administrative inquiry, they are found to have committed any of 10 acts, among them violating a taxpayer's constitutional or civil rights, threatening an audit for personal gain, making a false statement under oath, or falsifying or destroying documents to conceal mistakes. Employees terminated under the law have no right to appeal. It is a genuine cultural revolution, with many employees struggling to shift from an adversarial approach to the new customer-service mind-set. The result, current and former IRS officials said, is near paralysis in the agency's enforcement apparatus.[5] "Seizing property, for example, now requires a 54-step process that more than two dozen revenue officers have described as virtually impossible to navigate."[6]

The culprit is allegedly what has come to be called "The 10 deadly sins for which collection agents can be fired." For the benefit of all taxpayers, here they are:

1. Willfully seizing taxpayer assets without authorization.
2. Making false statements under oath about a taxpayer or taxpayer representative.
3. Violating the constitutional or civil rights of a taxpayer or taxpayer representative.
4. Falsifying or destroying documents to conceal mistakes.
5. Committing assault or battery on a taxpayer or taxpayer representative.
6. Retaliating against or harassing a taxpayer or taxpayer representative, in violation of the Tax Code or IRS rules.
7. Willfully misusing "confidentiality" rules to conceal information from a congressional inquiry.
8. Willfully failing to file tax returns.
9. Willfully understating tax liabilities.
10. Threatening to audit a taxpayer for personal gain.[7]

Add to this a 19 percent *decrease* in the number of tax collectors—to 6,800—and a 13 percent *increase* in the number of tax returns being filed—to 226 million—for 1999. Commissioner Rossotti has gone on record expressing his concern. And he should. It seems that in the collection area, things can't get much worse. The IRS is currently facing a situation where the number of tax delinquents going without paying their tax bill is so huge, billions of dollars are being left uncollected.

Is this just a sudden-death reaction to the change, and will the IRS response calm down in time? I see it as a period of adjustment. No doubt enforcement efforts will taper off during this time, but once the momentum of the new laws kicks in, with Rossotti spearheading the change, there should be a leveling off. Remember, these IRS agents have been doing it their way for 15 years or more. The new law threatens those ways. Some in the agency believe that all a taxpayer has to do is say, "I'm not paying," or offer $10 a week toward an installment agreement in lieu of thousands of tax dollars owed, or say the magic word, "harassment," and that will be the end of that. But that's probably just a front, the propaganda of resistance made more real by some IRS employees relaxing their efforts. What's worse—collection agents following new rules for seizing property, or a taxpayer being unfairly harassed by having a lien placed on his house?

In keeping with the 1998 legislation, here's another victory for taxpayers, and a direct hit at the IRS Collection Division. In July 1999, the IRS issued regulations aimed to provide greater relief from tax debts. Now people with overdue taxes will be able to keep their securities (stocks and bonds), businesses, and homes if they can show that they need these assets to pay for medical care or basic living expenses.

This is a real change from previous IRS collection methods of seizing a taxpayer's assets and selling them, usually at a great discount, in return for taxes owed, often with no questions asked—or allowed. Now, a taxpayer with a stock portfolio and a history of paying taxes on time until trouble struck might be able to wipe out or significantly reduce a tax bill if he or she could show that the assets were needed, for example, to pay medical bills.[8] It's another step toward taxpayers receiving greater due process under the law.

If collections and enforcement continue to drop, it will be interesting to see the steps the IRS and Congress will take. Some switch—creating a balance between fair and adequate collections and fair and decent treatment of taxpayers—is in the works!

Innocent Spouse Relief—Huge Backlog of Requests

From April 1998 until the passage of RRA '98, there were 3,000 innocent spouse claims waiting to be handled at the IRS. Since the passage of RRA '98 and May 2000, the IRS has received about 85,700 relief requests from about 45,000 taxpayers. Of those 85,700 claims, there were 30,451 relief requests still pending. Of the claims that met the requirements for being considered, about 45 percent were allowed in full, and 8 percent were partially allowed.[9] **Claims are continuing to rise at a rate of**

4,000 per month! Nevertheless, Commissioner Rossotti says that "this growth in claims is a good sign that America's taxpayers are learning about the innocent spouse provision from many sources, including our aggressive outreach program and the Taxpayer Advocates."[10] It seems that the current pileup is due to several factors: Thousands of taxpayers are becoming aware of the new law and how they can be helped by it, and IRS employees are needing more time to interpret the new law and to develop procedures to put the provisions into effect. Again, IRS staff from examination have been borrowed from auditing assignments to help reduce the backlog and to weed out ineligible taxpayers.

"In fact, the IRS has pulled about 500 auditors, more than 3 percent of its auditing force, to help with the huge backlog of innocent spouse requests. This represents at least one audit group of 10 to 15 auditors in each of the 33 IRS districts."[11]

Of the 73,777 requests filed between March 1999 through March 2000, approximately 15,500, or some 21 percent, were determined not to meet basic requirements for processing. Through its on-line E-mail issued April 26, 2000, the IRS announced the top five reasons for the delays in processing Form 8857 (Request for Innocent Spouse Relief):

1. The collection statute of limitations had already expired and there was no longer a balance due.
2. The taxpayer was an "injured spouse" and should have filed Form 8379 (Injured Spouse Claim and Allocation).
3. The requesting spouse did not file a joint federal tax return for the year relief was requested.
4. Incomplete information was submitted, and the requesting spouse did not respond to IRS requests for additional data.
5. The year for which relief was requested was not identified accurately on line 1 of Form 8857.

For anyone wishing to check eligibility for innocent spouse relief, try going on-line at www.irs.gov/ind_info/s_tree/index.html. In addition, the "Spousal Tax Relief Eligibility Explorer" is available as a link from the "Tax Info for You" page of the IRS website at www.irs.gov. This program offers an interactive prompt to help taxpayers determine if they qualify for relief from a joint tax liability with their current or former spouse. If it appears that you qualify, the program offers to download the appropriate application form.[12]

IRS Publication 3512, *Innocent Spouse Relief*, outlines eligibility for innocent spouse relief, gives information about the forms needed to be filed, and tells who to contact at the IRS.

These aids are certainly impressive, considering how quickly they have appeared since the law went into effect. No doubt they are examples of a newer, more responsive IRS under Commissioner Rossotti.

During an address to the American Institute of CPAs Tax Division, Commissioner Rossotti said that it's not just "innocent" spouses who are petitioning for a rollback in federal tax assessments, interest, and penalties. The requests are coming in from battered wives, individuals "separated" from their spouses because of military duty, and even the spouses of prison inmates. In some cases the IRS is receiving petitions for spousal relief from both parties in a failed marriage.

The innocent spouse provision is filling a tremendous need for spouses who have been wrongly accused and been made responsible for tax misdeeds not their own simply because they filed a joint return. To say that the situation has been pent up for years is obvious.

NOTE: For those filing these claims, make sure you select the correct one, either Form 8857 or Form 8379, and fill in the information as requested. Like all IRS forms, it may be confusing, so consider asking a tax pro for help.

Training—The Infrastructure of Change

Rather than trying to grab tight budget dollars for a quick fix of its systems (one of the most visible of IRS flaws)—an unfortunate habit of previous IRS commissioners—Mr. Rossotti seems to understand the value of training to effect real change. New laws, endless promises, and stacks of documents reiterating plans and ideas to improve the IRS are fine, but little will come to fruition unless staff—all of the almost 100,000 IRS employed—are trained to do their part. Besides the overwhelming demands required for changing the old IRS into its newly developed vision, there's a great deal more that needs to be handled. This includes the implementation of RRA '98 legislation, 423 tax code changes, 153 revised forms and 39 revised publications, 14 new regulations, and 8 revenue procedures.[13]

Accordingly, in his appearance before the Ways and Means Oversight Subcommittee regarding IRS reform in July 1999, Mr. Rossotti described the massive training effort currently under way. Since about 70 percent of IRS employees deal directly with taxpayers, he stated that "taxpayers have every right to expect that in every such encounter with an IRS employee, whether it is a phone call asking a question about how to fill out a return, or a meeting with a revenue agent in an audit, the IRS employee should understand the current tax law and have the skills to understand the facts and circumstances of that taxpayer."[14] To accomplish this, 60,000 employees are being given up to 1.5 million hours of formal implementation training on new statutory requirements and key procedures. About 75,000 employees are being given technical training. Overall, nearly everyone at the IRS will be provided with some form of essential training through a variety of measures. Individual training plans are being developed, involving testing and evaluation, for each IRS function, along with a certification process for completing the courses. Video courses have been developed on Collection Due Process, Installment Agreements, Offers in Compromise, Seizures, Innocent Spouse Relief, and more, and information is being constantly posted to the IRS's Corporate Education website, linked to the National Resource Center established in July 1998 to coordinate policy and program questions via IRS E-mail. The Center answers questions posed by IRS staff regarding RRA '98.

Of course this requires a great deal of coordinating, monitoring, and evaluating, and that appears to be what's happening. In addition to the National Resource Center, a network has been established of over 180 RRA '98 field coordinators in each IRS district, region, and service center identified and trained to be local points of contact for the training and education effort. For fiscal year 2000, the goal is for IRS employees to apply specific provisions of RRA '98 and the newly revised *Internal Revenue Manual* into their daily operations. The training operation is no doubt swallowing a large chunk of the IRS's budget and cutting down substantially on the time employees have to fulfill their normal workloads. That's one of the reasons why Rosotti made a grand plea before the Ways and Means Oversight Subcommittee hearing not to reduce the IRS budget. We won't know for a few more months.

Pervasive Weaknesses in the IRS

Despite what will surely be ongoing efforts to treat taxpayers fairly and to set about creating a new IRS, some things never do change, a fact the GAO has been witness to for decades through its periodic investigations of the IRS.

In an embarrassing about-face during a time in which taxpayers are supposed to envision the IRS moving urgently and valiantly ahead—in terms of progress, that is—federal auditors told Congress that the financial management weaknesses that plagued the IRS for years have returned with a vengeance. The new audit uncovered "pervasive weaknesses in the design and operation of the IRS's financial management systems accounting procedures, documentation, record keeping and internal controls," the U.S. General Accounting Office said in a report on the service's 1998 operations.

These are some of the major deficiencies cited:

- An inadequate financial reporting process that resulted in the IRS's inability to reliably prepare several of the required principal financial statements.
- Deficiencies in preventative controls that resulted in the disbursement of $17 million of fraudulent refunds.
- The lack of a subsidiary ledger to properly manage unpaid assets. (Roughly estimated, only about $26 billion of the $222 billion in unpaid taxes as of October 1998 is likely to be collected.)
- An inability to reconcile its fund balance with Treasury Department records.
- A failure to provide assurance that the agency's $8.1 billion budget is being properly accounted for, and
- An inability to safeguard its own property and equipment (keeping track of a $300,000 laser printer, laptop computers, televisions, VCRs, fax machines).[15] This also involves embezzlement by IRS employees from January 1995 to July 1997 amounting to $5.3 million, including an altered check that read "IRSmith" deposited in a personal checking account.[16]

Where will it end? Commissioner Rossotti must be asking himself. The IRS is incapable of doing inside its own house what it expects taxpayers across the country to do: basic record keeping and accounting.

The GAO also said that some of the procedures in place at the IRS are so defective that the confidentiality of taxpayer information may be in jeopardy. The GAO found serious flaws in the tax service's computer security procedures "that may allow unauthorized individuals to access, alter, or abuse proprietary IRS programs and data," as well as taxpayer information. This problem is not a new one.

IRS ON TRACK: DIRECTION—ELECTRONIC FILING— INDIVIDUAL RETURNS

These are the primary directions where the IRS is heading.

Electronic filing, which began in 1986, has developed to the point where taxpayers can sit in front of a computer in their home or office, type in numbers on a 1040 on their screen, make one telephone call, then transmit their 1040 via a modem and tax preparation software directly to the IRS computers. Initially, returns were filed not by taxpayers themselves, but by tax professionals whose equipment and software have been certified by the IRS for performing electronic filing for clients. But the IRS currently accepts several formats for "e-filing," as it is now called.

Electronic filing, which became nationwide in 1990, allows taxpayers' federal and state returns to be filed in one transmission to the IRS, which in turn relays the relevant data to state tax collectors.

What to Do About Electronic Filing

Lower Error Rate

The greatest benefit for taxpayers who file electronically is a dramatically lower error rate. Computer-assisted returns are generally far more accurate than those prepared by hand. The accuracy shows up in the mathematics and through general neatness. As a result, the error rate on electronic returns is about 2.8 percent, compared with 18 percent for paper returns.

This is what error reduction does for the average taxpayer:

- It ensures your anonymity.
- It helps you avoid a mismatch and subsequent flagging of your return for review.
- It eliminates the possibility of having your refund check delayed or of your being charged penalties that later have to be rectified.

Faster Refunds

Another benefit for people who file electronically is that a refund may arrive faster, in about three weeks or less. The reason for the time saved is not that an electronically filed return is processed more quickly than a paper 1040, but that the refund may be deposited in a taxpayer's bank account electronically, similarly to the way many Social Security payments are made.[17] A check sent through the mail may take six or eight weeks, according to the IRS.

Essentially, electronic filing is just another method for transmitting returns to the IRS. Tax preparers who do a high volume of returns are offering electronic filing for an extra fee. For some clients the extra fee is worth it.

Nationally, the number of electronic returns has increased steadily and dramatically, from 7.5 million in 1991 to 13.5 million in 1994, an 80 percent increase in three years. By 1997 it hit 19.1 million.[18] And preliminary data up through May 2000 shows it has risen another 19.2 percent, to almost 30 million returns. Sixty percent of returns were not filed electronically by the year 2000, as the IRS predicted. However, RRA '98 sets an even more ambitious goal of having 80 percent of returns filed electronically by 2007. That leaves 20 percent for paper returns!

The present strategy has resulted in a program that primarily attracts individuals who file simple returns, are due refunds, and are willing to pay fees, now only minimal, associated with electronic filing to get those refunds sooner. There is no doubt that electronic filing will be *the* filing method of the future.

DIRECTION—IRS E-FILE

In 1996, a pilot program for filing tax returns on a personal computer proved such a success, the IRS has become more gung ho for a completely paperless way to file. Meanwhile, here's how you too can get in on the act: First, complete your tax return using IRS-accepted software found at computer stores or downloaded from participating websites. Transmit the return to an on-line filing company or designated provider such as Nelco (1-920-339-1040; website address: http://www.nelcoinc.com), which converts the file to IRS specifications. The on-line company transmits the file to the IRS, and within 48 hours, you are supposed to be notified by the filing company if the return is accepted or, if it's not, which items you need to correct. After the return is accepted, you mail to the IRS a signed Form 8453-OL (U.S. Individual Income Tax Declaration for On-Line Service Electronic Filing), which is provided by either the tax preparation software or the on-line filing company.[19]

You no longer have to include W-2 forms with your mailing to the IRS, but the e-file provider is required to hold copies until the end of the calendar year.

Payment Methods for On-line Filers

Once you submit your return using IRS e-file, various payment methods are available for the payment of federal income tax.

Payment can be made using the following:

- Form 1040V (Payment Voucher): This form automatically prints out and will be sent to you when the IRS determines that you owe money based on the e-return you submitted. Simply follow the directions and return it with your payment.

- Through debiting your checking or savings account, or with
- A credit card, by calling U.S. Audiotex at 1-888-2PAYTAX, where you will be prompted for your credit card information, Social Security number, and verification of address. The companies signed on for this are NOVUS, American Express, MasterCard, and Discover. The fee is roughly 2.5 percent of your tax due, which you can determine in advance by going to www.usaudiotex.com. The entire amount owed must be paid in a single payment.

What to Do About Electronic Filing for Personal Computers
There is no cost to use this capability, though the filing company may charge a small transmission fee. This is a viable alternative to filing a paper return, especially for computer-knowledgeable people. For the 1999 filing season, computer returns increased by a whopping 161 percent, with over 2.4 million taxpayers choosing to do their taxes with software or on-line.[20] In 2000, this number doubled to 4.9 million.

Paperless Electronic Filing Programs
In working toward paperless filing, the IRS has initiated two signature pilots where a number can be used as the taxpayer's electronic signature. The number can be used in place of the paper signature documents, Forms 8453/8453-OL, and you don't even have to mail in your W-2 forms as is required in the usual on-line filing.[21]

Over 1.4 million taxpayers, more than double those of last year, participated in the On-line Signature Pilot, where the IRS distributed E-file Customer Numbers to taxpayers who used personal computers to prepare their returns in the past. These taxpayers prepared their own returns using tax preparation software and filed from their home computers.

Another 5.4 million taxpayers, a tenfold increase from last year, participated in the Practitioner Signature Pilot, where taxpayers chose a personal identification number (PIN) when filing through participating practitioners.

DIRECTION—TELEPHONE FILING (TELEFILING)

Initially instituted on a test basis with about 126,000 eligible taxpayers in Ohio, telephone filing was first tried during the 1992 tax season. By 1996 the IRS hoped that 23 million single taxpayers who filed 1040EZ now could file their returns using TeleFile in less than 10 minutes.[22] In fact, as of June 24, 1996, 2.8 million taxpayers filed by telephone, an increase of more than 300 percent over the number who filed one year prior. According to the Statistics of Income office of the IRS, by July 1998 that figure rose to almost 6 million, an increase of 114 percent, and dropped slightly for 1999. It's still a far cry from the 23 million the IRS hoped for, probably because of the dramatic increase in the use of computers by taxpayers to file their returns. Many of these computer users are the recipients of the more than 21 million invitations sent to taxpayers authorizing the use of the TeleFile option. Those eligible must meet all eight requirements for filing the 1040EZ. You must

1. File as single or, if married, jointly, and this is your same status as last year.
2. Have no dependents.
3. Be under 65 years of age on January 1, 2000, and not be blind at the end of 1999.
4. Have a total income less than $57,050 if single; less than $62,700 if married and filing jointly.
5. Derive your income from wages, salaries, tips, and taxable scholarship or fellowship grants, unemployment compensation, Alaska Permanent Fund dividends, or qualified state tuition program earnings, and have taxable interest income of $400 or less.
6. Have not received advanced payments of the Earned Income Credit, accelerated death benefits, or payments under a long-term insurance contract.
7. Have a married filing jointly status if you were a nonresident alien at any time in 1999.
8. Not claim a student loan interest deduction or education credit, not had a medical savings account in 1999, and not had a household employee for whom you owe employment taxes.

Taxpayers are limited to the standard deduction that is based on filing status (single, married, head of household): $4,400 for most single people and $7,350 for married taxpayers filing jointly. Therefore, if you have higher itemized deductions, it may be wiser to use Form 1040 unless you prefer the ease of filing offered through TeleFiling.

What to Do About TeleFiling
It's quick—about 10 minutes. Using your Touch-Tone phone, you simply enter your Social Security number, your employer's identification number (from your W-2 form), your wages, federal tax withheld, taxable interest, and unemployment compensation, if any. In seconds a voice tells you your

federal adjusted gross income, taxable income, and refund due or balance owed, followed by a confirmation number. You should receive a refund within three weeks, versus 40 days for mailed-in returns, which can be deposited directly into your bank account. The service is free. Try it.

If you don't own a computer, TeleFiling would be a logical choice. Beginning in 2000, you will be able to file your federal *and* state returns via TeleFile in Kentucky and Indiana.

Taxpayers who file using TeleFiling can now also use a charge card to pay their taxes. (See page 358.)

DIRECTION—ELECTRONIC FILING FOR BUSINESSES— ELECTRONIC FEDERAL TAX PAYMENT SYSTEM

The Electronic Federal Tax Payment System (EFTPS) was enacted as part of the North American Free Trade Agreement of 1993 (NAFTA). Designed to speed the flow of funds to the U.S. Treasury, EFTPS allows employers to deposit federal payroll taxes electronically.

It is best to enroll in the program immediately, since the process takes at least 10 weeks. Once you become part of the system, you can electronically pay business taxes owed not only on Form 941 (Employer's Quarterly Federal Tax Return) but also on Form 1120 (U.S. Corporate Income Tax Return), Form 940 (Employer's Annual Federal Unemployment—FUTA—Tax Return), and eight other infrequently used federal business tax returns.

You have four payment options:

1. Call your bank, which debits your account.
2. Call the IRS, which debits your bank account.
3. Use Fedwire, especially for companies required to make large deposits; it offers same-day debits.
4. Transmit from your own PC.

What to Do About EFTPS
My clients are extremely satisfied with the ease and simplicity of the system as well as with the reduced error rate and fewer penalties paid each year. EFTPS can save business taxpayers millions of dollars annually. Why? It eliminates all of the time and energy offices like mine spend answering IRS queries regarding inadequate or untimely deposits made with Form 941. We receive more questions from the IRS about this than in any other business-tax area. According to the IRS, the number of taxpayers currently enrolling in the system continues at

a rate of about 6,500 per week. As of September 1999, there were more than 2 million taxpayers enrolled in EFTPS and more than $1.2 trillion had been collected.[23]

Single Wage Reporting—Form W-2 (Wage and Tax Statement) Electronic Filing—Form 941 (Employer's Quarterly Federal Tax Return)—Form 941TeleFile Pilot

Currently, employers report annual employee wages on W-2's to numerous state and federal agencies. To simplify the multiple steps, paperwork, and time it takes for employers to complete a W-2 and send it to multiple agencies, the IRS and the Social Security Administration are each developing their own system.

What to Do About Single Wage Reporting

Over the years, employers have become accustomed to the W-2 format, which is easy to fill out. If the IRS wants to allocate money and slim down the wage-reporting process, there's no harm in it. But perhaps the money would be better directed to something that really needs work, such as K-1 reporting or the multiple reporting formats of 1099-B's. Remember? The ones that brokerage companies mail to taxpayers in any, usually unrecognizable, format they wish.

In any case, a 1995 initiative by the IRS, the Social Security Administration, and the Department of Labor to create the Simplified Tax and Wage Reporting System (STAWRS) to reduce the tax- and wage-reporting burden on employers while improving the efficiency and effectiveness of each agency's operations, never took off. There seemed to be no cooperation among the various government agencies to produce a prototype that would allow all major payroll reports to be filed simultaneously. So it is no surprise that separate efforts are in the works: The Social Security Administration (SSA) is developing an electronic filing option for Form W-2 (Wage and Tax Statement) covering employees, using a personal computer and modem; and the IRS's 1997 pilot program for electronically filing Form 941 (Employer's Quarterly Federal Tax Return) is now completely operational. (Employers are generally required to report both the federal income tax withheld and the employer and employee portions of the FICA tax on a quarterly return, Form 941.)

The Social Security Administration has developed the Online Wage Reporting Bulletin Board System (OWRBBS), dedicated exclusively to electronically filing Form W-2. Designed for small- to medium-size employers, OWRBBS can be accessed from 8:00 A.M. to 4:00 P.M. EST, by modem (dial 410-966-8450). The system is supposed to be easy to use;

an instruction booklet details steps to take, and there are specifications for diskette filers.

No costs are associated with registering or using the system except for a normal telephone line charge.

If help is needed during use, a systems operator is available on-line, or you can call 410-966-5549 Monday through Friday, 8:30 A.M. to 4:00 P.M. EST. The SSA's home page can be accessed at http:\\www.ssa.gov for further information.[24]

Another IRS project allows almost one million small businesses that meet certain qualifications to file their Form 941 by telephone, using a toll-free number. If you receive the special TeleFile package, give it a try. I did, and it's as easy as following a few instructions, calling the number, then going through the voice prompts. This free, fast paperless method automatically calculates the tax and any refund due or balance owed. Filers receive a confirmation number as verification of filing.[25]

Electronic filing is gradually being expanded into other business areas. According to the IRS, Form 1041 (U.S. Income Tax Return for Estates and Trusts) can be filed electronically or via magnetic media; Form 1065 (U.S. Partnership Return of Income) and Schedule K-1's can be filed electronically, via magnetic media or through a remote Bulletin Board System using modem-to-modem transmission; and Employee Benefit Plan 5500 series returns can be filed using magnetic media or electronically using a modem over telephone lines directly into IRS computers.

DIRECTION—INCREASING COMPLIANCE

In a genuine attempt to meet its goal of producing a more compliant taxpayer, the IRS has taken several initiatives. It has:

- Changed the rules for Form 4868 (Application for Automatic Extension of Time to File U.S. Individual Income Tax Return).
- Put in place revised approaches for negotiating monies owed.
- Tried to ease the taxpayer's burden through education and tax simplification.

AUTOMATIC EXTENSIONS—FORM 4868 (APPLICATION FOR AUTOMATIC EXTENSION OF TIME TO FILE U.S. INDIVIDUAL INCOME TAX RETURN)

With Form 4868 you are forced to make a conscientious effort to estimate your total tax liability by April 15. However, prior to the 1996 tax filing season, if you submitted less than the full amount of tax you had estimated you owed, your request could have been deemed invalid by the IRS. Therefore, once the completed 1040 was filed, the taxpayer might be facing a rejected extension and a late-filing penalty.

Furthermore, upon rejection you could be prevented from using several important tax breaks when the return is eventually filed. A self-employed person who files late without a valid extension cannot deduct contributions to a Keogh retirement account paid between April 16 and August 15. If you are subsequently audited, any tax assessed will be subject to greater penalties because your return was not filed in a timely manner (no extension).

Since the 1996 filing season, the extension has been deemed valid *even if* you do not pay the balance due by April 15, as long as you make a reasonable, conscientious effort to report on Form 4868 how much you think your total tax liability will be. The revised extension form doesn't even require a signature.

If, for example, your estimated total tax liability is $7,500 but the actual amount turns out to be $8,500, the IRS will probably accept your payment with no further recriminations.

What to Do About Automatic Extensions
What are the benefits of using Form 4868? Despite the leeway afforded by the IRS, I agree with current professional advice: If at all possible, rather than borrowing the money you owe from the government (by not paying the full tax that is due), borrow it instead from your family, a friend, or a bank. Hopefully the interest rate will be lower, and potential collection efforts should not be as severe.

For a major misconception regarding Form 4868, see pages 225–226.

FORM 1127 (APPLICATION FOR EXTENSION OF TIME FOR PAYMENT OF TAX)

When choosing Form 1127, you'd better know what's in store.

Form 1127 allows taxpayers to file a maximum extension of six months to pay the full amount of tax owed in a one-time payment. This form is *not* about installments. For the IRS to accept this form, taxpayers must, among other things:

- Prove undue hardship.
- Show they will experience substantial financial loss on the day the payment is due.

- Indicate they have no borrowing power except under terms that will cause severe difficulties.

The two major disadvantages to Form 1127 are:

- Taxpayers must disclose their full financial data, so that if you don't fulfill the terms of the agreement, the IRS will know exactly where to attack your assets.
- The IRS requests collateral, such as the deed to your house, on the amount promised. If you don't pay when Form 1127 states you will, the collateral is subject to a lien, seizure, and sale.

If Form 1127 does resurface, I recommend using it only if you are in dire financial straits.

HOW TO PAY WHAT YOU OWE—YOU CHOOSE

The essence of tax amnesty legislation is to encourage nonfilers to come forward and negotiate a means to pay or begin to pay what they owe over a period of time without being criminally prosecuted.

About six years ago the IRS finally took a good look at this situation and came up with some genuine amnesty-type measures for nonfilers based on the philosophy that it is more sensible to encourage taxpayers to come forward and offer some payment than to threaten them and receive nothing.

Payment Vehicles—Offer in Compromise (Form 656)

An Offer in Compromise (OIC) is used when the IRS agrees to settle for less than the amount owed because it seems unlikely that any more can be collected from the taxpayer. Since 1992, offers in compromise that were accepted increased in astounding numbers, from 4,356 to a record 27,673 in fiscal 1996. This represents an acceptance rate of 50 percent— about $287 million to settle debts totaling about $2.17 billion.[26] For 1999, the acceptance rate jumped to 62 percent. What has helped to accelerate the acceptance rate is that IRS attorneys are getting involved *only* if the amount owed is $50,000 or more, compared with $500 previously.

What to Do About an Offer in Compromise

- The IRS wants to get paid what it is owed.
- To realize this, it must encourage nonfilers to come in out of the cold.

Acceptance rates for offers in compromise had been slowed down because the IRS faced a growing backlog. The source of the problem seems to have been the national and local standards developed by the IRS to help revenue officers make decisions regarding allowances for living expenses—costs of housing, utilities, transportation, and such. Generally assets or income above these standard amounts are used to satisfy paying off the taxes owed. However, in basing a decision on these criteria, individual circumstances were being overlooked, making settlements more difficult and harder to come by.

In response, RRA '98 required the IRS to develop employee guidelines for taking into consideration the circumstances of *each* taxpayer and then considering whether the national and local allowances are appropriate. By putting the standards into this perspective, the IRS would help taxpayers end up in a better position to begin to settle their tax liabilities and still have the means to cover basic living expenses.

In late 1999, the IRS announced a new simplified approach to offers in compromise made possible by a combination of proposed new tax regulations effective July 19, 1999, that reflect changes made by RRA '98 and the Taxpayer Bill of Rights 2. The new regulations expand the grounds under which the IRS can accept an Offer in Compromise to include a determination that collecting the taxes owed would create an economic hardship for the taxpayer. The regulations also add provisions on

- Expanding the definition of basic living expenses.
- Allowing for evaluation of offers from low-income taxpayers.
- Reviewing rejected offers without requiring the taxpayer to go through Appeals (as done previously).
- Suspending examination and collection activities while offers in compromise are pending.
- Prohibiting notification of third parties when a taxpayer is targeted by the IRS. (See page 306.)

Taxpayers are eligible if their liability is greater than their assets and if they do not have earnings potential to pay off the amount owed over time. In the past, such offers were routinely denied if a taxpayer had certain assets such as equity in a home or a 401(k) plan, even if those assets couldn't be readily cashed in. Under this new approach, taxpayers would not necessarily have to liquidate such assets if doing so would create significant economic hardship, and they would also be eligible for the new fixed monthly payment options. The new fixed payment combines all debts, including interest, owed by the taxpayer under the

Offer in Compromise into a single payment that reflects the maximum the taxpayer can pay after covering basic living expenses.

Commissioner Rossotti claims that this common-sense approach eliminates headaches and uncertainty for taxpayers and tax practitioners by simplifying the process.[27]

All instructions for an Offer in Compromise will now be contained in a new Form 656 (Offer in Compromise) package. To apply, file Form 656 along with a financial statement on Form 433-A (Collection Information Statement for Individuals), and if you are self-employed, use Form 433-B (Collection Information Statement for Business.)

It is important to prepare your application carefully. More than half of the offers submitted in 1999 were too flawed to process, and it may take up to six months for the IRS to review your application.[28] Taxpayers need to make sure that they properly identify themselves on Form 656, that they state their tax liability correctly, that some amount of money is offered, and that their request includes the latest Form 656 along with Forms 433-A or 433-B.

NOTE: These new provisions are tailored for taxpayers entangled in very severe circumstances and are not designed to be a sweeping program for everyone with financial difficulties.

Disadvantages of Filing an Offer in Compromise

The key disadvantage is that when you file, the statute of limitations for the IRS to collect the tax you owe will automatically be extended from the usual 10-year collection period by as much as two additional years. If the statute of limitations is close to expiring before you submit, it is probably better if you simply wait for it to expire, at which point the IRS cannot legally collect the debt. For example, if your tax debt was assessed on June 15, 1990, the IRS is unable to collect after June 15, 2000. Generally, however, most taxpayers have several years left on the collection statute when they consider filing an Offer in Compromise. From a broad perspective, consider paying your debt, even if the collection period is extended. You walk away free and unencumbered.

YOUR TAX-SAVING STRATEGY.
Though the IRS has gone on record as being more sympathetic to taxpayers who owe back taxes, IRS specialists who accept or deny compromise offers seem to insist on one thing: If your income varies from year to year, which often happens to self-employed people, the IRS will average the past three or four years to obtain an average cash flow. This may inadvertently make it appear as if you are earning more than you actually are, which, in turn, will affect your OIC payments. You can op-

pose this averaging method by documenting that a higher income earned in a prior year is not likely to recur, giving a reason such as you lost your best customer or you've moved on to other clients.[29]

Reminder: Once an offer is signed and accepted, the IRS will retain any refunds or credits that you may be entitled to receive for 2000 or for earlier years. This includes refunds you receive in 2001 for any overpayments you made in 2000 or in earlier years. Also, you must stay up-to-date in filing and paying all required taxes for five years from the date of the offer, or the IRS can (and probably will) rescind the offer and go after you for the entire unpaid balance of the offer. Last, if you signed a joint offer with your spouse and you made all your payments in a timely fashion, but your spouse (or former spouse) fails to comply with the requirements, e.g., he or she didn't make payments on time, your offer will *not* be forfeited.

For 1997, the IRS made 25,052 compromise agreements, in which it wrote off $1.6 billion of $1.9 billion in overdue taxes, collecting $290 million, or 15 percent, of the tax bills.[30]

YOUR TAX-SAVING STRATEGY.
When evaluating an Offer in Compromise, for which you are solely responsible, the IRS takes into consideration your spouse's earnings. In so doing, more of your money, as they see it, is freed up to pay your obligation. If your spouse is female, it is up to you to argue that her earnings may not continue (e.g., because of having a child) and have her earnings eliminated from the computations. If your spouse is male, think of a different reason.

IRS lawyers who review offers in compromise are always on the lookout for taxpayers who transfer assets from one spouse to another in an attempt to hide these assets from a tax settlement. Be ready for your spouse to prove that her wealth came from her own earnings or inheritance, or was transferred from the other spouse *long* before the tax problems began.

Installment Agreement Request (Form 9465)
In the last few years the IRS has also accepted an increasing number of 9465 forms to create an installment agreement between the IRS and taxpayers who have balances due on their 1040's. Before the changeover to this form, taxpayers had to receive a tax bill *before* they could ask to set up a payment agreement.

Now taxpayers can attach Form 9465 to the 1040 and specify the amount of the proposed monthly payment. A response from the IRS to accept, deny, or request more information regarding the terms is supposed to arrive within 30 days. The terms of the agreement are negotiated between the IRS and the taxpayer.

Form 9465 actually offers an enormous advantage: The old form required taxpayers to disclose their current financial status to the IRS, about four pages of it, including a full list of all assets and liabilities. The new form omits this requirement for tax liabilities under $10,000. **Here are the advantages: taxpayers can pay their bills without disclosing their ready assets to the IRS, which could implicate them if they have sufficient means to pay their obligation in full.** A revenue officer can accept the terms of the agreement without going through a chain of command, and if taxpayers adhere to the terms of the payment schedule, no tax liens will be filed against the taxpayers' property.

The IRS says it has decided to take this approach to reduce the number of taxpayers who do not file at all because of money owed, and in the hope that taxpayers will file returns even if they cannot pay the balance due immediately.

Disadvantages to Filing an Installment Agreement

First, they are binding. Second, penalties and interest are due on the unpaid balance. Essentially, taxpayers who file Form 9465 are locked into a late-payment penalty of one quarter of one percent a month (down from one half a percent), effective January 1, 2000, plus interest on unpaid amounts. Taken together, the cost comes to about 15 percent a year. This is less interest than on a credit card, but you still need to think it through before you sign. You may end up owing more than you expect, and if you don't meet your monthly payment, the IRS will come after you. In addition, if your income goes up, the IRS can insist that monthly payments be increased. However, if your income drops, you must submit new financial information before the IRS will, *at its discretion*, consider lowering your payments, though the IRS is now required to notify taxpayers *before* changing the terms of an installment agreement. Finally, there is a $43 fee for setting up the installment agreement.

With Commissioner Rossotti's emphasis on customer service, you may stand a better chance these days of negotiating such an agreement where previously, despite laws and guidelines, the outcomes remained unknown.

Finally, according to RRA '98, if you request an installment agreement, you will generally be guaranteed one if the balance you owe is $10,000 or less and if you are up-to-date on filing your returns and paying your taxes.

A few years ago only the Collection Division could work with accounts over $5,000. Now all functions within the IRS have the authority to grant installment agreements up to $25,000. That means employees in Appeals, Employee Plans and Exempt Organizations, Examination, Problem Resolution, Returns Processing (in the service centers), and Taxpayer Service can help in resolving accounts.[31] Now, if you owe up to $25,000 and the IRS believes you can pay the amount within five years, your agreement will probably be accepted. If the IRS refuses to grant your installment request, investigate the possibility of making an Offer in Compromise. You can go to the IRS website for an online calculator to figure a reasonable monthly installment payment and to obtain the necessary forms.

How to Pay Off the IRS on Your Terms
Without Using IRS Installment Agreements

Rather than locking yourself into a 9465 installment agreement, I recommend the following short-term fix to ease out of tax money due:

- Send in some money as soon as you receive your first notice of tax due.
- Follow the payment up with some more money each time you receive another collection notice.
- With each notice, include a short note explaining why you cannot pay the full balance right now, such as illness or loss of your job.
- Be sure to tell the IRS that you will continue to try your best to pay as much as you can.

Using this method, you could get away with paying a fairly small amount for three to four months. **If you file a 9465, you will soon be strapped with a strict payment schedule that will be fraught with penalties if you don't make all the payments on time.** Hopefully, after the first few months you'll be in better shape to pay off the balance.

In 1997 $10.8 billion was collected in installment agreements, representing 2.8 million agreements struck. Those figures dropped slightly for 1998 and fell even more in the first six months of 1999 to only about $3.5 billion collected, or 778,000 installment agreements made.[32]

DIRECTION—THE IRS, THE INTERNET,
AND ELECTRONIC SERVICES

In August 1996, the IRS announced that it intended to enhance its offerings on the information superhighway to include the *Internal Revenue*

Manual; its Market Segment Specialization Program Audit Technique Guides (see pages 55 and 174–177); a database of tax-exempt organizations; news from local IRS offices; a list of 500,000 organizations to which contributions are considered tax deductible; and a downloadable tax calendar showing due dates for various forms.[33] The address for this service is: www.irs.gov.

In addition, the IRS has made available an interesting array of helpful electronic as well as Internet services on several of its websites.

- An electronic bulletin board can be reached via computer modem at 703-321-8020.
- To have IRS forms, publications, and *Tax Topic* information releases faxed to you, call the Tax Fax Service, 703-368-9694, from a fax machine and make your selection. Users can request up to three items per transmission.
- *Taxpayer Help and Education* will help you with TeleTax topics, frequently asked questions, and where to file. Submit a question at www.irs.gov/tax_edu/index.html.
- At *Tax Information For You* there's information on IRS Collection financial standards, Taxpayer Advocates, and Internal Revenue Bulletins. Check website www.irs.gov/ind_info/index.html.
- *IRS News Stand*, www.irs.gov/news/index.html, gives you the tax calendar for small businesses, news releases, and the electronic Freedom of Information Act, including excerpts from the *Internal Revenue Manual.*
- *Tax Professionals Corner,* www.irs.gov/bus_info/tax_pro, has information regarding IRS forms and publications, early release drafts of forms, CD-ROM products, fill-in forms, and administrative information and resources.
- **Appendix E contains a complete list of IRS websites.**
- IRS forms and instructions can now be downloaded from the IRS website. This represents a great improvement as well as a convenience to millions of taxpayers who formerly had to obtain these forms at an IRS office or public library. According to TRAC, Americans downloaded close to 90 million forms and instructions in 1999.

New CD-ROM

A new CD-ROM now available from the IRS is titled "Small Business Resource Guide 2000." It contains all IRS business forms and publications as well as instructions for preparing a business plan and obtaining business financing. One CD-ROM per person is being made available for free and can be ordered by calling 1-800-TAX-FORM or by visiting the IRS website at irs.gov.

For questions and comments about print publications or CD-ROM sales, you can also contact the U.S. Government Printing Office, Superintendent of Documents, Box 371954, Pittsburgh, PA 15250, or call 202-512-1800.

DIRECTION—PAYING TAXES WITH PLASTIC

Now for the tax law you've been waiting for. You can now use a credit or charge card for the payment of federal income taxes. Taxpayers who file Form 1040, 1040A, or 1040EZ on paper or electronically can call U.S. Audiotex at 1-888-2PAY-TAX, where they will be prompted for their credit card information, Social Security number, and verification of address. American Express, MasterCard, and Discover are all accepted. The fee is roughly 2.5 percent of your tax due, which you can determine in advance by going to www.usaudiotex.com. For the 1999 tax filing, as of April 15, 2000, 100,311 taxpayers charged their taxes, a 60 percent increase in just one year. The largest single payment was $7.2 million.

Although taxpayers using IRS e-file can use their credit card for the payment of federal income tax, take note: Don't even think about charging your tax bill and then not paying the credit card company. The U.S. Treasury is still responsible for such bad debts, which translates into the probability of an IRS revenue officer knocking at your front door demanding payment.

If you're the least bit tempted to have less federal tax withheld from your wages during the year so you'll be able to add up the sums and subsequently charge a large amount of tax due using your credit, debit, or charge card on April 15, this is unwise. The penalty for underpaying tax during the year will outweigh any frequent flier miles you receive.

LATEST TRENDS

Rise of Abusive Tax Shelters

Toward the end of the 1990's, the IRS believed it had conquered the power of abusive tax shelters, an effort that severely weakened the examination function for at least 10 years. Well, the IRS did accomplish that, at least for individual tax shelters, but the ugly beast has risen its head again. This time corporations are the culprits.

American corporations, whose profits have been consistently increasing, are now paying less in taxes because of well-conceived tax shelters. According to the IRS, less than 70 cents of each dollar of profit reported to shareholders in 1998 was reported by companies as taxable income, down from 91 cents in 1991.[34]

According to Treasury Secretary Lawrence H. Summers, "corporate tax shelters are our number one problem in enforcing the tax laws not just because they cost money, but because they breed disrespect for the tax system."[35] From a purely moral perspective, it appears that some of the largest companies have thrown their integrity out the window in their search for tax breaks that will enable them to hold on to greater profit. As discussed in chapter 4, tax shelters are considered abusive because they are not intended to make a profit, as a solid investment would be, but are designed specifically to allow for huge write-offs that reduce the amount of tax due. Though corporate profits reported to the IRS were 252 percent higher in 1998, taxes rose just 191 percent. It is estimated that abusive corporate tax shelters cost the government more than $10 billion a year, and that's a conservative figure.[36]

The government and IRS officials are calling for new laws that would require early disclosure of tax shelters and provide for a penalty tax on the promoters and buyers of such shelters. Meanwhile, corporations are still taking aggressive postures in their ongoing attempts to increase profits.

New Technology to Catch Cheaters

The IRS may be in an upheaval as it goes through a tremendous transition, with audit rates at an all-time low, but tax cheats beware. As the IRS pulls together, researching technology and designing computer systems that will perhaps one day do what the IRS has hoped for since the early 1990's, a new device is in the offing that taxpayers need to know about. Within the next few years, with the help of Computer Sciences Corporation of El Segundo, California, the IRS is hoping to initiate a technology to track tax cheats and to identify patterns of fraud. Of course, given its new accent on customer service, the IRS has said that this capability is only a small part of the whole. But that part will be a database technology that identifies the behavior patterns of customers, similar to what companies such as American Express and Citibank use to "decide which charges to approve and which advertisements to slip in the mail with monthly bills."[37] This capability, called "data mining," will enable the IRS to access information needed by auditors for examination purposes, as well as by Customer Service employees to help taxpayers at walk-in centers. So besides working to make things easier, quicker, and more efficient for taxpayers, data mining can also be designed to identify patterns of cheating. Once this is in place, the process of finding tax cheats and working through the administrative and clerical processes to seek them out will be substantially easier and quicker. Be forewarned.

Besides checking for tax cheats using specific technology, top IRS officials have recently admitted that the Internet contains a lot of personal information about taxpayers that is useful to the IRS. IRS auditors are using search engines to verify such things as new stories about taxpayers being audited and to obtain specific industry practices and statistics to compare with information provided by businesses that are undergoing an audit. The emphasis is currently on business audits, but you can be sure the use of the Internet will soon be expanded to individual audits as well. **Business owners should carefully review what information is available at their websites that would prove useful to an IRS auditor.**

Tax Delinquents Avoid Paying Tax Bills

Given the much publicized drop in IRS audits and collection activities, it appears that a growing number of tax cheats—those at high income levels and major corporations involved with abusive tax shelters (discussed above)—have established a new trend of tax delinquency. The first problem is insufficient IRS tax auditors to weed out the delinquents. The second is IRS tax collectors allegedly more worried about losing their jobs than going after known delinquents. The situation has resulted in billions of dollars of unpaid taxes. In the past, the IRS typically collected what it could from a taxpayer, and when the statute of limitations on collecting the debt was near, revenue officers would choose from its battery of weapons—liens, levies, or seizures to further collect on what was owed. With RRA '98, the IRS is supposed to negotiate all terms of the tax-collection agreement up front. "But what has been occurring is, if a taxpayer cannot agree to pay in full, collectors apply the label 'currently noncollectible,' which effectively closes the case."[38] Since the performance of revenue officers is no longer judged by the amount of penalties they collect (although the IRS has consistently denied use of quotas), but by the efficiency with which they close cases, you can see the problem.

Furthermore, if a taxpayer does not agree to an extension of the statute of limitations, or if regular payments would not cover 100 percent of the debt even with a five-year extension beyond the limitation on collecting the back taxes owed, the IRS is refusing to accept an installment agreement and it will suspend its collection efforts.[39] Then the taxpayer simply waits until the period of payment expires and—voilà!—no tax is paid. If the taxpayer attracts no undue attention by continuing to file tax returns and shows no evidence of an increase in income, there is minimal chance that his case will be revived in the time allotted for its settlement.

The biggest source of tax dollars being left unpaid comes from thousands of cases of withheld taxes owed by small businesses.

Commissioner Rossotti insists that once the collection staff is fully trained, seizures of property and all the rest of collection activity will resume.

Catching Nonfilers

According to TRAC, one area of collection activity that was sharply higher in 1999 involved the issuance of Tax Delinquent Return Investigations (TDIs). A TDI signals the IRS's preliminary decision to investigate why no return was filed by a taxpayer who had income that was taxable. In 1992, there were 877,966 TDIs; in 1999, that number nearly doubled to 1.58 million. IRS officials have stated that this increase is a result of a policy decision to place more emphasis on tracking down nonfilers. It also helps that the IRS continues to receive billions of income reports from third-party payers such as employers and banks, which tip off the IRS as to who the delinquent filers are.

If you're a nonfiler and need some advice, see pages 180–181.

Reducing Penalties Over the Internet

About one in seven payroll and income tax filings by employers are assessed penalties by the IRS due to late payments or underpayments. Though the average penalty is $900, the IRS often proposes a larger penalty than is required because of the complex rules involved in making the payments in a timely fashion.

New software developed by Time Value Software of Irvine, California, provides on-line calculation of penalties due. "The Software Company claims that 91 percent of their users have had their penalties reduced or eliminated with an average reduction of 44 percent."[40] Service is available at www.taxpenalty.com and the cost is $49 if penalty reduction is $500 or more. There is no fee if the penalty reduction is under $500.

Checkbox Initiative to Resolve Tax Problems

Beginning with the 2001 filing season, paid preparers, with their clients' permission, will be allowed to work directly with the IRS to resolve many tax return processing issues (e.g., leaving out a Social Security number, forgetting to attach a W-2, math errors). Using a checkbox on all series of Form 1040 returns (except TeleFile), taxpayers can select their own paid preparer to help resolve these matters. The IRS thinks that this step will resolve up to 90 percent of the issues normally resolved through telephone contact with paid preparers. Under this new initiative, the taxpayer's designee will have the ability to speak directly to IRS Customer Service people and to receive information about a refund or payment. For more serious issues, such as audit matters, underreported income, appeals, and collections notices, your tax adviser will still need a properly filled-in Form 2848 (Power of Attorney), signed by you.

THE BEST IRS EVER—MAYBE SOMEDAY

At this point, there's a glimmer that the IRS stands a good chance of becoming an agency that will work effectively and efficiently, and serve American taxpayers fairly, at least down the line. Commissioner Rossotti is going about it the right way: enlisting existing expertise from inside the IRS; recruiting executive skills from the outside; carefully designing next steps; creating vertical and horizontal communications networks across the agency; developing precise training programs; and focusing an enormous effort on adequately training IRS staff so that they are prepared to be emissaries, not adversaries.

He has made himself a visible IRS leader, ready to explore issues and concerns, and devoted to figuring out how to resolve them. Periodically, when he and his top-level staff appear before Congress, you can see how much progress has been made and the levels of change that are ongoing across the agency. He has created new linkages within the IRS and into the community by reaching out to the professional community not only by formalizing a separate Communications and Liaison Division (tried several times in the past), but also through IRS cosponsored seminars presented to leading tax practitioner groups. The lastest one of these is on the progress of the modernization system, i.e., the as yet unsolved technology behemoth. Mr. Rossotti has also done something never before done in the history of the IRS: He held a special three-day meeting in Chicago, summoning managers in the Collections Department, the group that seems the most confused or, should we say, hardest hit by the RRA '98. Rossotti needs revenue officers to get it right, so he insisted on the gathering to uncover where the problems are. Yes, collections have gone down, along with seizures, levies, and liens, and yes, audit rates are the lowest in history. Mr. Rossotti is concerned that enforcement has slipped too far, but during any transition, particularly one of this magnitude, morale will suffer, work will backslide, and jobs will go begging as people leave or are transferred from one location to another.

Restructuring at the IRS will take some time to bear fruit. Although some wrong turns are being made, the agency, headed by Mr. Rossotti, is clearly going where it should—in a direction that will be better for taxpayers, for the IRS, and, eventually, for compliance.

APPENDIXES

Appendix A: Most Important Tax Forms
Discussed in This Book
Appendix B: Guide to Free Tax Services
Appendix C: State Filing Authority
Telephone Numbers and Websites
Appendix D: Your Rights as a Taxpayer
Appendix E: Practitioner Hot Line
Telephone Numbers
Appendix F: Useful Websites

APPENDIX A: MOST IMPORTANT
TAX FORMS
DISCUSSED IN THIS BOOK

The IRS forms included in this book are for reference purposes only. If you need a specific form, it is best to obtain it and the accompanying instructions directly from the IRS. Call the taxpayer assistance telephone number for your area (listed in Appendix B, page 483).

Almost all IRS tax forms remain identical from year to year, except that a new year is printed on the form.

Form **1040**	Department of the Treasury — Internal Revenue Service **U.S. Individual Income Tax Return** **1999**	(99)	IRS Use Only — Do not write or staple in this space.

For the year Jan. 1 - Dec. 31, 1999, or other tax year beginning , 1999, ending , | OMB No. 1545-0074

Label
(See instructions on page 18.)

Use the IRS label. Otherwise, please print or type.

L A B E L   H E R E

Your first name and initial | Last name | Your social security number

If a joint return, spouse's first name and initial | Last name | Spouse's social security number

Home address (number and street). If you have a P.O. box, see page 18. | Apt. no.

City, town or post office, state, and ZIP code. If you have a foreign address, see page 18.

▲ **IMPORTANT!** ▲
You must enter your SSN(s) above.

Presidential Election Campaign
(See page 18.)

Do you want $3 to go to this fund? ....
If a joint return, does your spouse want $3 to go to this fund? ....

| | Yes | No | Note: Checking "Yes" will not change your tax or reduce your refund. |

Filing Status

Check only one box.

1 ☐ Single
2 ☐ Married filing joint return (even if only one had income)
3 ☐ Married filing separate return. Enter spouse's social security no. above and full name here. ▶
4 ☐ Head of household (with qualifying person). (See page 18.) If the qualifying person is a child but not your dependent, enter this child's name here. ▶
5 ☐ Qualifying widow(er) with dependent child (year spouse died ▶ 19). (See page 18.)

Exemptions

6a ☐ **Yourself.** If your parent (or someone else) can claim you as a dependent on his or her tax return, do not check box 6a ....
b ☐ **Spouse** ....
c **Dependents:**

(1) First name Last name	(2) Dependent's social security number	(3) Dependent's relationship to you	(4) ✔ if qualifying child for child tax credit (see page 19)
			☐
			☐
			☐
			☐
			☐
			☐

If more than six dependents, see page 19.

No. of boxes checked on 6a and 6b ____
No. of your children on 6c who:
• lived with you ____
• did not live with you due to divorce or separation (see page 19) ____
Dependents on 6c not entered above ____
Add numbers entered on lines above ▶ ☐

d Total number of exemptions claimed ....

Income

Attach Copy B of your Forms W-2 and W-2G here. Also attach Form(s) 1099-R if tax was withheld.

If you did not get a W-2, see page 20.

Enclose, but do not staple, any payment. Also, please use Form 1040-V.

7 Wages, salaries, tips, etc. Attach Form(s) W-2 .... | 7
8a **Taxable interest.** Attach Schedule B if required .... | 8a
b Tax-exempt interest. DO NOT include on line 8a .... | 8b
9 Ordinary dividends. Attach Schedule B if required .... | 9
10 Taxable refunds, credits, or offsets of state and local income taxes (see page 21) ..... | 10
11 Alimony received .... | 11
12 Business income or (loss). Attach Schedule C or C-EZ .... | 12
13 Capital gain or (loss). Attach Schedule D if required. If not required, check here ▶ ☐ | 13
14 Other gains or (losses). Attach Form 4797 .... | 14
15a Total IRA distributions .... | 15a | b Taxable amount (see page 22) . | 15b
16a Total pensions and annuities | 16a | b Taxable amount (see page 22) . | 16b
17 Rental real estate, royalties, partnerships, S corporations, trusts, etc. Attach Schedule E ...... | 17
18 Farm income or (loss). Attach Schedule F .... | 18
19 Unemployment compensation .... | 19
20a Social security benefits .... | 20a | b Taxable amount (see page 24) . | 20b
21 Other income. List type and amount (see page 24) _____ | 21
22 Add the amounts in the far right column for lines 7 through 21. This is your **total income** .... ▶ | 22

Adjusted Gross Income

23 IRA deduction (see page 26) .... | 23
24 Student loan interest deduction (see page 26) .... | 24
25 Medical savings account deduction. Attach Form 8853 .... | 25
26 Moving expenses. Attach Form 3903 .... | 26
27 One-half of self-employment tax. Attach Schedule SE .... | 27
28 Self-employed health insurance deduction (see page 28) ...... | 28
29 Keogh and self-employed SEP and SIMPLE plans .... | 29
30 Penalty on early withdrawal of savings .... | 30
31a Alimony paid b Recipient's SSN ▶ _____ | 31a
32 Add lines 23 through 31a .... | 32
33 Subtract line 32 from line 22. This is your **adjusted gross income** .... ▶ | 33

For Disclosure, Privacy Act, and Paperwork Reduction Act Notice, see page 54.
ISA
STF FED2611F.1

Form **1040** (1999)

Form 1040 (1999)

Page **2**

Tax and Credits	34	Amount from line 33 (adjusted gross income)	34
	35a	Check if: ☐ **You** were 65 or older, ☐ Blind; ☐ **Spouse** was 65 or older, ☐ Blind. Add the number of boxes checked above and enter the total here . . . . ▶ 35a	
	b	If you are married filing separately and your spouse itemizes deductions or you were a dual-status alien, see page 30 and check here . . . . ▶ 35b ☐	
Standard Deduction for Most People Single: $4,300 Head of household: $6,350 Married filing jointly or Qualifying widow(er): $7,200 Married filing separately: $3,600	36	Enter your **itemized deductions** from Schedule A, line 28, OR **standard deduction** shown on the left. **But see** page 30 to find your standard deduction if you checked any box on line 35a or 35b **or** if someone can claim you as a dependent	36
	37	Subtract line 36 from line 34	37
	38	If line 34 is $94,975 or less, multiply $2,750 by the total number of exemptions claimed on line 6d. If line 34 is over $94,975, see the worksheet on page 31 for the amount to enter	38
	39	**Taxable income.** Subtract line 38 from line 37. If line 38 is more than line 37, enter -0-	39
	40	Tax (see page 31). Check if any tax is from **a** ☐ Form(s) 8814 **b** ☐ Form 4972 . . . . . ▶	40
	41	Credit for child and dependent care expenses. Attach Form 2441 . . .	41	
	42	Credit for the elderly or the disabled. Attach Schedule R	42	
	43	Child tax credit (see page 33)	43	
	44	Education credits. Attach Form 8863	44	
	45	Adoption credit. Attach Form 8839	45	
	46	Foreign tax credit. Attach Form 1116 if required	46	
	47	Other. Check if from **a** ☐ Form 3800 **b** ☐ Form 8396 **c** ☐ Form 8801 **d** ☐ Form (specify) _____	47	
	48	Add lines 41 through 47. These are your **total credits**	48
	49	Subtract line 48 from line 40. If line 48 is more than line 40, enter -0- . . . . ▶	49
Other Taxes	50	Self-employment tax. Attach Schedule SE	50
	51	Alternative minimum tax. Attach Form 6251	51
	52	Social security and Medicare tax on tip income not reported to employer. Attach Form 4137	52
	53	Tax on IRAs, other retirement plans, and MSAs. Attach Form 5329 if required	53
	54	Advance earned income credit payments from Form(s) W-2	54
	55	Household employment taxes. Attach Schedule H	55
	56	Add lines 49 through 55. This is your **total tax** . . . . ▶	56
Payments	57	Federal income tax withheld from Forms W-2 and 1099	57	
	58	1999 estimated tax payments and amount applied from 1998 return .	58	
	59a	**Earned income credit.** Attach Sch. EIC if you have a qualifying child		
	b	Nontaxable earned income: amount . . . . . ▶ and type ▶	59a	
	60	Additional child tax credit. Attach Form 8812	60	
	61	Amount paid with request for extension to file (see page 48)	61	
	62	Excess social security and RRTA tax withheld (see page 48)	62	
	63	Other payments. Check if from **a** ☐ Form 2439 **b** ☐ Form 4136	63	
	64	Add lines 57, 58, 59a, and 60 through 63. These are your **total payments** . . . . ▶	64
Refund Have it directly deposited! See page 48 and fill in 66b, 66c, and 66d.	65	If line 64 is more than line 56, subtract line 56 from line 64. This is the amount you **OVERPAID**	65
	66a	Amount of line 65 you want **REFUNDED TO YOU** . . . . ▶	66a
	▶ b	Routing number ☐☐☐☐☐☐☐☐☐ ▶ c Type: ☐ Checking ☐ Savings	
	▶ d	Account number ☐☐☐☐☐☐☐☐☐☐☐☐☐☐☐☐☐	
	67	Amount of line 65 you want **APPLIED TO YOUR 2000 ESTIMATED TAX** ▶	67	
Amount You Owe	68	If line 56 is more than line 64, subtract line 64 from line 56. This is the **AMOUNT YOU OWE.** For details on how to pay, see page 49 . . . . ▶	68
	69	Estimated tax penalty. Also include on line 68	69	

Sign Here

Under penalties of perjury, I declare that I have examined this return and accompanying schedules and statements, and to the best of my knowledge and belief, they are true, correct, and complete. Declaration of preparer (other than taxpayer) is based on all information of which preparer has any knowledge.

Joint return?
See page 18.

Keep a copy for your records.

Your signature	Date	Your occupation	Daytime telephone number (optional)
Spouse's signature. If a joint return, BOTH must sign.	Date	Spouse's occupation	

Paid Preparer's Use Only

Preparer's signature	Date	Check if self-employed ☐	Preparer's SSN or PTIN
Firm's name (or yours if self-employed) and address			EIN ZIP code

STF FED2611F.2

Form **1040** (1999)

SCHEDULES A&B **(Form 1040)** Department of the Treasury Internal Revenue Service (99)	**Schedule A — Itemized Deductions** **(Schedule B is on back)** ▶ Attach to Form 1040. ▶ See Instructions for Schedules A and B (Form 1040).		OMB No. 1545-0074 **1999** Attachment Sequence No. **07**

Name(s) shown on Form 1040 | Your social security number

Medical and Dental Expenses		Caution. Do not include expenses reimbursed or paid by others.	
	1	Medical and dental expenses (see page A-1)	**1**
	2	Enter amount from Form 1040, line 34.	**2**	
	3	Multiply line 2 above by 7.5% (.075)	**3**
	4	Subtract line 3 from line 1. If line 3 is more than line 1, enter -0-.	**4**
Taxes You Paid (See page A-2.)	5	State and local income taxes	**5**
	6	Real estate taxes (see page A-2)	**6**
	7	Personal property taxes	**7**
	8	Other taxes. List type and amount ▶ _____	**8**
	9	Add lines 5 through 8	**9**
Interest You Paid (See page A-3.) **Note.** Personal interest is not deductible.	10	Home mortgage interest and points reported to you on Form 1098 . . .	**10**
	11	Home mortgage interest not reported to you on Form 1098. If paid to the person from whom you bought the home, see page A-3 and show that person's name, identifying no., and address ▶ _____	**11**
	12	Points not reported to you on Form 1098. See page A-3 for special rules	**12**
	13	Investment interest. Attach Form 4952 if required. (See page A-3.)	**13**
	14	Add lines 10 through 13	**14**
Gifts to Charity If you made a gift and got a benefit for it, see page A-4.	15	Gifts by cash or check. If you made any gift of $250 or more, see page A-4	**15**
	16	Other than by cash or check. If any gift of $250 or more, see page A-4. You **MUST** attach Form 8283 if over $500	**16**
	17	Carryover from prior year	**17**
	18	Add lines 15 through 17	**18**
Casualty and Theft Losses	19	Casualty or theft loss(es). Attach Form 4684. (See page A-5.)	**19**
Job Expenses and Most Other Miscellaneous Deductions (See page A-5 for expenses to deduct here.)	20	Unreimbursed employee expenses — job travel, union dues, job education, etc. You **MUST** attach Form 2106 or 2106-EZ if required. (See page A-5.) ▶ _____	**20**
	21	Tax preparation fees	**21**
	22	Other expenses — investment, safe deposit box, etc. List type and amount ▶ _____	**22**
	23	Add lines 20 through 22	**23**
	24	Enter amount from Form 1040, line 34.	**24**	
	25	Multiply line 24 above by 2% (.02)	**25**
	26	Subtract line 25 from line 23. If line 25 is more than line 23, enter -0-	**26**
Other Miscellaneous Deductions	27	Other — from list on page A-6. List type and amount ▶ _____	**27**
Total Itemized Deductions	28	Is Form 1040, line 34, over $126,600 (over $63,300 if married filing separately)? ☐ **No.** Your deduction is not limited. Add the amounts in the far right column for lines 4 through 27. Also, enter on Form 1040, line 36. } . . ▶ ☐ **Yes.** Your deduction may be limited. See page A-6 for the amount to enter.	**28**

For Paperwork Reduction Act Notice, see Form 1040 instructions.
ISA
STF FED2613F

Schedule A (Form 1040) 1999

Schedules A & B (Form 1040) 1999

OMB No. 1545-0074   Page **2**

Name(s) shown on Form 1040. Do not enter name and social security number if shown on other side.

Your social security number

Schedule B — Interest and Ordinary Dividends

Attachment
Sequence No. **08**

Part I

Interest

(See page B-1 and the instructions for Form 1040, line 8a.)

Note. If you received a Form 1099-INT, Form 1099-OID, or substitute statement from a brokerage firm, list the firm's name as the payer and enter the total interest shown on that form.

Note. If you had over $400 in taxable interest, you must also complete Part III.

1   List name of payer. If any interest is from a seller-financed mortgage and the buyer used the property as a personal residence, see page B-1 and list this interest first. Also, show that buyer's social security number and address ▶

	Amount

1

2   Add the amounts on line 1 . . . .   **2**

3   Excludable interest on series EE and I U.S. savings bonds issued after 1989 from Form 8815, line 14. You **MUST** attach Form 8815 . . . .   **3**

4   Subtract line 3 from line 2. Enter the result here and on Form 1040, line 8a . . ▶   **4**

Part II

Ordinary Dividends

(See page B-1 and the instructions for Form 1040, line 9.)

Note. If you received a Form 1099-DIV or substitute statement from a brokerage firm, list the firm's name as the payer and enter the total dividends shown on that form.

Note. If you had over $400 in ordinary dividends, you must also complete Part III.

5   List name of payer. Include only ordinary dividends. If you received any capital gain distributions, see the instructions for Form 1040, line 13 ▶

	Amount

5

6   Add the amounts on line 5. Enter the total here and on Form 1040, line 9 . . . . ▶   **6**

Part III

Foreign Accounts and Trusts

(See page B-2.)

You must complete this part if you **(a)** had over $400 of interest or ordinary dividends; **(b)** had a foreign account; or **(c)** received a distribution from, or were a grantor of, or a transferor to, a foreign trust.

		Yes	No
7a	At any time during 1999, did you have an interest in or a signature or other authority over a financial account in a foreign country, such as a bank account, securities account, or other financial account? See page B-2 for exceptions and filing requirements for Form TD F 90-22.1		
b	If "Yes," enter the name of the foreign country ▶		
8	During 1999, did you receive a distribution from, or were you the grantor of, or transferor to, a foreign trust? If "Yes," you may have to file Form 3520. See page B-2		

For Paperwork Reduction Act Notice, see Form 1040 instructions.
ISA
STF FED2614F

Schedule B (Form 1040) 1999

SCHEDULE C (Form 1040)		**Profit or Loss From Business** (Sole Proprietorship)	OMB No. 1545-0074
Department of the Treasury Internal Revenue Service (99)		▶ **Partnerships, joint ventures, etc., must file Form 1065 or Form 1065-B.** ▶ **Attach to Form 1040 or Form 1041.** ▶ **See Instructions for Schedule C (Form 1040).**	**1999** Attachment Sequence No. **09**

Name of proprietor	Social security number (SSN)

A Principal business or profession, including product or service (see page C-1)   **B** Enter code from pages C-8 & 9 ▶

C Business name. If no separate business name, leave blank.   **D** Employer ID number (EIN), if any

E Business address (including suite or room no.) ▶
City, town or post office, state, and ZIP code

F Accounting method: (1) ☐ Cash   (2) ☐ Accrual   (3) ☐ Other (specify) ▶

G Did you "materially participate" in the operation of this business during 1999? If "No," see page C-2 for limit on losses .... ☐ Yes ☐ No

H If you started or acquired this business during 1999, check here .... ▶ ☐

Part I   Income

1	Gross receipts or sales. **Caution:** *If this income was reported to you on Form W-2 and the "Statutory employee" box on that form was checked, see page C-2 and check here* .... ▶ ☐	**1**
2	Returns and allowances	**2**
3	Subtract line 2 from line 1	**3**
4	Cost of goods sold (from line 42 on page 2)	**4**
5	**Gross profit.** Subtract line 4 from line 3	**5**
6	Other income, including Federal and state gasoline or fuel tax credit or refund (see page C-3)	**6**
7	**Gross income.** Add lines 5 and 6 .... ▶	**7**

Part II   Expenses. Enter expenses for business use of your home **only** on line 30.

8	Advertising	**8**		19	Pension and profit-sharing plans	**19**
9	Bad debts from sales or services (see page C-3)	**9**		20	Rent or lease (see page C-4):	
10	Car and truck expenses (see page C-3)	**10**		**a**	Vehicles, machinery, and equipment	**20a**
				b	Other business property	**20b**
11	Commissions and fees	**11**		21	Repairs and maintenance......	**21**
12	Depletion	**12**		22	Supplies (not included in Part III)	**22**
13	Depreciation and section 179 expense deduction (not included in Part III) (see page C-3)	**13**		23	Taxes and licenses	**23**
				24	Travel, meals, and entertainment:	
				a	Travel	**24a**
14	Employee benefit programs (other than on line 19)	**14**		**b**	Meals and entertainment .	
15	Insurance (other than health) ...	**15**		**c**	Enter nondeductible amount included on line 24b (see page C-5)	
16	Interest:					
a	Mortgage (paid to banks, etc.)...	**16a**		**d**	Subtract line 24c from line 24b ..	**24d**
b	Other	**16b**		25	Utilities	**25**
17	Legal and professional services .	**17**		26	Wages (less employment credits)	**26**
18	Office expense	**18**		27	Other expenses (from line 48 on page 2)	**27**
28	**Total expenses** before expenses for business use of home. Add lines 8 through 27 in columns .... ▶	**28**				

29	Tentative profit (loss). Subtract line 28 from line 7	**29**
30	Expenses for business use of your home. Attach **Form 8829**	**30**

31	**Net profit or (loss).** Subtract line 30 from line 29.
	  • If a profit, enter on **Form 1040, line 12,** and ALSO on **Schedule SE, line 2** (statutory employees, see page C-6). Estates and trusts, enter on Form 1041, line 3.
	  • If a loss, you MUST go on to line 32.
		31

32	If you have a loss, check the box that describes your investment in this activity (see page C-6).
	  • If you checked 32a, enter the loss on **Form 1040, line 12,** and ALSO on **Schedule SE, line 2** (statutory employees, see page C-6). Estates and trusts, enter on Form 1041, line 3.
	  • If you checked 32b, you MUST attach **Form 6198.**
		32a ☐ All investment is at risk.
		32b ☐ Some investment is not at risk.

For Paperwork Reduction Act Notice, see Form 1040 instructions.   Schedule C (Form 1040) 1999

ISA
STF FED2615F.1

SCHEDULE C-EZ
(Form 1040)

Department of the Treasury
Internal Revenue Service   (99)

Net Profit From Business
(Sole Proprietorship)

▶ Partnerships, joint ventures, etc., must file Form 1065 or 1065-B.
▶ Attach to Form 1040 or Form 1041. ▶ See instructions.

OMB No. 1545-0074

1999

Attachment
Sequence No. **09A**

Name of proprietor

Social security number (SSN)

Part I   General Information

You May Use Schedule C-EZ Instead of Schedule C Only If You:

- Had business expenses or $2,500 or less.
- Use the cash method of accounting.
- Did not have an inventory at any time during the year.
- Did not have a net loss from your business.
- Had only one business as a sole proprietor.

And You:

- Had no employees during the year.
- Are not required to file Form 4562, Depreciation and Amortization, for this business. See the instructions for Schedule C, line 13, on page C-3 to find out if you must file.
- Do not deduct expenses for business use of your home.
- Do not have prior year unallowed passive activity losses from this business.

A   Principal business or profession, including product or service

B   Enter code from pages C-8 & 9 ▶

C   Business name. If no separate business name, leave blank.

D   Employer ID number (EIN), if any

E   Business address (including suite or room no.). Address not required if same as on Form 1040, page 1.

City, town or post office, state, and ZIP code

Part II   Figure Your Net Profit

1 **Gross receipts.** Caution: *If this income was reported to you on Form W-2 and the "Statutory employee" box on that form was checked, see* **Statutory Employees** *in the instructions for Schedule C, line 1, on page C-2 and check here* .... ▶ ☐ | **1**

2 **Total expenses.** If more than $2,500, you **must** use Schedule C. See instructions .... | **2**

3 **Net profit.** Subtract line 2 from line 1. If less than zero, you **must** use Schedule C. Enter on **Form 1040, line 12,** and ALSO on **Schedule SE, line 2.** (Statutory employees **do not** report this amount on Schedule SE, line 2. Estates and trusts, enter on Form 1041, line 3.) .... | **3**

Part III   Information on Your Vehicle. Complete this part **ONLY** if you are claiming car or truck expenses on line 2.

4   When did you place your vehicle in service for business purposes? (month, day, year) ▶ _____ .

5   Of the total number of miles you drove your vehicle during 1999, enter the number of miles you used your vehicle for:

a Business _____ b Commuting _____ c Other _____

6   Do you (or your spouse) have another vehicle available for personal use? .... ☐ Yes ☐ No

7   Was your vehicle available for use during off-duty hours? .... ☐ Yes ☐ No

8a Do you have evidence to support your deduction? .... ☐ Yes ☐ No

  b If "Yes," is the evidence written? .... ☐ Yes ☐ No

For Paperwork Reduction Act Notice, see Form 1040 instructions.

ISA

Schedule C-EZ (Form 1040) 1999

STF FED2617F

SCHEDULE D		Capital Gains and Losses				OMB No. 1545-0074

SCHEDULE D (Form 1040) (U)
Department of the Treasury
Internal Revenue Service

Capital Gains and Losses

▶ Attach to Form 1040.　　▶ See Instructions for Schedule D (Form 1040).

▶ Use Schedule D-1 for more space to list transactions for lines 1 and 8.

OMB No. 1545-0074

1999

Attachment
Sequence No. **12**

Name(s) shown on Form 1040

Your social security number

Part I   **Short-Term Capital Gains and Losses—Assets Held One Year or Less**

(a) Description of property (Example: 100 sh. XYZ Co.)	(b) Date acquired (Mo., day, yr.)	(c) Date sold (Mo., day, yr.)	(d) Sales price (see page D-5)	(e) Cost or other basis (see page D-5)	(f) GAIN or (LOSS) Subtract (e) from (d)
1					

2	Enter your short-term totals, if any, from Schedule D-1, line 2	**2**	
3	**Total short-term sales price amounts.** Add column (d) of lines 1 and 2	**3**	
4	Short-term gain from Form 6252 and short-term gain or (loss) from Forms 4684, 6781, and 8824	**4**	
5	Net short-term gain or (loss) from partnerships, S corporations, estates, and trusts from Schedule(s) K-1	**5**	
6	Short-term capital loss carryover. Enter the amount, if any, from line 8 of your 1998 Capital Loss Carryover Worksheet	**6**	( )
7	**Net short-term capital gain or (loss).** Combine lines 1 through 6 in column (f) ▶	**7**	

Part II   **Long-Term Capital Gains and Losses—Assets Held More Than One Year**

(a) Description of property (Example: 100 sh. XYZ Co.)	(b) Date acquired (Mo., day, yr.)	(c) Date sold (Mo., day, yr.)	(d) Sales price (see page D-5)	(e) Cost or other basis (see page D-5)	(f) GAIN or (LOSS) Subtract (e) from (d)	(g) 28% RATE GAIN or (LOSS) * (see instr. below)
8						

9	Enter your long-term totals, if any, from Schedule D-1, line 9	**9**	
10	**Total long-term sales price amounts.** Add column (d) of lines 8 and 9	**10**	
11	Gain from Form 4797, Part I; long-term gain from Forms 2439 and 6252; and long-term gain or (loss) from Forms 4684, 6781, and 8824	**11**	
12	Net long-term gain or (loss) from partnerships, S corporations, estates, and trusts from Schedule(s) K-1.	**12**	
13	Capital gain distributions. See page D-1	**13**	
14	Long-term capital loss carryover. Enter in both columns (f) and (g) the amount, if any, from line 13 of your 1998 Capital Loss Carryover Worksheet	**14**	( ) ( )
15	Combine lines 8 through 14 in column (g).	**15**	
16	**Net long-term capital gain or (loss).** Combine lines 8 through 14 in column (f) ▶ Next: Go to Part III on the back.	**16**	

*28% Rate Gain or Loss includes **all** "collectibles gains and losses" (as defined on page D-5) and up to 50% of the eligible gain on qualified small business stock (see page D-4).

For Paperwork Reduction Act Notice, see Form 1040 instructions.   Cat. No. 15787U   Schedule D (Form 1040) 1999

Schedule D (Form 1040) 1999   Page **2**

Part III   Summary of Parts I and II

17 Combine lines 7 and 16. If a loss, go to line 18. If a gain, enter the gain on Form 1040, line 13   **17**

     Next: Complete Form 1040 through line 39. Then, go to **Part IV** to figure your tax if:
- Both lines 16 and 17 are gains, **and**
- Form 1040, line 39, is more than zero.

18 If line 17 is a loss, enter here and as a (loss) on Form 1040, line 13, the **smaller** of these losses:
- The loss on line 17, **or**
- ($3,000) or, if married filing separately, ($1,500) . . . .   **18** (   )

     Next: Skip **Part IV** below. Instead, complete Form 1040 through line 37. Then, complete the **Capital Loss Carryover Worksheet** on page D-6 if:
- The loss on line 17 exceeds the loss on line 18, **or**
- Form 1040, line 37, is a loss.

Part IV   Tax Computation Using Maximum Capital Gains Rates

19 Enter your taxable income from Form 1040, line 39 . . . . . .   **19**

20 Enter the **smaller** of line 16 or line 17 of Schedule D **20**

21 If you are filing Form 4952, enter the amount from Form 4952, line 4e   **21**

22 Subtract line 21 from line 20. If zero or less, enter -0- **22**

23 Combine lines 7 and 15. If zero or less, enter -0- **23**

24 Enter the **smaller** of line 15 or line 23, but not less than zero . . .   **24**

25 Enter your unrecaptured section 1250 gain, if any, from line 16 of the worksheet on page D-7 . . . .   **25**

26 Add lines 24 and 25 . . . .   **26**

27 Subtract line 26 from line 22. If zero or less, enter -0- **27**

28 Subtract line 27 from line 19. If zero or less, enter -0- **28**

29 Enter the **smaller** of:
- The amount on line 19, **or**
- $25,750 if single; $43,050 if married filing jointly or qualifying widow(er);   } **29**
  $21,525 if married filing separately; or $34,550 if head of household

30 Enter the **smaller** of line 28 or line 29 . . . .   **30**

31 Subtract line 22 from line 19. If zero or less, enter -0- **31**

32 Enter the **larger** of line 30 or line 31 . . . . ▶   **32**

33 Figure the tax on the amount on line 32. Use the Tax Table or Tax Rate Schedules, whichever applies   **33**

     Note. If line 29 is less than line 28, go to line 38.

34 Enter the amount from line 29 . . . .   **34**

35 Enter the amount from line 28 . . . .   **35**

36 Subtract line 35 from line 34. If zero or less, enter -0- . . . ▶   **36**

37 Multiply line 36 by 10% (.10) **37**

     Note. If line 27 is more than zero **and** equal to line 36, go to line 52.

38 Enter the **smaller** of line 19 or line 27 . . . .   **38**

39 Enter the amount from line 36 . . . .   **39**

40 Subtract line 39 from line 38 . . . . ▶   **40**

41 Multiply line 40 by 20% (.20) **41**

     Note. If line 25 is zero or blank, skip lines 42 through 47 and read the note above line 48.

42 Enter the **smaller** of line 22 or line 25 . . . . . .   **42**

43 Add lines 22 and 32 . . . .   **43**

44 Enter the amount from line 19 . . . . .   **44**

45 Subtract line 44 from line 43. If zero or less, enter -0- **45**

46 Subtract line 45 from line 42. If zero or less, enter -0- . . . ▶   **46**

47 Multiply line 46 by 25% (.25) **47**

     Note. If line 24 is zero or blank, go to line 52.

48 Enter the amount from line 19 . . . .   **48**

49 Add lines 32, 36, 40, and 46 . . . .   **49**

50 Subtract line 49 from line 48 . . . .   **50**

51 Multiply line 50 by 28% (.28) **51**

52 Add lines 33, 37, 41, 47, and 51 . . . .   **52**

53 Figure the tax on the amount on line 19. Use the Tax Table or Tax Rate Schedules, whichever applies   **53**

54 **Tax on all taxable income (including capital gains).** Enter the **smaller** of line 52 or line 53 here and on Form 1040, line 40. . . . .   **54**

*U.S. GPO: 1999 — 456-554   ✪   *Printed on recycled paper*   Schedule D (Form 1040) 1999

SCHEDULE E	**Supplemental Income and Loss**	OMB No. 1545-0074
(Form 1040)	(From rental real estate, royalties, partnerships, S corporations, estates, trusts, REMICs, etc.)	**1999**
Department of the Treasury Internal Revenue Service (99)	▶ Attach to Form 1040 or Form 1041.　　▶ See Instructions for Schedule E (Form 1040).	Attachment Sequence No. **13**

Name(s) shown on return | Your social security number

| **Part I** | **Income or Loss From Rental Real Estate and Royalties**　Note: Report income and expenses from your business of renting personal property on **Schedule C** or **C-EZ** (see page E-1). Report farm rental income or loss from **Form 4835** on page 2, line 39. |

1 Show the kind and location of each **rental real estate property**:

A _____

B _____

C _____

2 For each rental real estate property listed on line 1, did you or your family use it during the tax year for personal purposes for more than the greater of:
- 14 days, **or**
- 10% of the total days rented at fair rental value?
(See page E-1.)

	Yes	No
A		
B		
C		

Income:

			Properties			Totals
			A	B	C	(Add columns A, B, and C.)
3	Rents received	**3**				**3**
4	Royalties received	**4**				**4**

Expenses:

5	Advertising	**5**				
6	Auto and travel (see page E-2) . . .	**6**				
7	Cleaning and maintenance	**7**				
8	Commissions	**8**				
9	Insurance	**9**				
10	Legal and other professional fees .	**10**				
11	Management fees	**11**				
12	Mortgage interest paid to banks, etc. (see page E-2)	**12**				**12**
13	Other interest	**13**				
14	Repairs	**14**				
15	Supplies	**15**				
16	Taxes	**16**				
17	Utilities	**17**				
18	Other (list)▶ _____	**18**				
19	Add lines 5 through 18	**19**				**19**
20	Depreciation expense or depletion (see page E-3)	**20**				**20**
21	Total expenses. Add lines 19 and 20	**21**				
22	Income or (loss) from rental real estate or royalty properties. Subtract line 21 from line 3 (rents) or line 4 (royalties). If the result is a (loss), see page E-3 to find out if you must file **Form 6198**	**22**				
23	Deductible rental real estate loss. **Caution:** Your rental real estate loss on line 22 may be limited. See page E-3 to find out if you must file **Form 8582.** Real estate professionals must complete line 42 on page 2 . .	**23**	( )	( )	( )	
24	**Income.** Add positive amounts shown on line 22. **Do not** include any losses				**24**	
25	**Losses.** Add royalty losses from line 22 and rental real estate losses from line 23. Enter total losses here				**25**	( )
26	Total rental real estate and royalty income or (loss). Combine lines 24 and 25. Enter the result here. If Parts II, III, IV, and line 39 on page 2 do not apply to you, also enter this amount on Form 1040, line 17. Otherwise, include this amount in the total on line 40 on page 2				**26**	

For Paperwork Reduction Act Notice, see Form 1040 instructions.　　ISA　　Schedule E (Form 1040) 1999

STF FED2623F.1

APPENDIX A

Schedule E (Form 1040) 1999   Attachment Sequence No. **13**   Page **2**

Name(s) shown on return. Do not enter name and social security number if shown on other side. | **Your social security number**

Note: *If you report amounts from farming or fishing on Schedule E, you must enter your gross income from those activities on line 41 below. Real estate professionals must complete line 42 below.*

Part II   **Income or Loss From Partnerships and S Corporations**   Note: *If you report a loss from an at-risk activity, you MUST check either column (e) or (f) on line 27 to describe your investment in the activity. See page E-5. If you check column (f), you must attach Form 6198.*

27	(a) Name	(b) Enter P for partnership; S for S corporation	(c) Check if foreign partnership	(d) Employer identification number	Investment At Risk? (e) All is at risk	(f) Some is not at risk
A						
B						
C						
D						
E						

	Passive Income and Loss		Nonpassive Income and Loss		
	(g) Passive loss allowed (attach **Form 8582** if required)	(h) Passive income from **Schedule K-1**	(i) Nonpassive loss from **Schedule K-1**	(j) Section 179 expense deduction from **Form 4562**	(k) Nonpassive income from **Schedule K-1**
A					
B					
C					
D					
E					
28a Totals					
b Totals					

29	Add columns (h) and (k) of line 28a	29	
30	Add columns (g), (i), and (j) of line 28b	30	( )
31	Total partnership and S corporation income or (loss). Combine lines 29 and 30. Enter the result here and include in the total on line 40 below	31	

Part III   **Income or Loss From Estates and Trusts**

32	(a) Name	(b) Employer identification number
A		
B		

	Passive Income and Loss		Nonpassive Income and Loss	
	(c) Passive deduction or loss allowed (attach **Form 8582** if required)	(d) Passive income from **Schedule K-1**	(e) Deduction or loss from **Schedule K-1**	(f) Other income from **Schedule K-1**
A				
B				
33a Totals				
b Totals				

34	Add columns (d) and (f) of line 33a	34	
35	Add columns (c) and (e) of line 33b	35	( )
36	Total estate and trust income or (loss). Combine lines 34 and 35. Enter the result here and include in the total on line 40 below	36	

Part IV   **Income or Loss From Real Estate Mortgage Investment Conduits (REMICs) — Residual Holder**

37	(a) Name	(b) Employer identification number	(c) Excess inclusion from Schedules Q, line 2c (see page E-6)	(d) Taxable income (net loss) from Schedules Q, line 1b	(e) Income from Schedules Q, line 3b

38	Combine columns (d) and (e) only. Enter the result here and include in the total on line 40 below	38	

Part V   **Summary**

39	Net farm rental income or (loss) from **Form 4835**. Also, complete line 41 below	39	
40	TOTAL income or (loss). Combine lines 26, 31, 36, 38, and 39. Enter the result here and on Form 1040, line 17 ▶	40	
41	**Reconciliation of Farming and Fishing Income.** Enter your **gross** farming and fishing income reported on Form 4835, line 7; Schedule K-1 (Form 1065), line 15b; Schedule K-1 (Form 1120S), line 23; and Schedule K-1 (Form 1041), line 14 (see page E-6)	41	
42	**Reconciliation for Real Estate Professionals.** If you were a real estate professional (see page E-4), enter the net income or (loss) you reported anywhere on Form 1040 from all rental real estate activities in which you materially participated under the passive activity loss rules	42	

Schedule E (Form 1040) 1999

STF FED2623F.2

379

SCHEDULE EIC
(Form 1040A or 1040)

(U)

Department of the Treasury
Internal Revenue Service

Earned Income Credit

Qualifying Child Information

1040A
1040
EIC

*Complete and attach to Form 1040A or 1040
only if you have a qualifying child.*

OMB No. 1545-0074

1999

Attachment
Sequence No. **43**

Name(s) shown on return

Your social security number

Before you begin: See the instructions for Form 1040A, lines 37a and 37b, or Form 1040, lines 59a and 59b, to make sure that (1) you can take the EIC and (2) you have a qualifying child.

⚠ CAUTION

- If you take the EIC even though you are not eligible, you may not be allowed to take the credit for up to 10 years. See back of schedule for details.
- It will take us longer to process your return and issue your refund if you do not fill in all lines that apply for each qualifying child.
- If you do not enter the child's correct social security number on line 4, at the time we process your return, we may reduce or disallow your EIC.

Qualifying Child Information

	Child 1		**Child 2**	
	First name / Last name		First name / Last name	
1 Child's name If you have more than two qualifying children, you only have to list two to get the maximum credit.				
2 Child's year of birth	Year ____ __ __ __ *If born after 1980, skip lines 3a and 3b; go to line 4.*		Year ____ __ __ __ *If born after 1980, skip lines 3a and 3b; go to line 4.*	
3 If the child was born before 1981— **a** Was the child under age 24 at the end of 1999 and a student?	☐ Yes. *Go to line 4.*	☐ No. *Continue*	☐ Yes. *Go to line 4.*	☐ No. *Continue*
b Was the child permanently and totally disabled during any part of 1999?	☐ Yes. *Continue*	☐ No. *The child is not a qualifying child.*	☐ Yes. *Continue*	☐ No. *The child is not a qualifying child.*
4 Child's social security number (SSN) The child must have an SSN as defined on page 42 of the Form 1040A instructions or page 41 of the Form 1040 instructions unless the child was born and died in 1999. If your child was born and died in 1999 and did not have an SSN, enter "Died" on this line and attach a copy of the child's birth certificate.				
5 Child's relationship to you (for example, son, daughter, grandchild, foster child, etc.)				
6 Number of months child lived with you in the United States during 1999 • If the child lived with you for more than half of 1999 but less than 7 months, enter "7". • If the child was born or died in 1999 and your home was the child's home for the entire time he or she was alive during 1999, enter "12".	____ months *Do not enter more than 12 months.*		____ months *Do not enter more than 12 months.*	

Do you want part of the EIC added to your take-home pay in 2000? To see if you qualify, get Form W-5 from your employer or by calling the IRS at 1-800-TAX-FORM (1-800-829-3676).

For Paperwork Reduction Act Notice, see Form 1040A or 1040 instructions.

Cat. No. 15788F

Schedule EIC (Form 1040A or 1040) 1999

APPENDIX A

SCHEDULE H
(Form 1040)

Department of the Treasury
Internal Revenue Service   (O)

Household Employment Taxes
(For Social Security, Medicare, Withheld Income, and Federal Unemployment (FUTA) Taxes)
▶ Attach to Form 1040, 1040NR, 1040NR-EZ, 1040-SS, or 1041.
▶ See separate instructions.

OMB No. 1545-0074

1999

Attachment
Sequence No. **44**

Name of employer

Social security number

Employer identification number

A Did you pay **any one** household employee cash wages of $1,100 or more in 1999? (If any household employee was your spouse, your child under age 21, your parent, or anyone under age 18, see the line A instructions on page 3 before you answer this question.)

☐ **Yes.** Skip lines B and C and go to line 1.
☐ **No.** Go to line B.

B Did you withhold Federal income tax during 1999 for any household employee?

☐ **Yes.** Skip line C and go to line 5.
☐ **No.** Go to line C.

C Did you pay **total** cash wages of $1,000 or more in **any** calendar **quarter** of 1998 or 1999 to household employees? (**Do not** count cash wages paid in 1998 or 1999 to your spouse, your child under age 21, or your parent.)

☐ **No.** **Stop.** Do not file this schedule.
☐ **Yes.** Skip lines 1-9 and go to line 10 on the back.

Part I   Social Security, Medicare, and Income Taxes

1 Total cash wages subject to social security taxes (see page 3)	**1**	
2 Social security taxes. Multiply line 1 by 12.4% (.124)	**2**	
3 Total cash wages subject to Medicare taxes (see page 3)	**3**	
4 Medicare taxes. Multiply line 3 by 2.9% (.029)	**4**	
5 Federal income tax withheld, if any	**5**	
6 **Total social security, Medicare, and income taxes** (add lines 2, 4, and 5)	**6**	
7 Advance earned income credit (EIC) payments, if any	**7**	
8 **Net taxes** (subtract line 7 from line 6)	**8**	

9 Did you pay **total** cash wages of $1,000 or more in **any** calendar **quarter** of 1998 or 1999 to household employees? (**Do not** count cash wages paid in 1998 or 1999 to your spouse, your child under age 21, or your parent.)

☐ **No.** **Stop.** Enter the amount from line 8 above on Form 1040, line 55. If you are not required to file Form 1040, see the line 9 instructions on page 4.

☐ **Yes.** Go to line 10 on the back.

For Paperwork Reduction Act Notice, see Form 1040 instructions.   Cat. No. 12187K   Schedule H (Form 1040) 1999

381

Form
1040A

Department of the Treasury—Internal Revenue Service

U.S. Individual Income Tax Return (99) **1999**

IRS Use Only—Do not write or staple in this space.

OMB No. 1545-0085

Label
(See page 19.)

Use the IRS label.

Otherwise, please print or type.

L A B E L   H E R E

Your first name and initial	Last name	Your social security number
If a joint return, spouse's first name and initial	Last name	Spouse's social security number

Home address (number and street). If you have a P.O. box, see page 20. | Apt. no.

City, town or post office, state, and ZIP code. If you have a foreign address, see page 20.

IMPORTANT!

You **must** enter your SSN(s) above.

Presidential Election Campaign Fund (See page 20.)

	Yes	No
Do you want $3 to go to this fund?		
If a joint return, does your spouse want $3 to go to this fund?		

Note. Checking "Yes" will not change your tax or reduce your refund.

Filing status

Check only one box.

1 ☐ Single

2 ☐ Married filing joint return (even if only one had income)

3 ☐ Married filing separate return. Enter spouse's social security number above and full name here.

4 ☐ Head of household (with qualifying person). (See page 21.) If the qualifying person is a child but not your dependent, enter this child's name here.

5 ☐ Qualifying widow(er) with dependent child (year spouse died 19). (See page 22.)

Exemptions

If more than seven dependents, see page 22.

6a ☐ **Yourself.** If your parent (or someone else) can claim you as a dependent on his or her tax return, **do not** check box 6a.

b ☐ **Spouse**

c Dependents: (1) First name Last name	(2) Dependent's social security number	(3) Dependent's relationship to you	(4) ✓ if qualifying child for child tax credit (see page 23)
			☐
			☐
			☐
			☐
			☐
			☐
			☐

No. of boxes checked on 6a and 6b

No. of your children on 6c who:
- lived with you
- did not live with you due to divorce or separation (see page 24)

Dependents on 6c not entered above

Add numbers entered on lines above

d Total number of exemptions claimed.

Income

Attach Copy B of your Form(s) W-2 here.

Also attach Form(s) 1099-R if tax was withheld.

If you did not get a W-2, see page 25.

Enclose, but do not staple, any payment.

7 Wages, salaries, tips, etc. Attach Form(s) W-2. | 7

8a **Taxable** interest. Attach Schedule 1 if required. | 8a

b **Tax-exempt** interest. DO NOT include on line 8a. | 8b

9 Ordinary dividends. Attach Schedule 1 if required. | 9

10a Total IRA distributions. 10a | **10b** Taxable amount (see page 25). | 10b

11a Total pensions and annuities. 11a | **11b** Taxable amount (see page 26). | 11b

12 Unemployment compensation, qualified state tuition program earnings, and Alaska Permanent Fund dividends. | 12

13a Social security benefits. 13a | **13b** Taxable amount (see page 28). | 13b

14 Add lines 7 through 13b (far right column). This is your **total income.** | 14

Adjusted gross income

15 IRA deduction (see page 30). | 15

16 Student loan interest deduction (see page 30). | 16

17 Add lines 15 and 16. These are your **total adjustments.** | 17

18 Subtract line 17 from line 14. This is your **adjusted gross income.** | 18

For Disclosure, Privacy Act, and Paperwork Reduction Act Notice, see page 53. Cat. No. 14089Z Form **1040A** (1999)

Taxable income	**19**	Enter the amount from line 18.			**19**	
	20a	Check if: ☐ **You** were 65 or older ☐ Blind ☐ **Spouse** was 65 or older ☐ Blind **Enter number of boxes checked** 20a ☐				
	b	If you are married filing separately and your spouse itemizes deductions, see page 32 and check here . . . . . . 20b ☐				
	21	Enter the **standard deduction** for your filing status. **But** see page 33 if you checked any box on line 20a or 20b **OR** if someone can claim you as a dependent. Single—$4,300 Married filing jointly or Qualifying widow(er)—$7,200 Head of household—$6,350 Married filing separately—$3,600			**21**	
	22	Subtract line 21 from line 19. If line 21 is more than line 19, enter -0-.			**22**	
	23	Multiply $2,750 by the total number of exemptions claimed on line 6d.			**23**	
	24	Subtract line 23 from line 22. If line 23 is more than line 22, enter -0-. This is your **taxable income.**			**24**	
Tax, credits, and payments	**25**	Find the tax on the amount on line 24 (see page 34).			**25**	
	26	Credit for child and dependent care expenses. Attach Schedule 2.	**26**			
	27	Credit for the elderly or the disabled. Attach Schedule 3.	**27**			
	28	Child tax credit (see page 35).	**28**			
	29	Education credits. Attach Form 8863.	**29**			
	30	Adoption credit. Attach Form 8839.	**30**			
	31	Add lines 26 through 30. These are your **total credits.**			**31**	
	32	Subtract line 31 from line 25. If line 31 is more than line 25, enter -0-.			**32**	
	33	Advance earned income credit payments from Form(s) W-2.			**33**	
	34	Add lines 32 and 33. This is your **total tax.**			**34**	
	35	Total Federal income tax withheld from Forms W-2 and 1099.	**35**			
	36	1999 estimated tax payments and amount applied from 1998 return.	**36**			
	37a	**Earned income credit.** Attach Schedule EIC if you have a qualifying child.	**37a**			
	b	Nontaxable earned income: amount and type				
	38	Additional child tax credit. Attach Form 8812.	**38**			
	39	Add lines 35, 36, 37a, and 38. These are your **total payments.**			**39**	
Refund Have it directly deposited! See page 47 and fill in 41b, 41c, and 41d.	**40**	If line 39 is more than line 34, subtract line 34 from line 39. This is the amount you **overpaid.**			**40**	
	41a	Amount of line 40 you want **refunded to you.**			**41a**	
	b	Routing number ☐☐☐☐☐☐☐☐☐ **c** Type: ☐ Checking ☐ Savings				
	d	Account number ☐☐☐☐☐☐☐☐☐☐☐☐☐☐☐☐☐				
	42	Amount of line 40 you want **applied to your 2000 estimated tax.**	**42**			
Amount you owe	**43**	If line 34 is more than line 39, subtract line 39 from line 34. This is the **amount you owe.** For details on how to pay, see page 48.			**43**	
	44	Estimated tax penalty (see page 48).	**44**			

Sign here

Joint return? See page 20.

Keep a copy for your records.

Under penalties of perjury, I declare that I have examined this return and accompanying schedules and statements, and to the best of my knowledge and belief, they are true, correct, and accurately list all amounts and sources of income I received during the tax year. Declaration of preparer (other than the taxpayer) is based on all information of which the preparer has any knowledge.

Your signature	Date	Your occupation	Daytime telephone number (optional) ( )
Spouse's signature. If joint return, BOTH must sign.	Date	Spouse's occupation	

Paid preparer's use only

Preparer's signature	Date	Check if self-employed ☐	Preparer's SSN or PTIN
Firm's name (or yours if self-employed) and address			EIN :
			ZIP code

♻ *Printed on recycled paper*

Form **1040A** (1999)

Department of the Treasury—Internal Revenue Service

Form 1040EZ (U)

Income Tax Return for Single and Joint Filers With No Dependents

1999

OMB No. 1545-0675

Use the IRS label here

Your first name and initial — Last name

If a joint return, spouse's first name and initial — Last name

Home address (number and street). If you have a P.O. box, see page 12. — Apt. no.

City, town or post office, state, and ZIP code. If you have a foreign address, see page 12.

Your social security number

Spouse's social security number

▲ **IMPORTANT!** ▲

You must enter your SSN(s) above.

Presidential Election Campaign (See page 12.)

Note. *Checking "Yes" will not change your tax or reduce your refund.*

Do you want $3 to go to this fund? ▶ Yes ☐ No ☐

If a joint return, does your spouse want $3 to go to this fund? ▶ Yes ☐ No ☐

Income

Attach Copy B of Form(s) W-2 here. Enclose, but do not staple, any payment.

1 Total wages, salaries, and tips. This should be shown in box 1 of your W-2 form(s). Attach your W-2 form(s). — 1

2 Taxable interest. If the total is over $400, you cannot use Form 1040EZ. — 2

3 Unemployment compensation, qualified state tuition program earnings, and Alaska Permanent Fund dividends (see page 14). — 3

4 Add lines 1, 2, and 3. This is your **adjusted gross income.** — 4

Note. You must check Yes or No.

5 Can your parents (or someone else) claim you on their return?

Yes. Enter amount from worksheet on back. ☐

No. If **single,** enter 7,050.00. If **married,** enter 12,700.00. See back for explanation. ☐ — 5

6 Subtract line 5 from line 4. If line 5 is larger than line 4, enter 0. This is your **taxable income.** ▶ 6

Payments and tax

7 Enter your Federal income tax withheld from box 2 of your W-2 form(s). — 7

8a **Earned income credit** (see page 15).

b Nontaxable earned income: enter type and amount below.

Type _____ $ _____ — 8a

9 Add lines 7 and 8a. These are your **total payments.** — 9

10 **Tax.** Use the amount on **line 6 above** to find your tax in the tax table on pages 24–28 of the booklet. Then, enter the tax from the table on this line. — 10

Refund

Have it directly deposited! See page 20 and fill in 11b, 11c, and 11d.

11a If line 9 is larger than line 10, subtract line 10 from line 9. This is your **refund.** — 11a

▶ b Routing number

▶ c Type: ☐ Checking ☐ Savings d Account number

Amount you owe

12 If line 10 is larger than line 9, subtract line 9 from line 10. This is the **amount you owe.** See page 21 for details on how to pay. — 12

Dollars | **Cents**

I have read this return. Under penalties of perjury, I declare that to the best of my knowledge and belief, the return is true, correct, and accurately lists all amounts and sources of income I received during the tax year.

Sign here

Keep copy for your records.

Your signature — Spouse's signature if joint return. See page 11.

Date — Your occupation — Date — Spouse's occupation

For Official Use Only

1 2 3 4 5 6 7 8 9 10

For Disclosure, Privacy Act, and Paperwork Reduction Act Notice, see page 23. Cat. No. 14090A

1999 Form 1040EZ

Form **1040X** (Rev. November 1999)	Department of the Treasury—Internal Revenue Service **Amended U.S. Individual Income Tax Return** ▶ See separate instructions.	OMB No. 1545-0091

This return is for calendar year ▶ _____ , **OR fiscal year ended** ▶ _____ , _____ .

Please print or type

Your first name and initial	Last name	Your social security number
If a joint return, spouse's first name and initial	Last name	Spouse's social security number
Home address (no. and street) or P.O. box if mail is not delivered to your home	Apt. no.	Telephone number (optional) ( )
City, town or post office, state, and ZIP code. If you have a foreign address, see page 2 of the instructions.		For Paperwork Reduction Act Notice, see page 6.

A If the name or address shown above is different from that shown on the original return, check here . . . . . ▶ ☐

B Has the original return been changed or audited by the IRS or have you been notified that it will be? . . ☐ **Yes** ☐ **No**

C Filing status. Be sure to complete this line. **Note.** You cannot change from joint to separate returns after the due date.

On original return ▶ ☐ Single ☐ Married filing joint return ☐ Married filing separate return ☐ Head of household ☐ Qualifying widow(er)

On this return ▶ ☐ Single ☐ Married filing joint return ☐ Married filing separate return ☐ Head of household* ☐ Qualifying widow(er)

* If the qualifying person is a child but not your dependent, see page 2.

USE PART II ON THE BACK TO EXPLAIN ANY CHANGES		**A. Original amount** or as previously adjusted (see page 2)	**B. Net change**—amount of increase or (decrease)—explain in Part II	**C. Correct amount**
Income and Deductions (see pages 2–5)				
1 Adjusted gross income (see page 3)	**1**			
2 Itemized deductions or standard deduction (see page 3). .	**2**			
3 Subtract line 2 from line 1	**3**			
4 Exemptions. If changing, fill in Parts I and II on the back .	**4**			
5 Taxable income. Subtract line 4 from line 3	**5**			
6 Tax (see page 4). Method used in col. C_____	**6**			
7 Credits (see page 4)	**7**			
8 Subtract line 7 from line 6. Enter the result but not less than zero .	**8**			
9 Other taxes (see page 4)	**9**			
10 Total tax. Add lines 8 and 9	**10**			
11 Federal income tax withheld and excess social security and RRTA tax withheld. If changing, see page 4	**11**			
12 Estimated tax payments, including amount applied from prior year's return	**12**			
13 Earned income credit	**13**			
14 Additional child tax credit from Form 8812	**14**			
15 Credits from Form 4136 or Form 2439	**15**			
16 Amount paid with request for extension of time to file (see page 4)			**16**	
17 Amount of tax paid with original return plus additional tax paid after it was filed			**17**	
18 Total payments. Add lines 11 through 17 in column C			**18**	
Refund or Amount You Owe				
19 Overpayment, if any, as shown on original return or as previously adjusted by the IRS . . .			**19**	
20 Subtract line 19 from line 18 (see page 5).			**20**	
21 **AMOUNT YOU OWE.** If line 10, column C, is more than line 20, enter the difference and see page 5			**21**	
22 If line 10, column C, is less than line 20, enter the difference			**22**	
23 Amount of line 22 you want **REFUNDED TO YOU**			**23**	
24 Amount of line 22 you want **APPLIED TO YOUR ESTIMATED TAX | 24**				

Sign Here

Joint return? See page 2. Keep a copy for your records.

Under penalties of perjury, I declare that I have filed an original return and that I have examined this amended return, including accompanying schedules and statements, and to the best of my knowledge and belief, this amended return is true, correct, and complete. Declaration of preparer (other than taxpayer) is based on all information of which the preparer has any knowledge.

▶ Your signature	Date	▶ Spouse's signature. If a joint return, BOTH must sign.	Date

Paid Preparer's Use Only

Preparer's signature ▶	Date	Check if self-employed ☐	Preparer's SSN or PTIN
Firm's name (or yours if self-employed) and address ▶			EIN
			ZIP code

Cat. No. 11360L   Form **1040X** (Rev. 11-99)

APPENDIX A

Application for Employer Identification Number

Form **SS-4**

(Rev. April 2000)

Department of the Treasury
Internal Revenue Service

(For use by employers, corporations, partnerships, trusts, estates, churches, government agencies, certain individuals, and others. See instructions.)

▶ Keep a copy for your records.

EIN

OMB No. 1545-0003

Please type or print clearly.

1 Name of applicant (legal name) (see instructions)

2 Trade name of business (if different from name on line 1)

3 Executor, trustee, "care of" name

4a Mailing address (street address) (room, apt., or suite no.)

5a Business address (if different from address on lines 4a and 4b)

4b City, state, and ZIP code

5b City, state, and ZIP code

6 County and state where principal business is located

7 Name of principal officer, general partner, grantor, owner, or trustor—SSN or ITIN may be required (see instructions) ▶

8a Type of entity (Check only one box.) (see instructions)

Caution: *If applicant is a limited liability company, see the instructions for line 8a.*

☐ Sole proprietor (SSN) _____
☐ Partnership
☐ REMIC
☐ State/local government
☐ Church or church-controlled organization
☐ Other nonprofit organization (specify) ▶ _____
☐ Other (specify) ▶

☐ Personal service corp.
☐ National Guard
☐ Farmers' cooperative

☐ Estate (SSN of decedent) _____
☐ Plan administrator (SSN) _____
☐ Other corporation (specify) ▶ _____
☐ Trust
☐ Federal government/military

(enter GEN if applicable) _____

8b If a corporation, name the state or foreign country (if applicable) where incorporated

State

Foreign country

9 Reason for applying (Check only one box.) (see instructions)
☐ Started new business (specify type) ▶ _____
☐ Hired employees (Check the box and see line 12.)
☐ Created a pension plan (specify type) ▶

☐ Banking purpose (specify purpose) ▶ _____
☐ Changed type of organization (specify new type) ▶ _____
☐ Purchased going business
☐ Created a trust (specify type) ▶ _____
☐ Other (specify) ▶

10 Date business started or acquired (month, day, year) (see instructions)

11 Closing month of accounting year (see instructions)

12 First date wages or annuities were paid or will be paid (month, day, year). **Note:** *If applicant is a withholding agent, enter date income will first be paid to nonresident alien. (month, day, year)* . . . . ▶

13 Highest number of employees expected in the next 12 months. **Note:** *If the applicant does not expect to have any employees during the period, enter -0-. (see instructions)* . . . . . ▶

Nonagricultural	Agricultural	Household

14 Principal activity (see instructions) ▶

15 Is the principal business activity manufacturing? . . . . ☐ Yes ☐ No
If "Yes," principal product and raw material used ▶

16 To whom are most of the products or services sold? Please check one box.   ☐ Business (wholesale)
☐ Public (retail)   ☐ Other (specify) ▶   ☐ N/A

17a Has the applicant ever applied for an employer identification number for this or any other business? . . . . ☐ Yes ☐ No
Note: *If "Yes," please complete lines 17b and 17c.*

17b If you checked "Yes" on line 17a, give applicant's legal name and trade name shown on prior application, if different from line 1 or 2 above.
Legal name ▶   Trade name ▶

17c Approximate date when and city and state where the application was filed. Enter previous employer identification number if known.

Approximate date when filed (mo., day, year)	City and state where filed	Previous EIN

Under penalties of perjury, I declare that I have examined this application, and to the best of my knowledge and belief, it is true, correct, and complete.

Business telephone number (include area code)
(   )

Fax telephone number (include area code)
(   )

Name and title (Please type or print clearly.) ▶

Signature ▶   Date ▶

Note: *Do not write below this line. For official use only.*

Please leave blank ▶	Geo.	Ind.	Class	Size	Reason for applying

For Privacy Act and Paperwork Reduction Act Notice, see page 4.

Cat. No. 16055N

Form **SS-4** (Rev. 4-2000)

| Form **SS-8**
(Rev. June 1997)
Department of the Treasury
Internal Revenue Service | **Determination of Employee Work Status
for Purposes of Federal Employment Taxes
and Income Tax Withholding** | OMB No. 1545-0004 |

Paperwork Reduction Act Notice

We ask for the information on this form to carry out the Internal Revenue laws of the United States. You are required to give us the information. We need it to ensure that you are complying with these laws and to allow us to figure and collect the right amount of tax.

You are not required to provide the information requested on a form that is subject to the Paperwork Reduction Act unless the form displays a valid OMB control number. Books or records relating to a form or its instructions must be retained as long as their contents may become material in the administration of any Internal Revenue law. Generally, tax returns and return information are confidential, as required by Code section 6103.

The time needed to complete and file this form will vary depending on individual circumstances. The estimated average time is: **Recordkeeping, 34 hr., 55 min.; Learning about the law or the form, 12 min.;** and **Preparing and sending the form to the IRS, 46 min.** If you have comments concerning the accuracy of these time estimates or suggestions for making this form simpler, we would be happy to hear from you. You can write to the Tax Forms Committee, Western Area Distribution Center, Rancho Cordova, CA 95743-0001. **DO NOT** send the tax form to this address. Instead, see **General Information** for where to file.

Purpose

Employers and workers file Form SS-8 to get a determination as to whether a worker is an employee for purposes of Federal employment taxes and income tax withholding.

General Information

Complete this form carefully. If the firm is completing the form, complete it for **ONE** individual who is representative of the class of workers whose status is in question. If you want a written determination for more than one class of workers, complete a separate Form SS-8 for one worker

from each class whose status is typical of that class. A written determination for any worker will apply to other workers of the same class if the facts are not materially different from those of the worker whose status was ruled upon.

Caution: *Form SS-8 is **not** a claim for refund of social security and Medicare taxes or Federal income tax withholding. Also, a determination that an individual is an employee does not necessarily reduce any current or prior tax liability. A worker must file his or her income tax return even if a determination has not been made by the due date of the return.*

Where to file.—In the list below, find the state where your legal residence, principal place of business, office, or agency is located. Send Form SS-8 to the address listed for your location.

Location:	Send to:
Alaska, Arizona, Arkansas, California, Colorado, Hawaii, Idaho, Illinois, Iowa, Kansas, Minnesota, Missouri, Montana, Nebraska, Nevada, New Mexico, North Dakota, Oklahoma, Oregon, South Dakota, Texas, Utah, Washington, Wisconsin, Wyoming	Internal Revenue Service SS-8 Determinations P.O. Box 1231, Stop 4106 AUSC Austin, TX 78767
Alabama, Connecticut, Delaware, District of Columbia, Florida, Georgia, Indiana, Kentucky, Louisiana, Maine, Maryland, Massachusetts, Michigan, Mississippi, New Hampshire, New Jersey, New York, North Carolina, Ohio, Pennsylvania, Rhode Island, South Carolina, Tennessee, Vermont, Virginia, West Virginia, All other locations not listed	Internal Revenue Service SS-8 Determinations Two Lakemont Road Newport, VT 05855-1555
American Samoa, Guam, Puerto Rico, U.S. Virgin Islands	Internal Revenue Service Mercantile Plaza 2 Avenue Ponce de Leon San Juan, Puerto Rico 00918

Name of firm (or person) for whom the worker performed services	Name of worker
Address of firm (include street address, apt. or suite no., city, state, and ZIP code)	Address of worker (include street address, apt. or suite no., city, state, and ZIP code)
Trade name	Telephone number (include area code) ( )	Worker's social security number
Telephone number (include area code) ( )	Firm's employer identification number	

Check type of firm for which the work relationship is in question:

☐ **Individual**   ☐ **Partnership**   ☐ **Corporation**   ☐ **Other** (specify) ▶ ....

Important Information Needed To Process Your Request

This form is being completed by: ☐ Firm   ☐ Worker

If this form is being completed by the worker, the IRS **must** have your permission to disclose your name to the firm.

Do you object to disclosing your name and the information on this form to the firm? . . . .   ☐ Yes   ☐ No

If you answer "Yes," the IRS cannot act on your request. **Do not complete the rest of this form unless the IRS asks for it.**

Under section 6110 of the Internal Revenue Code, the information on this form and related file documents will be open to the public if any ruling or determination is made. However, names, addresses, and taxpayer identification numbers will be removed before the information is made public.

Is there any other information you want removed? . . . .   ☐ Yes   ☐ No

If you check "Yes," we cannot process your request unless you submit a copy of this form and copies of all supporting documents showing, in brackets, the information you want removed. Attach a separate statement showing which specific exemption of section 6110(c) applies to each bracketed part.

Cat. No. 16106T   Form **SS-8** (Rev. 6-97)

Form SS-8 (Rev. 6-97)

This form is designed to cover many work activities, so some of the questions may not apply to you. **You must answer ALL items or mark them "Unknown" or "Does not apply."** *If you need more space, attach another sheet.*

Total number of workers in this class. (Attach names and addresses. If more than 10 workers, list only 10.) ▶ _____

This information is about services performed by the worker from _____ to _____
(month, day, year)   (month, day, year)

Is the worker still performing services for the firm? . . . . ☐ **Yes** ☐ **No**

● If "No," what was the date of termination? ▶ _____
(month, day, year)

1a Describe the firm's business ....

b Describe the work done by the worker ....

2a If the work is done under a written agreement between the firm and the worker, attach a copy.

b If the agreement is not in writing, describe the terms and conditions of the work arrangement ....
....
....

c If the actual working arrangement differs in any way from the agreement, explain the differences and why they occur ....
....

3a Is the worker given training by the firm? . . . . ☐ **Yes** ☐ **No**
● If "Yes," what kind? ....
● How often? ....

b Is the worker given instructions in the way the work is to be done (exclusive of actual training in 3a)? . ☐ **Yes** ☐ **No**
● If "Yes," give specific examples ....

c Attach samples of any written instructions or procedures.

d Does the firm have the right to change the methods used by the worker or direct that person on how to
do the work? . . . . ☐ **Yes** ☐ **No**
● Explain your answer ....
....

e Does the operation of the firm's business require that the worker be supervised or controlled in the
performance of the service? . . . . ☐ **Yes** ☐ **No**
● Explain your answer ....

4a The firm engages the worker:
☐ To perform and complete a particular job only
☐ To work at a job for an indefinite period of time
☐ Other (explain) ....

b Is the worker required to follow a routine or a schedule established by the firm? . . . . ☐ **Yes** ☐ **No**
● If "Yes," what is the routine or schedule? ....
....

c Does the worker report to the firm or its representative?. . . . . ☐ **Yes** ☐ **No**
● If "Yes," how often? ....
● For what purpose? ....
● In what manner (in person, in writing, by telephone, etc.)? ....
● Attach copies of any report forms used in reporting to the firm.

d Does the worker furnish a time record to the firm? . . . . ☐ **Yes** ☐ **No**
● If "Yes," attach copies of time records.

5a State the kind and value of tools, equipment, supplies, and materials furnished by:
● The firm ....
....
● The worker ....
....

b What expenses are incurred by the worker in the performance of services for the firm? ....
....

c Does the firm reimburse the worker for any expenses? . . . . ☐ **Yes** ☐ **No**
● If "Yes," specify the reimbursed expenses ....

6a Will the worker perform the services personally? . . . . ☐ **Yes** ☐ **No**

  b Does the worker have helpers? . . . . ☐ **Yes** ☐ **No**
- If "Yes," who hires the helpers? ☐ **Firm** ☐ **Worker**
- If the helpers are hired by the worker, is the firm's approval necessary? . . . . ☐ **Yes** ☐ **No**
- Who pays the helpers? ☐ **Firm** ☐ **Worker**
- If the worker pays the helpers, does the firm repay the worker? . . . . ☐ **Yes** ☐ **No**
- Are social security and Medicare taxes and Federal income tax withheld from the helpers' pay? . . . ☐ **Yes** ☐ **No**
- If "Yes," who reports and pays these taxes? ☐ **Firm** ☐ **Worker**
- Who reports the helpers' earnings to the Internal Revenue Service? ☐ **Firm** ☐ **Worker**
- What services do the helpers perform? ....

7 At what location are the services performed? ☐ Firm's ☐ Worker's ☐ Other (specify) ....

8a Type of pay worker receives:
  ☐ Salary ☐ Commission ☐ Hourly wage ☐ Piecework ☐ Lump sum ☐ Other (specify) ....

  b Does the firm guarantee a minimum amount of pay to the worker? . . . . ☐ **Yes** ☐ **No**

  c Does the firm allow the worker a drawing account or advances against pay? . . . . ☐ **Yes** ☐ **No**
- If "Yes," is the worker paid such advances on a regular basis? . . . . ☐ **Yes** ☐ **No**

  d How does the worker repay such advances? ....

9a Is the worker eligible for a pension, bonus, paid vacations, sick pay, etc.? . . . . ☐ **Yes** ☐ **No**
- If "Yes," specify ....

  b Does the firm carry worker's compensation insurance on the worker? . . . . ☐ **Yes** ☐ **No**

  c Does the firm withhold social security and Medicare taxes from amounts paid the worker? . . . . . ☐ **Yes** ☐ **No**

  d Does the firm withhold Federal income tax from amounts paid the worker? . . . . ☐ **Yes** ☐ **No**

  e How does the firm report the worker's earnings to the Internal Revenue Service?
  ☐ Form W-2 ☐ Form 1099-MISC ☐ Does not report ☐ Other (specify) ....
- Attach a copy.

  f Does the firm bond the worker? . . . . ☐ **Yes** ☐ **No**

10a Approximately how many hours a day does the worker perform services for the firm? ....

  b Does the firm set hours of work for the worker? . . . . ☐ **Yes** ☐ **No**
- If "Yes," what are the worker's set hours? _____ a.m./p.m. to _____ a.m./p.m. (Circle whether a.m. or p.m.)

  c Does the worker perform similar services for others? . . . . ☐ **Yes** ☐ **No** ☐ **Unknown**
- If "Yes," are these services performed on a daily basis for other firms? . . . . . ☐ **Yes** ☐ **No** ☐ **Unknown**
- Percentage of time spent in performing these services for:
  This firm .... % Other firms .... % ☐ **Unknown**
- Does the firm have priority on the worker's time? . . . . ☐ **Yes** ☐ **No**
- If "No," explain ....

  d Is the worker prohibited from competing with the firm either while performing services or during any later period? . . . . ☐ **Yes** ☐ **No**

11a Can the firm discharge the worker at any time without incurring a liability? . . . . ☐ **Yes** ☐ **No**
- If "No," explain ....

  b Can the worker terminate the services at any time without incurring a liability? . . . . ☐ **Yes** ☐ **No**
- If "No," explain ....

12a Does the worker perform services for the firm under:
  ☐ The firm's business name ☐ The worker's own business name ☐ Other (specify) ....

  b Does the worker advertise or maintain a business listing in the telephone directory, a trade journal, etc.? . . . . ☐ **Yes** ☐ **No** ☐ **Unknown**
- If "Yes," specify ....

  c Does the worker represent himself or herself to the public as being in business to perform the same or similar services? . . . . ☐ **Yes** ☐ **No** ☐ **Unknown**
- If "Yes," how? ....

  d Does the worker have his or her own shop or office? . . . . ☐ **Yes** ☐ **No** ☐ **Unknown**
- If "Yes," where? ....

  e Does the firm represent the worker as an employee of the firm to its customers? . . . . ☐ **Yes** ☐ **No**
- If "No," how is the worker represented? ....

  f How did the firm learn of the worker's services? ....

13 Is a license necessary for the work? . . . . ☐ **Yes** ☐ **No** ☐ **Unknown**
- If "Yes," what kind of license is required? ....
- Who issues the license? ....
- Who pays the license fee?

Form SS-8 (Rev. 6-97)   Page **4**

14 Does the worker have a financial investment in a business related to the services performed?. . . . . ☐ Yes ☐ No ☐ Unknown
   • If "Yes," specify and give amount of the investment . . . .

15 Can the worker incur a loss in the performance of the service for the firm? . . . . ☐ Yes ☐ No
   • If "Yes," how? . . . .

16a Has any other government agency ruled on the status of the firm's workers? . . . . ☐ Yes ☐ No
   • If "Yes," attach a copy of the ruling.

   b Is the same issue being considered by any IRS office in connection with the audit of the worker's tax return or the firm's tax return, or has it been considered recently? . . . . ☐ Yes ☐ No
   • If "Yes," for which year(s)? . . . .

17 Does the worker assemble or process a product at home or away from the firm's place of business? ☐ Yes ☐ No
   • If "Yes," who furnishes materials or goods used by the worker? ☐ Firm   ☐ Worker   ☐ Other
   • Is the worker furnished a pattern or given instructions to follow in making the product? . . . . . ☐ Yes ☐ No
   • Is the worker required to return the finished product to the firm or to someone designated by the firm? ☐ Yes ☐ No

18 Attach a detailed explanation of any other reason why you believe the worker is an employee or an independent contractor.

Answer items 19a through o only if the worker is a salesperson or provides a service directly to customers.

19a Are leads to prospective customers furnished by the firm?. . . . . ☐ Yes ☐ No ☐ Does not apply
   b Is the worker required to pursue or report on leads? . . . . ☐ Yes ☐ No ☐ Does not apply
   c Is the worker required to adhere to prices, terms, and conditions of sale established by the firm? . . ☐ Yes ☐ No
   d Are orders submitted to and subject to approval by the firm? . . . . ☐ Yes ☐ No
   e Is the worker expected to attend sales meetings?. . . . . ☐ Yes ☐ No
   • If "Yes," is the worker subject to any kind of penalty for failing to attend?. . . . . ☐ Yes ☐ No
   f Does the firm assign a specific territory to the worker? . . . . ☐ Yes ☐ No
   g Whom does the customer pay?   ☐ Firm   ☐ Worker
   • If worker, does the worker remit the total amount to the firm? . . . . ☐ Yes ☐ No
   h Does the worker sell a consumer product in a home or establishment other than a permanent retail establishment? . . . . ☐ Yes ☐ No
   i List the products and/or services distributed by the worker, such as meat, vegetables, fruit, bakery products, beverages (other than milk), or laundry or dry cleaning services. If more than one type of product and/or service is distributed, specify the principal one . . . .
   j Did the firm or another person assign the route or territory and a list of customers to the worker? . . ☐ Yes ☐ No
   • If "Yes," enter the name and job title of the person who made the assignment . . . .
   k Did the worker pay the firm or person for the privilege of serving customers on the route or in the territory? ☐ Yes ☐ No
   • If "Yes," how much did the worker pay (not including any amount paid for a truck or racks, etc.)? $ . . . .
   • What factors were considered in determining the value of the route or territory? . . . .
   l How are new customers obtained by the worker? Explain fully, showing whether the new customers called the firm for service, were solicited by the worker, or both . . . .
   m Does the worker sell life insurance? . . . . ☐ Yes ☐ No
   • If "Yes," is the selling of life insurance or annuity contracts for the firm the worker's entire business activity?. . . . . ☐ Yes ☐ No
   • If "No," list the other business activities and the amount of time spent on them . . . .
   n Does the worker sell other types of insurance for the firm? . . . . ☐ Yes ☐ No
   • If "Yes," state the percentage of the worker's total working time spent in selling other types of insurance . . . . %
   • At the time the contract was entered into between the firm and the worker, was it their intention that the worker sell life insurance for the firm: ☐ on a full-time basis   ☐ on a part-time basis
   • State the manner in which the intention was expressed . . . .
   o Is the worker a traveling or city salesperson? . . . . ☐ Yes ☐ No
   • If "Yes," from whom does the worker principally solicit orders for the firm? . . . .
   • If the worker solicits orders from wholesalers, retailers, contractors, or operators of hotels, restaurants, or other similar establishments, specify the percentage of the worker's time spent in the solicitation . . . . %
   • Is the merchandise purchased by the customers for resale or for use in their business operations? If used by the customers in their business operations, describe the merchandise and state whether it is equipment installed on their premises or a consumable supply

---

Under penalties of perjury, I declare that I have examined this request, including accompanying documents, and to the best of my knowledge and belief, the facts presented are true, correct, and complete.

Signature ▶   Title ▶   Date ▶

If the firm is completing this form, an officer or member of the firm must sign it. If the worker is completing this form, the worker must sign it. If the worker wants a written determination about services performed for two or more firms, a separate form must be completed and signed for each firm. Additional copies of this form may be obtained by calling 1-800-TAX-FORM (1-800-829-3676).

✳ *Printed on recycled paper*   *U.S. Government Printing Office: 1997 - 417-677/60200

a Control number				
	OMB No. 1545-0008			

b Employer identification number	1 Wages, tips, other compensation	2 Federal income tax withheld
c Employer's name, address, and ZIP code	3 Social security wages	4 Social security tax withheld
	5 Medicare wages and tips	6 Medicare tax withheld
	7 Social security tips	8 Allocated tips
d Employee's social security number	9 Advance EIC payment	10 Dependent care benefits
e Employee's name, address, and ZIP code	11 Nonqualified plans	12 Benefits included in box 1
	13 See instrs. for box 13	14 Other

15 Statutory employee ☐	Deceased ☐	Pension plan ☐	Legal rep. ☐	Deferred compensation ☐

16 State Employer's state I.D. no.	17 State wages, tips, etc.	18 State income tax	19 Locality name	20 Local wages, tips, etc.	21 Local income tax

Form **W-2** **Wage and Tax Statement** **1999**

(O)

Copy B To Be Filed With Employee's FEDERAL Tax Return

Department of the Treasury—Internal Revenue Service

This information is being furnished to the Internal Revenue Service.

Notice to Employee

Refund. Even if you do not have to file a tax return, you should file to get a refund if box 2 shows Federal income tax withheld, or if you can take the earned income credit.

Earned income credit (EIC). You must file a tax return if any amount is shown in box 9.

You may be able to take the EIC for 1999 if **(1)** you do not have a qualifying child and you earned less than $10,200, **(2)** you have one qualifying child and you earned less than $26,928, or **(3)** you have more than one qualifying child and you earned less than $30,580. You and any qualifying children must have valid social security numbers (SSNs). You cannot claim the EIC if your investment income is more than $2,350. **Any EIC that is more than your tax liability is refunded to you, but only if you file a tax return.** If you have at least one qualifying child, you may get as much as $1,387 of the EIC in advance by completing **Form W-5,** Earned Income Credit Advance Payment Certificate.

Clergy and religious workers. If you are not subject to social security and Medicare taxes, see **Pub. 517,** Social Security and Other Information for Members of the Clergy and Religious Workers.

Corrections. If your name, SSN, or address is incorrect, correct Copies B, C, and 2 and ask your employer to correct your employment record. Be sure to ask the employer to file **Form W-2c,** Corrected Wage and Tax Statement, with the Social Security Administration (SSA) to correct any name, SSN, or amount error reported to the SSA on Form W-2. If your name and SSN are correct but are not the same as shown on your social security card, you should ask for a new card at any SSA office or call 1-800-772-1213.

Credit for excess taxes. If you had more than one employer in 1999 and more than $4,501.20 in social security and/or tier 1 railroad retirement (RRTA) taxes were withheld, you may be able to claim a credit for the excess against your Federal income tax. If you had more than one railroad employer and more than $2,631.30 in tier 2 RRTA tax was withheld, you also may be able to claim a credit. See your Form 1040 or 1040A instructions and **Pub. 505,** Tax Withholding and Estimated Tax.

(Also, see **Instructions** on back of Copy C.)

391

Form W-4 (2000)

Purpose. Complete Form W-4 so your employer can withhold the correct Federal income tax from your pay. Because your tax situation may change, you may want to refigure your withholding each year.

Exemption from withholding. If you are exempt, complete only lines 1, 2, 3, 4, and 7, and sign the form to validate it. Your exemption for 2000 expires February 16, 2001.

Note: *You cannot claim exemption from withholding if (1) your income exceeds $700 and includes more than $250 of unearned income (e.g., interest and dividends) and (2) another person can claim you as a dependent on their tax return.*

Basic instructions. If you are not exempt, complete the **Personal Allowances Worksheet** below. The worksheets on page 2 adjust your withholding allowances based on itemized deductions, adjustments to income, or two-earner/two-job situations. Complete all worksheets that apply. They will help you figure the number of withholding allowances you are entitled to claim. **However, you may claim fewer (or zero) allowances.**

Child tax and higher education credits. For details on adjusting withholding for these and other credits, see **Pub. 919,** How Do I Adjust My Tax Withholding?

Head of household. Generally, you may claim head of household filing status on your tax return only if you are unmarried and pay more than 50% of the costs of keeping up a home for yourself and your dependent(s) or other qualifying individuals. See line **E** below.

Nonwage income. If you have a large amount of nonwage income, such as interest or dividends, you should consider making estimated tax payments using **Form 1040-ES,** Estimated Tax for Individuals. Otherwise, you may owe additional tax.

Two earners/two jobs. If you have a working spouse or more than one job, figure the total number of allowances you are entitled to claim on all jobs using worksheets from only one Form W-4. Your withholding usually will be most accurate when all allowances are claimed on the Form W-4 prepared for the highest paying job and zero allowances are claimed for the others.

Check your withholding. After your Form W-4 takes effect, use Pub. 919 to see how the dollar amount you are having withheld compares to your projected total tax for 2000. Get Pub. 919 especially if you used the **Two-Earner/Two-Job Worksheet** on page 2 and your earnings exceed $150,000 (Single) or $200,000 (Married).

Recent name change? If your name on line 1 differs from that shown on your social security card, call 1-800-772-1213 for a new social security card.

Personal Allowances Worksheet (Keep for your records.)

A Enter "1" for **yourself** if no one else can claim you as a dependent . . . . **A** _____

B Enter "1" if:
- You are single and have only one job; or
- You are married, have only one job, and your spouse does not work; or
- Your wages from a second job or your spouse's wages (or the total of both) are $1,000 or less.

. . **B** _____

C Enter "1" for your **spouse.** But, you may choose to enter -0- if you are married and have either a working spouse or more than one job. (Entering -0- may help you avoid having too little tax withheld.) . . . . **C** _____

D Enter number of **dependents** (other than your spouse or yourself) you will claim on your tax return . . . . **D** _____

E Enter "1" if you will file as **head of household** on your tax return (see conditions under **Head of household** above) . **E** _____

F Enter "1" if you have at least $1,500 of **child or dependent care expenses** for which you plan to claim a credit . . **F** _____

G **Child Tax Credit:**
- If your total income will be between $18,000 and $50,000 ($23,000 and $63,000 if married), enter "1" for each eligible child.
- If your total income will be between $50,000 and $80,000 ($63,000 and $115,000 if married), enter "1" if you have two eligible children, enter "2" if you have three or four eligible children, or enter "3" if you have five or more eligible children. **G** _____

H Add lines A through G and enter total here. **Note:** *This may be different from the number of exemptions you claim on your tax return.* ► **H** _____

For accuracy, complete all worksheets that apply.
- If you plan to **itemize or claim adjustments to income** and want to reduce your withholding, see the **Deductions and Adjustments Worksheet** on page 2.
- If you are **single,** have **more than one job** and your combined earnings from all jobs exceed $34,000, OR if you are **married** and have a **working spouse or more than one job** and the combined earnings from all jobs exceed $60,000, see the **Two-Earner/Two-Job Worksheet** on page 2 to avoid having too little tax withheld.
- If **neither** of the above situations applies, **stop here** and enter the number from line H on line 5 of Form W-4 below.

-------------------- Cut here and give Form W-4 to your employer. Keep the top part for your records. --------------------

Form **W-4**	**Employee's Withholding Allowance Certificate**	OMB No. 1545-0010
Department of the Treasury Internal Revenue Service	► **For Privacy Act and Paperwork Reduction Act Notice, see page 2.**	2000

1 Type or print your first name and middle initial	Last name	**2** Your social security number

Home address (number and street or rural route)	**3** ☐ Single ☐ Married ☐ Married, but withhold at higher Single rate. Note: *If married, but legally separated, or spouse is a nonresident alien, check the Single box.*
City or town, state, and ZIP code	**4** If your last name differs from that on your social security card, check here. **You must call 1-800-772-1213 for a new card** . . . ► ☐

5 Total number of allowances you are claiming (from line **H** above **OR** from the applicable worksheet on page 2) **5** _____

6 Additional amount, if any, you want withheld from each paycheck . . . . **6** $ _____

7 I claim exemption from withholding for 2000, and I certify that I meet **BOTH** of the following conditions for exemption:
- Last year I had a right to a refund of **ALL** Federal income tax withheld because I had **NO** tax liability **AND**
- This year I expect a refund of **ALL** Federal income tax withheld because I expect to have **NO** tax liability.

If you meet both conditions, write "EXEMPT" here . . . . ► **7** _____

Under penalties of perjury, I certify that I am entitled to the number of withholding allowances claimed on this certificate, or I am entitled to claim exempt status.

Employee's signature
(Form is not valid unless you sign it) ► _____ Date ► _____

8 Employer's name and address (Employer: Complete lines 8 and 10 only if sending to the IRS.)	**9** Office code (optional)	**10** Employer identification number

Cat. No. 10220Q

APPENDIX A

Deductions and Adjustments Worksheet

Note: *Use this worksheet only if you plan to itemize deductions or claim adjustments to income on your 2000 tax return.*

1   Enter an estimate of your 2000 itemized deductions. These include qualifying home mortgage interest, charitable contributions, state and local taxes, medical expenses in excess of 7.5% of your income, and miscellaneous deductions. (For 2000, you may have to reduce your itemized deductions if your income is over $128,950 ($64,475 if married filing separately). See **Worksheet 3** in Pub. 919 for details.) . . .   **1** $ _____

2   Enter: { $7,350 if married filing jointly or qualifying widow(er)
                $6,450 if head of household
                $4,400 if single
                $3,675 if married filing separately } . . . .   **2** $ _____

3   **Subtract** line 2 from line 1. If line 2 is greater than line 1, enter -0- . . . .   **3** $ _____

4   Enter an estimate of your 2000 adjustments to income, including alimony, deductible IRA contributions, and student loan interest   **4** $ _____

5   **Add** lines 3 and 4 and enter the total (Include any amount for credits from **Worksheet 7** in Pub. 919.) .   **5** $ _____

6   Enter an estimate of your 2000 nonwage income (such as dividends or interest) . . . .   **6** $ _____

7   **Subtract** line 6 from line 5. Enter the result, but not less than -0- . . . .   **7** $ _____

8   **Divide** the amount on line 7 by $3,000 and enter the result here. Drop any fraction . . . . . .   **8**   _____

9   Enter the number from the **Personal Allowances Worksheet**, line H, page 1 . . . .   **9**   _____

10   **Add** lines 8 and 9 and enter the total here. If you plan to use the **Two-Earner/Two-Job Worksheet**, also enter this total on line 1 below. Otherwise, **stop here** and enter this total on Form W-4, line 5, page 1 .   **10**   _____

Two-Earner/Two-Job Worksheet

Note: *Use this worksheet only if the instructions under line H on page 1 direct you here.*

1   Enter the number from line H, page 1 (or from line 10 above if you used the **Deductions and Adjustments Worksheet**)   **1**   _____

2   Find the number in **Table 1** below that applies to the **LOWEST** paying job and enter it here . . . .   **2**   _____

3   If line 1 is **MORE THAN OR EQUAL TO** line 2, subtract line 2 from line 1. Enter the result here (if zero, enter -0-) and on Form W-4, line 5, page 1. **Do not** use the rest of this worksheet . . . . . .   **3**   _____

Note: *If line 1 is **LESS THAN** line 2, enter -0- on Form W-4, line 5, page 1. Complete lines 4–9 below to calculate the additional withholding amount necessary to avoid a year end tax bill.*

4   Enter the number from line 2 of this worksheet . . . .   **4**   _____

5   Enter the number from line 1 of this worksheet . . . .   **5**   _____

6   **Subtract** line 5 from line 4 . . . .   **6**   _____

7   Find the amount in **Table 2** below that applies to the **HIGHEST** paying job and enter it here . . . .   **7** $ _____

8   **Multiply** line 7 by line 6 and enter the result here. This is the additional annual withholding needed . .   **8** $ _____

9   Divide line 8 by the number of pay periods remaining in 2000. For example, divide by 26 if you are paid every other week and you complete this form in December 1999. Enter the result here and on Form W-4, line 6, page 1. This is the additional amount to be withheld from each paycheck . . . .   **9** $ _____

Table 1: Two-Earner/Two-Job Worksheet

Married Filing Jointly				All Others			
If wages from **LOWEST** paying job are—	Enter on line 2 above	If wages from **LOWEST** paying job are—	Enter on line 2 above	If wages from **LOWEST** paying job are—	Enter on line 2 above	If wages from **LOWEST** paying job are—	Enter on line 2 above
$0 - $4,000	0	41,001 - 45,000	8	$0 - $5,000	0	65,001 - 80,000	8
4,001 - 7,000	1	45,001 - 55,000	9	5,001 - 11,000	1	80,001 - 100,000	9
7,001 - 13,000	2	55,001 - 63,000	10	11,001 - 17,000	2	100,001 and over	10
13,001 - 19,000	3	63,001 - 70,000	11	17,001 - 22,000	3		
19,001 - 25,000	4	70,001 - 85,000	12	22,001 - 27,000	4		
25,001 - 31,000	5	85,001 - 100,000	13	27,001 - 40,000	5		
31,001 - 37,000	6	100,001 - 110,000	14	40,001 - 50,000	6		
37,001 - 41,000	7	110,001 and over	15	50,001 - 65,000	7		

Table 2: Two-Earner/Two-Job Worksheet

Married Filing Jointly		All Others	
If wages from **HIGHEST** paying job are—	Enter on line 7 above	If wages from **HIGHEST** paying job are—	Enter on line 7 above
$0 - $50,000	$420	$0 - $30,000	$420
50,001 - 100,000	780	30,001 - 60,000	780
100,001 - 130,000	870	60,001 - 120,000	870
130,001 - 250,000	1,000	120,001 - 270,000	1,000
250,001 and over	1,100	270,001 and over	1,100

Privacy Act and Paperwork Reduction Act Notice. We ask for the information on this form to carry out the Internal Revenue laws of the United States. The Internal Revenue Code requires this information under sections 3402(f)(2)(A) and 6109 and their regulations. Failure to provide a **properly** completed form will result in your being treated as a single person who claims no withholding allowances; **providing fraudulent information may also subject you to penalties.** Routine uses of this information include giving it to the Department of Justice for civil and criminal litigation, to cities, states, and the District of Columbia for use in administering their tax laws, and for use in the National Directory of New Hires.

You are not required to provide the information requested on a form that is subject to the Paperwork Reduction Act unless the form displays a valid OMB control number. Books or records relating to a form or its instructions must be retained as long as their contents may become material in the administration of any Internal Revenue law. Generally, tax returns and return information are confidential, as required by Code section 6103.

The time needed to complete this form will vary depending on individual circumstances. The estimated average time is: **Recordkeeping** 46 min., **Learning about the law or the form** 13 min., **Preparing the form** 59 min. If you have comments concerning the accuracy of these time estimates or suggestions for making this form simpler, we would be happy to hear from you. You can write to the Tax Forms Committee, Western Area Distribution Center, Rancho Cordova, CA 95743-0001. **DO NOT** send the tax form to this address. Instead, give it to your employer.

 Printed on recycled paper   *U.S. Government Printing Office: 1999 — 456-119

Form **211** (Rev. June 1997) Department of the Treasury Internal Revenue Service	**Application for Reward for Original Information**	OMB Clearance No. 1545-0409
		Claim No.

This application is voluntary and the information requested enables us to determine and pay rewards. We use the information to record a claimant's reward as taxable income and to identify any tax outstanding (including taxes on a joint return filed with a spouse) against which the reward would first be applied. We need taxpayer identification numbers, i.e., social security number (SSN) or employer identification number (EIN), as applicable, in order to process it. Failure to provide the information requested may result in suspension of processing this application. Our authority for asking for the information on this form is 26 USC 6001, 6011, 6109, 7602, 7623, 7802, and 5 USC 301

Name of claimant. If an individual, provide date of birth	Date of Birth			Claimant's Tax Identification Number, SSN or EIN:
	Month	Day	Year	
Name of spouse (if applicable)	Date of Birth			Social Security Number
	Month	Day	Year	

Address of claimant, including zip code, and telephone number (telephone number is optional)

I am applying for a reward, in accordance with the law and regulations, for original information furnished, which led to the detection of a violation of the internal revenue laws of the United States and the collection of taxes, penalties, and fines. I was not an employee of the Department of the Treasury at the time I came into possession of the information nor at the time I divulged it.

Name of IRS employee to whom violation was reported	Title of IRS employee	Date violation reported (Month/day/year)

Method of reporting the information—check applicable box   [ ] Telephone   [ ] Mail   [ ] In person

Name of taxpayer who committed the violation and, if known, the taxpayer's SSN or EIN

Address of taxpayer, including zip code if known

Relative to information I furnished on the above taxpayer, the Internal Revenue Service made the following payments to me or on my behalf:

Date of payment	Amount	Name of Person/Entity to Whom Payment was made

Under penalties of perjury, I declare that I have examined this application and my accompanying statements, if any, and to the best of my knowledge and belief, they are true, correct, and complete. I understand the amount of any reward will represent what the District or Service Center Director considers appropriate in this particular case. I agree to repay the reward, or an appropriate percentage thereof, if the collection on which it is based is subsequently reduced.

Signature of Claimant	Date

The following is to be completed by the Internal Revenue Service

Authorization of Reward

District/Service Center/Assistant Commissioner (International)	Sum recovered $	Amount of Reward $

In consideration of the original information that was furnished by the claimant named above, which concerns a violation of the internal revenue laws and which led to the collection of taxes, penalties, and fines in the sum shown above, I approve payment of a reward in the amount stated.

Signature of the Service Center Director	Date

MAIL COMPLETED FORM TO THE APPROPRIATE ADDRESS SHOWN ON THE BACK

Cat. No. 16571S

Form 211 (Rev. 6-97)

Form **433-A**
(Rev. September 1995)

Department of the Treasury — Internal Revenue Service

Collection Information Statement for Individuals

NOTE: Complete all blocks, except shaded areas, Write "N/A" *(not applicable)* in those blocks that do not apply.
Instructions for certain line items are in Publication 1854.

1. Taxpayer(s) name(s) and address	2. Home phone number ( )	3. Marital status
County _____	4.a. Taxpayer's social security number	b. Spouse's social security number

Section I.   Employment Information

5. Taxpayer's employer or business *(name and address)*	a. How long employed	b. Business phone number ( )	c. Occupation
	d. Number of exemptions claimed on Form W-4 _____	e. Pay period: ☐ Weekly ☐ Bi-weekly ☐ Monthly ☐ _____ Payday: _____ (Mon - Sun)	f. *(Check appropriate box)* ☐ Wage earner ☐ Sole proprietor ☐ Partner
6. Spouse's employer or business *(name and address)*	a. How long employed	b. Business phone number ( )	c. Occupation
	d. Number of exemptions claimed on Form W-4 _____	e. Pay period: ☐ Weekly ☐ Bi-weekly ☐ Monthly ☐ _____ Payday: _____ (Mon - Sun)	f. *(Check appropriate box)* ☐ Wage earner ☐ Sole proprietor ☐ Partner

Section II.   Personal Information

7. Name, address and telephone number of next of kin or other reference	8. Other names or aliases	9. Previous address(es)

10. Age and relationship of dependents living in your household *(exclude yourself and spouse)*

11. Date of Birth	a. Taxpayer	b. Spouse	12. Latest filed income tax return *(tax year)*	a. Number of exemptions claimed	b. Adjusted Gross Income

Section III.   General Financial Information

13. Bank accounts *(include savings & loans, credit unions, IRA and retirement plans, certificates of deposit, etc.)* Enter bank <u>loans</u> in item 28.

Name of Institution	Address	Type of Account	Account No.	Balance
			Total *(Enter in Item 21)*	

Cat. No. 20312N

Form **433-A** (Rev. 9-95)

APPENDIX A

Section III - *continued*   General Financial Information

14. Charge cards and lines of credit from banks, credit unions, and savings and loans. List all other charge accounts in item 28.

Type of Account or Card	Name and Address of Financial Institution	Monthly Payment	Credit Limit	Amount Owed	Credit Available
Totals *(Enter in Item 27)* ▶					

15. Safe deposit boxes rented or accessed *(List all locations, box numbers, and contents)*

16. **Real Property** *(Brief description and type of ownership)*	Physical Address
a.	County _____
b.	County _____
c.	County _____

17. **Life Insurance** *(Name of Company)*	Policy Number	Type	Face Amount	Available Loan Value
		☐ Whole ☐ Term		
		☐ Whole ☐ Term		
		☐ Whole ☐ Term		
	Total *(Enter in Item 23)* ▶			

18. Securities *(stocks, bonds, mutual funds, money market funds, government securities, etc.)*:

Kind	Quantity or Denomination	Current Value	Where Located	Owner of Record

19. Other information relating to your financial condition. If you check the yes box, please give dates and explain on page 4, Additional Information or Comments:

a. Court proceedings	☐ Yes ☐ No	b. Bankruptcies	☐ Yes ☐ No
c. Repossessions	☐ Yes ☐ No	d. Recent sale or other transfer of assets for less than full value	☐ Yes ☐ No
e. Anticipated increase in income	☐ Yes ☐ No	f. Participant or beneficiary to trust, estate, profit sharing, etc.	☐ Yes ☐ No

Form **433-A**   **page 2**   (Rev. 9-95)

396

Section IV.   Assets and Liabilities

Description	Current Market Value	Current Amount Owed	Equity in Asset	Amount of Monthly Payment	Name and Address of Lien/Note Holder/Lender	Date Pledged	Date of Final Payment
20. Cash							
21. Bank accounts *(from Item 13)*					·		
22. Securities *(from Item 18)*							
23. Cash or loan value of insurance							
24. Vehicles *(model, year, license, tag#)*							
a.							
b.							
c.							
25. Real property *(From Section III, item 16)* a.							
b.							
c.							
26. Other assets							
a.							
b.							
c.							
d.							
e.							
27. Bank revolving credit *(from Item 14)*							
28. Other Liabilities *(Including bank loans, judgments, notes, and charge accounts not entered in Item 13.)* a.							
b.							
c.							
d.							
e.							
f.							
g.							
29. Federal taxes owed (prior years)							
30. **Totals**			$	$			

Internal Revenue Service Use Only Below This Line

Financial Verification/Analysis

Item	Date Information or Encumbrance Verified	Date Property Inspected	Estimated Forced Sale Equity
Personal Residence			
Other Real Property			
Vehicles			
Other Personal Property			
State Employment *(Husband and Wife)*			
Income Tax Return			
Wage Statements *(Husband and Wife)*			
Sources of Income/Credit *(D&B Report)*			
Expenses			
Other Assets/Liabilities			

Form **433-A**   **page 3**   (Rev. 9-95)

Section V.   Monthly Income and Expense Analysis

Total Income			Necessary Living Expenses		
Source	**Gross**			**Claimed**	*(IRS use only)* **Allowed**
31. Wages/Salaries *(Taxpayer)*	$		42. National Standard Expenses[1]	$	$
32. Wages/Salaries *(Spouse)*			43. Housing and utilities[2]		
33. Interest - Dividends			44. Transportation[3]		
34. Net business income *(from Form 433-B)*			45. Health care		
35. Rental Income			46. Taxes *(income and FICA)*		
36. Pension *(Taxpayer)*			47. Court ordered payments		
37. Pension *(Spouse)*			48. Child/dependent care		
38. Child Support			49. Life insurance		
39. Alimony			50. Secured or legally-perfected debts *(specify)*		
40. Other			51. Other expenses *(specify)*		
41. **Total Income**	$		52. **Total Expenses**	$	$
			53. *(IRS use only)* Net difference *(income less necessary living expenses)*	$	

Certification   Under penalties of perjury, I declare that to the best of my knowledge and belief this statement of assets, liabilities, and other information is true, correct, and complete.

54. Your signature	55. Spouse's signature *(if joint return was filed)*	56. Date

Notes

1. Clothing and clothing services, food, housekeeping supplies, personal care products and services, and miscellaneous.

2. Rent or mortgage payment for the taxpayer's principal residence. Add the average monthly payment for the following expenses if they are *not* included in the rent or mortgage payment: property taxes, homeowner's or renter's insurance, parking, necessary maintenance and repair, homeowner dues, condominium fees and utilities. Utilities includes gas, electricity, water, fuel oil, coal, bottled gas, trash and garbage collection, wood and other fuels, septic cleaning and telephone.

3. Lease or purchase payments, insurance, registration fees, normal maintenance, fuel, public transportation, parking and tolls.

Additional information or comments:

Internal Revenue Service Use Only Below This Line

Explain any difference between Item 53 and the installment agreement payment amount:

Name of originator and IDRS assignment number: Date

Form **433-A**   page 4   (Rev. 9-95)   ☆ U.S. GPO:1997-432-213/71716

Form **433-B**
(Rev. June 1991)

Department of the Treasury — Internal Revenue Service

Collection Information Statement for Businesses

(If you need additional space, please attach a separate sheet)

NOTE: Complete all blocks, except shaded areas. Write "N/A" *(not applicable)* **in those blocks that do not apply.**

1. Name and address of business	2. Business phone number ( )
	3. *(Check appropriate box)*
	☐ Sole proprietor ☐ Other *(specify)*
	☐ Partnership
County_____	☐ Corporation

4. Name and title of person being interviewed	5. Employer Identification Number	6. Type of business

7. Information about owner, partners, officers, major shareholder, etc.

Name and Title	Effective Date	Home Address	Phone Number	Social Security Number	Total Shares or Interest

Section I.

General Financial Information

8. Latest filed income tax return ▶	Form	Tax Year ended	Net income before taxes

9. Bank accounts *(List all types of accounts including payroll and general, savings, certificates of deposit, etc.)*

Name of Institution	Address	Type of Account	Account Number	Balance
		Total *(Enter in Item 17)* ▶		

10. Bank credit available *(Lines of credit, etc.)*

Name of Institution	Address	Credit Limit	Amount Owed	Credit Available	Monthly Payments
Totals *(Enter in Items 24 or 25 as appropriate)*		▶			

11. Location, box number, and contents of all safe deposit boxes rented or accessed

Page 1	Form 433-B (Rev. 6-91)

Section I - *continued*   **General Financial Information**

12. Real property

Brief Description and Type of Ownership	Physical Address
a.	County _____
b.	County _____
c.	County _____
d.	County _____

13. Life insurance policies owned with business as beneficiary

Name Insured	Company	Policy Number	Type	Face Amount	Available Loan Value
		Total (Enter in Item 19)		▶	

14a. Additional information regarding financial condition *(Court proceedings, bankruptcies filed or anticipated, transfers of assets for less than full value, changes in market conditions, etc.; include information regarding company participation in trusts, estates, profit-sharing plans, etc.)*

b. If you know of any person or organization that borrowed or otherwise provided funds to pay net payrolls:	a. Who borrowed funds?
	b. Who supplied funds?

15. Accounts/Notes receivable *(Include current contract jobs, loans to stockholders, officers, partners, etc.)*

Name	Address	Amount Due	Date Due	Status
		$		
	Total (Enter in Item 18) ▶	$		

    Form **433-B** (Rev. 6-91)

Section II.   Asset and Liability Analysis

Description (a)	Cur. Mkt. Value (b)	Liabilities Bal. Due (c)	Equity in Asset (d)	Amt. of Mo. Pymt. (e)	Name and Address of Lien/Note Holder/Obligee (f)	Date Pledged (g)	Date of Final Pymt. (h)
16. Cash on hand							
17. Bank accounts							
18. Accounts/Notes receivable							
19. Life insurance loan value							
20. Real property (from Item 12) a.							
b.							
c.							
d.							
21. Vehicles (Model, year, and license) a.							
b.							
c.							
22. Machinery and equipment (Specify) a.							
b.							
c.							
23. Merchandise inventory (Specify) a.							
b.							
24. Other assets (Specify) a.							
b.							
25. Other liabilities (Including notes and judgments) a.							
b.							
c.							
d.							
e.							
f.							
g.							
h.							
26. Federal taxes owed							
27. Total							

Form 433-B (Rev. 6-91)

Section III.   Income and Expense Analysis

The following information applies to income and expenses during the period _____ to _____

Accounting method used

Income			Expenses	
28. Gross receipts from sales, services, etc.	$		34. Materials purchased	$
29. Gross rental income			35. Net wages and salaries Number of Employees _____	
30. Interest			36. Rent	
31. Dividends			37. Allowable installment payments *(IRS use only)*	
32. Other income *(Specify)*			38. Supplies	
			39. Utilities/Telephone	
			40. Gasoline/Oil	
			41. Repairs and maintenance	
			42. Insurance	
			43. Current taxes	
			44. Other *(Specify)*	
33. Total Income ▶	$		45. Total Expenses *(IRS use only)* ▶	$
			46. Net difference *(IRS use only)* ▶	$

Certification   Under penalties of perjury, I declare that to the best of my knowledge and belief this statement of assets, liabilities, and other information is true, correct, and complete.

47. Signature	48. Date

Internal Revenue Service Use Only Below This Line

Financial Verification/Analysis

Item	Date Information or Encumbrance Verified	Date Property Inspected	Estimated Forced Sale Equity
Sources of Income/Credit (D&B Report)			
Expenses			
Real Property			
Vehicles			
Machinery and Equipment			
Merchandise			
Accounts/Notes Receivable			
Corporate Information, if Applicable			
U.C.C. : Senior/Junior Lienholder			
Other Assets/Liabilities:			

Explain any difference between Item 46 (or P&L) and the installment agreement payment amount:

Name of Originator and IDRS assignment number	Date

How to prepare a
Collection Information Statement (Form 433-A)

Complete all blocks, except shaded areas. Write "N/A" (Not Applicable) in those blocks that do not apply to you. *If you don't complete the form, we won't be able to help determine the best method for you to pay the amount due.* The areas explained below are the ones we have found to be the most confusing to people completing the form.

Section III
Item 13 - Bank Accounts
Enter all accounts even if there is currently no balance. *Do Not* enter bank loans.

Item 14 - Bank Charge Cards, Lines of Credit, etc.
Enter only credit issued by a bank, credit union, or savings and loan (MasterCard, Visa, overdraft protection, etc.). List other charge accounts such as oil companies and department stores in Item 28.

Item 16 - Real Property Description and Ownership
List all real property that you own or are purchasing. Include the address, county, and type of buildings on the property. List the names of all owners and type of ownership (such as joint tenants, tenant in common, etc.).

Section IV
Items 24 thru 26 - Vehicles, Real Property, and Other Assets

Current Market Value - Indicate the amount you could sell the asset for today.

Equity in Asset - Subtract liability (current amount owed) from current market value.

Data Pledged - Enter the date the loan was originally taken out or property given as security.

Date of Final Payment - Enter the date the loan will be fully paid. If you are behind in payments, enter "Behind."

List other assets you own such as campers, boats, jewelry, antiques, etc., in item 26.

Item 28 - Other Liabilities
List all other liabilities, including charge accounts, bank loans and notes, personal loans, medical bills, etc.

Section V
If only one spouse has a tax liability, but both have income, list the total household income and expenses.

Items 31 and 32 - Wages and Salaries
Enter your *gross* monthly wages and/or salaries. Do not deduct withholding or allotments you elect to take out of your pay such as insurance payments, credit union deductions, car payments, etc. List these expenses in Section IV and Section V.

Item 34 - Net Business Income
Enter your monthly *net* business income, that is what you earn after you have paid your ordinary and necessary monthly business expenses.

Necessary Living Expenses
To be necessary, expenses must provide for the health and welfare of you and your family and/or provide for the production of income, and must be reasonable in amount. You may be asked to provide substantiation of certain expenses.

Item 42 - National Standard Expenses
This category includes clothing and clothing services, food, housekeeping supplies, personal care products and services, and miscellaneous. Enter the amount you are allowed, based on your total monthly gross income and the size of your family, from the chart on the back of these instructions. If you claim a higher amount, you must substantiate why a higher amount is necessary for each item included in a category.

Item 43 - Housing and Utilities
Enter the monthly rent or mortgage payment for your principal residence. Add the average monthly payment for the following expenses if they are *not* included in your rent or mortgage payments: property taxes, homeowner's or renters insurance, parking, necessary maintenance and repair, homeowner dues, condominium fees, and utilities. Utilities includes gas, electricity, water, fuel oil, coal, bottled gas, trash and garbage collection, wood and other fuels, septic cleaning and telephone.

Item 44 - Transportation
Enter your average monthly transportation expenses. Transportation expenses include: lease or purchase payments, insurance, registration fees, normal maintenance, fuel, public transportation, parking and tolls.

Item 50 - Secured or Legally-Perfected Debts
Do not enter mortgage payment entered in Item 43, or lease or purchase payments entered in Item 44.

Item 51 - Other Expenses
Enter your average monthly payments for any other *necessary* expenses.

Item 53 - Not Difference
Do not show an entry in this space. IRS use only.

Certification
For joint income tax liabilities, both husband and wife should sign the statement.

Department of the Treasury
Internal Revenue Service

www.irs.ustreas.gov

Publication 1854 (Rev. 1-1999)

STF FED1060I.1

APPENDIX A

Collection Financial Analysis: Total Monthly National Standards (Rev. 7-98)

Total Gross Monthly Income	Number of Persons				
	One	Two	Three	Four	Over Four
Less than $830	341	461	573	717	+125
$830 to $1,249	387	520	639	753	+135
$1,250 to $1,669	429	622	728	790	+145
$1,670 to $2,499	521	675	771	819	+155
$2,500 to $3,329	548	758	851	912	+165
$3,330 to $4,169	612	818	935	1,049	+175
$4,170 to $5,829	761	944	1,004	1,154	+185
$5,830 and over	977	1,218	1,379	1,453	+195

Expenses include: Housekeeping supplies
Apparel and services
Personal care products and services
Food
Miscellaneous

To find the amount you are allowed, read down the Total Gross Monthly Income Column until you find your income, then read across to the column for the number of persons in your family.

If there are more than four persons in your family, multiply the number of additional persons by the amount in the "Over Four" column and add the result to the amount in the "Four" column. (For example, total monthly income of $830 to $1,249 for six persons would equal a monthly national standard of 753 + 135 + 135, + or 1023.)

Normally, expenses should be allowed only for persons who can be claimed as exemptions on your income tax return.

Dollar amounts are derived from the Bureau of Labor Statistics (BLS) Consumer Expenditure Survey.

Publication 1854 (Rev. 1-1999)

STF FED1060L2

Form 656

Offer in Compromise

Department of the Treasury
Internal Revenue Service

www.irs.gov

Form 656 (Rev. 1-2000)
Catalog Number 16728N

Item 1 — Taxpayer's Name and Home or Business Address

Name

Name

Street Address

City   State   ZIP Code

Mailing Address *(if different from above)*

Street Address

City   State   ZIP Code

Item 2 — Social Security Numbers

(a) Primary _____

(b) Secondary _____

Item 3 — Employer Identification Number *(included in offer)*

_____

Item 4 — Other Employer Identification Numbers *(not included in offer)*

_____

_____

_____

Item 5 — To: Commissioner of Internal Revenue Service

I/We (includes all types of taxpayers) submit this offer to compromise the tax liabilities plus any interest, penalties, additions to tax, and additional amounts required by law (tax liability) for the tax type and period marked below: (Please mark an "X" in the box for the correct description and fill-in the correct tax period(s), adding additional periods if needed).

❑ **1040/1120 Income Tax** — Year(s) _____
_____

❑ **941 Employer's Quarterly Federal Tax Return** — Quarterly period(s) _____
_____

❑ **940 Employer's Annual Federal Unemployment (FUTA) Tax Return** — Year(s) _____
_____

❑ **Trust Fund Recovery Penalty** as a responsible person of (enter corporation name) _____
_____ ,
for failure to pay withholding and Federal Insurance Contributions Act Taxes (Social Security taxes), for period(s) ending _____ .

❑ **Other Federal Tax(es)** [specify type(s) and period(s)] _____

_____

Note: *If you need more space, use another sheet titled "Attachment to Form 656 Dated _____ ." Sign and date the attachment following the listing of the tax periods.*

Item S — I/we submit this offer for the reason(s) checked below:

❑ **Doubt as to Liability** — "I do not believe I owe this amount." You must include a detailed explanation of the reason(s) why you believe you do not owe the tax in Item 9.

❑ **Doubt as to Collectibility** — "I have insufficient assets and income to pay the full amount." You must include a complete financial statement, Form 433-A and/or Form 433-B.

❑ **Effective Tax Administration** — "I owe this amount and have sufficient assets to pay the full amount, but due to my exceptional circumstances, requiring full payment would cause an economic hardship or would be unfair and inequitable." You must include a complete financial statement, Form 433-A and/or Form 433B and complete Item 9.

Item 7

I/we offer to pay $ _____

❑ Paid in full with this offer.

❑ Deposit of $ _____ is attached to this offer.

❑ No deposit.

Note: Make all checks payable to: The United States Treasury

Check one of the following:

❑ **Cash Offer (Offered amount will be paid in 90 days or less.)**

Balance to be paid in: _____ 10, _____ 30, _____ 60, or _____ 90 days from notice of acceptance of the offer. If more than one payment will be made during the time frame checked, provide the amount and date of the payment on the line below.

_____

❑ **Short Term Deferred Payment Offer (Offered amount paid in more than 90 days but within 24 months.)**

Amount of monthly payment _____

Monthly payment date _____

Date offered amount will be paid in full _____

Other terms for payment _____

❑ **Deferred Payment Offer (Offered amount will be paid over the life of the collection statute.)**

Amount of monthly payment _____

Monthly payment date _____

Other terms for payment _____

APPENDIX A

Item 8 — By submitting this offer, I/we understand and agree to the following conditions:

(a) I/we voluntarily submit all payments made on this offer.

(b) The IRS will apply payments made under the terms of this offer in the best interest of the government.

(c) If the IRS rejects or returns the offer or I/we withdraw the offer, the IRS will return any amount paid with the offer. If I/we agree in writing, IRS will apply the amount paid with the offer to the amount owed. If I/we agree to apply the payment, the date the IRS received the offer remittance will be considered the date of payment. I/we understand that the IRS will not pay interest on any amount I/we submit with the offer.

(d) **I/we will comply with all provisions of the Internal Revenue Code relating to filing my/our returns and paying my/our required taxes for 5 years or until the offered amount is paid in full, whichever is longer. In the case of a jointly submitted offer to compromise joint tax liabilities, I/we understand that default with respect to the compliance provisions described in this paragraph by one party to this agreement will not result in the default of the entire agreement. The default provisions described in Item 8(o) of this agreement will be applied only to the party failing to comply with the requirements of this paragraph. This provision does not apply to offers based on Doubt as to Liability.**

(e) I/we waive and agree to the suspension of any statutory periods of limitation (time limits provided for by law) for the IRS assessment of the tax liability for the tax periods identified in Item 5. I/we understand that the statute of limitations for collection will be suspended during the period an offer is considered pending by the IRS (paragraph (m) defines pending).

(f) The IRS will keep all payments and credits made, received or applied to the total original tax liability before submission of this offer. The IRS may keep any proceeds from a levy served prior to submission of the offer, but not received at the time the offer is submitted. If I/we have an installment agreement prior to submitting the offer, I/we must continue to make the payments as agreed while this offer is pending. Installment agreement payments will not be applied against the amount offered.

(g) **The IRS will keep any refund, including interest, due to me/us because of overpayment of any tax or other liability, for tax periods extending through the calendar year that the IRS accepts the offer. I/we may not designate an overpayment ordinarily subject to refund, to which the IRS is entitled, to be applied to estimated tax payments for the following year. This condition does not apply if the offer is based on Doubt as to Liability.**

(h) I/we will return to the IRS any refund identified in (g) received after submission of this offer. This condition does not apply to offers based on Doubt as to Liability.

(i) The IRS cannot collect more than the full amount of the tax liability under this offer.

(j) I/we understand that I/we remain responsible for the full amount of the tax liability, unless and until the IRS accepts the offer in writing and I/we have met all the terms and conditions of the offer. The IRS will not remove the original amount of the tax liability from its records until I/we have met all the terms of the offer.

(k) I/we understand that the tax I/we offer to compromise is and will remain a tax liability until I/we meet all the terms and conditions

406

of this offer. If I/we file bankruptcy before the terms and conditions of this offer are completed, any claim the IRS files in the bankruptcy proceedings will be a tax claim.

(l) Once the IRS accepts the offer in writing, I/we have no right to contest, in court or otherwise, the amount of the tax liability.

(m) The offer is pending starting with the date an authorized IRS official signs this form. The offer remains pending until an authorized IRS official accepts, rejects, returns or acknowledges withdrawal of the offer in writing. If I/we appeal an IRS rejection decision on the offer, the IRS will continue to treat the offer as pending until the Appeals Office accepts or rejects the offer in writing. If I/we don't file a protest within 30 days of the date the IRS notifies me/us of the right to protest the decision, I/we waive the right to a hearing before the Appeals Office about the offer in compromise.

(n) The waiver and suspension of any statutory periods of limitation for assessment of the tax liability described in Item 5, continue to apply:

- while the offer is pending [see (m) above]
- during the time I/we have not paid all of the amount offered
- during the time I/we have not completed all terms and conditions of the offer
- for one additional year beyond each of the time periods identified in this paragraph

(o) If I/we fail to meet any of the terms and conditions of the offer and the offer defaults, then the IRS may:

- immediately file suit to collect the entire unpaid balance of the offer
- immediately file suit to collect an amount equal to the original amount of the tax liability as liquidating damages, minus any payment already received under the terms of this offer
- disregard the amount of the offer and apply all amounts already paid under the offer against the original amount of the tax liability
- file suit or levy to collect the original amount of the tax liability, without further notice of any kind.

(p) The IRS generally files a Notice of Federal Tax Lien to protect the Government's interest on deferred payment offers. This tax lien will be released when the payment terms of the offer agreement have been satisfied.

(q) I/we understand that Internal Revenue Service employees may contact third parties in order to respond to this request, and I authorize such contacts to be made. Further, by authorizing the Internal Revenue Service to contact third parties, I understand that I will not receive notice pursuant to section 7602(c) of the Internal Revenue Code of third parties contacted in connection with this request.

Item 9 — Explanation of Circumstances

I am requesting an offer in compromise for the reason(s) listed below:

Note: *If you are requesting compromise based on doubt as to liability, explain why you don't believe you owe the tax.*
If you believe you have special circumstances affecting your ability to fully pay the amount due, explain your situation.
You may attach additional sheets if necessary.

_____
_____
_____
_____
_____
_____
_____
_____
_____
_____
_____
_____
_____
_____
_____
_____
_____

Item 10

If I/we submit this offer on a substitute form, I/we affirm that this form is a verbatim duplicate of the official Form 656, and I/we agree to be bound by all the terms and conditions set forth in the official Form 656.

Under penalties of perjury, I declare that I have examined this offer, including accompanying schedules and statements, and to the best of my knowledge and belief, it is true, correct and complete.

_____
10(a) Signature of Taxpayer — proponent

_____
Date

_____
10(b) Signature of Taxpayer — proponent

_____
Date

For Official Use Only

_____
Signature of Authorized Internal Revenue Service Official

_____
Title

_____
Date

OFFICIAL USE ONLY

What You Need to Know Before Submitting an Offer in Compromise

What is an Offer In Compromise?

An *Offer In Compromise* (OIC) is an agreement between a taxpayer and the Internal Revenue Service (IRS) that resolves the taxpayer's tax liability. The IRS has the authority to settle, or compromise, federal tax liabilities by accepting less than full payment under certain circumstances. The IRS may legally compromise for one of the following reasons:

■ **Doubt as to Liability** — Doubt exists that the assessed tax is correct.

■ **Doubt as to Collectibility** — Doubt exists that you could ever pay the full amount of tax owed.

■ **Effective Tax Administration** — There is no doubt the tax is correct and no doubt the amount owed could be collected, but an exceptional circumstance exists that allows us to consider your offer. To be eligible for compromise on this basis, you must demonstrate that collection of the tax would create an economic hardship or would be unfair and inequitable.

Form 656, Offer In Compromise, and Substitute Forms

Form 656, *Offer In Compromise,* is the official compromise agreement. Substitute forms, whether computer-generated or photocopies, must affirm that:

1. The substitute form is a verbatim duplicate of the official Form 656, and

2. You agree to be bound by all terms and conditions set forth in the official Form 656.

You must initial and date all pages of the substitute form, in addition to signing and dating the signature page.

You can get Form 656 by calling 1-800-829-1040, by visiting your local Internal Revenue Service (IRS) office, or by accessing our web site at www.irs.gov

Am I Eligible for Consideration of an Offer In Compromise?

You may be eligible for consideration of an Offer In Compromise if:

1. In your judgment, you don't owe the tax liability **(Doubt as to Liability).** You must submit a detailed written statement explaining why you believe you don't owe the tax liability you want to compromise. You won't be required to submit a financial statement if you're submitting an offer on this basis alone.

2. In your judgment, you can't pay the entire tax liability in full **(Doubt as to Collectibility).** You must submit a statement showing your current financial situation.

3. You agree the tax liability is correct and you're able to pay the balance due in full, but you have exceptional circumstances you'd like us to consider **(Effective Tax Administration).** To receive consideration on this basis, you must submit:

a. A financial statement, and

b. A detailed written narrative. The narrative must explain your exceptional circumstances and why paying the tax liability in full would either create an economic hardship or would be unfair and inequitable.

We'll also consider your overall history of filing and paying taxes.

Note: If you request consideration on the basis of effective tax administration, we're first required to establish that there is no doubt as to liability and no doubt as to collectibility. We can only consider an offer on the basis of effective tax administration after we've determined the liability is correct and collectible.

APPENDIX A

When Am I Not Eligible for Consideration of an Offer In Compromise?	You are not eligible for consideration of an Offer In Compromise on the basis of **doubt as to collectibility or effective tax administration** if: 1. You haven't filed all federal tax returns, or 2. You're involved in an open bankruptcy proceeding.

Note: If you are an in-business taxpayer, you must have timely filed and timely deposited all employment taxes for the two prior quarters before the offer was submitted. You must have also timely made all federal tax deposits during the quarter in which the offer is being submitted.

What We Need to Process Your Offer In Compromise	For us to process your offer, you must provide a complete and correct Form 656 and:

- Form 433-A, *Collection Information Statement for Individuals,* if you're submitting an offer as an **individual.**

- Forms 433-A and 433-B, *Collection Information Statement for Businesses,* if you're submitting an offer as a **self-employed** taxpayer.

- Form 433-B, if you're submitting an offer as a **corporation or other business** taxpayer. We may also require Forms 433-A from corporate officers or individual partners.

For a more detailed explanation of the information required to complete these forms, see the section entitled "Financial Information" on page 4.

Note: We don't need a financial statement for an offer based solely on doubt as to liability.

Please complete all applicable items on Form 656 and provide all required documentation. We may contact you for any missing required information. If you don't respond to our request or provide the required information, we won't recommend your offer for acceptance and will return your Form 656 to you by mail. We will explain our reason(s) for returning your offer in our letter. The reasons for return are:

- The pre-printed terms and conditions listed on Form 656 have changed

- A taxpayer name is missing
- A Social Security Number or Employer Identification Number is missing, incomplete, or incorrect
- An offer amount or payment term is unstated
- A signature is missing
- A financial statement (Form 433-A or Form 433-B) is missing or incomplete, if your offer is based on doubt as to collectibility or effective tax administration
- Requested financial statement verification isn't provided
- Our records show you don't have a tax liability
- Your offer is submitted solely to delay collection or if a delay will jeopardize our ability to collect the tax

Note: You should personally sign your offer as well as any required collection information statements unless unusual circumstances prevent you from doing so. If an authorized power of attorney signs your offer because of unusual circumstances, you must include a completed Form 2848, Power of Attorney and Declaration of Representative, with your offer.

What You Should Do If You Want to Submit an Offer In Compromise

Determine Your Offer Amount

All offer amounts **(doubt as to liability, doubt as to collectibility,** or **effective tax administration)** must exceed $0.00.

- **Doubt as to Liability**

  Complete Item 9, *Explanation of Circumstances,* on Form 656, explaining why, in your judgment, you don't owe the tax liability you want to compromise. Offer the correct tax, penalty, and interest owed based on your judgment.

- **Doubt as to Collectibility**

  Complete Form 433-A, *Collection Information Statement for Individuals* (and if applicable, Form 433-B, *Collection Information Statement for Businesses*) and attach to your Form 656. To figure your offer amount, complete the worksheet on pages 8 - 10 and enter this amount on Item 7 of Form 656.

  You must offer an amount greater than or equal to the "reasonable collection potential" (RCP). The RCP equals the net equity of your assets plus the amount we could collect from your future income. Please see page 8, **Terms and Definitions,** for more detailed definitions of these and other terms.

  If special circumstances cause you to offer an amount less than the RCP, you must also complete Item 9, *Explanation of Circumstances,* on Form 656, explaining your situation. Special circumstances may include advanced age, serious illness from which recovery is unlikely, or other circumstances that you believe are unusual.

- **Effective Tax Administration**

  Complete Form 433-A (and Form 433-B, if applicable) and attach to Form 656.

  Complete Item 9, *Explanation of Circumstances,* on Form 656, explaining your exceptional circumstances and why requiring payment of the tax liability in full would either create an economic hardship or would be unfair and inequitable.

  Enter your offer amount on Item 7 of Form 656.

Financial Information

You must provide financial information when you submit offers on the bases of **doubt as to collectibility and effective tax administration.**

If you're submitting an offer as an individual, you must file Form 433-A, Collection Information Statement for Individuals, with your Form 656. If you're a self-employed taxpayer, you must also file Form 433-B, Collection Information Statement for Businesses. If you're a corporate or other business taxpayer, you must file Form 433-B. We may also request Forms 433-A from corporate officers or individual partners.

You must send us current information that reflects your financial situation for at least the past six months. Financial statements must show all your assets and income, even those unavailable to us through direct collection action, because you can use them to fund your offer. The offer examiner needs this information to evaluate your offer and may ask you to update it or verify certain financial information. We may also return offer packages without complete financial statements.

Note: Do not include information about unsecured creditors when reporting your liabilities on Form 433-A, line 28, or Form 433-B, line 25. For example, don't include amounts you owe on credit cards or on loans not backed by assets as security.

When only one spouse has a tax liability but both have incomes, only the spouse responsible for the debt is required to prepare the necessary financial statements. In states with community property laws, however, we require financial statements from both spouses. We may also request financial information on the non-liable spouse for offer verification purposes, even when community property laws do not apply.

Determine Your Payment Terms

You can pay in three ways:

- Cash (paid in 90 days or less)
- Short-Term Deferred Payment (more than 90 days, up to 24 months)
- Deferred Payment (offers with payment terms over the remaining statutory period for collecting the tax)

Cash Offer

You must pay cash offers within 90 days of acceptance.

You should offer the realizable value of your assets plus the total amount we could collect over 48 months of payments (or the remainder of the ten-year statutory period for collection, whichever is less).

Note: We require full payment of accepted doubt as to liability offers at the time of mutual agreement of the corrected liability. If you're unable to pay the corrected amount, you must also request compromise on the basis of doubt as to collectibility.

Short-Term Deferred Payment Offer

This option requires you to pay the offer within two years of acceptance.

The offer must include the realizable value of your assets plus the amount we could collect over 60 months of payments (or the remainder of the ten-year statutory period for collection, whichever is less).

We may file a Notice of Federal Tax Lien on tax liabilities compromised under short-term deferred payment offers.

Deferred Payment Offer

This payment option requires you to pay the offer amount over the remaining statutory period for collecting the tax.

The offer must include the realizable value of your assets plus the amount we could collect through monthly payments during the remaining life of the collection statute.

The deferred payment plan has three options:

Option One

- Full payment of the realizable value of your assets within 90 days from the date we accept your offer, and
- Your future income in monthly payments during the remaining life of the collection statute.

Option Two

- Cash payment for a portion of the realizable value of your assets within 90 days from the date we accept your offer, and
- Monthly payments during the remaining life of the collection statute for both the balance of the realizable value and your future income.

Option Three

- The entire offer amount in monthly payments over the life of the collection statute.

Just as with short-term deferred payment offers, we may file a Notice of Federal Tax Lien.

Note: The worksheet on page 10 instructs you how to figure the appropriate amount for a Cash, Short-Term Deferred Payment, or Deferred Payment Offer.

How We Consider Your Offer	An offer examiner will evaluate your offer and may request additional documentation from you to verify financial or other information you provide. The examiner will then make a recommendation to accept or reject the offer.	The examiner may also return your offer if you don't provide the requested information. The examiner may decide that a larger offer amount is necessary to justify acceptance. You'll have the opportunity to amend your offer.
Additional Agreements	When you submit certain offers, we may also request that you sign an additional agreement requiring you to: ■ Pay a percentage of your future earnings	■ Waive certain present or future tax benefits ■ Link separate offers based on the same reasonable collection potential
Withholding Collection Activities	We will withhold collection activities while we consider your offer. We will not act to collect the tax liability: ■ While we investigate and evaluate your offer ■ For 30 days after we reject an offer ■ While you appeal an offer rejection	The above don't apply if we find any indication that you submitted your offer to delay collection or if a delay will jeopardize our ability to collect the tax. If you currently have an installment agreement when you submit an offer, you must continue making the agreed upon monthly payments while we consider your offer.
Suspension of the Statute of Limitations	The collection statute of limitation is suspended for all tax periods on your offer during the period your offer is pending. Your offer is considered pending: ■ While we investigate and evaluate your offer ■ For 30 days after we reject an offer ■ While you appeal on offer rejection	When you sign the offer, you agree to suspend the assessment statute of limitation for all tax periods included in your offer. Your signature extends this statute: ■ During the timeframes listed above ■ While the amount you agreed to pay under an accepted agreement remains unpaid. ■ While any other term or condition of the offer remains unsatisfied

If We Accept Your Offer

If we accept your offer, we'll notify you by mail. When you receive your acceptance letter, you must:

- Promptly pay any unpaid amounts that become due under the terms of the offer agreement
- Comply with all the terms and conditions of the offer, along with those of any additional agreement
- Promptly notify us of any change of address until you meet the conditions of your offer. Your acceptance letter will indicate which IRS office to contact if your address changes. Your notification allows us to contact you immediately regarding the status of your offer.

We will release all Notices of Federal Tax Lien when you satisfy the payment terms of the offered amount. For an immediate release of a lien, you can submit certified funds with a request letter.

In the future, not filing returns or paying taxes when due could result in the default of an accepted offer (see Form 656, Item 8(d), the future compliance provision). If you default your agreement, we will reinstate the unpaid amount of the original tax liability, file a Notice of Federal Tax Lien on any tax liability without a lien, and resume collection activities. The future compliance provision applies to offers based on **doubt as to collectibility.** In certain cases, the future compliance provision may apply to offers based on **effective tax administration.**

We won't default your offer agreement when you've filed a joint offer with your spouse or ex-spouse as long as you've kept or are keeping all the terms of the agreement, even if your spouse or ex-spouse violates the future compliance provision.

Except for offers based on **doubt as to liability,** the offer agreement requires you to forego certain refunds, and you must return erroneous refunds to us. These conditions are also listed on Form 656, Items 8(g) and 8(h).

Note: The law requires us to make certain information from accepted Offers In Compromise available for public inspection and review in your IRS District Office. Therefore, information regarding your Offer In Compromise may become publicly known.

If We Reject Your Offer

We'll notify you by mail if we reject your offer. In our letter, we will explain our reason for the rejection. If your offer is rejected, you have the right to:

- Appeal our decision to the Office of Appeals within thirty days from the date of our letter. The letter will include detailed instructions on how to appeal the rejection.
- Submit another offer. You must increase an offer we've rejected as being too low, when your financial situation remains unchanged. However, you *must* provide updated financial information when your financial situation has changed or when the original offer is more than six months old.

Worksheet to Calculate an Offer Amount Using Forms 433-A and/or 433-B

You need to prepare a financial statement before you can determine the amount you should offer. We use Form 433-A or Form 433-B, *Collection Information Statement,* for most purposes. Individual taxpayers should prepare a Form 433-A using Publication 1854 for instructions. Self-employed taxpayers should prepare a Form 433-A and a Form 433-B, the statement we use for businesses; Corporations and other types of businesses should prepare a Form 433-B. Remember to calculate the monthly net income from your business on Form 433-B and transfer that amount to line 34 of your Form 433-A.

Terms and Definitions

An understanding of the following terms and conditions will help you to prepare your offer.

Fair Market Value (FMV) — The amount you could reasonably expect from the sale of an asset. Provide an accurate valuation of each asset. Determine value from realtors, used car dealers, publications, furniture dealers, or other experts on specific types of assets. Please include a copy of any written estimate with your financial statement.

Quick Sale Value (QSV) — The amount you could reasonably expect from the sale of an asset if you sold it quickly, typically in ninety days or less. This amount generally is less than fair market value, but may be equal to or higher, based on local circumstances.

Realizable Value — The quick sale value amount minus what you owe to a secured creditor. The creditor must have priority over a filed Notice of Federal Tax Lien before we allow a subtraction from the asset's value.

Future Income — We generally determine the amount we could collect from your future income by subtracting necessary living expenses from your monthly income over a set number of months. For a cash offer, you must offer what you could pay in monthly payments over forty-eight months (or the remainder of the ten-year statutory period for collection, whichever is less). For a short-term deferred offer, you must offer what you could pay in monthly payments over sixty months (or the remainder of the statutory period for collection, whichever is less). For a deferred payment offer, you must offer what you could pay in monthly payments during the remaining time we could legally receive payments.

Reasonable Collection Potential (RCP) — The total realizable value of your assets plus your future income. The total is generally your minimum offer amount.

Necessary Expenses — The allowable payments you make to support you and your family's health and welfare and/or the production of income. This expense allowance does not apply to business entities. Our Publication 1854 explains the National Standard Expenses and gives the allowable amounts. We derive these amounts from the Bureau of Labor Statistics (BLS) Consumer Expenditure Survey. We also use information from the Bureau of the Census to determine local expenses for housing, utilities, and transportation.

Note: If the IRS determines that the facts and circumstances of your situation indicate that using the scheduled allowance of necessary expenses is inadequate, we will allow you an adequate means for providing basic living expenses. However, you must provide documentation that supports a determination that using national and local expense standards leaves you an inadequate means of providing for basic living expenses.

Expenses Not Generally Allowed — We typically do not allow you to claim tuition for private schools, public or private college expenses, charitable contributions, voluntary retirement contributions, payments on unsecured debts such as credit card bills, cable television charges and other similar expenses as necessary living expenses. However, we can allow these expenses when you can prove that they are necessary for the health and welfare of you or your family or for the production of income.

APPENDIX A

WORKSHEET

1. Enter the total amount of cash you currently have available. Include cash, savings, checking account balances minus your monthly necessary living expenses, cash value in life insurance policies, and securities (Items 20, 21, 22, and 23 of Form 433-A and/or Items 16, 17, 18, & 19 of Form 433-B).

Line 1 Total $_____

2. Enter the value of any retirement plans (*e.g.,* IRA, 401-K, etc.) from which you can cash out or borrow funds minus the amount of tax (federal, state and local) and early withdrawal penalty you would incur by withdrawing these funds.

Line 2 Total $_____

3. The following schedule helps you calculate the realizable value of your assets:

   ■ Enter the current Fair Market Value (FMV) in column (B) for each asset listed on Form 433-A, Items 24, 25, and 26, and/or Form 433-B, Items 20 through 24

   ■ *Multiply the amounts in column (B) by 80% (.80) and enter the results in column (C)*

   ■ Enter the amounts owed (liability) to any secured creditor in column (D)

   ■ Subtract the amounts in column (D) from the amounts in column (C) and enter the results in column (E)

Don't show negative values on assets for which you owe more than their worth. Show realizable value as $0.00 for cases like these.

Note: We may not allow the amount owed to a secured creditor as a liability unless it has priority over a filed Notice of Federal Tax Lien.

(A) ASSET	(B) FMV	(C) QSV	(D) LIABILITY	(E) REALIZABLE VALUE
1998 truck	20,000	16,000	12,000	$4,000
Real property	100,000	80,000	96,000	0
			TOTAL	$4,000

ASSET	FMV	QSV	LIABILITY	REALIZABLE VALUE

(Attach Additional Sheets if Needed)

Line 3 Total $_____

APPENDIX A

Note: __Individuals__ may exclude the value of the following:

- *$6,250 of the value of your furniture or personal effects in your household, items of personal use, livestock or poultry. Don't include the value of your vehicle in this exclusion.*

- *$3,125 of the value of trade or business tools.*

4. To calculate monthly payments:
    a. Enter total monthly income (Item 41, Form 433-A) here $_____$
    b. Enter necessary monthly living expenses (Item 52) here $_____$
    c. Subtract b from a: enter the result here   **Line 4C Total** $_____$
        (This amount cannot be less than $0)

Note: Decide now to make either a Cash, Short Term Deferred or a Deferred Payment Offer.

5. For a **Cash Offer,** multiply line 4c by 48 (or the remainder of the ten-year statutory period for collection, whichever is less) and enter amount in total. This amount represents the total amount of future income for a cash offer.

            Line 5 Total $_____$

6. For a **Short-Term Deferred Payment Offer,** multiply line 4c by 60 (or the remainder of the ten-year statutory period for collection, whichever is less). This amount represents the total amount of future income for a Short-Term Deferred Payment offer.

            Line 6 Total $_____$

7. For a **Deferred Payment Offer,** we will help you determine your future income amount. To compute this amount, we must calculate the remaining time left on the collection statute for each period of tax liability.

Call your local IRS office or 1-800-829-1040 to assist you in this calculation.

- Multiply the amount on **line 4c** by the number of months remaining on the collection statute, and enter on line 7.

            Line 7 Total $_____$

8. **AMOUNT OF OFFER** (Add lines 1, 2, 3 and either 5, 6, or 7) $_____$

Completing Form 656, Offer In Compromise

We have included two *Offer In Compromise* forms. Use one form to submit your offer in compromise. You may use the other form as a worksheet and retain it for your personal records.

Note: Direct any questions that arise in completing this form to 1-800-829-1040 or your local IRS office. We may return your offer if you don't follow these instructions.

Item 1: Enter your name and home or business address. You should also include a mailing address, if it is different from your street address.

Show both names on joint offers for joint liabilities. If you owe one liability by yourself (such as employment taxes), and other liabilities jointly (such as income taxes), but only you are submitting an offer, list all tax liabilities on one Form 656. If you owe one liability yourself and another jointly, and both parties submit an offer, **complete two Forms 656,** one for the individual liability and one for the joint liability.

Item 2: Enter the Social Security Number(s) for the person(s) submitting the offer. For example, enter the Social Security Number of both spouses when submitting a joint offer for a joint tax liability. However, when only one spouse submits an offer, enter only that spouse's Social Security Number.

Item 3: Enter the Employer Identification Number for offers from businesses.

Item 4: Show the Employer Identification Numbers for all other businesses (excluding corporate entities) that you own or in which you have an ownership interest.

Item 5: Identify your tax liability and enter the tax year or period. Letters and notices from us and Notices of Federal Tax Lien show the tax periods for trust fund recovery penalties.

Item 6: Check the appropriate box(es) describing the basis for your offer.

Doubt as to Liability offers require a statement describing in detail why you think you do not owe the liability. Complete Item 9, "Explanation of Circumstances", explaining your situation and enter your offer amount on Item 7.

Doubt as to Collectibility offers require you to complete a *Collection Information Statement*: a Form 433-A for individuals and/or a Form 433-B for businesses. Enter your offer amount on Item 7.

Effective Tax Administration offers require you to complete a Form 433A for individuals and/or a Form 433-B for businesses. Complete Item 9, "Explanation of Circumstances" and enter your offer amount on Item 7.

Item 7:	Enter the total amount of your offer. (See page 10, Amount of Offer). Your offer amount can't include a refund we owe you or amounts you've already paid. *Note: We don't require a deposit. The law requires us to hold any deposits you make in a special non-interest bearing account. However, should we reject or return your offer and you decide to apply a deposit towards the liability, you will receive credit on the deposit from the date we received it.*	Check the appropriate payment box (cash, short-term deferred payment or deferred payment). We have provided some specific payment periods. If these are inapplicable, describe your proposed payment terms on the line provided. For example, for offers with 7 years remaining on the statutory period for collection and a total offer of $25,000, you might propose to pay $10,000 (equity) within 90 days and the balance of $15,000 in 84 monthly installments of $179. You could also pay the same offer in 84 monthly installments of $298.
Item 8:	It is important that you understand the requirements listed in this section. Pay particular attention to Items 8(d) and 8(g), as	they address the future compliance provision and refunds.
Item 9:	Explain your reason(s) for submitting your offer in the "Explanation of Circumstances."	You may attach additional sheets if necessary.
Item 10:	All persons submitting the offer must sign and date Form 656. Include titles of authorized	corporate officers, executors, trustees, Powers of Attorney, etc. where applicable.
Where to File	File your offer in compromise at the IRS district office in your area. To get the address	of the local office nearest you, call the toll free number at 1-800-829-1040.

419

Form **709**	**United States Gift (and Generation-Skipping Transfer) Tax Return**	OMB No. 1545-0020
	(Section 6019 of the Internal Revenue Code) (For gifts made during calendar year 1999)	**1999**
Department of the Treasury Internal Revenue Service	▶ **See separate instructions. For Privacy Act Notice, see the Instructions for Form 1040.**	

Part 1—General Information

1 Donor's first name and middle initial	2 Donor's last name	3 Donor's social security number
4 Address (number, street, and apartment number)		5 Legal residence (domicile) (county and state)
6 City, state, and ZIP code		7 Citizenship

		Yes	No
8	If the donor died during the year, check here ▶ ☐ and enter date of death............... , ...		
9	If you received an extension of time to file this Form 709, check here ▶ ☐ and attach the Form 4868, 2688, 2350, or extension letter		
10	Enter the total number of separate donees listed on Schedule A—count each person only once. ▶		
11a	Have you (the donor) previously filed a Form 709 (or 709-A) for any other year? If the answer is "No," do not complete line 11b .		
11b	If the answer to line 11a is "Yes," has your address changed since you last filed Form 709 (or 709-A)?		
12	Gifts by husband or wife to third parties.—Do you consent to have the gifts (including generation-skipping transfers) made by you and by your spouse to third parties during the calendar year considered as made one-half by each of you? (See instructions.) (If the answer is "Yes," the following information must be furnished and your spouse must sign the consent shown below. **If the answer is "No," skip lines 13–18 and go to Schedule A.**)		
13	Name of consenting spouse **14** SSN		
15	Were you married to one another during the entire calendar year? (see instructions)		
16	If the answer to 15 is "No," check whether ☐ married ☐ divorced or ☐ widowed, and give date (see instructions) ▶		
17	Will a gift tax return for this calendar year be filed by your spouse?		
18	**Consent of Spouse**—I consent to have the gifts (and generation-skipping transfers) made by me and by my spouse to third parties during the calendar year considered as made one-half by each of us. We are both aware of the joint and several liability for tax created by the execution of this consent.		

Consenting spouse's signature ▶   Date ▶

Part 2—Tax Computation

1	Enter the amount from Schedule A, Part 3, line 15	1	
2	Enter the amount from Schedule B, line 3	2	
3	Total taxable gifts (add lines 1 and 2)	3	
4	Tax computed on amount on line 3 (see Table for Computing Tax in separate instructions). . .	4	
5	Tax computed on amount on line 2 (see Table for Computing Tax in separate instructions). . .	5	
6	Balance (subtract line 5 from line 4)	6	
7	Maximum unified credit (nonresident aliens, see instructions)	7	211,300 00
8	Enter the unified credit against tax allowable for all prior periods (from Sch. B, line 1, col. C) . .	8	
9	Balance (subtract line 8 from line 7)	9	
10	Enter 20% (.20) of the amount allowed as a specific exemption for gifts made after September 8, 1976, and before January 1, 1977 (see instructions)	10	
11	Balance (subtract line 10 from line 9)	11	
12	Unified credit (enter the smaller of line 6 or line 11)	12	
13	Credit for foreign gift taxes (see instructions)	13	
14	Total credits (add lines 12 and 13)	14	
15	Balance (subtract line 14 from line 6) (do not enter less than zero)	15	
16	Generation-skipping transfer taxes (from Schedule C, Part 3, col. H, Total)	16	
17	Total tax (add lines 15 and 16)	17	
18	Gift and generation-skipping transfer taxes prepaid with extension of time to file	18	
19	If line 18 is less than line 17, enter BALANCE DUE (see instructions)	19	
20	If line 18 is greater than line 17, enter AMOUNT TO BE REFUNDED	20	

Under penalties of perjury, I declare that I have examined this return, including any accompanying schedules and statements, and to the best of my knowledge and belief it is true, correct, and complete. Declaration of preparer (other than donor) is based on all information of which preparer has any knowledge.

Donor's signature ▶   Date ▶

Preparer's signature (other than donor) ▶   Date ▶

Preparer's address (other than donor) ▶

Attach check or money order here.

For Paperwork Reduction Act Notice, see page 8 of the separate instructions for this form.   Cat. No. 16783M   Form **709** (1999)

SCHEDULE A	Computation of Taxable Gifts (Including Transfers in Trust)

A Does the value of any item listed on Schedule A reflect any valuation discount? If the answer is "Yes," see instructions .... Yes ☐ No ☐

B ☐ ◄ Check here if you elect under section 529(c)(2)(B) to treat any transfers made this year to a qualified state tuition program as made ratably over a 5-year period beginning this year. See instructions. Attach explanation.

Part 1 — Gifts Subject Only to Gift Tax. *Gifts less political organization, medical, and educational exclusions — see instructions*

A Item number	B <ul><li>Donee's name and address</li><li>Relationship to donor (if any)</li><li>Description of gift</li><li>If the gift was made by means of a trust, enter trust's identifying number and attach a copy of the trust instrument</li><li>If the gift was of securities, give CUSIP number</li></ul>	C Donor's adjusted basis of gift	D Date of gift	E Value at date of gift
1				

Total of Part 1 (add amounts from Part 1, column E) .... ►

Part 2 — Gifts That are Direct Skips and are Subject to Both Gift Tax and Generation-Skipping Transfer Tax. You must list the gifts in chronological order. *Gifts less political organization, medical, and educational exclusions — see instructions. (Also list here direct skips that are subject only to the GST tax at this time as the result of the termination of an "estate tax inclusion period." See instructions.)*

A Item number	B <ul><li>Donee's name and address</li><li>Relationship to donor (if any)</li><li>Description of gift</li><li>If the gift was made by means of a trust, enter trust's identifying number and attach a copy of the trust instrument</li><li>If the gift was of securities, give CUSIP number</li></ul>	C Donor's adjusted basis of gift	D Date of gift	E Value at date of gift
1				

Total of Part 2 (add amounts from Part 2, column E) .... ►

Part 3 — Taxable Gift Reconciliation

1	Total value of gifts of donor (add totals from column E of Parts 1 and 2)	1	
2	One-half of items _____ attributable to spouse (see instructions)	2	
3	Balance (subtract line 2 from line 1)	3	
4	Gifts of spouse to be included (from Schedule A, Part 3, line 2 of spouse's return — see instructions)	4	
	If any of the gifts included on this line are also subject to the generation-skipping transfer tax, check here ► ☐ and enter those gifts also on Schedule C, Part 1.		
5	Total gifts (add lines 3 and 4)	5	
6	Total annual exclusions for gifts listed on Schedule A (including line 4, above) (see instructions)	6	
7	Total included amount of gifts (subtract line 6 from line 5)	7	

Deductions (see instructions)

8	Gifts of interests to spouse for which a marital deduction will be claimed, based on items _____ of Schedule A	8		
9	Exclusions attributable to gifts on line 8	9		
10	Marital deduction — subtract line 9 from line 8	10		
11	Charitable deduction, based on items _____ less exclusions .	11		
12	Total deductions — add lines 10 and 11		12	
13	Subtract line 12 from line 7		13	
14	Generation-skipping transfer taxes payable with this Form 709 (from Schedule C, Part 3, col. H, Total)		14	
15	Taxable gifts (add lines 13 and 14). Enter here and on line 1 of the Tax Computation on page 1		15	

(If more space is needed, attach additional sheets of same size.)

Form **709** (1999)

STF FED1435F.2

Form **872**	Department of the Treasury—Internal Revenue Service	In Reply Refer To:
(Rev. August 1988)	**Consent to Extend the Time to Assess Tax**	SSN or EIN

_____
(Name(s))

taxpayer(s) of _____
(Number, Street, City or Town, State, ZIP Code)

and the District Director of Internal Revenue or Regional Director of Appeals consent and agree to the following:

(1) The amount of any Federal _____ tax due on any return(s) made by
(Kind of tax)
or for the above taxpayer(s) for the period(s) ended _____

_____

may be assessed at any time on or before _____ . However, if
(Expiration date)
a notice of deficiency in tax for any such period(s) is sent to the taxpayer(s) on or before that date, then the time for assessing the tax will be further extended by the number of days the assessment was previously prohibited, plus 60 days.

(2) This agreement ends on the earlier of the above expiration date or the assessment date of an increase in the above tax that reflects the final determination of tax and the final administrative appeals consideration. An assessment for one period covered by this agreement will not end this agreement for any other period it covers. Some assessments do not reflect a final determination and appeals consideration and therefore will not terminate the agreement before the expiration date. Examples are assessments of: (a) tax under a partial agreement; (b) tax in jeopardy; (c) tax to correct mathematical or clerical errors; (d) tax reported on amended returns; and (e) advance payments. In addition, unassessed payments, such as amounts treated by the Service as cash bonds and advance payments not assessed by the Service, will not terminate this agreement before the expiration date.

This agreement ends on the above expiration date regardless of any assessment for any period includible in a report to the Joint Committee on Taxation submitted under section 6405 of the Internal Revenue Code.

(3) The taxpayer(s) may file a claim for credit or refund and the Service may credit or refund the tax within 6 months after this agreement ends.

(SIGNATURE INSTRUCTIONS AND SPACE FOR SIGNATURE ARE ON THE BACK OF THIS FORM)   Form **872** (Rev. 8-88)

Cat.No. 20755I

Form **872-A** (Rev. October 1987)	Department of the Treasury — Internal Revenue Service ## Special Consent to Extend the Time to Assess Tax	In reply refer to: SSN or EIN

(Name(s))

taxpayer(s) of _____

(Number, Street, City or Town, State, ZIP Code)

and the District Director of Internal Revenue or Regional Director of Appeals consent and agree as follows:

(1) The amount(s) of any Federal_____tax due on any return(s) made by or

(Kind of tax)

for the above taxpayer(s) for the period(s) ended_____

may be assessed on or before the 90th (ninetieth) day after: (a) the Internal Revenue Service office considering the case receives Form 872-T, Notice of Termination of Special Consent to Extend the Time to Assess Tax, from the taxpayer(s); or (b) the Internal Revenue Service mails Form 872-T to the taxpayer(s); or (c) the Internal Revenue Service mails a notice of deficiency for such period(s); except that if a notice of deficiency is sent to the taxpayer(s), the time for assessing the tax for the period(s) stated in the notice of deficiency will end 60 days after the period during which the making of an assessment is prohibited. A final adverse determination subject to declaratory judgment under sections 7428, 7476, or 7477 of the Internal Revenue Code will not terminate this agreement.

(2) This agreement ends on the earlier of the above expiration date or the assessment date of an increase in the above tax or the overassessment date of a decrease in the above tax that reflects the final determination of tax and the final administrative appeals consideration. An assessment or overassessment for one period covered by this agreement will not end this agreement for any other period it covers. Some assessments do not reflect a final determination and appeals consideration and therefore will not terminate the agreement before the expiration date. Examples are assessments of: (a) tax under a partial agreement; (b) tax in jeopardy; (c) tax to correct mathematical or clerical errors; (d) tax reported on amended returns; and (e) advance payments. In addition, unassessed payments, such as amounts treated by the Service as cash bonds and advance payments not assessed by the Service, will not terminate this agreement before the expiration date determined in (1) above. This agreement ends on the date determined in (1) above regardless of any assessment for any period includible in a report to the Joint Committee on Taxation submitted under section 6405 of the Internal Revenue Code.

(3) This agreement will not reduce the period of time otherwise provided by law for making such assessment.

(4) The taxpayer(s) may file a claim for credit or refund and the Service may credit or refund the tax within 6 (six) months after this agreement ends.

(Signature instructions and space for signature are on the back of this form)   Form **872-A** (Rev. 10-87)

OMB No. 1545-1504

Department of the Treasury – Internal Revenue Service

A TAXPAYER **ADVOCATE** SERVICE

Application for Taxpayer Assistance Order (ATAO)

Form **911**
(Rev. 3-2000)

Section I.	Taxpayer Information

1. Name(s) as shown on tax return	4. Your Social Security Number	6. Tax Form(s)
	5. Social Security No. of Spouse	7. Tax Period(s)
2. Current mailing address (Number, Street & Apartment Number)	8. Employer Identification Number (if applicable)	
	9. E-Mail address	
3. City, Town or Post Office, State and ZIP Code	10. Fax number	
11. Person to contact	12. Daytime telephone number	13. Best time to call

14. Please describe the problem and the significant hardship it is creating. *(If more space is needed, attach additional sheets.)*

15. Please describe the relief you are requesting. *(If more space is needed, attach additional sheets.)*

I understand that Taxpayer Advocate employees may contact third parties in order to respond to this request and I authorize such contacts to be made. Further, by authorizing the Taxpayer Advocate Service to contact third parties, I understand that I will not receive notice, pursuant to section 7602(c) of the Internal Revenue Code, of third parties contacted in connection with this request.

16. Signature of taxpayer or corporate officer	17. Date	18. Signature of spouse	19. Date

Section II.	Representative Information (if applicable)

1. Name of Authorized Representative	3. Centralized Authorization File Number (CAF)
	4. Daytime telephone number
2. Mailing Address	5. Fax number
6. Signature of Representative	7. Date

Cat. No. 16965S

Form **911** (Rev. 3-2000)

Instructions

When to use this form: Use this form to request relief if any of the following apply to you:
1. You are suffering or about to suffer a significant hardship;
2. You are facing an immediate threat of adverse action;
3. You will incur significant costs, including fees for professional representation, if relief is not granted;
4. You will suffer irreparable injury or long-term adverse impact if relief is not granted;
5. You experienced an IRS delay of more than 30 calendar days in resolving an account-related problem or inquiry;
6. You did not receive a response or resolution to your problem by the date promised;
7. A system or procedure has either failed to operate as intended or failed to resolve your problem or dispute with the IRS.

If an IRS office will not grant the relief requested or will not grant the relief in time to avoid the significant hardship, you may submit this form. No enforcement action will be taken while we are reviewing your application.

Where to Submit This Form: Submit this application to the Taxpayer Advocate office located in the state or city where you reside. For the address of the Taxpayer Advocate in your state or city or for additional information call the National Taxpayer Advocate Toll-Free Number 1-877-777-4778.

Third Party Contact: You should understand that in order to respond to this request you are also authorizing the Taxpayer Advocate Service to contact third parties when necessary and that you will not receive further notice regarding contacted parties. See IRC 7602(c).

Overseas Taxpayers: Taxpayers residing overseas can submit this application by mail to the Taxpayer Advocate, Internal Revenue Service, PO Box 193479, San Juan, Puerto Rico 00919 or in person at 2 Ponce de Leon Avenue, Mercantil Plaza Building, Room GF05A, Hato Rey PR 00918. The application can also be faxed to (787) 759-4535.

Caution: Incomplete applications or applications submitted to an Advocate office outside of your geographical location may result in delays. If you do not hear from us within one week of submitting Form 911, please contact the Taxpayer Advocate office where you originally submitted your application.

Section I Instructions--Taxpayer Information
1. Enter your name(s) as shown on the tax return that relates to this application for relief.
2. Enter your current mailing address, including street number and name and apartment number.
3. Enter your city, town or post office, state and ZIP code.
4. Enter your Social Security Number.
5. Enter the Social Security Number of your spouse if this application relates to a jointly filed return.
6. Enter the number of the Federal tax return or form that relates to this application. For example, an individual taxpayer with an income tax issue would enter Form 1040.
7. Enter the quarterly, annual or other tax period that relates to this application. For example, if this request involves an income tax issue, enter the calendar or fiscal year; if an employment tax issue, enter the calendar quarter.
8. Enter your Employer Identification Number if this relief request involves a business or non-individual entity (e.g.; a partnership, corporation, trust, self-employed individual with employees).
9. Enter your E-mail address.
10. Enter your fax number including the area code.
11. Enter the name of the individual we should contact. For partnerships, corporations, trusts, etc., enter the name of the individual authorized to act on the entity's behalf.
12. Enter your daytime telephone number including the area code.
13. Indicate the best time to call you. Please specify a.m. or p.m. hours.
14. Describe the problem and the significant hardship it is creating for you. Specify the actions that the IRS has taken (or not taken) to cause the problem and ensuing hardship. **If the problem involves an IRS delay of more than 30 days in resolving your issue, indicate the date you first contacted the IRS for assistance in resolving your problem.**
15. Describe the relief you are seeking. Specify the actions that you want taken and that you believe necessary to relieve the significant hardship. Furnish if applicable any relevant proof and corroboration as to why relief is warranted or why you cannot or should not meet current IRS demands to satisfy your tax obligations.
16.&18. If this application is a joint relief request relating to a joint tax liability, both spouses should sign in the appropriate blocks. If only one spouse is requesting relief relating to a joint tax liability, only the requesting spouse has to sign the application. If this application is being submitted for another individual, only a person authorized and empowered to act on that individual's behalf should sign the application.
NOTE: The signing of this application allows the IRS by law to suspend, for the period of time it takes the Advocate to review and decide upon your request, any applicable statutory periods of limitation relating to the assessment or collection of taxes..
17.&19. Enter the date the application was signed.

Section II Instructions--Representative Information
Taxpayers: If you wish to have a representative act on your behalf, you must give him/her power of attorney or tax information authorization for the tax return(s) and period(s)involved. For additional information see Form 2848, Power of Attorney and Declaration of Representative or Form 8821, Tax Information Authorization, and the accompanying instructions.

Representatives: If you are an authorized representative submitting this request on behalf of the taxpayer identified in Section I, complete Blocks 1 through 7 of Section II. Attach a copy of Form 2848, Form 8821 or other power of attorney. Enter your Centralized Authorization File (CAF) number in Block 3 of Section II. The CAF number is the unique number that the IRS assigns to a representative after Form 2848 or Form 8821 is filed with an IRS office.

Paperwork Reduction Act Notice: We ask for the information on this form to carry out the Internal Revenue laws of the United States. Your response is voluntary. You are not required to provide the information requested on a form that is subject to the Paperwork Reduction Act unless the form displays a valid OMB control number. Books or records relating to a form or its instructions must be retained as long as their contents may become material in the administration of any Internal Revenue law. Generally, tax returns and return information are confidential, as required by Code section 6103. Although the time needed to complete this form may vary depending on individual circumstances, the estimated average time is 30 minutes. Should you have comments concerning the accuracy of this time estimate or suggestions for making this form simpler, please write to the Internal Revenue Service, Attention: Tax Forms Committee, Western Area Distribution Center, Rancho Cordova, CA 95743-0001.

Cat. No. 16065S

Form 911 (Rev. 3-2000)

*U.S. GPO: 2000-461-017/21525

Form **941** (Rev. January 2000) Department of the Treasury Internal Revenue Service (O)	**Employer's Quarterly Federal Tax Return** ▶ See separate instructions for information on completing this return. Please type or print.

Enter state code for state in which deposits were made ONLY if different from state in address to the right ▶ ⬚⋮ (see page 2 of instructions).	Name (as distinguished from trade name)	Date quarter ended	OMB No. 1545-0029
	Trade name, if any	Employer identification number	T FF FD
	Address (number and street)	City, state, and ZIP code	FP I T

If address is different from prior return, check here ▶ ⬚

IRS Use

```
1 1 1 1 1 1 1 1 1 1     2     3 3 3 3 3 3 3 3     4 4 4     5 5 5
  6   7   8 8 8 8 8 8 8 8     9 9 9 9 9     10 10 10 10 10 10 10 10 10
```

If you do not have to file returns in the future, check here ▶ ⬚ and enter date final wages paid ▶

If you are a seasonal employer, see **Seasonal employers** on page 1 of the instructions and check here ▶

1 Number of employees in the pay period that includes March 12th . ▶	1	
2 Total wages and tips, plus other compensation	**2**	
3 Total income tax withheld from wages, tips, and sick pay	**3**	
4 Adjustment of withheld income tax for preceding quarters of calendar year	**4**	
5 Adjusted total of income tax withheld (line 3 as adjusted by line 4—see instructions) . . .	**5**	

6 Taxable social security wages	**6a**		× 12.4% (.124) =	**6b**	
Taxable social security tips	**6c**		× 12.4% (.124) =	**6d**	
7 Taxable Medicare wages and tips . . .	**7a**		× 2.9% (.029) =	**7b**	

8 Total social security and Medicare taxes (add lines 6b, 6d, and 7b). Check here if wages are not subject to social security and/or Medicare tax . . . . ▶ ⬚	**8**	
9 Adjustment of social security and Medicare taxes (see instructions for required explanation) Sick Pay $ _____ ± Fractions of Cents $ _____ ± Other $ _____ =	**9**	
10 Adjusted total of social security and Medicare taxes (line 8 as adjusted by line 9—see instructions)	**10**	
11 **Total taxes** (add lines 5 and 10)	**11**	
12 Advance earned income credit (EIC) payments made to employees	**12**	
13 Net taxes (subtract line 12 from line 11). If **$1,000 or more, this must equal line 17, column (d) below (or line D of Schedule B (Form 941))**	**13**	
14 Total deposits for quarter, including overpayment applied from a prior quarter	**14**	
15 **Balance due** (subtract line 14 from line 13). See instructions	**15**	
16 **Overpayment.** If line 14 is more than line 13, enter excess here ▶ $ _____ and check if to be: ⬚ Applied to next return **OR** ⬚ Refunded.		

- **All filers:** If line 13 is less than $1,000, you need not complete line 17 or Schedule B (Form 941).
- **Semiweekly schedule depositors:** Complete Schedule B (Form 941) and check here . . . . ▶ ⬚
- **Monthly schedule depositors:** Complete line 17, columns (a) through (d), and check here. . . . . ▶ ⬚

17 Monthly Summary of Federal Tax Liability. Do not complete if you were a semiweekly schedule depositor.			
(a) First month liability	(b) Second month liability	(c) Third month liability	(d) Total liability for quarter

Sign Here	Under penalties of perjury, I declare that I have examined this return, including accompanying schedules and statements, and to the best of my knowledge and belief, it is true, correct, and complete.		
	Signature ▶	Print Your Name and Title ▶	Date ▶

For Privacy Act and Paperwork Reduction Act Notice, see back of Payment Voucher.   Cat. No. 17001Z   Form **941** (Rev. 1-2000)

Department of the Treasury
Internal Revenue Service
(Rev. January 1999)
RQ 13-3240231

941TeleFile Tax Record

▶ **Call TeleFile 24 hours a day at 1-800-583-5345.**

Do Not Mail

OMB No. 1545-1509

150852*** ***** ECRLOT** C-007
                S19   CT

016-0051

I..IIII...II....I.II.I.I.I.I.II....II.I.I.I..I..I.II

If your name, address, or EIN as shown is incorrect, you **CANNOT** use TeleFile.

Information You Provide	Information Provided by TeleFile

A Enter the total deposits (line 14) reported on your **1998 third** quarter Form 941 (or 941TeleFile Tax Record)

B Enter the numerical code for the state in which deposits were made only if the state is different from that shown in your address above (see page TEL-3)

C Is this your final return?   Yes ☐   No ☐
If yes, enter date final wages paid . . . .

*Line numbers correspond to Form 941. See the **Instructions for Form 941.***

1 Number of employees (except household employees) employed in the pay period that includes March 12th (first quarter only) — **1**

2 Total wages and tips, plus other compensation — **2**

3 Total income tax withheld from wages, tips, and sick pay — **3**

6 Taxable social security wages — **6a** | **6b**

Taxable social security tips — **6c** | **6d**

7 Taxable Medicare wages and tips — **7a** | **7b**

9 Fractions of cents adjustment only (+/–) — **9**

10 Adjusted total of social security and Medicare taxes — **10**

12 Advance earned income credit (EIC) payments made to employees — **12**

13 Net taxes. **If $1,000 or more, this amount must equal line 17d below.** — **13**

14 Total deposits for quarter, including overpayment applied from a prior quarter — **14**

15 Balance due — **15**

16 Overpayment (applied to next return) — **16**

17 Monthly summary of Federal tax liability

17a First month liability	17b Second month liability	17c Third month liability	17d Total liability for quarter

D **Signature:** You will be required to make the following declaration: *Under penalties of perjury, I declare that, to the best of my knowledge and belief, the return information I provided is true, correct, and complete.*
Before you call, enter the numbers on your phone for the first five letters of your last name (see item 2 on page TEL-2). **Caution: See Who must sign the return on page TEL-2.**

Name (numbers)

Stay on the line until TeleFile tells you your return has been accepted and gives you a 6-digit confirmation number and filing date.

Confirmation Number

/ /
Filing Date

The IRS considers this Tax Record, including the confirmation number, to be the record of information used to file your tax return.

For Privacy Act and Paperwork Reduction Act Notice, see back of Form 941.   Cat. No. 22389E   941TeleFile Tax Record (Rev. 1-99)

B18-19-000140725

Here's How To File by Phone

1. Check to see if you can use 941TeleFile before you call (the requirements are listed on page TEL-1).

2. Complete the 941TeleFile Tax Record (unshaded column) before you call.

   Line A. Total deposits from 1998 third quarter Form 941. Enter the total deposits reported on line 14 of your 1998 third quarter Form 941 (or 941TeleFile Tax Record). This information is required for security reasons.

   Line B. State code box. If you deposited your Form 941 taxes in a state other than the one shown in your address on the Tax Record, enter the numerical code for the state where you made deposits from the **State Code Table** on page TEL-3. Do not use the two-letter postal abbreviation used on Form 941.

   Line C. Final return. If you have gone out of business or stopped paying wages and this is your final return, mark the "Yes" box and enter the date final wages were paid. See **Dates** under item 4 below.

   Lines 1 through 17. Fill in the entry spaces in the unshaded column. (941TeleFile will provide the amounts for the entry spaces in the shaded column.) See the separate **Instructions for Form 941.**

   Caution: If you are reporting advance earned income credit payments, do not use line 13 to determine your deposit schedule. You will need the line 11 (total taxes) amount to determine your deposit schedule (monthly or semiweekly). 941TeleFile will not compute line 11 for this quarter, and the Tax Record does not include an entry space for this amount. You may figure line 11 (line 3 plus line 10) after the TeleFile call. If you do not have any advance earned income credit payments (line 12), line 11 will equal line 13, which is provided by TeleFile.

   Line D. Signature. Before you call, enter the numbers on your phone corresponding to the first five letters of your last name in section D of the Tax Record.

   Note: You will be required to enter your social security number (SSN) when you call, but you are **not** required to write your SSN on the Tax Record.

   During the call, after you have completed the entries for line 17, you will be required to make the following declaration:

   Under penalties of perjury, I declare that, to the best of my knowledge and belief, the return information I provided is true, correct, and complete.

   To make this declaration and sign your return, 941TeleFile will ask you to:

   a) Enter **your** SSN (not the business' EIN) and

   b) Enter the first five letters of **your** last name (not your business name). Enter the letters of your last name by pressing the numbers corresponding to the letters. (Enter "7" for "Q" and "9" for "Z.")

   For example, John Doe (SSN: 123-00-6789) would sign the return for Cedar Inc. as follows: (a) Enter 123006789 and (b) enter 363# (the corresponding number keys for DOE).

   Who must sign the return:

   - **Sole proprietorships.** The individual owning the business.
   - **Corporations.** The president, vice president, or other principal officer.
   - **Partnerships or unincorporated organizations.** A responsible and duly authorized member or officer having knowledge of its affairs.
   - **Trusts or estates.** The fiduciary.

   The return may also be signed by a duly authorized agent of the taxpayer if a valid power of attorney is on file.

**Call TeleFile
24 Hours a Day**

1-800-583-5345

**If you get
a busy signal,
please try again.**

**During the call,
skip through
familiar instructions
to speed up input.**

Form **1041**	Department of the Treasury—Internal Revenue Service **U.S. Income Tax Return for Estates and Trusts**	19**99**

For calendar year 1999 or fiscal year beginning _____ , 1999, and ending _____ , | OMB No. 1545-0092

A Type of entity:	Name of estate or trust (If a grantor type trust, see page 8 of the instructions.)	**C** Employer identification number
☐ Decedent's estate		
☐ Simple trust		**D** Date entity created
☐ Complex trust		
☐ Grantor type trust	Name and title of fiduciary	**E** Nonexempt charitable and split-interest trusts, check applicable boxes (see page 10 of the instructions):
☐ Bankruptcy estate–Ch. 7		
☐ Bankruptcy estate–Ch. 11	Number, street, and room or suite no. (If a P.O. box, see page 8 of the instructions.)	
☐ Pooled income fund		☐ Described in section 4947(a)(1)
B Number of Schedules K-1 attached (see instructions) ▶	City or town, state, and ZIP code	☐ Not a private foundation ☐ Described in section 4947(a)(2)

F Check applicable boxes:	☐ Initial return ☐ Final return ☐ Amended return ☐ Change in fiduciary's name ☐ Change in fiduciary's address	**G** Pooled mortgage account (see page 10 of the instructions): ☐ Bought ☐ Sold Date:

Income	1	Interest income	1	
	2	Ordinary dividends	2	
	3	Business income or (loss) (attach Schedule C or C-EZ (Form 1040))	3	
	4	Capital gain or (loss) (attach Schedule D (Form 1041))	4	
	5	Rents, royalties, partnerships, other estates and trusts, etc. (attach Schedule E (Form 1040))	5	
	6	Farm income or (loss) (attach Schedule F (Form 1040))	6	
	7	Ordinary gain or (loss) (attach Form 4797)	7	
	8	Other income. List type and amount	8	
	9	**Total income.** Combine lines 1 through 8 . . . . ▶	9	

Deductions	10	Interest. Check if Form 4952 is attached ▶ ☐	10	
	11	Taxes	11	
	12	Fiduciary fees	12	
	13	Charitable deduction (from Schedule A, line 7)	13	
	14	Attorney, accountant, and return preparer fees	14	
	15a	Other deductions NOT subject to the 2% floor (attach schedule)	15a	
	b	Allowable miscellaneous itemized deductions subject to the 2% floor	15b	
	16	**Total.** Add lines 10 through 15b	16	
	17	Adjusted total income or (loss). Subtract line 16 from line 9. Enter here and on Schedule B, line 1 ▶	17	
	18	Income distribution deduction (from Schedule B, line 15) (attach Schedules K-1 (Form 1041))	18	
	19	Estate tax deduction (including certain generation-skipping taxes) (attach computation) . .	19	
	20	Exemption	20	
	21	**Total deductions.** Add lines 18 through 20 . . . . ▶	21	

Tax and Payments	22	Taxable income. Subtract line 21 from line 17. If a loss, see page 14 of the instructions	22	
	23	**Total tax** (from Schedule G, line 8)	23	
	24	**Payments: a** 1999 estimated tax payments and amount applied from 1998 return . . .	24a	
	b	Estimated tax payments allocated to beneficiaries (from Form 1041-T)	24b	
	c	Subtract line 24b from line 24a	24c	
	d	Tax paid with extension of time to file: ☐ Form 2758 ☐ Form 8736 ☐ Form 8800	24d	
	e	Federal income tax withheld. If any is from Form(s) 1099, check ▶ ☐	24e	
		Other payments: **f** Form 2439 .... ; **g** Form 4136 .... ; Total ▶	24h	
	25	**Total payments.** Add lines 24c through 24e, and 24h . . . . ▶	25	
	26	Estimated tax penalty (see page 15 of the instructions)	26	
	27	**Tax due.** If line 25 is smaller than the total of lines 23 and 26, enter amount owed . .	27	
	28	**Overpayment.** If line 25 is larger than the total of lines 23 and 26, enter amount overpaid	28	
	29	Amount of line 28 to be: **a Credited to 2000 estimated tax** ▶ _____ ; **b Refunded** ▶	29	

Please Sign Here

Under penalties of perjury, I declare that I have examined this return, including accompanying schedules and statements, and to the best of my knowledge and belief, it is true, correct, and complete. Declaration of preparer (other than fiduciary) is based on all information of which preparer has any knowledge.

▶		▶	
Signature of fiduciary or officer representing fiduciary	Date	EIN of fiduciary if a financial institution (see page 5 of the instructions)	

Paid Preparer's Use Only	Preparer's signature ▶	Date	Check if self-employed ▶ ☐	Preparer's SSN or PTIN
	Firm's name (or yours if self-employed) and address ▶		EIN ▶	
			ZIP code ▶	

For Paperwork Reduction Act Notice, see the separate instructions.   Cat. No. 11370H   Form **1041** (1999)

Form **1065**	**U.S. Partnership Return of Income**	OMB No. 1545-0099
Department of the Treasury Internal Revenue Service	For calendar year 1999, or tax year beginning .... , 1999, and ending .... , ... · ▶ **See separate instructions.**	**1999**

A Principal business activity	Use the IRS label. Other-wise, please print or type.	Name of partnership	D Employer identification number
B Principal product or service		Number, street, and room or suite no. If a P.O. box, see page 12 of the instructions.	E Date business started
C Business code number		City or town, state, and ZIP code	F Total assets (see page 12 of the instructions) $

G · Check applicable boxes: **(1)** ☐ Initial return **(2)** ☐ Final return **(3)** ☐ Change in address **(4)** ☐ Amended return

H Check accounting method: **(1)** ☐ Cash **(2)** ☐ Accrual **(3)** ☐ Other (specify) ▶..............................

I Number of Schedules K-1. Attach one for each person who was a partner at any time during the tax year ▶.............................

Caution: *Include **only** trade or business income and expenses on lines 1a through 22 below. See the instructions for more information.*

Income

1a Gross receipts or sales	**1a**		
b Less returns and allowances.	**1b**	**1c**	
2 Cost of goods sold (Schedule A, line 8)		**2**	
3 Gross profit. Subtract line 2 from line 1c.		**3**	
4 Ordinary income (loss) from other partnerships, estates, and trusts *(attach schedule)* . . .		**4**	
5 Net farm profit (loss) *(attach Schedule F (Form 1040))*		**5**	
6 Net gain (loss) from Form 4797, Part II, line 18.		**6**	
7 Other income (loss) *(attach schedule)*		**7**	
8 **Total income (loss).** Combine lines 3 through 7		**8**	

Deductions (see page 14 of the instructions for limitations)

9 Salaries and wages (other than to partners) (less employment credits)		**9**	
10 Guaranteed payments to partners		**10**	
11 Repairs and maintenance.		**11**	
12 Bad debts		**12**	
13 Rent		**13**	
14 Taxes and licenses		**14**	
15 Interest		**15**	
16a Depreciation (if required, attach Form 4562)	**16a**		
b Less depreciation reported on Schedule A and elsewhere on return	**16b**	**16c**	
17 Depletion **(Do not deduct oil and gas depletion.)**		**17**	
18 Retirement plans, etc.		**18**	
19 Employee benefit programs		**19**	
20 Other deductions *(attach schedule)*		**20**	
21 **Total deductions.** Add the amounts shown in the far right column for lines 9 through 20 .		**21**	

22 **Ordinary income (loss)** from trade or business activities. Subtract line 21 from line 8 . .	**22**	

Please Sign Here	Under penalties of perjury, I declare that I have examined this return, including accompanying schedules and statements, and to the best of my knowledge and belief, it is true, correct, and complete. Declaration of preparer (other than general partner or limited liability company member) is based on all information of which preparer has any knowledge.	
	▶ Signature of general partner or limited liability company member	▶ Date

Paid Preparer's Use Only	Preparer's signature ▶	Date	Check if self-employed ▶ ☐	Preparer's SSN or PTIN
	Firm's name (or yours if self-employed) and address ▶		EIN ▶	
			ZIP code ▶	

For Paperwork Reduction Act Notice, see separate instructions. Cat. No. 11390Z Form **1065** (1999)

APPENDIX A

SCHEDULE K-1 (Form 1065) Department of the Treasury Internal Revenue Service	**Partner's Share of Income, Credits, Deductions, etc.** ▶ See separate instructions. For calendar year 1999 or tax year beginning _____ , 1999, and ending _____	OMB No. 1545-0099 **1999**

Partner's identifying number ▶ | Partnership's identifying number ▶

Partner's name, address, and ZIP code | Partnership's name, address, and ZIP code

A This partner is a ☐ general partner ☐ limited partner
☐ limited liability company member
B What type of entity is this partner? ▶ ....
C Is this partner a ☐ domestic or a ☐ foreign partner?
D Enter partner's percentage of: (i) Before change or termination (ii) End of year
Profit sharing . . . . % .... %
Loss sharing . . . . % .... %
Ownership of capital . . . . % .... %
E IRS Center where partnership filed return:

F Partner's share of liabilities (see instructions):
Nonrecourse . . . . $ ....
Qualified nonrecourse financing . $ ....
Other . . . . $ ....
G Tax shelter registration number . ▶ ....
H Check here if this partnership is a publicly traded partnership as defined in section 469(k)(2) . . . . . ☐
I Check applicable boxes: (1) ☐ Final K-1 (2) ☐ Amended K-1

J Analysis of partner's capital account:

(a) Capital account at beginning of year	(b) Capital contributed during year	(c) Partner's share of lines 3, 4, and 7, Form 1065, Schedule M-2	(d) Withdrawals and distributions	(e) Capital account at end of year (combine columns (a) through (d))
			( )	

	(a) Distributive share item		(b) Amount	(c) 1040 filers enter the amount in column (b) on:
Income (Loss)	**1** Ordinary income (loss) from trade or business activities . . .	**1**		See page 6 of Partner's Instructions for Schedule K-1 (Form 1065).
	2 Net income (loss) from rental real estate activities	**2**		
	3 Net income (loss) from other rental activities	**3**		
	4 Portfolio income (loss):			
	a Interest	**4a**		Sch. B, Part I, line 1
	b Ordinary dividends	**4b**		Sch. B, Part II, line 5
	c Royalties	**4c**		Sch. E, Part I, line 4
	d Net short-term capital gain (loss)	**4d**		Sch. D, line 5, col. (f)
	e Net long-term capital gain (loss):			
	(1) 28% rate gain (loss)	**e(1)**		Sch. D, line 12, col. (g)
	(2) Total for year.	**e(2)**		Sch. D, line 12, col. (f)
	f Other portfolio income (loss) *(attach schedule)*	**4f**		Enter on applicable line of your return.
	5 Guaranteed payments to partner	**5**		See page 6 of Partner's Instructions for Schedule K-1 (Form 1065).
	6 Net section 1231 gain (loss) (other than due to casualty or theft) .	**6**		
	7 Other income (loss) *(attach schedule)*	**7**		Enter on applicable line of your return.
Deductions	**8** Charitable contributions (see instructions) *(attach schedule)* . .	**8**		Sch. A, line 15 or 16
	9 Section 179 expense deduction	**9**		See pages 7 and 8 of Partner's Instructions for Schedule K-1 (Form 1065).
	10 Deductions related to portfolio income *(attach schedule)* . . .	**10**		
	11 Other deductions *(attach schedule)*	**11**		
Credits	**12a** Low-income housing credit:			
	(1) From section 42(j)(5) partnerships for property placed in service before 1990	**a(1)**		
	(2) Other than on line 12a(1) for property placed in service before 1990	**a(2)**		Form 8586, line 5
	(3) From section 42(j)(5) partnerships for property placed in service after 1989	**a(3)**		
	(4) Other than on line 12a(3) for property placed in service after 1989	**a(4)**		
	b Qualified rehabilitation expenditures related to rental real estate activities	**12b**		
	c Credits (other than credits shown on lines 12a and 12b) related to rental real estate activities.	**12c**		See page 8 of Partner's Instructions for Schedule K-1 (Form 1065).
	d Credits related to other rental activities	**12d**		
	13 Other credits.	**13**		

For Paperwork Reduction Act Notice, see Instructions for Form 1065. | Cat. No. 11394R | Schedule K-1 (Form 1065) 1999

APPENDIX A

☐ CORRECTED (if checked)

RECIPIENT'S/LENDER'S name, address, and telephone number	* **Caution:** *The amount shown may not be fully deductible by you. Limits based on the loan amount and the cost and value of the secured property may apply. Also, you may only deduct interest to the extent it was incurred by you, actually paid by you, and not reimbursed by another person.*	OMB No. 1545-0901 **2000** Form **1098**	**Mortgage Interest Statement**
RECIPIENT'S Federal identification no.	PAYER'S social security number	1 Mortgage interest received from payer(s)/borrower(s)* $	**Copy B For Payer**
PAYER'S/BORROWER'S name		2 Points paid on purchase of principal residence (See **Box 2** on back.) $	The information in boxes 1, 2, and 3 is important tax information and is being furnished to the Internal Revenue Service. If you are required to file a return, a negligence penalty or other
Street address (including apt. no.)		3 Refund of overpaid interest (See **Box 3** on back.) $	sanction may be imposed on you if the IRS determines that an
City, state, and ZIP code		4	underpayment of tax results because you overstated a deduction for this mortgage interest or for these points
Account number (optional)			or because you did not report this refund of interest on your return.

Form **1098**   (Keep for your records.)   Department of the Treasury - Internal Revenue Service

Instructions for Payer/Borrower

A person (including a financial institution, a governmental unit, and a cooperative housing corporation) who is engaged in a trade or business and, in the course of such trade or business, received from you at least $600 of mortgage interest (including certain points) on any one mortgage in the calendar year must furnish this statement to you.

If you received this statement as the payer of record on a mortgage on which there are other borrowers, please furnish each of the other borrowers with information about the proper distribution of amounts reported on this form. Each borrower is entitled to deduct only the amount he or she paid and points paid by the seller that represent his or her share of the amount allowable as a deduction for mortgage interest and points. Each borrower may have to include in income a share of any amount reported in box 3.

If your mortgage payments were subsidized by a government agency, you may not be able to deduct the amount of the subsidy.

Box 1. Shows the mortgage interest received by the interest recipient during the year. This amount includes interest on any obligation secured by real property, including a home equity, line of credit, or credit card loan. This amount does not include points, government subsidy payments, or seller payments on a "buy-down" mortgage. Such amounts are deductible by you only in certain circumstances. **Caution:** *If you prepaid interest in 2000 that accrued in full by January 15, 2001, this prepaid interest may be included in box 1. However, you cannot deduct the prepaid amount in 2000 even though it may be included in box 1.* If you hold a mortgage credit certificate and can claim the

mortgage interest credit, see **Form 8396,** Mortgage Interest Credit. If the interest was paid on a mortgage, home equity, line of credit, or credit card loan secured by your personal residence, you may be subject to a deduction limitation. For example, if a home equity loan exceeds $100,000 ($50,000 if married filing separately) or, together with other home loans, exceeds the fair market value of your home (such as in a high loan-to-value loan), your interest deduction may be limited. For more information, see **Pub. 936,** Home Mortgage Interest Deduction.

Box 2. Not all points are reportable to you. Box 2 shows points you or the seller paid this year for the purchase of your principal residence that are required to be reported to you. Generally, these points are fully deductible in the year paid, but you must subtract seller-paid points from the basis of your residence. Other points not reported in this box may also be deductible. See Pub. 936 or your Schedule A (Form 1040) instructions.

Box 3. Do not deduct this amount. It is a refund (or credit) for overpayment(s) of interest you made in a prior year or years. If you itemized deductions in the year(s) you paid the interest, include the total amount shown in box 3 on the "Other income" line of your 2000 Form 1040. However, do not report the refund as income if you did not itemize deductions in the year(s) you paid the interest. No adjustment to your prior year(s) tax return(s) is necessary. For more information, see "Recoveries" in **Pub. 525,** Taxable and Nontaxable Income.

Box 4. The interest recipient may use this box to give you other information, such as real estate taxes or insurance paid from escrow.

432

APPENDIX A

☐ CORRECTED (if checked)

RECIPIENT'S/LENDER'S name, address, and telephone number		OMB No. 1545-1576	**Student Loan Interest Statement**
		2000	
		Form **1098-E**	

RECIPIENT'S Federal identification no.	BORROWER'S social security number	1 Student loan interest received by lender	**Copy B**
		$	**For Borrower**
BORROWER'S name			This is important tax information and is being furnished to the Internal Revenue Service. If you are required to file a return, a negligence penalty or other sanction may be imposed on you if the IRS determines that an underpayment of tax results because you overstated a deduction for student loan interest.
Street address (including apt. no.)			
City, state, and ZIP code			
Account number (optional)			

Form **1098-E**   (Keep for your records.)   Department of the Treasury - Internal Revenue Service

Instructions for Borrower

A person (including a financial institution, a governmental unit, and an educational institution) that is engaged in a trade or business and, in the course of such trade or business, received interest of $600 or more during the year on a student loan used solely to pay for qualified higher education expenses must furnish this statement to you.

You may be able to deduct student loan interest on your income tax return if the interest payments were made during the first 60 months the interest payments were required. However, the interest reported on this statement may be different from the interest you may deduct. See the "Student Loan Interest Deduction Worksheet" in your Form 1040 or 1040A instructions. Also, see **Pub. 970,** Tax Benefits for Higher Education, for more information.

Box 1. Shows the interest received by the lender during the year on this student loan.

APPENDIX A

☐ CORRECTED (if checked)

FILER'S name, street address, city, state, ZIP code, and telephone number	1	OMB No. 1545-1574	**Tuition Payments Statement**
	2	2000 Form **1098-T**	
FILER'S Federal identification no.	STUDENT'S social security number		**Copy B** **For Student**
STUDENT'S name Street address (including apt. no.) City, state, and ZIP code			This is important tax information and is being furnished to the Internal Revenue Service.
Account number (optional)	3 At least half-time student (if checked) ☐	4 Graduate student (if checked) . . ☐	

Form **1098-T** (Keep for your records.) Department of the Treasury - Internal Revenue Service

Instructions for Student

An eligible educational institution, such as your college or university, that receives qualified tuition and related expenses on your behalf must furnish this statement to you. This information will help to determine whether you, or the person who may claim you as a dependent, may claim an income tax credit for the Hope credit or lifetime learning credit on **Form 8863,** Education Credits. For information about these credits, see **Pub. 970,** Tax Benefits for Higher Education.

Caution: *If you are claimed as a dependent by another person (including your parent(s)), you cannot claim the Hope credit or lifetime learning credit. However, the person claiming you may be entitled to the credit on his or her tax return.*

Boxes 1 and 2. The reporting institution is not required to but may provide information in these boxes.

Box 3. Shows whether you are considered to be carrying at least one-half the normal full-time work load for your course of study at the reporting institution. If you are at least a half-time student for at least one academic period beginning during the year, you meet one of the requirements for the Hope credit. You do not have to be a half-time student to qualify for the lifetime learning credit.

Box 4. Shows whether you are considered to be enrolled exclusively in a program leading to a graduate degree, graduate-level certificate, or other recognized graduate-level educational credential. If you are enrolled exclusively in a graduate program, you are not eligible for the Hope credit, but you may qualify for the lifetime learning credit.

434

☐ CORRECTED (if checked)

PAYER'S name, street address, city, state, ZIP code, and telephone no.		1a Date of sale	OMB No. 1545-0715	Proceeds From Broker and Barter Exchange Transactions
		1b CUSIP No.	20**00** Form **1099-B**	
		2 Stocks, bonds, etc. $	Reported to IRS } ☐ Gross proceeds ☐ Gross proceeds less commissions and option premiums	
PAYER'S Federal identification number	RECIPIENT'S identification number	3 Bartering $	4 Federal income tax withheld $	**Copy B** **For Recipient**
RECIPIENT'S name		5 Description		This is important tax information and is being furnished to the Internal Revenue Service. If you are required to file a return, a negligence penalty or other sanction may be imposed on you if this income is taxable and the IRS determines that it has not been reported.
		Regulated Futures Contracts		
Street address (including apt. no.)		6 Profit or (loss) realized in 2000 $	7 Unrealized profit or (loss) on open contracts—12/31/99 $	
City, state, and ZIP code		8 Unrealized profit or (loss) on open contracts—12/31/2000 $	9 Aggregate profit or (loss) $	
Account number (optional)				

Form **1099-B**   (Keep for your records.)   Department of the Treasury - Internal Revenue Service

Instructions for Recipient

Brokers and barter exchanges must report proceeds from transactions to you and to the Internal Revenue Service. This form is used to report these proceeds.

Box 1a. Shows the trade date of the transaction. For aggregate reporting, no entry will be present.

Box 1b. For broker transactions, may show the CUSIP (Committee on Uniform Security Identification Procedures) number of the item reported.

Box 2. Shows the proceeds from transactions involving stocks, bonds, other debt obligations, commodities, or forward contracts. Losses on forward contracts are shown in parentheses. This box does not include proceeds from regulated futures contracts. The broker must indicate whether gross proceeds or gross proceeds less commissions and option premiums were reported to the IRS. Report this amount on **Schedule D (Form 1040)**, Capital Gains and Losses.

Box 3. Shows the fair market value of any trade credits or scrip credited to your account for exchanges of property or services as well as cash received through a barter exchange. Report bartering income in the proper part of Form 1040. See **Pub. 525**, Taxable and Nontaxable Income, for information on how to report this income.

Box 4. Shows backup withholding. For example, persons not furnishing their taxpayer identification number to the payer become subject to backup withholding at a 31% rate on certain payments. See **Form W-9**, Request for Taxpayer Identification Number and Certification, for information on backup withholding. **Include this amount on your income tax return as tax withheld.**

Box 5. Shows a brief description of the item or service for which the proceeds or bartering income is being reported. For regulated futures contracts and forward contracts, "RFC" or other appropriate description may be shown.

Box 6. Shows the profit or (loss) realized on regulated futures or foreign currency contracts closed during 2000.

Box 7. Shows any year-end adjustment to the profit or (loss) shown in box 6 due to open contracts on December 31, 1999.

Box 8. Shows the unrealized profit or (loss) on open contracts held in your account on December 31, 2000. These are considered sold as of that date. This will become an adjustment reported in box 7 in 2001.

Box 9. Boxes 6, 7, and 8 are used to figure the aggregate profit or (loss) on regulated futures or foreign currency contracts for the year. Include this figure on your 2000 **Form 6781**, Gains and Losses From Section 1256 Contracts and Straddles.

APPENDIX A

☐ CORRECTED (if checked)

PAYER'S name, street address, city, state, ZIP code, and telephone no.	1 Ordinary dividends $	OMB No. 1545-0110	**Dividends and Distributions**
	2a Total capital gain distr. $	**2000** Form **1099-DIV**	
PAYER'S Federal identification number	RECIPIENT'S identification number	2b 28% rate gain $	2c Unrecap. sec. 1250 gain $	**Copy B** **For Recipient**
RECIPIENT'S name		2d Section 1202 gain $	3 Nontaxable distributions $	This is important tax information and is being furnished to the Internal Revenue Service. If you are required to file a return, a negligence penalty or other sanction may be imposed on you if this income is taxable and the IRS determines that it has not been reported.
Street address (including apt. no.)		4 Federal income tax withheld $	5 Investment expenses $	
City, state, and ZIP code		6 Foreign tax paid $	7 Foreign country or U.S. possession	
Account number (optional)		8 Cash liquidation distr. $	9 Noncash liquidation distr. $	

Form **1099-DIV**   (Keep for your records.)   Department of the Treasury - Internal Revenue Service

Instructions for Recipient

Caution: *if an amount appears in box 2a, you must file Form 1040. You may not file Form 1040A.*

Box 1. Ordinary dividends, which include any net short-term capital gains from a mutual fund, are fully taxable. Include this amount on the "Ordinary dividends" line of Form 1040 or 1040A. Also report it on Schedule B (Form 1040) or Schedule 1 (Form 1040A), if required. This amount includes any amount shown in box 5.

The amount shown may be a distribution from an employee stock ownership plan (ESOP). Report it as a dividend on your income tax return, but treat it as a plan distribution, not as investment income, for any other purpose.

Box 2a. Shows total capital gain distributions (long-term) from a regulated investment company or real estate investment trust. Amounts shown in boxes 2b, 2c, and 2d are included in box 2a. Report the amount in box 2a on Schedule D (Form 1040), Part II. But, if **no amount** is shown in boxes 2b–2d **and** your **only** capital gains and losses are capital gain distributions, you may be able to report the amount in box 2a on the "Capital gain or (loss)" line of Form 1040 rather than on Schedule D (Form 1040). See the Form 1040 instructions.

Box 2b. Shows 28% rate gain from sales or exchange of collectibles. Report this amount on Schedule D (Form 1040), Part II.

Box 2c. Shows unrecaptured section 1250 gain from certain depreciable real property. Report this amount on the **Unrecaptured Section 1250 Gain Worksheet** in the Instructions for Schedule D (Form 1040).

Box 2d. Section 1202 gain from certain small business stock may be subject to a 50% exclusion. See the Schedule D (Form 1040) instructions.

Box 3. This part of the distribution is nontaxable because it is a return of your cost (or other basis). You must reduce your cost (or other basis) by this amount for figuring gain or loss when you sell your stock. But if you get back all your cost (or other basis), report future nontaxable distributions as capital gains, even though this form shows them as nontaxable. See **Pub. 550,** Investment Income and Expenses.

Box 4. Shows backup withholding. For example, persons not furnishing their taxpayer identification number to the payer become subject to backup withholding at a 31% rate on certain payments. See **Form W-9,** Request for Taxpayer Identification Number and Certification, for information on backup withholding. **Include this amount on your income tax return as tax withheld.**

Box 5. Any amount shown is your share of expenses of a nonpublicly offered regulated investment company, generally a nonpublicly offered mutual fund. If you file Form 1040, you may deduct these expenses on the "Other expenses" line on Schedule A (Form 1040) subject to the 2% limit. This amount is included in box 1.

Box 6. You may be able to claim this foreign tax as a deduction or a credit on Form 1040. See your Form 1040 instructions.

Boxes 8 and 9. Show cash and noncash liquidation distributions.

Nominees. If this form includes amounts belonging to another person, you are considered a nominee recipient. You must file Form 1099-DIV with the IRS for each of the other owners to show their share of the income, and you must furnish a Form 1099-DIV to each. A husband or wife is not required to file a nominee return to show amounts owned by the other. See the **2000 General Instructions for Forms 1099, 1098, 5498, and W-2G.**

☐ CORRECTED (if checked)

PAYER'S name, street address, city, state, ZIP code, and telephone no.	1 Unemployment compensation $	OMB No. 1545-0120	Certain Government and Qualified State Tuition Program Payments
	2 State or local income tax refunds, credits, or offsets $	19**99** Form **1099-G**	
PAYER'S Federal identification number	RECIPIENT'S identification number	3 Box 2 amount is for tax year	4 Federal income tax withheld $	Copy B
RECIPIENT'S name		5 Qualified state tuition program earnings $	6 Taxable grants $	For Recipient
Street address (including apt. no.)		7 Agriculture payments $	8 The amount in box 2 applies to income from a trade or business ▶ ☐	This is important tax information and is being furnished to the Internal Revenue Service. If you are required to file a return, a negligence penalty or other sanction may be imposed on you if this income is taxable and the IRS determines that it has not been reported.
City, state, and ZIP code				
Account number (optional)				

Form **1099-G**   (Keep for your records.)   Department of the Treasury - Internal Revenue Service

Instructions for Recipient

Box 1. Shows the total unemployment compensation paid to you this year. Report this amount as income on the unemployment compensation line of your income tax return. If you expect to receive these benefits in the future, you can ask the payer to withhold Federal income tax from each payment Or, you can make estimated tax payments using **Form 1040-ES,** Estimated Tax for Individuals.

Box 2. Shows refunds, credits, or offsets of state or local income tax you received. It may be taxable to you if you deducted the state or local income tax paid as an itemized deduction on your Federal income tax return. Even if you did not receive the amount shown, for example, because it was credited to your state or local estimated tax, it is still taxable if it was deducted. Any interest received on this must be reported as interest income on your tax return. See the instructions for your tax return.

Box 3. Identifies the tax year for which the refunds, credits, or offsets shown in box 2 were made. If there is no entry in this box, the refund is for 1998 taxes.

Box 4. Shows backup withholding or withholding you requested on unemployment compensation, Commodity Credit Corporation loans, or certain crop disaster payments. Generally, a payer must backup withhold on certain payments at a 31% rate if you did not give your taxpayer identification number to the payer.

See **Form W-9,** Request for Taxpayer Identification Number and Certification, for information on backup withholding. **Include this on your income tax return as tax withheld.**

Box 5. Shows the earnings part of any distribution (including in-kind distributions) from a qualified state tuition program. Report this amount as income on the qualified state tuition program earnings line of your income tax return.

Box 6. Shows the amount of taxable grants you received from the Federal, state, or local government.

Box 7. Shows the amount of Department of Agriculture payments that are taxable to you. If the payer shown is anyone other than the Department of Agriculture, it means the payer has received a payment, as a nominee, that is taxable to you. This may represent the entire agricultural subsidy payment received on your behalf by the nominee, or it may be your pro rata share of the original payment. See **Pub. 225,** Farmers Tax Guide, and the Instructions for **Schedule F (Form 1040)** Profit or Loss From Farming, for information about where to report this income.

Box 8. If this box is checked, the refunds, credits, or offsets in box 2 are attributable to an income tax that applies exclusively to income from a trade or business and is not a tax of general application. If taxable, report the amount in box 2 on Schedule C, C-EZ, or F (Form 1040), as appropriate.

☐ CORRECTED (if checked)

PAYER'S name, street address, city, state, ZIP code, and telephone no.	Payer's RTN (optional)	OMB No. 1545-0112	
		20**00** Interest Income	
		Form **1099-INT**	

PAYER'S Federal identification number	RECIPIENT'S identification number	1 Interest income not included in box 3 $	**Copy B** **For Recipient**
RECIPIENT'S name		2 Early withdrawal penalty $	3 Interest on U.S. Savings Bonds and Treas. obligations $	This is important tax information and is being furnished to the Internal Revenue Service. If you are required to file a return, a negligence penalty or other sanction may be imposed on you if this income is taxable and the IRS determines that it has not been reported.

RECIPIENT'S name

Street address (including apt. no.)

| 4 Federal income tax withheld $ | 5 Investment expenses $ |
| 6 Foreign tax paid | 7 Foreign country or U.S. possession |

City, state, and ZIP code

Account number (optional) $

Form **1099-INT**   (Keep for your records.)   Department of the Treasury - Internal Revenue Service

Instructions for Recipient

Box 1. Shows interest paid to you during the calendar year by the payer. This does not include interest shown in box 3.

If you receive a Form 1099-INT for interest paid on a tax-exempt obligation, see the instructions for your income tax return.

Box 2. Shows interest or principal forfeited because of early withdrawal of time savings. You may deduct this on the "Penalty on early withdrawal of savings" line of **Form 1040.**

Box 3. Shows interest on U.S. Savings Bonds, Treasury bills, Treasury bonds, and Treasury notes. This may or may not be all taxable. See **Pub. 550,** Investment Income and Expenses. This interest is exempt from state and local income taxes. **This interest is not included in box 1.**

Box 4. Shows backup withholding. For example, persons not furnishing their taxpayer identification number to the payer become subject to backup withholding at a 31% rate. See **Form W-9,** Request for Taxpayer Identification Number and Certification, for information on backup withholding. **Include this amount on your income tax return as tax withheld.**

Box 5. Any amount shown is your share of investment expenses of a single-class REMIC. If you file Form 1040, you may deduct these expenses on the "Other expenses" line of **Schedule A (Form 1040)** subject to the 2% limit. This amount is included in box 1.

Box 6. Shows foreign tax paid. You may be able to claim this tax as a deduction or a credit on your Form 1040. See your Form 1040 instructions.

Nominees. If this form includes amounts belonging to another person, you are considered a nominee recipient. You must file Form 1099-INT for each of the other owners showing the income allocable to each. You must also furnish a Form 1099-INT to each of the other owners. File Form(s) 1099-INT with **Form 1096,** Annual Summary and Transmittal of U.S. Information Returns, with the Internal Revenue Service Center for your area. On each Form 1099-INT, list yourself as the "payer" and the other owner as the "recipient." On Form 1096, list yourself as the "filer." A husband or wife is not required to file a nominee return to show amounts owned by the other.

APPENDIX A

☐ CORRECTED (if checked)

| PAYER'S name, street address, city, state, ZIP code, and telephone no. | 1 Gross long-term care benefits paid $ | OMB No. 1545-1519 | Long-Term Care and Accelerated Death Benefits |
| | 2 Accelerated death benefits paid $ | 2000 Form **1099-LTC** | |

PAYER'S Federal identification number	POLICYHOLDER'S identification number	3 ☐ Per diem ☐ Reimbursed amount	INSURED'S social security no.	**Copy B** **For Policyholder**
POLICYHOLDER'S name		INSURED'S name		This is important tax information and is being furnished to the Internal Revenue Service. If you are required to file a return, a negligence penalty or other sanction may be imposed on you if this item is required to be reported and the IRS determines that it has not been reported.
Street address (including apt. no.)		Street address (including apt. no.)		
City, state, and ZIP code		City, state, and ZIP code		
Account number (optional)		4 (optional) ☐ Chronically ill ☐ Terminally ill	Date certified	

Form **1099-LTC** (Keep for your records.) Department of the Treasury - Internal Revenue Service

Instructions for Policyholder

A payer, such as an insurance company or a viatical settlement provider, must give this form to you for payments made under a long-term care insurance contract or for accelerated death benefits. Payments include those made directly to you (or to the insured) and those made to third parties.

A long-term care insurance contract provides coverage of expenses for long-term care services for an individual who has been certified by a licensed health care practitioner as chronically ill. A life insurance company or viatical settlement provider may pay accelerated death benefits if the insured has been certified by either a physician as terminally ill or by a licensed health care practitioner as chronically ill.

Long-term care insurance contract. Amounts received under a **qualified** long-term care insurance contract are excluded from your income. However, if payments are made on a per diem basis, the amount you may exclude is limited. The per diem exclusion limit must be allocated among all policyholders who own qualified long-term care insurance contracts for the same insured. See **Pub. 502,** Medical and Dental Expenses, and **Form 8853,** Medical Savings Accounts and Long-Term Care Insurance Contracts, for more information.

Per diem basis. This means payments made on a periodic basis without regard to the actual expenses incurred during the period to which the payments relate.

Accelerated death benefits. Amounts paid as accelerated death benefits are fully excludable from your income if the insured has been certified by a physician as terminally ill. Accelerated death benefits paid on behalf of individuals who are certified as chronically ill are excludable from income to the same extent they would be if paid under a qualified long-term care insurance contract.

Box 1. Shows the gross benefits paid under a long-term care insurance contract during the year.

Box 2. Shows the gross accelerated death benefits paid during the year.

Box 3. Shows whether the amount in box 1 or 2 was paid on a per diem basis or was reimbursement of actual long-term care expenses. This box may not be marked if the insured was terminally ill.

Box 4. May show whether the insured was certified chronically ill or terminally ill, and the latest date certified.

439

☐ CORRECTED (if checked)

PAYER'S name, street address, city, state, ZIP code, and telephone no.	1 Rents $	OMB No. 1545-0115	
	2 Royalties $	**2000**	**Miscellaneous Income**
	3 Other income $	Form **1099-MISC**	
PAYER'S Federal identification number RECIPIENT'S identification number	4 Federal income tax withheld $	5 Fishing boat proceeds $	**Copy B** **For Recipient**
RECIPIENT'S name	6 Medical and health care payments $	7 Nonemployee compensation $	This is important tax information and is being furnished to the
Street address (including apt. no.)	8 Substitute payments in lieu of dividends or interest $	9 Payer made direct sales of $5,000 or more of consumer products to a buyer (recipient) for resale ▶ ☐	Internal Revenue Service. If you are required to file a return, a negligence penalty or other sanction may be
City, state, and ZIP code	10 Crop insurance proceeds $	11 State income tax withheld $	imposed on you if this income is taxable and the IRS determines that
Account number (optional)	12 State/Payer's state number	13 $	it has not been reported.

Form **1099-MISC**   (Keep for your records.)   Department of the Treasury - Internal Revenue Service

Amounts shown on this form may be subject to self-employment tax. If your net income from self-employment is $400 or more, you must file a return and compute your self-employment tax on **Schedule SE (Form 1040).** See **Pub. 533,** Self-Employment Tax, for information on self-employment income. If no income or social security and Medicare taxes were withheld by the payer, you may have to make estimated tax payments if you are still receiving these payments. See **Form 1040-ES,** Estimated Tax for Individuals.

If you are an individual, report the taxable amounts shown on this form on Form 1040, as explained below. (Others, such as corporations, fiduciaries, or partnerships, report the amounts on the proper line of your tax return.)

Boxes 1 and 2. Report rents from real estate on Schedule E (Form 1040). If you provided significant services to the tenant, sold real estate as a business, or rented personal property as a business, report on Schedule C or C-EZ (Form 1040). For royalties on timber, coal, and iron ore, see **Pub. 544,** Sales and Other Dispositions of Assets.

Box 3. Generally, report on the "Other income" line of Form 1040 and identify the payment. If it is trade or business income, report this amount on Schedule C, C-EZ, or F (Form 1040). The amount shown may be payments you received as the beneficiary of a deceased employee, prizes, awards, taxable damages, Indian gaming profits, or other taxable income.

Box 4. Shows backup withholding or withholding on Indian gaming profits. Generally, a payer must backup withhold at a 31% rate if you did not furnish your taxpayer identification number to the payer. See **Form W-9,** Request for Taxpayer Identification Number and Certification, for information on backup withholding. **Include this on your income tax return as tax withheld.**

Box 5. An amount in this box means the fishing boat operator considers you self-employed. Report this amount on Schedule C or C-EZ (Form 1040). See **Pub. 595,** Tax Highlights for Commercial Fishermen.

Box 6. Report on Schedule C or C-EZ (Form 1040).

Box 7. Generally shows nonemployee compensation. If you are in the trade or business of catching fish, box 7 may show cash you received for the sale of fish. Generally, payments reported in this box are income from self-employment. Since you received this form, rather than Form W-2, the payer may have considered you self-employed and did not withhold social security or Medicare taxes. Report self-employment income on Schedule C, C-EZ, or F (Form 1040), **and compute the self-employment tax on Schedule SE (Form 1040).** However, if you are not self-employed, report this amount on the "Wages, salaries, tips, etc." line of Form 1040. Call the IRS for information about how to report any social security and Medicare taxes.

Box 8. Shows substitute payments in lieu of dividends or tax-exempt interest received by your broker on your behalf after transfer of your securities for use in a short sale. Report on the "Other income" line of Form 1040.

Box 9. If marked, sales to you of consumer products on a buy-sell, deposit-commission, or any other basis for resale have amounted to $5,000 or more. The person filing this return does not have to show a dollar amount in this box. Generally, report any income from your sale of these products on Schedule C or C-EZ (Form 1040).

Box 10. Report on the "Crop insurance proceeds. . ." line on Schedule F (Form 1040).

Box 13. "A" or "EPP" may be shown to identify the income you received:

A—Gross proceeds paid to an attorney in connection with legal services. Report only the taxable part as income on your return.

EPP—Excess golden parachute payments subject to a 20% excise tax. See your Form 1040 instructions for the "Total Tax" line. The amount in box 7 is your total compensation.

Other information may be provided to you in box 13 without "A" or "EPP."

☐ CORRECTED (if checked)

PAYER'S name, street address, city, state, and ZIP code		OMB No. 1545-1517	**Distributions From an MSA or Medicare+Choice MSA**
		19**99**	
		Form **1099-MSA**	

PAYER'S Federal identification number	RECIPIENT'S identification number	1 Gross distribution $	2 Earnings on excess contributions $	**Copy B** **For Recipient**
RECIPIENT'S name		3 Distribution code	4 FMV on date of death $	
Street address (including apt. no.)		5 Medicare+Choice MSA . . . . ☐		This information is being furnished to the Internal Revenue Service.
City, state, and ZIP code				
Account number (optional)				

Form **1099-MSA**   (Keep for your records.)   Department of the Treasury - Internal Revenue Service

Instructions for Recipient

Distributions from a medical savings account (MSA) or Medicare+Choice MSA (M+C MSA) are reported to recipients on Form 1099-MSA. You must file **Form 8853**, Medical Savings Accounts and Long-Term Care Insurance Contracts, with your Form 1040, to report a distribution from an MSA or M+C MSA.

The payer is not required to compute the taxable amount of any distribution. An MSA distribution is not taxable if you used it to pay qualified medical expenses of the account holder and family or you rolled it over to another MSA. However, see **Box 2** below. If you did not use the MSA distribution for qualified medical expenses or you did not roll it over, you must include the distribution in your income on Form 8853, and you may owe a 15% penalty.

An M+C MSA distribution is not taxable if you used it to pay qualified medical expenses of the account holder only. However, if you did not use the M+C MSA distribution for qualified medical expenses, you must include the distribution in your income on Form 8853, and you may owe a 50% penalty if you did not maintain a minimum account balance.

Spouse beneficiary. If you inherited an MSA or M+C MSA because of the death of your spouse, special rules apply. See Form 8853 and its instructions.

Estate beneficiary. If the MSA or M+C MSA account holder dies and the estate is the beneficiary, the fair market value (FMV) of the account on the date of death is includible in the account holder's gross income on the account holder's final income tax return.

Nonspouse beneficiary. If you inherited the MSA or M+C MSA from someone who was not your spouse, you must report as income on Form 8853 the FMV of the account on the date of death. Report the FMV on your tax return for the year the account owner died even if you received the distribution from the account in a later year. Any earnings on the account after the date of death (box 1 minus box 4) are taxable.

Box 1. Shows the amount you received this year. The amount may have been a direct payment to the medical service provider or distributed to you.

Box 2. Shows the earnings on any excess contributions you withdrew from an MSA by the due date of your income tax return. If you withdrew the excess, plus any earnings, by the due date of your income tax return, you must include the earnings in your income in the year you received the distribution even if you used it to pay qualified medical expenses. This amount is included in box 1.

Box 3. These codes identify the distribution you received:

1—Normal distribution

2—Excess contributions

3—Disability

4—Death distribution other than code 6

5—Prohibited transaction

6—Death distribution after year of death to a nonspouse beneficiary

Box 4. If the account holder died, shows the fair market value (FMV) of the account on the date of death.

Box 5. If this box is checked, the distribution was from a Medicare+Choice MSA.

441

☐ VOID   ☐ CORRECTED

PAYER'S name, street address, city, state, and ZIP code	1 Gross distribution $	OMB No. 1545-0119	Distributions From Pensions, Annuities, Retirement or Profit-Sharing Plans, IRAs, Insurance Contracts, etc.
	2a Taxable amount $	2000 Form 1099-R	
	2b Taxable amount not determined ☐	Total distribution ☐	Copy 1 For State, City, or Local Tax Department
PAYER'S Federal identification number / RECIPIENT'S identification number	3 Capital gain (included in box 2a) $	4 Federal income tax withheld $	
RECIPIENT'S name	5 Employee contributions or insurance premiums $	6 Net unrealized appreciation in employer's securities $	
Street address (including apt. no.)	7 Distribution code	IRA/SEP/SIMPLE ☐	8 Other $ %
City, state, and ZIP code	9a Your percentage of total distribution %	9b Total employee contributions $	
Account number (optional)	10 State tax withheld $ / $	11 State/Payer's state no.	12 State distribution $ / $
	13 Local tax withheld $ / $	14 Name of locality	15 Local distribution $ / $

Form **1099-R**   Department of the Treasury - Internal Revenue Service

Instructions for Recipient

Generally, distributions from pensions, annuities, profit-sharing and retirement plans, IRAs, insurance contracts, etc., are reported to recipients on Form 1099-R.

Qualified plans. If your annuity starting date is after 1997, you must use the simplified method to figure your taxable amount if your payer did not show the taxable amount in box 2a. See **Pub. 575,** Pension and Annuity Income.

IRAs. For distributions from a traditional individual retirement arrangement (IRA), simplified employee pension (SEP), or savings incentive match plan for employees (SIMPLE), generally the payer is not required to compute the taxable amount. Therefore, the amounts in boxes 1 and 2a will be the same most of the time. See the Form 1040 or 1040A instructions to determine the taxable amount. If you are at least age 70½, you must take minimum distributions from your IRA. If you do not, you may be subject to a 50% excise tax on the amount that should have been distributed. See **Pub. 590,** Individual Retirement Arrangements (IRAs), and **Pub. 560,** Retirement Plans for Small Business (SEP, Keogh, and SIMPLE Plans), for more information on IRAs.

Roth and education IRAs. For distributions from a Roth IRA or an education IRA (Ed IRA), generally the payer is not required to compute any taxable amount. You must compute any taxable amount. Report on **Form 8606,** Nondeductible IRAs. An amount shown in box 2a may be taxable earnings on an excess contribution.

Loans treated as distributions. If you borrow money from a qualified plan, tax-sheltered annuity, or government plan, you may have to treat the loan as a distribution and include all or part of the amount borrowed in your income. There are exceptions to this rule. If your loan is taxable, Code L will be shown in box 7. See Pub. 575.

Box 1. Shows the total amount you received this year. The amount may have been a direct rollover, a transfer or conversion to a Roth IRA, a recharacterized IRA contribution, or you may have received it as periodic payments, as nonperiodic payments, or as a total distribution. Report this amount on Form 1040 or 1040A on the line for "Total IRA distributions" or "Total pensions and annuities" (or the line for "Taxable amount"), or on Form 8606, whichever applies, unless this is a lump-sum distribution and you are using **Form 4972,** Tax on Lump-Sum Distributions. However, if you have not reached minimum retirement age, report your disability payments on the line

for "Wages, salaries, tips, etc." Also report on that line corrective distributions of excess deferrals, excess contributions, or excess aggregate contributions.

If you received a death benefit payment made by an employer but not made from the employer's pension, profit-sharing, or retirement plan, see **Pub. 525,** Taxable and Nontaxable Income.

If a life insurance, annuity, or endowment contract has been transferred tax free to another trustee or contract issuer, an amount will be shown in this box and Code 6 will be shown in box 7. You need not report this on your tax return.

Box 2a. This part of the distribution is generally taxable. If there is no entry in this box, the payer may not have all the facts needed to figure the taxable amount. In that case, the first box in box 2b should be marked. You may want to get one of the following publications from the IRS to help you figure the taxable amount: **Pub. 571,** Tax-Sheltered Annuity Programs for Employees of Public Schools and Certain Tax-Exempt Organizations, **Pub. 575, Pub. 590, Pub. 721,** Tax Guide to U.S. Civil Service Retirement Benefits, or **Pub. 939,** General Rule for Pensions and Annuities. For an IRA distribution, see **IRAs** and **Roth and education IRAs** above. For a direct rollover, zero should be shown, and you must enter zero (-0-) on the "Taxable amount" line of your tax return.

If this is a total distribution from a qualified plan and you were at least age 59½ on the date of distribution (or you are the beneficiary of someone who had reached age 59½ or someone born before 1936), you may be eligible for the 5- or 10-year tax option. See Form 4972 for more information. The 5- or 10-year tax option does not apply to any IRA or to tax-sheltered annuities.

Box 2b. If the first checkbox is marked, the payer was unable to determine the taxable amount, and box 2a should be blank unless this is a traditional IRA, SEP, or SIMPLE distribution. If the second checkbox is marked, the distribution was a total distribution that closed out your account.

Box 3. If you received a lump-sum distribution from a qualified plan and you were born before 1936 (or you are the beneficiary of someone born before 1936), you may be able to elect to treat this amount as a capital gain on Form 4972 (not on Sch. D (Form 1040)). See the **Instructions for Form 4972.** For a charitable gift annuity, report as a long-term capital gain on Schedule D (Form 1040) instead of on Form 1040.

(Continued on the back of Copy C.)

442

Form **1120**	U.S. Corporation Income Tax Return	OMB No. 1545-0123
Department of the Treasury Internal Revenue Service	For calendar year 1999 or tax year beginning ...., 1999, ending ...., ... ▶ **Instructions are separate. See page 1 for Paperwork Reduction Act Notice.**	**19 99**

A Check if a:			**B** Employer identification number
1 Consolidated return (attach Form 851) ☐	Use IRS label. Other- wise, print or type.	Name	
2 Personal holding co. (attach Sch. PH) ☐		Number, street, and room or suite no. (If a P.O. box, see page 5 of instructions.)	**C** Date incorporated
3 Personal service corp. (as defined in Temporary Regs. sec. 1.441-4T— see instructions) ☐		City or town, state, and ZIP code	**D** Total assets (see page 6 of instructions)

E Check applicable boxes: (1) ☐ Initial return (2) ☐ Final return (3) ☐ Change of address $

Income	1a	Gross receipts or sales	**b** Less returns and allowances	**c** Bal ▶	**1c**	
	2	Cost of goods sold (Schedule A, line 8)	**2**	
	3	Gross profit. Subtract line 2 from line 1c	**3**	
	4	Dividends (Schedule C, line 19)	**4**	
	5	Interest	**5**	
	6	Gross rents	**6**	
	7	Gross royalties	**7**	
	8	Capital gain net income (attach Schedule D (Form 1120)) . . .	**8**	
	9	Net gain or (loss) from Form 4797, Part II, line 18 (attach Form 4797) .	**9**	
	10	Other income (see page 7 of instructions—attach schedule) . . .	**10**	
	11	**Total income.** Add lines 3 through 10 . . . . ▶	**11**	

Deductions (See instructions for limitations on deductions.)	12	Compensation of officers (Schedule E, line 4)	**12**	
	13	Salaries and wages (less employment credits)	**13**	
	14	Repairs and maintenance	**14**	
	15	Bad debts	**15**	
	16	Rents	**16**	
	17	Taxes and licenses	**17**	
	18	Interest	**18**	
	19	Charitable contributions (see page 9 of instructions for 10% limitation) .	**19**	
	20	Depreciation (attach Form 4562)	**20**		**21b**	
	21	Less depreciation claimed on Schedule A and elsewhere on return . . .	**21a**	
	22	Depletion	**22**	
	23	Advertising	**23**	
	24	Pension, profit-sharing, etc., plans	**24**	
	25	Employee benefit programs	**25**	
	26	Other deductions (attach schedule)	**26**	
	27	**Total deductions.** Add lines 12 through 26 . . . . . . ▶	**27**	
	28	Taxable income before net operating loss deduction and special deductions. Subtract line 27 from line 11	**28**	
	29	**Less:** **a** Net operating loss (NOL) deduction (see page 11 of instructions)	**29a**		
		b Special deductions (Schedule C, line 20)	**29b**		**29c**	

Tax and Payments	30	**Taxable income.** Subtract line 29c from line 28	**30**	
	31	**Total tax** (Schedule J, line 12)	**31**	
	32	**Payments: a** 1998 overpayment credited to 1999	**32a**		
	b	1999 estimated tax payments . .	**32b**		
	c	Less 1999 refund applied for on Form 4466	**32c** (	**d** Bal ▶	**32d**	
	e	Tax deposited with Form 7004	**32e**	
	f	Credit for tax paid on undistributed capital gains (attach Form 2439) . .	**32f**	
	g	Credit for Federal tax on fuels (attach Form 4136). See instructions	**32g**		**32h**	
	33	Estimated tax penalty (see page 12 of instructions). Check if Form 2220 is attached . . . ▶ ☐	**33**	
	34	**Tax due.** If line 32h is smaller than the total of lines 31 and 33, enter amount owed . .	**34**	
	35	**Overpayment.** If line 32h is larger than the total of lines 31 and 33, enter amount overpaid . . .	**35**	
	36	Enter amount of line 35 you want: **Credited to 2000 estimated tax** ▶ **Refunded** ▶	**36**	

Sign Here

Under penalties of perjury, I declare that I have examined this return, including accompanying schedules and statements, and to the best of my knowledge and belief, it is true, correct, and complete. Declaration of preparer (other than taxpayer) is based on all information of which preparer has any knowledge.

▶ _____   ▶ _____
Signature of officer   Date   Title

Paid Preparer's Use Only	Preparer's signature ▶		Date		Check if self-employed ☐	Preparer's SSN or PTIN
	Firm's name (or yours if self-employed) and address ▶				EIN ▶	
					ZIP code ▶	

Cat. No. 11450Q   Form **1120** (1999)

Form **1120S**

U.S. Income Tax Return for an S Corporation

▶ Do not file this form unless the corporation has timely filed Form 2553 to elect to be an S corporation.

▶ See separate instructions.

Department of the Treasury
Internal Revenue Service

OMB No. 1545-0130

1999

For calendar year 1999, or tax year beginning _____ , 1999, and ending _____ ,

A Effective date of election as an S corporation	Use IRS label. Other-wise, please print or type.	Name		C Employer identification number
		Number, street, and room or suite no. (If a P.O. box, see page 10 of the instructions.)		D Date incorporated
B Business code no. (see pages 26–28)		City or town, state, and ZIP code		E Total assets (see page 10) $

F Check applicable boxes: (1) ☐ Initial return (2) ☐ Final return (3) ☐ Change in address (4) ☐ Amended return

G Enter number of shareholders in the corporation at end of the tax year . . . . ▶

Caution: *Include only trade or business income and expenses on lines 1a through 21. See page 10 of the instructions for more information.*

Income

1a	Gross receipts or sales	**b** Less returns and allowances	**c** Bal ▶	1c
2	Cost of goods sold (Schedule A, line 8)			2
3	Gross profit. Subtract line 2 from line 1c			3
4	Net gain (loss) from Form 4797, Part II, line 18 *(attach Form 4797)*			4
5	Other income (loss) *(attach schedule)*			5
6	**Total income (loss).** Combine lines 3 through 5 . . . . ▶			6

Deductions (see page 11 of the instructions for limitations)

7	Compensation of officers			7
8	Salaries and wages (less employment credits)			8
9	Repairs and maintenance.			9
10	Bad debts			10
11	Rents			11
12	Taxes and licenses.			12
13	Interest			13
14a	Depreciation *(if required, attach Form 4562)*	14a		
b	Depreciation claimed on Schedule A and elsewhere on return . .	14b		
c	Subtract line 14b from line 14a			14c
15	Depletion **(Do not deduct oil and gas depletion.)**			15
16	Advertising			16
17	Pension, profit-sharing, etc., plans			17
18	Employee benefit programs			18
19	Other deductions *(attach schedule)*			19
20	**Total deductions.** Add the amounts shown in the far right column for lines 7 through 19 . ▶			20
21	Ordinary income (loss) from trade or business activities. Subtract line 20 from line 6			21

Tax and Payments

22	Tax: **a** Excess net passive income tax *(attach schedule)*. . .	22a		
	b Tax from Schedule D (Form 1120S)	22b		
	c Add lines 22a and 22b (see page 14 of the instructions for additional taxes)			22c
23	**Payments: a** 1999 estimated tax payments and amount applied from 1998 return	23a		
	b Tax deposited with Form 7004	23b		
	c Credit for Federal tax paid on fuels *(attach Form 4136)*	23c		
	d Add lines 23a through 23c			23d
24	Estimated tax penalty. Check if Form 2220 is attached . . . . ▶ ☐			24
25	**Tax due.** If the total of lines 22c and 24 is larger than line 23d, enter amount owed. See page 4 of the instructions for depository method of payment . . . . ▶			25
26	**Overpayment.** If line 23d is larger than the total of lines 22c and 24, enter amount overpaid ▶			26
27	Enter amount of line 26 you want: **Credited to 2000 estimated tax** ▶	**Refunded** ▶		27

Please Sign Here

Under penalties of perjury, I declare that I have examined this return, including accompanying schedules and statements, and to the best of my knowledge and belief, it is true, correct, and complete. Declaration of preparer (other than taxpayer) is based on all information of which preparer has any knowledge.

▶ _____ _____ ▶ _____
Signature of officer   Date   Title

Paid Preparer's Use Only

Preparer's signature ▶		Date	Check if self-employed ▶ ☐	Preparer's SSN or PTIN
Firm's name (or yours if self-employed) and address ▶			EIN ▶	
			ZIP code ▶	

For Paperwork Reduction Act Notice, see the separate instructions.   Cat. No. 11510H   Form **1120S** (1999)

APPENDIX A

Schedule A   **Cost of Goods Sold** (see page 15 of the instructions)

1	Inventory at beginning of year	1	
2	Purchases	2	
3	Cost of labor	3	
4	Additional section 263A costs *(attach schedule)*	4	
5	Other costs *(attach schedule)*	5	
6	**Total.** Add lines 1 through 5	6	
7	Inventory at end of year	7	
8	**Cost of goods sold.** Subtract line 7 from line 6. Enter here and on page 1, line 2	8	

9a Check all methods used for valuing closing inventory:
   (i) ☐ Cost as described in Regulations section 1.471-3
   (ii) ☐ Lower of cost or market as described in Regulations section 1.471-4
   (iii) ☐ Other (specify method used and attach explanation) ▶ ....

b Check if there was a writedown of "subnormal" goods as described in Regulations section 1.471-2(c) . . . . ▶ ☐

c Check if the LIFO inventory method was adopted this tax year for any goods *(if checked, attach Form 970)*. . . . . . ▶ ☐

d If the LIFO inventory method was used for this tax year, enter percentage (or amounts) of closing
inventory computed under LIFO . . . . | **9d** | |

e Do the rules of section 263A (for property produced or acquired for resale) apply to the corporation?. . . . . ☐ Yes ☐ No

f Was there any change in determining quantities, cost, or valuations between opening and closing inventory? . . ☐ Yes ☐ No
If "Yes," attach explanation.

Schedule B   **Other Information**

		Yes	No
1	Check method of accounting: **(a)** ☐ Cash **(b)** ☐ Accrual **(c)** ☐ Other (specify) ▶..........................		
2	Refer to the list on pages 26 through 28 of the instructions and state the corporation's principal:
(a) Business activity ▶ .... **(b)** Product or service ▶		
3	Did the corporation at the end of the tax year own, directly or indirectly, 50% or more of the voting stock of a domestic corporation? (For rules of attribution, see section 267(c).) If "Yes," attach a schedule showing: **(a)** name, address, and employer identification number and **(b)** percentage owned.		
4	Was the corporation a member of a controlled group subject to the provisions of section 1561?		
5	At any time during calendar year 1999, did the corporation have an interest in or a signature or other authority over a financial account in a foreign country (such as a bank account, securities account, or other financial account)? (See page 15 of the instructions for exceptions and filing requirements for Form TD F 90-22.1.) . . . . If "Yes," enter the name of the foreign country ▶		
6	During the tax year, did the corporation receive a distribution from, or was it the grantor of, or transferor to, a foreign trust? If "Yes," the corporation may have to file Form 3520. See page 15 of the instructions.		
7	Check this box if the corporation has filed or is required to file **Form 8264,** Application for Registration of a Tax Shelter . . . . ▶ ☐		
8	Check this box if the corporation issued publicly offered debt instruments with original issue discount . . ▶ ☐ If so, the corporation may have to file **Form 8281,** Information Return for Publicly Offered Original Issue Discount Instruments.		
9	If the corporation: **(a)** filed its election to be an S corporation after 1986, **(b)** was a C corporation before it elected to be an S corporation **or** the corporation acquired an asset with a basis determined by reference to its basis (or the basis of any other property) in the hands of a C corporation, and **(c)** has net unrealized built-in gain (defined in section 1374(d)(1)) in excess of the net recognized built-in gain from prior years, enter the net unrealized built-in gain reduced by net recognized built-in gain from prior years (see page 15 of the instructions) . . . . . ▶ $		
10	Check this box if the corporation had accumulated earnings and profits at the close of the tax year (see page 16 of the instructions) . . . . ▶ ☐		

Form **1120S** (1999)

SCHEDULE K-1 (Form 1120S)	Shareholder's Share of Income, Credits, Deductions, etc.	OMB No. 1545-0130

Department of the Treasury
Internal Revenue Service

▶ See separate instructions.

For calendar year 1999 or tax year
beginning _____, 1999, and ending _____,

1999

Shareholder's identifying number ▶	Corporation's identifying number ▶
Shareholder's name, address, and ZIP code	Corporation's name, address, and ZIP code

A Shareholder's percentage of stock ownership for tax year (see instructions for Schedule K-1) . . . . ▶ .... %

B Internal Revenue Service Center where corporation filed its return ▶ ....

C Tax shelter registration number (see instructions for Schedule K-1) . . . . ▶ ....

D Check applicable boxes: **(1)** ☐ Final K-1 **(2)** ☐ Amended K-1

(a) Pro rata share items		(b) Amount	(c) Form 1040 filers enter the amount in column (b) on:
Income (Loss) 1 Ordinary income (loss) from trade or business activities . . .	1		See pages 4 and 5 of the Shareholder's Instructions for Schedule K-1 (Form 1120S).
2 Net income (loss) from rental real estate activities	2		
3 Net income (loss) from other rental activities	3		
4 Portfolio income (loss):			
a Interest	4a		Sch. B, Part I, line 1
b Ordinary dividends	4b		Sch. B, Part II, line 5
c Royalties	4c		Sch. E, Part I, line 4
d Net short-term capital gain (loss).	4d		Sch. D, line 5, col. (f)
e Net long-term capital gain (loss):			
(1) 28% rate gain (loss)	e(1)		Sch. D, line 12, col. (g)
(2) Total for year	e(2)		Sch. D, line 12, col. (f)
f Other portfolio income (loss) *(attach schedule)*	4f		*(Enter on applicable line of your return.)*
5 Net section 1231 gain (loss) (other than due to casualty or theft)	5		See Shareholder's Instructions for Schedule K-1 (Form 1120S).
6 Other income (loss) *(attach schedule)*	6		*(Enter on applicable line of your return.)*
Deductions 7 Charitable contributions *(attach schedule)*	7		Sch. A, line 15 or 16
8 Section 179 expense deduction	8		See page 6 of the Shareholder's Instructions for Schedule K-1 (Form 1120S).
9 Deductions related to portfolio income (loss) *(attach schedule)* .	9		
10 Other deductions *(attach schedule)*	10		
Investment Interest 11a Interest expense on investment debts	11a		Form 4952, line 1
b (1) Investment income included on lines 4a, 4b, 4c, and 4f above	b(1)		See Shareholder's Instructions for Schedule K-1 (Form 1120S).
(2) Investment expenses included on line 9 above	b(2)		
Credits 12a Credit for alcohol used as fuel	12a		Form 6478, line 10
b Low-income housing credit:			
(1) From section 42(j)(5) partnerships for property placed in service before 1990.	b(1)		Form 8586, line 5
(2) Other than on line 12b(1) for property placed in service before 1990	b(2)		
(3) From section 42(j)(5) partnerships for property placed in service after 1989	b(3)		
(4) Other than on line 12b(3) for property placed in service after 1989	b(4)		
c Qualified rehabilitation expenditures related to rental real estate activities	12c		See page 7 of the Shareholder's Instructions for Schedule K-1 (Form 1120S).
d Credits (other than credits shown on lines 12b and 12c) related to rental real estate activities	12d		
e Credits related to other rental activities.	12e		
13 Other credits	13		

For Paperwork Reduction Act Notice, see the Instructions for Form 1120S.   Cat. No. 11520D   **Schedule K-1 (Form 1120S) 1999**

Schedule K-1 (Form 1120S) (1999)   Page **2**

(a) Pro rata share items		(b) Amount	(c) Form 1040 filers enter the amount in column (b) on:
Adjustments and Tax Preference Items	**14a** Depreciation adjustment on property placed in service after 1986 **14a**		See page 7 of the Shareholder's Instructions for Schedule K-1 (Form 1120S) and Instructions for Form 6251
	b Adjusted gain or loss **14b**		
	c Depletion (other than oil and gas) **14c**		
	d (1) Gross income from oil, gas, or geothermal properties **d(1)**		
	(2) Deductions allocable to oil, gas, or geothermal properties **d(2)**		
	e Other adjustments and tax preference items *(attach schedule)* **14e**		
Foreign Taxes	**15a** Type of income ▶		Form 1116, Check boxes
	b Name of foreign country or U.S. possession ▶		
	c Total gross income from sources outside the United States *(attach schedule)* **15c**		Form 1116, Part I
	d Total applicable deductions and losses *(attach schedule)* **15d**		
	e Total foreign taxes (check one): ▶ ☐ Paid ☐ Accrued **15e**		Form 1116, Part II
	f Reduction in taxes available for credit *(attach schedule)* **15f**		Form 1116, Part III
	g Other foreign tax information *(attach schedule)* **15g**		See Instructions for Form 1116
Other	**16** Section 59(e)(2) expenditures: **a** Type ▶		See Shareholder's Instructions for Schedule K-1 (Form 1120S)
	b Amount **16b**		
	17 Tax-exempt interest income **17**		Form 1040, line 8b
	18 Other tax-exempt income **18**		
	19 Nondeductible expenses **19**		See pages 7 and 8 of the Shareholder's Instructions for Schedule K-1 (Form 1120S).
	20 Property distributions (including cash) other than dividend distributions reported to you on Form 1099-DIV **20**		
	21 Amount of loan repayments for "Loans From Shareholders" **21**		
	22 Recapture of low-income housing credit:		
	a From section 42(j)(5) partnerships **22a**		Form 8611, line 8
	b Other than on line 22a **22b**		

23 Supplemental information required to be reported separately to each shareholder *(attach additional schedules if more space is needed)*:

Supplemental Information

....

....

....

....

....

....

....

....

....

....

....

....

....

....

....

APPENDIX A

Form **1127**
(Rev. 11-93)
Department of the Treasury
Internal Revenue Service

APPLICATION FOR EXTENSION OF TIME FOR PAYMENT OF TAX

(ATTN: *This type of payment extension is rarely <u>granted</u> because the legal requirements are so strict. Please read the conditions on the back carefully before continuing.)*

Taxpayer's Name (include spouse if your extension request is for a joint return)	Social Security Number or Employer Identification Number
Present Address	Spouse's Social Security Number if this is for a joint return
City, Town or Post Office, State, and Zip Code	

District Director of Internal Revenue at _____
(Enter City and State where IRS Office is located)

I request an extension from _____ , 19 _____ , to_____ , 19 _____.
(Enter Due Date of Return)

to pay tax of $ _____ for the year ended _____ , 19 _____ .

This extension is necessary because *(If more space is needed, please attach a separate sheet):* _____
_____
_____
_____

I can't borrow to pay the tax because: _____
_____
_____

To show the need for the extension. I am attaching: (1) a statement of my assets and liabilities at the end of last month (showing book and market values of assets and whether securities are listed or unlisted); and (2) an itemized list of money I received and spent for 3 months before the date the tax is due.

I propose to secure this liability as follows:
_____
_____

Under penalties of perjury, I declare that I have examined this application, including any accompanying schedules and statements, and to the best of my knowledge and belief it is true, correct, and complete.

_____   _____
SIGNATURE (BOTH SIGNATURES IF YOUR EXTENSION REQUEST IS FOR A JOINT RETURN)   *(DATE)*

The District Director will let you know whether the extension is approved or denied and will tell you if you need some form of security. However, the Director can't consider an application if it is filed after the due date of the return. We will send you a list of approved surety companies if you ask for it.

(The following will be filled in by the IRS.)

This application is ☐ approved   for the following reasons:
.   ☐ denied
_____
_____

Interest _____   Date of assessment _____   Identifying no._____

Penalty _____   _____   _____
                              (SIGNATURE)   *(DATE)*

CAT. NO. 172380   *(over)*   Form **1127** (Rev. 11-93)

448

Form **2120**
(Rev. January 1997)

Department of the Treasury
Internal Revenue Service

Multiple Support Declaration

▶ Attach to Form 1040 or Form 1040A of person claiming the dependent.

OMB No. 1545-0071

Attachment
Sequence No. **50**

Name of person claiming the dependent

Social security number

During the calendar year 19 ...., I paid over 10% of the support of

....
Name of person

I could have claimed this person as a dependent except that I did not pay over half of his or her support. I understand that the person named above is being claimed as a dependent on the income tax return of

....
Name

....
Address

I agree not to claim this person as a dependent on my Federal income tax return for any tax year that began in this calendar year.

....
Your signature

....
Your social security number

....
Address (number, street, apt. no.)

....
Date

....
City, state, and ZIP code

Instructions

Paperwork Reduction Act Notice

We ask for the information on this form to carry out the Internal Revenue laws of the United States. You are required to give us the information. We need it to ensure that you are complying with these laws and to allow us to figure and collect the right amount of tax.

You are not required to provide the information requested on a form that is subject to the Paperwork Reduction Act unless the form displays a valid OMB control number. Books or records relating to a form or its instructions must be retained as long as their contents may become material in the administration of any Internal Revenue law. Generally, tax returns and return information are confidential, as required by Internal Revenue Code section 6103.

The time needed to complete and file this form will vary depending on individual circumstances. The estimated average time is: **Recordkeeping,** 7 minutes; **Learning about the law or the form,** 3 minutes; **Preparing the form,** 7 minutes; and **Copying, assembling, and sending the form to the IRS,** 10 minutes.

If you have comments concerning the accuracy of these time estimates or suggestions for making this form simpler, we would be happy to hear from you. See the instructions for the tax return with which this form is filed.

Purpose of Form

When two or more persons together pay over half of another person's support, only one of them can claim the person they support as a dependent for tax purposes.

Each person who does not claim the dependent completes and signs a Form 2120 (or similar statement containing the same information required by the form) and gives the form (or statement) to the person claiming the dependent. That person attaches all the forms or statements to his or her tax return. See **How To File** on this page.

Who Can Claim the Dependent

Generally, to claim someone as a dependent, you must pay over half of that person's living expenses (support). However, even if you did not meet this support test, you might still be able to claim him or her as a dependent if **all five** of the following apply:

1. You and one or more other eligible person(s) (see below) together paid over half of another person's support.

2. You paid over 10% of the support.

3. No one alone paid over half of the person's support.

4. The other four dependency tests are met. See **Dependents** in the Form 1040 or Form 1040A instructions.

5. Each other eligible person who paid over 10% of the support agrees not to claim the dependent by completing a **Form 2120** or similar statement.

An **eligible person** is someone who could have claimed another person as a dependent except that he or she did not pay over half of that person's support.

How To File

The person claiming the dependent must attach all the completed and signed Form(s) 2120 or similar statement(s) to his or her tax return. The name and social security number of the person claiming the dependent must be at the top of each Form 2120 or similar statement.

Additional Information

See **Pub. 501,** Exemptions, Standard Deduction, and Filing Information, for details.

*U.S. Government Printing Office: 1997 — 417-677/60026

Cat. No. 11712F

Form **2120** (Rev. 1-97)

 Printed on recycled paper

Form 2553
(Rev. September 1997)

Department of the Treasury
Internal Revenue Service

Election by a Small Business Corporation
(Under section 1362 of the Internal Revenue Code)
▶ For Paperwork Reduction Act Notice, see page 2 of instructions.
▶ See separate instructions.

OMB No. 1545-0146

Notes:
1. *This election to be an S corporation can be accepted only if all the tests are met under **Who May Elect** on page 1 of the instructions; all signatures in Parts I and III are originals (no photocopies); and the exact name and address of the corporation and other required form information are provided.*
2. *Do not file **Form 1120S**, U.S. Income Tax Return for an S Corporation, for any tax year before the year the election takes effect.*
3. *If the corporation was in existence before the effective date of this election, see **Taxes an S Corporation May Owe** on page 1 of the instructions.*

Part I — Election Information

Please Type or Print

Name of corporation (see instructions)	**A** Employer identification number
Number, street, and room or suite no. (If a P.O. box, see instructions.)	**B** Date incorporated
City or town, state, and ZIP code	**C** State of incorporation

D Election is to be effective for tax year beginning (month, day, year) . . . . ▶ / /

E Name and title of officer or legal representative who the IRS may call for more information

F Telephone number of officer or legal representative
( )

G If the corporation changed its name or address after applying for the EIN shown in **A** above, check this box . . . . ▶ ☐

H If this election takes effect for the first tax year the corporation exists, enter month, day, and year of the **earliest** of the following: (1) date the corporation first had shareholders, (2) date the corporation first had assets, or (3) date the corporation began doing business . . . . ▶ / /

I Selected tax year: Annual return will be filed for tax year ending (month and day) ▶..................................
If the tax year ends on any date other than December 31, except for an automatic 52-53-week tax year ending with reference to the month of December, you **must** complete Part II on the back. If the date you enter is the ending date of an automatic 52-53-week tax year, write "52-53-week year" to the right of the date. See Temporary Regulations section 1.441-2T(e)(3).

J Name and address of each shareholder; shareholder's spouse having a community property interest in the corporation's stock; and each tenant in common, joint tenant, and tenant by the entirety. (A husband and wife (and their estates) are counted as one shareholder in determining the number of shareholders without regard to the manner in which the stock is owned.)	K Shareholders' Consent Statement. Under penalties of perjury, we declare that we consent to the election of the above-named corporation to be an S corporation under section 1362(a) and that we have examined this consent statement, including accompanying schedules and statements, and to the best of our knowledge and belief, it is true, correct, and complete. We understand our consent is binding and may not be withdrawn after the corporation has made a valid election. (Shareholders sign and date below.)		L Stock owned		M Social security number or employer identification number (see instructions)	N Shareholder's tax year ends (month and day)
	Signature	Date	Number of shares	Dates acquired		

Under penalties of perjury, I declare that I have examined this election, including accompanying schedules and statements, and to the best of my knowledge and belief, it is true, correct, and complete.

Signature of officer ▶   Title ▶   Date ▶

See Parts II and III on back.   Cat. No. 18629R   Form **2553** (Rev. 9-97)

APPENDIX A

Form 2848
(Rev. December 1997)
Department of the Treasury
Internal Revenue Service

Power of Attorney
and Declaration of Representative

▶ See the separate instructions.

OMB No. 1545-0150

For IRS Use Only
Received by:
Name _____
Telephone _____
Function _____
Date ___ / ___ / ___

Part I Power of Attorney (Please type or print.)

1 Taxpayer information (Taxpayer(s) must sign and date this form on page 2, line 9.)

Taxpayer name(s) and address	Social security number(s)	Employer identification number
	Daytime telephone number	Plan number (if applicable)

hereby appoint(s) the following representative(s) as attorney(s)-in-fact:

2 Representative(s) (Representative(s) must sign and date this form on page 2, Part II.)

Name and address
CAF No. ....
Telephone No. ....
Fax No. ....
Check if new: Address ☐   Telephone No. ☐

Name and address
CAF No. ....
Telephone No. ....
Fax No. ....
Check if new: Address ☐   Telephone No. ☐

Name and address
CAF No. ....
Telephone No. ....
Fax No. ....
Check if new: Address ☐   Telephone No. ☐

to represent the taxpayer(s) before the Internal Revenue Service for the following tax matters:

3 Tax matters

Type of Tax (Income, Employment, Excise, etc.)	Tax Form Number (1040, 941, 720, etc.)	Year(s) or Period(s)

4 Specific use not recorded on Centralized Authorization File (CAF). If the power of attorney is for a specific use not recorded on CAF, check this box. (See instruction for **Line 4—Specific uses not recorded on CAF.**) . . . . ▶ ☐

5 Acts authorized. The representatives are authorized to receive and inspect confidential tax information and to perform any and all acts that I (we) can perform with respect to the tax matters described on line 3, for example, the authority to sign any agreements, consents, or other documents. The authority does not include the power to receive refund checks (see line 6 below), the power to substitute another representative unless specifically added below, or the power to sign certain returns (see instruction for **Line 5—Acts authorized**).

List any specific additions or deletions to the acts otherwise authorized in this power of attorney: ....
....
....

Note: *In general, an unenrolled preparer of tax returns cannot sign any document for a taxpayer. See Revenue Procedure 81-38, printed as Pub. 470, for more information.*

Note: *The tax matters partner of a partnership is not permitted to authorize representatives to perform certain acts. See the instructions for more information.*

6 Receipt of refund checks. If you want to authorize a representative named on line 2 to receive, **BUT NOT TO ENDORSE OR CASH**, refund checks, initial here _____ and list the name of that representative below.

Name of representative to receive refund check(s) ▶

For Paperwork Reduction and Privacy Act Notice, see the separate instructions.   Cat. No. 11980J   Form **2848** (Rev. 12-97)

Form **4506** (Rev. May 1997) Department of the Treasury Internal Revenue Service	**Request for Copy or Transcript of Tax Form** ▶ Read instructions before completing this form. ▶ Type or print clearly. Request may be rejected if the form is incomplete or illegible.	OMB No. 1545-0429

Note: *Do not* use this form to get *tax account information.* Instead, see instructions below.

1a Name shown on tax form. If a joint return, enter the name shown first.	1b **First social security number on tax form or employer identification number** (see instructions)
2a If a joint return, spouse's name shown on tax form	2b **Second social security number on tax form**

3 Current name, address (including apt., room, or suite no.), city, state, and ZIP code

4 Address, (including apt., room, or suite no.), city, state, and ZIP code shown on the last return filed if different from line 3

5 If copy of form or a tax return transcript is to be mailed to someone else, enter the third party's name and address

6 If we cannot find a record of your tax form and you want the payment refunded to the third party, check here . . . . . ▶ ☐

7 If name in third party's records differs from line 1a above, enter that name here (see instructions) ▶

8 Check only one box to show what you want. There is **no charge** for items 8a, b, and c:
 a ☐ Tax return transcript of Form 1040 series filed during the **current calendar year** and the **3 prior calendar years** (see instructions).
 b ☐ Verification of nonfiling.
 c ☐ Form(s) W-2 information (see instructions).
 d ☐ Copy of tax form and all attachments (including Form(s) W-2, schedules, or other forms). **The charge is $23 for each period requested.**
    Note: *If these copies must be certified for court or administrative proceedings, see instructions and check here* . . . . . ▶ ☐

9 If this request is to meet a requirement of one of the following, check all boxes that apply.
 ☐ Small Business Administration ☐ Department of Education ☐ Department of Veterans Affairs ☐ Financial institution

10 **Tax form number** (Form 1040, 1040A, 941, etc.)	12 Complete only if **line 8d** is checked. Amount due:		
	a Cost for each period	$	23.00
11 **Tax period(s)** (year or period ended date). If more than four, see instructions.	b Number of tax periods requested on line 11		
	c Total cost. Multiply line 12a by line 12b. .	$	
	Full payment must accompany your request. Make check or money order payable to "Internal Revenue Service."		

Caution: *Before signing, make sure all items are complete and the form is dated.*

I declare that I am either the taxpayer whose name is shown on line 1a or 2a, or a person authorized to obtain the tax information requested. I am aware that based upon this form, the IRS will release the tax information requested to any party shown on line 5. The IRS has no control over what that party does with the information.

Please Sign Here	Signature. See instructions. If other than taxpayer, attach authorization document.	Date	Telephone number of requester ( )
	Title (if line 1a above is a corporation, partnership, estate, or trust)		Best time to call
	Spouse's signature	Date	**TRY A TAX RETURN TRANSCRIPT** (see line 8a instructions)

Instructions

Section references are to the Internal Revenue Code.

TIP: If you had your tax form filled in by a paid preparer, check first to see if you can get a copy from the preparer. This may save you both time and money.

Purpose of Form.—Use Form 4506 to get a tax return transcript, verification that you did not file a Federal tax return, Form W-2 information, or a copy of a tax form. Allow 6 weeks after you file a tax form before you request a copy of it or a transcript. For W-2

information, wait 13 months after the end of the year in which the wages were earned. For example, wait until Feb. 1999 to request W-2 information for wages earned in 1997.

Do not use this form to request Forms 1099 or tax account information. See this page for details on how to get these items.

Note: *Form 4506 must be received by the IRS within 60 calendar days after the date you signed and dated the request.*

How Long Will It Take?—You can get a tax return transcript or verification of nonfiling within 7 to 10 workdays after the IRS receives your request. It can take up to 60 calendar

days to get a copy of a tax form or W-2 information. To avoid any delay, be sure to furnish all the information asked for on Form 4506.

Forms 1099.—If you need a copy of a Form 1099, contact the payer. If the payer cannot help you, call or visit the IRS to get Form 1099 information.

Tax Account Information.—If you need a statement of your tax account showing any later changes that you or the IRS made to the original return, request tax account information. Tax account information lists *(Continued on back)*

For Privacy Act and Paperwork Reduction Act Notice, see back of form. Cat. No. 41721E Form **4506** (Rev. 5-97)

Form **4562**	**Depreciation and Amortization**	OMB No. 1545-0172
(U)	**(Including Information on Listed Property)**	19**99**
Department of the Treasury Internal Revenue Service	▶ See separate instructions. ▶ Attach this form to your return.	Attachment Sequence No. **67**
Name(s) shown on return	Business or activity to which this form relates	Identifying number

Part I   Election To Expense Certain Tangible Property (Section 179) (Note: *If you have any "listed property," complete Part V before you complete Part I.*)

1	Maximum dollar limitation. If an enterprise zone business, see page 2 of the instructions . .	**1**	$19,000
2	Total cost of section 179 property placed in service. See page 2 of the instructions	**2**	
3	Threshold cost of section 179 property before reduction in limitation	**3**	$200,000
4	Reduction in limitation. Subtract line 3 from line 2. If zero or less, enter -0-	**4**	
5	Dollar limitation for tax year. Subtract line 4 from line 1. If zero or less, enter -0-. If married filing separately, see page 2 of the instructions	**5**	

(a) Description of property	(b) Cost (business use only)	(c) Elected cost	
6			

7	Listed property. Enter amount from line 27.	**7**	
8	Total elected cost of section 179 property. Add amounts in column (c), lines 6 and 7 . . .	**8**	
9	Tentative deduction. Enter the smaller of line 5 or line 8	**9**	
10	Carryover of disallowed deduction from 1998. See page 2 of the instructions	**10**	
11	Business income limitation. Enter the smaller of business income (not less than zero) or line 5 (see instructions)	**11**	
12	Section 179 expense deduction. Add lines 9 and 10, but do not enter more than line 11 . .	**12**	
13	Carryover of disallowed deduction to 2000. Add lines 9 and 10, less line 12 ▶	**13**	

Note: *Do not use Part II or Part III below for listed property (automobiles, certain other vehicles, cellular telephones, certain computers, or property used for entertainment, recreation, or amusement). Instead, use Part V for listed property.*

Part II   MACRS Depreciation for Assets Placed in Service ONLY During Your 1999 Tax Year (Do Not Include Listed Property.)

Section A—General Asset Account Election

14   If you are making the election under section 168(i)(4) to group any assets placed in service during the tax year into one or more general asset accounts, check this box. See page 3 of the instructions . . . . ▶ ☐

Section B—General Depreciation System (GDS) (See page 3 of the instructions.)

(a) Classification of property	(b) Month and year placed in service	(c) Basis for depreciation (business/investment use only—see instructions)	(d) Recovery period	(e) Convention	(f) Method	(g) Depreciation deduction
15a 3-year property						
b 5-year property						
c 7-year property						
d 10-year property						
e 15-year property						
f 20-year property						
g 25-year property			25 yrs.		S/L	
h Residential rental property			27.5 yrs.	MM	S/L	
			27.5 yrs.	MM	S/L	
i Nonresidential real property			39 yrs.	MM	S/L	
				MM	S/L	

Section C—Alternative Depreciation System (ADS) (See page 5 of the instructions.)

16a Class life					S/L	
b 12-year			12 yrs.		S/L	
c 40-year			40 yrs.	MM	S/L	

Part III   Other Depreciation (Do Not Include Listed Property.) (See page 5 of the instructions.)

17	GDS and ADS deductions for assets placed in service in tax years beginning before 1999 .	**17**	
18	Property subject to section 168(f)(1) election	**18**	
19	ACRS and other depreciation	**19**	

Part IV   Summary (See page 6 of the instructions.)

20	Listed property. Enter amount from line 26.	**20**	
21	**Total.** Add deductions on line 12, lines 15 and 16 in column (g), and lines 17 through 20. Enter here and on the appropriate lines of your return. Partnerships and S corporations—see instructions . .	**21**	
22	For assets shown above and placed in service during the current year, enter the portion of the basis attributable to section 263A costs . .	**22**	

For Paperwork Reduction Act Notice, see page 9 of the instructions.   Cat. No. 15789Q   Form **4562** (1999)

Examination Workpapers

Taxpayer's name, address, SSN *(Use pre-addressed label or show changes for both spouses if a joint return audit)*	Date		Year(s)	
	Examiner		Grade	
	Taxpayer(s)	Home Phone		Work Phone
	Reviewer			

A

Initial Interview

1. Examination technique: ☐ Correspondence
   ☐ Undeliverable mail ☐ No show
   ☐ Interview with:

2. Receipt of Publication 1 ☐
3. Appeal rights and Privacy Act explained ☐
4. Innocent spouse (Pub. 971) ☐
5. Continue on Form 4700-A, B or C

Representative - Power of Attorney ☐ Yes ☐ No
Name

B

Closed No Change

Issue: ☐ Letter 590 ☐ Letter 1156 ☐ Other

Examiner

C

EQMS Auditing Standards (Rev. 5/95) — IRM Exhibit 4910-1

1. Consideration of Large, Unusual, or Questionable items
2. Probes for Unreported Income
3. Required Filing Checks
4. Examination Depth and Records Examined
5. Continue on Form 4700-A, B or C

6. Penalties Properly Considered
7. Workpapers Support Conclusions
8. Report Writing Procedures Followed
9. Time Span/Time Charged

Was consideration given to all applicable auditing standards?
YES
If no, indicate the standard(s) not given consideration, and the reasons why consideration was not given: _____

Service Center Tax Examiners — Refer to Center Examination Quality Measurement System (CEQMS) Auditing Standards in IRM Exhibit 4010-2

D

Examination Reminders

1. Proforma Worksheets utilized where applicable
2. Alternate minimum tax
3. Inspection of prior and subsequent year return, IRM 4215
4. Probe for unreported deductions and credits
5. Scope of Examination, IRM 4253.2
6. Automatic adjustments resulting from AGI change(s)
7. "Burned Out" Tax Shelters - IRM 4236(13)
8. Amounts claimed for See/Special Fuels - IRC 6426/6421
9. Health Care Continuation Coverage Under COBRA - IRC 49908

Case Processing Reminders

1. Claim Case - Forms 2297 and 3363
2. Information Reports (IRM 4219) - Form 5346
3. FICA, Self-Employment or Tip Income Adjustments
   Forms 885-E, 885-F, and 885-T
4. Inequities, Abuses, Loopholes - Form 3558
5. Inadequate Records Notices (IRM 4271)
6. Special Handling Notice 3198

E

Required Filing Checks - IRM 4034	CHECK COMPLETED			COMMENT IN:	
	YES	NO	N/A	F4700 SUPPLEMENT	F4700 BUSINESS SUPPLEMENT
1. All Required Returns (of THIS T/P)					
. . Prior					
. . Subsequent					
. . Compliance Items:					
Information Returns					
Questionable W-4's					
Forms 8300					
Any Other Returns					
2. All Related Returns (of ANOTHER T/P)					

Form **4700** (Rev. 1-99) Department of the Treasury — **Internal Revenue Service**
ISA
STF FED5169F.1

APPENDIX A

Form **4822** (Rev. 6-83)	Department of the Treasury - Internal Revenue Service **STATEMENT OF ANNUAL ESTIMATED PERSONAL AND FAMILY EXPENSES**

TAXPAYER'S NAME AND ADDRESS	TAX YEAR ENDED

	ITEM	BY CASH	BY CHECK	TOTAL	REMARKS
1. PERSONAL EXPENSES	Groceries and outside meals				
	Clothing				
	Laundry and dry cleaning				
	Barber, beauty shop, and cosmetics				
	Education *(tuition, room, board, books, etc.)*				
	Recreation, entertainment, vacations				
	Dues *(clubs, lodge, etc.)*				
	Gifts and allowances				
	Life and accident insurance				
	Federal taxes *(income, FICA, etc.)*				
2. HOUSEHOLD EXPENSES	Rent				
	Mortgage payments *(including interest)*				
	Utilities *(electricity, gas, telephone, water, etc.)*				
	Domestic help				
	Home insurance				
	Repairs and improvements				
	Child care				
3. AUTO EXPENSES	Gasoline, oil, grease, wash				
	Tires, batteries, repairs, tags				
	Insurance				
	Auto payments *(including interest)*				
	Lease of auto				
4. DEDUCTIBLE ITEMS	Contributions				
	Medical Expenses — Insurance				
	Medical Expenses — Drugs				
	Medical Expenses — Doctors, hospitals, etc.				
	Taxes — Real estate *(not included in 2. above)*				
	Taxes — Personal property				
	Taxes — Income *(State and local)*				
	Interest *(not included in 2. and 3. above)*				
	Miscellaneous — Alimony				
	Miscellaneous — Union dues				
5. PERSONAL ASSETS, ETC.	Stocks and bonds				
	Furniture, appliances, jewelry				
	Loans to others				
	Boat				
	TOTALS ▶				

Cat. No. 23460C   *U.S. Government Printing Office: 1996 - 405-506/33726   Form 4822 (Rev. 6-83)

455

Form **4852** (Revised May 1996)	Department of the Treasury - Internal Revenue Service **Substitute for Form W-2, Wage and Tax Statement or Form 1099R, Distributions From Pensions, Annuities, Retirement or Profit-Sharing Plans, IRA's, Insurance Contracts, Etc.** Attach to Form 1040, 1040A, 1040EZ or 1040X	**OMB No.** 1545-0458

1. Name *(First , middle, last)*   2. Social security number *(SSN)*

3. Address *(Number, street, city, state, ZIP code)*

4. **Please fill in the year at the end of the statement:** I have been unable to obtain (or have received an incorrect) Form W-2, Wage and Tax Statement, or Form 1099R, Distributions From Pensions, Annuities, Retirement or Profit-Sharing Plans IRA's, Insurance Contracts, etc., from my employer or payer named below. I have notified the Internal Revenue Service of this fact. The amounts shown below are my best estimates of all wages or payments paid to me and Federal taxes withheld by this employer or payer during 19 ——————.

5. Employer's or payer's name, address and ZIP code

6. Employer's or payer's
identification number *(if known)*

7. Enter wages, compensations and taxes withheld

   a. Wages *(Note: Include (1) the total wages paid, (2) noncash payments, (3) tips /reported, and (4) all other compensation before deductions for taxes, insurance, etc.)* ——————

   f. Federal income tax withheld ——————

   g. State tax withheld ——————
   (Name of state) ——————

   b. Social security wages ——————

   c. Medicare wages ——————

   h. Local tax withheld ——————
   (Name of locality) ——————

   d. Advance EIC payments ——————

   i. Social security tax withheld ——————

   e. Social security tips ——————

   j. Medicare tax withheld ——————

8. How did you determine the amounts in item 7 above ?

9. Explain your efforts to obtain Form W-2, 1099R, or W-2c, Statement of Corrected Income and Tax Amounts.

Important Notice: If your employer has ceased operations or filed for bankruptcy, you may wish to send a copy of this form to the Social Security Administration office listed in your telephone directory to ensure proper social security credit.

Paperwork Reduction Act Notice :
We ask for the information on this form to carry out the Internal Revenue laws of the United States. You are required to give us the information. We need it to ensure that you are complying with these laws and to allow us to figure and collect the right amount of tax. The time needed to complete this form will vary depending on individual circumstances. The estimated average time is 18 minutes. If you have any comments concerning the accuracy of this time estimate or suggestions for making this form simpler; we would be happy to hear from you. You can write to the Internal Revenue Service, Attn: Reports Clearance Officer, T:FP, Washington, DC 20224. **Do Not** send form to this office. Instead, attach it to your tax return.

Under penalties of perjury, I declare that I have examined this statement, and to the best of my knowledge and belief, it is true, correct, and complete.

10. Your signature   11. Date *(mmddyy)*

Catalog No. 42058U   *U.S.GPO:1996-715-016/54260   Form **4852** (Rev. 5-96)

Form **4868**		**Application for Automatic Extension of Time**	OMB No. 1545-0188
Department of the Treasury Internal Revenue Service	(O)	**To File U.S. Individual Income Tax Return**	19**99**

General Instructions

A Change To Note

You may be able to use a credit card to get an extension of time to file without sending in Form 4868. See **Extension of Time To File Using a Credit Card** below for more details.

Purpose of Form

Use Form 4868 to apply for 4 more months to file **Form 1040EZ, Form 1040A, Form 1040, Form 1040NR-EZ,** or **Form 1040NR.**

To get the extra time you **MUST:**

- Properly estimate your 1999 tax liability using the information available to you,
- Enter your tax liability on line 9 of Form 4868, **AND**
- File Form 4868 by the regular due date of your return.

You are not required to make a payment of the tax you estimate as due. But remember, Form 4868 does not extend the time to pay taxes. If you do not pay the amount due by the regular due date, you will owe interest. You may also be charged penalties. For more details, see **Interest** and **Late Payment Penalty** on page 3. Any remittance you make with your application for extension will be treated as a payment of tax.

You do not have to explain why you are asking for the extension. We will contact you only if your request is denied.

Do not file Form 4868 if you want the IRS to figure your tax or you are under a court order to file your return by the regular due date.

If you need an additional extension, see **If You Need Additional Time** on page 3.

Note: Generally, an extension of time to file your 1999 **calendar year** income tax return also extends the time to file a gift or generation-skipping transfer (GST) tax return **(Form 709** or **709-A)** for 1999. Special rules apply if the donor dies during the year in which the gifts were made. See the Instructions for Form 709.

Extension of Time To File Using a Credit Card

You generally can get an extension by phone if you pay part or all of your estimate of income tax due by using a credit card (American Express® Card, MasterCard®, or Discover® Card). To pay by credit card, call **1-888-2PAY-TAX** (1-888-272- 9829) toll free by April 17, 2000, and follow the instructions. Your payment must be at least $1 to use this system. Before you call, fill in Form 4868 as a worksheet. You will be asked to enter certain items from the form during the call. A convenience fee will be charged by the credit card processor based on the amount you are paying. You will be told what the fee is when you call and you will have the option to either continue or cancel the call. You can also find out what the fee will be on the Internet at **www.8882paytax.com.**

You will be given a confirmation number at the end of the call. Keep the confirmation number with your records. Once you receive your confirmation number, you have completed the requirements for requesting an extension of time to file. **Do not** send in Form 4868.

Note: Although an extension of time to file your income tax return also extends the time to file Form 709 or 709-A, you cannot make payments of the gift or GST tax with a credit card. To make a payment of the gift or GST tax, send a check or money order to the service center where the donor's income tax return will be filed. Enter "1999 Form 709" and the donor's name and social security number on the payment. **Do not** send in Form 4868.

Out of the Country

If you already had 2 extra months to file because you were a U.S. citizen or resident and were out of the country, use this form to obtain an additional 2 months to file. Write "Taxpayer Abroad" across the top of Form 4868. "Out of the country" means either **(a)** you live outside the United States and Puerto Rico **and** your main place of work is outside the United States and Puerto Rico, **or (b)** you are in military or naval service outside the United States and Puerto Rico.

For Privacy Act and Paperwork Reduction Act Notice, see page 4.   Cat. No. 13141W   Form **4868** (1999)

▼ DETACH HERE ▼

Form **4868**	**Application for Automatic Extension of Time**	OMB No. 1545-0188
Department of the Treasury Internal Revenue Service	**To File U.S. Individual Income Tax Return** For calendar year 1999, or other tax year beginning ,1999, ending ,	19**99**

Part I Identification

1 Your name(s) (see instructions)

Address (see instructions)

City, town or post office, state, and ZIP code

2 Your social security number   3 Spouse's social security number

Part II Complete ONLY If Filing Gift/GST Tax Return

This form also extends the time for filing a gift or generation-skipping transfer (GST) tax return if you file a calendar (not fiscal) year income tax return. Enter your gift or GST tax payment(s) in Part IV and:

Check this box ▶ ☐ if you are requesting a **GIFT or GST TAX** return extension.

Check this box ▶ ☐ if your spouse is requesting a **GIFT or GST TAX** return extension.

Checking box(es) may result in correspondence if Form 709 or 709-A is not filed.

Part III Individual Income Tax

4 Total tax liability on your income tax return for 1999 $ _____

5 Total 1999 payments . . . . . _____

6 **Balance.** Subtract 5 from 4 . . . . _____

Part IV Gift/GST Tax—If you are **not filing** a gift or GST tax return, go to Part V now. See the instructions.

7 Your gift or GST tax payment. . . $ _____

8 **Your spouse's** gift/GST tax payment . _____

Part V Total

9 **Total liability.** Add lines 6, 7, and 8 $ _____

10 Amount you are paying. . . . . ▶ _____

If line 10 is less than line 9, you may be liable for interest and penalties. See page 3.

Form **4868** (1999)

APPENDIX A

<table>
<tr><td>Form 5213
(Rev. August 1997)
Department of the Treasury
Internal Revenue Service</td><td>Election To Postpone Determination
as To Whether the Presumption Applies That an
Activity Is Engaged in for Profit
▶ To be filed by individuals, estates, trusts, partnerships, and S corporations.</td><td>OMB No. 1545-0195</td></tr>
</table>

Name(s) as shown on tax return	Identifying number as shown on tax return

Address (number and street, apt. no., rural route) (or P.O. box number if mail is not delivered to street address)

City, town or post office, state, and ZIP code

The taxpayer named above elects to postpone a determination as to whether the presumption applies that the activity described below is engaged in for profit. The determination is postponed until the close of:
- The 6th tax year, for an activity that consists mainly of breeding, training, showing, or racing horses; or
- The 4th tax year for any other activity,

after the tax year in which the taxpayer first engaged in the activity.

1 Type of taxpayer engaged in the activity (check the box that applies):

☐ Individual ☐ Partnership ☐ S corporation ☐ Estate or trust

2a Description of activity for which you elect to postpone a determination

2b First tax year you engaged in activity described in 2a

Under penalties of perjury, I declare that I have examined this election, including accompanying schedules, and to the best of my knowledge and belief, it is true, correct, and complete.

(Signature of taxpayer or fiduciary)	(Date)

(Signature of taxpayer's spouse, if joint return was filed)	(Date)

(Signature of general partner authorized to sign partnership return)	(Date)

(Signature and title of officer, if an S corporation)	(Date)

For Paperwork Reduction Act Notice, see instructions.

ISA
STF FED5383F

Form **5213** (Rev. 8-97)

Form **6251**	**Alternative Minimum Tax—Individuals**	OMB No. 1545-0227
	▶ See separate instructions.	**19**99
Department of the Treasury Internal Revenue Service (O)	▶ **Attach to Form 1040 or Form 1040NR.**	Attachment Sequence No. **32**
Name(s) shown on Form 1040		Your social security number

Part I   Adjustments and Preferences

1	If you itemized deductions on Schedule A (Form 1040), go to line 2. Otherwise, enter your standard deduction from Form 1040, line 36, here and go to line 6	1	
2	Medical and dental. Enter the smaller of Schedule A (Form 1040), line 4 **or** 2½% of Form 1040, line 34	2	
3	Taxes. Enter the amount from Schedule A (Form 1040), line 9	3	
4	Certain interest on a home mortgage **not** used to buy, build, or improve your home	4	
5	Miscellaneous itemized deductions. Enter the amount from Schedule A (Form 1040), line 26 .	5	
6	Refund of taxes. Enter any tax refund from Form 1040, line 10 or line 21	6	( )
7	Investment interest. Enter difference between regular tax and AMT deduction	7	
8	Post-1986 depreciation. Enter difference between regular tax and AMT depreciation	8	
9	Adjusted gain or loss. Enter difference between AMT and regular tax gain or loss	9	
10	Incentive stock options. Enter excess of AMT income over regular tax income	10	
11	Passive activities. Enter difference between AMT and regular tax income or loss	11	
12	Beneficiaries of estates and trusts. Enter the amount from Schedule K-1 (Form 1041), line 9 .	12	
13	Tax-exempt interest from private activity bonds issued after 8/7/86	13	
14	Other. Enter the amount, if any, for each item below and enter the total on line 14.		

a Circulation expenditures .		**h** Loss limitations			
b Depletion		**i** Mining costs			
c Depreciation (pre-1987) .		**j** Patron's adjustment . .			
d Installment sales . . .		**k** Pollution control facilities .			
e Intangible drilling costs .		**l** Research and experimental			
f Large partnerships . . .		**m** Section 1202 exclusion . .			
g Long-term contracts . .		**n** Tax shelter farm activities .			
		o Related adjustments . .		14	

15	**Total Adjustments and Preferences.** Combine lines 1 through 14 . . . . ▶	15	

Part II   Alternative Minimum Taxable Income

16	Enter the amount from **Form 1040, line 37.** If less than zero, enter as a (loss) . . . . . ▶	16	
17	Net operating loss deduction, if any, from Form 1040, line 21. Enter as a positive amount .	17	
18	If Form 1040, line 34, is over $126,600 (over $63,300 if married filing separately), and you itemized deductions, enter the amount, if any, from line 9 of the worksheet for Schedule A (Form 1040), line 28	18	( )
19	Combine lines 15 through 18 . . . . ▶	19	
20	Alternative tax net operating loss deduction. See page 6 of the instructions	20	
21	**Alternative Minimum Taxable Income.** Subtract line 20 from line 19. (If married filing separately and line 21 is more than $165,000, see page 7 of the instructions.) . . . . ▶	21	

Part III   Exemption Amount and Alternative Minimum Tax

22	**Exemption Amount.** (If this form is for a child under age 14, see page 7 of the instructions.)		

IF your filing status is . . .	AND line 21 is not over . . .	THEN enter on line 22 . . .	
Single or head of household	$112,500	. . . . . . $33,750	
Married filing jointly or qualifying widow(er) .	150,000	 45,000	22
Married filing separately.	75,000	 22,500	

If line 21 is **over** the amount shown above for your filing status, see page 7 of the instructions.

23	Subtract line 22 from line 21. If zero or less, enter -0- here and on lines 26 and 28 . . . . . ▶	23	
24	If you reported capital gain distributions directly on Form 1040, line 13, **or** you completed Schedule D (Form 1040) and have an amount on line 25 or line 27 (or would have had an amount on either line if you had completed Part IV) (as refigured for the AMT, if necessary), go to Part IV of Form 6251 to figure line 24. **All others:** If line 23 is $175,000 or less ($87,500 or less if married filing separately), multiply line 23 by 26% (.26). Otherwise, multiply line 23 by 28% (.28) and subtract $3,500 ($1,750 if married filing separately) from the result . . . . ▶	24	
25	Alternative minimum tax foreign tax credit. See page 7 of the instructions	25	
26	Tentative minimum tax. Subtract line 25 from line 24	26	
27	Enter your tax from Form 1040, line 40 (minus any tax from Form 4972 and any foreign tax credit from Form 1040, line 46)	27	
28	**Alternative Minimum Tax.** Subtract line 27 from line 26. If zero or less, enter -0-. Enter here and on Form 1040, line 51 . . . . ▶	28	

For Paperwork Reduction Act Notice, see page 8 of the instructions.   Cat. No. 13600G   Form **6251** (1999)

Form **8082**	**Notice of Inconsistent Treatment or Administrative Adjustment Request (AAR)**	OMB No. 1545-0790
(Rev. January 2000)	(For use by partners, S corporation shareholders, estate and domestic trust beneficiaries, foreign trust owners and beneficiaries, REMIC residual interest holders, and TMPs)	Attachment Sequence No. **84**
Department of the Treasury Internal Revenue Service	▶ See separate instructions.	

Name(s) shown on return	Identifying number

Part I   General Information

1 Check boxes that apply: **(a)** ☐ Notice of inconsistent treatment   **(b)** ☐ Administrative adjustment request (AAR)

2 If you are a TMP filing an AAR on behalf of the pass-through entity, are you requesting substituted return treatment? (see instructions) . . . . ☐ Yes ☐ No

3 Check applicable box to identify type of pass-through entity:

(a) ☐ Partnership   **(b)** ☐ Electing large partnership   **(c)** ☐ S corporation   **(d)** ☐ Estate   **(e)** ☐ Trust   **(f)** ☐ REMIC

4 Identifying number of pass-through entity	**6** Tax shelter registration number (if applicable) of pass-through entity
5 Name, address, and ZIP code of pass-through entity	**7** Internal Revenue Service Center where pass-through entity filed its return
	8 Tax year of pass-through entity / / to / /
	9 Your tax year / / to / /

Part II   Inconsistent or Administrative Adjustment Request (AAR) Items

(a) Description of inconsistent or administrative adjustment request (AAR) items (see instructions)	(b) Inconsistency is in, or AAR is to correct (check boxes that apply)		(c) Amount as shown on Schedule K-1, Schedule Q, or similar statement, a foreign trust statement, or your return, whichever applies (see instructions)	(d) Amount you are reporting	(e) Difference between (c) and (d)
	Amount of item	Treatment of item			
10					
11					
12					
13					

Part III   Explanations—Enter the Part II item number before each explanation. If more space is needed, continue your explanations on the back.

For Paperwork Reduction Act Notice, see separate instructions.	Cat. No. 49975G	Form **8082** (Rev. 1-2000)

Form **8275**

(Rev. March 1998)

Department of the Treasury
Internal Revenue Service

Disclosure Statement

Do not use this form to disclose items or positions that are contrary to Treasury
regulations. Instead, use Form 8275-R, Regulation Disclosure Statement.
See separate instructions.

▶ Attach to your tax return.

OMB No. 1545-0889

Attachment
Sequence No. **92**

Name(s) shown on return	Identifying number shown on return

Part I   General Information (see instructions)

(a) Rev. Rul., Rev. Proc., etc.	(b) Item or Group of Items	(c) Detailed Description of Items	(d) Form or Schedule	(e) Line No.	(f) Amount
1					
2					
3					

Part II   Detailed Explanation (see instructions)

1

2

3

Part III   **Information About Pass-Through Entity.** To be completed by partners, shareholders, beneficiaries, or
residual interest holders.

Complete this part only if you are making adequate disclosure for a pass-through item.

Note: *A pass-through entity is a partnership, S corporation, estate, trust, regulated investment company, real estate investment trust,
or real estate mortgage investment conduit (REMIC).*

1 Name, address, and ZIP code of pass-through entity	2 Identifying number of pass-through entity
	3 Tax year of pass-through entity to
	4 Internal Revenue Service Center where the pass-through entity filed its return

For Paperwork Reduction Act Notice, see separate instructions.
ISA
STF FED6516F.1

Form **8275** (Rev. 3-98)

APPENDIX A

Form **8275-R**

(Rev. March 1998)

Department of the Treasury
Internal Revenue Service

Regulation Disclosure Statement

Use this form only to disclose items or positions that are contrary to Treasury regulations.
For other disclosures, use Form 8275, Disclosure Statement. See separate instructions.
▶ Attach to your tax return.

OMB No. 1545-0889

Attachment
Sequence No. **92A**

Name(s) shown on return

Identifying number shown on return

Part I   **General Information** (See instructions.)

(a) Regulation Section	(b) Item or Group of Items	(c) Detailed Description of Items	(d) Form or Schedule	(e) Line No.	(f) Amount
1					
2					
3					

Part II   **Detailed Explanation** (See instructions.)

1

2

3

Part III   **Information About Pass-Through Entity.** To be completed by partners, shareholders, beneficiaries, or residual interest holders.

Complete this part only if you are making adequate disclosure for a pass-through item.

Note: *A pass-through entity is a partnership, S corporation, estate, trust, regulated investment company, real estate investment trust, or real estate mortgage investment conduit (REMIC).*

1 Name, address, and ZIP code of pass-through entity	2 Identifying number of pass-through entity
	3 Tax year of pass-through entity to
	4 Internal Revenue Service Center where the pass-through entity filed its return

For Paperwork Reduction Act Notice, see separate instructions.

Form **8275-R** (Rev. 3-98)

ISA
STF FED6520F.1

462

Form **8283**
(Rev. October 1998)

Department of the Treasury
Internal Revenue Service

Noncash Charitable Contributions

▶ Attach to your tax return if you claimed a total deduction
of over $500 for all contributed property.

▶ See separate instructions.

OMB No. 1545-0908

Attachment
Sequence No. **55**

Name(s) shown on your income tax return

Identifying number

Note: *Figure the amount of your contribution deduction before completing this form. See your tax return instructions.*

Section A—List in this section **only** items (or groups of similar items) for which you claimed a deduction of $5,000 or less. Also, list certain publicly traded securities even if the deduction is over $5,000 (see instructions).

Part I   **Information on Donated Property**—If you need more space, attach a statement.

1	(a) Name and address of the donee organization	(b) Description of donated property
A		
B		
C		
D		
E		

Note: *If the amount you claimed as a deduction for an item is $500 or less, you do not have to complete columns (d), (e), and (f).*

	(c) Date of the contribution	(d) Date acquired by donor (mo., yr.)	(e) How acquired by donor	(f) Donor's cost or adjusted basis	(g) Fair market value	(h) Method used to determine the fair market value
A						
B						
C						
D						
E						

Part II   **Other Information**—Complete line 2 if you gave less than an entire interest in property listed in Part I. Complete line 3 if conditions were attached to a contribution listed in Part I.

2   If, during the year, you contributed less than the entire interest in the property, complete lines a–e.

a   Enter the letter from Part I that identifies the property ▶ _____. If Part II applies to more than one property, attach a separate statement.

b   Total amount claimed as a deduction for the property listed in Part I: **(1)** For this tax year   ▶ _____.

  (2) For any prior tax years   ▶ _____.

c   Name and address of each organization to which any such contribution was made in a prior year (complete only if different from the donee organization above):

Name of charitable organization (donee)

Address (number, street, and room or suite no.)

City or town, state, and ZIP code

d   For tangible property, enter the place where the property is located or kept ▶ _____

e   Name of any person, other than the donee organization, having actual possession of the property ▶ _____

3   If conditions were attached to any contribution listed in Part I, answer questions a – c and attach the required statement (see instructions).

		Yes	No
a	Is there a restriction, either temporary or permanent, on the donee's right to use or dispose of the donated property?		
b	Did you give to anyone (other than the donee organization or another organization participating with the donee organization in cooperative fundraising) the right to the income from the donated property or to the possession of the property, including the right to vote donated securities, to acquire the property by purchase or otherwise, or to designate the person having such income, possession, or right to acquire?		
c	Is there a restriction limiting the donated property for a particular use?		

For Paperwork Reduction Act Notice, see page 4 of separate instructions.

Cat. No. 62299J

Form **8283** (Rev. 10-98)

Form 8283 (Rev. 10-98)   Page **2**

Name(s) shown on your income tax return	Identifying number

Section B—Appraisal Summary—List in this section only items (or groups of similar items) for which you claimed a deduction of more than $5,000 per item or group. **Exception.** Report contributions of certain publicly traded securities only in Section A.

If you donated art, you may have to attach the complete appraisal. See the **Note** in Part I below.

Part I   **Information on Donated Property**—To be completed by the taxpayer and/or appraiser.

4   Check type of property:

☐ Art* (contribution of $20,000 or more)   ☐ Real Estate   ☐ Gems/Jewelry   ☐ Stamp Collections

☐ Art* (contribution of less than $20,000)   ☐ Coin Collections   ☐ Books   ☐ Other

*Art includes paintings, sculptures, watercolors, prints, drawings, ceramics, antique furniture, decorative arts, textiles, carpets, silver, rare manuscripts, historical memorabilia, and other similar objects.

Note: *If your total art contribution deduction was $20,000 or more, you must attach a complete copy of the signed appraisal. See instructions.*

5	(a) Description of donated property (if you need more space, attach a separate statement)	(b) If tangible property was donated, give a brief summary of the overall physical condition at the time of the gift	(c) Appraised fair market value
A			
B			
C			
D			

	(d) Date acquired by donor (mo., yr.)	(e) How acquired by donor	(f) Donor's cost or adjusted basis	(g) For bargain sales, enter amount received	See instructions	
					(h) Amount claimed as a deduction	(i) Average trading price of securities
A						
B						
C						
D						

Part II   **Taxpayer (Donor) Statement**—List each item included in Part I above that the appraisal identifies as having a value of $500 or less. See instructions.

I declare that the following item(s) included in Part I above has to the best of my knowledge and belief an appraised value of not more than $500 (per item). Enter identifying letter from Part I and describe the specific item. See instructions. ▶ _____

Signature of taxpayer (donor) ▶ _____   Date ▶ _____

Part III   **Declaration of Appraiser**

I declare that I am not the donor, the donee, a party to the transaction in which the donor acquired the property, employed by, or related to any of the foregoing persons, or married to any person who is related to any of the foregoing persons. And, if regularly used by the donor, donee, or party to the transaction, I performed the majority of my appraisals during my tax year for other persons.

Also, I declare that I hold myself out to the public as an appraiser or perform appraisals on a regular basis; and that because of my qualifications as described in the appraisal, I am qualified to make appraisals of the type of property being valued. I certify that the appraisal fees were not based on a percentage of the appraised property value. Furthermore, I understand that a false or fraudulent overstatement of the property value as described in the qualified appraisal or this appraisal summary may subject me to the penalty under section 6701(a) (aiding and abetting the understatement of tax liability). I affirm that I have not been barred from presenting evidence or testimony by the Director of Practice.

Sign Here   Signature ▶ _____   Title ▶ _____   Date of appraisal ▶ _____

Business address (including room or suite no.)	Identifying number
City or town, state, and ZIP code	

Part IV   **Donee Acknowledgment**—To be completed by the charitable organization.

This charitable organization acknowledges that it is a qualified organization under section 170(c) and that it received the donated property as described in Section B, Part I, above on ▶ _____
(Date)

Furthermore, this organization affirms that in the event it sells, exchanges, or otherwise disposes of the property described in Section B, Part I (or any portion thereof) within 2 years after the date of receipt, it will file **Form 8282**, Donee Information Return, with the IRS and give the donor a copy of that form. This acknowledgment does not represent agreement with the claimed fair market value.

Does the organization intend to use the property for an unrelated use? . . . . ▶ ☐ Yes   ☐ No

Name of charitable organization (donee)	Employer identification number
Address (number, street, and room or suite no.)	City or town, state, and ZIP code

Authorized signature	Title	Date

✪ *Printed on recycled paper*   *U.S. Government Printing Office: 1999 — 455-238/10042

APPENDIX A

Form 8300

(Rev. August 1997)

Department of the Treasury
Internal Revenue Service

Report of Cash Payments Over $10,000 Received in a Trade or Business

▶ See instructions for definition of cash.
▶ Use this form for transactions occurring after July 31, 1997.
Please type or print.

OMB No. 1545-0892

1 Check appropriate box(es) if: **a** ☐ Amends prior report; **b** ☐ Suspicious transaction.

Part I   Identity of Individual From Whom the Cash Was Received

2 If more than one individual is involved, check here and see instructions .... ▶ ☐

3 Last name | **4** First name | **5** M.I. | **6** Taxpayer identification number

7 Address (number, street, and apt. or suite no.) | **8** Date of birth .... ▶ M M D D Y Y Y Y (see instructions)

9 City | **10** State | **11** ZIP code | **12** Country (if not U.S.) | **13** Occupation, profession, or business

14 Document used to verify identity: **a** Describe identification ▶
b Issued by | **c** Number

Part II   Person on Whose Behalf This Transaction Was Conducted

15 If this transaction was conducted on behalf of more than one person, check here and see instructions .... ▶ ☐

16 Individual's last name or Organization's name | **17** First name | **18** M.I. | **19** Taxpayer identification number

20 Doing business as (DBA) name (see instructions) | Employer identification number

21 Address (number, street, and apt. or suite no.) | **22** Occupation, profession, or business

23 City | **24** State | **25** ZIP code | **26** Country (if not U.S.)

27 Alien identification: **a** Describe identification ▶
b Issued by | **c** Number

Part III   Description of Transaction and Method of Payment

28 Date cash received M M D D Y Y Y Y | **29** Total cash received $ .00 | **30** If cash was received in more than one payment, check here .... ▶ ☐ | **31** Total price if different from item 29 $ .00

32 Amount of cash received (in U.S. dollar equivalent) (must equal item 29) (see instructions):
a U.S. currency $ .00 (Amount in $100 bills or higher $ .00)
b Foreign currency $ .00 (Country ▶)
c Cashier's check(s) $ .00 } Issuer's name(s) and serial number(s) of the monetary instrument(s) ▶
d Money order(s) $ .00
e Bank draft(s) $ .00
f Traveler's checks $ .00

33 Type of transaction
a ☐ Personal property purchased
b ☐ Real property purchased
c ☐ Personal services provided
d ☐ Business services provided
e ☐ Intangible property purchased
f ☐ Debt obligations paid
g ☐ Exchange of cash
h ☐ Escrow or trust funds
i ☐ Bail bond
j ☐ Other (specify) ▶

34 Specific description of property or service shown in 33. (Give serial or registration number, address, docket number, etc.) ▶

Part IV   Business That Received Cash

35 Name of business that received cash | **36** Employer identification number

37 Address (number, street, and apt. or suite no.) | Social security number

38 City | **39** State | **40** ZIP code | **41** Nature of your business

42 Under penalties of perjury, I declare that to the best of my knowledge the information I have furnished above is true, correct, and complete.

Signature of authorized official | Title of authorized official

43 Date of signature M M D D Y Y Y Y | **44** Type or print name of contact person | **45** Contact telephone number

For Paperwork Reduction Act Notice, see page 4.
ISA
STF FED6581F.1

Form **8300** (Rev. 8-97)

APPENDIX A

<table>
<tr><td>Form 8332
(Rev. June 1996)
Department of the Treasury
Internal Revenue Service</td><td><h2>Release of Claim to Exemption
for Child of Divorced or Separated Parents</h2>▶ ATTACH to noncustodial parent's return EACH YEAR exemption claimed.</td><td>OMB No. 1545-0915

Attachment
Sequence No. 51</td></tr>
</table>

Name(s) of parent claiming exemption | Social security number

Part I Release of Claim to Exemption for Current Year

I agree not to claim an exemption for_____
Name(s) of child (or children)

for the tax year 19_____ .

_____
Signature of parent releasing claim to exemption | Social security number | Date

If you choose not to claim an exemption for this child (or children) for future tax years, complete Part II.

Part II Release of Claim to Exemption for Future Years (If completed, see Noncustodial Parent below.)

I agree not to claim an exemption for_____
Name(s) of child (or children)

for the tax year(s)_____ .
(Specify. See instructions.)

_____
Signature of parent releasing claim to exemption | Social security number | Date

General Instructions

Paperwork Reduction Act Notice.—We ask for the information on this form to carry out the Internal Revenue laws of the United States. You are required to give us the information. We need it to ensure that you are complying with these laws and to allow us to figure and collect the right amount of tax.

You are not required to provide the information requested on a form that is subject to the Paperwork Reduction Act unless the form displays a valid OMB control number. Books or records relating to a form or its instructions must be retained as long as their contents may become material in the administration of any Internal Revenue law. Generally, tax returns and return information are confidential, as required by Internal Revenue Code section 6103.

The time needed to complete and file this form will vary depending on individual circumstances. The estimated average time is: **Recordkeeping,** 7 min.; **Learning about the law or the form,** 5 min.; **Preparing the form,** 7 min.; and **Copying, assembling, and sending the form to the IRS,** 14 min.

If you have comments concerning the accuracy of these time estimates or suggestions for making this form simpler, we would be happy to hear from you. See the instructions for the tax return with which this form is filed.

Purpose of Form.—If you are a **custodial parent,** you may use this form to release your claim to your child's exemption. To do so, complete this form and give it to the **noncustodial parent** who will claim the child's exemption. Then, the noncustodial parent must attach this form or a similar statement to his or her tax return EACH YEAR the exemption is claimed.

You are the **custodial parent** if you had custody of the child for most of the year. You are the **noncustodial parent** if you had custody for a shorter period of time or did not have custody at all.

Instead of using this form, you (the custodial parent) may use a similar statement as long as it contains the same information required by this form.

Children of Divorced or Separated Parents.—Special rules apply to determine if the support test is met for children of parents who are divorced or legally separated under a decree of divorce or separate maintenance or separated under a written separation agreement. The rules also apply to children of parents who did not live together at any time during the last 6 months of the year, even if they do not have a separation agreement.

The general rule is that the custodial parent is treated as having provided over half of the child's support if:

1. The child received over half of his or her total support for the year from both of the parents, **AND**

2. The child was in the custody of one or both of his or her parents for more than half of the year.

Note: Public assistance payments, such as Aid to Families with Dependent Children, are not support provided by the parents.

If both **1** and **2** above apply, and the other four dependency tests in your tax return instruction booklet are also met, the custodial parent can claim the child's exemption.

Exception. The general rule does not apply if **any** of the following apply:

● The custodial parent agrees not to claim the child's exemption by signing this form or similar statement. The noncustodial parent **must** attach this form or similar statement to

his or her tax return for the tax year. See **Custodial Parent** later.

● The child is treated as having received over half of his or her total support from a person under a multiple support agreement (**Form 2120,** Multiple Support Declaration).

● A pre-1985 divorce decree or written separation agreement states that the noncustodial parent can claim the child as a dependent. But the noncustodial parent must provide at least $600 for the child's support during the year. This rule does not apply if the decree or agreement was changed after 1984 to say that the noncustodial parent cannot claim the child as a dependent.

Additional Information.—For more details, get **Pub. 504,** Divorced or Separated Individuals.

Specific Instructions

Custodial Parent.—You may agree to release your claim to the child's exemption for the current tax year or for future years, or both.

● Complete **Part I** if you agree to release your claim to the child's exemption for the current tax year.

● Complete **Part II** if you agree to release your claim to the child's exemption for any or all future years. If you do, write the specific future year(s) or "all future years" in the space provided in Part II.

Noncustodial Parent.—Attach Form 8332 or similar statement to your tax return for the tax year in which you claim the child's exemption. You may claim the exemption **only** if the other four dependency tests in your tax return instruction booklet are met.

Note: If the custodial parent completed Part II, you **must** attach a copy of this form to your tax return for each future year in which you claim the exemption.

*U.S. Government Printing Office: 1999 — 455-238/10002 | Cat. No. 13910F | Form **8332** (Rev. 6-96)

 Printed on recycled paper

466

Form **8379** (Rev. January 1999) Department of the Treasury Internal Revenue Service	**Injured Spouse Claim and Allocation**	OMB No. 1545-1210
		Attachment Sequence No. **104**
Name(s) shown on return		Your social security number

Are You an Injured Spouse?

You are an injured spouse if you file a joint return and all or part of your share of the overpayment was, or is expected to be, applied against your spouse's past-due Federal tax, child support, or Federal nontax debt, such as a student loan. All or part of an overpayment that would be refunded after 1999 may be applied to past-due state income tax. Complete Form 8379 if **all three** of the following apply and you want your share of the overpayment shown on the joint return refunded to you. **But** if your main home was in a community property state (see line 6 below), you may file Form 8379 if only item 1 below applies.

1. You are not required to pay the past-due amount.

2. You reported income such as wages, taxable interest, etc. on the joint return.

3. You made and reported payments such as Federal income tax withheld from your wages or estimated tax payments, OR you claimed the earned income credit or other refundable credit, on the joint return.

Note: *The Treasury Department's Financial Management Service (FMS) is authorized to apply all or part of the joint refund to the past-due child support or Federal nontax debt before the IRS can process your claim. If this happens, you will receive a notice from the FMS. If you also owe child support or a Federal nontax debt, the FMS will apply all or part of your share of the refund to that debt.*

How Do You File Form 8379?

● If you have not filed your joint return, attach Form 8379 behind your return in the order of the attachment sequence number. Enter "Injured Spouse" in the upper left corner of the return.

● If you have already filed the joint tax return, mail Form 8379 by itself to the Internal Revenue Service Center for the place where you lived when you filed the joint return. See your tax return instruction booklet for the address. **Be sure** to include copies of all W-2 forms of both spouses and any Forms 1099-R showing income tax withheld. The processing of your claim may be delayed if you do not include these copies.

Note: *Please allow at least 8 weeks from the time the refund is applied to the past-due debt for the IRS to process this claim.*

Part I   **Information About the Joint Tax Return for Which This Claim Is Filed**

1   **Enter the following information exactly as it is shown on the tax return for which you are filing this claim. The spouse's name and social security number shown first on that tax return must also be shown first below.**

First name, initial, and last name shown first on the return	Social security number shown first	If Injured Spouse, check here ▶ ☐
First name, initial, and last name shown second on the return	Social security number shown second	If Injured Spouse, check here ▶ ☐

If you are filing Form 8379 with your tax return, skip to line 5.

2   **Enter the tax year for which you are filing this claim (for example, 1999)** ▶ _____

3

Current home address	City	State	ZIP code

4   Is the address on your joint return different from the address shown above? . . . .   ☐ **Yes**   ☐ **No**

5   Check this box only if you are divorced or separated from the spouse with whom you filed the joint return and you want your refund issued in your name only   . . . .   ☐

6   Was your main home in a community property state (Arizona, California, Idaho, Louisiana, Nevada, New Mexico, Texas, Washington, or Wisconsin) at any time during the year entered on line 2? . . . . . .   ☐ **Yes**   ☐ **No**
    If "Yes," which community property state(s)? _____
    Note: *Overpayments involving community property states will be allocated by the IRS according to state law.*

Go to Part II on the back.

Privacy Act and Paperwork Reduction Act Notice.—Our legal right to ask for the information on this form is Internal Revenue Code sections 6001, 6011, 6109, and 6402 and their regulations. You are required to give us the information so that we can process your claim for refund of your share of an overpayment shown on the joint return with your spouse. We need it to ensure that you are allocating items correctly and to allow us to figure the correct amount of your claim for refund. If you do not provide all of the information, we may not be able to process your claim. We may give this information to the Department of Justice as provided by law. We may also give it to cities, states, and the District of Columbia to carry out their tax laws.

You are not required to provide the information requested on a form that is subject to the Paperwork Reduction Act unless the form displays a valid OMB control number. Books or records relating to a form or its instructions must be retained as long as their contents may become material in the administration of any Internal Revenue law. Generally, tax returns and return information are confidential, as required by Code section 6103.

The time needed to complete and file this form will vary depending on individual circumstances. The estimated average time is: **Recordkeeping,** 13 min.; **Learning about the law or the form,** 8 min.; **Preparing the form,** 58 min.; and **Copying, assembling, and sending the form to the IRS,** 31 min.

If you have comments concerning the accuracy of these time estimates or suggestions for making this form simpler, we would be happy to hear from you. You can write to the Tax Forms Committee, Western Area Distribution Center, Rancho Cordova, CA 95743-0001. **Do not** send the form to this address. Instead, see **How Do You File Form 8379?** above.

Cat. No. 62474Q   Form **8379** (Rev. 1-99)

Part II   Allocation Between Spouses of Items on the Joint Tax Return

Allocated Items	(a) Amount shown on joint return	(b) Allocated to injured spouse	(c) Allocated to other spouse
7 **Income.** Enter the separate income that each spouse earned. Allocate joint income, such as interest earned on a joint bank account, as you determine. But be sure to allocate **all** income shown on the joint return.			
a Wages.			
b All other income. Identify the type and amount ▶			
_____			
_____			
_____			
_____			
_____			
8 **Adjustments to income.** Enter each spouse's separate adjustments, such as an IRA deduction. Allocate other adjustments as you determine.			
9 **Standard deduction.** If you itemized your deductions, go to line 10. Otherwise, enter in both columns **(b)** and **(c)** ½ of the amount shown in column **(a)** and go to line 11 . .			
10 **Itemized deductions.** Enter each spouse's separate deductions, such as employee business expenses. Allocate other deductions as you determine			
11 **Number of exemptions.** Allocate the exemptions claimed on the joint return to the spouse who would have claimed them if separate returns had been filed. Enter whole numbers only (for example, you **cannot** allocate 3 exemptions by giving 1.5 exemptions to each spouse) .			
12 **Credits.** Allocate any child tax credit, child and dependent care credit, and additional child tax credit to the spouse who was allocated the dependent's exemption. **Do not** include any earned income credit here; the IRS will allocate it based on each spouse's income. Allocate business credits based on each spouse's interest in the business. Allocate any other credits as you determine . . .			
13 **Other taxes.** Allocate self-employment tax to the spouse who earned the self-employment income. Allocate any alternative minimum tax as you determine.			
14 **Federal income tax withheld.** Enter Federal income tax withheld from each spouse's income as shown on Forms W-2 and 1099-R. **Be sure to attach copies of these forms to your tax return, or to Form 8379 if you are filing it by itself.** (Also, include on this line any excess social security and RRTA tax withheld.)			
15 **Payments.** Allocate joint estimated tax payments as you determine			

Note: The IRS will figure the amount of any refund due the injured spouse.

Part III   Signature. Complete this part only if you are filing Form 8379 by itself and not with your tax return.

Under penalties of perjury, I declare that I have examined this form and any accompanying schedules or statements and to the best of my knowledge and belief, they are true, correct, and complete. Declaration of preparer (other than taxpayer) is based on all information of which preparer has any knowledge.

Keep a copy of this form for your records	Injured spouse's signature	Date	Phone number (optional) ( )

Paid Preparer's Use Only	Preparer's signature ▶	Date	Check if self-employed ☐	Preparer's social security no.
	Firm's name (or yours if self-employed) and address ▶		EIN	
			ZIP code	

Declaration Control Number (DCN)

| 0 0 | – | | | | | | | – | | | | | – | 0 | |

IRS Use Only—Do not write or staple in this space.

Form **8453-OL**

Department of the Treasury
Internal Revenue Service

U.S. Individual Income Tax Declaration
for an *e-file* On-Line Return
For the year January 1–December 31, 1999
▶ See instructions on back.

OMB No. 1545-1397

1999

Use the
IRS label.
Otherwise,
please
print or
type.

L
A
B
E
L

H
E
R
E

Your first name and initial	Last name	Your social security number
If a joint return, spouse's first name and initial	Last name	Spouse's social security number
Home address (number and street). If a P.O. box, see instructions.	Apt. no.	▲ **IMPORTANT!** ▲ You **must** enter your SSN(s) above.
City, town or post office, state, and ZIP code		Telephone number (optional) ( )

Part I   Tax Return Information (Whole dollars only)

1 Total income (Form 1040, line 22; Form 1040A, line 14; Form 1040EZ, line 4) **1**

2 Total tax (Form 1040, line 56; Form 1040A, line 34; Form 1040EZ, line 10) **2**

3 Federal income tax withheld (Form 1040, line 57; Form 1040A, line 35; Form 1040EZ, line 7) . .   **3**

4 Refund (Form 1040, line 66a; Form 1040A, line 41a; Form 1040EZ, line 11a) **4**

5 Amount you owe (Form 1040, line 68; Form 1040A, line 43; Form 1040EZ, line 12). See instructions   **5**

Part II   Declaration of Taxpayer

6a ☐ I consent that my refund be directly deposited as designated in the electronic portion of my 1999 Federal income tax return. If I have filed a joint return, this is an irrevocable appointment of the other spouse as an agent to receive the refund.

b ☐ I do not want direct deposit of my refund **or** I am not receiving a refund.

c ☐ I authorize the U.S. Treasury and its designated Financial Agents to initiate an ACH debit (automatic withdrawal) entry to my financial institution account indicated for payment of my Federal taxes owed, and my financial institution to debit the entry to my account. This authorization is to remain in full force and effect until the U.S. Treasury's Financial Agents receive notification from me of the termination. To revoke this payment authorization, I must contact the U.S. Treasury Financial Agent at **1-888-353-4537** no later than 2 business days prior to the payment (settlement) date. I also authorize the financial institutions involved in the processing of my electronic payment of taxes to receive confidential information necessary to answer inquiries and resolve issues related to my payment.

If I have filed a balance due return, I understand that if the IRS does not receive full and timely payment of my tax liability, I will remain liable for the tax liability and all applicable interest and penalties. If I have filed a joint Federal and state tax return and there is an error on my state return, I understand my Federal return will be rejected.

Under penalties of perjury, I declare that the information I have given my on-line service provider and/or transmitter and the amounts in Part I above agree with the amounts on the corresponding lines of the electronic portion of my 1999 Federal income tax return. To the best of my knowledge and belief, my return is true, correct, and complete.

Sign Here ▶

| Your signature | Date | ▶ Spouse's signature. If a joint return, BOTH must sign. | Date |

For Paperwork Reduction Act Notice, see back of form.   Cat. No. 15907C   Form **8453-OL** (1999)

Form **8582**	**Passive Activity Loss Limitations**	OMB No. 1545-1008
Department of the Treasury (O) Internal Revenue Service	► See separate instructions. ► Attach to Form 1040 or Form 1041.	**19 99** Attachment Sequence No. **88**
Name(s) shown on return		Identifying number

Part I   **1999 Passive Activity Loss**

Caution: *See the instructions for Worksheets 1 and 2 on page 7 before completing Part I.*

Rental Real Estate Activities With Active Participation (For the definition of active participation see **Active Participation in a Rental Real Estate Activity** on page 3.)

1a Activities with net income (enter the amount from Worksheet 1, column (a)). **1a**

  b Activities with net loss (enter the amount from Worksheet 1, column (b)). . . . .   **1b** ( )

  c Prior years unallowed losses (enter the amount from Worksheet 1, column (c)). . . . .   **1c** ( )

  d Combine lines 1a, 1b, and 1c **1d**

All Other Passive Activities

2a Activities with net income (enter the amount from Worksheet 2, column (a)). **2a**

  b Activities with net loss (enter the amount from Worksheet 2, column (b)). . . . .   **2b** ( )

  c Prior years unallowed losses (enter the amount from Worksheet 2, column (c)). . . . .   **2c** ( )

  d Combine lines 2a, 2b, and 2c **2d**

3 Combine lines 1d and 2d. If the result is net income or zero, all losses are allowed, including any prior year unallowed losses entered on line 1c or 2c. **Do not** complete Form 8582. Take the losses to the form or schedule you normally report them on. If this line and line 1d are losses, go to Part II. Otherwise, enter -0- on line 9 and go to line 10 .   **3**

Part II   **Special Allowance for Rental Real Estate With Active Participation**

Note: *Enter all numbers in Part II as positive amounts. See page 7 for examples.*

Note: *If your filing status is married filing separately and you lived with your spouse at any time during the year,* **do not** *complete Part II. Instead, enter -0- on line 9 and go to line 10.*

4 Enter the **smaller** of the loss on line 1d or the loss on line 3 . . . .   **4**

5 Enter $150,000. If married filing separately, see page 7 . . . .   **5**

6 Enter modified adjusted gross income, but not less than zero (see page 7) **6**

Note: *If line 6 is greater than or equal to line 5, skip lines 7 and 8, enter -0- on line 9, and go to line 10. Otherwise, go to line 7.*

7 Subtract line 6 from line 5 . . . .   **7**

8 Multiply line 7 by 50% (.5). **Do not** enter more than $25,000. If married filing separately, see page 8 . . . .   **8**

9 Enter the **smaller** of line 4 or line 8 . . . .   **9**

Part III   **Total Losses Allowed**

10 Add the income, if any, on lines 1a and 2a and enter the total **10**

11 **Total losses allowed from all passive activities for 1999.** Add lines 9 and 10. See page 9 to find out how to report the losses on your tax return **11**

For Paperwork Reduction Act Notice, see page 11.   Cat. No. 63704F   Form **8582** (1999)

Form 8582 (1999)   Page **2**

Caution: *The worksheets are not required to be filed with your tax return and may be detached before filing Form 8582. Keep a copy of the worksheets for your records.*

Worksheet 1—For Form 8582, Lines 1a, 1b, and 1c (See page 7.)

Name of activity	Current year		Prior years	Overall gain or loss	
	(a) Net income (line 1a)	(b) Net loss (line 1b)	(c) Unallowed loss (line 1c)	(d) Gain	(e) Loss
Total. Enter on Form 8582, lines 1a, 1b, and 1c. . . . . ▶				/////	/////

Worksheet 2—For Form 8582, Lines 2a, 2b, and 2c (See page 7.)

Name of activity	Current year		Prior years	Overall gain or loss	
	(a) Net income (line 2a)	(b) Net loss (line 2b)	(c) Unallowed loss (line 2c)	(d) Gain	(e) Loss
Total. Enter on Form 8582, lines 2a, 2b, and 2c. . . . . ▶				/////	/////

Worksheet 3—Use this worksheet if an amount is shown on Form 8582, line 9 (See page 8.)

Name of activity	Form or schedule to be reported on	(a) Loss	(b) Ratio	(c) Special allowance	(d) Subtract column (c) from column (a)
Total . . . . ▶			1.00		

Worksheet 4—Allocation of Unallowed Losses (See page 8.)

Name of activity	Form or schedule to be reported on	(a) Loss	(b) Ratio	(c) Unallowed loss
Total . . . . ▶			1.00	

Worksheet 5—Allowed Losses (See page 8.)

Name of activity	Form or schedule to be reported on	(a) Loss	(b) Unallowed loss	(c) Allowed loss
Total . . . . ▶				

Form **8582** (1999)

Form **8582-CR**

Department of the Treasury
Internal Revenue Service

Passive Activity Credit Limitations

▶ See separate instructions.
▶ Attach to Form 1040 or 1041.

OMB No. 1545-1034

1999

Attachment
Sequence No. **89**

Name(s) shown on return

Identifying number

Part I   **1999 Passive Activity Credits**

Caution: *If you have credits from a publicly traded partnership, see **Publicly Traded Partnerships (PTPs)** on page 15 of the instructions.*

Credits From Rental Real Estate Activities With Active Participation (Other Than Rehabilitation Credits and Low-Income Housing Credits) (See Lines 1a through 1c on page 9.)

1a Credits from Worksheet 1, column (a)	**1a**	
b Prior year unallowed credits from Worksheet 1, column (b)	**1b**	
c Add lines 1a and 1b		**1c**

Rehabilitation Credits from Rental Real Estate Activities and Low-Income Housing Credits for Property Placed in Service Before 1990 (or From Pass-Through Interests Acquired Before 1990) (See Lines 2a through 2c on page 9.)

2a Credits from Worksheet 2, column (a)	**2a**	
b Prior year unallowed credits from Worksheet 2, column (b)	**2b**	
c Add lines 2a and 2b		**2c**

Low-Income Housing Credits for Property Placed in Service After 1989 (See Lines 3a through 3c on page 9.)

3a Credits from Worksheet 3, column (a)	**3a**	
b Prior year unallowed credits from Worksheet 3, column (b)	**3b**	
c Add lines 3a and 3b		**3c**

All Other Passive Activity Credits (See Lines 4a through 4c on page 9.)

4a Credits from Worksheet 4, column (a)	**4a**	
b Prior year unallowed credits from Worksheet 4, column (b)	**4b**	
c Add lines 4a and 4b		**4c**
5 Add lines 1c, 2c, 3c, and 4c		**5**
6 Enter the tax attributable to net passive income (see page 9)		**6**
7 Subtract line 6 from line 5. If line 6 is more than or equal to line 5, enter -0- and see page 10		**7**

Note: *If your filing status is married filing separately and you lived with your spouse at any time during the year, do not complete Part II, III, or IV. Instead, go to line 37.*

Part II   **Special Allowance for Rental Real Estate Activities With Active Participation**

Note: *Complete this part only if you have an amount on line 1c. Otherwise, go to Part III.*

8 Enter the smaller of line 1c or line 7		**8**
9 Enter $150,000. If married filing separately, see page 10	**9**	
10 Enter modified adjusted gross income, but not less than zero (see page 10). If line 10 is equal to or greater than line 9, skip lines 11 through 15 and enter -0- on line 16	**10**	
11 Subtract line 10 from line 9	**11**	
12 Multiply line 11 by 50% (.50). Do not enter more than $25,000. If married filing separately, see page 11	**12**	
13 Enter the amount, if any, from line 9 of Form 8582	**13**	
14 Subtract line 13 from line 12	**14**	
15 Enter the tax attributable to the amount on line 14 (see page 11).........................		**15**
16 Enter the **smaller** of line 8 or line 15		**16**

For Paperwork Reduction Act Notice, see page 16.

Form **8582-CR** (1999)

ISA
STF FED6787F.1

Form **8586**	**Low-Income Housing Credit**	OMB No. 1545-0984
Department of the Treasury Internal Revenue Service	▶ **Attach to your return.**	**1999** Attachment Sequence No. **36b**
Name(s) shown on return		Identifying number

Part I   Current Year Credit (See instructions.)

1	Number of Forms 8609 attached .... ▶		
2	Eligible basis of building(s) (total from attached Schedules(s) A (Form 8609), line 1)	**2**	
3a	Qualified basis of low-income building(s) (total from attached Schedule(s) A (Form 8609), line 3) ...	**3a**	
b	Has there been a decrease in the qualified basis of any building(s) since the close of the preceding tax year? ☐ **Yes** ☐ **No** If "Yes," enter the building identification number (BIN) of the building(s) that had a decreased basis. If more space is needed, attach a schedule to list the BINs.		
	(i) _____ (ii) _____ (iii) _____ (iv)_____		
4	Current year credit (total from attached Schedule(s) A (Form 8609), see instructions)	**4**	
5	Credits from flow-through entities (if from more than one entity, see instructions):		

If you are a —	Then enter total of current year housing credit(s) from —		
a Shareholder	Schedule K-1 (Form 1120S), lines 12b(1) through (4)		
b Partner	Schedule K-1 (Form 1065), lines 12a(1) through (4), or Schedule K-1 (Form 1065-B), box 8		**5**
c Beneficiary	Schedule K-1 (Form 1041), line 14	EIN of flow-through entity	

6	Add lines 4 and 5. (See instructions to find out if you complete lines 7 through 17 or file Form 3800.).	**6**	
7	**Passive activity credit** or **total current year credit** for 1999 (see instructions)	**7**	

Part II   Tax Liability Limit

8	Regular tax before credits: • Individuals. Enter amount from Form 1040, line 40 .... • Corporations. Enter amount from Form 1120, Schedule J, line 3 (or Form 1120-A, Part I, line 1) ...... • Other filers. Enter regular tax before credits from your return		**8**	
9a	Credit for child and dependent care expenses (Form 2441, line 9)	**9a**		
b	Credit for the elderly or the disabled (Schedule R (Form 1040), line 20) ..	**9b**		
c	Child tax credit (Form 1040, line 43)...........................	**9c**		
d	Education credits (Form 8863, line 18).........................	**9d**		
e	Mortgage interest credit (Form 8396, line 11)	**9e**		
f	Adoption credit (Form 8839, line 15)	**9f**		
g	District of Columbia first-time homebuyer credit (Form 8859, line 11)	**9g**		
h	Foreign tax credit	**9h**		
i	Possessions tax credit (Form 5735, line 17 or 27)	**9i**		
j	Credit for fuel from a nonconventional source.....................	**9j**		
k	Qualified electric vehicle credit (Form 8834, line 19)..................	**9k**		
l	Add lines 9a through 9k		**9l**	
10	Net regular tax. Subtract line 9l from line 8		**10**	
11	Alternative minimum tax: • Individuals. Enter amount from Form 6251, line 28 .... • Corporations. Enter amount from Form 4626, line 15............... • Estates and trusts. Enter amount from Form 1041, Schedule I, line 39		**11**	
12	Net income tax. Add lines 10 and 11................................		**12**	
13	Tentative minimum tax (see instructions): • Individuals. Enter amount from Form 6251, line 26 .... • Corporations. Enter amount from Form 4626, line 13............. • Estates and trusts. Enter amount from Form 1041, Schedule I, line 37	**13**		
14	If line 10 is more than $25,000, enter 25% (.25) of the excess (see instructions)	**14**		
15	Enter the greater of line 13 or line 14		**15**	
16	Subtract line 15 from line 12. If zero or less, enter -0-.......................		**16**	
17	**Low-income housing credit allowed for current year.** Enter the **smaller** of line 7 or line 16. Enter here and on Form 1040, line 47; Form 1120, Schedule J, line 4d; Form 1120-A, Part I, line 2a; Form 1041, Schedule G, line 2c; or the applicable line of your return		**17**	

General Instructions

Section references are to the Internal Revenue Code.

Purpose of Form

An owner of a residential rental building in a qualified low-income housing project uses Form 8586 to claim the low-income housing credit.

The low-income housing credit determined under section 42 is a credit of 70% of the qualified basis of each new low-income building placed in service after 1986 (30% for certain federally subsidized new buildings or existing

For Paperwork Reduction Act Notice, see back of form.
ISA
STF FED6835F.1

Form **8586** (1999)

Form **8615**

Department of the Treasury
Internal Revenue Service (O)

Tax for Children Under Age 14
Who Have Investment Income of More Than $1,400

▶ Attach ONLY to the child's Form 1040, Form 1040A, or Form 1040NR.

OMB No. 1545-0998

1999

Attachment
Sequence No. **33**

Child's name shown on return	Child's social security number

A Parent's name (first, initial, and last). **Caution:** See instructions on back before completing.	**B** Parent's social security number

C Parent's filing status (check one):

☐ Single ☐ Married filing jointly ☐ Married filing separately ☐ Head of household ☐ Qualifying widow(er)

Part I   Child's Net Investment Income

1	Enter the child's investment income, such as taxable interest and dividends. See instructions. If this amount is $1,400 or less, **stop;** do not file this form	1	
2	If the child **did not** itemize deductions on **Schedule A** (Form 1040 or Form 1040NR), enter $1,400. If the child **did** itemize deductions, see instructions	2	
3	Subtract line 2 from line 1. If the result is zero or less, **stop;** do not complete the rest of this form but **do** attach it to the child's return	3	
4	Enter the child's **taxable income** from Form 1040, line 39; Form 1040A, line 24; or Form 1040NR, line 38	4	
5	Enter the **smaller** of line 3 or line 4	5	

Part II   Tentative Tax Based on the Tax Rate of the Parent Listed on Line A

6	Enter the parent's **taxable income** from Form 1040, line 39; Form 1040A, line 24; Form 1040EZ, line 6; TeleFile Tax Record, line K; Form 1040NR, line 38; or Form 1040NR-EZ, line 14. If less than zero, enter -0-	6	
7	Enter the total net investment income, if any, from Forms 8615, line 5, of **all other** children of the parent identified above. **Do not** include the amount from line 5 above	7	
8	Add lines 5, 6, and 7	8	
9	Enter the tax on line 8 based on the **parent's** filing status. See instructions. If the **Capital Gain Tax Worksheet** or **Schedule D** or **J** (Form 1040) is used to figure the tax, check here ▶ ☐	9	
10	Enter the parent's tax from Form 1040, line 40; Form 1040A, line 25; Form 1040EZ, line 10; TeleFile Tax Record, line K; Form 1040NR, line 39; or Form 1040NR-EZ, line 15. If any tax is from **Form 4972** or **8814,** see instructions. If the **Capital Gain Tax Worksheet** or **Schedule D** or **J** (Form 1040) was used to figure the tax, check here . . . . ▶ ☐	10	
11	Subtract line 10 from line 9 and enter the result. If line 7 is blank, also enter this amount on line 13 and go to **Part III**	11	
12a	Add lines 5 and 7 . . . . [12a]		
b	Divide line 5 by line 12a. Enter the result as a decimal (rounded to at least three places) . .	12b	× .
13	Multiply line 11 by line 12b	13	

Part III   Child's Tax—If lines 4 and 5 above are the same, enter -0- on line 15 and go to line 16.

14	Subtract line 5 from line 4 . . . . [14]		
15	Enter the tax on line 14 based on the **child's** filing status. See instructions. If the **Capital Gain Tax Worksheet** or **Schedule D** or **J** (Form 1040) is used to figure the tax, check here ▶ ☐	15	
16	Add lines 13 and 15	16	
17	Enter the tax on line 4 based on the **child's** filing status. See instructions. If the **Capital Gain Tax Worksheet** or **Schedule D** or **J** (Form 1040) is used to figure the tax, check here ▶ ☐	17	
18	Enter the **larger** of line 16 or line 17 here and on Form 1040, line 40; Form 1040A, line 25; or Form 1040NR, line 39	18	

General Instructions

Purpose of Form

For children under age 14, investment income over $1,400 is taxed at the parent's rate if the parent's rate is higher than the child's rate. If the child's investment income is more than $1,400, use this form to figure the child's tax.

See Pub. 929, Tax Rules for Children and Dependents, if the child, the parent, or any of the parent's other children under age 14 received capital gain distributions or farm income. It has information on how

to figure the tax using the **Capital Gain Tax Worksheet** or **Schedule D** or **J,** which may result in less tax.

Investment Income

For this form, "investment income" includes all taxable income other than earned income as defined on page 2. It includes taxable interest, dividends, capital gains, rents, royalties, etc. It also includes taxable social security benefits, pension and annuity income, and income (other than earned income) received as the beneficiary of a trust.

Who Must File

Generally, Form 8615 must be filed for any child who was under age 14 on January 1, 2000, had more than $1,400 of investment income, and is required to file a tax return. But if neither parent was alive on December 31, 1999, do not use Form 8615. Instead, figure the child's tax in the normal manner.

Note: *The parent may be able to elect to report the child's interest and dividends (including capital gain distributions) on the parent's return. If the parent makes this election, the child will not have to file a return or Form 8615. However, the Federal*

For Paperwork Reduction Act Notice, see back of form.

Cat. No. 64113U

Form **8615** (1999)

Form **8822**
(Rev. Oct. 1997)
Department of the Treasury
Internal Revenue Service

Change of Address

▶ Please type or print.

▶ See instructions on back.   ▶ Do not attach this form to your return.

OMB No. 1545-1163

Part I   Complete This Part To Change Your Home Mailing Address

Check **ALL** boxes this change affects:

1 ☐ Individual income tax returns (Forms 1040, 1040A, 1040EZ, 1040NR, etc.)

▶ If your last return was a joint return and you are now establishing a residence separate
from the spouse with whom you filed that return, check here . . . . ▶ ☐

2 ☐ Gift, estate, or generation-skipping transfer tax returns (Forms 706, 709, etc.)

▶ For Forms 706 and 706-NA, enter the decedent's name and social security number below.

▶ Decedent's name   ▶ Social security number

3a Your name (first name, initial, and last name)	3b Your social security number
4a Spouse's name (first name, initial, and last name)	4b Spouse's social security number

5 Prior name(s). See instructions.

6a Old address (no., street, city or town, state, and ZIP code). If a P.O. box or foreign address, see instructions.	Apt. no.
6b Spouse's old address, if different from line 6a (no., street, city or town, state, and ZIP code). If a P.O. box or foreign address, see instructions.	Apt. no.
7 New address (no., street, city or town, state, and ZIP code). If a P.O. box or foreign address, see instructions.	Apt. no.

Part II   Complete This Part To Change Your Business Mailing Address or Business Location

Check **ALL** boxes this change affects:

8 ☐ Employment, excise, and other business returns (Forms 720, 940, 940-EZ, 941, 990, 1041, 1065, 1120, etc.)
9 ☐ Employee plan returns (Forms 5500, 5500-C/R, and 5500-EZ). See instructions.
10 ☐ Business location

11a Business name	11b Employer identification number
12 Old mailing address (no., street, city or town, state, and ZIP code). If a P.O. box or foreign address, see instructions.	Room or suite no.
13 New mailing address (no., street, city or town, state, and ZIP code). If a P.O. box or foreign address, see instructions.	Room or suite no.
14 New business location (no., street, city or town, state, and ZIP code). If a foreign address, see instructions.	Room or suite no.

Part III   Signature

Daytime telephone number of person to contact (optional) ▶ (   )

**Please
Sign
Here**

▶ _____   _____
Your signature   Date

▶ _____   _____
If Part II completed, signature of owner, officer, or representative   Date

▶ _____   _____
If joint return, spouse's signature   Date

Title

For Privacy Act and Paperwork Reduction Act Notice, see back of form.   Cat. No. 12081V   Form **8822** (Rev. 10-97)

475

Form **8829**	**Expenses for Business Use of Your Home**	OMB No. 1545-1266
	► File only with Schedule C (Form 1040). Use a separate Form 8829 for each home you used for business during the year.	**19 99**
Department of the Treasury Internal Revenue Service (O)	► See separate instructions.	Attachment Sequence No. **66**

Name(s) of proprietor(s)	Your social security number

Part I   Part of Your Home Used for Business

1	Area used regularly and exclusively for business, regularly for day care, or for storage of inventory or product samples. See instructions	**1**	
2	Total area of home	**2**	
3	Divide line 1 by line 2. Enter the result as a percentage	**3**	%
	• **For day-care facilities not used exclusively for business, also complete lines 4–6.**		
	• **All others, skip lines 4–6 and enter the amount from line 3 on line 7.**		
4	Multiply days used for day care during year by hours used per day . **4** ____ hr.		
5	Total hours available for use during the year (365 days × 24 hours). See instructions **5** 8,760 hr.		
6	Divide line 4 by line 5. Enter the result as a decimal amount . . . **6** .		
7	Business percentage. For day-care facilities not used exclusively for business, multiply line 6 by line 3 (enter the result as a percentage). All others, enter the amount from line 3 . . . . ►	**7**	%

Part II   Figure Your Allowable Deduction

		(a) Direct expenses	(b) Indirect expenses	
8	Enter the amount from Schedule C, line 29, **plus** any net gain or (loss) derived from the business use of your home and shown on Schedule D or Form 4797. If more than one place of business, see instructions			**8**
	See instructions for columns (a) and (b) before completing lines 9–20.			
9	Casualty losses. See instructions	**9**		
10	Deductible mortgage interest. See instructions .	**10**		
11	Real estate taxes. See instructions	**11**		
12	Add lines 9, 10, and 11	**12**		
13	Multiply line 12, column (b) by line 7 . . .		**13**	
14	Add line 12, column (a) and line 13			**14**
15	Subtract line 14 from line 8. If zero or less, enter -0- .			**15**
16	Excess mortgage interest. See instructions . .	**16**		
17	Insurance	**17**		
18	Repairs and maintenance	**18**		
19	Utilities	**19**		
20	Other expenses. See instructions	**20**		
21	Add lines 16 through 20	**21**		
22	Multiply line 21, column (b) by line 7 . . .	**22**		
23	Carryover of operating expenses from 1998 Form 8829, line 41 . . .	**23**		
24	Add line 21 in column (a), line 22, and line 23			**24**
25	Allowable operating expenses. Enter the **smaller** of line 15 or line 24			**25**
26	Limit on excess casualty losses and depreciation. Subtract line 25 from line 15			**26**
27	Excess casualty losses. See instructions	**27**		
28	Depreciation of your home from Part III below	**28**		
29	Carryover of excess casualty losses and depreciation from 1998 Form 8829, line 42	**29**		
30	Add lines 27 through 29			**30**
31	Allowable excess casualty losses and depreciation. Enter the **smaller** of line 26 or line 30 . .			**31**
32	Add lines 14, 25, and 31			**32**
33	Casualty loss portion, if any, from lines 14 and 31. Carry amount to **Form 4684**, Section B . .			**33**
34	Allowable expenses for business use of your home. Subtract line 33 from line 32. Enter here and on Schedule C, line 30. If your home was used for more than one business, see instructions ►			**34**

Part III   Depreciation of Your Home

35	Enter the **smaller** of your home's adjusted basis or its fair market value. See instructions . .	**35**	
36	Value of land included on line 35	**36**	
37	Basis of building. Subtract line 36 from line 35	**37**	
38	Business basis of building. Multiply line 37 by line 7	**38**	
39	Depreciation percentage. See instructions	**39**	%
40	Depreciation allowable. Multiply line 38 by line 39. Enter here and on line 28 above. See instructions	**40**	

Part IV   Carryover of Unallowed Expenses to 2000

41	Operating expenses. Subtract line 25 from line 24. If less than zero, enter -0-	**41**	
42	Excess casualty losses and depreciation. Subtract line 31 from line 30. If less than zero, enter -0- .	**42**	

For Paperwork Reduction Act Notice, see page 4 of separate instructions.   Cat. No. 13232M   Form **8829** (1999)

✳ Printed on recycled paper   *U.S. Government Printing Office: 1999 — 456-551

Form **8853**	**Medical Savings Accounts and Long-Term Care Insurance Contracts**	OMB No. 1545-1561
Department of the Treasury Internal Revenue Service	▶ Attach to Form 1040. ▶ See separate instructions.	19**99** Attachment Sequence No. **39**

Name(s) shown on return	Social security number of MSA account holder. If both spouses have MSAs, see page 1 ▶

Section A. Medical Savings Accounts (MSAs).

If you only have a Medicare+Choice MSA, skip Section A and complete Section B.

Part I **General Information.** You MUST complete this part if you (or your spouse, if married filing jointly) established a new MSA for 1999 (even if the contributions to the MSA were made by an employer).

		Yes	No
1a	Did you establish a new MSA for 1999? **1a**		
b	If "Yes," were you a previously uninsured account holder (see page 2 of the instructions for definition)? **1b**		
c	If line 1a is "Yes," indicate coverage under high deductible health plan: ☐ Self-Only **or** ☐ Family		
2a	If you were married, did your spouse establish a new MSA for 1999? **2a**		
b	If "Yes," was your spouse a previously uninsured account holder (see page 2 of the instructions)? . . . **2b**		
c	If line 2a is "Yes," indicate coverage under high deductible health plan: ☐ Self-Only **or** ☐ Family		

Part II **MSA Contributions and Deductions.** See page 2 of the instructions before completing this part.
If you and your spouse each have high deductible health plans with self-only coverage, check here ▶ ☐
If you check this box, complete a separate Part II for each spouse (see page 2 of the instructions).

3a	Were any employer contributions made to your MSA(s)? . . . . . . ☐ **Yes** ☐ **No**	
b	Enter all employer contributions to your MSA(s) for 1999 ▶	
4	Enter MSA contributions that you made for 1999, including those made from January 1, 2000, through April 17, 2000, that were for 1999. Do not include rollovers (see page 2 of the instructions) . . .	**4**
5	Enter your limitation from the worksheet on page 3 of the instructions	**5**
6	Enter your compensation (see page 2 of the instructions) from the employer maintaining the high deductible health plan. If you (and your spouse, if married filing jointly) have more than one plan, see **How To Complete Part II** on page 2 of the instructions. (If self-employed, enter your earned income from the trade or business under which the high deductible health plan was established.)	**6**
7	**MSA deduction.** Enter the **smallest** of line 4, 5, or 6 here and on Form 1040, line 25 . . .	**7**

Note: *If line 4 is more than line 7, you may have to pay an additional tax. See page 3 of the instructions for details.*

Part III **MSA Distributions**

8a	Enter the total MSA distributions you and your spouse received from all MSAs during 1999 (see page 4 of the instructions).	**8a**
b	Enter any distributions included on line 8a that you rolled over to another MSA (see page 4 of the instructions). Also include any excess contributions (and the earnings on those excess contributions) included on line 8a that were withdrawn by the due date of your return	**8b**
c	Subtract line 8b from line 8a	**8c**
9	Enter your total unreimbursed qualified medical expenses (see page 4 of the instructions) . .	**9**
10	**Taxable MSA distributions.** Subtract line 9 from line 8c. If zero or less, enter -0-. Also include this amount in the total on Form 1040, line 21. On the dotted line next to line 21, enter "MSA" and show the amount	**10**
11a	If you meet any of the **Exceptions to the 15% Tax** (see page 4 of the instructions), check ▶ ☐	
b	If you do not meet any of the exceptions, enter 15% (.15) of line 10 here and also include it in the total on Form 1040, line 56. On the dotted line next to line 56, enter "MSA" and the amount	**11b**

Section B. Medicare+Choice MSA Distributions.

If you are married filing jointly and both you and your spouse received distributions from a Medicare+Choice MSA in 1999, complete a separate Section B for each spouse. See page 4 of the instructions.

12	Enter the total distributions you received from all Medicare+Choice MSAs in 1999	**12**
13	Enter your total unreimbursed qualified medical expenses (see page 5 of the instructions) . .	**13**
14	**Taxable Medicare+Choice MSA Distributions.** Subtract line 13 from line 12. If zero or less, enter -0-. Also include this amount in the total on Form 1040, line 21. On the dotted line next to line 21, enter "Med+MSA" and show the amount	**14**
15a	If you meet any of the **Exceptions to the 50% Tax** (see page 5 of the instructions), check ▶ ☐	
b	If you do not meet any of the exceptions, enter 50% (.5) of line 14 here and include it in the total on Form 1040, line 56. On the dotted line next to line 56, enter "Med+MSA" and the amount	**15b**

For Paperwork Reduction Act Notice, see page 8 of the instructions.   Cat. No. 24091H   Form **8853** (1999)

477

Form **8857**	**Request for Innocent Spouse Relief**	
(Rev. October 1999)	(And Separation of Liability and Equitable Relief)	OMB No. 1545-1596
Department of the Treasury Internal Revenue Service	▶ Do not file with your tax return. ▶ See instructions.	

Your name		Your social security number
Your current address		Apt. no.
City, town or post office, state, and ZIP code. If a foreign address, see instructions.		Daytime phone no. (optional) ( )

Do not file this form if all or part of your overpayment was (or is expected to be) applied against your spouse's past-due debt (such as child support). Instead, file **Form 8379,** Injured Spouse Claim and Allocation, to have your share of the overpayment refunded to you.

TIP *The IRS can help you with your request. If you are working with an IRS employee, you can ask that employee, or you can call 1-800-829-1040.*

Part I

1 Enter the year(s) for which you are requesting relief from liability of tax . . . . . ▶ ....

2 Information about the person to whom you were married as of the end of the year(s) on line 1.

See
**Spousal
Notification**
on page 3.

Name		Social security number
Current home address (number and street). If a P.O. box, see instructions.		Apt. no.
City, town or post office, state, and ZIP code. If a foreign address, see instructions.		Daytime phone no. (if known) ( )

3 Do you have an **Understatement of Tax** (that is, the IRS has determined there is a difference between the tax shown on your return and the tax that should have been shown)?

☐ **Yes.** Go to Part II. ☐ **No.** Go to Part IV.

Part II

4 Are you divorced from the person listed on line 2 (or has that person died)?
☐ **Yes.** Go to line 7. ☐ **No.** Go to line 5.

5 Are you legally separated from the person listed on line 2?
☐ **Yes.** Go to line 7. ☐ **No.** Go to line 6.

6 Have you lived apart from the person listed on line 2 at all times during the 12-month period prior to filing this form?
☐ **Yes.** Go to line 7. ☐ **No.** Go to Part III.

7 If line **4, 5,** or **6** is **Yes,** you may request **Separation of Liability** by **attaching a statement** (see page 3). Check here ▶ ☐ and go to Part III below.

Part III

8 Is the understatement of tax due to the **Erroneous Items** of your spouse (see page 4)?

☐ **Yes.** You may request **Innocent Spouse Relief** by **attaching a statement** (see page 4). Go to Part IV below.

☐ **No.** You may request **Equitable Relief** for the understatement of tax. Check **Yes** in Part IV below.

Part IV

9 Do you have an **Underpayment of Tax** (that is, tax that is properly shown on your return but not paid) or another tax liability that qualifies for **Equitable Relief** (see page 4)?

☐ **Yes.** You may request **Equitable Relief** by **attaching a statement** (see page 4).

☐ **No.** You cannot file this form unless line 3 is **Yes.**

Under penalties of perjury, I declare that I have examined this form and any accompanying schedules and statements, and to the best of my knowledge and belief, they are true, correct, and complete. Declaration of preparer (other than taxpayer) is based on all information of which preparer has any knowledge.

Sign Here Keep a copy of this form for your records. ▶	Your signature			Date

Paid Preparer's Use Only	Preparer's signature ▶	Date	Check if self-employed ☐	Preparer's SSN or PTIN
	Firm's name (or yours if self-employed) and address ▶			EIN
				ZIP code

For Privacy Act and Paperwork Reduction Act Notice, see page 4. Cat. No. 24647V Form **8857** (Rev. 10-99)

APPENDIX A

Form **8863**	**Education Credits** (Hope and Lifetime Learning Credits)	OMB No. 1545-1618
Department of the Treasury Internal Revenue Service	▶ See instructions on pages 3 and 4. ▶ Attach to Form 1040 or Form 1040A.	**1999** Attachment Sequence No. **51**

Name(s) shown on return | Your social security number

Part I Hope Credit

1

(a) Student's name First, Last	(b) Student's social security number	(c) Qualified expenses (but **do not** enter more than $2,000 for each student). See instructions	(d) Enter the **smaller** of the amount in column (c) or $1,000	(e) Subtract column (d) from column (c)	(f) Enter one-half of the amount in column (e)

2 Add the amounts in columns (d) and (f) . . . . . | **2** | | |

3 Add the amounts on line 2, columns (d) and (f) . . . . ▶ | **3** |

Part II Lifetime Learning Credit

4

Caution: *You cannot take the Hope credit and the lifetime learning credit for the same student.*

(a) Student's name First Last	(b) Student's social security number	(c) Qualified expenses. See instructions

5 Add the amounts on line 4, column (c), and enter the total . . . . | **5** |
6 Enter the **smaller** of line 5 or $5,000 . . . . | **6** |

7 Multiply line 6 by 20% (.20) . . . . ▶ | **7** |

Part III Allowable Education Credits

8 Add lines 3 and 7. . . . . | **8** |
9 Enter: $100,000 if married filing jointly; $50,000 if single, head of household, or qualifying widow(er) . . . . . . | **9** |
10 Enter the amount from Form 1040, line 34 (or Form 1040A, line 19)* | **10** |
11 Subtract line 10 from line 9. If line 10 is equal to or more than line 9, **stop;** you cannot take any education credits . . . . . | **11** |
12 Enter: $20,000 if married filing jointly; $10,000 if single, head of household, or qualifying widow(er) . . . . | **12** |
13 If line 11 is equal to or more than line 12, enter the amount from line 8 on line 14 and go to line 15. If line 11 is less than line 12, divide line 11 by line 12. Enter the result as a decimal (rounded to at least three places). . . . . | **13** | × . |
14 Multiply line 8 by line 13 . . . . ▶ | **14** |
15 Enter your tax from Form 1040, line 40 (or Form 1040A, line 25) . . . . | **15** |
16 Enter the total, if any, of your credits from Form 1040, lines 41 and 42 (or from Form 1040A, lines 26 and 27) . . . . | **16** |
17 Subtract line 16 from line 15. If line 16 is equal to or more than line 15, **stop;** you cannot take any education credits . . . . | **17** |
18 **Education credits.** Enter the **smaller** of line 14 or line 17 here and on Form 1040, line 44 (or Form 1040A, line 29) . . . . ▶ | **18** |

*See Pub. 970 for the amount to enter if you are filing Form 2555, 2555-EZ, or 4563, or you are excluding income from Puerto Rico.

For Paperwork Reduction Act Notice, see page 4.   Cat. No. 25379M   Form **8863** (1999)

479

Form **9465**
(Rev. January 1996)
Department of the Treasury
Internal Revenue Service

Installment Agreement Request

▶ **See instructions below and on back.**

OMB No. 1545-1350

Note: *Do not file this form if you are currently making payments on an installment agreement. You must pay your other Federal tax liabilities in full or you will be in default on your agreement.*

If you can't pay the full amount you owe, you can ask to make monthly installment payments. If we approve your request, you will be charged a $43 fee. **Do not include the fee with this form.** We will deduct the fee from your first payment after we approve your request, unless you choose **Direct Debit** (see the line 13 instructions). We will usually let you know within 30 days after we receive your request whether it is approved or denied. But if this request is for tax due on a return you filed after March 31, it may take us longer than 30 days to reply.

To ask for an installment agreement, complete this form. Attach it to the front of your return when you file. If you have already filed your return or you are filing this form in response to a notice, see **How Do I File Form 9465?** on page 2. If you have any questions about this request, call 1-800-829-1040.

Caution: *A Notice of Federal Tax Lien may be filed to protect the government's interest until you pay in full.*

1	Your first name and initial	Last name	Your social security number
	If a joint return, spouse's first name and initial	Last name	Spouse's social security number
	Your current address (number and street). If you have a P.O. box and no home delivery, show box number.		Apt. number
	City, town or post office, state, and ZIP code. If a foreign address, show city, state or province, postal code, and full name of country.		

2   If this address is new since you filed your last tax return, check here . . . . ▶ ☐

3   (_____) _____   _____
      Your home phone number   Best time for us to call

4   (_____) _____   _____   _____
      Your work phone number   Ext.   Best time for us to call

5   Name of your bank or other financial institution:

6   Your employer's name:

Address

Address

City, state, and ZIP code

City, state, and ZIP code

7   Enter the tax return for which you are making this request (for example, Form 1040). But if you are filing this form in response to a notice, don't complete lines 7 through 9. Instead, attach the bottom section of the notice to this form and go to line 10 . . . . ▶ _____

8   Enter the tax year for which you are making this request (for example, 1995) . . . . ▶ _____

9   Enter the total amount you owe as shown on your tax return . . . . ▶ $ _____

10   Enter the amount of any payment you are making with your tax return (or notice). See instructions . ▶ $ _____

11   Enter the amount you can paym each month. **Make your payments as large as possible to limit interest and penalty charges.** The charges will continue until you pay in full . . . . ▶ $ _____

12   Enter the date you want to make your payment each month. Do not enter a date later than the 28th ▶ _____

13   If you would like to make your monthly payments using **Direct Debit** (automatic withdrawals from your bank account), check here. . . . . ▶ ☐

Your signature	Date	Spouse's signature. If a joint return, BOTH must sign.	Date

Privacy Act and Paperwork Reduction Act Notice.—Our legal right to ask for the information on this form is Internal Revenue Code sections 6001, 6011, 6012(a), 6109, and 6159 and their regulations. We will use the information to process your request for an installment agreement. The reason we need your name and social security number is to secure proper identification. We require this information to gain access to the tax information in our files and properly respond to your request. If you do not enter the information, we may not be able to process your request. We may give this information to the Department of Justice as provided by law. We may also give it to cities, states, and the District of Columbia to carry out their tax laws.

Cat. No. 14842Y

Form **9465** (Rev. 1-96)

The time needed to complete and file this form will vary depending on individual circumstances. The estimated average time is: **Learning about the law or the form,** 2 min.; **Preparing the form,** 24 min.; and **Copying, assembling, and sending the form to the IRS,** 20 min.

If you have comments concerning the accuracy of this time estimate or suggestions for making this form simpler, we would be happy to hear from you. You can write to the Tax Forms Committee, Western Area Distribution Center, Rancho Cordova, CA 95743-0001. **DO NOT** send the form to this address. Instead, see **How Do I File Form 9465?** on this page.

General Instructions

If you cannot pay the full amount you owe shown on your tax return (or on a notice we sent you), you can ask to make monthly installment payments. But before requesting an installment agreement, you should consider other less costly alternatives, such as a bank loan.

You will be charged interest and may be charged a late payment penalty on any tax not paid by its due date, even if your request to pay in installments is granted. To limit interest and penalty charges, file your return on time and pay as much of the tax as possible with your return (or notice).

You will be charged a $43 fee if your request is approved. **Do not include the fee with this form.** We will send you a letter telling you your request has been approved, how to pay the fee, and how to make your first installment payment. After we receive each payment, we will send you a letter showing the remaining amount you owe, and the due date and amount of your next payment.

By approving your request, we agree to let you pay the tax you owe in monthly installments instead of immediately paying the amount in full. In return, you agree to make your monthly payments on time. **You also agree to meet all your future tax liabilities.** This means that you must have adequate withholding or estimated tax payments so that your tax liability for future years is paid in full when you timely file your return. If you do not make your payments on time or have an outstanding past-due amount in a future year, you will be in default on your agreement and we may take enforcement actions to collect the entire amount you owe.

Bankruptcy—Offer-in-Compromise.—If you are in bankruptcy or we have accepted your offer-in-compromise, **do not** file this form. Instead, call your local IRS District Office Special Procedures function. You can get the number by calling 1-800-829-1040.

Specific Instructions

Line 1

If you are making this request for a joint tax return, show the names and SSNs in the same order as on your tax return.

Line 10

Even if you can't pay the full amount you owe now, you should pay as much of it as possible to limit penalty and interest charges. If you are filing this form with your tax return, make the payment with your return. If you are filing this form by itself, for example, in response to a notice, include a check or money order payable to the Internal Revenue Service with this form. **Do not** send cash. On your payment, write your name, address, social security number, daytime phone number, and the tax year and tax return for which you are making this request (for example, "1995 Form 1040").

Line 11

You should try to make your payments large enough so that your balance due will be paid off by the due date of your next tax return.

Line 12

You can choose the date your monthly payment is due. For example, if your rent or mortgage payment is due on the first of the month, you may want to make your installment payments on the 15th. When we approve your request, we will tell you the month and date that your first payment is due. If we have not replied by the date you choose for your first payment, you may send the first payment to the Internal Revenue Service Center at the address shown on this page for the place where you live. Make your check or money order payable to the Internal Revenue Service. See the instructions for line 10 for what to write on your payment.

Line 13

Check the box on line 13 if you want your monthly payments automatically deducted **(Direct Debit)** from your bank account. If your installment agreement request is approved, we will send you the required Direct Debit enrollment form and you must include the $43 fee when you return it.

How Do I File Form 9465?

- If you haven't filed your return, attach Form 9465 to the front of your return.

- If you have already filed your return, you are filing your return electronically, or you are filing this form in response to a notice, mail it to the **Internal Revenue Service Center** at the address shown below for the place where you live. No street address is needed.

If you live in:	Use this address:
Florida, Georgia, South Carolina	Atlanta, GA 39901
New Jersey, New York (New York City and counties of Nassau, Rockland, Suffolk, and Westchester)	Holtsville, NY 00501
New York (all other counties), Connecticut, Maine, Massachusetts, New Hampshire, Rhode Island, Vermont	Andover, MA 05501
Illinois, Iowa, Minnesota, Missouri, Wisconsin	Kansas City, MO 64999
Delaware, District of Columbia, Maryland, Pennsylvania, Virginia	Philadelphia, PA 19255
Indiana, Kentucky, Michigan, Ohio, West Virginia	Cincinnati, OH 45999
Kansas, New Mexico, Oklahoma, Texas	Austin, TX 73301
Alaska, Arizona, California (counties of Alpine, Amador, Butte, Calaveras, Colusa, Contra Costa, Del Norte, El Dorado, Glenn, Humboldt, Lake, Lassen, Marin, Mendocino, Modoc, Napa, Nevada, Placer, Plumas, Sacramento, San Joaquin, Shasta, Sierra, Siskiyou, Solano, Sonoma, Sutter, Tehama, Trinity, Yolo, and Yuba), Colorado, Idaho, Montana, Nebraska, Nevada, North Dakota, Oregon, South Dakota, Utah, Washington, Wyoming	Ogden, UT 84201
California (all other counties), Hawaii	Fresno, CA 93888
Alabama, Arkansas, Louisiana, Mississippi, North Carolina, Tennessee	Memphis, TN 37501
American Samoa Guam: Nonpermanent residents only* Puerto Rico (or if excluding income under section 933) Virgin Islands: Nonpermanent residents only* Foreign country (or if a dual-status alien): U.S. citizens and those filing Form 2555, 2555-EZ, or 4563 All APO and FPO addresses	Philadelphia, PA 19255

*Permanent residents of Guam and the Virgin Islands cannot use Form 9465.

☆ U.S. GPO:1998-715-016/64543

Printed on recycled paper

Request for a Collection Due Process Hearing

Use this form to request a hearing with the IRS Office of Appeals only when you receive a **Notice of Federal Tax Lien Filing & Your Right To A Hearing Under IRC 6320**, a **Final Notice - Notice Of Intent to Levy & Your Notice Of a Right To A Hearing**, or a **Notice of Jeopardy Levy and Right of Appeal**. Complete this form and send it to the address shown on your lien or levy notice for expeditious handling. Include a copy of your lien or levy notice(s) to ensure proper handling of your request.

(Print) Taxpayer Name(s):_____

(Print) Address: _____

Daytime Telephone Number:_____ Type of Tax/Tax Form Number(s):_____

Taxable Period(s):_____

Social Security Number/Employer Identification Number(s):_____

Check the IRS action(s) that you do not agree with. Provide specific reasons why you don't agree. If you believe that your spouse or former spouse should be responsible for all or a portion of the tax liability from your tax return, check here [___] and attach Form 8857, Request for Innocent Spouse Relief, to this request.

_____ **Filed Notice of Federal Tax Lien (Explain why you don't agree. Use extra sheets if necessary.)**

_____ **Notice of Levy/Seizure (Explain why you don't agree. Use extra sheets if necessary.)**

I/we understand that the statutory period of limitations for collection is suspended during the Collection Due Process Hearing and any subsequent judicial review.

Taxpayer's or Authorized Representative's Signature and Date:_____

Taxpayer's or Authorized Representative's Signature and Date:_____

IRS Use Only:

IRS Employee *(Print)*: _____ IRS Received Date:_____

Employee Telephone Number: _____

Form **12153** (01-1999)   Catalog Number 26685D   Department of the Treasury – Internal Revenue Service

(Over)

APPENDIX B:
GUIDE TO FREE TAX SERVICES

Guide to Free Tax Services

Guide to Free Tax Services identifies the many IRS tax materials and services available to you, and how, when, and where you can get them. Most materials and programs are free and most are available year-round through the IRS. Internet, telephone, and fax access of tax materials; filing options; tax publications; tax education and assistance programs; and tax tips are covered in this Guide. Publication 910 also gives direction to access recorded tax information and automated refund information. Please read on to see which IRS tax services will help make your tax filing easier.

Customer Service

Customer Service — *taxpayer rights and good service and still collect the taxes* — The *Restructuring and Reform Act* was truly a landmark in the history of the IRS. It laid out a fundamentally new direction for the agency — the first one since Harry Truman was in the White House. And since there are many detailed and complex provisions in the Bill, including 71 new taxpayer rights, it's easy to get lost in specifics and overlook the whole picture. Through this *Act*, the IRS was given a new direction and a new challenge, namely to measure its success or failure in terms of its effect on the people it serves as well as the taxes it collects. This new direction relies heavily on improved management, improved business practices, and improved technology.

Taxpayer Rights
The *IRS Restructuring and Reform Act of 1998*, signed into law on July 22, 1998, contains the *Taxpayer Bill of Rights 3*. The *Taxpayer Bill of Rights 3* preserves the balance between safeguarding the rights of the individual taxpayers and enabling the Internal Revenue Service to administer the tax laws efficiently, fairly, and with the least amount of burden to the taxpayer.

Under this Bill, taxpayer rights were expanded in several areas:

- The burden of proof shifted to the IRS in certain court proceedings.
- In certain cases, taxpayers may be awarded damages and fees, and get liens released.
- Penalties will be eased when the IRS exceeds specified time limits between when a return is filed and when the taxpayer is notified of a tax liability.
- Interest will be eliminated in certain cases involving federally-declared disaster areas.
- There are new rules for collection actions by levy.
- Innocent spouse relief provisions are strengthened.
- In certain situations, taxpayer-requested installment agreements must be accepted. Taxpayers will get annual status reports of their installment agreements.

The IRS revised Publications 1, *Your Rights as a Taxpayer*, and 1SP, *Derechos del Contribuyente*, to incorporate *Taxpayer Bill of Rights 3* with some of the most important rights. These publications can be downloaded from the IRS Web site (www.irs.gov) or ordered through the IRS by calling 1-800-829-3676.

Good Service
In conjunction with the implementation of new taxpayer rights, the IRS has made many improvements in customer service. The Agency expanded hours of operations nationwide for both its tax assistance toll-free lines and its walk-in assistance at convenient locations. The Agency further increased options for filing and paying electronically, improved access to the taxpayer advocate, and set up 'problem solving days' in communities nationwide to resolve particularly difficult tax cases.

Still Collect the Taxes
The IRS works around the clock to provide revised tax materials to taxpayers. Publications, forms, instructions, booklets, brochures, CD-ROMs, videos, and etc., reflect the latest tax legislation. These products are available to help taxpayers meet their tax responsibilities. Publication 553, *Highlights of 1999 Tax Changes*, is a collection of the latest tax law changes that may affect you this filing season. You can download Publication 553 and nearly 100 other tax publications listed in this booklet from the IRS Web site (www.irs.gov), and you can request a free copy of any IRS tax publication by calling the IRS at 1-800-829-3676.

Advances in technology have provided new tools and new skills and have enabled significant improvements in operating processes and procedures. Currently, the IRS is capitalizing on these advances and is undertaking the enormous job of modernizing and replacing information computer systems designed in the early '60s. These improvements will greatly enhance the Agency's ability to achieve its goal of top quality service including timely and accurate responses to the taxpayers.

Restructuring a new IRS that meets new expectations of the public and the Congress will require years of sustained effort. The new IRS mission statement, *"Provide America's taxpayers top quality service by helping them understand and meet their tax responsibilities and by applying the tax law with integrity and fairness to all,"* clearly points to the Agency's new direction. In the past twelve months, the IRS has clarified its direction, developed a new attitude, and created new and exciting business practices. The IRS has taken the first bold steps toward achieving the goals as directed in the IRS Restructuring and Reform Act of 1998.

APPENDIX B

Tax Information — Where to Get It

The Internal Revenue Service produces and provides publications, forms, and other tax materials and information to help taxpayers meet their tax responsibilities. In addition to getting these materials over the telephone, through the mail, at local IRS offices, and at community locations, most materials can be obtained electronically — via the Internet, through a fax machine, and on CD-ROM.

Tax Information Available Electronically

From a computer, you can download and print any of 700 federal tax forms with instructions, approximately 100 tax publications, and other tax materials. Also for your convenience, you can request and receive forms through a fax machine or you can order the *Federal Tax Products on CD-ROM* of IRS forms and publications.

IRS Home Page: The IRS home page offers convenient access to information 24 hours a day, 7 days a week. The Web site has tax forms with instructions, publications, the latest tax law changes, and specific tax information for individuals and businesses. Access the IRS Web site at www.irs.gov

IRS Tax Fax: To get a faxed index of nearly 100 more frequently requested IRS tax forms, dial (703) 368-9694 from a fax machine. Follow the voice prompts and key in your response. You may select up to three (3) items to order during a single call. The forms are generally available for fax transmission at all times. Your order will be faxed back to you through your fax machine.

IRS CD-ROM: Publication 1796, *Federal Tax Products on CD-ROM*, of current and prior year tax publications and forms can be purchased from the National Technical Information Service (NTIS). Order by calling toll free 1-877-233-6767 (1-877-CDFORMS) or via the Internet at www.irs.gov/cdorders. (Cost is less when ordered through the Internet.)

IRS Community-Based Outlet Programs

The IRS and local community businesses across the United States are working together to increase accessibility of tax publications, forms, and other tax materials for your convenience. In addition to community outlets listed below, the IRS supplies tax forms and publications to a number of technical schools, military bases, prisons, and community colleges nationwide. Most banks are no longer tax form distribution outlets. However, banks that participate in the electronic filing program or are a VITA/TCE site may distribute tax forms. For businesses that would like to participate in one or more of these programs, call the IRS at 916-636-7703. Post offices and libraries need to call the IRS at 1-800-829-2765.

IRS Post Office Program: The IRS supplies free tax materials to many post offices nationwide. Most post offices stock Forms 1040 (*U.S. Individual Income Tax Return*), 1040A, and 1040EZ with the instructions and related schedules.

IRS Library Program: Members of the American Library Association and the Public Library Association continue to partner with the IRS to provide taxpayers access to a wide variety of tax products. Currently, over 14,000 libraries participate in this program. There may be a nominal fee if you need to reproduce a tax form where stock is not available.

IRS Copy Center Program: Each year, the IRS furnishes thousands of copy centers (nationwide) either the IRS Publication 1796, *Federal Tax Products on CD-ROM*, or IRS Publication 3195, *Laminated Tax Forms*. Through this program, quick copy centers and office supply stores can offer taxpayers a wide variety of IRS forms with instructions for copying. It may be a good idea to call the store nearest you prior to visiting since not all copy centers have this material. There is often a nominal charge associated with making copies.

IRS Corporate Partnership Program: The IRS and employers with 100 or more employees are working together to get tax materials to their employees. Upon request, the IRS provides employers with a free copy of Publication 1796, *Federal Tax Products on CD-ROM*, that contains tax forms with instructions and publications. The employer can then load this information on their Intranet or local area network so their employees can access the tax information. Employees will be able to view and print more than 700 current IRS tax forms with instructions and publications. Prior-year forms, tax regulations, IR bulletins are also available on the CD. For companies that have employees that do not have computer access, the IRS can provide a free copy of Publication 1132, *Reproducible Copies of Federal Tax Forms*. This publication is a compilation of over 150 tax forms with instructions that can be photocopied and used. The forms are in camera-ready format for better quality reproduction.

IRS Credit Union Program: The IRS and credit unions are partnering to offer credit union members another outlet to access tax forms. Through this program, credit unions can get a free copy of IRS tax products on CD-ROM and IRS reproducible tax forms (Publications 1132, 1132L, and 3194). Credit unions also have the option to load the CD-ROM on their Internet site or they can link to the IRS Web site. Then credit union members can obtain tax materials at work or at home via their credit union Internet Web site or they can photocopy forms at their credit union.

IRS Grocery Store Program: Grocery store chains across the nation are partnering with the IRS to get tax forms to their customers. IRS provides Publication 3194, *Laminated Tax Forms*, to these stores. Then grocery stores may attach this Publication to a self-service copy machine so customers can make copies.

IRS Newspaper Supplement Program: Through this program, the IRS provides print media outlets with a package of the most frequently used IRS tax forms. The IRS will provide requested quantities of this package to insert in newspapers. Newspapers can also obtain a free copy of Publication 1796, *Federal Tax Products on CD-ROM*, to load to their Web site. And, when a newspaper is affiliated with a TV or radio station, the TV or radio station may want to take advantage of loading Publication 1796 on their Web site.

Tax Publications

The IRS produces many free publications to help you fill out your tax return and to answer your tax questions. All IRS publications and forms can be downloaded from the Internet or ordered at no charge by calling the IRS at 1-800-829-3676. You can also get forms faxed to you. See section IRS Tax Fax under **Tax Information Available Electronically.**

Tax Publications and Related Forms: You may want to get one or more of the publications listed below for information on a specific topic. Where the publication title may not be enough to describe the contents of the publication, there is a brief description. Forms and schedules related to the contents of each publication are shown after each listing.

Most Popular Publications!

Pub 17, *Your Federal Income Tax (For Individuals)* — can help you prepare your individual tax return. This publication takes you step-by-step through each part of the return. It explains the tax law in a way that will help you better understand your taxes so that you pay only as much as you owe and no more. This publication also includes information on various kinds of credits you may be able to take to reduce your tax. **(Note to Tax Professionals only: There is a fee to order this publication.)**
  Forms 1040 (Schedules A,B,D,E,EIC,R) 1040A, 1040EZ, 2106, 2119, 2441, 3903, W-2.

Pub 334, *Tax Guide for Small Business (For Individuals Who Use Schedule C or C-EZ)* — explains federal tax laws that apply to sole proprietors and statutory employees. **(Note to Tax Professionals only: There is a fee for this publication.)**
  Forms 1040 (Schedule C, C-EZ, SE), 4562.

Pub 553, *Highlights of 1999 Tax Changes* — provides detailed information about tax law changes that may affect you this filing season. There were a number of tax law changes that occurred in the Taxpayer Relief Act of 1997 and the IRS Restructuring and Reform Act of 1998 that may apply to many individuals and business owners over the next few years. Pub 553 includes these tax law changes.

Pub 579SP, *Cómo Preparar la Declaración de Impuesto Federal* (How to Prepare the Federal Income Tax Return) —
  Forms 1040, 1040A, (Schedules 1 and 2), 1040EZ, and Schedule EIC.

Pub 1, *Your Rights as a Taxpayer* — explains some of your most important rights as a taxpayer. It also explains the examination, appeal, collection, and refund processes. To ensure that you always receive fair treatment in tax matters, you should know what your rights are.

Pub 1SP, *Derechos del Contribuyente* (Your Rights as a Taxpayer) — (Publication 1 in Spanish.)

Pub 3, *Armed Forces Tax Guide* — gives information about the special tax situations of active members of the Armed Forces. This publication contains information on items that are included in and excluded from gross income, combat zone exclusion, alien status, dependency exemptions, sale of residence, itemized deductions, tax liability, extension of deadline, and filing returns.
  Forms 1040, 1040A, 1040EZ, 1040NR, 1040X, 1310, 2106, 2688, 2848, 3903, 4868, 8822, 9465, W-2.

Pub 4, *Student's Guide to Federal Income Tax* — explains the federal tax laws that are of particular interest to high school and college students. It describes student's responsibilities to pay taxes and file returns and explains how to file and get help, if needed.
  Forms 1040 (Schedules C-EZ and SE), 1040EZ, 4070, W-2, W-4.

Pub 15, *Circular E, Employer's Tax Guide* — Forms 940, 941.

Pub 15-A, *Employer's Supplemental Tax Guide*

Pub 51, *Circular A, Agricultural Employer's Tax Guide* — Form 943.

Pub 54, *Tax Guide for U.S. Citizens and Resident Aliens Abroad* — explains the special tax rules for U.S. citizens and resident aliens who live and work abroad or who have income earned in foreign countries. In particular, this publication explains the rules for excluding income and excluding or deducting certain housing costs.
  Forms 1040, 1116, 2555, 2555-EZ.

Pub 80, *Federal Tax Guide for Employers in the Virgin Islands, Guam, American Samoa, and the Commonwealth of the Northern Mariana Islands (Circular SS)* —
  Forms 940, 941SS, 943.

Pub 179, *Guía Contributiva Federal Para Patronos Puertorriqueños (Circular PR)* (Federal Tax Guide for Employers in Puerto Rico) —
  Forms 940PR, 941PR, 943PR, W-3PR.

Pub 225, *Farmer's Tax Guide* — identifies the kind of farm income you must report and the different deductions you can take.
  Forms 1040 (Schedules F,J,SE), 4562, 4684, 4797.

Pub 378, *Fuel Tax Credits and Refunds* — explains the credit or refund that may be allowable for the federal excise taxes on certain fuels. Also discusses the alcohol fuel credit.
  Forms 720, 4136, 6478, 8849.

1-800 Tax Assistance Telephone Number

If you cannot answer your tax question by reading the tax form instructions or our free tax publications, please call the IRS for assistance at 1-800-829-1040 beginning January 3, 2000, 24 hours a day, seven (7) days a week. To check on the status of your refund, call TeleTax at 1-800-829-4477.

Before You Call

IRS representatives care about the quality of service you get. We can better provide you with accurate and complete answers to your tax questions if you have the following information available.

- ✓ The tax form, schedule, or notice to which your question relates.

- ✓ The facts about your particular situation. (The answer to the same question often varies from one taxpayer to another because of differences in their age, income, whether they can be claimed as a dependent, etc.)

- ✓ The name of any IRS publication or other source of information that you used to look for the answer.

To protect and maintain your individual account security, you may also be asked for your social security number (SSN), date of birth, or personal identification number (PIN) if you have one. You may also need to provide the amount of your refund, filing status shown on your tax return, the "caller ID number" shown at the top of any notice you received, the numbers in your street address, or your ZIP code.

If you are asking for an *installment agreement* to pay your tax, you will be asked for the highest amount you can pay each month and the date on which you can pay it.

NOTE: *Toll-free Spanish Assistance Available — Beginning January 3, 2000, Spanish speaking assistance will be available by calling 1-800-829-1040.*

Making the Call

Call 1-800-829-1040. If you are using a pulse or rotary dial phone, stay on the line and an IRS assistor will answer. If you are using a Touch-Tone telephone to dial the number, you can then press 1 to enter the IRS automated telephone system. Listen for and press the number for a specific topic of interest. Selecting the correct topic helps us serve you faster and more efficiently. The system allows you to order tax forms and publications; to find out the status of your refund or what you owe; to find out if we adjusted your account or received your payment; or to request a transcript of your account.

Before You Hang Up

If you do not fully understand the answer you receive, or you feel the IRS representative may not fully understand your question, the representative needs to know. The representative will be happy to take additional time to be sure he or she has answered your question fully.

By law, you are responsible for paying your fair share of federal income tax. If we should make an error in answering your question, you are still responsible for the payment of the correct tax. Should this occur, however, you will not be charged any penalty.

The IRS uses different methods to evaluate the quality of this telephone service. To make sure that IRS representatives give accurate and courteous answers, a second IRS representative sometimes listens in. And some callers are asked to complete a short survey at the end of the call.

Explore IRS *e-file*

Join the 30 million Americans who file their tax returns electronically using an IRS *e-file* option. IRS *e-file* is the quickest and most accurate way to file your taxes. It offers a fast refund (twice as fast as filing on paper, even faster with direct deposit); a better likelihood for an error-free return (IRS *e-file* has less than 1% error rate); the opportunity to file your federal and state tax returns together; proof within 48 hours that your return has been accepted; privacy; and security. If you have a balance due, you may choose to file now and pay later (up until April 17, 2000) using a direct debit from your checking or savings account or using a credit card. To pay by credit card, call 888-2pay-tax (1-888-272-9829). Check out the IRS Web site at www.irs.gov for more information on electronic filing.

Here's how you can IRS *e-file*:

IRS *e-file* Through an Authorized Provider
(Look for an "Authorized IRS *e-file* Provider" sign)

Many tax professionals file returns electronically for their clients. **You can prepare** your return and have a professional transmit it electronically to the IRS; or you **can have a professional prepare** your return and transmit it for you electronically. Tax professionals may charge a fee to IRS *e-file*. Fees may vary depending on the professional and the specific services rendered.

Thirty million Americans use IRS *e-file*. Get your federal tax refund in less than half the usual time. Or, if you owe tax, e-file early but wait until April 17th to pay. Visit our Web site: www.irs.gov

IRS *e-file* Using a Personal Computer

If you have a modem, a personal computer, and tax preparation software, **you** can *e-file* your tax return. Tax preparation software that offers the IRS *e-file* option is available at computer retailers and through various Web sites over the Internet. Access a list of participating software companies via the Internet at www.irs.gov, click on "Electronic Services," and then click on "On-Line Filing Companies." You can also find a list of IRS partners that provide free or low-cost IRS *e-file* options by clicking on "Electronic Services," and then on "IRS *e-file* Partners." By using your personal computer, IRS *e-file* is available 24 hours a day, 7 days a week.

IRS *e-file* Using a Touch-Tone Telephone

For millions of eligible taxpayers, TeleFile is the easiest way to file. TeleFile allows you to file your simple federal tax return using a Touch-Tone telephone. **If you are eligible to use TeleFile,** the IRS will automatically send you a TeleFile tax package through the mail. Just fill in the tax record in the booklet, pick up a telephone, and call the toll-free number listed in the tax package, any time — day or night. TeleFile is completely paperless — there are no forms to mail. It usually takes about 10 minutes and is absolutely free.

> *Parents!*
> *If your children receive a TeleFile Tax Package in the mail, please encourage them to use TeleFile.*

IRS *e-file* Through Employers and Financial Institutions

Some businesses offer e-filing services to their employees for free. Others offer it to their customers for a fee. See if your employer or financial institution offers IRS *e-file* to employees, members, or customers. If they don't, ask them to provide IRS *e-file* as a service this filing season.

IRS *e-file* at Authorized VITA and TCE Sites

Volunteer Income Tax Assistance (VITA) and Tax Counseling for the Elderly (TCE) sites are open to assist individuals with low income, individuals with special needs, and the elderly. Both programs are free and can be found in community locations, such as libraries, colleges, universities, shopping malls, and retirement and senior centers. Ask for IRS *e-file* at these sites.

Business Tax Services and Information

The IRS has many publications containing information about the federal tax laws that apply to businesses. Publication 334, *Tax Guide for Small Business*, is a good place to start to learn more about sole proprietors and statutory employees. Publication 583, *Starting a Business and Keeping Records*, covers basic tax information for those who are starting a business. Look in section **Tax Publications** for other materials that can explain your business tax responsibilities. For electronic assistance, you may go to the *IRS Digital Daily* Web site at www.irs.gov and access "Electronic Services." Then look for "IRS *e-file* Options for Business."

IRS *e-file* Programs for Businesses

File Form 941 by Telephone

Employers nationwide have the opportunity to file Form 941, *Employer's Quarterly Federal Tax Return*, using a Touch-Tone telephone, toll-free telephone number, and simple instructions. Businesses that meet certain qualifications are invited to participate in the paperless, 941TeleFile program. Eligible filers will receive a special 941TeleFile Tax Record and instructions with their Form 941 tax package.

If you receive the purple tax package in the mail with your traditional Form 941 and meet the qualifications in the instructions, you can use 941TeleFile. It's easy and **Free**. File your 941 in three easy steps:

- complete the 941TeleFile Tax Record
- with a Touch-Tone telephone, call the toll-free TeleFile number provided in the 941TeleFile tax package
- keep the 941TeleFile Tax Record as part of your permanent business records.

The 941TeleFile system automatically calculates your tax liability and any overpayment or balance due during the call. It also gives you a confirmation number as proof of filing your return. The call only takes about 10 minutes. The system is available 24 hours a day, 7 days a week. And, there is nothing to mail to the IRS.

File Form 941 Using a Reporting Agent

The 941*e-file* program accepts and processes Forms 941, Employer's Quarterly Federal Tax Return in the Electronic Data Interchange (EDI) format. Returns are transmitted nationwide via dial-up phone lines and menu-driven software directly to the IRS where they are processed at the Tennessee Computing Center (TCC) or the Austin Service Center (AUSC). An electronic acknowledgment is returned within 48 hours of receipt of the return. 941*e-file* accepts both timely filed returns, and late filed returns for the current tax year as well as for one (1) preceding tax year.

Large payroll processing companies, bulk-filer reporting agents, and/or large businesses capable of developing their own software are ideally suited to participate in this 941*e-file* program. Small businesses or reporting agents may also participate by developing their own software or by purchasing off-the-shelf software. With the appropriate software, almost any 941 filer can transmit his/her return.

To file using the IRS 941*e-file* program, an applicant should obtain a copy of Publication 1911, *Instructions for Preparing and Submitting Form 8655, Reporting Agent Authorization*, and Publication 3062, *Requirements of the Electronic Filing Program for Reporting of Form 941, Employer's Quarterly Federal Tax Return*. You can order these items free of charge through an IRS Area Distribution Center by calling the IRS at 1-800-829-3676. Additional information on how to participate in 941*e-file* can be obtained by contacting the IRS electronic filing TCC Help Desk on 901-546-2690, ext 7519 or the AUSC Help Desk on 512-460-4069.

File Form 941 Using a Personal Computer

Businesses that have a computer, modem, and off-the-shelf tax preparation software can transmit tax return information to a third party transmitter. The third party transmitter will batch, and then electronically forward, the return to the Austin Service Center. This program accepts and processes Form 941 in Electronic Data Interchange (EDI) format. The program also automatically conducts security checks, sends acknowledgments, and formats records to be processed by current IRS computer systems.

Business filers are responsible for obtaining a personal identification number (PIN) to be used as the electronic signature. You may request a PIN through a *Letter of Application*. The *Letter of Application* is included in the software and can be electronically transmitted to the Austin Service Center via the third party transmitter.

Payment options are available through the Federal Tax Deposit (FTD) coupon system or through the Electronic Federal Tax Payment System (EFTPS). For more information on the newer EFTPS system, see the EFTPS section below.

Electronic Federal Tax Payment System (EFTPS)

Several year ago, the U.S. Department of Treasury designed EFTPS to modernize 'making tax payments' — from a paper-based payment system to an electronic one. Today, 2.5M business taxpayers are enrolled in EFTPS. This tax payment system helps individuals and business owners save time and money in paying their federal business taxes

APPENDIX B

and in making their federal tax payments electronically — either by telephone, personal computer, or through the transfer of funds offered by their financial institution. **All** federal tax payments (including payroll taxes, corporate income taxes, partnership, and fiduciary taxes) can be made using EFTPS.

You will find that EFTPS is easy to use, convenient, accurate, fast, and economical.

- Individuals and business owners can use **EFTPS-Direct** to make their tax payments by telephone or personal computer, 24 hours a day, seven days a week. For your computer, free Windows-based software is available when you enroll in EFTPS and use EFTPS-Direct. Using EFTPS-Direct only takes a few minutes — no check writing; no trips to the bank; and no courier, checks, stamps, and envelope expenses. And as an added convenience, EFTPS-Direct lets taxpayers **'warehouse'** their tax payment instructions up to 30 days in advance of a tax due date to **automatically make their payments on the tax due date.**
- Financial institutions are integrating EFTPS into the many services they offer their clients. Under the client's direction, funds can be transferred from the client's account into Treasury's account on a specified date.
- Tax professionals have a number of options to make federal tax payments for their clients:
  ✓ EFTPS Voice Response System — make multiple payments with a single telephone call
  ✓ EFTPS PC Debit — use Windows-based software to send payments
  ✓ EFTPS Batch — use Windows-based software to send batches of payments electronically
  ✓ EFTPS Bulk — make frequent consolidated payments from an EDI-compatible system

To participate in EFTPS, you must first enroll. For an enrollment form and for more information on EFTPS, call EFTPS Customer Service at 1-800-945-8400 or 1-800-555-4477. En Espanol communication, call 1-800-945-8600 or 1-800-244-4829. With access to teletypewriter/telecommunications device for the deaf (TTY/TDD) equipment only, call 1-800-945-8900 or 1-800-733-4829.

The IRS produces a number of print materials that can provide you with additional information on EFTPS. You can order these forms and publications free through the IRS Area Distribution Centers by calling 1-800-829-3676.

- Form 9779, *Business Enrollment Form and Instructions*
- Form 9783, *Individual Enrollment Form and Instructions*
- Publication 966, *The Easiest Way to Pay Your Federal Taxes*
- Publication 3110, *EFTPS Information Stuffer*
- Publication 3127, *EFTPS Fact Sheet*
- Publication 3425, *4 Easy Ways to Use EFTPS* — for tax professionals, accountants, and payroll companies

Some forms can be downloaded from the IRS Web site at www.irs.gov, and you can also get some forms via the IRS Tax Fax by dialing (703) 368-9694 from a fax machine and following the voice prompts to get tax forms faxed back to you.

Independent Contractor or Employee

For Federal tax purposes, this is an important distinction. Worker classification affects how you pay your Federal income tax, social security and Medicare taxes, and how you file your return. Classification affects your eligibility for employer and social security and Medicare benefits and your tax responsibilities.

A worker is either an **independent contractor** or an **employee**. The classification is determined by relevant facts that fall into three main categories: behavioral control; financial control; and relationship of the parties. In each case, it is very important to consider all the facts — no single fact provides the answer.

Publication 1779, *Independent Contractor or Employee*, has detailed information about these facts.

- An independent contractor will usually maintain an office and staff, advertise, and have a financial investment risk. Independent contractors will generally file a Schedule C and may be able to deduct certain expenses that an employee would not.
- Generally, an **employee** is controlled by an employer in ways that a true independent contractor is not. If the employer has the legal right to control the details of how the services are performed, the worker is generally an employee, not an independent contractor.

Those who should be classified as employees, but aren't, may lose out on social security and Medicare benefits, workers' compensation, unemployment benefits, and, in many cases, group insurance (including life and health), and retirement benefits.

If you are not sure whether you are an independent contractor or an employee, get Form SS-8, *Determination of Employee Work Status for Purposes of Federal Employment Taxes and Income Tax Withholding.*

Publication 1779, *Independent Contractor or Employee*, and Publication 15-A, *Employer's Supplemental Tax Guide*, provide additional information on independent contractor or employee status.

IRS publications and forms can be downloaded from the Internet at www.irs.gov. You can also order a free copy of IRS publications and forms when you call the IRS at 1-800-829-3676.

Publication 1518, *Year 2000 Tax Calendar for Small Businesses*

Business owners who are opening their doors for the first time or are hiring their first employees may benefit from this 12-month wall calendar. Publication 1518 shows all the 2000 due dates for making payroll deposits, paying estimated taxes, and for filing business tax forms. It also includes general information on basic business tax law, where to go for assistance, helpful bookkeeping and recordkeeping hints, and facts about IRS notices and penalties. Call the IRS at 1-800-829-3676 to order a free copy of this calendar.

Office of Public Liaison and Small Business Affairs

As a national public liaison for small businesses, this office maintains daily contact and exchanges business tax information with IRS external stakeholders — national organizations representing tax professionals, payroll processors, volunteers and social services, electronic commerce, state departments of revenue, small business organizations, and large corporate taxpayers. This office also works with the Small Business Administration and other government agencies to initiate and foster programs and actions to reduce small business burdens government-wide.

The Office of Public Liaison and Small Business Affairs provides 'one-stop' service for sharing 'small business' information. Some of these services include:

- working to establish partnering opportunities
- providing forums to discuss new ideas and feedback
- tracking issues and sharing information
- coordinating liaison meetings
- coordinating IRS participation at meetings and conferences

You can write to the IRS Office of Public Liaison and Small Business Affairs if you have **suggestions regarding tax laws, regulations, or policy.**

Internal Revenue Service
The Office of Public Liaison and
  Small Business Affairs CL:PL
IR Room 7559
1111 Constitution Avenue NW
Washington, DC 20224
*public_liaison@m1.irs.gov

This office **does not** handle small business owners' individual tax problems. If a problem has not been resolved after repeated attempts through normal IRS

channels, small business owners should contact their local IRS Taxpayer Advocate Service for assistance. See section in this booklet on Taxpayer Advocate Service (TAS) under **Taxpayer Assistance Programs** for more information.

The IRS produces a number of print and electronic information materials to help new businesses. The following IRS tax publications and small business CD-ROM can be ordered free through the IRS by calling 1-800-829-3676.

- Publication 334, *Tax Guide for Small Business (For Individuals Who Use Schedule C or C-EZ)*
- Publication 583, *Starting a Business and Keeping Records*
- Publication 1066, *Small Business Tax Workshop* (booklet), provides general information about different types of business organizations, record-keeping requirements, and business tax returns. This booklet is used as an education tool in small business workshops given by local IRS offices.
- Publication 1518, *Year 2000 Tax Calendar for Small Businesses*, notes the most common tax filing dates. A specific tax tip is highlighted each month, in the calendar, to help small businesses not only during the tax-filing season, but also throughout the year.
- Publication 1853, *Small Business Talk*, tells of the Office of Public Liaison and Small Business Affairs, and lists services and tax materials available to small businesses.
- Publication 3207, *Small Business Resource Guide 2000: What You Need to Know About Taxes and Other Topics* (CD-ROM). This CD-ROM includes tax information, provided by multiple government agencies, to help small business entrepreneurs meet regulatory requirements.

Many IRS information products are also available on the small business corner of the IRS Web site @ www.irs.gov/prod/bus_info/sm_bus/index.html.

SSA/IRS *(Social Security Administration/Internal Revenue Service) Reporter* (newsletter)

If you are an employer and have not been receiving a copy of the *SSA/IRS Reporter*, tell your local IRS Public Affairs Officer/Communications Manager.

The *SSA/IRS Reporter* is a quarterly newsletter that keeps you up-to-date on changes to taxes and employee wage obligations. This newsletter, produced jointly by the Social Security Administration and the IRS, is mailed to approximately seven million employers along with each quarterly Form 941, *Employer's Quarterly Federal Tax Return*, and instructions.

Small Business Tax Education Program (STEP)

Small business owners and other self-employed individuals can learn about business taxes through a unique partnership between the IRS and local organizations. Through workshops or in-depth tax courses, instructors provide training on starting a business, recordkeeping, preparing business tax returns, self-employment tax issues, and employment taxes.

Some courses are offered free as a community service. Courses given by an educational facility may include costs for materials and tuition. Other courses may have a nominal fee to offset administrative costs of sponsoring organizations.

Your Business Tax Kit (YBTK)

The *YBTK*, in booklet format, contains various IRS business tax forms and publications that may be used to prepare and file business tax returns. Besides forms and publications, the kit includes information on quick and easy access to IRS tax help. To order, call 1-800-829-3676 and ask for Publication 454, *Your Business Tax Kit*.

- inform individuals (whose second language is English) of their tax rights and responsibilities

The grants **are not available to individuals.** However, through this grant program, the IRS awards qualifying **organizations** grants of up to $100,000 per year to develop, expand, and continue low-income taxpayer clinics. The clinics are administered and sponsored by accredited law, business, and accounting schools where students represent taxpayers in tax controversies before the IRS or before the courts. In addition, the clinics may be administered and sponsored by non-profit organizations that meet program requirements.

To learn more about the **Low-Income Taxpayer Clinics Grant Program,** call your local IRS office and ask to speak to the Taxpayer Education Coordinator. You can also call the IRS at 1-800-829-3676 and order a free copy of Publication 3319, *LITC Grant Application Package and Guidelines.* Each year, Publication 3319 is revised to provide the *current year application deadline date.* This product is available on the IRS Web site.

Taxpayer Advocate Service

If you have an ongoing tax issue with the IRS, that has not been resolved through normal channels, you may contact the Taxpayer Advocate Service (formerly the Problem Resolution Program) for assistance. The Taxpayer Advocate Service has the ability to cut through red tape and can often help with delayed refunds, unanswered inquiries, and incorrect billing notices. Generally, the Taxpayer Advocate can help if, as a result of the administration of the tax laws, you:

- are suffering, or are about to suffer, a significant hardship
- are facing an immediate threat of adverse action (penalties, interest, liens)
- will incur significant costs (including fees for professional representation)
- will suffer irreparable injury or long-term adverse impact
- have experienced a delay of more than 30 days to resolve an issue
- have not received a response or resolution through normal channels by the date promised

Hardship situations and other issues that are referred to the Taxpayer Advocate are reviewed on the individual merits of each case. It is important to remember, that the Taxpayer Advocate is not a substitute for established IRS procedures or the formal appeals process. The Taxpayer Advocate cannot reverse legal or technical tax determinations.

To reach a Taxpayer Advocate, call 1-877-777-4778. You can also call the IRS at 1-800-829-1040 and ask for Taxpayer Advocate assistance. Deaf and hearing-impaired, with access to teletype-writer/telecommunication device for the deaf (TTY/TDD) equipment, may call the IRS at 1-800-829-4059.

For more information about Taxpayer Advocate Service and for a list of Taxpayer Advocate telephone numbers and addresses, listen to TeleTax topic #104 (See **Table of Contents** in this booklet for TeleTax page number), or call the IRS at 1-800-829-3676 for a copy of Publication 1546, *The Taxpayer Advocate Service of the Internal Revenue Service.* You may also download this publication from the IRS Web site at www.irs.gov

Taxpayer Education Programs

The IRS has year-round education programs designed to help you understand the tax laws and IRS procedures. Volunteers trained by the IRS are an important part of these programs. For times and locations of the available services in your community, or to become a volunteer, call the IRS office in your area and ask for the Taxpayer Education Coordinator or the Public Affairs Officer/Communications Manager.

Community Outreach Tax Education

Through this program, IRS staff or trained volunteers will speak to groups of people (retirees, farmers, small business owners, and employees) with common tax concerns. This program offers two kinds of assistance.

- line-by-line self-help income tax return preparation
- tax seminars on various tax topics

Outreach sessions may be co-sponsored by community organizations and other government agencies.

Understanding Taxes Program for Students

Understanding Taxes consists of four separate tax education courses designed to teach students about their federal tax rights and responsibilities and the economics and history on

which our tax system is based.

- The eighth grade program, *Taxes in U.S. History*, details the roles that taxes have played in our nation's history. It is designed for U.S. history classes. Students learn how tax policies of the past have contributed to tax policies in effect today. Teachers can integrate the program into standard curricula.

- The high school program, *Understanding Taxes*, explains how to prepare and file a simple tax return and teaches about the history, politics, and economics of our tax system. The variety of topics covered in their modular format allows the course to be used in a number of different classes, such as history, economics, consumer education, social studies, government, civics, and business education.

- TAX Interactive (TAXi) is an on-line learning lab designed for high school student and teacher use. Visit TAX Interactive on the IRS Web site at www.irs.gov/taxi for an educational and entertaining way to learn about tax rights and responsibilities.

- The post-secondary program, *Taxes and You*, is designed to assist adult learners in becoming responsible participants in the tax system. Students will learn how taxes affect people and the economy and how to interpret and prepare tax forms. By learning how to pay only what is owed, managing personal finances will become a lot easier.

Practitioner Education

Through this program, training is provided to people who prepare tax returns and counsel taxpayers for a fee. Classes are held in every state in cooperation with the state bureau of revenue, colleges, universities, and professional accounting groups. Tax professional institutes alert participants of the tax law changes and work with participants to improve the quality of return preparation to reduce errors.

Important Tax Subjects You Should Know About

The IRS has many programs and processes that can reduce anxieties of taxes. A description of some of the more popular ones follows. In most cases, the description lists free IRS publications for additional information.

Amending a Return

If you find that you made a mistake on your tax return, you can correct it by filing a Form 1040X, *Amended U.S. Individual Income Tax Return.* Generally, you must file this form within three years from the date you filed your original return or within two years from the date you paid your tax, whichever is later. File Form 1040X with the Internal Revenue Service Center for your area. (Your **state tax** liability may be affected by a change made on your federal income tax return. For more information on this, contact your state tax authority.)

Adoption Taxpayer Identification Number (ATIN)

If you are in the process of adopting a child and are able to claim the child as your dependent or are able to claim the child care credit, you may need an ATIN for your adoptive child. The Internal Revenue Service can issue an ATIN as a temporary taxpayer identification number for children who are being adopted. Parents will use the ATIN to identify the child on their Federal Income Tax Return while final adoption is pending. See FORM W-7A, *Application for Taxpayer Identification Number for Pending U.S. Adoptions,* in this section.

Collection Process

When the IRS sends you a notice of tax due, do not ignore it — pay the amount owed, or contact your local IRS office by telephone or through written correspondence about the notice. If you believe a bill from the IRS is incorrect, you will need to provide information showing why you think the bill is wrong. If the IRS agrees with you, then your account will be corrected. However, if the bill is correct, interest and penalties will be charged on the amount owed until the full amount due is paid.

If you are not able to pay the taxes you owe in full, IRS staff will work with you to find the best way to meet your tax obligations. This may include an installment agreement or acceptance of an offer to settle the account. If taxes, interest, and penalties are not paid in full, a Federal tax lien may also be filed. Under certain conditions, the IRS may enforce collection and seize personal assets, including income and other property. The collection process can be stopped at any stage if the amount owed is paid in full.

More information about your rights and the collection process are found in Publication 1, *Your Rights as a Taxpayer,* and Publication 594, *What You Should Know About the IRS Collection Process.* Both publications are available in Spanish.

Copies Of Prior Year Returns

There are occasions when you may need a copy of your prior year(s) Federal Tax Forms 1040, 1040A, and 1040EZ, a transcript of return, or account information.

A *transcript of return* contains information from the original return. It does not contain information regarding amended returns or subsequent payments. If amended returns or subsequent payment summary is needed, account information can be secured.

Examples of when you may need a copy of a return or a transcript of return include applying for a home mortgage loan or financial aid for education. While there is a fee for requesting a photocopy of a return, transcripts are free of charge. Make sure a transcript is acceptable by the company or establishment needing your income information.

- You can get a *copy* of a prior year(s) tax return by completing Form 4506, *Request for Copy or Transcript of Tax Form,* and mailing it to the IRS address for your area. See **"Where to File" Your Taxes for Tax Year 1999** on last page. There is a fee of $23 for each return requested. Please allow up to 60 days to receive your copy.
- For a *transcript* that reflects most items from your return, send a completed Form 4506 to the IRS address where the return was filed. There is no charge at this time. You should receive the transcript within 7 - 10 workdays from the IRS office's receipt of your request.
- For tax *account information,* you can visit an IRS office or call the IRS toll-free number listed in your telephone directory. This list of basic tax data, like marital status, type of return filed, adjusted gross income, and taxable income, is available free of charge. Do not use Form 4506 to request this information. Please allow 15 days for delivery.

To obtain Form 4506, download from the IRS Web site, use IRS Tax Fax system (See IRS Tax Fax under **Tax Information Available Electronically**), or order by calling the IRS at 1-800-829-3676.

Credits

The tax laws include a number of credits you may be entitled to take. The following are several of the more popular credits available.

- adoption credit
- child and dependent care credit
- child tax credit
- earned income tax credit
- education credits: Hope, lifetime learning
- foreign tax credit
- mortgage interest

Turn to the **Index of Topics and Related Publications** section and look under "Credits" for a list of the credits and the related publications for details.

Disaster/Casualty Losses

When property is damaged or lost in a hurricane, earthquake, fire, flood, or similar event that is sudden, unexpected, or unusual, it is called a casualty. Your unreimbursed loss from a casualty may be deductible on your tax return for the year the casualty occurred. If the loss happened in an area the President designated as a disaster area, you may not have to wait until the end of the year to file a tax return and claim a loss. You may be able to file an amended return for last year right now and get a refund of taxes you have already paid. If you were located in a Presidentially-declared disaster area, there will be no interest on taxes due for the length of any extension granted for filing your tax return. For details, get Publication 547, *Casualties, Disasters, and Thefts (Business and Nonbusiness)*. You can also download a copy of Publication 1600, *Disaster Losses — Help From the IRS*, from the IRS Web site.

Estimated Tax

If you are self-employed or have other income not subject to income tax withholding, you may have to make estimated tax payments. For details on who must pay estimated taxes and how and when to make payments, get Publication 505, *Tax Withholding and Estimated Tax*.

Examination of Returns

If your return is selected for examination, you may be asked to show records such as canceled checks, receipts, or other supporting documents to verify entries on your return. You can appeal if you disagree with the examination results. Your appeal rights will be explained to you.

You may act on your own behalf or have an attorney, a certified public accountant, or an individual (enrolled to practice before the IRS) represent or accompany you. The Student Tax Clinic Program is available in some areas to help people during examination and appeal proceedings. Call your local IRS office and ask the Taxpayer Education Coordinator or the Public Affairs Officer/Communications Manager about this program.

For more information on the examination of returns, get Publication 556, *Examination of Returns, Appeal Rights, and Claims for Refund*, and Publication 1, *Your Rights as a Taxpayer*. Also see Publication 947, *Practice Before the IRS and Power of Attorney*. Publication 1 is available in Spanish.

Form W-4, *Employee's Withholding Allowance Certificate*

Each time you start working for an employer, you should complete a Form W-4. The information you provide will help your employer know how much federal tax to withhold from your wages. If your tax situation changes, complete a new Form W-4 so that the correct amount of tax will be withheld. For more information on tax withholding, get Publication 919, *Is My Withholding Correct for 2000?*

How do you qualify for the Earned Income Tax Credit?

If you work hard but don't earn a high income, EITC can mean you'll pay less tax, no tax or even get a refund.

You may be eligible if you have two qualifying children and earnings under $30,580 in 1999. Or one qualifying child and earnings under $26,928. Or no child and earnings under $10,200.

To get all the facts, call **1-800-829-3676** for IRS Pub. 596, *Earned Income Credit.*

IRS Web site: **www.irs.gov**

The Internal Revenue Service — Working to put service first

Form W-5, *Earned Income Credit Advance Payment Certificate*

In 2000, you may be able to file a Form W-5 with your employer for the Advance EITC if:

1) you expect you will be eligible for the Earned Income Tax Credit (EITC), and

2) if you will have a qualifying child on your 2000 Federal Tax Return.

Filing for the Advance EITC will allow you to receive partial payment of the EITC during the year rather than only when you file your tax return. The amount of the Advance EITC payments you receive will be shown on your Form W-2, *Wage and Tax Statement*. For more information, get Publication 596, *Earned Income Credit*. This publication is available in Spanish.

Form W-7, *Application for IRS Individual Taxpayer Identification Number*

If you are required to have an identifying number for federal tax purposes, but cannot obtain a social security number (SSN), the IRS will issue an individual taxpayer identification number (ITIN). The IRS will issue this number for a nonresident or resident alien who **does not have** and **is not eligible** to get an SSN issued by the Social Security Administarion (SSA). To apply for an ITIN, file Form W-7 with the IRS.

> NOTE: An ITIN is for tax use only. It does not entitle you to social security benefits or change your employment or immigration status under U.S. law.

Form W-7A, *Application for Taxpayer Identification Number for Pending U.S. Adoptions*

If you have a child placed in your home for legal adoption, the adoption is not yet final, and you cannot obtain an SSN for that child, you must get an adoption taxpayer identification number (ATIN) if you want to claim various tax benefits (but not the earned income tax credit). When the adoption is final, you should no longer use the ATIN. Instead, you must obtain a social security number issued by the Social Security Administration and use it.

Late (Overdue) Returns

Sometimes people do not file their tax return(s) because of personal problems, no money to pay, lost records, or confusion over complex tax rules.

If you have not filed your federal income tax return for a year or more and should have filed, IRS staff will work with you to help you get back on track. Copies of missing documents like Form W-2, *Wage and Tax Statement*, can often be retrieved. If you owe taxes, the IRS will explain your payment options. And if you have a refund coming, they will explain the time limit on getting it.

Call your local IRS office or call toll-free 1-800-829-1040 for assistance. Remember, interest and penalties are adding up if you owe taxes, and time is running out if you are due a refund.

Social Security Number (SSN)

Your SSN **is not** posted anywhere in your tax package. So...**make sure** you write your SSN on your Form 1040, 1040A, or 1040EZ and on each supporting schedule or form that you include with your return when you file it. List the complete and correct SSN issued by the Social Security Administration (SSA) for yourself, spouse, and each dependent on your tax return.

Name Change

If your name has changed for some reason, like marriage or divorce, notify the Social Security Administration (SSA) immediately.

If the name and social security number you show on your tax return does not match the one SSA has on record, there can be a processing delay, which could hold up your refund.

Dependent's SSN

If you claim an exemption for a dependent, you are required to show his or her social security number on your tax return.

If you do not list a complete and correct social security number issued by the SSA, the IRS may disallow the exemption for that dependent.

To get a social security number, contact the nearest Social Security Administration office to get Form SS-5, *Application for a Social Security Card.*

If you are not eligible to obtain a social security number from the SSA, use an IRS individual taxpayer identification number (ITIN) instead of a social security number. To get an ITIN, contact the IRS to get Form W-7, *Application for IRS Individual Taxpayer Identification Number.*

Tips When Filing Your Return

Gathering forms, receipts, and other paperwork to file your taxes is only half the battle. Once you've completed your forms, it is equally important to double-check your figures, information, and packaging procedures (as applicable to your filing method).

Make certain that you include your social security number (SSN) on each page of your return and supporting schedules and forms when you file your return. (If you use your tax package, remember your SSN is not pre-printed on the address label or the forms.) Always review your filing entries for misprinted or overlooked data. And with a paper return, also review your forms for miscalculations. Any mistake can cause processing delays that may hold up your refund. When mailing a paper return, make sure you have enough postage and your complete return address on the IRS envelope to avoid mailing delays. If you owe taxes, remember any delay could cause you notices, penalties, and interest charges.

The tips below can serve as your checklist to prevent filing mistakes.

Important Parts of Your Return

■ **Enter Social Security Number(S)?**
Make sure your social security number *is on your return and all supporting schedules and forms.*

■ **Check Age/Blindness Box?**
If you are age 65 or older or blind, or your spouse is age 65 or older or blind, make sure you notate the appropriate box(es) on Form 1040 or Form 1040A.

■ **Claim Child Tax Credit?**
If you have income below a certain level, and a child under age 17, you may be able to claim this credit. Read about this credit in your Forms 1040 or 1040A Instructions.

■ **Claim Earned Income Credit; Figure Correctly?**
This tax credit can help some people who work and have income below a certain level. For more information on whether you qualify and how to figure the credit, get Publication 596, *Earned Income Credit*, or Publication 596SP, *Crédito por Ingreso del Trabajo.*

■ **Enter Federal Income Tax Withheld, not Social Security Tax, on the Return?** Form W-2, *Wage and Tax Statement*, shows both the federal income tax and FICA (social security tax) withheld. Remember to use the amount for federal income tax withheld on your return to calculate your total income tax payments.

■ **Enter Correct Standard Deduction Amount?**
If you do not itemize deductions, use the correct standard deduction chart to find the right amount.

■ **Check Refund or Balance Due Amount?**
On paper return, check your addition and subtraction. If your total payments are more than your total tax, you are due a refund. A balance due is figured when your taxes due are more than the amount you have already paid. If you make a payment by check, you should make the check out to the *United States Treasury.*

■ **Take Correct Tax from Tax Table?**
When using the tax table, first you have to take the amount shown on the taxable income line of your Form 1040, 1040A, or 1040EZ and find the line in the tax table showing that amount. Next, find the column for your marital status (married filing joint, single, etc.) and read down the column. The amount shown where the income line and filing status column meet is your tax.

Important Double-Checks on Your Paper Return Before Mailing

■ Attach Copy B of all Forms W-2.
■ Attach all required **forms** and related **schedules. Write your** SSN (and spouse's if filing joint) on your return form and supporting schedules and forms.
■ Place preprinted **address label** on your return and **make any necessary changes** on it.
■ **Sign** and **date** your **return** (both husband and wife must sign a joint return).

■ If you owe tax, **include** your check or money order **payable to United States Treasury.** Write your **social security number,** daytime **telephone number, tax form number,** and tax year on your check or money order.
■ **Make a copy** of the return for your records.

Important Mailing Procedures

■ **Use preprinted envelope** that came in the tax package to mail your return. If you do not have one, address an envelope to the Internal Revenue Service Center for your state.

■ **Write** your **complete return address** on the envelope.

■ **Attach** the **correct postage.**

'Where to File' Your Taxes for Tax Year 1999

This filing season (for Tax Year 1999) most 1040 tax packages will contain an envelope with two labels. The two labels will enable the IRS to more efficiently sort the refund returns from the remittance returns.

These labels will contain the address of the IRS Service Center and separate zip+4 zip codes and PostNet barcodes. One of the labels will be used by taxpayers filing for a refund, or the other label will be used by taxpayers filing a balance due return and remittance.

In addition, the 'Where to File' instructions will have the same service center addresses with the same two zip codes. This will allow the taxpayers or practitioners to place a handwritten address on their tax return envelope and the U.S. Postal Service will imprint the proper PostNet barcode on the face of the envelope. Barcodes will permit the tax returns to be sorted.

If You Are Requesting a Refund, use the IRS Service Center mailing address below for your area:	
Internal Revenue Service Atlanta GA 39901-0102	Internal Revenue Service Fresno CA 93888-0102
Internal Revenue Service Andover MA 05501-0102	Internal Revenue Service Kansas City MO 64999-0102
Internal Revenue Service Austin TX 73301-0102	Internal Revenue Service Memphis TN 37501-0102
Internal Revenue Service Holtsville NY 00501-0102	Internal Revenue Service Ogden UT 84201-0102
Internal Revenue Service Cincinnati OH 45999-0102	Internal Revenue Service Philadelphia PA 19255-0102

If You ARE NOT Requesting a REFUND, use the IRS Service Center mailing address below for your area:	
Internal Revenue Service Atlanta GA 39901-0002	Internal Revenue Service Fresno CA 93888-0002
Internal Revenue Service Andover MA 05501-0002	Internal Revenue Service Kansas City MO 64999-0002
Internal Revenue Service Austin TX 73301-0002	Internal Revenue Service Memphis TN 37501-0002
Internal Revenue Service Holtsville NY 00501-0002	Internal Revenue Service Ogden UT 84201-0002
Internal Revenue Service Cincinnati OH 45999-0002	Internal Revenue Service Philadelphia PA 19255-0002

APPENDIX C:
STATE FILING AUTHORITY
TELEPHONE NUMBERS AND WEBSITES

Below is a listing of all the states and the telephone numbers and websites for you to order state forms and where your questions can be answered regarding your state filing requirements. A few toll-free numbers are for in-state calls only. Further information about electronic and fax services plus forms for all states is available at **www.1040.com** and **www.taxweb.com**.

STATE	FORM NUMBER	INFORMATION NUMBERS	WEBSITE ADDRESSES (ALL START WITH WWW. EXCEPT KENTUCKY)
Alabama	334/242–9681	334/242–9681	ADOR.STATE.AL.US
Alaska	907/465–2320	907/465–2320	REVENUE.STATE.AK.US
Arizona	602/542–4260	602/255–3381	REVENUE.STATE.AZ.US
Arkansas	501/682–7255	501/682–7250	STATE.AR.US/DFA/
California	800/852–5711	800/338–0505	FTB.CA.GOV
Colorado	303/232–2414	303/232–2414	STATE.CO.US
Connecticut	860/297–5962	800/382–9463	CGA.STATE.CT.US
Delaware	302/577–3300	302/577–3300	STATE.DE.US/GOVERN/AGENCIES/ REVENUE/REVENUE.HTM
District of Columbia	202/727–6170	202/727–6104	DCCFO.COM
Florida	904/488–6800	904/488–6800	FCN.STATE.FL.US
Georgia	404/656–4293	404/656–4071	STATE.GA.US/DEPARTMENTS/DOR
Hawaii	800/222–7572	800/222–3229	HAWAII.GOV/ICSD/TAX/TAX.HTM
Idaho	208/334–7660	208/334–7660	STATE.ID.US/TAX/TAXFORMS.HTM
Illinois	800/356–6302	800/732–8866	REVENUE.STATE.IL.US
Indiana	317/486–5103	317/232–2240	AI.ORG/DOR
Iowa	515/281–7239	515/281–3114	STATE.IA.US/GOVERNMENT/DRF/ INDEX.HTML
Kansas	913/296–4937	913/296–0222	INK.ORG/PUBLIC/KDOR
Kentucky	502/564–3658	502/564–4580	REVWEB@MAIL.STATE.KY.US
Louisiana	504/925–7532	504/925–4611	REV.STATE.LA.US
Maine	207/624–7894	207/626–8475	STATE.ME.US/TAXATION
Maryland	410/974–3981	800/638–2937	COMP.STATE.MD.US
Massachusetts	617/887–6367	617/887–6367	MAGNET.STATE.MA.US/DOR/ DORPG.HTM
Michigan	800/367–6263	517/373–3200	TREAS.STATE.MI.US
Minnesota	800/657–3676	800/652–9094	TAXES.STATE.MN.US

Mississippi	601/923–7000	601/923–7000	MSTC.STATE
Missouri	573/751–4695	573/751–4450	STATE.MO.US/DOR/TAX
Montana	406/444–0290	406/444–2837	MT.GOV/REVENUE/REV.HTM
Nebraska	800/626–7899	402/471–2971	NOL.ORG/REVENUE
Nevada	702/687–4820	702/687–4892	STATE.NV.US/TAXATION/
New Hampshire	603/271–2192	603/271–2186	STATE.NH.US/
New Jersey	609/588–2200	800/323–4400	STATE.NJ.US/TREASURY/TAXATION/
New Mexico	505/827–2260	505/827–0700	STATE.NM.US/TAX
New York City	718/935–6114	718/935–6000	CI.NYC.NY.US/FINANCE
New York State	800/462–8100	800/225–5829	STATE.NY.US
North Carolina	919/715–0397	919/733–4682	SIPS.STATE.NC.US
North Dakota	701/328–3017	701/328–2770	STATE.ND.US/TAXDPT
Ohio	614/846–6712	614/846–6712	STATE.OH.US/TAX/
Oklahoma	405/521–3108	405/521–3160	OKTAX.STATE.OK.US
Oregon	503/378–4988	503/378–4988	DOR.STATE.OR.US
Pennsylvania	800/362–2050	717/787–8201	REVENUE.STATE.PA.US
Puerto Rico	787/721–2020	787/721–2020	
Rhode Island	401/277–3934	401/277–2905	TAX.STATE.RI.US
South Carolina	803/737–5085	803/737–4761	STATE.SC.US/DOR/DOR.HTML
South Dakota	605/773–3311	605/773–3311	STATE.SD.US/STATE/EXECUTIVE/ REVENUE/REVENUE.HTML
Tennessee	615/741–4466	615/741–2594	STATE.TN.US/REVENUE
Texas	512/463–4600	512/463–4600	WINDOW.STATE.TX.US
Utah	801/297–6700	801/297–2200	TAX.EX.STATE.UT.US
Vermont	802/828–2515	802/828–2501	STATE.VT.US/TAX
Virginia	804/367–8205	804/367–2062	STATE.VA.US/TAX/TAX.HTML
Washington	800/647–7706	800/647–7706	GA.GOV/DOR/WADOR.HTM
West Virginia	304/344–2068	304/558–3333	STATE.WV.US/TAXDIV/
Wisconsin	608/266–1961	608/266–2486	DOR.STATE.WI.US
Wyoming	307/777–7961	307/777–7961	STATE.WI.US

APPENDIX D:
YOUR RIGHTS AS A TAXPAYER
(TAXPAYER BILL OF RIGHTS)

The first part of this publication explains some of your most important rights as a taxpayer. The second part explains the examination, appeal, collection, and refund processes.

IRS

Department of the Treasury
Internal Revenue Service

Publication 1
(Rev. December 1998)

Catalog Number 64731W

www.irs.ustreas.gov

THE IRS MISSION

PROVIDE AMERICA'S TAXPAYERS TOP QUALITY SERVICE BY HELPING THEM UNDERSTAND AND MEET THEIR TAX RESPONSIBILITIES AND BY APPLYING THE TAX LAW WITH INTEGRITY AND FAIRNESS TO ALL.

Declaration of Taxpayer Rights

I. Protection of Your Rights

IRS employees will explain and protect your rights as a taxpayer throughout your contact with us.

II. Privacy and Confidentiality

The IRS will not disclose to anyone the information you give us, except as authorized by law. You have the right to know why we are asking you for information, how we will use it, and what happens if you do not provide requested information.

III. Professional and Courteous Service

If you believe that an IRS employee has not treated you in a professional, fair, and courteous manner, you should tell that employee's supervisor. If the supervisor's response is not satisfactory, you should write to your IRS District Director or Service Center Director.

IV. Representation

You may either represent yourself or, with proper written authorization, have someone else represent you in your place. Your representative must be a person allowed to practice before the IRS, such as an attorney, certified public accountant, or enrolled agent. If you are in an interview and ask to consult such a person, then we must stop and reschedule the interview in most cases.

You can have someone accompany you at an interview. You may make sound recordings of any meetings with our examination, appeal, or collection personnel, provided you tell us in writing 10 days before the meeting.

V. Payment of Only the Correct Amount of Tax

You are responsible for paying only the correct amount of tax due under the law — no more, no less. If you cannot pay all of your tax when it is due, you may be able to make monthly installment payments.

VI. Help With Unresolved Tax Problems

The National Taxpayer Advocate's Problem Resolution Program can help you if you have tried unsuccessfully to resolve a problem with the IRS. Your local Taxpayer Advocate can offer you special help if you have a significant hardship as a result of a tax problem. For more information, call toll-free 1–877–777–4778 (1–800–829–4059 for TTY/TDD users) or write to the Taxpayer Advocate at the IRS office that last contacted you.

VII. Appeals and Judicial Review

If you disagree with us about the amount of your tax liability or certain collection actions, you have the right to ask the Appeals Office to review your case. You may also ask a court to review your case.

VIII. Relief From Certain Penalties and Interest

The IRS will waive penalties when allowed by law if you can show you acted reasonably and in good faith or relied on the incorrect advice of an IRS employee. We will waive interest that is the result of certain errors or delays caused by an IRS employee.

Examinations, Appeals, Collections, and Refunds

Examinations (Audits)

We accept most taxpayer's returns as filed. If we inquire about your return or select it for examination, it does not suggest that you are dishonest. The inquiry or examination may or may not result in more tax. We may close your case without change; or, you may receive a refund.

The process of selecting a return for examination usually begins in one of two ways. First, we use computer programs to identify returns that may have incorrect amounts. These programs may be based on information returns, such as Forms 1099 and W-2, on studies of past examinations, or on certain issues identified by compliance projects. Second, we use information from outside sources that indicates that a return may have incorrect amounts. These sources may include newspapers, public records, and individuals. If we determine that the information is accurate and reliable, we may use it to select a return for examination.

Publication 556, *Examination of Returns, Appeal Rights, and Claims for Refund,* explains the rules and procedures that we follow in examinations. The following sections give an overview of how we conduct examinations.

By Mail

We handle many examinations and inquiries by mail. We will send you a letter with either a request for more information or a reason why we believe a change to your return may be needed. You can respond by mail or you can request a personal interview with an examiner. If you mail us the requested information or provide an explanation, we may or may not agree with you, and we will explain the reasons for any changes. Please do not hesitate to write to us about anything you do not understand.

By Interview

If we notify you that we will conduct your examination through a personal interview, or you request such an interview, you have the right to ask that the examination take place at a reasonable time and place that is convenient for both you and the IRS. If our examiner proposes any changes to your return, he or she will explain the reasons for the changes. If you do not

agree with these changes, you can meet with the examiner's supervisor.

Repeat Examinations

If we examined your return for the same items in either of the 2 previous years and proposed no change to your tax liability, please contact us as soon as possible so we can see if we should discontinue the examination.

Appeals

If you do not agree with the examiner's proposed changes, you can appeal them to the Appeals Office of IRS. Most differences can be settled without expensive and time-consuming court trials. Your appeal rights are explained in detail in both Publication 5, *Appeal Rights and Preparation of Protests for Unagreed Cases,* and Publication 556, *Examination of Returns, Appeal Rights, and Claims for Refund.*

If you do not wish to use the Appeals Office or disagree with its findings, you may be able to take your case to the U.S. Tax Court, U.S. Court of Federal Claims, or the U.S. District Court where you live. If you take your case to court, the IRS will have the burden of proving certain facts if you kept adequate records to show your tax liability, cooperated with the IRS, and meet certain other conditions. If the court agrees with you on most issues in your case, and finds that our position was largely unjustified, you may be able to recover some of your administrative and litigation costs. You will not be eligible to recover these costs unless you tried to resolve your case administratively, including going through the appeals system, and you gave us the information necessary to resolve the case.

Collections

Publication 594, *The IRS Collection Process,* explains your rights and responsibilities regarding payment of federal taxes. It describes:

- What to do when you owe taxes. It describes what to do if you get a tax bill and what to do if you think your bill is wrong. It also covers making installment payments, delaying collection action, and submitting an offer in compromise.

- IRS collection actions. It covers liens, releasing a lien, levies, releasing a levy, seizures and sales, and release of property.

Publication 1660, *Collection Appeal Rights for Liens, Levies, Seizures, and Installment Agreement Terminations,* explains your collection appeal rights.

Innocent Spouse Relief

Generally, both you and your spouse are responsible, jointly and individually, for paying the full amount of any tax, interest, or penalties due on your joint return. However, you may not have to pay the tax, interest, and penalties related to your spouse (or former spouse).

New tax law changes make it easier to qualify for innocent spouse relief and add two other ways for you to get relief. For more information, see Publication 971, *Innocent Spouse Relief,* and Form 8857, *Request for Innocent Spouse Relief (And Separation of Liability and Equitable Relief).*

Refunds

You may file a claim for refund if you think you paid too much tax. You must generally file the claim within 3 years from the date you filed your original return or 2 years from the date you paid the tax, whichever is later. The law generally provides for interest on your refund if it is not paid within 45 days of the date you filed your return or claim for refund. Publication 556, *Examination of Returns, Appeal Rights, and Claims for Refund,* has more information on refunds.

Tax Information

The IRS provides a great deal of free information. The following are sources for forms, publications, and additional information.

- *Tax Questions: 1–800–829–1040* (1–800–829–4059 for TTY/TDD users)

- *Forms and Publications: 1–800–829–3676* (1–800–829–4059 for TTY/TDD users)

- *Internet:* www.irs.ustreas.gov

- *TaxFax Service:* From your fax machine, dial *703–368–9694.*

- *Small Business Ombudsman:* If you are a small business entity, you can participate in the regulatory process and comment on enforcement actions of IRS by calling *1–888–REG–FAIR.*

- *Treasury Inspector General for Tax Administration:* If you want to confidentially report misconduct, waste, fraud, or abuse by an IRS employee, you can call *1–800–366–4484* (1–800–877–8339 for TTY/TDD users). You can remain anonymous.

Your Appeal Rights and How To Prepare a Protest If You Don't Agree

Department of the Treasury
Internal Revenue Service

www.irs.ustreas.gov

Publication 5 (Rev. 01-1999)
Catalog Number 46074I

Introduction

This Publication tells you how to appeal your tax case if you don't agree with the Internal Revenue Service (IRS) findings.

If You Don't Agree

If you don't agree with any or all of the IRS findings given you, you may request a meeting or a telephone conference with the supervisor of the person who issued the findings. If you still don't agree, you may appeal your case to the Appeals Office of IRS.

If you decide to do nothing and your case involves an examination of your income, estate, gift, and certain excise taxes or penalties, you will receive a formal Notice of Deficiency. The Notice of Deficiency allows you to go to the Tax Court and tells you the procedure to follow. If you do not go to the Tax Court, we will send you a bill for the amount due.

If you decide to do nothing and your case involves a trust fund recovery penalty, or certain employment tax liabilities, the IRS will send you a bill for the penalty. If you do not appeal a denial of an offer in compromise or a denial of a penalty abatement, the IRS will continue collection action.

If you don't agree, we urge you to appeal your case to the Appeals Office of IRS. The Office of Appeals can settle most differences without expensive and time-consuming court trials. [Note: Appeals can not consider your reasons for not agreeing if they don't come within the scope of the tax laws (for example, if you disagree solely on moral, religious, political, constitutional, conscientious, or similar grounds.)]

The following general rules tell you how to appeal your case.

Appeals Within the IRS

Appeals is the administrative appeals office for the IRS. You may appeal most IRS decisions with your local Appeals Office. The Appeals Office is separate from - and independent of - the IRS Office taking the action you disagree with. The Appeals Office is the only level of administrative appeal within the IRS.

Conferences with Appeals Office personnel are held in an informal manner by correspondence, by telephone or at a personal conference. There is no need for you to have representation for an Appeals conference, but if you choose to have a representative, see the requirements under *Representation.*

If you want an Appeals conference, follow the instructions in our letter to you. Your request will be sent to the Appeals Office to arrange a conference at a convenient time and place. You or your representative should prepare to discuss all issues you don't agree with at the conference. Most differences are settled at this level.

In most instances, you may be eligible to take your case to court if you don't reach an agreement at your Appeals conference, or if you don't want to appeal your case to the IRS Office of Appeals. See the later section *Appeals To The Courts.*

Protests

When you request an appeals conference, you may also need to file a formal written protest or a small case request with the office named in our letter to you. Also, see the special appeal request procedures in Publication 1660, Collection Appeal Rights, if you disagree with lien, levy, seizure, or denial or termination of an installment agreement.

You need to file a written protest:

- In all employee plan and exempt organization cases without regard to the dollar amount at issue.

- In all partnership and S corporation cases without regard to the dollar amount at issue.

- In all other cases, unless you qualify for the small case request procedure, or other special appeal procedures such as requesting Appeals consideration of liens, levies, seizures, or installment agreements. See Publication 1660.

How to prepare a protest:

When a protest is required, **send it within the time limit specified in the letter you received.** Include in your protest:

1) Your name and address, and a daytime telephone number,

2) A statement that you want to appeal the IRS findings to the Appeals Office,

3) A copy of the letter showing the proposed changes and findings you don't agree with (or the date and symbols from the letter),

4) The tax periods or years involved,

5) A list of the changes that you don't agree with, and why you don't agree.

6) The facts supporting your position on any issue that you don't agree with,

7) The law or authority, if any, on which you are relying.

8) You must sign the written protest, stating that it is true, under the penalties of perjury as follows:

> **"Under the penalties of perjury, I declare that I examined the facts stated in this protest, including any accompanying documents, and, to the best of my knowledge and belief, they are true, correct, and complete."**

If your representative prepares and signs the protest for you, he or she must substitute a declaration stating:

1) That he or she submitted the protest and accompanying documents and

2) Whether he or she knows personally that the facts stated in the protest and accompanying documents are true and correct.

We urge you to provide as much information as you can, as this will help us speed up your appeal. This will save you both time and money.

Small Case Request:

If the total amount for any tax period is not more than $25,000, you may make a small case request instead of filing a formal written protest. In computing the total amount, include a proposed increase or decrease in tax (including penalties), or claimed refund. For an offer in compromise, in calculating the total amount, include total unpaid tax, penalty and interest due. For a small case request, follow the instructions in our letter to you by: sending a letter requesting Appeals consideration, indicating the changes you don't agree with, and the reasons why you don't agree.

Representation

You may represent yourself at your appeals conference, or you may have an attorney, certified public accountant, or an individual enrolled to practice before the IRS represent you. Your representative must be qualified to practice before the IRS. If you want your representative to appear without you, you must provide a properly completed power of attorney to the IRS before the representative can receive or inspect confidential information. Form 2848, Power of Attorney and Declaration of Representative, or any other properly written power of attorney or authorization may be used for this purpose. You can get copies of Form 2848 from an IRS office, or by calling 1-800-TAX-FORM (1-800-829-3676).

You may also bring another person(s) with you to support your position.

Appeals To The Courts

If you and Appeals don't agree on some or all of the issues after your Appeals conference, or if you skipped our appeals system, you may take your case to the United States Tax Court, the United States Court of Federal Claims, or your United States District Court, after satisfying certain procedural and jurisdictional requirements as described below under each court. (However, if you are a nonresident alien, you cannot take your case to a United States District Court.) These courts are independent judicial bodies and have no connection with the IRS.

Tax Court

If your disagreement with the IRS is over whether you owe additional income tax, estate tax, gift tax, certain excise taxes or penalties related to these proposed liabilities, you can go to the United States Tax Court. (Other types of tax controversies, such as those involving some employment tax issues or manufacturers' excise taxes, cannot be heard by the Tax Court.) You can do this after the IRS issues a formal letter, stating the amounts that the IRS believes you owe. This letter is called a notice of deficiency. You have 90 days from the date this notice is mailed to you to file a petition with the Tax Court (or 150 days if the notice is addressed to you outside the United States). The last date to file your petition will be entered on the notice of deficiency issued to you by the IRS. If you don't file the petition within the 90-day period (or 150 days, as the case may be), we will assess the proposed liability and send you a bill. You may also have the right to take your case to the Tax Court in some other situations, for example, following collection action by the IRS in certain cases. See Publication 1660.

If you discuss your case with the IRS during the 90-day period (150-day period), the discussion will not extend the period in which you may file a petition with the Tax Court.

The court will schedule your case for trial at a location convenient to you. You may represent yourself before the Tax Court, or you may be represented by anyone permitted to practice before that court.

Note: If you don't choose to go to the IRS Appeals Office before going to court, normally you will have an opportunity to attempt settlement with Appeals before your trial date.

If you dispute not more than $50,000 for any one tax year, there are simplified procedures. You can get information about these procedures and

other matters from the Clerk of the Tax Court, 400 Second St. NW, Washington, DC 20217.

Frivolous Filing Penalty

Caution: If the Tax Court determines that your case is intended primarily to cause a delay, or that your position is frivolous or groundless, the Tax Court may award a penalty of up to $25,000 to the United States in its decision.

District Court and Court of Federal Claims

If your claim is for a refund of any type of tax, you may take your case to your United States District Court or to the United States Court of Federal Claims. Certain types of cases, such as those involving some employment tax issues or manufacturers' excise taxes, can be heard only by these courts.

Generally, your District Court and the Court of Federal Claims hear tax cases only after you have paid the tax and filed a claim for refund with the IRS. You can get information about procedures for filing suit in either court by contacting the Clerk of your District Court or the Clerk of the Court of Federal Claims.

If you file a formal refund claim with the IRS, and we haven't responded to you on your claim within 6 months from the date you filed it, you may file suit for a refund immediately in your District Court or the Court of Federal Claims. If we send you a letter that proposes disallowing or disallows your claim, you may request Appeals review of the disallowance. If you wish to file a refund suit, you must file your suit no later than 2 years from the date of our notice of claim disallowance letter.

Note: Appeals review of a disallowed claim doesn't extend the 2 year period for filing suit. However, it may be extended by mutual agreement.

Recovering Administrative and Litigation Costs

You may be able to recover your reasonable litigation and administrative costs if you are the prevailing party, and if you meet the other requirements. You must exhaust your administrative remedies within the IRS to receive reasonable litigation costs. You must not unreasonably delay the administrative or court proceedings.

Administrative costs include costs incurred on or after the date you receive the Appeals decision letter, the date of the first letter of proposed deficiency, or the date of the notice of deficiency, whichever is earliest.

Recoverable litigation or administrative costs may include:

- Attorney fees that generally do not exceed $125 per hour. This amount will be indexed for a cost of living adjustment.

- Reasonable amounts for court costs or any administrative fees or similar charges by the IRS.

- Reasonable expenses of expert witnesses.

- Reasonable costs of studies, analyses, tests, or engineering reports that are necessary to prepare your case.

You are the prevailing party if you meet all the following requirements:

- You substantially prevailed on the amount in controversy, or on the most significant tax issue or issues in question.

- You meet the net worth requirement. For individuals or estates, the net worth cannot exceed $2,000,000 on the date from which costs are recoverable. Charities and certain cooperatives must not have more than 500 employees on the date from which costs are recoverable. And taxpayers other than the two categories listed above must not have net worth exceeding $7,000,000 and cannot have more than 500 employees on the date from which costs are recoverable.

You are not the prevailing party if:

- The United States establishes that its position was substantially justified. If the IRS does not follow applicable published guidance, the United States is presumed to not be substantially justified. This presumption is rebuttable. Applicable published guidance means regulations, revenue rulings, revenue procedures, information releases, notices, announcements, and, if they are issued to you, private letter rulings, technical advice memoranda and determination letters. The court will also take into account whether the Government has won or lost in the courts of appeals for other circuits on substantially similar issues, in determining if the United States is substantially justified.

You are also the prevailing party if:

- The final judgment on your case is less than or equal to a "qualified offer" which the IRS rejected, and if you meet the net worth requirements referred to above.

A court will generally decide who is the prevailing party, but the IRS makes a final determination of liability at the administrative level. This means you may receive administrative costs from the IRS without going to court. You must file your claim for administrative costs no later than the 90th day after the final determination of tax, penalty or interest is mailed to you. The Appeals Office makes determinations for the IRS on administrative costs. A denial of administrative costs may be appealed to the Tax Court no later than the 90th day after the denial.

☆U.S. GPO: 1999-455-262/91705

COLLECTION APPEAL RIGHTS

You can appeal many IRS collection actions. If you receive a **Notice of Federal Tax Lien Filing & Your Right To a Hearing Under IRC 6320** (Lien Notice), a **Final Notice - Notice of Intent to Levy And Your Notice of a Right to A Hearing**, or **Notice of Jeopardy Levy and Right of Appeal** (Levy Notices), you can appeal under Due Process procedures. You have 30 days to request a hearing with the IRS Office of Appeals and you can go to court if you object to Appeals' determination. Under the Collection Appeals Program (CAP) you can appeal any IRS collection action at any time but you cannot proceed to court if you object to Appeals' determination. Appeals will try to give you a decision within five business days after they receive the appeal on a CAP case. If you are told by a Collection employee that a Notice of Federal Tax Lien will be filed, you can appeal that action under CAP <u>before</u> the Notice of Federal Tax Lien is filed. A Due Process appeal is available only <u>after</u> the Notice of Federal Tax Lien is filed.

HEARING AVAILABLE UNDER DUE PROCESS
For Lien and Levy Notices

The law provides you the right to a fair hearing by the IRS Office of Appeals after a Notice of Federal Tax Lien is filed and before a levy on your property is issued. You also have the right to contest Appeals' determination in Tax Court or U.S. District Court, as appropriate. Under Due Process, you may request a hearing for each taxable period for one or both of the following IRS actions:

LIEN Notice. IRS is required to notify you that a Notice of Federal Tax Lien has been filed within 5 days after filing. You then have 30 days from the date of the lien notice to request a hearing with the IRS Office of Appeals.

LEVY Notice. IRS is required to notify you of its intention to collect a tax liability by taking your property or rights to property. The IRS does this by sending you a levy notice. No levy or seizure can occur within 30 days from the date of mailing of the levy notice or the date the levy notice is given to you or left at your home or business. During that 30 day period, you may request a hearing with the IRS Office of Appeals. There are two exceptions to this levy or seizure notice provision. When the collection of tax is in jeopardy or when the IRS issues a levy to collect from a state tax refund, the IRS may issue a levy without sending a levy notice or waiting 30 days after it sends the notice.

How to Request a Hearing under Due Process with the Office of Appeals

- Complete Form 12153, Request for a Collection Due Process Hearing, and send it to us at the address shown on your lien or levy notice within 30 days. Identify the IRS action(s) you disagree with (levy and/or lien notice) and explain why you disagree. You may appeal both actions, if you received both a lien and levy notice. You must identify all of your reasons for disagreement with the IRS at this time.

- To preserve your right to go to court, you must send us the Form 12153 within 30 days. Include a copy of your lien and/or levy notice. List all tax(es) and taxable periods for which you are requesting a hearing. You are entitled to only one hearing under Due Process for each taxable period. If you receive a subsequent lien or levy notice after you request a hearing on a lien or levy notice, Appeals can consider both matters at the same time. You can obtain Form 12153 by calling 1-800-829-3676.

504

- At the hearing, you may raise any relevant issue relating to the unpaid tax including
    1. Appropriateness of collection actions;
    2. Collection alternatives such as installment agreement, offer in compromise, posting a bond or substitution of other assets;
    3. Appropriate spousal defenses;
    4. The existence or amount of the tax, but only if you did not receive a notice of deficiency or did not have an opportunity to dispute the tax liability.

- You may not, however, raise an issue that was raised and considered at a prior administrative or judicial hearing, if you participated meaningfully in the prior hearing or proceeding.

- Before you formally appeal a lien or levy notice by sending us Form 12163, you may be able to work out a solution with the Collection function that proposed the action. To do so, contact the IRS employee whose name appears on the lien or levy notice and explain why you disagree with the action. This contact, however, does NOT extend the 30 day period to request an appeal.

What will happen when you request a hearing with the Office of Appeals?

- Unless we have reason to believe that collection of the tax is in jeopardy, we will stop collection action during the 30 days after the levy notice and, if your appeal is timely, during the appeal process. We will also suspend the collection statute of limitations, which is 10 years, from the date we receive a timely filed Form 12153, until the date the determination is final. Your appeal is timely if you mail your request for a hearing on or before the 30th day after the date of our lien or levy notice.

- If your appeal request is not timely, you will be allowed a hearing, but there will be no statutory suspension of collection action and you cannot go to court if you disagree with Appeals' determination.

- Appeals will contact you to schedule a hearing, either in person or by telephone. At the conclusion of the hearing, Appeals will issue a written determination letter. If you agree with Appeals' decision, both you and the IRS are required to live up to the terms of the decision.

- If you do not agree with Appeals' decision, you may request judicial review of the decision by initiating a case in a court of proper jurisdiction (United States Tax Court or United States District Court, depending on the circumstances) on or before the 30th day after the date of Appeals' decision. Once the Court rules, its decision will be binding on both you and the IRS.

The IRS Office of Appeals will retain jurisdiction over its determinations and how they are carried out. You may also return to Appeals if your circumstances change and impact the original decision. However, you must exhaust your administrative remedies first.

You may represent yourself at your Due Process hearing or you may be represented by an attorney, certified public accountant or a person enrolled to practice before the IRS. If you want your representative to appear without you, you must provide a properly completed Form 2848, Power of Attorney and Declaration of Representative.

ADMINISTRATIVE COLLECTION APPEAL RIGHTS
COLLECTION APPEALS PROGRAM (CAP)

For Liens, Levies, Seizures and Installment Agreements
Under the CAP procedure, you do not have the right to a judicial review of Appeals' decision

The IRS CAP procedure is available under more circumstances than the Due Process hearing procedure. It is important to note, however, that you cannot obtain judicial review of Appeals' decision following a CAP hearing.

IRS Collection Actions You Can Appeal

- *Notice of Federal Tax Lien* - You may appeal before or after IRS files a lien. You may also appeal denied requests to withdraw a Notice of Federal Tax Lien, and denied discharges, subordinations, and non-attachments of a lien. If IRS files a Notice of Federal Tax Lien, you may have additional Due Process appeal rights. See the preceding information regarding Hearing Available Under Due Process.

- *Notice of Levy* - You may appeal before or after the IRS places a levy on your wages, bank account or other property. Before a levy is issued, you may have additional Due Process appeal rights. See the preceding information regarding Hearing Available Under Due Process.

- *Seizure of Property* - You may appeal before or after IRS makes a seizure. However, if you request an appeal after IRS makes a seizure, you must appeal to the Collection manager within 10 business days after the Notice of Seizure is provided to you or left at your home or business.

- *Denial or Termination of Installment Agreement* - You may appeal when you are notified that IRS intends to deny you an installment agreement or terminate your installment agreement.

How to Appeal One of These IRS Collection Actions If Your Only Collection Contact Has Been A Notice or Telephone Call

1. Call the IRS at the telephone number shown on your notice. Be prepared to explain which action(s) you disagree with and why you disagree. You must also offer your solution to your tax problem.

2. If you cannot reach an agreement with the IRS employee, tell the employee that you want to appeal their decision. The employee must honor your request, and will refer you to a manager. The manager will either speak with you then, or will return your call within 24 hours.

3. Explain which action(s) you disagree with and why you disagree to the manager. The manager will make a decision on the case. If you do not agree with the manager's decision, we will send your case to an Appeals Officer for review.

How to Appeal One of These IRS Collection Actions If You Have Been Contacted By A Revenue Officer

1. If you disagree with the decision of the Revenue Officer, and wish to appeal under CAP, you must first request a conference with a Collection manager.

2. If you do not resolve your disagreement with the Collection manager, you may request Appeals consideration by completing Form 9423, Collection Appeal Request .

3. On the Form 9423, check the action(s) you disagree with and explain why you disagree. You must also explain your solution to resolve your tax problem. WE MUST RECEIVE YOUR REQUEST FOR AN APPEAL WITHIN 2 DAYS OF YOUR CONFERENCE WITH THE COLLECTION MANAGER OR WE RESUME COLLECTION ACTION.

What will happen when you appeal your case:

Normally, we will stop collection action related to the IRS action(s) you disagree with until the Appeals Officer makes a determination, unless we have reason to believe that collection of the amount owed is at risk.

You may have a representative

You may represent yourself at your Appeals conference or you may be represented by an attorney, certified public accountant or a person enrolled to practice before the IRS. If you want your representative to appear without you, you must provide a properly completed Form 2848, Power of Attorney and Declaration of Representative. You can obtain Form 2848 from your local IRS office or by calling 1-800-829-3676.

Decision on the appeal

Once the Appeals Officer makes a decision on your case, that decision is binding on both you and the IRS. This means that both you and the IRS are required to accept the decision and live up to its terms. You cannot obtain judicial review of Appeals Officer decision following a CAP hearing.

Note: If you provide false information, fail to provide all pertinent information, or fraud will void Appeals' decision.

Department of the Treasury
Internal Revenue Service

www.irs.ustreas.gov

Publication 1660 (Rev. 01-1999)
Catalog Number 14376Z

☆U.S.GPO:1998-448-032

IRS Mission:

Provide America's taxpayers top quality service by helping them understand and meet their tax responsibilities and by applying the tax law with integrity and fairness to all.

What You Should Know About

The IRS Collection Process

Keep this publication for future reference   **Publication 594**

We usually send this publication to taxpayers along with a final bill for taxes they owe. If you owe the tax shown on the bill we sent you, please arrange to pay it immediately. If you believe the bill is incorrect, call us now so that we may correct the mistake. We urge you to settle your tax account now so that we don't have to take any further action to collect the taxes you owe.

This publication tells you the steps the Internal Revenue Service (IRS) may take to collect overdue taxes. It also includes a summary of your rights and responsibilities concerning paying your federal taxes.

Inside you will find a number of titles of IRS forms and publications that apply to the various situations discussed. For a complete list of these documents, see page 12. For copies of these documents, please call us, write to us, visit your local library or IRS office, or contact us at our web site. See the next page for the phone numbers and addresses that you'll need. Please contact us right away; we will work with you to solve your tax problem.

Please note that the information in this document applies to all taxpayers— for example, individuals who owe income tax and employers who owe employment tax. Special rules that apply only to employers are in separate sections at the end.

This document is for information only. Although it discusses the legal authority that allows the IRS to collect taxes, it is not a precise and technical analysis of the law.

IRS

Department of the Treasury
Internal Revenue Service

Publication 594 (Rev.1-1999)
Catalog Number 46596B

---

en español
Existe una versión de esta publicación en español, la Publicación 594S, que puede obtener en la oficina local del Servicio de Impuestos Internos.

What's inside...

Do you have questions or need help right away? Call us. We're here to help you.

For tax information and help:

Call the number on the bill you received or call us toll free at:

1-800-829-1040
1-800-829-4059 / TDD

For tax forms and publications:

1-800-829-3676
1-800-829-4059 / TDD

Internet: http://www.irs.ustreas.gov

FTP-ftp.irs.ustreas.gov
Telnet-iris.irs.ustreas.gov

You'll find answers to frequently asked tax questions, tax forms online, searchable publications, hot tax issues and news, and help through e-mail.

If you prefer to write to us...

Enclose a copy of your tax bill. Print your name, Social Security number or taxpayer identification number, and the tax form and period shown on your bill. Write to us at the address shown on your tax bill.

You can also visit your nearest IRS office.
You'll find the exact address in your local phone book under *U.S. Government.*

What to Do When You Receive a Bill from the IRS

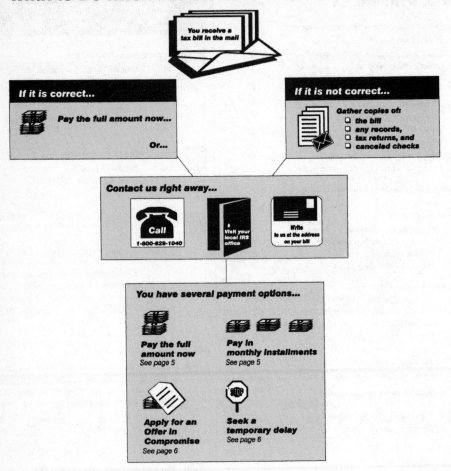

Avoid Having Overdue Taxes Next Year

▼ If you owe taxes because not enough money was withheld from your wages, claim a lower number of withholding allowances on your W-4 form. See Publication 919, *Is My Withholding Correct?*

▼ If you are self-employed and owe tax, increase your estimated tax payments. See Publication 505, *Tax Withholding and Estimated Tax.*

▼ If you are an employer, see Publication 15, *Circular E, Employer's Tax Guide.*

— 3 —

Important Information You Should Know

By law, you have the right to be treated professionally, fairly, promptly, and courteously by IRS employees. Among other things, you have the right to:

- disagree with your tax bill,

- meet with an IRS manager if you disagree with the IRS employee who handles your tax case,

- appeal most IRS collection actions,

- transfer your case to a different IRS office,

- be represented by someone when dealing with IRS matters, and

- receive a receipt for any payment you make.

For details about your rights, see Publication 1, *Your Rights as a Taxpayer*. You received a copy of it with your first bill.

If you disagree with our decisions...

If you disagree with the decision of an IRS employee at any time during the collection process, you can ask that employee's manager to review your case.

When you ask for a review, the employee will refer you to a manager. The manager will either speak with you then or will return your call by the next work day.

If you disagree with the manager's decision, you have the right to file an appeal under the Collection Appeals Program. This program enables you to appeal most collection actions we may take, including filing a lien, placing a levy on your wages or bank account, or seizing your property. See Publication 1660, *Collection Appeal Rights* for more information.

If you want someone to represent you...

When dealing with the IRS, you may choose to represent yourself, or you may have an attorney, a certified public accountant, an enrolled agent, or any person enrolled to practice before the IRS represent you. For example, you may want your tax preparer to respond to a tax bill that you believe is incorrect.

If your representative appears without you, he or she must file a Form 2848, *Power of Attorney and Declaration of Representative*, or Form 8821, *Tax Information Authorization*, before being allowed to receive or inspect confidential material.

We have a special program to help you with tax problems that cannot be resolved through normal IRS channels...

The **Problem Resolution Program** ensures that taxpayers' problems are handled promptly and properly. If you've made repeated attempts to work out your tax problems with the IRS but have been unsuccessful, first ask any IRS employee or manager to help you.

If the problem continues, ask for the **Taxpayer Advocate** in your local IRS office or **call 1-800-829-1040.** The Taxpayer Advocate determines whether you qualify for the Problem Resolution Program.

Other items to note...

▼ **The IRS can share your tax information** — By law, the IRS can share your tax information with city and state tax agencies and, in some cases, with the Department of Justice, other federal agencies, and people you authorize. We can also share it with certain foreign governments under tax treaty provisions.

▼ **We may contact a third party** — The law allows us to contact someone else, such as neighbors, banks, employers, or employees, to investigate your case.

▼ **If you are involved in bankruptcy proceedings** — Contact your local IRS office. While the proceeding may not eliminate your tax debt, it may temporarily stop IRS enforcement action from collecting a debt related to the bankruptcy.

▼ **Spousal defenses** — In some cases, you may not be liable for taxes, interest, and penalties on a joint income tax return. Contact your local IRS office for more information.

▼ **If you owe child support** — If you are entitled to a federal or state tax refund while you still owe unpaid taxes or child support, we may automatically apply the refund toward your debt. We will send you the remaining balance, if there is any.

— 4 —

What to Do When You Owe Taxes

Pay Your Taxes — or Tell Us Why You Can't

When you file your tax return, we check to see if the math is accurate and if you have paid the correct amount. If you have not paid all you owe, we send a bill called a *Notice of Tax Due and Demand for Payment*. (You may have already received it if you did not pay your taxes or if your payment was incorrect.) The bill includes the taxes, plus penalties and interest. We encourage you to pay your bill by check or money order as quickly as possible.

If you have received a bill for unpaid taxes, you should pay the entire amount — or tell us right away why you cannot. Call the office that sent you the bill. There are several different ways that you can pay.

If you do not pay the taxes you owe and if you make no effort to pay them, we can ask you to take action to pay your taxes, such as selling or mortgaging any assets you have or getting a loan. If you still make no effort to pay your bill or to work out a payment plan, we may also take more serious action, such as seizing your bank account, levying your wages, or taking your other income or assets. (See pages 7-10 for more information about liens and levies.)

What if you believe your bill is wrong?

If you believe your bill is wrong, let us know as soon as possible. Call the number on your bill, write to the IRS office that sent you the bill, call 1-800-829-1040, or visit your local IRS office, if you prefer.

To help us correct the problem, gather a copy of the bill along with copies of any records, tax returns, and canceled checks, etc., that will help us understand why you believe your bill is wrong.

If you write to us, tell us why you believe your bill is wrong. With your letter, include copies of all the documents you gathered to explain your case. Please do not send original documents. If we find you are correct, we will adjust your account and, if necessary, send you a corrected bill.

If you cannot pay all that you owe now, there's still something you can do...

If you cannot pay all your taxes now, pay as much as you can. By paying now, you reduce the amount of interest and penalty you will owe. Then, immediately call, write, or visit the nearest IRS office to explain your situation.

After you explain your problem, we may ask you to fill out a *Collection Information Statement* to help us compare your monthly income with your expenses and to figure out the amount you can pay. We can then help you work out a payment plan that fits your problem. Based on your situation, we will work with you to consider several different ways to pay what you owe:

- You may be able to make monthly payments through an installment agreement,

- You may be able to apply for an Offer in Compromise, or

- You may qualify for a temporary delay or your case may be considered a significant hardship.

Set Up an Installment Agreement

Installment agreements allow the full payment of your debt in smaller, more manageable amounts. Installment agreements generally require equal monthly payments. The amount of your installment payment will be based on the amount you owe and your ability to pay that amount within the time available to the IRS to collect the tax debt from you. An installment agreement is a reasonable payment option for some taxpayers.

You should be aware, however, that an installment agreement is more costly to you than paying all the taxes you owe now and may be more costly than borrowing funds to pay the amount you owe. Why? Because the IRS charges interest and penalties on the tax you owe, and charges interest on the unpaid penalties and interest that have been charged to your tax account. So, while you are making payments on your tax debt through an installment agreement, IRS continues to

— 5 —

charge interest and penalties on the unpaid portion of that debt. The interest rate on a bank loan or cash advance on your credit card may be lower than the combination of penalties and interest that IRS charges.

You should know about another cost associated with an installment agreement: To set up your installment agreement, we will charge you a $43 user fee.

If you would like to pay off your tax debt through an installment agreement and...

▸ **You owe less $10,000 or less in tax,** just call the number on your bill to set up your plan now. We'll tell you what you have to do to begin today.

▸ **You owe more than $10,000 in tax,** we may still be able to set up an installment agreement for you, but you may have to fill out Form 433-F, *Collection Information Statement.*

Even though you agree to an installment agreement, we may still file a *Notice of Federal Tax Lien* to secure the government's interest until you make a final payment. (See *Liens* on page 7.) However, we cannot levy against your property while your request for an installment agreement is being considered, while your agreement is in effect, for 30 days after your request for an agreement has been rejected, or for any period while an appeal of the rejection is being evaluated by the IRS.

If you do arrange for an installment agreement, you can pay with personal or business checks, money orders, or certified funds; payroll deductions that your employer takes from your salary and regularly sends to the IRS; or electronic transfers from your bank account or other similar means.

Your agreement is based on your financial situation. If a change in your financial situation makes it necessary to change your agreement, we will send you a letter 30 days before we change your plan. *If you have an installment agreement, you must pay on time. If you cannot, tell us immediately.*

Caution   We may end the agreement if you don't give us updated financial information when we ask for it, or if you don't meet the terms of the agreement. Your agreement could end if you pay late, miss a payment, or don't file or pay all required tax returns. In that case, we may take enforced collection action. See page 7 for more information.

Apply for an Offer in Compromise

In some cases, we may accept an Offer in Compromise to settle an unpaid tax account, including any interest and penalties. With this type of arrangement, we accept less than the amount you owe when it is doubtful we will be able to collect all the debt in the near future.

To file for an Offer in Compromise, see Form 656, *Offer in Compromise.*

Temporarily Delay the Collection Process

If we determine that you cannot pay *any* of your tax debt, we may temporarily delay collection until your financial condition improves. You should know that if we do delay collecting from you, your debt will increase because penalties and interest are charged until you pay the full amount. During a temporary delay, we will again review your ability to pay. We may also file a *Notice of Federal Tax Lien* (see page 7) to protect the government's interest in your assets.

If you have a significant hardship...

Your case may be considered a significant hardship if paying your taxes would mean that you cannot afford to maintain the necessities to live day to day, such as food, clothing, shelter, transportation, and medical treatment.

In addition, other cases may be considered as significant hardship by law: an immediate threat of adverse action, a delay of more than 30 days in resolving taxpayer account problems, the incurring of significant costs (including fees for professional representation) if relief is not granted, and irreparable injury to, or long-term adverse impact on, the taxpayer if relief is not granted.

To apply for emergency relief if you are facing a significant hardship, call **1-800-829-1040** or visit your district's **Taxpayer Advocate.** If you qualify, they can help you fill out Form 911, *Application for Taxpayer Assistance Order.*

— 6 —

About IRS Collection Actions

Before we take any action explained in this section, we will contact you to give you a chance to voluntarily pay what you owe. But if you do not pay your taxes in full and do not contact us to let us know why you cannot pay or why you disagree with our decision to take enforcement action, the law requires us to take action. We may:

▸ **File a lien** against your property (Make a legal claim to your property as security or payment for your tax debt) (*See the information below*).

▸ **Serve a levy** on your property or salary (Legally seize your property to satisfy a tax debt) (*See page 8*).

▸ **Assess a trust fund recovery penalty**, for employment taxes (*See page 11*).

These *enforced collection actions* are the means by which we can enforce the *Notice and Demand for Tax Payment*. On the following pages, we explain these collection actions and the rules that govern them.

Liens

Liens give us a legal claim to your property as security or payment for your tax debt. A *Notice of Federal Tax Lien* may be filed only after:

▸ We assess the liability;

▸ We send you a *Notice and Demand for Payment* — a bill that tells you how much you owe in taxes; and

▸ You neglect or refuse to fully pay the debt within 10 days after we notify you about it.

Once these requirements are met, a lien is created for the amount of your tax debt. By filing this notice, your creditors are publicly notified that we have a claim against all your property, including property you acquire after the lien was filed.

The lien attaches to all your property (such as your house or car) and to all your rights to property (such as your accounts receivable, if you are an employer).

Caution Once a lien is filed, your credit rating may be harmed. You may not be able to get a loan to buy a house or a car, get a new credit card, or sign a lease.

Releasing a lien

We will issue a *Release of the Notice of Federal Tax Lien*:

▸ Within 30 days after you satisfy the tax due (including interest and other additions) by paying the debt or by having it adjusted, or

▸ Within 30 days after we accept a bond that you submit, guaranteeing payment of the debt.

In addition, you must pay all fees that a state or other jurisdiction charges you to file and release the lien. These fees will be added to the amount you owe. See Publication 1450, *Request for Release of Federal Tax Lien*.

Usually 10 years after a tax is assessed, a lien releases automatically if we have not filed it again. If we knowingly or negligently do not release a *Notice of Federal Tax Lien* when it should be released, you may sue the federal government, but not IRS employees, for damages.

Applying for a discharge of a federal tax lien

If you are giving up ownership of property, such as when you sell your home, you may apply for a *Certificate of Discharge*. Each application for a discharge of a tax lien releases the effects of the lien against one piece of property. Note that when certain conditions exist, a third party may also request a *Certificate of Discharge*. See Publication 783, *Instructions on How to Apply for a Certificate of Discharge of Property from the Federal Tax Lien*.

Making the IRS lien secondary to another lien

In some cases, a federal tax lien can be made secondary to another lien. That process is called *subordination*. See Publication 784, *How to Prepare Application for Certificate of Subordination of Federal Tax Lien*.

Withdrawing liens

By law, a filed notice of tax lien can be withdrawn if:

- the notice was filed too soon or not according to IRS procedures,
- you entered into an installment agreement to pay the debt on the notice of lien (unless the agreement provides otherwise),
- withdrawal will speed collecting the tax, or
- withdrawal would be in your best interest (as determined by the Taxpayer Advocate) and the best interest of the government.

We will give you a copy of the withdrawal and, if you write to us, we will send a copy to other institutions you name.

Appealing the filing of a lien

The law requires us to notify you in writing within 5 business days after the filing of a lien. We may give you this notice in person, leave it at your home or your usual place of business, or send it by certified or registered mail to your last known address. You may ask an IRS manager to review your case or you may file an appeal with the IRS Office of Appeals. You must file your appeal within 30 days of the date of the notice. Some of the issues you may discuss include:

- You paid all you owed before we filed the lien,

- We assessed the tax and filed the lien when you were in bankruptcy and subject to the automatic stay during bankruptcy,
- We made a procedural error in an assessment,
- The time to collect the tax (called the *statute of limitations*) expired before we filed the lien,
- You did not have an opportunity to dispute the assessed liability,
- You wish to discuss the collection options, or
- You wish to make spousal defenses.

At the conclusion of your appeal, the IRS Office of Appeals will issue a determination. That determination may support the continued existence of the filed federal tax lien or it may determine that the lien should be released or withdrawn. You will have a 30-day period, starting with the date of the determination, to bring a suit to contest the determination. See Publication 1660, *Collection Appeal Rights*, for more information.

Levies

A levy is a legal seizure of your property to satisfy a tax debt. Levies are different from liens. A lien is a *claim used as security* for the tax debt, while a levy actually *takes the property* to satisfy the tax debt.

If you do not pay your taxes (or make arrangements to settle your debt), the IRS may seize and sell any type of real or personal property that you own or have an interest in. For instance,

- We could seize and sell property that you hold (such as your car, boat, or house), or
- We could levy property that is yours but is held by someone else (such as your wages, retirement accounts, dividends, bank accounts, licenses, rental income, accounts receivables, the cash value of your life insurance, or commissions).

We usually levy only after these three requirements are met:

- We assessed the tax and sent you a *Notice and Demand for Payment*,
- You neglected or refused to pay the tax, and

We sent you a *Final Notice of Intent to Levy* and a *Notice of Right to Hearing* (levy notice) at least 30 days before the levy. We may give you this notice in person, leave it at your home or your usual place of business, or send it to your last known address by certified mail, return receipt requested.

If your property is levied or seized, contact the IRS employee who took the action. You may also ask an IRS manager to review your case, or you may file an appeal with the IRS Office of Appeals. You must file your appeal within 30 days of the date of the *Final Notice of Intent to Levy and a Notice of Right to Hearing*. Some of the issues you may discuss include:

- You paid all you owed before we sent the levy notice,
- We assessed the tax and sent the levy notice when you were in bankruptcy and subject to the automatic stay during bankruptcy,
- We made a procedural error in an assessment,
- The time to collect the tax (called *the statute of limitations*) expired before we sent the levy notice,
- You did not have an opportunity to dispute the assessed liability,
- You wish to discuss the collection options, or
- You wish to make spousal defenses.

At the conclusion of your appeal, the IRS Office of Appeals will issue a determination. That determination may support the levy action or it may determine that the levy should be released. You will have a 30-day period, starting with the date of determination to bring a suit to contest the determination. See Publication 1660, *Collection Appeal Rights*, for more information.

Levying your wages or your bank account

If we levy your salary or wages, the levy will end when:

- The levy is released,
- You pay your tax debt, or
- The time expires for legally collecting the tax.

If we levy your bank account, for 21 days your bank must hold funds you have on deposit — up to the amount you owe. This period allows you time to solve any problems from the levy or to make other arrangements to pay. After 21 days, the bank must send the money, plus interest if it applies, to the IRS.

To discuss your case, call the IRS employee whose name is shown on the *Notice of Levy*.

Filing a claim for reimbursement when we made a mistake in levying your account

If you paid bank charges because of a mistake we made when we levied your account, you may be entitled to a reimbursement. To be reimbursed, you must file a claim with us within 1 year after your bank charged you the fee. Use Form 8546, *Claim for Reimbursement of Bank Charges Incurred Due to Erroneous Service Levy or Misplaced Payment Check*.

Releasing a levy

We must release your levy if any of the following occur:

- You pay the tax, penalty, and interest you owe.
- We discover that the time for collection ended (the *statute of limitations*) before the levy was served.
- You provide documentation proving that releasing the levy will help us collect the tax.
- You have, or are about to enter into, an approved, current installment agreement, unless the agreement says the levy does not have to be released.
- We determine that the levy is creating a significant economic hardship for you.
- The expense of selling the property would be more than the tax debt.

Releasing your property

Before the sale date, we may release the property if:

- You pay the amount of the government's interest in the property,
- You enter into an escrow arrangement,
- You furnish an acceptable bond,
- You make an acceptable agreement for paying the tax, or
- The expense of selling your property would be more than the tax debt.

— 9 —

Returning levied property

We can consider returning levied property if:

► We levy before we send you the 2 required notices or before your time for responding to them has passed (10 days for the *Notice and Demand*; 30 days for the *Notice of Intent to Levy* and the *Notice of Right to Hearing*).

► It was determined that we did not follow our own procedures.

► We agree to let you pay in installments, but we still levy, and the agreement does not say that we can do so.

► Returning the property will help you pay your taxes.

► Returning the property is in your best interest and the government's.

Selling your property

After your property is seized, we must usually wait 60 days before we sell it. We will post a public notice of a pending sale, usually in local newspapers or flyers. We will deliver the original notice of sale to you or send it to you by certified mail.

After placing the notice, we must wait at least 10 days before conducting the sale, unless the property is perishable and must be sold immediately.

Before the sale, we will compute a *minimum bid price*. This bid is usually 80% or more of the forced sale value of the property, after subtracting any liens.

If you disagree with this price, you can appeal it. Ask that the price be computed again by either an IRS or private appraiser.

You may also ask that we sell the seized property within 60 days. For information about how to do so, call the IRS employee who made the seizure. We will grant your request, unless it is in the government's best interest to keep the property. We will send you a letter telling you of our decision about your request. After the sale, we first use the proceeds to pay the expenses of the levy and sale. Then we use any remaining amount to pay the tax bill.

► **If the proceeds of the sale are less than the total of the tax bill and the expenses of levy and sale**, you will still have to pay the unpaid tax.

► **If the proceeds of the sale are more than the total of the tax bill and the expenses of the levy and sale**, we will notify you about the surplus money and will tell you how to ask for a refund. However, if someone, such as a mortgagee or other lienholder, makes a claim that is superior to yours, we will pay that claim before we refund any money to you.

Redeeming your real estate

You (or anyone with an interest in the property) may redeem your real estate within 180 days after the sale. You must pay the purchaser the amount paid for the property, plus interest at 20% annually.

Some property cannot be levied or seized

By law, some property cannot be levied or seized. We may not seize any of your property when the expense of selling the property would be more than the tax debt. In addition, we may not seize or levy your property on the day you attend a collection interview because of a summons.

Other items we may not levy or seize include:

► School books and certain clothing;

► Fuel, provisions, furniture, and personal effects for a head of household, totaling $6,250;

► Books and tools you use in your trade, business, or profession, totaling $3,125;

► Unemployment benefits;

► Undelivered mail;

► Certain annuity and pension benefits;

► Certain service-connected disability payments;

► Workmen's compensation;

► Salary, wages, or income included in a judgment for court-ordered child support payments;

► Certain public assistance payments;

► A minimum weekly exemption for wages, salary, and other income.

Use Publication 1494, *Table of Figuring Amount Exempt from Levy on Wages, Salary and Other Income* (Forms 668-W(c)(DO)and 668-W(c)), to determine the amount of earned income exempt from levy.

— 10 —

517

Employment Taxes for Employers

To encourage prompt payment of withheld income and employment taxes, including Social Security taxes, railroad retirement taxes, or collected excise taxes, Congress passed a law that provides for the trust fund recovery penalty. (These taxes are called *trust fund taxes* because you actually hold the employee's money in trust until you make a federal tax deposit in that amount.)

If we plan to assess you for the trust fund recovery penalty, we will send you a letter stating that you are the *responsible* person. You have 60 days after you receive our letter to appeal our proposal. If you do not respond to our letter, we will assess the penalty against you and send you a *Notice and Demand for Payment*. Also, we can apply this penalty whether or not you are out of business.

A responsible person is a person or group of people who has the duty to perform and the power to direct the collecting, accounting, and paying of trust fund taxes. This person may be:

- an officer or an employee of a corporation,
- a member or employee of a partnership,
- a corporate director or shareholder,
- a member of a board of trustees of a nonprofit organization, or
- another person with authority and control over funds to direct their disbursement.

Assessing the trust fund recovery penalty

We may assess the penalty against anyone:

- who is responsible for collecting or paying withheld income and employment taxes, or for paying collected excise taxes, and

- who willfully fails to collect or pay them.

For willfulness to exist, the responsible person must:

- Have known about the unpaid taxes, and

- Have used the funds to keep the business going or allowed available funds to be paid to other creditors.

Especially for Employers...

Employment taxes are:

- The amount you should withhold from your employees for both income and Social Security tax, plus

- The amount of Social Security tax you pay on behalf of each employee.

Caution

If you ignore the federal tax deposit and filing requirements, the amount you owe can increase dramatically.

If you do not pay your employment taxes on time, or if you were required to and did not include your payment with your return, we will charge you interest and penalties on any unpaid balance. We may charge you penalties of up to 15% of the amount not deposited, depending on how many days late you are.

If you do not pay withheld trust fund taxes, we may take additional collection action. We may require you to:

- File and pay your taxes monthly rather than quarterly, or

- Open a special bank account for the withheld amounts, under penalty of prosecution. See Form 8109, *Federal Tax Deposit Coupon*; Circular E, *Employer's Tax Guide*; and Notice 109, *Information About Depositing Employment and Excise Taxes*.

Figuring the penalty amount

The amount of the penalty is equal to the unpaid balance of the trust fund tax. The penalty is computed based on:

- The unpaid income taxes withheld, plus
- The employee's portion of the withheld FICA taxes.

For collected taxes, the penalty is based on the unpaid amount of collected excise taxes.

Caution

Once we assert the penalty, we can take collection action against your personal assets. For instance, we can file a federal tax lien if you are the responsible person.

Appealing the decision

You have the right to appeal our decision to recommend that you pay the trust fund recovery penalty amount.

See Publication 5, *Your Appeal Rights and How to Prepare a Protest if You Don't Agree*, for a clear outline of the appeals process.

We offer you a number of free publications and forms...

These IRS forms and publications mentioned in this document give you more information about the various situations discussed. For copies of these documents, call us, write to us, visit your local library or IRS office, or contact us at our website at **www.irs.ustreas.gov**.

Forms

- Form 433-F, *Collection Information Statement*
- Form 911, *Application for Taxpayer Assistance Order*
- Form 656, *Offer in Compromise*
- Form 2848, *Power of Attorney and Declaration of Representative*
- Form 8109, *Federal Tax Deposit Coupon*
- Form 8821, *Tax Information Authorization*
- Form 8546, *Claim for Reimbursement of Bank Charges Incurred Due to Erroneous Service Levy or Misplaced Payment Check*

Publications

- Publication 1, *Your Rights as a Taxpayer*
- Publication 5, *Your Appeal Rights and How to Prepare a Protest if You Don't Agree*

- Publication 783, *Instructions on How to Apply for a Certificate of Discharge of Property from the Federal Tax Lien*
- Publication 784, *How to Prepare Application for Certificate of Subordination of Federal Tax Lien*
- Publication 919, *Is My Withholding Correct?*
- Publication 1459, *Request for Release of Federal Tax Lien*
- Publication 1494, *Table of Figuring Amount Exempt from Levy on Wages, Salary and Other Income*
- Publication 1660, *Collection Appeal Rights*
- Circular E, *Employer's Tax Guide*
- Notice 109, *Information About Depositing Employment and Excise Taxes*

*U.S. Government Printing Office: 1998 — 448-085

APPENDIX E:
PRACTITIONER HOT LINE
TELEPHONE NUMBERS

Account-related inquiries on individual and business tax accounts will be accepted from tax practitioners when representing a client. A valid authorization must be on file with the IRS for the taxpayer, type of tax, and tax period involved.

District	*Hot Line Phone*	*Hours*
REGION: NORTHEAST		
Brooklyn	718-488-2250	8:15 A.M.–4:30 P.M.
Manhattan	212-719-6045/46	8:30 A.M.–5:00 P.M.
Upstate New York	716-961-5151 (Buffalo)	8:00 A.M.–4:30 P.M.
	518-427-4228 (Albany)	8:30 A.M.–4:00 P.M.
Conn./R.I.	860-240-4101 (Connecticut)	8:00 A.M.–4:30 P.M.
	401-528-4033/34 (Rhode Island)	7:30 A.M.–4:30 P.M.
Ohio	513-241-2929/30 (Cincinnati)	8:30 A.M.–4:30 P.M.
	216-623-1338 (Cleveland)	7:30 A.M.–4:30 P.M.
Michigan	313-961-4609	8:00 A.M.–4:15 P.M.
New England	617-536-0739	8:30 A.M.–4:30 P.M.
New Jersey	201-645-2231 201-645-3271	8:15 A.M.–4:15 P.M.

| Pennsylvania | 215-440-1524
(Philadelphia) | 8:30 A.M.–4:00 P.M. |
| | 412-281-0281
(Pittsburgh) | 8:30 A.M.–4:00 P.M. |

REGION: SOUTHEAST

Md./Delaware	410-727-7965	8:00 A.M.–4:30 P.M.
Va./W. Va.	804-698-5010	8:00 A.M.–4:30 P.M.
Ky./Tenn.	615-781-4826	8:00 A.M.–4:30 P.M.
Gulf States	504-558-3050 (New Orleans)	8:00 A.M.–4:30 P.M.
	601-965-4134 (Jackson)	8:00 A.M.–4:30 P.M.
	205-912-5150 (Birmingham)	8:00 A.M.–4:30 P.M.
Georgia	678-530-7799	7:30 A.M.–5:30 P.M.
Indiana	317-377-0027	8:00 A.M.–4:30 P.M.
N. Florida	904-358-3572	8:00 A.M.–4:30 P.M.
S. Florida	305-982-5242 (Ft. Lauderdale)	8:00 A.M.–4:30 P.M.
	954-423-7763 (Miami)	8:00 A.M.–4:30 P.M.
N./S. Carolina	910-378-2157 (Greensboro)	8:00 A.M.–4:30 P.M.
	803-253-3231 (Columbia)	8:00 A.M.–4:30 P.M.

REGION: MIDSTATES

Kansas/Mo.	314-342-9325	7:30 A.M.–5:30 P.M.
North Texas	214-767-2440 (Accounts)	7:30 A.M.–5:30 P.M.
	214-767-1501 (Technical)	7:30 A.M.–5:30 P.M.

REGION: WESTERN

L.A.	213-894-3706	8:00 A.M.–4:15 P.M.
Central Calif.	408-494-8113	9:00 A.M.–3:00 P.M.
N. Calif.	510-271-0781	8:00 A.M.–5:00 P.M.
S. Calif.	714-360-2185	8:00 A.M.–4:30 P.M.
Pacific Northwest	206-220-5786 (Washington)	8:00 A.M.–5:00 P.M.
	503-222-7562 (Oregon)	8:00 A.M.–5:00 P.M.
Rocky Mtn.	303-820-3940	8:00 A.M.–5:30 P.M.

Southwest	602-640-3935 (Arizona)	8:00 A.M.–4:30 P.M.
	505-837-5749 (New Mexico)	8:00 A.M.–4:30 P.M.
	702-455-1201 (Nevada)	8:00 A.M.–4:30 P.M.

SERVICE CENTERS:

Andover	617-720-4147	8:00 A.M.–4:00 P.M.
Atlanta	678-530-7799	8:00 A.M.–5:00 P.M.
Austin	*NO HOT LINE*	
Brookhaven	631-447-4960 631-447-4297 (fax)	9:00 A.M.–3:00 P.M.
Cincinnati	513-241-2929	
Fresno	559-452-4210	8:00 A.M.–3:30 P.M.
Kansas City	314-342-9325	
Memphis	901-546-4213/4212	
Ogden	801-620-6339	6:00 A.M.–4:30 P.M.
Philadelphia	215-516-2000	

APPENDIX F:
USEFUL WEBSITES

TAX-RELATED WEBSITES

What the IRS Doesn't Want You to Know: The author's own website will provide you with a wealth of information: monthly tax tips, the ability to ask Marty a tax question, and links to other sites.
www.irsmaven.com

Internal Revenue Service (Home Page)
www.irs.gov

Court Decisions Online: From the U.S. House of Representatives, federal court decisions and rules, plus links to various law libraries and other sources of court cases.
www.http://uscode.house.gov/

Essential Links: Very comprehensive listing for tax information and resources plus current tax news.
www.el.com/elinks/taxes

General Accounting Office: Overseer of the IRS. The financial operations of the IRS are reviewed in detail.
www.gao.gov

Help & Education: Will help you with TeleTax topics, frequently asked questions, and where to file. Questions can be submitted.
www.irs.gov/tax_edu/index.html

Independent Contractor Audit Guide: Find out what to expect *before* audit starts.
www.irs.gov/bus_info/tax_pro/tax-law.html

Local Offices of IRS: To obtain information directly from IRS specialists.
www.irs.gov/where_file/

MSSP Audit Guides: Many of the most popular guides are available for downloading.
www.irs.gov/prod/bus_info/mssp/index.html

Market Segment Understandings (MSU)
www.irs.gov/bus_info/msu-info.html

NewsStand: Gives you the calendar for small businesses; news releases; electronic Freedom of Information Act; excerpts from the *Internal Revenue Manual*.
www.irs.gov/news/index.html

Penalty Box: Enter tax liabilities in order to calculate lower tax penalties that are determined by alternative calculations permitted by the IRS.
www.taxpenalty.com

Roth IRAs: Comprehensive site updated with Roth IRA information and has calculator utilities. Although much of the information is designed for tax pros, there is lots of useful stuff for ordinary people.
www.rothira.com

Statistics of Income: Contains a great deal of information on IRS audit results and collections.
www.irs.gov/prod/tax_stats/index.html

Tax History: An overview of the history of taxes from the seventeenth century to now. Bonus: Form 1040 of presidents, from FDR to Clinton, plus Al Gore.
www.taxhistory.tax.org

Tax Information for Business: Retirement plans, business library, tax calendars, market segment guides, and market segment understandings.
www.irs.gov/bus_info/index.html

Tax Information for You: Information on IRS collection financial standards, taxpayer advocates, and Internal Revenue Bulletins.
www.irs.gov/ind_info/index.html

Tax Professionals Corner: Has information regarding IRS forms and publications, early release drafts of forms, CD-ROM products, fill-in forms, and administrative information and resources.
www.irs.gov/bus_info/tax_pro/

Tax Publications for Business: An excellent library of publications for businesses and farms.
www.irs.gov/bus_info/library.html

Tax Wire: Daily tax news including IRS updates.
www.tax.org/taxwire/taxwire.htm

Taxsites (Federal): Gateway to a wide range of tax and accounting information. Has links to on-line tax services such as Commerce Clearing House and Research Institute of America.
www.taxsites.com

Taxsites (States): Comprehensive list of tax resources for all states, including links to state tax agencies.
www.taxsites.com/state.html

Taxweb: Broad collection of links to federal and state agencies, including tax discussion groups.
www.taxweb.com

1040.COM: Good site for forms, instructions, publications, and bulletins in PDF format. Allows quick access and download, and is kept current.
www.1040.com

Transactional Records Access Clearinghouse (Syracuse University): Thousands of facts and statistics about the IRS.
www.trac.syr.edu

What's New: On the IRS website. New forms and publications and much more.
www.irs.gov/help/newmail/maillist.html

FINANCIAL AND BUSINESS WEBSITES

American Institute of Philanthropy: How charities spend their money, plus ratings of charities.
www.charitywatch.org

Appraisers: FAQs about appraisals and contact information for appraisers.
www.appraisers.org

CNNFN: A supermarket of financial news.
www.cnnfn.com

Motley Fool: Portfolio tracking, financial news, and lots more, written in plain, easy-to-understand language.
www.fool.com

Human Resources: Human resources topics, including sexual harassment and age bias.
www.hr-esource.com

Morningstar Finance: All about mutual funds.
www.morningstar.com

N.Y. State College Tuition Program
www.osc.state.ny.us

Prophet Finance: The place to go for conducting simple or sophisticated technical analysis of stocks.
www.prophetfinance.com

S & P Equity Investor Services
www.stockinfo.standardpoor.com

Small Business Administration: Excellent information source about starting and maintaining a business. Loaded with on-line tutorials, helpful software, and information about SBA applications and assistance programs.
www.sba.gov

Small Business Owners: Buying and selling a business, franchising, marketing, and more.
www.helpbizowners.com

Small Cap Center: Information about earnings and investments, as well as computer-related and telecommunications news.
www.smallcapcenter.com

Social Security Administration: Useful for requesting earnings and benefit statements.
www.ssa.gov

Social Security Administration—Retire: A retirement planner that walks you through the retirement application.
www.ssa.gov/retire

State College Savings Plans
www.collegesavings.org

Supreme Court of the U.S.: Includes the Court schedule, opinions, rules, and a visitors guide.
www.supremecourtus.gov

NOTES

All IRS publications are issued by the Department of the Treasury and published by the U.S. Government Printing Office in Washington, D.C. Please see the Bibliography, page 509, for further information on these publications.

1. WHY EVERY TAXPAYER MUST READ THIS BOOK

1. David Cay Johnston, "Man Pursued by IRS Wins $75,000 to Pay His Lawyer," *The New York Times*, Feb. 9, 1999, A:12:1.

2. THE IRS PERSONALITY: PLAYING IT TO YOUR ADVANTAGE

1. Kevin McCormally, "How a Dumb Idea Became a Law," *Kiplinger's Personal Finance*, July 1993, pp. 44–47.
2. Ken Rankin, "And the Award for Tax Headache of the Year: AMT," *Accounting Today*, May 1–21, 2000, p. 5.
3. Don Van Natta, Jr., "11 Officers Are Accused of Failure to Pay Taxes," *The New York Times*, July 17, 1996, B:3:5.
4. *IRS 1980 Annual Report*, pp. 10–11.
5. *IRS 1998 Data Book*, advance draft, Table 1.
6. Jerold L. Waltman, *Political Origins of the U.S. Income Tax* (Jackson, Miss.: University Press of Mississippi, 1985), p. 17.
7. Ibid., p. 113.
8. Gregg Hitt, "Favored Companies Get 11th-Hour Tax Breaks," *The Wall Street Journal*, July 30, 1997, A:2.
9. *IRS Data Book*, 1997 and 1998, advance draft, Table 1.
10. Mary A. Turville, "Treasury Proposes Crackdown on EITC Errors," *National Public Accountant*, July 1997, p. 8 ("Capital Corridors").
11. *IRS 1996 Data Book*, advance draft, Table 9; *IRS 1997 Data Book*, Table 9.
12. Lillian Doris, ed., *The American Way in Taxation: Internal Revenue, 1862–1963* (Englewood Cliffs, N.J.: Prentice-Hall, 1963), p. 39.

13. Gerald Carson, *The Golden Egg: The Personal Income Tax—Where It Came From, How It Grew* (Boston: Houghton Mifflin, 1977), p. 210.

14. Clayton Knowles, "Nunan Mentioned in Tax Cut Case," *The New York Times*, Feb. 15, 1952, 10:5.

15. Clayton Knowles, "Nunan Accused Before the Senate of Complicity in 4 New Tax Cases," *The New York Times*, Feb. 22, 1952, 1:2.

16. John C. Chommie, *The Internal Revenue Service* (New York: Praeger, 1970), p. 94.

17. *IRS 1997 Data Book*, Table 23.

18. *IRS 1998 Data Book*, advance draft, Table 19.

19. *IRS 1995 Data Book*, advance draft, Table 18; *IRS Data Book*, 1996 and 1997, advance draft, Table 19.

3. WHO RUNS THE SHOW: WHAT YOU'RE UP AGAINST

1. IRS, *Tax Hints 1999*, p. 3.

2. IRS, *Guide to the Internal Revenue Service for Congressional Staff*, p. 29.

3. *Tax Hotline*, "Discriminate Function Hotline, IRS Audit Lottery," May 1999, p. 11.

4. "IRS Briefing," *Practical Accountant*, August 1999, p. 17.

5. *IRS 1998 Data Book*, advance draft, Table 11.

6. *IRS 1998 Data Book*, advance draft, Table 20.

7. IRS, *Guide*, p. 31.

8. Ibid., p. 33.

9. *IRS 1998 Data Book*, advance draft, Table 21.

10. IRS, *Internal Revenue Service Manual*, p. 4231–161.

11. *IRS 1993–94 Data Book*, advance draft, Table 28; *IRS Data Book*, 1996 and 1997, Table 29.

12. *IRS 1995 Data Book*, advance draft, Table 20; *IRS Data Book*, 1996, 1997, and 1998, advance draft, Table 21.

13. *IRS Data Book*, 1997 and 1998, advance draft, Table 21.

14. IRS, *Guide*, p. 10.

15. Ibid., pp. 10–11.

16. *IRS Data Book*, 1995, 1996, and 1997, advance draft, Table 10.

4. IRS PEOPLE

1. David Burnham, *A Law Unto Itself: Power, Politics and the IRS* (New York: Random House, 1989), p. 22.

2. Ibid., p. 23.

3. Eugene C. Steuerle, *Who Should Pay for Collecting Taxes?* (Washington, D.C.: American Institute for Public Policy Research, 1986), p. 15.

4. Ibid.

5. *Journal of Accountancy*, "IRS Forced to Operate With Less, to See a Decline in Service," Oct. 1996, p. 32 ("Tax Matters").

6. IRS, *Guide to the IRS for Congressional Staff*, p. 8.

7. Commerce Clearing House, *1998 Tax Legislation, IRS Restructuring and Reform Law, Explanation and Analysis*, June 1998, Sec. 1316, pp. 344, 345.

5. NEUTRALIZING THE IRS'S POWER

1. David Burnham, *A Law Unto Itself: Power, Politics and the IRS* (New York: Random House, 1989), p. 21.
2. Jeff A. Schnepper, *Inside IRS* (New York: Stein and Day, 1987), p. 57.
3. General Accounting Office, GAO Month in Review: April 1999, Tax Policy and Administration, "Confidentiality of Tax Data: IRS Implementation of the Taxpayer Browsing Protection Act," GAO/GGD-99-43, March 31, 1999, p. 10.
4. Andrea Adelson, "IRS Is Getting a Look at Some Mortgage Applications," *The New York Times*, Dec. 29, 1996, 11:2.
5. Kenneth Harney, "IRS Casts High-Tech Net to Snare Mortgage Frauds," *Newsday*, Nov. 1, 1996, D:2:1.
6. Burnham, *A Law Unto Itself*, p. 313.
7. IRS, *Guide to the IRS for Congressional Staff*, p. 38.
8. *IRS Data Book*, 1994–1996 and 1997, Tables 31, 34.
9. Ibid.
10. IRS, *Guide*, p. 38.
11. Ibid.
12. Ibid.
13. *IRS Data Book*, 1994–1996, advance draft, Tables 31, 34.
14. IRS, *Guide*, p. 38.
15. Ibid.
16. *IRS Data Book*, 1994–1996 and 1997, Tables 31, 34.
17. As quoted in Burnham, *A Law Unto Itself*, p. 303.
18. John C. Chommie. *The Internal Revenue Service* (New York: Praeger, 1970), p. 177.
19. Seymour Hersh, "IRS Said to Balk Inquiry on Rebozo," *The New York Times*, April 21, 1974, 1:3; and "Ervin Unit to Get Rebozo Tax Data," *The New York Times*, April 24, 1974, 1:4.
20. U.S. Congress House Committee on Government Operations, fourth report, *A Citizen's Guide on Using the Freedom of Information Act and the Privacy Act of 1974 to Request Government Records*, House Report 102-146 (Washington, D.C.: GPO, 1991), p. 2.
21. Ibid., pp. 5–6.
22. George S. Alberts, *Tax Loopholes* (Springfield, N.J.: Boardroom Classics, 1994), p. 34.
23. Randy Bruce Blaustein, *How to Do Business with the IRS—Taxpayer's Edition* (Englewood Cliffs, N.J.: Prentice-Hall, 1984), p. 13.
24. *The New York Times*, "Nuclear War Plan by IRS," March 28, 1989, D:16:6.
25. Preliminary IRS data, Tables 1, 15.
26. Joseph A. Pechman, *Federal Tax Policy*, 4th ed., Studies of Government Finance (Washington, D.C.: Brookings Institution, 1983), p. 61.
27. David Cay Johnston, "IRS Bolstering Efforts to Curb Cheating on Taxes," *The New York Times*, Feb. 13, 2000, A:6:1.
28. Burnham, *A Law Unto Itself*, p. 308.
29. Kip Dellinger, Audit and Accounting Forum, "Is Asking for Honesty Undermining the Tax System?" *Accounting Today*, Aug. 25–Sept. 7, 1997, p. 12.

6. IRS TECHNOLOGY

1. *IRS 1991 Annual Report*, p. 10.
2. *IRS 1997 Data Book*, Table 19.
3. Ibid., Tables 1, 2.
4. Ibid., Tables 11, 19, 20.
5. *NSPA Washington Reporter*, "IRS, NSPA Meet to Review '92 Tax Form Changes," August 1991, p. 3.
6. *Practical Accountant*, "Inside the IRS," June 1991, p. 22.
7. Ingrid Eisenstadter, "Insufficient Funds and the IRS," *The New York Times*, May 17, 1998, 3:12.
8. David Cay Johnston, "Computers Clogged, IRS Seeks to Hire Outside Processors," *The New York Times*, Jan. 31, 1997, 1:1.
9. Ibid.
10. David Cay Johnston, "Leaders of IRS Panel Urge Sweeping Overhaul of Agency," *The New York Times*, Feb. 1, 1997, 8:4.

7. IRS TARGETS AND WHAT TO DO IF YOU'RE ONE OF THEM

1. Arthur Fredheim, "Audits Digging Deeper Beneath the Surface," *Practical Accountant*, March 1996, p. 20; taken from IRS commissioner Margaret Milner Richardson's speech to New York State Bar Association, Albany, N.Y., January 24, 1995.
2. Marguerite T. Smith, "Who Cheats on Their Income Taxes," *Money*, April 1991, pp. 101–102.
3. Ibid., p. 104.
4. Statistics of Income Division, Individual Income Tax Returns, Analytical Table C, 1996.
5. Alan R. Sumutka and James Volpi, "Benefits and Rewards of the 'New' Home Office Deduction," *The CPA Journal*, Feb. 2000, p. 27.
6. Jan M. Rosen, "Trained on Home Offices: Secret Weapon 8829," *The New York Times*, March 1, 1992, F:21:1.
7. Randall W. Roth and Andrew R. Biebl, "How to Avoid Getting Caught in the IRS Crackdown," *Journal of Accountancy*, May 1991, p. 35.
8. Natwar M. Gandi, "Issues in Classifying Workers as Employees or Independent Contractors," Testimony before the Subcommittee on Oversight, Committee on Ways and Means, June 20, 1996. U.S. GAO, p. 3.
9. Ibid., p. 12.
10. Barry H. Frank, "What You Can Do About the IRS's All-Out Attack on Independent Contractors," *Practical Accountant*, April 1991, p. 34.
11. Ibid., p. 35.
12. Commerce Clearing House, *1998 Tax Legislation, IRS Restructuring and Reform Law, Explanation and Analysis*, June 1998, Sec. 1126, p. 270.
13. Roth and Biebl, "How to Avoid," p. 35.
14. *Standard Federal Tax Reporter*, CCH Comments (Chicago: Commerce Clearing House), March 21, 1996, Sec. 79,354 and Sec. 79,355, pp. 48,725–48,726.
15. Kathy Krawczyk, Lorraine M. Wright, and Roby B. Sawyers, "Independent Contractor: The Consequences of Reclassification," *Journal of Accountancy*, Jan. 1996, p. 48.

16. Ibid.
17. *Standard Federal Tax Reporter,* CCH Comments, Aug. 1, 1996, p. 4.
18. *Tax Hotline,* "IRS Abuse Hotline," Dec. 1997, p. 13.
19. Richard Byllott, "Compliance 2000 and Cash Transaction Reporting," *Nassau Chapter Newsletter* (published by New York State Society of Certified Public Accountants), vol. 36, no. 4 (Dec. 1992), p. 10.
20. *Social Security Administration/IRS Reporter,* "Market Segment Specialization in the Examination Division," Summer 1995, p. 2.
21. *Practical Accountant,* "Latest IRS Audit Technique Guides," Jan. 1996, p. 52 ("Inside the IRS").
22. *Practical Accountant,* "MSSP Guides Issued on Architects and Cancellation of RTC Debt," April 1995, p. 16 ("Inside the IRS").
23. Materials handed out at IRS's Financial Status Audits Conference, presented by Donald Caterraccio, IRS Brooklyn District; Denis Bricker, IRS Brooklyn District; Jack Angel, CPA, The Tax Institute, College of Management, Long Island University/C. W. Post Campus, July 11, 1996.
24. IRS, MSSP Garment Manufacturers, Training 3147-103, April 1997, TPDS84302H, p. 1–4.
25. Ibid.
26. IRS, MSSP Bars and Restaurants, Training 3149-118, Feb. 1998, TPDS 83849L, pp. 2–1, 2–3, 2–5.
27. "AMT, NOL and Garden Supplies MSSPs," IRS Briefing, *Practical Accountant,* June 2000, p. 18.
28. *Social Security Administration/IRS Reporter,* "Market Segment Understanding Program Provides Guidelines," Fall 1995, p. 2.
29. *Tax Wise Money,* June 1993, p. 8.
30. *IRS 1992 Annual Report,* p. 10.

8. HOW TO AVOID AN AUDIT COMPLETELY

1. *IRS 1980 Annual Report,* p. 52; *IRS 1991 Annual Report,* p. 26; *IRS 1997 Data Book,* advance draft, Table 11.
2. *IRS 1993 Annual Report,* advance draft, Table 11.
3. Ibid., Tables 11, 13, 14, 16, and 17 (footnotes).
4. *IRS 1998 Data Book* and 1999 advance draft, Table 11.
5. *IRS 1996 Data Book,* Table 11.
6. David Cay Johnston, "IRS More Likely to Audit the Poor and Not the Rich," *The New York Times,* April 16, 2000, A:1:32.
7. *Tax Hotline,* "IRS Audit Rate Still Falling" (Tax Points), Sept. 2000, p. 1.
8. *IRS 1998 Data Book,* advance draft, Table 11.
9. *IRS 1976 Annual Report,* p. 99, Table 2.
10. *IRS Data Book,* 1997 and 1998, advance draft, Table 11.
11. Alan E. Weiner, *All About Limited Liability Companies & Partnerships* (Melville, N.Y.: Holtz Rubenstein & Co., 1994), p. 4.
12. IRS, MSSP Garment Manufacturers, Training, 3147-103, April 1997, TPDS84302H, p. 7–13.
13. Ibid., p. 7–16.
14. Ibid., p. 7–14.

NOTES

11. TEN GROUND RULES NEVER TO BREAK TO WIN WITH THE IRS

1. *Tax Hotline*, March 1999, p. 4.
2. Robert D. Hershey, Jr., "Taxpayers, Defeated by Schedule D, Surrender to the Experts, *The New York Times*, March 29, 1998, Bu:1:11.
3. *National Public Accountant*, "How to Communicate with Your Members of Congress," June–July 1995, p. 35 ("Client Report").
4. John M. Peterson, *Tax Hotline*, January 2000, p. 9.

12. NEW TAX LEGISLATION—WHAT TO WATCH OUT FOR, HOW TO BENEFIT

1. Margaret O. Kirk, "Medical Accounts: Mixed Reviews," *The New York Times*, July 5, 1998, Bu:6:3.
2. Joe Catalano, "New Tax Laws Create Need for Fresh Thinking by Homeowners," *Newsday*, Dec. 5, 1997, C:1:1.
3. Commerce Clearing House, *1998 Tax Legislation, IRS Restructuring and Reform Law, Explanation and Analysis*, June 1998, Sec. 846, p. 223.
4 Ibid.
5. Grace W. Weinstein, "No More Income Gap for Retirees Over 65," *Investor's Business Daily*, May 19, 2000, p. 4.
6. "Clinton Signs New Law Ending Earnings Limits for 60-somethings," *The Leader-Herald* (Johnstown, N.Y.), April 8, 2000, p. 1.
7. Diana Furchtgott-Ross, "Left with the Bill: Women, Not Men, Carry the Largest Estate Tax Burden," *Investor's Business Daily*, July 20, 2000, p. 26 ("Issues and Insights").
8. Ibid.

13. THE NEW IRS

1. Commerce Clearing House, *1998 Tax Legislation, IRS Restructuring and Reform Law, Explanation and Analysis*, June 1998, Sec. 821, p. 212.
2. Tracey Miller-Segarra, "IRS Gets Down to Business with Rossotti," *Accounting Today*, July 13–26, 1998, p. 45.

14. WHERE THE IRS IS (OR ISN'T) GOING
AND WHAT *to* DO, OR *not* DO, ABOUT IT

1. Lizette Alvarez, "Senate Hearings Open with Talk of a Sweeping IRS Shakeup," *The New York Times*, Jan. 29, 1998, A:13:10.
2. "IRS Horror Stories Told by Senators," *Newsday*, Sept. 24, 1997, A:7:1.
3. Melissa Klein, "Roth Reports IRS Reprisals Against Whistle-blowers," *Accounting Today*, May 10–23, 1999, p. 5.
4. David Cay Johnston, "IRS More Likely to Audit the Poor and Not the Rich," *The New York Times*, April 16, 2000, A:1:32.
5. David Cay Johnston, "Fearing for Jobs, IRS Workers Relax Effort to Get Unpaid Taxes," *The New York Times*, May 18, 1999, A:1:1.
6. Johnston, *The New York Times*, April 16, 2000.
7. Frederick Daily, "Big Problems at the IRS," *Tax Hotline*, March 7, 2000, p. 8.
8. David Cay Johnston, "IRS May Be Slower to Seize Some Assets," *The New York Times*, July 20, 1999, C:8:3.

9. *The Wall Street Journal*, "Tax Report," July 21, 2000, p. 1.
10. Charles O. Rossotti, prepared testimony before the Ways and Means Oversight Committee on IRS Restructuring and Reform Act Hearing, July 22, 1999.
11. David Cay Johnston, "Innocent Spouse Claims to IRS Soar Under New Law," *The New York Times*, Dec. 29, 1999, C:1:2.
12. *Practical Accountant*, "Innocent Spouse Test," June 2000, p. 20 ("IRS Briefing").
13. Rosotti, testimony, July 22, 1999.
14. Ibid.
15. Ken Rankin, "GAO Auditors Expose IRS's 'Pervasive Weaknesses,'" *Accounting Today*, April 26–May 9, 1999, p. 5.
16. "Audit Says Employees for IRS Stole $5.3 Million," *Newsday*, Nov. 17, 1998, C:8:1.
17. Matthew L. Wald, "The Latest Pitch: 1040PC and the Promise of a Speedy Refund," *The New York Times*, Feb. 28, 1993, "Your Taxes," 17:1.
18. *National Public Accountant*, "Easier Transactions Through Electronic Methods," Dec. 1997, p. 27.
19. *Standard Federal Tax Reports* (Chicago: Commerce Clearing House), "Electronic Filing for Personal Computer Users," Feb. 13, 1997, p. 3 ("Taxes on Parade").
20. John Fuller, "IRS Tallies Up Record-Setting Tax Season for E-filing," *Accounting Today*, June 7–20, 1999, p. 4.
21. Michael Stroh, "Accountant in a Box," *Newsday*, Feb. 10, 1999, C:8:1.
22. Robert D. Hershey, Jr., "A Technological Overhaul of IRS Is Called a Fiasco," *The New York Times*, April 15, 1996, 8:5.
23. www.irs.gov website.
24. *NPA Journal*, "SSA Develops Electronic Filing Option for Employees," July 1997, p. 10 ("Practitioner Communiqué").
25. *Standard Federal Tax Reports*, "IRS Announces Telefile Pilot for Filing Quarterly Payroll Tax Returns," CCH, March 3, 1997, p. 3 ("Taxes on Parade").
26. Tom Herman, "A Special Summary and Forecast of Federal and State Tax Developments," *The Wall Street Journal*, March 26, 1997, A:1:5.
27. Jeffrey L. Winograd, "Washington Alert," *Federal Taxes Weekly Alert*, Jan. 6, 2000, p. 23.
28. *Money*, "Tax Redemption," May 2000, p. 146.
29. *Tax Hotline*, "Offer in Compromise Strategy," June 15, 2000, p. 15.
30. Johnston, "IRS May Be Slower to Seize Some Assets."
31. IRS, *Taxnotes*, 1993, p. 2 ("Procedural Changes for Granting Installment Agreements").
32. George G. Jones and Mark A. Luscombe, "Do Lower IRS Collection Stats Warrant Aggressive Strategies?," *Accounting Today*, June 21–July 4, 1999, p. 8.
33. *Journal of Accountancy*, "IRS Announces Possible New Features for Web Site," Aug. 1996, p. 32 ("Tax Matters").
34. David Cay Johnston, Corporations' Taxes Are Falling Even As Individuals' Burden Rises," *The New York Times*, Feb. 20, 2000, 1:1:1.
35. Ibid.

36. Ibid.
37. David Cay Johnston, "New Tools for the IRS to Sniff Out Tax Cheats," *The New York Times*, Jan 3, 2000, C:1:5.
38. David Cay Johnston, "IRS Is Allowing More Delinquents to Avoid Tax Bill," *The New York Times*, Oct. 10, 1999, 1:1:6.
39. Ibid.
40. David Cay Johnston, "Compressed Data Web Site Offers Help with IRS Penalties," *The New York Times*, Jan. 10, 2000, C:4:1.

BIBLIOGRAPHY

All IRS publications are listed under the Department of the Treasury.

Adelson, Andrea. "IRS Is Getting a Look at Some Mortgage Applications." *The New York Times*, Dec. 29, 1996, 11:2

Alvarez, Lizette. "Senate Hearings Open with Talk of a Sweeping IRS Shake-up." *The New York Times*, Jan. 29, 1998, A:13:10.

Audit and Accounting Forum. "Is Asking for Honesty Undermining the Tax System?" Aug. 25–Sept. 7, 1997, p. 12.

Blaustein, Randy Bruce. *How to Do Business with the IRS. Taxpayer's Edition.* Englewood Cliffs, N.J.: Prentice-Hall, 1984.

(Boardroom Classics). *Tax Loopholes.* Springfield, N.J.: Boardroom Classics, 1994.

Burnham, David. *A Law Unto Itself: Power, Politics and the IRS.* New York: Random House, 1989.

Bylott, Richard. "Compliance 2000 and Cash Transaction Reporting." *Nassau Chapter Newsletter.* Published by New York State Society of Certified Public Accountants, vol. 36, no. 4 (Dec. 1992).

Carlson, Robert C., ed. *Tax Wise Money*, vol. 2, no. 6 (June 1993).

Catalano, Joe. "New Tax Laws Create Need for Fresh Thinking by Homeowners." *Newsday*, Dec. 5, 1997, C:1:1.

Chommie, John C. *The Internal Revenue Service.* New York: Praeger, 1970.

(Commerce Clearing House). *1998 Tax Legislation, IRS Restructuring and Reform Law, Explanation and Analysis.* June 1998. *Standard Federal Tax Reporter, Internal Revenue Code,* "Historical Note." Chicago: Commerce Clearing House, Inc., 1994.

Daily, Frederick W. *Stand Up to the IRS: How to Handle Audits, Tax Bills and Tax Court.* Berkeley: Nolo Press, 1992.

Davis, Shelley, L. *IRS Historical Fact Book: A Chronology, 1646–1992.* Washington, D.C.: U.S. Government Printing Office, 1993.

Dellinger, Kip; Audit and Accounting Forum. "Is Asking for Honesty Undermining the Tax System?" *Accounting Today*, Aug. 25–Sept. 7, 1997, p. 12.

Department of the Treasury, Internal Revenue Service. *1998 Tax Hints*. Brookhaven Service Center. Washington, D.C.: GPO, 1999.

———. *Guide to the Internal Revenue Service for Congressional Staff*. Legislative Affairs Division, Publication 1273. Washington, D.C.: GPO, 1991.

———. *Internal Revenue Service Manual*. Sections 912, 913, 940. Washington, D.C.: GPO, 1981.

———. *IRS 1993–94 Data Book* (advance report). Washington, D.C.: GPO, 1994.

———. *IRS 1995 Data Book* (advance report). Washington, D.C.: GPO, 1995.

———. *IRS 1996 Data Book* (advance report). Washington, D.C.: GPO, 1996.

———. *IRS 1997 Data Book* (advance report). Washington, D.C.: GPO, 1997.

———. *IRS 1976 Annual Report, IRS 1980 Annual Report, IRS 1990 Annual Report, IRS 1991 Annual Report, IRS 1992 Annual Report, IRS 1993 Annual Report* (advance draft). Washington, D.C.: GPO, 1977, 1981, 1991, 1992, 1993.

———. IRS Market Segment Specialization Program. Garment Manufacturers, Training 3147-1093, TPDS84302H. Washington, D.C., GPO, 1997.

———. Bars and Restaurants, Training 3149-118, TPDS83849L. Washington, D.C., GPO, 1998.

———. *IRS Service*. Washington, D.C.: GPO, 1990.

———. Statistics of Income Division, Individual Tax Returns, Analytical Table C, 1996.

———. *Taxnotes*, 1993, p. 2 ("Procedure Changes for Granting Installment Agreements").

Doris, Lillian, ed. *The American Way in Taxation: Internal Revenue, 1862–1963*. Englewood Cliffs, N.J.: Prentice-Hall, 1963.

Eisenstadter, Ingrid. "Insufficient Funds and the IRS." *The New York Times*, May 17, 1998, 3:12:4.

Frank, Barry H. "What You Can Do About the IRS's All-Out Attack on Independent Contractors." *Practical Accountant*, April 1991, pp. 33–37.

Furchtgott-Ross, Diana. "Left with the Bill: Women, Not Men, Carry the Largest Estate Tax Burden." *Investor's Business Daily*, July 20, 2000, p. 26.

Gandi, Natwar M. "Issues in Classifying Workers as Employees or Independent Contractors." Testimony before the Subcommittee on Oversight, Committee on Ways and Means, June 20, 1996. Washington, D.C.: GPO, 1996.

General Accounting Office, *GAO Month in Review:* April 1999, Tax Policy Administration, "Confidentiality of Tax Data: IRS Implementation of the Taxpayer Browsing Protection Act," GAO/GGD-99-43, March 31, 1999, p. 10.

Hersh, Seymour M. "IRS Said to Balk Inquiry on Rebozo." *The New York Times*, April 21, 1974, 1:3.

———. "Ervin Unit to Get Rebozo Tax Data." *The New York Times*, April 24, 1974, 1:4.

Hershey, Robert D., Jr. "Taxpayers, Defeated by Schedule D, Surrender to Experts," *The New York Times*, March 29, 1998, Bu:1:1.

———. "A Technological Overhaul of IRS Is Called a Fiasco." *The New York Times*, April 15, 1996, 8:5.

Hitt, Greg. "Favored Companies Get 11th-Hour Tax Breaks." *The Wall Street Journal*, July 30, 1997, A:2.

Horrock, Nicholas M. "IRS Trained Its Agents in Drinking." *The New York Times*, April 14, 1975, 1:3.

Investor's Business Daily. "Gap for Retirees Over 65," May 19, 2000, p. 4.

irs.gov website.

Johnston, David Cay. "Compressed Data Web Site Offers Help with IRS Penalties." *The New York Times*, Jan. 10, 2000, C:4:1.

———. "Computers Clogged, IRS Seeks to Hire Outside Processors." *The New York Times*, Jan. 31, 1997, 1:1.

———. Corporations' Taxes Are Falling Even as Individuals' Burden Rises." *The New York Times*, Feb. 20, 2000, 1:1:1.

———. "Fearing for Jobs, IRS Workers Relax Efforts to Get Unpaid Taxes." *The New York Times*, May 18, 1999, A:1:1.

———. "Innocent Spouse Claims to IRS Soar Under New Law." *The New York Times*, Dec. 29, 1999, C:1:2.

———. "IRS Bolstering Efforts to Curb Cheating on Taxes." *The New York Times*, Feb. 13, 2000, A:6:1.

———. "IRS Is Allowing More Delinquents to Avoid Tax Bills." *The New York Times*, Oct. 10, 1999, 1:1:6.

———. "IRS May Be Slower to Seize Some Assets." *The New York Times*, July 20, 1999, C:8:3.

———. "IRS More Likely to Audit the Poor and Not the Rich." *The New York Times*, April 16, 2000, A:1:32.

———. "Leaders of IRS Panel Urge Sweeping Overhaul of Agency." *The New York Times*, Feb. 1, 1997, 8:4.

———. "Man Pursued by IRS Wins $75,000 to Pay His Lawyers." *The New York Times*, Feb. 9, 1999, A:12:1.

———. "New Tools for the IRS to Sniff Out Tax Cheats." *The New York Times*, Jan. 3, 2000, C:1:15.

Jones, George G., and Mark A. Luscombe. "Do Lower IRS Collection Stats Warrant Aggressive Strategies?" *Accounting Today*, June 21–July 4, 1999, p. 8.

Journal of Accountancy. "CPAs Recommend Simplifying Earned Income Tax Credit ("Tax Matters"), July 1995, p. 36; "IRS Audits Focus on Market Segments" ("Tax Matters"), Aug. 1995, p. 21; "Independent Contractor: The Consequences of Reclassification," Jan. 1996, p. 47.

Kirk, Margaret O. "Medical Accounts: Mixed Reviews." *The New York Times*, July 5, 1998, Bu:6:3.

Klein, Melissa. "Roth Reports IRS Reprisals Against Whistle-blowers." *Accounting Today*, May 10–23, 1999, p. 5.

Knowles, Clayton. "Nunan Accused Before the Senate of Complicity in 4 New Tax Cases." *The New York Times*, Feb. 22, 1952, 1:2.

———. "Nunan Mentioned in Tax Cut Case." *The New York Times*, Feb. 15, 1952, 10:5.

The Leader Herald (Johnstown, N.Y.). "Clinton Signs New Law Ending Earnings Limits for 60-somethings," April 18, 2000, p. 1.

Lewis, Peter H. "In the Home Office, Equipment May Still Be Deductible." *The New York Times*, Jan. 24, 1993, F:8:1.

McCormally, Kevin. "How a Dumb Idea Became a Law." *Kiplinger's Personal Finance*, July 1993, pp. 44–47.

Miller-Segarra, Tracey. "IRS Gets Down to Business with Rossotti." *Accounting Today*, July 13–26, 1998, p. 45.

Money. "Tax Redemption," May 2000, p. 146.

National Public Accountant. "How to Communicate with Your Members of Congress" ("Client Report"), June/July 1995, p. 35; "Treasury Proposes Crackdown on EITC Errors" ("Capital Corridors"), July 1997, p. 8.

NPA Journal. "SSA Develops Electronic Filing Option for Employees" ("Practioner Communiqué"), July 1997, p. 10.

(New York State Society of Certified Public Accountants). "New IRS Audit Approach Sending Tremors Through the CPA Profession." *Tax and Regulatory Bulletin,* vol. 5, no. 2 (Aug./Sept. 1995), p. 1.

The New York Times. "Tax Breaks for the Few Hinge on Access to Power," July 19, 1976, A:1:2; "Nuclear War Plan by IRS," March 28, 1989, D:16:6; "You Work at Home: Does the Town Board Care?," July 14, 1996, B:1:1.

Newsday. "Audit Says Employees for IRS Stole $5.3 Million," Nov. 17, 1998, C:8:1; "IRS Casts High-Tech Net to Snare Mortgage Frauds," Nov. 1, 1996, D:2:1; "IRS Horror Stories Told by Senators," Sept. 24, 1997, A:7:1.

NSPA Washington Reporter. Mary Beth Loutinsky, ed. Published by National Society of Public Accountants, Alexandria, Va. "IRS, NSPA Meet to Review '92 Tax Form Changes," August 1991; "TaxLink Foreshadows Future," Aug. 6, 1993; "Ways and Means Subcommittee Hears Testimony on IRS Troubles," Nov. 19, 1993.

Pechman, Joseph A. *Federal Tax Policy.* 4th ed. Studies of Government Finance. Washington, D.C.: Brookings Institution, 1983.

Practical Accountant. "Alternative Filing Up This Year," April 1993, p. 20; "Inside the IRS," June 1991, p. 22; "IRS Briefs" ("Inside the IRS"), August 1995, p. 54; "Audits Digging Deeper Beneath the Surface," March 1996, p. 20; "Latest IRS Audit Technique Guides." Jan. 1996, p. 62; "MSSP Guides Issued on Architects and Cancellation of RTC Debt," April 1995, p. 16; "IRS Briefing," August 1999, p. 17; "AMT, NOL, and Garden Supplies MSSPs," June 2000, p. 18; "IRS Briefing," June 2000, p. 20.

Rankin, Ken. "And the Award for Tax Headache of the Year: AMT." *Accounting Today,* May 1–21, 2000, p. 5.

———. "GAO Auditors Expose IRS's 'Pervasive Weaknesses,'" *Accounting Today,* April 26–May 9, 1999, p. 5.

(Research Institute of America). *A Guide for Securing Independent Contractor Status for Workers.* New York: Research Institute of America, 1991.

Rosen, Jan M. "Trained on Home Offices: Secret Weapon 8829." *The New York Times,* March 1, 1992, F:21:1.

Rossotti, Charles O. Prepared testimony before the Ways and Means Oversight Committee on IRS Restructuring and Reform Act Hearing, July 22, 1999.

Roth, Randall W., and Andrew R. Biebl. "How to Avoid Getting Caught in the IRS Crackdown." *Journal of Accountancy,* May 1991, pp. 35–37.

Schmeckebier, Lawrence F., and Francis X. A. Eble. *The Bureau of Internal Revenue: Its History, Activities and Organization.* Baltimore: Johns Hopkins Press, 1923.

Schnepper, Jeff A. *Inside IRS.* New York: Stein and Day, 1987.

Sloane, Leonard. "Home Offices: Tough, Not Impossible." *The New York Times,* Feb. 28, 1993, F:20:1.

Smith, Marguerite T. "Who Cheats on Their Income Taxes." *Money,* April 1991, pp. 101–108.

Social Security Administration/IRS Reporter. "Market Segment Specialization in the Examination Division," Summer 1995, p. 2; "Market Segment Understanding Program Provides Guidelines," Fall 1995, p. 2.

Standard Federal Tax Reporter, CCH Comments. March 21, 1996, Sec. 79.354 and Sec. 79.355, pp. 48,725–726; Aug. 1, 1996, p. 4; March 3, 1997, p. 3.

Standard Federal Tax Reports. "Electronic Filing for Personal Computer Users" (Chicago: Commerce Clearing House), p. 3 ("Taxes on Parade").

Stern, Philip M. *The Best Congress Money Can Buy.* New York: Pantheon, 1988.

———. *The Rape of the Taxpayer.* New York: Random House, 1972.

Steuerle, Eugene C. *Who Should Pay for Collecting Taxes?* Washington, D.C.: American Institute for Public Policy Research, 1986.

Strassels, Paul N., with Robert Wool. *All You Need to Know About the IRS: A Taxpayer's Guide.* New York: Random House, 1979.

Stroh, Michael. "Accountant in a Box," *Newsday,* Feb. 10, 1999, C:8:1.

Tax Hotline. David Ellis and James Glass, eds. Published by Boardroom Reports, Inc., New York, N.Y. Feb. 1992, Dec. 1997, March 1999, May 1999, March 7, 2000, June 15, 2000.

Tax Points. "IRS Audit Rate Still Falling," Sept. 2000, p. 1; "Offer in Compromise Strategy," June 15, 2000, p. 15; John M. Peterson, Jan. 2000, p. 9.

U.S. Congress. House Committee on Government Operations. *A Citizen's Guide on Using the Freedom of Information Act and the Privacy Act of 1974 to Request Government Records.* Fourth Report. House Report 102-146. Washington, D.C.: GPO, 1991.

———. *The Public Statutes at Large of the United States of America from the Organization of the Government in 1789 to March 3, 1845.* Ed. Richard Peters. Vol. 1. Boston: Charles C. Little and James Brown, 1850.

Van Natta, Don, Jr. "11 Officers Are Accused of Failure to Pay Taxes." *The New York Times,* July 17, 1996, B:3:5.

Wald, Matthew L. "The Latest Pitch: 1040PC and the Promise of a Speedy Refund." *The New York Times,* Feb. 28, 1993, "Your Taxes," 17:1.

Walker, Jack L. *Mobilizing Interest Groups in America: Patrons, Professions, and Social Movements.* Ann Arbor: University of Michigan Press, 1991.

The Wall Street Journal. "A Special Summary and Forecast of Federal and State Tax Developments," March 26, 1997, A:1:5; "Favored Companies Get 11th-Hour Tax Breaks," July 30, 1997, A:2; "Tax Report," July 21, 2000, p. 1.

Waltman, Jerold L. *Political Origins of the U.S. Income Tax.* Jackson, Miss.: University Press of Mississippi, 1985.

The Washington Post. "Computer Problems Taxing IRS," March 15, 1996, 1:5.

Weiner, Alan E. *All About Limited Liability Companies & Partnerships.* Melville, N.Y.: Holtz Rubenstein & Co., 1994.

Winograd, Jeffrey L. "Washington Alert." *Federal Taxes Weekly Alert,* Jan. 6, 2000, p. 23.

Witnah, Donald R., ed. *The Greenwood Encyclopedia of American Institutions.* S.V. "Government Agencies." Westport, Conn., and London: Greenwood Press, 1983.

Zorack, John L. *The Lobbying Handbook.* Washington, D.C.: Professional Lobbying and Consulting Center, 1990.

INDEX

INDEX

state tuition programs, 281–82
Statutory Notice of Deficiency, 249
Stedman, Ellen, 152–53
stock transactions, 56
  with cash-intensive businesses, 173
  ground rules for reporting of, 242
  IRS technology and, 136–38
  overlooked credits and deductions on, 237
  taxpayer misconceptions about, 227
  see also dividends
straight line method, 154
Student Loan Interest Statement (Form 1098-E),
  433
student loans, 280–81
subpoenas, 69–70, 93
Substitute for Form W-2, Wage and Tax Statement
  or Form 1099R, Distributions from Pensions,
  Annuities, Retirement or Profit-Sharing Plans,
  IRAs, Insurance Contracts, etc. (Form 4852),
  456
summonses:
  cash-intensive businesses and, 56
  in collections, 63
  in criminal investigations, 92
  in future, 308
Supplemental Income and Loss (Schedule E), 193,
  200, 239, 251, 253–55, 259–60, 319, 378–79
Supreme Court, U.S., 22, 93, 110, 115, 169

tax brackets, 16–18, 272
  in audits, 99
  Examination Division on, 80
  in future, 285
  in gray area deductions, 252
  in hiring dependents, 270–71
  S corporations and, 199–200
  in self-employment, 155
  taxpayer misconceptions about, 216–17
Tax Counseling for the Elderly (TCE), 47
Tax Court, U.S., 70, 74, 76, 80–81, 94–95, 100, 107,
  115, 205, 246, 298, 305–6
tax credits, 469, 493
  in audits, 186, 189
  and complexity of tax forms, 263–64
  EIC, 38–39
  Examination Division on, 80
  in future, 277–83, 287–91, 298
  IRS technology and, 135
  overlooked, 237–41
  unused, 237
Tax Delinquent Return Investigations, 361
taxes:
  avoidance of, 71
  cuts in, 278
  evasion of, 6, 22, 44, 71–73, 148, 190
  experts on, 3–14
  history of, 15–16, 22–23, 32
  increases in, 16–22, 128, 235
  information on, 3–14, 44, 76–77, 84, 265, 483–97
  literature on, 3, 28–29, 31

minimizing of, 8
  overdue, 62, 65–66
  revenues generated by, 16–18, 22, 32, 119, 148
  underpayment of, 106
tax education incentives, 278–83
tax-exempt businesses and groups, 133, 317–19,
  320
Tax Exempt and Government Entities Division,
  322
Tax for Children Under Age 14 Who Have
  Investment Income of More Than $1,400
  (Form 8615), 261, 264–65, 474
Tax Guide for Small Business (IRS Publication
  334), 155, 488
tax laws:
  complexity of, 28–29, 43, 82–83, 233–34, 310–11
  favoritism in, 25–28
  IRS in interpreting and acting on, 12
  new, 277–316
  see also specific tax laws
Tax Loopholes (Alberts), 117
Tax Modernization System, 274
Taxpayer Advocates (TAs), 328–30
Taxpayer Assistance Orders (TAOs), 330–31
Taxpayer Bill of Rights, 61, 167, 330, 500–507
Taxpayer Bill of Rights 2 (TBOR 2), 167
Taxpayer Bill of Rights 3 (TBOR 3), 167, 483
Taxpayer Browsing Protection Act, 105
Taxpayer Compliance Measurement Program
  (TCMP), 48–50, 138, 307
Taxpayer Help and Education, 357
taxpayer identification numbers (TINs), 39
Taxpayer Information Program, 77
Taxpayer Relief Act of 1997 (TRA '97), 28, 82, 167,
  262, 283, 277–94, 493–95
Taxpayer Services, 76–77
taxpayers:
  as client types, 10–12, 74, 88
  commonsense tools for, 8–9
  cooperativeness of, 73
  empowerment of, 8–10, 12
  errors of, 127, 132, 141, 143, 224
  high-profile, 44
  in interviews with IRS, 307
  IRS feared by, 3–4, 68
  lifestyles of, 55, 64
  as perceived by IRS, 46
  records kept by, 190–91, 298, 310
  relationship between IRS and, 15–43, 102–20,
  333
  rights of, 61, 73, 75, 103–7, 112, 115–17, 120, 167,
  181, 297–311, 323, 330, 483, 500–507
Tax Payment Act of 1943, 32–33, 242
Tax Reform Act of 1976 (TRA '76), 115
Tax Reform Act of 1986 (TRA '86), 80, 82, 112,
  233–34
tax shelters, *see* shelters, tax
Tax Systems Modernization (TSM), 121–22, 145
Tax Topic, 357
tax year, 145, 212

556

ABOUT THE AUTHORS

MARTIN KAPLAN has been a certified public accountant for over thirty years. For over twenty years, Mr. Kaplan operated his own New York City public-accounting firm. He is now a member of the accounting firm of Geller, Marzano, and Co., CPAs, P.C., and his clients include wholesalers, manufacturers, and service industries. The firm performs audit and accounting work but focuses its attention on the tax-planning opportunities available to its clients and on representation in IRS matters.

NAOMI WEISS writes fiction and nonfiction on a broad range of subjects. As president of her own firm, she also writes and produces marketing and communications materials for clients, from small businesses to multinationals. She has received awards from the National Council of Family Relations, the International Association of Business Communicators, and the Art Directors Club.

DISCARDED

DISCARDED

ADAMSVILLE-COLLIER HEIGHTS

343.73052   Kaplan, Marty.
KAPLAN

What the IRS doesn't want
you to know

ATLANTA-FULTON PUBLIC LIBRARY